THE HUMAN DIALOGUE

Edited by
FLOYD W. MATSON
and
ASHLEY MONTAGU

Fp

the

human

dialogue

PERSPECTIVES ON

COMMUNICATION

THE FREE PRESS, *New York*

COLLIER-MACMILLAN LIMITED, *London*

Collier-Macmillan Canada, Ltd., Toronto, Ontario

Library of Congress Catalog Card Number: 66-10383

Second printing March 1968

The Civilization of the Dialogue

*is the only civilization worth having and the only civilization in which
the whole world can unite. It is, therefore, the only civilization
we can hope for, because the world must unite or be blown to bits.
The Civilization of the Dialogue requires communication. It requires a
common language and a common stock of ideas. It assumes that
every man has reason and that every man can use it. It preserves to every
man his independent judgment and, since it does so, it deprives any
man or any group of men of the privilege of forcing their
judgment upon any other man or group of men. The Civilization of the
Dialogue is the negation of force. We have reached the point, in any event,
when force cannot unite the world; it can merely destroy it.
Through continuing and enriching the Great Conversation higher
education not only does its duty by morals and religion,
it not only performs its proper intellectual task: it also supports and
symbolizes the highest hopes and the highest aspirations of mankind.*

ROBERT M. HUTCHINS

Of the making of books about communication, it sometimes seems, there is no end. The total output to date on this most protean of subjects would not only fill a library; it would occupy most of the categories of the Dewey Decimal System. Nearly every organized field of thought and scholarship, from particle physics to parapsychology, has its implicit or explicit theory of communication—and, more often than not, its several competing theories.

There is, for example, a five-foot shelf of books on communication composed largely in the language of mathematics and seemingly in the interests of engineering—a literature derived from the physical sciences, pure and applied, and subdivided into technical specialities bearing such names as cybernetics, telecommunication, mathematical information theory, and the like. On the wall opposite is another collection of books, older and more expensively bound, treating of communication in what may be called the "classical" vein—studies of rhetoric and dialectic, grammar and poetic, allegory and myth, which discourse upon discourse in endless variations on a theme by Aristotle.

Then there are books on the psychological shelves that treat all human behavior, including the private experience of perceiving, as communication (or "transaction"); and there are books by other psychologists that approach communication as the helping or healing art: in a word, as therapy. There are also books, by prodigal anthropologists returned from the Antipodes, that define *culture* as communication ("the silent language"); and there are parallel books, by sociologists, that discuss *society* as communication ("symbolic interaction"). There are philosophical works that contemplate existence as dialogue and truth as communicability; and there are political tomes that describe communication as the groundwork of democracy and the highroad to the good society.

But in all this wealth of perspectives on communication, curiously enough, there is a remarkable poverty of synthesis or even of comparative discussion. The jealous conventions of academic specialism, which tend to convert new pathways into exclusive provinces, operate nowhere with more constricting effect than in the study of human communication. To be sure, there are occasional efforts at interdisciplinary "teamwork" among neighboring departments—as in the empiricist persuasion that has come to be known as the behavioral approach. Unfortunately what this teamwork often means in practice is that like-minded students of symbolic behavior, variously positioned in the social sciences but sharing a common methodology and assumptive framework, carve up a carefully delimited subject among themselves; starting out in intellectual congeniality, they end up in predictable consensus and mutual confirmation. They have described a circle, but have not significantly widened it. There are many such monadic circles, touching and recoiling but rarely interpenetrating, in the discursive universe of communication study and research.

The present volume does not claim to be the creative synthesis that will give unity and coherence to this fragmented realm. Nor does it purport to be fully comprehensive or undiscriminatingly eclectic. All selection (and not least that of anthologists) is governed by a point of view, which it is well to recognize at the outset—not in order to make a virtue of a defect (if that is what it is) but rather to let the reader in on the orientation of the enterprise and to cast some light both upon what has been selectively included and what has been selectively left out.

The point of view of this book is set forth at length in the introductory essay, "The Unfinished Revolution." That essay not only presents an overview of the general subject but also advances a deliberately provocative thesis: that the field of communication is today more than ever a battleground contested by two opposing conceptual forces—those of *monologue* and *dialogue*. The "monological" approach, which defines communication as essentially the transmission and reception of symbolic stimuli (messages or commands), finds its classical formulation in the art and science of rhetoric and its characteristic modern expressions in cybernetics, combative game theory, and the repertoires of mass persuasion. The "dialogical" approach, which regards communication as the path to communion and the ground of self-discovery, found its original champion in Socrates and has its spokesmen today in such diverse currents of thought as religious existentialism, post-Freudian psychotherapy, and sociological interactionism.

The bias of the editors—the principle of organization underlying this anthology—distinctly favors all those ideas and activities, metaphors and models, which give promise of vitalizing the human dialogue. Within the limitations of that outlook, we have sought to bring together as wide and representative a variety as possible of the current perspectives on communication to be found in the major disciplines concerned with the subject.

Psychology and psychotherapy, sociology and anthropology, political science and international relations, linguistic philosophy and existentialism, mass culture and mass media studies, cybernetics and information theory—these fields offer the principal frames of heuristic reference on which we have relied for the forty-nine contributions that make up this volume.

By way of acknowledgment, our thanks go first to all the contributing authors, whose generous cooperation has made this undertaking possible. We are grateful to our editor, Emanuel Geltman of the Free Press, for his sustained encouragement and understanding. To students, colleagues, and friends too numerous to mention who have helped to shape and sharpen our own perspectives, we owe a substantial debt of appreciation. And finally to our wives, Carla Matson and Marjorie Montagu, we make an offering of this book in token return for the gift of love that unravels the mystery and comprehends the miracle of dialogue.

Floyd W. Matson
Ashley Montagu

CONTRIBUTORS

Gordon W. Allport, who has taught psychology at Harvard University since 1926, is a personality theorist whose influence upon American clinical psychologists is (by their own testimony) second only to that of Freud. His recent works include *Personality and Social Encounter*, *The Nature of Prejudice*, and *Becoming: Basic Considerations for a Psychology of Personality.*

Hannah Arendt is a political and social philosopher who received her Ph.D. degree from Heidelberg University and has taught at several American universities since coming to this country in 1941. She is currently at Princeton University. She is the author, among other books, of *Eichmann in Jerusalem*, *The Origins of Totalitarianism*, *The Human Condition*, and *On Revolution.*

Jacques Barzun, provost of Columbia University, is a cultural historian, social critic, educator, and interpreter of the arts whose intellectual range is suggested by a few of his titles: *Science: The Glorious Entertainment*, *The House of Intellect*, *The Energies of Art*, *Teacher in America*, *Race: A Study in Modern Superstition*, *Darwin, Marx, Wagner*, and *Romanticism and the Modern Ego.*

Martin Buber, who died in Israel in 1965 at the age of eighty-seven, was a philosopher and theologian whose early book, *I and Thou*, introduced in 1923 the dialogical principle that came to underlie all his subsequent writing. Among his influential volumes are *Between Man and Man*, *Paths in Utopia*, *Pointing the Way*, *Israel and the World*, and *At the Turning.*

Albert Camus, novelist and philosopher, was active in the French Resistance during the Second World War and became, with Jean-Paul Sartre, a leader in the nonreligious wing of French existentialist thought. Recipient of the Nobel Prize for Literature in 1957, he was killed in an automobile accident in 1960. His works include *The Rebel*, *The Myth of Sisyphus*, *The Stranger*, and *The Plague*.

Hadley Cantril is president of the Institute for International Social Research in Princeton, New Jersey. A noted psychologist, his publications include *The Politics of Despair*, *The "Why" of Man's Experience*, and (with C. H. Bumstead) *Reflections on the Human Venture*.

Pierre Teilhard de Chardin, born in France in 1881, was both a Jesuit father and an eminent paleontologist. Much of his scientific work was carried on in China, where, as director of the National Geologic Survey, he was instrumental in the discovery of Pekin Man. His major work, *The Phenomenon of Man*, was published shortly after his death in 1955.

Robert Coles is a graduate of Harvard University and of Columbia University's College of Physicians and Surgeons who is presently on the psychiatric staff of the Harvard University Health Services.

Hanna Colm, who died in 1965, was a psychoanalyst in Washington, D.C., whose writing and practice evinced a strong interest in existentialist psychotherapy and a commitment to humanistic psychology.

John Dewey, 1859–1952, whose instrumentalist philosophy and social psychology incorporated a comprehensive "contextualist" theory of human communication, was the author among numerous other works of *Experience and Nature*, *Human Nature and Conduct*, and *Reconstruction in Philosophy*.

Hugh Dalziel Duncan is a sociologist presently teaching at Southern Illinois University. His important study, *Communication and the Social Order*, is being revised and expanded for a new edition.

Franklin Fearing, who died suddenly in 1962, was a psychologist with a special interest in social and mass communication. He taught at the University of California at Los Angeles.

Leon Festinger, a social psychologist at Stanford University, is the author of the influential *A Theory of Cognitive Dissonance*.

Erich Fromm, born in Germany in 1900, is a renowned psychoanalyst with additional training in sociology and philosophy. His many seminal works include *Escape From Freedom*, *Man for Himself*, *The Sane Society*, *The Art of Loving*, and *The Heart of Man*.

Hans H. Gerth, co-author with C. Wright Mills of *Character and Social Structure*, is a sociologist in the tradition of Max Weber who teaches at the University of Wisconsin.

Howard Luck Gossage, a partner in the San Francisco advertising firm of Freeman and Gossage, has published articles on mass communication in *Harper's* and other magazines (including *Ramparts*, of which he is an editor). He has taught and lectured at various universities, among them Pennsylvania State University and the University of California.

Edward T. Hall is an anthropologist who teaches at the Armour Institute, Chicago. He is the author of *The Silent Language* and *The Hidden Dimension*.

F. A. Hayek is a social theorist whose distinguished contributions embrace the fields of economics, philosophy, political science, and psychology. Among his books are *The Sensory Order*, *The Counterrevolution of Science*, and *The Road to Serfdom*. He is presently associated with the University of Freiburg.

William Ernest Hocking, born in 1873, was the dean of American philosophers, having retired as Alford Professor at Harvard in 1943. His first book, *The Meaning of God in Human Experience*, published in 1912, was the outgrowth of his Harvard doctoral dissertation—which bore the title, "Philosophy of Communication: Part I." His doctrine of "intersubjectivity" has had a deep influence upon today's existentialist philosophers, notably Gabriel Marcel. He died in 1966.

Oliver Wendell Holmes, Jr., became known as "the great dissenter" for his eloquent defenses of free speech and civil liberties during his thirty-year tenure on a dominantly conservative Supreme Court, to which he was appointed by Theodore Roosevelt in 1902.

Reuel L. Howe is an American theologian whose book *The Miracle of Dialogue* embodies the Kellogg Lectures, which he delivered at the Episcopal Theological School in Cambridge, Massachusetts. He is also the author of *Man's Need and God's Action*, *The Creative Years*, and *Herein Is Love*.

Robert M. Hutchins is the director of the Center for the Study of Democratic Institutions, Santa Barbara, California. Previously chancellor of the University of Chicago, he is the author of numerous books on education, including *The University of Utopia* and *Education for Freedom*.

William H. Ittelson is a psychologist specializing in perception, who has been closely associated with the transactionalist point of view developed by Adelbert Ames and Hadley Cantril, among others. He is the author of *Visual Space Perception* and (with Professor Cantril) *Perception: A Transactional Approach*.

Karl Jaspers, born in 1883, is a distinguished German existentialist thinker who received an M.D. degree but later turned from psychiatry to philosophy. Among his works available in English are *The Perennial Scope of Philosophy, Existentialism and Humanism, The Way to Wisdom, Reason and Existenz*, and *Man in the Modern Age*.

Weston La Barre is the author of *The Human Animal* and other works in anthropology and social science. He has been a research intern at the Menninger Clinic and taught anthropology at several universities prior to accepting his present professorship at Duke University.

Susanne K. Langer received her B.A., M.A., and Ph.D. degrees from Radcliffe College. Among her well-known philosophical works are *Philosophy in a New Key, Feeling and Form, Introduction to Symbolic Logic*, and *Reflections on Art*. Since 1954, she has taught philosophy at Connecticut College.

Leo Lowenthal is a sociologist of international reputation who is equally at home in philosophy, history, and literary criticism. Now teaching at the University of California (Berkeley), he is the author of *Literature and the Image of Man, Literature, Popular Culture, and Society, Prophets of Deceit* (with Norbert Guterman), and *Culture and Social Behavior* (with Seymour M. Lipset).

Gabriel Marcel, French philosopher and theologian, is a former playwright (with more than forty dramatic works to his credit) who became a convert to Catholicism. Like Martin Buber and William Ernest Hocking, his philosophy rests upon an "intersubjective" theory of human communication. His books include *The Mystery of Being, The Philosophy of Existentialism, Man Against Mass Society*, and *Metaphysical Journal*.

Abraham H. Maslow, who teaches at Brandeis University, is one of the leaders of the contemporary school of humanistic psychology that has come to be known as the "third force" (in contradistinction to behaviorism and orthodox psychoanalysis). Trained in anthropology and psychoanalysis as well as in academic psychology, he is the author of *Motivation and Personality, Toward a Psychology of Being*, and *Religions, Values, and Peak-Experiences*.

Floyd W. Matson took his B.A. degree in the study of communications and his Ph.D. degree in political science, both from the University of California (Berkeley), where he taught speech and communications from 1952 to 1965. He is presently director of the social sciences program at the University of Hawaii. He is the author of *The Broken Image, Hope Deferred: Public Welfare and the Blind* (with Jacobus tenBroek), and *Prejudice, War, and the Constitution* (with Jacobus tenBroek and E. N. Barnhart), and is editor of *Voices of Crisis*.

Marshall McLuhan is director of the Center for Culture and Technology at the University of Toronto. He was born in Canada and received his Ph.D. degree in English literature at Cambridge University. His books are *The Mechanical Bride*, *The Gutenberg Galaxy*, and *Understanding Media: The Extensions of Man*.

George Herbert Mead, who died in 1931, was a leading figure in the development of American pragmatism, along with his close colleague John Dewey. His thought is preserved mainly in three posthumous volumes assembled from lecture notes by his students: *Mind, Self, and Society*, *The Philosophy of the Act*, and *Movements of Thought in the Nineteenth Century*.

Joost A. M. Meerloo is a Dutch psychoanalyst, whose books include *The Rape of the Mind* and *Conversation and Communication*.

C. Wright Mills, who died in 1963, was an American sociologist whose widely influential writings in political sociology and social psychology include *The Power Elite*, *White Collar*, *The New Men of Power*, *The Sociological Imagination*, and (with Hans H. Gerth) *Character and Social Structure*.

Ashley Montagu, born in England and educated at the University of London, the University of Florence, and Columbia University, is an anthropologist and social biologist whose thirty books cover a broad range of social and natural science. Among them are *The Direction of Human Development*, *Man in Process*, *Human Heredity*, *Man's Most Dangerous Myth: The Fallacy of Race*, *The Natural Superiority of Women*, and *The Science of Man*.

Pope Paul VI succeeded to the papacy in 1963 after the death of Pope John XXIII. His first encyclical, *Ecclesiam Suam*, was issued in August, 1964.

J. R. Pierce received his B.S., M.S., and Ph.D. degrees from the California Institute of Technology and has been associated with the Bell Telephone Laboratories, Inc., since 1936. He is co-author of *Man's World of Sound* and the author of *Electrons, Waves and Messages* and *Symbols, Signals and Noise*.

Anatol Rapoport is a mathematician and philosopher whose career includes a childhood phase as a musical prodigy. Among his books are *Operational Philosophy*, *Science and the Goals of Man*, *Fights, Games, and Debates*, and *Strategy and Conscience*.

Carl R. Rogers is a distinguished American psychologist whose writings have had a profound effect upon the progress of psychotherapy and social work. His books include *Counseling and Psychotherapy*, *Client-Centered*

Therapy, and *On Becoming a Person*. He is presently associated with the Western Behavioral Science Institute at La Jolla, California.

Jerome Rothstein is a physicist educated at Columbia University and The City College of New York, who has been associated since 1942 with the Signal Corps Engineering Laboratories. He is the author of more than sixty articles on scientific subjects, as well as of *Communication, Organization, and Science*.

Jurgen Ruesch, a psychiatrist who teaches at the University of California School of Medicine, has long specialized in problems of human communication. Among his authoritative works are *Therapeutic Communication, Nonverbal Communication, Disturbed Communication*, and *Communication: The Social Matrix of Psychiatry* (with Gregory Bateson).

Ludwig von Bertalanffy is an eminent biologist, who has taught at the University of Vienna and is presently with the University of Alberta. He is the author of *Problems of Life* and *Modern Theories of Development* and is co-editor of the *General Systems Yearbooks*.

Paul Weiss is a philosopher at Yale University whose concern with the human venture is indicated by such books as *The Nature of Man* and *Man's Freedom*.

E. B. White is the famous essayist, humorist, and social commentator whose "Notes and Comments" in *The New Yorker* have been required reading for the literate since the 1930s. Some of his books are *The Wild Flag, The Second Tree From the Corner, One Man's Meat*, and *Quo Vadimus?*

Norbert Wiener, who died in 1964, was the mathematical genius who developed cybernetics and pioneered in the construction of current scientific theories of communication and information. He taught for many years at the Massachusetts Institute of Technology and was the author of *Cybernetics, The Human Use of Human Beings, Nonlinear Problems in Random Theory*, two autobiographical volumes, and a novel.

CONTENTS

Part Two.   COMMUNICATION AS DIALOGUE

Part Three.   PERSON TO PERSON:
                 PSYCHOLOGICAL APPROACHES

Part Four.　　DEMOCRATIC DIALOGUE:
　　　　　　　THE POLITICS OF COMMUNICATION

Part Five.　　THE MODERN PERSUASION:
　　　　　　　THE RHETORICS OF MASS SOCIETY

INTRODUCTION: THE UNFINISHED REVOLUTION

Floyd W. Matson and Ashley Montagu

*I*t is a thoroughly familiar remark of recent years that the field of human communication, both in theory and in practice, has undergone a revolution. Like most truisms, this one is true enough but as outdated as it is imprecise. It would be more accurate to say that the realm of communications, like the modern world it accurately reflects, has undergone a succession of revolutions—or (to do justice to the truism) a single continuing revolution of recurrent active phases, already more than a century old, the end of which is yet beyond our vision or prevision.

The communications revolution has not only proceeded by historical stages; it has also exploded simultaneously upon various plateaus of thought and action. The most conspicuous of its many phases is also the most fundamental: that is, the technological transformation of the means and media of communication, from telegraph and telephone to television and Telstar. In this primary respect, the revolution in communications is a peculiarly potent expression of the encompassing industrial-technological revolution of the last century. The vast and cumulative changes that have occurred in the means of communication run parallel to changes in the means of production, with consequences that are equally parallel—and equally ambiguous. Indeed, the phenomenon of mass communication may plausibly be viewed as a peculiar form of mass production: that is, the production and distribution of *messages*, regarded as symbolic commodities.

The parallel may be carried further. Just as we are accustomed to referring to the first and second industrial revolutions, so we may distinguish between the first and second communications revolutions. The earlier of these eruptions represented the triumph of scientific invention and mechanical engineering; it gave us, typically, the telephone, the radio, and the giant printing press. The second communications revolution is a triumph of scientific *theory* and *human* engineering; and it has given us,

I

typically, cybernetics and mass motivation research. The heroes of the first communications revolution were such men as Thomas Edison and Alexander Graham Bell; the heroes (some might say the antiheroes) of the second revolution are such men as Norbert Wiener and Ernest Dichter.[1]

To put the distinction another way, the first revolution in communications was predominantly a practical and mechanical matter; like the first industrial revolution (or any large-scale natural phenomenon), it simply *happened* to society—and it was left to succeeding generations, standing amid the ruins of traditional folkways and institutions, to analyze, rationalize, and ideologize its import. By contrast, the second communications revolution, the advent of which we are still uncertainly celebrating, is as theoretical and "philosophical" as it is practical. It is revolutionary not only technically but intellectually as well—a thoroughly articulate, self-conscious, and sophisticated affair.

This point may be illuminated by reference to one of the master symbols of the second communications revolution: the concept of cybernetics. On its face, this idea is a rich and complicated one—as complicated as the mind of its gifted creator, the late Norbert Wiener. Something of its ambitious sweep may be gleaned from Wiener's delineation of the province his concept was intended to embrace: "Besides the electrical engineering theory of the transmission of messages, there is a larger field which includes not only the study of language but the study of messages as a means of controlling machinery and society [*sic*], the development of computing machines and other such automata, certain reflections upon psychology and the nervous system, and a tentative new theory of scientific method."[1]

As this complex sentence suggests, the range of innovation signified by the concept of cybernetics is not restricted to the spheres of mechanical invention and industrial engineering but spills over lavishly into the humane studies of linguistics and rhetoric ("the study of language"); of sociology ("the study of messages as a means of controlling . . . society"); of psychology; and of at least one branch of philosophy. As a matter of fact, the impact of cybernetics as a tool of observation and a style of thought —with its intricately elaborated logical theory of information and communication—has come to be deeply and disturbingly felt in nearly every department of the social sciences and the humanities.[2]

The extent and significance of that impact, as well as of its limitations and hazards, form the problematic theme under discussion in the first part of this volume ("Communication as Science")—and indirectly of all the remaining parts as well. At least one dimension of the problem may be briefly anticipated here, once again by reference to the influential writings of Wiener. For it was Wiener who, with one hand, charted in remarkable

detail and candor the future path of his scientific theory of communication
—and who, with the other hand, sounded the alarm against it.

In his curiously titled discussion of the interrelations of cybernetics and
society, *The Human Use of Human Beings*, Wiener took pains to emphasize
that his theoretical program of communication was also, intrinsically and
irresistibly, a theory and program of *control*. Indeed, from the point of
view of cybernetics—based upon the observation of communicative processes in those supremely sophisticated automata, the giant computers—
all communication is conducted in the imperative mood. To transmit a
message to the machine is to give it a command—not a proposition to be
entertained or argued with but an order to be obeyed. But is the machine
any different after all, in this respect, from man? "When I give an order
to a machine," said Wiener, "the situation is not essentially different from
that which arises when I give an order to a person." In society as in the
laboratory, "*communication and control* [*go*] *together*." Wiener could thus
speak in a single breath of the new "theory of control in engineering,
whether human or animal or mechanical . . ."[3]

It is apparent from this description that the cybernetic theory of communication—like the rhetorical theory shared by the ancient sophists and
the postmodern "engineers of consent"—is inherently *monological* and
directive. For all its attention to the responsive mechanisms of feedback,
its map of the communicative process is essentially that of a one-way
street—what Franklin Fearing in the present volume calls the "trans-
mission-belt" theory[4]—with all the traffic moving in an unbroken stream
from the message center to the receiving station. It is, in purest form, the
model of the monologue—as opposed to that of the dialogue. (It may be
recalled that the sustained opposition of Socrates to the rhetorical sophists,
as expressed most notably in the encounter with Gorgias and Callicles,
was that of the dialogical spirit confronted with the aggressive designs of
the monological persuader.)

This point brings us to the newest (as well as, perhaps, the oldest)
theoretical development in the field of communications—one sufficiently
profound and pervasive to deserve the label "the third revolution." It is,
simply put, the view of human communication as *dialogue*. But before
turning to an examination of this competing perspective, let us follow the
founder of cybernetics somewhat further along the astonishing path of
speculation that he has opened up. Even more noteworthy than Wiener's
frankness in spelling out the logical implications of his theory of communication was his vivid premonition of its antisocial potentialities—a fearful
anticipation of the inhuman use of human beings through a kind of applied
"social cybernetics." For even if it be granted that the channels of communication between man and machine are one-way control circuits, it does
not follow that the directional flow of the messages (commands) must

necessarily proceed only *from* man *to* the machine. What Wiener came to suspect, with a degree of concern that assumed almost the proportions of obsession, was that the flow of commands might eventually reverse direction, proceeding (with all its former authority) *from machine to man.*

Wiener's apprehension was not, of course, that the computer would suddenly develop a "mind of its own" and turn like a Frankenstein monster upon its custodians; it was rather that the *principle of mechanization* itself might take command, as men came to confer ever greater authority and prestige upon the bloodless ratiocinations of their electronic oracles. His point (argued forcibly in the second of two articles in this volume) was that the mechanical style of thought—the very literalness of the automaton in executing its technical assignments—must, if unchecked, give rise to programmatic solutions and directives for action suited well enough to the makeup of automata but disastrous to the deepest needs and aspirations of human beings.[5]

Our immediate concern is not to reinforce the premonitions and prophecies voiced by Wiener but instead to take note of the marked tendency of his theory of communication to manifest coercive and manipulative properties—and so to raise doubts on all sides concerning its ultimate fruitfulness both as theory and as program. Nor was Wiener alone in his sober second thoughts regarding the denouement of cybernetic reasoning; more recently another distinguished mathematician and philosopher, Anatol Rapoport, has been led to express quite similar apprehensions about the consequences to man and his civilization of the continued reliance by political decision-makers upon that coolly objective style of strategic thinking derived from the mathematical theory of games—a theory, be it noted, to which both Rapoport and Wiener have made significant contributions.

In the title of his deeply concerned study of the problem, *Strategy and Conscience*, Rapoport implicitly redefines the familiar thesis of the "two cultures"—of two divergent realms of discourse, styles of thought, and modes of communication—that presently divide mankind, not geographically (into east and west or north and south), but intellectually and psychologically. On one side are the devotees of strategic gamesmanship and combative role-playing—those who maintain, in the courage of their resolution to "think about the unthinkable," that politics is the continuation of war by other means. On the other side are the advocates of the human conscience—those who believe that politics is the art of reaching consensus: the continuation of the Great Conversation by the same means. "It is extremely difficult for one who subscribes to this orientation," writes Rapoport, "to join in a dialogue with a strategist, even with the best intentions. The basic question in the strategist's mind is this: 'In a conflict how can I gain an advantage over him?' The critic cannot disregard the question,

'If I gain an advantage over him, what sort of person will I become?' "[6]

This condition of strategic blindness is, furthermore, but one of the dilemmas into which the second revolution in communications, the revolution of steersmanship and gamesmanship, appears to have been seduced by the directives of its own logic. What holds for the scientific theory of interpersonal communication holds also for the quasi-scientific theory of mass communication. The claims and credentials of that well-publicized school of applied rhetoric that finds its characteristic expression in the mystique of "mass motivation research" are examined at some length in our section entitled "The Modern Persuasion: The Rhetorics of Mass Society." It is enough here to emphasize that the theoretical assumptions underlying the work of the mass persuaders (whether hidden or all too visible) are transparently monological and manipulative. The very conception of the audience for such communication as a "mass" heightens the impression of a process in which all power and initiative are on one side, with the other reduced to pliant inertness and susceptibility. The late C. Wright Mills, for one, regarded it as "not surprising under such conditions that there should arise a conception of public opinion as a mere reaction—we cannot say 'response'—to the content of the mass media. In this view, the public is merely the collectivity of individuals each rather passively exposed to the mass media and rather helplessly opened up to the suggestions and manipulations that flow from these media."[7]

If it is reasonable to regard the phenomena of cybernetics and mass motivation research as twin symbols of the second communications revolution, it becomes less difficult to understand the basis for the third revolution—the counterrevolution of dialogue. There is, to be sure, a multiplicity of points of view assembled under that banner, in what may seem here and there to be a strange bedfellowship. The concept of "dialogue," for all its recency as a movement of thought, has already begun to suffer the inevitable fate of fashionable acceptance—that of dilution and distortion. But there is also something to be said on behalf of this popular currency: The favorable reception that the dialogical theory of communication is receiving, in so many differing circles of thought and influence, is surely an index of its relevance—both to the felt needs of men and to the felt lacks of conventional theory.

If the Jewish theologian and philosopher Martin Buber is to be accredited as the earliest contemporary spokesman of the theory of dialogue, a more recent spokesman from the side of religion is the most prominent and authoritative: Pope Paul VI. His first encyclical, *Ecclesiam Suam*, issued in August, 1964, constitutes a remarkable endorsement of the principle of dialogue, both as a practical mission of the Church and as a norm for all interhuman encounter. The influence of this powerful testimonial is certain to be far-reaching, not only among Catholics or even within

Christendom alone, but also wherever men still respond to the voice that speaks of *agape* and tolerance. The very event of this encyclical serves to enforce a renewed and sympathetic attention to the humane theory of communication that the dialogical viewpoint offers to the world as an alternative—or successor—to the technical-strategic theory of the second revolution.

As the roster of contributors to the present volume attests, the deepest wellspring from which the dialogical philosophy draws inspiration is the body of writings of a number of contemporary thinkers often classified together as "religious existentialists": specifically, Martin Buber, Gabriel Marcel, Paul Tillich, and (by a liberal extension of the adjective "religious") Karl Jaspers. Although there are indeed important differences separating these four philosophers (not least of all in their spiritual commitments), there are also certain common denominators and chords of agreement—of which perhaps the most significant is the theory of communication broadly shared among them all. It is not too much to say that this conceptual framework is the essential premise of each of their respective philosophies, for it maintains no less than that existence (in its authentic form) *is* communication—that life is dialogue.[8] One distinctive service of the religious existentialists is to have repudiated the technological model of communication as an inexhaustible monologue, addressed to everyone and no one in the form of "mass communication." These writers have made us aware that human communication, wherever it is genuine, is always a person-to-person call—never a transcribed message from an anonymous answering service to whomever it may concern. The symbolic paradigm of this interpersonal encounter, formulated independently by both Marcel and Buber, is the relation of *I* and *Thou*. To be sure, neither in content nor in phraseology is this idea entirely original with the present-day philosophers of existence; its intellectual antecedents may be traced at least to the great nineteenth-century advocate of human understanding, Wilhelm Dilthey—and in its deepest intuition the concept is as old as the human family and the social community.[9]

But the contemporary religious existentialists speak directly to our time, for our time, and even (where necessary) against our time. They bespeak the dawning awareness of an age of alienation and anxiety—an awareness cutting across the planes of social science and social action—that the end of human communication is not to *command* but to *commune*; and that knowledge of the highest order (whether of the world, of oneself, or of the other) is to be sought and found not through detachment but through connection, not by objectivity but by intersubjectivity, not in a state of estranged aloofness but in something resembling an act of love.

The theory of communication upon which these thinkers proceed, then, is also a theory of knowledge. It has to do with the manner in which we gain understanding of the world—in particular, the world of other selves. But it has equally to do with the manner in which we gain *self*-understanding; and it may be that this is the crucial point of the theory. It is the insight suggested by Dilthey when he spoke of "the rediscovery of the I in the Thou." More directly, it is the message conveyed by Marcel through his distinctive conception of *intersubjectivity*. "My experience," according to Marcel, "is in a real communication with other experiences. I cannot be cut off from the one without being cut off from the other. . . . The fact is that we can understand ourselves by starting from the other, or from others, and only by starting from them."[10]

It is worth remarking the similarity of Marcel's language to the statement of Karl Jaspers that "we are what we are only through the community of mutually conscious understandings. There can be no man who is a man for himself alone, as a mere individual." No one in our time has given greater emphasis than has Jaspers to the crucial role of communication both in thought and in existence. As every human life begins in communication, he bids us regard it as "the universal condition of man's being. It is so much his comprehensive essence that both what man is and what is for him are in some sense bound up with communication."[11]

But genuine communication, for Jaspers, is not guaranteed by the mere presence of speech in man. Still less does it consist in the unilateral monologue of persuasive rhetoric by which one of us gains power over another. Authentic communication is a mutual struggle for common ground between two distinct and inviolable identities—a "loving contest in which each man surrenders his weapons to the other." And communication, not incidentally, is also the beginning and end of philosophy—of the act of concerned thinking. "The basic philosophical attitude of which I am speaking," wrote Jaspers in *The Way to Wisdom*, "is rooted in distress at the absence of communication, in the drive to authentic communication, and in the possibility of the loving contest which profoundly unites self and self. . . . Communication then is the aim of philosophy, and in communication all its other aims are ultimately rooted: awareness of being, illumination through love, attainment of peace."[12]

This existential approach to human communication is at once empirically descriptive (or "phenomenological") and unabashedly normative. On the descriptive side, it seeks to isolate and scrutinize the concrete facts and acts of existence, just as they are; and it proposes, as a primary fact about us all, that we exist *in the world* and that we exist *with others*. "Human existence," as John Wild has summarized the view, "is transmissive. Each individual, whether he wills it or not, is constantly radiating signs to others, and receiving signs from them. He is bathed in an atmosphere filled with the light of translucent communication."[13] It may well turn out to be the most impressive contribution of present-day existentialists to have compelled a new recognition of this profound but easily neglected aspect of common experience. To quote Wild further:

> Modern thought has ignored the complex phenomena of human communication. The existentialists have rightly called our attention to them as an essential phase of human existence, and have begun the arduous task of describing them as they actually occur, and distinguishing their major types. . . . The existentialist thinkers have laid the first foundations for a sound phenomenology of human communication. . . . The disciplined study of this obscure and complex process, which underlies the whole social life of man, and which has been completely neglected by modern logic, will be a primary concern of the philosophy of the future.[14]

But the existentialist theory of communication is also more, much more, than a phenomenological report of things as they are. On its normative side, this point of view holds that genuine communication between man and man—like wisdom, love, or self-realization—is a *task* to be achieved rather than an omnipresent feature of conventional behavior. This argument is indeed the salient point of that great consensual theme that, more than any other, links the writings of all the major existentialists from Kierkegaard to Sartre: the theme of authenticity *vs.* inauthenticity, of the distinction between the spurious and the genuine in conduct, between the role-playing performer and the "existential subject." In terms of communication, this distinction may be expressed in the contrast between the polar styles of monologue and dialogue—or, to use the graphic image of Heidegger, between the impersonal and well-armored atmosphere of "talk" (as at a cocktail party) and the intimate rapport of true conversation. "I cannot converse with my authoritarian-minded friend," writes Joost A. M. Meerloo. "His looks are too serious and he dictates the subject matter at dinner. The play of conversation must be a collective action; it must be speaking in such a way that the listener is able to receive the words and to know how to deal with them. It must remain a mutual experience, for only so is it real communication."[15]

It is not surprising that, philosophy aside, the field in which these themes of existentialism—and more particularly its underlying theory of communication—have had their deepest and most seminal influence is that of psychotherapy and psychoanalysis. The therapeutic encounter is a uniquely modern paradigm of the human dialogue: a dyad instituted expressly for the purpose of helping and healing through discussion, a relationship of peculiar intimacy and (on one side at least) sustained self-revelation. It does not seem excessive to suggest, following Sullivan and others, that the central problem of psychotherapy is that of interpersonal communication, both within and beyond the consulting room—but most of all within it, in terms of the reciprocating roles and attitudes of the partners in therapy.[16]

This introduction is not the place to review in depth the voluminous literature that has accumulated at an ever accelerating rate since at least the turn of the century on the issue of therapeutic communication. (For details, the reader may refer to the selected bibliography at the conclusion of this volume, as well as to the articles under Part Three, "Person to Person.") It is pertinent, however, to observe that the dominant trend of thought in the field, over more than a generation, has been unmistakably in the direction of closer, more personal, and more open engagement not only of "the one who seeks" but also of "the one who answers." In the professional transaction of the therapeutic hour, there is doubtless still room for objective analysis as well as for subjective free-associating. But the movement of therapy today is toward the higher ground, the *meeting ground*, of unreserved dialogue—in the interest of the cause symbolized by Tillich's concept of "healing as participation" and Hans Trueb's equivalent title, "Healing through Meeting."[17] The most graphic expression of the point, as might be expected, has been voiced by Martin Buber: "On the far side of the subjective, on this side of the objective, on the narrow ridge, where *I* and *Thou* meet, there is the realm of 'between.' "[18]

Beyond psychology, meanwhile, in other notable departments of human relations, the conception of dialogue or genuine conversation as a prototype of all communication has been gaining recognition. It was not by whim that Robert M. Hutchins selected as an appropriate designation for the living heritage of Western culture the simple term "the Great Conversation"—or that Joseph Wood Krutch was led to refer to the same tradition as "the Discourse."[19] Increasingly, in our day historians of culture—and historians of history—have come to regard their enterprise as a kind of conversation, or communion, of the present with the past. For surely the writing of history, when it is more than a mere clerical accounting or tabulation of data, entails a sympathetic involvement with and an imaginative reconstruction of past experience—that is, an act of communication in which the historian addresses his distant scene and cast interrogatively and, if the Muse Clio is with him, receives an answer that is not entirely feedback.

But it is not, of course, only in the accents of history that our culture speaks to us. In its anthropological sense, the concept of *culture* itself has come to represent for many scholars almost a synonym for communication (as in the forthright title, "Culture Is Communication," with which Edward T. Hall begins a salient chapter of his popular classic, *The Silent Language*). In fact the reawakened interest in communication that is prominently on display throughout the social sciences today reflects a new and inspiriting awareness—virtually a shocked recognition—of the critical importance of the *symbol* for an adequate understanding of every social institution, if not of every human act. In academic philosophy, especially in England and the

United States, this recognition has led to an absorption with the problems of language (both scientific and ordinary) that borders on fascination if it does not at times pass understanding. In anthropology and psychology, it has resulted among other things in a deep reassessment of the function and meaning of myth (and dream) as symbolic expression. In sociology and social psychology—even apart from their attention to the dramatistic enactments of art and religion—this emphasis has nourished the contemporary school of thought that defines the study of society as essentially the appraisal of men in symbolic interaction (see Part Six).

One final editors' note: If the deepest significance of the third revolution in the study of communication is its sensitivity to the *ends* of human discourse—in contradistinction to the scientific-engineering focus upon *means* and media—there is still another frame of reference in which that message is immediately clear and present. This area is identified in the present volume as "the politics of communication" and more pertinently as "the democratic dialogue." It was John Dewey who observed that "there is more than a verbal tie between the words common, community, and communication." Just so there is more than an alliterative connection between the terms *democracy* and *dialogue*. At a moment when the oral and written traditions of civility and tolerance that have sustained the improbable adventure of a free society are being strained to the point of rupture—and when for the first time in history it may be said with unqualified assurance that such a rupture can never be repaired—there may be slight additional justification for a volume like this one, which seeks to celebrate those thin symbolic pillars on which we may yet some day build, not perhaps the Great Society of a statesman's dream, but the reasonably good society that one of our contributing authors bids us recognize as the Civilization of the Dialogue.

NOTES

1. See his article, "Cybernetics and Society," pp. 15-23.
2. See, for an account of this influence, the article by Jurgen Ruesch, "Clinical Science and Communication Theory," pp. 51-66.
3. Wiener, *op. cit.*
4. Franklin Fearing, "Toward a Psychological Theory of Human Communication," pp. 179-194.
5. In addition to his article in the present volume, "Some Communication Machines and Their Future," see Norbert Wiener, *Cybernetics: Or Control and Communication in the Animal and the Machine* (rev. ed. Cambridge: The M.I.T. Press, 1961), Chapter IX. *Cf.* Norbert Wiener, "The Brain and the Machine," in Sidney Hook, ed., *Dimensions of Mind* (New York: Collier Books, 1960), pp. 109-112.
6. See his article, "Strategy and Conscience," pp. 79-96.
7. C. Wright Mills, *The Power Elite* (New York: Oxford Galaxy Books, 1959), p. 305.

8. *Cf.* Maurice Friedman, *Martin Buber: The Life of Dialogue* (New York: Harper Torchbooks, 1960), especially Part Three. See also Calvin O. Schrag, *Existence and Freedom* (Evanston: Northwestern University Press, 1961), pp. 40 ff., 200 ff.

9. On Dilthey, see H. P. Rickman, ed., *Wilhelm Dilthey: Pattern and Meaning in History* (New York: Harper Torchbooks, 1962), pp. 37 ff., 67 ff., 113 ff.

10. Gabriel Marcel, *The Mystery of Being*, 2 (Chicago: Gateway Edition, 1960), p. 9.

11. Karl Jaspers, "Truth as Communicability," pp. 518–538.

12. Karl Jaspers, *The Way to Wisdom* (New Haven: Yale University Press, 1960), pp. 26-7.

13. John Wild, *The Challenge of Existentialism* (Bloomington: Indiana University Press, 1955), p. 79.

14. *Ibid.*, pp. 79, 214.

15. See Meerloo's article, "Conversation and Communication," pp. 141–147.

16. *Cf.* Sullivan *The Psychiatric Interview* (New York: Norton, 1954); and Sullivan, *The Interpersonal Theory of Psychiatry* (New York: Norton, 1953.)

17. On Tillich, see the article by Hanna Colm, "Healing as Participation: Tillich's 'Therapeutic Theology,'" pp. 267–284. *Cf.* Hans Trueb, *Heilung aus der Begegnung*, edited by Ernst Michel and Arie Sborowitz (Stuttgart: Ernst Klett Verlag, 1952).

18. Martin Buber, *Between Man and Man* (Boston: Beacon Press, 1955), p. 204.

19. Joseph Wood Krutch, *The Measure of Man* (New York: Grosset Universal Library, 1953), Chapter 10, "The Function of Discourse."

part one

COMMUNICATION AS SCIENCE

A. Models and Mechanisms

B. Dilemmas and Dissents

CYBERNETICS AND SOCIETY*

Norbert Wiener

Since the end of World War II, I have been working on the many ramifications of the theory of messages. Besides the electrical engineering theory of the transmission of messages, there is a larger field which includes not only the study of language but the study of messages as a means of controlling machinery and society, the development of computing machines and other such automata, certain reflections upon psychology and the nervous system, and a tentative new theory of scientific method. This larger theory of messages is a probabilistic theory, an intrinsic part of the movement that owes its origin to Willard Gibbs and which I have described in the introduction.

Until recently, there was no existing word for this complex of ideas, and in order to embrace the whole field by a single term, I felt constrained to invent one. Hence "Cybernetics," which I derived from the Greek word *kubernētēs*, or "steersman," the same Greek word from which we eventually derive our word "governor." Incidentally, I found later that the word had already been used by Ampère with reference to political science, and had been introduced in another context by a Polish scientist, both uses dating from the earlier part of the nineteenth century.

I wrote a more or less technical book entitled *Cybernetics* which was published in 1948. In response to a certain demand for me to make its ideas acceptable to the lay public, I published the first edition of *The Human Use of Human Beings* in 1950. Since then the subject has grown from a few ideas shared by Drs. Claude Shannon, Warren Weaver, and myself, into an established region of research. Therefore, I take this opportunity occasioned by the reprinting of my book to bring it up to date, and to remove certain defects and inconsequentialities in its original structure.

* From *The Human Use of Human Beings*, pp. 15–27, by Norbert Wiener. Copyright 1950, and 1954 by Norbert Wiener. Reprinted by permission of the publisher, Houghton Mifflin Company.

In giving the definition of Cybernetics in the original book, I classed communication and control together. Why did I do this? When I communicate with another person, I impart a message to him, and when he communicates back with me he returns a related message which contains information primarily accessible to him and not to me. When I control the actions of another person, I communicate a message to him, and although this message is in the imperative mood, the technique of communication does not differ from that of a message of fact. Furthermore, if my control is to be effective I must take cognizance of any messages from him which may indicate that the order is understood and has been obeyed.

It is the thesis of this book that society can only be understood through a study of the messages and the communication facilities which belong to it; and that in the future development of these messages and communication facilities, messages between man and machines, between machines and man, and between machine and machine, are destined to play an ever-increasing part.

When I give an order to a machine, the situation is not essentially different from that which arises when I give an order to a person. In other words, as far as my consciousness goes I am aware of the order that has gone out and of the signal of compliance that has come back. To me, personally, the fact that the signal in its intermediate stages has gone through a machine rather than through a person is irrelevant and does not in any case greatly change my relation to the signal. Thus the theory of control in engineering, whether human or animal or mechanical, is a chapter in the theory of messages.

Naturally there are detailed differences in messages and in problems of control, not only between a living organism and a machine, but within each narrower class of beings. It is the purpose of Cybernetics to develop a language and techniques that will enable us indeed to attack the problem of control and communication in general, but also to find the proper repertory of ideas and techniques to classify their particular manifestations under certain concepts.

The commands through which we exercise our control over our environment are a kind of information which we impart to it. Like any form of information, these commands are subject to disorganization in transit. They generally come through in less coherent fashion and certainly not more coherently than they were sent. In control and communication we are always fighting nature's tendency to degrade the organized and to destroy the meaningful; the tendency, as Gibbs has shown us, for entropy to increase.

Much of this book concerns the limits of communication within and among individuals. Man is immersed in a world which he perceives through his sense organs. Information that he receives is co-ordinated through his

brain and nervous system until, after the proper process of storage, colla-
tion, and selection, it emerges through effector organs, generally his
muscles. These in turn act on the external world, and also react on the
central nervous system through receptor organs such as the end organs of
kinaesthesia; and the information received by the kinaesthetic organs is
combined with his already accumulated store of information to influence
future action.

Information is a name for the content of what is exchanged with the
outer world as we adjust to it, and make our adjustment felt upon it. The
process of receiving and of using information is the process of our adjusting
to the contingencies of the outer environment, and of our living effectively
within that environment. The needs and the complexity of modern life
make greater demands on this process of information than ever before, and
our press, our museums, our scientific laboratories, our universities, our
libraries and textbooks, are obliged to meet the needs of this process or fail
in their purpose. To live effectively is to live with adequate information.
Thus, communication and control belong to the essence of man's inner life,
even as they belong to his life in society.

The place of the study of communication in the history of science is
neither trivial, fortuitous, nor new. Even before Newton such problems
were current in physics, especially in the work of Fermat, Huygens, and
Leibnitz, each of whom shared an interest in physics whose focus was not
mechanics but optics, the communication of visual images.

Fermat furthered the study of optics with his principle of minimization
which says that over any sufficiently short part of its course, light follows
the path which it takes the least time to traverse. Huygens developed the
primitive form of what is now known as "Huygens' Principle" by saying
that light spreads from a source by forming around that source something
like a small sphere consisting of secondary sources which in turn propagate
light just as the primary sources do. Leibnitz, in the meantime, saw the
whole world as a collection of beings called "monads" whose activity consisted in the perception of one another on the basis of a pre-established
harmony laid down by God, and it is fairly clear that he thought of this
interaction largely in optical terms. Apart from this perception, the monads
had no "windows," so that in his view all mechanical interaction really
becomes nothing more than a subtle consequence of optical interaction.

A preoccupation with optics and with message, which is apparent in
this part of Leibnitz's philosophy, runs through its whole texture. It plays
a large part in two of his most original ideas: that of the *Characteristica
Universalis,* or universal scientific language, and that of the *Calculus
Ratiocinator,* or calculus of logic. This Calculus Ratiocinator, imperfect
as it was, was the direct ancestor of modern mathematical logic.

Leibnitz, dominated by ideas of communication, is, in more than one way, the intellectual ancestor of the ideas of this book, for he was also interested in machine computation and in automata. My views in this book are very far from being Leibnitzian, but the problems with which I am concerned are most certainly Leibnitzian. Leibnitz's computing machines were only an offshoot of his interest in a computing language, a reasoning calculus which again was, in his mind, merely an extension of his idea of a complete artificial language. Thus, even in his computing machine, Leibnitz's preoccupations were mostly linguistic and communicational.

Toward the middle of the last century, the work of Clerk Maxwell and of his precursor, Faraday, had attracted the attention of physicists once more to optics, the science of light, which was now regarded as a form of electricity that could be reduced to the mechanics of a curious, rigid, but invisible medium known as the ether, which, at the time, was supposed to permeate the atmosphere, interstellar space and all transparent materials. Clerk Maxwell's work on optics consisted in the mathematical development of ideas which had been previously expressed in a cogent but non-mathematical form by Faraday. The study of ether raised certain questions whose answers were obscure, as, for example, that of the motion of matter through the ether. The famous experiment of Michelson and Morley, in the nineties, was undertaken to resolve this problem, and it gave the entirely unexpected answer that there simply was no way to determine the motion of matter through the ether.

The first satisfactory solution to the problems aroused by this experiment was that of Lorentz, who pointed out that if the forces holding matter together were conceived as being themselves electrical or optical in nature, we should expect a negative result from the Michelson-Morley experiment. However, Einstein in 1905 translated these ideas of Lorentz into a form in which the unobservability of absolute motion was rather a postulate of physics than the result of any particular structure of matter. For our purposes, the important thing is that in Einstein's work, light and matter are on an equal basis, as they had been in the writings before Newton; without the Newtonian subordination of everything else to matter and mechanics.

In explaining his views, Einstein makes abundant use of the observer who may be at rest or may be moving. In his theory of relativity it is impossible to introduce the observer without also introducing the idea of message, and without, in fact, returning the emphasis of physics to a quasi-Leibnitzian state, whose tendency is once again optical. Einstein's theory of relativity and Gibbs' statistical mechanics are in sharp contrast, in that Einstein, like Newton, is still talking primarily in terms of an absolutely rigid dynamics not introducing the idea of probability. Gibbs' work, on the other hand, is probabilistic from the very start, yet both directions of work represent a shift in the point of view of physics in which the world as it actually exists is replaced in some sense or other by the world as it happens to be observed, and the old naïve realism of physics gives way to something on which Bishop Berkeley might have smiled with pleasure.

At this point it is appropriate for us to review certain notions pertaining to entropy which have already been presented in the introduction. As we have said, the idea of entropy represents several of the most important departures of Gibbsian mechanics from Newtonian mechanics. In Gibbs' view we have a physical quantity which belongs not to the outside world as such, but to certain sets of possible outside worlds, and therefore to the answer to certain specific questions which we can ask concerning the outside world. Physics now becomes not the discussion of an outside universe which may be regarded as the total answer to all the questions concerning it, but an account of the answers to much more limited questions. In fact, we are now no longer concerned with the study of all possible outgoing and incoming messages which we may send and receive, but with the theory of much more specific outgoing and incoming messages; and it involves a measurement of the no-longer infinite amount of information that they yield us.

Messages are themselves a form of pattern and organization. Indeed, it is possible to treat sets of messages as having an entropy like sets of states of the external world. Just as entropy is a measure of disorganization, the information carried by a set of messages is a measure of organization. In fact, it is possible to interpret the information carried by a message as essentially the negative of its entropy, and the negative logarithm of its probability. That is, the more probable the message, the less information it gives. Clichés, for example, are less illuminating than great poems.

I have already referred to Leibnitz's interest in automata, an interest incidentally shared by his contemporary, Pascal, who made real contributions to the development of what we now know as the desk adding-machine. Leibnitz saw in the concordance of the time given by clocks set at the same time, the model for the pre-established harmony of his monads. For the technique embodied in the automata of his time was that of the clockmaker. Let us consider the activity of the little figures which dance on the top of a music box. They move in accordance with a pattern, but it is a pattern which is set in advance, and in which the past activity of the figures has practically nothing to do with the pattern of their future activity. The probability that they will diverge from this pattern is nil. There is a message, indeed; but it goes from the machinery of the music box to the figures, and stops there. The figures themselves have no trace of communication with the outer world, except this one-way stage of communication with the pre-established mechanism of the music box. They are blind, deaf and dumb, and cannot vary their activity in the least from the conventionalized pattern.

Contrast with them the behavior of man, or indeed of any moderately intelligent animal such as a kitten. I call to the kitten and it looks up. I have sent it a message which it has received by its sensory organs, and which it registers in action. The kitten is hungry and lets out a pitiful wail. This time it is the sender of a message. The kitten bats at a swinging spool. The spool swings to its left, and the kitten catches it with its left paw. This time messages of a very complicated nature are both sent and received within the kitten's own nervous system through certain nerve end-bodies in its joints, muscles, and tendons; and by means of nervous messages sent by these organs, the animal is aware of the actual position and tensions of its tissues. It is only through these organs that anything like a manual skill is possible.

I have contrasted the prearranged behavior of the little figures on the music box on the one hand, and the contingent behavior of human beings and animals on the other. But we must not suppose that the music box is typical of all machine behavior.

The older machines, and in particular the older attempts to produce automata, did in fact function on a closed clockwork basis. But modern automatic machines such as the controlled missile, the proximity fuse, the automatic door opener, the control apparatus for a chemical factory, and the rest of the modern armory of automatic machines which perform military or industrial functions, possess sense organs; that is, receptors for messages coming from the outside. These may be as simple as photoelectric cells which change electrically when a light falls on them, and which can tell light from dark, or as complicated as a television set. They may measure a tension by the change it produces in the conductivity of a wire exposed to it, or they may measure temperature by means of a thermocouple, which is an instrument consisting of two distinct metals in contact with one another through which a current flows when one of the points of contact is heated. Every instrument in the repertory of the scientific-instrument maker is a possible sense organ, and may be made to record its reading remotely through the intervention of appropriate electrical apparatus. Thus the machine which is conditioned by its relation to the external world, and by the things happening in the external world, is with us and has been with us for some time.

The machine which acts on the external world by means of messages is also familiar. The automatic photoelectric door opener is known to every person who has passed through the Pennsylvania Station in New York, and is used in many other buildings as well. When a message consisting of the interception of a beam of light is sent to the apparatus, this message actuates the door, and opens it so that the passenger may go through.

The steps between the actuation of a machine of this type by sense organs and its performance of a task may be as simple as in the case of the electric door; or it may be in fact of any desired degree of complexity within the limits of our engineering techniques. A complex action is one in which the data introduced, which we call the *input*, to obtain an effect on the outer world, which we call the *output*, may involve a large number of combinations. These are combinations, both of the data put in at the moment and of the records taken from the past stored data which we call the *memory*. These are recorded in the machine. The most complicated machines yet made which transform input data into output data are the high-speed electrical computing machines, of which I shall speak later in more detail. The determination of the mode of conduct of these machines is given through a special sort of input, which frequently consists of punched cards or tapes or of magnetized wires, and which determines the way in which the machine is going to act in one operation, as distinct from the way in which it might have acted in another. Because of the frequent use of punched or magnetic tape in the control, the data which are fed in, and which indicate the mode of operation of one of these machines for combining information, are called the *taping*.

I have said that man and the animal have a kinaesthetic sense, by which they keep a record of the position and tensions of their muscles. For any machine subject to a varied external environment to act effectively it is necessary that information concerning the results of its own action be furnished to it as part of the information on which it must continue to act. For example, if we are running an elevator, it is not enough to open the outside door because the orders we have given should make the elevator be at that door at the time we open it. It is important that the release for opening the door be dependent on the fact that the elevator is actually at the door; otherwise something might have detained it, and the passenger might step into the empty shaft. This control of a machine on the basis of its *actual* performance rather than its *expected* performance is known as *feedback*, and involves sensory members which are actuated by motor members and perform the function of *tell-tales* or *monitors*—that is, of elements which indicate a performance. It is the function of these mechanisms to control the mechanical tendency toward disorganization; in other words, to produce a temporary and local reversal of the normal direction of entropy.

I have just mentioned the elevator as an example of feedback. There are other cases where the importance of feedback is even more apparent. For example, a gun-pointer takes information from his instruments of observation, and conveys it to the gun, so that the latter will point in such a direction that the missile will pass through the moving target at a certain time. Now, the gun itself must be used under all conditions of weather. In some of these the grease is warm, and the gun swings easily and rapidly. Under other conditions the grease is frozen or mixed with sand, and the gun is slow to answer the orders given to it. If these orders are reinforced by an extra push given when the gun fails to respond easily to the orders and lags behind them, then the error of the gun-pointer will be decreased. To obtain a performance as uniform as possible, it is customary to put into the gun a control feedback element which reads the lag of the gun behind the position it should have according to the orders given it, and which uses this difference to give the gun an extra push.

It is true that precautions must be taken so that the push is not too hard, for if it is, the gun will swing past its proper position, and will have to be pulled back in a series of oscillations, which may well become wider and wider, and lead to a disastrous instability. If the feedback system is itself controlled—if, in other words, its own entropic tendencies are checked by still other controlling mechanisms—and kept within limits sufficiently stringent, this will not occur, and the existence of the feedback will increase the stability of performance of the gun. In other words, the performance will become less dependent on the frictional load; or what is the same thing, on the drag created by the stiffness of the grease.

Something very similar to this occurs in human action. If I pick up my cigar, I do not will to move any specific muscles. Indeed in many cases, I do not know what those muscles are. What I do is to turn into action a certain feedback mechanism; namely, a reflex in which the amount by which I have yet failed to pick up the cigar is turned into a new and increased order to the lagging muscles, whichever they may be. In this way, a fairly uniform voluntary command will enable the same task to be performed from widely varying initial positions, and irrespective of the decrease of contraction due to fatigue of the muscles. Similarly, when I drive a car, I do not follow out a series of commands dependent simply on a mental image of the road and the task I am doing. If I find the car swerving too much to the right, that causes me to pull it to the left. This depends on the actual performance of the car, and not simply on the road; and it allows me to drive with nearly equal efficiency a light Austin or a heavy truck, without having formed separate habits for the driving of the two. I shall have more to say about this in the chapter in this book on special machines, where we shall discuss the service that can be done to neuropathology by the study of machines with defects in performance similar to those occurring in the human mechanism.

It is my thesis that the physical functioning of the living individual and the operation of some of the newer communication machines are precisely parallel in their analogous attempts to control entropy through feedback. Both of them have sensory receptors as one stage in their cycle of operation: that is, in both of them there exists a special apparatus for collecting information from the outer world at low energy levels, and for making it available in the operation of the individual or of the machine. In both cases these external messages are not taken *neat*, but through the internal transforming powers of the apparatus, whether it be alive or dead. The information is then turned into a new form available for the further stages of performance.

In both the animal and the machine this performance is made to be effective on the outer world. In both of them, their *performed* action on the outer world, and not merely their *intended* action, is reported back to the central regulatory apparatus. This complex of behavior is ignored by the average man, and in particular does not play the role that it should in our habitual analysis of society; for just as individual physical responses may be seen from this point of view, so may the organic responses of society itself. I do not mean that the sociologist is unaware of the existence and complex nature of communications in society, but until recently he has tended to overlook the extent to which they are the cement which binds its fabric together.

We have seen in this chapter the fundamental unity of a complex of ideas which until recently had not been sufficiently associated with one another, namely, the contingent view of physics that Gibbs introduced as a modification of the traditional, Newtonian conventions, the Augustinian attitude toward order and conduct which is demanded by this view, and the theory of the message among men, machines, and in society as a sequence of events in time which, though it itself has a certain contingency, strives to hold back nature's tendency toward disorder by adjusting its parts to various purposive ends.

LANGUAGE AND MEANING*

J. R. Pierce

*T*he two great triumphs of information theory are establishing the channel capacity and, in particular, the number of binary digits required to transmit information from a particular source and showing that a noisy communication channel has an information rate in bits per character or bits per second up to which errorless transmission is possible despite the noise. In each case, the results must be demonstrated for discrete and for continuous sources and channels.

After four chapters of by no means easy preparation, we were finally ready to essay in the previous chapter the problem of the number of binary digits required to transmit the information generated by a truly ergodic discrete source. Were this book a text on information theory, we would proceed to the next logical step, the noisy discrete channel, and then on to the ergodic continuous channel.

At the end of such a logical progress, however, our thoughts would necessarily be drawn back to a consideration of the message sources of the real world, which are only approximately ergodic, and to the estimation of their entropy and the efficient encoding of the messages they produce.

Rather than proceeding further with the strictly mathematical aspects of communication theory at this point, is it not more attractive to pause and consider that chief form of communication, language, in the light of communication theory? And, in doing so, why should we not let our thoughts stray a little in viewing an important part of our world from the small eminence we have attained? Why should we not see whether even the broad problems of language and meaning seem different to us in the light of what we have learned?

In following such a course the reader should heed a word of caution.

So far the main emphasis has been on what we *know*. What we know is the hard core of science. However, scientists find it very difficult to share the things that they know with laymen. To understand the sure and the reasonably sure knowledge of science takes the sort of hard thought which I am afraid was required of the reader in the last few chapters.

There is, however, another and easier though not entirely frivolous side to science. This is a peculiar type of informed ignorance. The scientist's ignorance is rather different from the layman's ignorance, because the background of established fact and theory on which the scientist bases his peculiar brand of ignorance excludes a wide range of nonsense from his speculations. In the higher and hazier reaches of the scientist's ignorance, we have scientifically informed ignorance about the origin of the universe, the ultimate basis of knowledge, and the relation of our present scientific knowledge to politics, free will, and morality. In this particular chapter we will dabble in what I hope to be scientifically informed ignorance about language.

The warning is, of course, that much of what will be put forward here about language is no more than informed ignorance. The warning seems necessary because it is very hard for laymen to tell scientific ignorance from scientific fact. Because the ignorance is necessarily expressed in broader, sketchier, and less qualified terms than is the fact, it is easier to assimilate. Because it deals with grand and unsolved problems, it is more romantic. Generally, it has a wider currency and is held in higher esteem than is scientific fact.

However hazardous such ignorance may be to the layman, it is valuable to the scientist. It is this vision of unattained lands, of unscaled heights, which rescues him from complacency and spurs him beyond mere plodding. But when the scientist is airing his ignorance he usually knows what he is doing, while the unwarned layman apparently often does not and is left scrambling about on cloud mountains without ever having set foot on the continents of knowledge.

With this caution in mind, let us return to what we have already encountered concerning language and proceed thence.

In what follows we will confine ourselves to a discussion of grammatical English. We all know (and especially those who have had the misfortune of listening to a transcription of a seemingly intelligible conversation or technical talk) that much spoken English appears to be agrammatical, as, indeed, much of Gertrude Stein is. So are many conventions and clichés. "Me heap big chief" is perfectly intelligible anywhere in the country, yet it is certainly not grammatical. Purists do not consider the inverted word order which is so characteristic of second-rate poetry as being grammatical.

Thus, a discussion of grammatical English by no means covers the field of spoken and written communication, but it charts a course which we can follow with some sense of order and interest.

We have noted before that, if we are to write what will be accepted as English text, certain constraints must be obeyed. We cannot simply set down any word following any other. A complete grammar of a language would have to express all of these constraints fully. It should allow within its rules the construction of any sequence of English words which will be accepted, at some particular time and according to some particular standard, as grammatical.

The matter of acceptance of constructions as grammatical is a difficult and hazy one. The translators who produced the King James Bible were free to say "fear not," "sin not," and "speak not" as well as "think not," "do not," or "have not," and we frequently repeat the aphorism "want not, waste not." Yet in our everyday speech or writing we would be constrained to say "do not fear," "do not sin," or "do not speak," and we might perhaps say, "If you are not to want, you should not waste." What is grammatical certainly changes with time. Here we can merely notice this and pass on to other matters.

Certainly, a satisfactory grammar must prescribe certain rules which allow the construction of all possible grammatical utterances and of grammatical utterances only. Besides doing this, satisfactory rules of grammar should allow us to analyze a sentence so as to distinguish the features which were determined merely by the rules of grammar from any other features.

If we once had such rules, we would be able to make a new estimate of the entropy of English text, for we could see what part of sentence structure is a mere mechanical following of rules and what part involves choice or uncertainty and hence contributes to entropy. Further, we could transmit English efficiently by transmitting as a message only data concerning the choices exercised in constructing sentences : at the receiver, we could let a grammar machine build grammatical sentences embodying the choices specified by the received message.

Even grammar, of course, is not the whole of language, for a sentence can be very odd even if it is grammatical. We can imagine that, if a machine capable of producing only grammatical sentences made its choices at random, it might perhaps produce such a sentence as "The chartreuse semiquaver skinned the feelings of the manifold." A man presumably makes his choices in some other way if he says, "The blue note flayed the emotions of the multitude." The difference lies in what choices one makes while following grammatical rules, not in the rules themselves. An understanding of grammar would not unlock to us all of the secrets of language, but it would take us a long step forward.

What sort of rules will result in the production of grammatical sentences only and of all grammatical sentences, even when choices are made at random? In Chapter III we saw that English-like sequences of words can be produced by choosing a word at random according to its probability of succeeding a preceding sequence of words some M words long. An example of a second-order word approximation, in which a word is chosen on the basis of its succeeding the previous word, was given.

One can construct higher-order word approximations by using the knowledge of English which is stored in our heads. One can, for instance, obtain a fourth-order word approximation by simply showing a sequence of three connected words to a person and asking him to think up a sentence in which the sequence of words occurs and to add the next word. By going from person to person a long string of words can be constructed, for instance:

1. When morning broke after an orgy of wild abandon he said here head shook vertically aligned in a sequence of words signifying what.

2. It happened one frosty look of trees waving gracefully against the wall.

3. When cooked asparagus has a delicious flavor suggesting apples.

4. The last time I saw him when he lived.

These "sentences" are as sensible as they are because selections of words were not made at random but by thinking beings. The point to be noted is how astonishingly grammatical the sentences are, despite the fact that rules of grammar (and sense) were applied to only four words at a time (the three shown to each person and the one he added). Still, example 4 is perhaps dubiously grammatical.

If Shannon is right and there is in English text a choice of about 1 bit per symbol, then choosing among a group of 4 words could involve about 22 binary choices, or a choice among some 10 million 4-word combinations. In principle, a computer could be made to add words by using such a list of combinations, but the result would not be assuredly grammatical, nor could we be sure that this cumbersome prodecure would produce all possible grammatical sequences of words. There probably are sequences of words which could form a part of a grammatical sentence in one case and could not in another case. If we included such a sequence, we would produce some nongrammatical sentences, and, if we excluded it, we would fail to produce all grammatical sentences.

If we go to combinations of more than four words, we will favor grammar over completeness. If we go to fewer than four words, we will favor completeness over grammar. We can't have both.

The idea of a finite-state machine recurs at this point. Perhaps at each point in a sentence a sentence-producing machine should be in a particular state, which allows it certain choices as to what state it will go to next. Moreover, perhaps such a machine can deal with certain classes or sub-classes of words, such as singular nouns, plural nouns, adjectives, adverbs,

verbs of various tense and number, and so on, so as to produce grammatical structures into which words can be fitted rather than sequences of particular words.

The idea of grammar as a finite-state machine is particularly appealing because a mechanist would assert that man must be a finite-state machine, because he consists of only a finite number of cells, or of atoms if we push the matter further.

Noam Chomsky, a brilliant and highly regarded modern linguist, rejects the finite-state machine as either a possible or a proper model of grammatical structure. Chomsky points out that there are many rules for constructing sequences of characters which cannot be embodied in a finite-state machine. For instance, the rule might be, choose letters at random and write them down until the letter Z shows up, then repeat all the letters since the preceding Z in reverse order, and then go on with a new set of letters, and so on. This process will produce a sequence of letters showing clear evidence of long-range order. Further, there is no limit to the possible length of the sequence between Z's. No finite-state machine can simulate this process and this result.

Chomsky points out that there is no limit to the possible length of grammatical sentences in English and argues that English sentences are organized in such a way that this is sufficient to rule out a finite-state machine as a source of all possible English text. But, can we really regard a sentence miles long as grammatical when we know darned well that no one ever has or will produce such a sentence and that no one could understand it if it existed?

To decide such a question, we must have a standard of being grammatical. While Chomsky seems to refer being or not being grammatical, and some questions of punctuation and meaning as well, to spoken English, I think that his real criterion is: a sentence is grammatical if, in reading or saying it aloud with a natural expression and thoughtfully but ingenuously it is deemed grammatical by a person who speaks it, or perhaps by a person who hears it. Some problems which might plague others may not bother Chomsky because he speaks remarkably well-connected and grammatical English.

Whether or not the rules of grammar can be embodied in a finite-state machine, Chomsky offers persuasive evidence that it is wrong and cumbersome to try to generate a sentence by basing the choice of the next word entirely and solely on words already written down. Rather, Chomsky considers the course of sentence generation to be something of this sort:

We start with one of several general forms the sentence might take; for example, a noun phrase followed by a verb phrase. Chomsky calls such a particular form of sentence a *kernel sentence*. We then invoke rules for expanding each of the parts of the kernel sentence. In the case of a noun phrase we may first describe it as an article plus a noun and finally as "the man." In the case of a verb phrase we may describe it as a verb plus an object, the object as an article plus a noun, and, in choosing particular words, as "hit the ball." Proceeding in this way from the kernel sentence, noun phrase plus verb phrase, we arrive at the sentence, "The man hit the ball." At any stage we could have made other choices. By making other choices at the final stages we might have arrived at "A girl caught a cat."

Here we see that the element of choice is not exercised sequentially along the sentence from beginning to end. Rather, we choose an over-all skeletal plan or scheme for the whole final sentence at the start. That scheme or plan is the kernel sentence. Once the kernel sentence has been chosen, we pass on to parts of the kernel sentence. From each part we proceed to the constituent elements of that part and from the constituent elements to the choice of particular words. At each branch of this treelike structure growing from the kernel sentence, we exercise choice in arriving at the particular final sentence, and, of course, we chose the kernel sentence to start with.

Here I have indicated Chomsky's ideas very incompletely and very sketchily. For instance, in dealing with irregular forms of words Chomsky will first indicate the root word and its particular grammatical form, and then he will apply certain obligatory rules in arriving at the correct English form. Thus, in the branching construction of a sentence, use is made both of optional rules, which allow choice, and of purely mechanical, deterministic obligatory rules, which do not.

To understand this approach further and to judge its merit, one must refer to Chomsky's book,[1] and to the references he gives.

Chomsky must, of course, deal with the problem of ambiguous sentences, such as, "The lady scientist made the robot fast while she ate." The author of this sentence, a learned information theorist, tells me that, allowing for the vernacular, it has at least four different meanings. It is perhaps too complicated to serve as an example for detailed analysis.

We might think that ambiguity arises only when one or more words can assume different meanings in what is essentially the same grammatical structure. This is the case in "he was mad" (either angry or insane) or "the pilot was high" (in the sky or in his cups). Chomsky, however, gives a simple example of a phrase in which the confusion is clearly grammatical. In "the shooting of the hunters," the noun hunters may be either the subject, as in "the growling of lions" or the object, as in "the growing of flowers."

Chomksy points out that different rules of transformation applied to different kernel sentences can lead to the same sequence of grammatical elements. Thus, "the picture was painted by a real artist" and "the picture was painted by a new technique" seem to correspond grammatically word for word, yet the first sentence could have arisen as a transformation of "a real artist painted the picture" while the second could not have arisen as a transformation of a sentence having this form. When the final words as well as the final grammatical elements are the same, the sentence is ambiguous.

Chomsky also faces the problem that the distinction between the provinces of grammar and meaning is not clear. Shall we say that grammar allows adjectives but not adverbs to modify nouns? This allows "colorless green." Or should grammar forbid the association of some adjectives with some nouns, of some nouns with some verbs, and so on? With one choice, certain constructions are grammatical but meaningless; with the other they are ungrammatical.

We see that Chomsky has laid out a plan for a grammar of English which involves at each point in the synthesis of a sentence certain steps which are either obligatory or optional. The processes allowed in this grammar cannot be carried out by a finite-state machine, but they can be carried out by a more general machine called a *Turing machine*, which is a finite-state machine plus an infinitely long tape on which symbols can be written and from which symbols can be read or erased. The relation of Chomsky's grammar to such machines is a proper study for those interested in automata.

We should note, however, that if we arbitrarily impose some bound on the length of a sentence, even if we limit the length to 1,000 or 1 million words, then Chomsky's grammar *does* correspond to a finite-state machine. The imposition of such a limit on sentence length seems very reasonable in a practical way.

Once a general specification or model of a grammar of the sort Chomsky proposes is set up, we may ask under what circumstances and how can an entropy be derived which will measure the choice or uncertainty of a message source that produces text according to the rules of the grammar? This is a question for the mathematically skilled information theorist.

Much more important is the production of a plausible and workable grammar. This might be a *phrase-structure* grammar, as Chomsky proposes, or it might take some other form. Such a grammar might be incomplete in that it failed to produce or analyze some constructions to be found in grammatical English. It seems more important that its operation should correspond to what we know of the production of English by human beings. Further, it should be simple enough to allow the generation and analysis of text by means of an electronic computer. I believe that computers must be used in attacking problems of the structure and statistics of English text.

While a great many people are convinced that Chomsky's phrase-structure approach is a very important aspect of grammar, some feel that his picture of the generation of sentences should be modified or narrowed if it is to be used to describe the actual generation of sentences by human beings. Subjectively, in speaking or listening to a speaker one has a strong impression that sentences are generated largely from beginning to end. One also gets the impression that the person generating a sentence doesn't have a very elaborate pattern in his head at any one time but that he elaborates the pattern as he goes along.

I suspect that studies of the form of grammars and of the statistics of their use as revealed by language will in the not distant future tell us many new things about the nature of language and about the nature of men as well. But, to say something more particular than this, I would have to out-reach present knowledge—mine and others'.

A grammar must specify not only rules for putting different types of words together to make grammatical structures; it must divide the actual words of English into classes on the basis of the places in which they can appear in grammatical structures. Linguists make such a division purely on the basis of grammatical function without invoking any idea of meaning. Thus, all we can expect of a grammar is the generation of grammatical sentences, and this includes the example given earlier: "The chartreuse semiquaver skinned the feelings of the manifold." Certainly the division of words into grammatical categories such as nouns, adjectives, and verbs is not our sole guide concerning the use of words in producing English text.

What does influence the choice among words when the words used in constructing grammatical sentences are chosen, not at random by a machine, but rather by a live human being who, through long training, speaks or writes English according to the rules of the grammar? This question is not to be answered by a vague appeal to the word *meaning*. Our criteria in producing English sentences can be very complicated indeed. Philosophers and psychologists have speculated about and studied the use of words and language for generations, and it is as hard to say anything entirely new about this as it is to say anything entirely true. In particular, what Bishop Berkeley wrote in the eighteenth century concerning the use of language is so sensible that one can scarcely make a reasonable comment without owing him credit.

Let us suppose that a poet of the scanning, rhyming school sets out to write a grammatical poem. Much of his choice will be exercised in selecting words which fit into the chosen rhythmic pattern, which rhyme, and which have alliteration and certain consistent or agreeable sound values. This is particularly notable in Poe's "The Bells," "Ulalume," and "The Raven."

Further, the poet will wish to bring together words which through their sound as well as their sense arouse related emotions or impressions in

the reader or hearer. The different sections of Poe's "The Bells" illustrate
this admirably. There is a marked contrast between:

> How they tinkle, tinkle, tinkle,
> In the icy air of night!
> While the stars that oversprinkle
> All the heavens, seem to twinkle
> In a crystalline delight; . . .

and

> Through the balmy air of night
> How they ring out their delight!
> From the molten-golden notes,
> And all in tune,
> What a liquid ditty floats . . .

Sometimes, the picture may be harmonious, congruous, and moving
without even the trivial literal meaning of this verse of Poe's, as in Blake's
two lines:

> Tyger, Tyger, burning bright
> In the forests of the night . . .

In instances other than poetry, words may be chosen for euphony, but
they are perhaps more often chosen for their associations with and ability
to excite passions such as those listed by Berkeley: fear, love, hatred, admiration, disdain. Particular words or expressions move each of us to such
feelings. In a given culture, certain words and phrases will have a strong
and common effect on the majority of hearers, just as the sights, sounds or
events with which they are associated do. The words of a hymn or psalm
can induce a strong religious emotion; political or racial epithets, a sense of
alarm or contempt, and the words and phrases of dirty jokes, sexual
excitement.

One emotion which Berkeley does not mention is a sense of understanding. By mouthing commonplace and familiar patterns of words in
connection with ill-understood matters, we can associate some of our
emotions of familiarity and insight with our perplexity about history, life,
the nature of knowledge, consciousness, death, and Providence. Perhaps
such philosophy as makes use of common words should be considered in
terms of assertion of a reassurance concerning the importance of man's
feelings rather than in terms of meaning.

One could spend days on end examining examples of motivation in the
choice of words, but we do continually get back to the matter of meaning.
Whatever meaning may be, all else seems lost without it. A Chinese poem,
hymn, deprecation, or joke will have little effect on me unless I understand
Chinese in whatever sense those who know a language understand it.

Though Colin Cherry, a well-known information theorist, appears to object, I think that it is fair to regard meaningful language as a sort of code of communication. It certainly isn't a simple code in which one mechanically substitutes a word for a deed. It's more like those elaborate codes of early cryptography, in which many alternative code words were listed for each common letter or word (in order to suppress frequencies). But in language, the listings may overlap. And one person's code book may have different entries from another's, which is sure to cause confusion.

If we regard language as an imperfect code of communication, we must ultimately refer meaning back to the intent of the user. It is for this reason that I ask, "What do you mean?" even when I have heard your words. Scholars seek the intent of authors long dead, and the Supreme Court seeks to establish the intent of Congress in applying the letter of the law.

Further, if I become convinced that a man is lying, I interpret his words as meaning that he intends to flatter or deceive me. If I find that a sentence has been produced by a computer, I interpret it to mean that the computer is functioning very cleverly.

I don't think that such matters are quibbles; it seems that we are driven to such considerations in connection with meaning if we do regard language as an imperfect code of communication, and as one which is sometimes exploited in devious ways. We are certainly far from any adequate treatment of such problems.

Grammatical sentences do, however, have what might be called a formal meaning, regardless of intent. If we had a satisfactory grammar, a machine should be able to establish the relations between the words of a sentence, indicating subject, verb, object, and what modifying phrases or clauses apply to what other words. The next problem beyond this in seeking such formal meaning in sentences is the problem of associating words with objects, qualities, actions, or relations in the world about us, including the world of man's society and of his organized knowledge.

In the simple communications of everyday life, we don't have much trouble in associating the words that are used with the proper objects, qualities, actions, and relations. No one has trouble with "close the east window" or "Henry is dead," when he hears such a simple sentence in simple, unambiguous surroundings. In a familiar American room, anyone can point out the window; we have closed windows repeatedly, and we know what direction east is. Also, we know Henry (if we don't get Henry Smith mixed up with Henry Jones), and we have seen dead people. If the sentence is misheard or misunderstood, a second try is almost sure to succeed.

Think, however, how puzzling the sentence about the window would be, even in translation, to a shelterless savage. And we can get pretty puzzled ourselves concerning such a question as, is a virus living or dead?

It appears that much of the confusion and puzzlement about the associations of words with things of the world arose through an effort by philosophers from Plato to Locke to give meaning to such ideas as window, cat, or dead by associating them with general ideas or ideal examples. Thus, we are presumed to identify a window by its resemblance to a general idea of a window, to an ideal window, in fact, and a cat by its resemblance to an ideal cat which embodies all the attributes of cattiness. As Berkeley points out, the abstract idea of a (or the ideal) triangle must at once be "neither oblique, rectangle, equilateral, equicrural nor scaleron, but all and none of these at once."

Actually, when a doctor pronounces a man dead he does so on the basis of certain observed *signs* which we would be at a loss to identify in a virus. Further, when a doctor makes a diagnosis, he does not start out by making an over-all comparison of the patient's condition with an ideal picture of a disease. He first looks for such signs as appearance, temperature, pulse, lesions of the skin, inflammation of the throat, and so on, and he also notes such *symptoms* as the patient can describe to him. Particular combinations of signs and symptoms indicate certain diseases, and in differential diagnoses further tests may be used to distinguish among diseases producing similar signs and symptoms.

In a similar manner, a botanist identifies a plant, familiar or unfamiliar, by the presence or absence of certain qualities of size, color, leaf shape and disposition, and so on. Some of these qualities, such as the distinction between the leaves of monocotyledonous and dicotyledonous plants, can be decisive; others, such as size, can be merely indicative. In the end, one is either sure he is right or perhaps willing to believe that he is right; or the plant may be a new species.

Thus, in the workaday worlds of medicine and botany, the ideal disease or plant is conspicuous by its absence as any actual useful criterion. Instead, we have lists of qualities, some decisive and some merely indicative.

The value of this observation has been confirmed strongly in recent work toward enabling machines to carry out tasks of recognition or classification. Early workers, perhaps misled by early philosophers, conceived the idea of matching a letter to an ideal pattern of a letter or the spectrogram of a sound to an ideal spectrogram of the sound. The results were terrible. Audrey, a patternmatching machine with the bulk of a hippo and brains beneath contempt, could recognize digits spoken by one voice or a selected group of voices, but Audrey was sadly fallible. We should, I think, conclude that human recognition works this way in very simple cases only, if at all.

Later and more sophisticated workers in the field of recognition look for significant features. Thus, as a very simple example, rather than having an ideal pattern of a capital Q, one might describe Q as a closed curve without corners or reversals of curvature and with something attached between four and six o'clock.

In 1959, L. D. Harmon built at the Bell Laboratories a simple device weighing a few pounds which almost infallibly recognizes the digits from one to zero written out as words in longhand. Does this gadget match the handwriting against patterns? You bet it doesn't! Instead, it asks such questions as, how many times did the stylus go above or below certain lines? Were I's dotted or T's crossed?

Certainly, no one doubts that words refer to classes of objects, actions, and so on. We are surrounded by and involved with a large number of classes and subclasses of objects and actions which we can usefully associate with words. These include such objects as plants (peas, sunflowers . . .), animals (cats, dogs . . .), machines (autos, radios . . .), buildings (houses, towers . . .), clothing (skirts, socks . . .), and so on. They include such very complicated sequences of actions as dressing and undressing (the absentminded, including myself, repeatedly demonstrate that they can do this unconsciously), tying one's shoes (an act which children have considerable difficulty in learning), eating, driving a car, reading, writing, adding figures, playing golf or tennis (activities involving a host of distinct subsidiary skills), listening to music, making love, and so on and on and on.

It seems to me that what delimits a particular class of objects, qualities, actions, or relations is not some sort of ideal example. Rather, it is a list of qualities. Further, the list of qualities cannot be expected to enable us to divide experience up into a set of logical, sharply delimited, and all-embracing categories. The language of science may approach this in dealing with a narrow range of experience, but the language of everyday life makes arbitrary, overlapping, and less than all-inclusive divisions of experience. Yet, I believe that it is by means of such lists of qualities that we identify doors, windows, cats, dogs, men, monkeys, and other objects of daily life. I feel also that this is the way in which we identify common actions such as running, skipping, jumping, and tying, and such symbols as words, written and spoken, as well.

I think that it is only through such an approach that we can hope to make a machine classify objects and experience in terms of language, or recognize and interpret language in terms of other language or of action. Further, I believe that when a word cannot offer a table of qualities or signs whose elements can be traced back to common and familiar experiences, we have a right to be wary of the word.

If we are to understand language in such a way that we can hope some day to make a machine which will use language successfully, we must have a grammar and we must have a way of relating words to the world about us, but this is, of course, not enough. If we are to regard sentences as meaningful, they must in some way correspond to life as we live it.

Our lives do not present fresh objects and fresh actions each day. They are made up of familiar objects and familiar though complicated sequences of actions presented in different groupings and orders. Sometimes we learn by adding new objects, or actions, or combinations of objects or sequences of actions to our stock, and so we enrich or change our lives. Sometimes we forget objects and actions.

Our particular actions depend on the objects and events about us. We dodge a car (a complicated sequence of actions). When thirsty, we stop at the fountain and drink (another complicated but recurrent sequence). In a packed crowd we may shoulder someone out of the way as we have done before. But our information about the world does not all come from direct observation, and our influence on others is happily not confined to pushing and shoving. We have a powerful tool for such purposes: language and words.

We use words to learn about relations among objects and activities and to remember them, to instruct others or to receive instruction from them, to influence people in one way or another. For the words to be useful, the hearer must understand them in the same sense that the speaker means them, that is, insofar as he associates them with nearly enough the same objects or skills. It's no use, however, to tell a man to read or to add a column of figures if he has never carried out these actions before, so that he doesn't have these skills. It is no use to tell him to shoot the aardvark and not the gnu if he has never seen either.

Further, for the sequences of words to be useful, they must refer to real or possible sequences of events. It's of no use to advise a man to walk from London to New York in the forenoon immediately after having eaten a seven o'clock dinner.

Thus, in some way the meaningfulness of language depends not only on grammatical order and on a workable way of associating words with collections of objects, qualities, and so on; it also depends on the structure of the world around us. Here we encounter a real and an extremely serious difficulty with the idea that we can in some way translate sentences from one language into another and accurately preserve the "meaning."

One obvious difficulty in trying to do this arises from differences in classification. We can refer to either the foot or the lower leg; the Russians have one word for the foot plus the lower leg. Hungarians have twenty fingers (or toes), for the word is the same for either appendage. To most of us today, a dog is a dog, male or female, but men of an earlier era distinguished sharply between a dog and a bitch. Eskimos make, it is said, many distinctions among snow which in our language would call for descriptions, and for us even these descriptions would have little real content of importance or feeling, because in our lives the distinctions have not been important. Thus, the parts of the world which are common and meaningful to those speaking different languages are often divided into somewhat different classes. It may be impossible to write down in different languages words or simple sentences that specify exactly the same range of experience.

There is a graver problem than this, however. The range of experience to which various words refer is not common among all cultures. What is one to do when faced with the problem of translating a novel containing the phrase, "tying one's shoelace," which as we have noted describes a complicated action, into the language of a shoeless people? An elaborate description wouldn't call up the right thing at all. Perhaps some cultural equivalent (?) could be found. And how should one deal with the fact that "he built a house" means personal tree cutting and adzing in a pioneer novel, while it refers to the employment of an architect and a contractor in a contemporary story?

It is possible to make some sort of translation between closely related languages on a word-for-word or at least phrase-for-phrase basis, though this is said to have led from "out of sight, out of mind" to "blind idiot." When the languages and cultures differ in major respects, the translator has to think what the words mean in terms of objects, actions, or emotions and then express this meaning in the other language. It may be, of course, that the culture with which the language is associated has no close equivalents to the objects or actions described in the passage to be translated. Then the translator is really stuck.

How, oh how is the man who sets out to build a translating machine to cope with a problem such as this? He certainly cannot do so without in some way enabling the machine to deal effectively with what we refer to as understanding. In fact, we see understanding at work even in situations which do not involve translation from one language into another. A screen writer who can quite accurately transfer the essentials of a scene involving a dying uncle in Omsk to one involving a dying father in Dubuque will repeatedly make complete nonsense in trying to rephrase a simple technical statement. This is clearly because he understands grief but not science.

Having grappled painfully with the word *meaning*, we are now faced with the word *understanding*. This seems to have two sides. If we understand algebra or calculus, we can use their manipulations to solve problems we haven't encountered before or to supply proofs of theorems we haven't seen proved. In this sense, understanding is manifested by a power to do, to create, not merely to repeat. To some degree, an electronic computer which proves theorems in mathematical logic which it has not encountered before (as computers can be programmed to do) could perhaps be said to understand the subject. But there is an emotional side to understanding, too. When we can prove a theorem in several ways and fit it together with other theorems or facts in various manners, when we can view a field from many aspects and see how it all fits together, we say that we understand the subject deeply. We attain a warm and confident feeling about our ability to cope with it. Of course, at one time or another most of us have felt the warmth without manifesting the ability. And how disillusioned we were at the critical test!

In discussing language from the point of view of information theory, we have drifted along a tide of words, through the imperfectly charted channels of grammar and on into the obscurities of meaning and understanding. This shows us how far ignorance can take one. It would be absurd to assert that information theory, or anything else, has enabled us to solve the problems of linguistics, of meaning, of understanding, of philosophy, of life. At best, we can perhaps say that we are pushing a little beyond the mechanical constraints of language and getting at the amount of choice that language affords. This idea suggests views concerning the use and function of language, but it does not establish them. The reader may share freely my offered ignorance concerning these matters, or he may prefer his own sort of ignorance.

NOTES

1. Noam Chomsky, *Syntactic Structures*, Mouton and Co., 's-Gravenhage, 1957.

THE RELATION OF ENVIRONMENT TO ANTI-ENVIRONMENT

Marshall McLuhan

a recent study by Leo Marx is entitled *The Machine in the Garden: Technology and the Pastoral Ideal in America.*[1] We are beginning to be more aware of the relation of technology and invention to cultural origins and cultural change. That may be why we tend more and more to recover the recognition of the pastoral as a primary social base upon which variations can be played. In James Joyce's *Finnegans Wake*, for example, there is the recurrent theme of the wheel without spokes that bespeaks the primordial technology of the mirror and reflection. The mythical mirror of Narcissus has been taken in various senses. Joyce, in choosing to stress that mirror as a wheel that conveys the human image, regards it as a technological extension of man. Man is fed into the mirror and is fed back as well. That is the cycle of reflection, of cognition and recognition, that initiates an individualizing and fragmenting process of detribalization in society. In a sense all technology is a mirror of man's bodily powers. Joyce does not fail to point out that all extensions of man create new environments. Indeed he calls the extensions of man, whether in weaponry or in clothing, the "extinsions of man." For every extension not only colors and enlarges our lives but also extinguishes a part of us. The extensions as extinctions present a paradox for *Homo faber*. For each extension, in the very act of enlarging the scope of one physical power, serves by "closure" to suppress a variety of human perceptions and actions. For example, in the act of acquiring our mother tongue we extend our experience and powers beyond measure. At the same time we lose the power ever to acquire any other language with the same immediacy and delicacy of sense involvement.

In *Finnegans Wake* Joyce confronted language itself as the most massive of all sensory environments and undertook to reveal its powers of social and psychic structuring, as it were. He saw that language in the electronic age faced "the abnihilization of the etym." That is, electric technology transcends classified, semantic data in favor of the pattern recognition of syntactical structures. It is not by visual or classified means that the child first encounters the complex structures of speech and language.

Eric Havelock's *Preface to Plato* is a study of the stages by which the Greeks shifted from "the tribal encyclopedia" of oral poets to the classified data of the ideas and the categories of literate culture. James Joyce saw that, under conditions of electronic data processing, the Western world was playing that classical tape backwards. The tribal or Finn cycle was waking again, but man would now go into tribal, integrated life wide awake. It was in the pastoral form of poetry that classical poets devoted themselves to studying the causes of change. The pastoral poets from Theocritus to Ovid were concerned with etiology. And in the process of isolating and recognizing the causes of change, these poets used almost exclusively the technique of "plot" and "subplot" or of environment and "anti-environment." If one observes that "King Cadmus sowed the dragon's teeth and they sprang up armed men," he is noting causal relationships. In this case it is the phonetic alphabet that is recognized as the source of military enterprise and imperial structures. The alphabet is cast in the role of the main plot, the environmental fact. The armed men are the subplot, both the content and the consequences of the main plot. While the main plot or environment is pervasive, it is the subplot or content that is most perceived. Knowing this psychological principle, the pastoral and mythic poets used the subplot systematically as a means of developing perception in the direction of the environmental or imperceptible area of technical and social change. The rise of military forces and bureaucracies was the obvious fact. What was too obvious to be perceived was the psychic and social effects of phonetic literacy in creating military structures.

The power of the subplot or anti-environment to intensify human awareness seems to be the principle on which Western artists and poets have reared their art forms. But does not the same principle apply to all the models of perception fostered in the educational establishment? In philosophy and the sciences as well? When any of these areas begins to repeat the environment instead of creating anti-environments, do we not rightly fear that men are being sunk in unawareness? The pastoral poets are erudite and esoteric precisely because they deal with those pervasive and environmental forms that Harold Innis referred to as "the bias of communication."

It is precisely those extensions of ourselves, whether in speech, clothing, script, or radio, that are most imperceptible to us as they initiate new social and sensory environments. Our technologies as corporate and institutional forms of "dress" and "clothing" are a major theme in *Finnegans Wake*. Joyce never tired of ringing the changes on "clothes" and "close" or *closure*. For he regarded the progressive, corporate clothing or "prankings" of man as always effecting "closure" of new psychic and social patterns of perception and association. Like the ancient poets of the pastoral mode, Joyce directed our perceptions to the environmental aspects of technology, whether ancient or modern. His perceptions had revealed to him that today, as in the past, the obvious is usually invisible and that the incidental content of any new environmental process can be counted on to exhaust human attention, blanking out awareness of the radically effective factors. This matter has had much consideration in our time under the heading of the "unconscious." Consciousness itself appears more and more a response to largely unconscious components in what we have long assumed to be the intransigent and "natural" configuration of our "private consciousness." Inevitably, as our electronic technology has extended not simply our bodies but also our nervous systems, we have become more deeply involved in other lives as portions of our own "unconscious." Greater awareness of our actual relation to the corporate life of mankind has bred the utmost doubts concerning the "private" character of our own consciousness. Indeed the quest for identity has become the obsession of the Western world during the past century.

In the world of corporate business not less than in that of personal recognition, the concern has been increasingly with the problems of identity and responsibility. New kinds of self-critical analysis have developed in business as in politics, education, and religion. Under the heading, "What exists is likely to be misallocated," Peter Drucker, in *Managing For Results*, discusses the structure of social situations. "Business enterprise is not a phenomenon of nature but one of society. In a social situation, however, events are not distributed according to the 'normal distribution' of a natural universe (that is, they are not distributed according to the bell-shaped Gaussian curve). In a social situation a very small number of events *at one extreme*—the first 10 per cent to 20 per cent at most—account for 90 per cent of all results; whereas the great majority of events accounts for 10 per cent or so of the results." What Drucker is discussing here is the environment as it presents itself for human attention and action. He confronts the phenomenon of the imperceptibility of the environment as such. Edward T. Hall also tackles this factor in *The Silent Language*. The ground rules, the pervasive structure, the over-all pattern elude perception except insofar as there is an anti-environment or a countersituation constructed to provide a means of direct attention. Paradoxically, the 10% of the typical situation that Drucker designates as the area of effective cause and as the area of opportunity—this small factor—is the environment. The 90% area is the area of problems generated by the active power of the 10% environment. For the environment is an active process pervading and impinging upon all the components of the situation. It is easy to illustrate this point.

Any new technology, any extension or amplification of human faculties given material embodiment, tends to create a new environment. This observation is as true of clothing as of speech or script or wheel. The process is more easily observed in our own time when several new environments have been created. To take only the latest one, television, we find a handful of engineers and technicians in the 10% area, as it were, creating a set of radical changes in the 90% area of daily life. The new television environment is an electric circuit that takes as its content the earlier environment, the photograph and the movie in particular. It is in the interplay between the old and the new environments that there is generated an innumerable series of problems and confusions. They extend all the way from how to allocate the time of children and adults to the problem of pay-television and television in the classroom. The new medium as an environment creates new occupations. As an environment it is imperceptible except in terms of its content. That is, all that is seen or noticed is the old environment, the movie. But even the effects of television on the movie go unnoticed, and the effects of the television environment in altering the entire character of human sensibility and sensory ratios are completely ignored.

The content of any system or organization naturally consists partly of the preceding system or organization and, in that degree, acts as a control on the new environment. It is useful to view all the arts and sciences as acting in the role of anti-environments that enable us to perceive the environment. In a business civilization we have long considered liberal study as providing necessary means of orientation and perception. When the arts and sciences themselves become environments under conditions of electric circuitry, conventional liberal studies, whether in the arts or in the sciences, will no longer serve as an anti-environment. When we live in a museum without walls or have music as a structural part of our sensory environment, new strategies of attention and perception have to be created. When the highest scientific knowledge creates the environment of the atom bomb, new controls for the scientific environment have to be discovered, if only in the interest of survival.

The structural examples of the relation of environment to anti-environment need to be multiplied as a means of understanding the principles of perception and activity involved. The Balinese say, "We have no art—we do everything as well as possible." This remark is not ironic but merely factual. In a preliterate society, art serves as a means of merging the individual and the environment, not as a means of training perception upon the environment. Archaic or primitive art seems to us a magical control built into the environment. To put the artifacts from such a culture into a museum or anti-environment is thus an act of nullification rather than of revelation. Today what is called "pop art" is the use of some object in our own daily environment as if it were anti-environmental. Pop art serves to remind us, however, that we have fashioned for ourselves a world of artifacts and images that are intended not to train perception or awareness but to be merged with them as the primitive man merges with his environment. The world of modern advertising is a magical environment constructed to produce effects for the total economy but not designed to increase human awareness. We have designed schools as anti-environments to develop the perception and judgment of the printed word. There are no means of training provided to develop similar perception and judgment of any of the new environments created by electric circuitry. This omission is not accidental. From the development of phonetic script to the invention of the electric telegraph, human technology tended strongly toward the furtherance of detachment and objectivity, detribalization and individuality. Electric circuitry has had quite the contrary effect. It involves in depth. It merges the individual and the mass environment. To create an anti-environment for such electric technology would seem to require a technological extension of consciousness itself. The awareness and opposition of the individual are in these circumstances as irrelevant as they are futile.

The structural features of environment and anti-environment appear in the age-old clash between professionalism and amateurism, whether in sport or in studies. Professional sport is environmental, and amateur sport is anti-environmental. Professional sport fosters the merging of the individual in the mass and in the patterns of the total environment. Amateur sport seeks rather the development of critical awareness of the individual and, most of all, critical awareness of the ground rules of the society as such. The same contrast exists for studies. The professional tends to specialize and to merge his being uncritically in the mass. The ground rules provided by the mass response of his colleagues serve as a pervasive environment of which he is uncritical and unaware.

The party system of government affords a familiar image of the relations of environment and anti-environment. The government as environment needs the opposition as anti-environment in order to be aware of itself. The role of the opposition seems to parallel that of the arts and sciences in creating perception. As the government environment becomes more cohesively involved in a world of instant information, opposition seems to become increasingly necessary but also intolerable. Opposition begins to assume the rancorous and hostile character of a Dew Line or a Distant Early Warning System. It is important, however, to consider the role of the arts and sciences as Early Warning Systems in the social environment. The models of perception provided in the arts and sciences alike can serve as indispensable means of orientation to future problems well before those problems become troublesome.

The story of Humpty Dumpty suggests a parallel to the 10%–90% distribution of causes and effects. The impact that resulted in his fall brought into play a massive response from the social bureaucracy. But all the king's horses and all the king's men could not put Humpty Dumpty together again. They could not recreate the old environment; they could only create a new one. Our typical response to a disruptintg new technology is to recreate the old environment instead of heeding the opportunities of the new environment. Failure to notice new opportunities is also failure to understand the new powers. We therefore fail to develop the necessary controls or anti-environments for the new environment. This failure leaves us in the role of automata merely.

W. T. Easterbrook, the economic historian, has done extensive exploration of the relations of bureaucracy and enterprise, discovering that, as soon as one element becomes the environment, the other becomes an anti-environment. They seem to bicycle along through history alternating their roles with all the dash and vigor of Tweedledum and Tweedledee. In the eighteenth century, when *realism* became a new method in literature, the external environment was put in the place of anti-environment. The ordinary world was given the role of art object by Daniel Defoe and others. The environment began to be used as a perceptual probe. It became self-conscious. It became what Harold Rosenberg calls an "anxious object" instead of an unperceived and pervasive pattern. Environment used as probe or art object is satirical because it draws attention to itself. The romantic poets extended this technique to external nature transforming nature into an art object. Beginning with Baudelaire and Rimbaud and continuing with Hopkins, Eliot, and Joyce, the poets turned their attention to language as a probe. Long used as an environment, language became an instrument of exploration and research. It became an anti-environment. It became pop art as in jabberwocky.

In the spring issue of the Toronto University *Varsity Graduate* (1965), Glenn Gould discusses the effects of recorded music on performance and composition. One of his main points is that, as recorded music creates a new environment, the audience in effect becomes participant both in performance and in composition. This process is a reversal or chiasmus of form, which occurs in any situation in which an environment is highly intensified or highly defined by technological change. A reversal of characteristics occurs, as in the case of bureaucracy and enterprise. An environment is naturally of low intensity or low definition, which is why it escapes observation. Anything that raises the environment to high intensity, whether it be a storm in nature or violent change resulting from a new technology, turns the environment into an object of attention. When an environment becomes an object of attention it assumes the character of an anti-environment or an art object. When the social environment is stirred up to exceptional intensity by technological change and becomes a focus of much attention, we apply the terms "war" and "revolution." All the components of "war" are present in any environment whatever. The recognition of war depends upon their being stepped up to high definition.

Under electric conditions of instant information-movement, both the concept and the reality of war become manifest in many situations of daily life. We have long been accustomed to war as what goes on between publics or nations. Publics and nations were the creations of print technology. With electric circuitry the publics and nations became the content of the new technology: "The mass audience is not a public as environment but a public as content of a new electric environment." And whereas "the public" as an environment created by print technology consisted of separate individuals with varying points of view, the mass audience consists of the same individuals involved in depth in one another and involved in the creative process of the art or educational situation that is presented to them. Art and education were presented to the *public* as consumer packages for its instruction and edification. The new mass audience is involved immediately in art and education, as participants and cocreators rather than as consumers. Art and education become new forms of experience, new environments, rather than new anti-environments. Pre-electric art and education were anti-environments in the sense that they were the contents of various environments. Under electric conditions the content tends, however, toward becoming environmental itself. This paradox Malraux describes in *The Museum Without Walls* and Glenn Gould finds in recorded music. Music in the concert hall had been an anti-environment. The same music recorded is *music without halls*, as it were.

Another paradoxical aspect of this change is that, when music becomes environmental by electric means, it becomes more and more the concern of the private individual. By the same token and complementary to the same paradox, the pre-electric music of the concert hall (music for a public instead of for a mass audience) was a corporate ritual for the group rather than for the individual. This paradox extends to all electrical technology whatever. The same means that permit, for example, a universal and centralized thermostat do in effect encourage a private thermostat for individual manipulation. The age of the mass audience is thus far more individualistic than was the preceding age of the *public*. It is this paradoxical dynamic that confuses every issue about "conformity," "separatism," and "integration" today. Profoundly contradictory actions and directions prevail in all these situations. This phenomenon is not surprising in an age of circuitry succeeding the age of the wheel. The feedback loop plays all sorts of tricks to confound the single-plane and one-way direction of thought and action as they had been constituted in the pre-electric age of the machine.

As our new electronic technology extends our nervous systems, as it were, it creates an environment of information. Whether it be recognized as radio or television or Telstar or the bomb, the new environment of mankind is scarcely "hardware" or physical so much as it is information and the configurations of codified data. We continue to talk of "explosions" of populations when we mean the disappearance of the spaces between people and the elimination of the time between events. We go on trying to read new events according to old patterns. The very nature of an electronic environment structured by information, turns all previous environments into content or anti-environments. The planet itself becomes the content of television and of Telstar. But this new role for old environments ensures that they will be intensely stirred and activated. They are now moved into sharp definition and stark patterns of crisis. This state characterizes all communities and situations that had previously been casually environmental. All that had been taken for granted, the position of women and children in society or the role of the unconscious in private identity, for example, have now become very much matters of immediate concern. The dimension of immediacy is, naturally enough, the dominant environmental factor in the age of electric circuitry, for circuitry is instant feedback and involvement in depth.

To put the present Negro question in this perspective, we may note that the agrarian South has long tended to regard the Negro as environmental. As such, the Negro is a challenge, a threat, a burden. The very phrase "white supremacy," quite as much as the phrase "white trash," registers this environmental attitude. The environment is the enemy that must be subdued. To the rural man the conquest of nature is an unceasing challenge. It was the southerner who contributed the cowboy to the frontier. The Virginian, the archetypal cowboy as it were, confronted the environment as if it were a hostile, natural force. To man on the frontier, other men were environmental and hostile. By contrast, to the townsman, men appear not as environmental but as content of the urban environment.

The American North tended to confront nature less directly than did the South. For the northerner, man tended to be the content of a technological environment. To the urban man integration seems fairly natural because black and white alike live in a city environment that contains them both. Physically, at least, city men do not think of themselves as environmental. But to the rural man the human figure and the human being are elemental. They create the environment.

There are already many problems parallel to the Negro question, and there are likely to be very many more. For example, French Canada now regards English Canada as a problem. English Canada has been the French Canadian environment, politically and technologically, for more than a century. (During the same time the United States, more than England, has been the social and technological environment of English Canada.) French Canada can no longer *feel* English Canada as an environmental fact; it can only confront the problem of English Canada. English Canada as the environment is the area of unawareness. French Canada as the anti-environment, or as the content of confederation, is very much aware of itself.

French Canada as the content of confederation has had a strongly defined identity that English Canadians have wistfully noted to be lacking among themselves. By treating English Canada as a social and political problem, the French Canadians may be able to create the identity long lacking for English Canadians. In quite the reverse way, as the United States becomes a kind of world environment by means of electric circuitry, it will encounter an ever increasing blur and uncertainty where before had been the definite boundaries of identity and purpose. For strongly marked contours and configurations do not characterize environments so much as their contents.

NOTES

1. New York: Oxford University Press, Inc., 1964.

MEASUREMENT AND COMMUNICATION*

Jerome Rothstein

*L*et us try to define what is meant by information in physics. Observation (measurement, experiment) is the only admissible means for obtaining valid information about the world. Measurement is a more quantitative variety of observation; e.g., we observe that a book is near the right side of the table, but we measure its position and orientation relative to two adjacent table edges. When we make a measurement, we use some kind of procedure and apparatus for choosing a given result or results from the ensemble of possible results. For measurement of length, for example, this ensemble of a priori possible results might consist in (a) too small to measure, (b) an integer multiple of a smallest perceptible interval, (c) too large to measure. It is usually assumed that cases *a* and *c* have been excluded by selection of instruments having a suitable range (on the basis of preliminary observation or prior knowledge). We can define an entropy for this a priori ensemble, expressing how uncertain we are initially about what the outcome of the measurement will be. The measurement is made, but because of experimental errors there is an ensemble of values, any one of which could have given rise to the result observed. An entropy can also be defined for this a posteriori ensemble, expressing how much uncertainty is left unresolved after the measurement. We can define the quantity of physical information obtained from the measurement as the difference between initial (a priori) and final (a posteriori) entropies. We can speak of position entropy, angular entropy, etc., and note that *we now have a quantitative measure of the information yield of an experiment*. A given measuring procedure can, a priori, provide a set of alternatives. Interaction between the object of interest and the measuring apparatus selects a subset thereof. When the results become known to the observer, the measurement has been completed.

* Reprinted from Jerome Rothstein, *Communication, Organization, and Science*, Falcon's Wing Press, 1958.

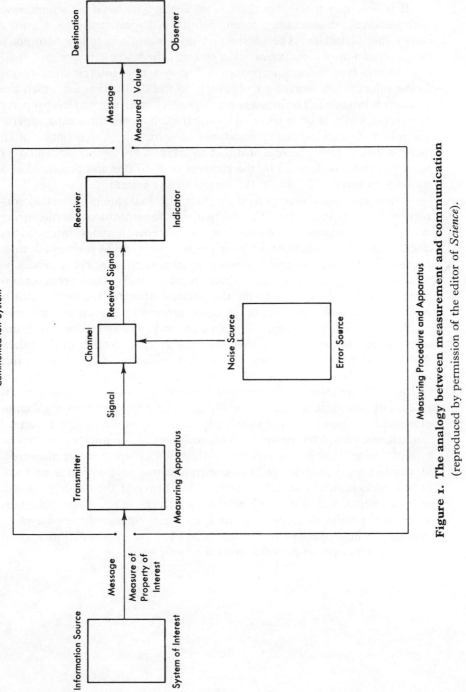

Figure 1. The analogy between measurement and communication
(reproduced by permission of the editor of *Science*).

It is now easy to see that there is an analogy between communication and measurement amounting to an identity in logical structure. Figure 1 shows this pictorially. The blocks and upper captions follow Shannon's characterization of a communication system; the lower captions give analogous terms for a measuring apparatus. The system of interest corresponds to the information source; the observer, to the destination for which the message is intended. The message corresponds to a measure of the property of interest, which is often encoded by the transmitter or measuring apparatus into information-bearing variations of some physical quantity often quite different from the one of direct interest. This signal, corrupted by noise or errors, is decoded by the receiver or indicator and presented as a message or measured value at the output of the system.

Calibration in measurement is, in part, the analogue of distortion correction in communication. In practice a communication or measuring system often consists of a number of sub-systems in series, intermediate ones serving as destinations for their predecessors and as sources for their successors. The sensory and nervous apparatus of the observer can best be considered the ultimate system, which, together with instruments, operations, and apparatus, constitute the means whereby the mind of the scientist communicates with, or acquires information about, the universe.

An immediate consequence of the common logical structure of communication and measurement is that progress in either will help the other. A "dictionary" can be written to permit translation of results from one field to the other. The statistical theory of errors, first attacked by Gauss, is basically the same as the statistical theory of noise. This, in turn, is essentially the same as the theory of the Brownian motion of a galvanometer mirror hung on an exceedingly fine suspension; the mechanical fluctuations caused by molecular bombardment of the mirror constitute a type of "noise" limiting the accuracy with which a current can be measured. Optimal experimental design has a communication analogy in the problem of best utilization of channel capacity. The theory of the resolving power of instruments, and that of the minimum detectable signal are analogous, as are the theories of accuracy in measurement and signal-to-noise ratio. Any measuring apparatus is characterized by a "noise level" and a band width, just as a communication system is, and so on.

CLINICAL SCIENCE
AND COMMUNICATION THEORY*

Jurgen Ruesch

Our forefathers simply communicated with each other and took the process for granted, but as children of our age we no longer are content to exercise our faculties and to develop our skills, we have to know how things work. The engineers who developed radio, television, photography, motion pictures, recording devices and computers laid the foundations for what today has become the communications industry. But this technological ingenuity was not the only element that contributed to progress. The owners and directors of the infant industry soon became aware that in order to utilize effectively communication machinery for political or commercial purposes a knowledge of people is indispensable. As a result, advertisers and social scientists, whose interests range from language to learning theory and from public opinion polls to group behavior, began to study audience and consumer responses and helped to put the communications industry into its present prominent position.

Today communication is studied and utilized by innumerable disciplines (table I). The more academic approaches range from basic to applied science and include physical, social and biological aspects of human behavior. The practical approaches range from advertising and brainwashing to psychotherapy and education. Broadly speaking, communication experts fall into three groups: the mathematically oriented engineers build the communication machines; the empirically oriented biological and social scientists study specialized aspects of human behavior and the person-oriented operators and clinicians experiment with influencing people in a given direction. While these groups share in common their interest in communicative behavior, they also are divergent in that each has developed its own concepts, vocabulary and procedures.

* Reprinted from *Disorders of Communication*, Vol. XLII, Research Publications A.R.N.M.D., pp. 247–261.

Table I.* The Varieties of Approaches to Communication

Discipline or field	Subject and area of specialization	Review of subject and summary of literature
The technological disciplines		
Cybernetics	Steersmanship and feed back in biological and social systems	Wiener (88, 89)
Mathematical theory of communication	Information theory	Shannon and Weaver (74); Brillouin (10)
Engineering	Computers, automata and control devices	Nagel (50); Latil (39)
History and scientific philosophy		
History of language	Development of language over the centuries	Pei (56); Revesz (60); Hoselitz (33)
History of instruments of communication	Development of communication technology	Cherry (12); Foerster *et al.* (17)
Epistemology of various fields	Assumptions made in scientific procedures	International Encyclopedia of Unified Science (34); Frank (18); Ruesch and Bateson (66); Horowitz (32)
Unified theory	Communication as general systems theory	Ashby (3); Bertalanffy (8); Ruesch (62)
The psychophysiological disciplines		
Neuropsychology	Correlation of organs and functions of communication. Model construction	Miller *et al.* (47); Walter (86); MacKay (43); George (20)
Psychophysiology	Sensory processes and performance	Stevens (79); Paillard (55); Teuber (83)
Psychopharmacology	Influence on communication through drugs	Kalinowsky and Hoch (35)
The psychological disciplines		
General psychology	Perception, transmission, decision-making, memory	Broadbent (11); Churchman (13); Kilpatrick (37); G. A. Miller (46)

* Table XVII.I in original source.

Table I—*Continued*

Discipline or field	Subject and area of specialization	Review of subject and summary of literature
Clinical psychology	Verbal behavior; complex patterns of behavior	Skinner (75); Garner (19)
Ethology	Communications of animals	J. P. Scott (72)
The social disciplines		
Social psychology	Communication in small groups	Hartley and Hartley (28)
Sociology	Mass communication	Klapper (38); Riley and Riley (61)
The language disciplines		
Speech and linguistics	Phonetics, language codes	Osgood and Sebeok (52); Sebeok (73)
Significs	The meaning of signs and signals	Hayakawa (29); Morris (49)
Cultural anthropology	Symbolic systems, verbal and nonverbal	Hall (25); Whorf (87)
The commercial disciplines		
Propaganda and advertising	Influencing people to act	Packard (54)
Political thought reform	Influencing people to believe	Lifton (42); Hinkle and Wolff (31)
Business organization	Improvement of efficiency of communication	Redfield (59); Haney (26)
The clinical disciplines		
Child and family psychiatry	Communicative difficulties inside family	Spitz (77); Ackerman (2); Spiegel (76)
Adult psychiatry	Disturbed communication of patient	Bateson *et al.* (6); Ruesch (63)
Psychoanalysis and psychotherapy	Understanding of communications of the patient	Feldman (15); Meerloo (44); Ruesch 64
Mental hygiene	Community organization	Leighton (41)
Neurology and neurosurgery	Pathology or organs of communication	Ashby (5); Pribram 57; Walter (85)

Table I—*Continued*

Discipline or field	*Subject and area of specialization*	*Review of subject and summary of literature*
The fine arts Painting & sculpture Dance Theatre Music	Expression of inner events through shape, color, movement, texture and sound, resulting in the creation of nonverbal signals and signs to which others respond	Gombrich (21); Sachs (69); Stanislavsky (78); Ostwald (53); Meyer (45)
The useful arts Architecture Decorative arts Cabinetmaking Handcrafts Interior decoration Fashion design	Shaping of the material environment embodies the assumptions and conventions of a particular period. Architectural structures and objects become symbols used in communicative exchange of people with each other and with posterity	Ruesch and Kees (67); G. Scott (71); Laver 40; Train (84); Gorsline (22)
The social games Law Sports Politics Special social 　occasions	Stylized message exchange by participants who assume certain roles and abide by well-established rules. Behavior then can be analyzed as if it were a game or a play	Neiman and Hughes (51); Rapoport (58); Sarbin (70); Szasz (82)

THE EPISTEMOLOGICAL POSITIONS OF COMMUNICATION EXPERTS

The physical scientist seeks truth; for this purpose he relies upon careful experimental design, well-stated hypotheses, control of as many variables as possible and precise measurement. He may use expensive equipment and his procedures may require a lot of personnel. At the expense of much effort and money he learns a great deal about a very few aspects of nature; and his knowledge usually stands the test of time—at least for a few years. The engineer in turn utilizes the data accumulated by the basic scientist in order to build machines which extend man's power to perceive, to express, to remember and to make decisions.

The empiricist—be he biologist, social scientist, linguist, or language expert—studies living things and naturally existing conditions. He neither constructs from materials nor influences people directly. Instead he gathers data about organisms, societies or social functions in order to derive knowledge which will enable him to predict behavior. Although essentially an observer, he may on occasion be experimentally inclined or rely upon statistical methods to validate his data.

The clinician, finally, is a task-oriented person who seeks to reach a previously defined goal. In this sense he is not an observer but an operator, and for him the proof of the pudding is in the eating. He considers his knowledge and procedures valid if they lead to the desired objective. In research, therefore, the clinician tends to abstain from elaborate control measures (24), time-consuming data processing and complicated theories, inasmuch as measurements and evaluations have to remain simple if they are to be used in action. Unfortunately the clinician's success and his subsequent empirical generalizations often are situation-bound and may not stand up in other places and at other times (65). In spite of the fact that clinical knowledge is not as easily transferable as other knowledge, it is the basis upon which the majority of life and death decisions about health are made.

Although physicist, engineer, naturalist, sociologist and clinician possess widely divergent epistemological positions, they influence one another to a considerable extent. The question naturally arises as to what they can accept from one another and what they have to reject. The clinician, for example, who deals with the practical aspects of communication, may raise the question : "What, if any, of the theoretical and technological advances made by mathematicians, engineers or social scientists can I use in my daily work?" Let us attempt to answer this question, beginning with the field of cybernetics—the science of control and communication in the animal and the machine.

THE INFLUENCE OF CYBERNETICS UPON CLINICAL WORK

The concept of steersmanship, which is mainly based on the notion of feedback, has had an enormous impact upon clinical work (4). As Kety (36) remarks : ". . . we do not always get closer to the truth as we slice and homogenize and isolate—that which we gain in precision and in the rigorous control of variables we sometimes lose in relevance to normal function, and . . . in the case of certain diseases or problems, the fundamental process may often be lost in the cutting." Well, the notion of feedback avoids these shortcomings and leaves organized patterns intact. The concept merely indicates that the output of a complex organism or machine may produce certain results which in turn influence the information held at the source. The combination of the notions of feedback (88) and probability (9) has provided the scientist with a tool to deal with complex patterns ; and this approach is indeed fundamental to almost all biological and social processes. As a result, biologists, psychologists, psychiatrists and sociologists have changed their views of causation; simple systems have been replaced by more complex ones; and, above all, the interaction of individuals and groups has been more satisfactorily conceptualized.

The principal reason that still prevents clinicians from wholeheartedly adopting communication theory in their daily work is tied to one of the fundamental assumptions of science: the anonymity of the entity under study (18). The scientist deals with anonymous entities whose externally observable characteristics are shared with other entities of the same class. Thus within each class all units are presumed to be the same. The specific relation of one particle to another, the specialized action patterns they might have and the past history of each particle the scientist can conveniently neglect. Science thus works only if not too much is known about the differences between particles. The clinician, in turn, deals with identified people or groups and with specifically labeled social situations, and he uses words which have multiple meanings; for him, no two people, situations, or verbal expressions are completely alike. If they were, his services would soon become obsolete.

Communication between persons and between automata also differs significantly with regard to impact of messages and attribution of meaning. In the case of robots and automata, messages may have impact but no meaning; and they have impact only if receiver is matched to sender, the code is consistent and the machine has been properly programmed (16). In the human situation, messages not only have impact, but this impact may change the referential property of the symbols, if not the code itself. In social situations both the sender's and the receiver's interpretations of symbols are forever undergoing modification over both the short and the longer term. Because externally similar people internally are not attributing the same meaning to symbols and are changing the meaning in somewhat unpredictable directions, the laws of thermodynamics and concepts such as entropy, which are based upon the assumption of similarity and stability of particles, cannot be applied to social communication.

The same goes for information theory, which is concerned with the quantitative, statistical and mathematical evaluation of coding and transmitting information. Clinicians who work with people and who use the communication process in its original form—that is, in face-to-face encounters—cannot apply information theory to the human situation directly. In face-to-face relations noise, for example, cannot be identified because we cannot separate the intentional signals that emanate from a person from the accidental signals that arise in the surroundings. In social situations we deal with multiple means of transmission; the channels are not discrete and their capacity is unknown. Also we cannot determine the set of possible messages in any given situation; the amount of information transmitted hence is unknown and information theory is hardly applicable.

But the very fact that communication theory does not deal with identified people or the idiosyncratic interpretation of words makes it admirably suitable as a general systems theory (23). In order to transcend the different scientific universes, biologists, physiologists and psychologists have followed the lead of the cyberneticists and have attempted to view people and animals as being made up of systems of reception, transmission, evaluation and storage. In modern vernacular, perception has become input; action is viewed as output and judgment is transformed into decision-making. The modern models of human functioning no longer are based on pressure analogies (psychohydraulics), or on energy analogies (psychothermodynamics), but more and more they tend to be based upon machine analogies (psycho-electronics).

SOCIAL AND BIOLOGICAL CONTRIBUTIONS TO COMMUNICATION

There are a number of older and well-established disciplines which for centuries in one way or another have been concerned with symbolic systems and actions of people. The humanists and the social scientists believe that one person is linked to another by a number of complex processes subsumed under the word "social," which in effect denotes relatedness based on an exchange of messages. These older disciplines (33) are concerned with concepts such as language, symbols, values, roles and rules. While the mathematicians and engineers emphasize the technical aspects of sending, receiving and evaluating, the social scientists are concerned with the persons who send and interpret messages. And indeed notions such as rules, roles and status (51, 70) are helpful in understanding and describing what is going on in the family, the school, the hospital or the corporation. Although these concepts do not lend themselves for direct measurement, they are testable by rating methods, and can be used independently of the abstract societal theories of the sociologists; therefore they appeal to a number of clinicians. That the social scientists have succeeded in influencing the clinicians can be seen in the latest trends of medicine which are concerned with topics such as human ecology and social psychiatry (90).

But the humanities and the social sciences were not the only representatives outside of engineering that dealt with communication. Medicine has been concerned with the problems of aphasia, apraxia, agnosia, peripheral and central lesions of the sensory system, paralysis, involuntary movements, thinking and memory disorders, disturbances of consciousness, emotional expression and judgment for hundreds of years. The older attempts of neuropsychology were essentially directed at establishing direct correlations between structure and function or between pathology and dysfunction. But these simple correlations of organ deficit and communicative disturbance apply only in extreme cases and we lack at the present time conceptual bridges that will tie neuropathology to the complex deviations in overall communicative behavior. Cyberneticists have offered the suggestion that if model construction replaces verbal speculations, one might find answers to this complex problem (57). Reenactment or simulation of natural phenomena is the path on which advances are currently made. "The program for a computer that reenacts a process is becoming just as acceptable a theory of that process as the equation describing it" (47). Although model construction has greatly enhanced our knowledge of central nervous system functioning, the understanding of abnormal processes still leaves much to be desired. Disease or trauma affecting the nervous system interferes with a variety of feedback within the organism and sometimes with the social communication of the person as a whole (63).

Although neuropsychologists (14, 81) have made great strides in elucidating the detailed problems of human input, output, decision-making and storage of information, it was the ethologists and animal biologists who contributed most significantly to communication at an organismic level. They taught us that the study of temporal and spatial configurations of communicative behavior may yield such notions as imprinting (30), that experiments with animal substitutes such as the monkey's wire mother may lead to notions of infant deprivation (27) and that operant conditioning techniques in which the responses of one individual are replaced by those of a machine may yield information on learning (80). These experiments as well as the empirical observation of communication between animals (72) have underlined the fact that formal determinants of communication are as relevant as, if not more relevant than, content (48).

A UNITARY APPROACH TO COMMUNICATION

After many years of cross-fertilization of disciplines and interdisciplinary study of communication, we now have reached the point where we need a more unitary approach to communication. What then are the difficulties? High-level cybernetic theories enhance the clinician's personal understanding of communication, but application of mathematical and electronic concepts to social data is limited. Engineers and mathematicians show little if any concern with the source and destination of messages—that is, with the persons who send and interpret messages. The social scientists, in turn, tend to neglect the technical aspects of communication in the organism and in the machine. The result is that the high-level theories stem from physical scientists and the empirical notions from the clinical disciplines. The question then arises whether or not it is possible to combine the abstractions of the mathematicians with the empirical notions of biologists and sociologists. In order to answer this question, let us consider for a moment a discrete statement which originates in a speaker and finds its way to a listener, and let us analyze what is needed to study these events.

The *"who"* and the *"to whom"* of any communication must be described in sociological terms. People are known by name and address, by age and sex and by their role, status and function in a group. In analyzing a communication network the task is to identify out of a pool of thousands of people the one person who actually sent or received a given message. However, the answer to the question of who sent the message is found not only in the social characteristics of the sender but also in the message itself. The way a message is coded, phrased and timed frequently identifies the sender—a fact which is made use of in detective and intelligence work. These additional metacommunicative aspects of a message (66) which help to decipher the principal message can be considered intentional or unintentional, conscious or unconscious instructions of the sender to the receiver. Thus we come to recognize that the social characteristics of a person are nothing else but signs of communicative behavior that inevitably enter the message and influence its interpretation. For example, a signal given by a uniformed traffic officer is a command; the same signal given by a 10-year-old child may be entirely ignored. Social role, status and position of the speaker or the receiver thus may annotate, amplify, condense or alter the fate of a message in certain predictable ways.

The *"what"* of a communication indicates the referential property of the symbols used. Signs and symbols presuppose the existence of a dictionary. Each word in the dictionary is defined by other words in the same dictionary. *Webster's International Dictionary*, for example, constitutes a closed system which purportedly is able to represent whatever exists in the world. But unfortunately the "what" refers not only to Webster but to a multitude of other informal and often unprinted dictionaries. Mothers and babies, husbands and wives and sports teams develop private languages. A message thus can be interpreted in many ways, depending upon the dictionary used. The broad conventions that regulate this process of attribution is the domain of language experts and cultural anthropologists; the narrower conventions are studied by group psychologists; and in the case of two- or three-person systems the psychiatrist and the psychoanalyst are the professionals who decipher the idiosyncratic and particularistic languages of patients and people. Recently, some new approaches to content analysis have been suggested (7).

The *"how"* of a message is the domain of the code specialist and the engineer. In the human field the engineer is the linguist, the speech specialist and the neurophysiologist. His task is to discover how nervous impulses or sounds are made and received and how they are recorded. The linguist also is joined by the gesture expert and all those artists and craftsmen who specialize in nonverbal codes (67). Much is known in this area, but the knowledge has not been systematized and no theoretical model exists which would facilitate analysis.

The "*where*" and the "*when*" of a message deal with the wider network in which a communication takes place. Again the social scientists provide us with concepts to analyze the transaction. Identification of the context or the occasion leads to a label of the situation which enables the bystander or the participant to consult the rule book. This in brief states: who can talk to whom, about what, in what manner, for how long and what happens in case the rules are violated (68).

An initial statement, whether it emanates from a person or from a group, may be followed by a statement of another person. A statement becomes a message only when it is followed by a *reply*, or if the information transmitted is acted upon. After repeated exchange back and forth, the identity of the participants, the instructions for interpretation, the rules of proceeding and the referential properties of the symbols are clarified. Also, the exchange may change the intentions or anticipations of the participants to the extent that they may no longer remember what they had in mind in the first place.

The final consideration in analyzing a message exchange is the study of the *effect* it has had upon action. Evaluation of effects is as a rule undertaken by advertisers, propaganda agents, traffic experts and clinicians. The procedure consists of correlating the information contained in a message with subsequent action. If the interval between message and action is short, a relationship may be established easily. If the interval is long, feedback is difficult to evaluate so that the results remain inconclusive. The task then is left to the historian.

In developing an over-all theory of communication the greatest need at present revolves around inclusion of the communicating persons. Secondly, we must develop ways of coping with content and the ever-changing meaning of symbols. Only in third place should we bother with the technology of communication—that is, the building of machines that amplify the human functions of reception, transmission, storage and decision-making. Although it is fascinating to extend message transmission in space and time and to augment the capacity of individual brains, the advances made in the technology of communication have not diminished the incidence of disturbances of communication; instead they probably have increased it.

DISTURBANCES OF COMMUNICATION

Until recently, communication pathology has been almost entirely the domain of psychiatry. Because of the magnitude of the problem and the slowness of progress, psychiatry over the last 150 years has frequently been the subject of rescue operations (1). Neuropathology, neurophysiology, neurochemistry, neurology, experimental and clinical psychology, psychoanalysis and now sociology and cybernetics have been supposed to elevate clinical psychiatry to lofty theoretical heights; thereafter psychiatry was expected to produce spectacular practical results. What usually happened was that at the time the new ideas and theories emerged, their applicability appeared to be unlimited. After a few decades the initial optimism receded, the hypotheses were tested, the work became more technical, limitations were recognized and reasoning by analogy diminished.

Today we know for sure that the formulations of neuropathology, psychopathology, psychoanalysis, clinical psychology, endocrinology and biochemistry have not solved the problem of mental disease. They have not prevented disturbances of communicative behavior from arising, nor have they been successful in outlining cures. Whether modern social trends in psychiatry will do more than simply introduce democratic practices in the autocratic hospital environment and shift the emphasis from family and institutional centered care to community and group care remains to be seen. In all likelihood, sociology and cybernetics will join—naturally with honorable mention—the other disciplines in the rogues' gallery of past fashion trends; and their epitaph might read: "Ingenious theories, but they did not improve health nor did they save life."

In spite of this somewhat gloomy prediction I believe that cybernetics and sociology have had an extremely salutary effect upon the clinician. They have given him, first and above all, a basic science of communicative behavior. And the thesis that some of the solutions to the problems of mental disease and disruptive social behavior lie in the study of man's communicative behavior and its disturbances is more than just a fancy idea. In thousands of offices and hospitals all around the world doctors are busy to assess disturbed behavior and to influence the patients in the desired direction. This may take the form of psychotherapy, group therapy, pharmacotherapy, electroshock therapy, or psychosurgery; but regardless of its nature, it is always directed at influencing and rectifying the communicative behavior of the patient. From these empirical facts the clinician eventually has to create the theoretical foundations upon which he can understand disturbed behavior and successfully influence it.

Disturbed communication is not confined to individuals. In politics erroneous assessment of instructions and misunderstandings of content can lead to major crises, and among the military an unrestrained paranoid character or a paranoid group which suffers from disturbed communication might exterminate us all. Abnormal behavior is, in effect, always disturbed communicative behavior, regardless of whether it occurs at the molecular, organ, organismic or societal level of organization. It is indeed sensible and realistic to formulate disturbed behavior at all levels of organization in terms of communication; but one also should think of remedial measures in terms of control devices that steer information and, subsequently, action. The difficulties we are faced with are related to the fact that although we have theories of communication, we do not possess theories of disturbed communication (63). There is to my knowledge no theory that explains machine failure except in terms of defective component parts or functions. Most medical theories proceed in the same way. But when we consider life and behavior we must postulate that the whole is more than the sum of the parts and at this point we seem to fail theoretically.

While the communication engineers, the experts of mass media, the sociologists, the physiologists and the biologists have developed theories to fit their approaches, the clinicians have been laggard in this task. We have to face the fact that we must fit our theories to our approaches and abandon the absurd practice of talking about one thing and doing another. The psychoanalyst and the psychotherapist talk about postulated intrapsychic processes when they actually engage in a communicative exchange with the patient. The socially oriented psychiatrists talk about institutions, communities and other equally abstract entities when in effect they are trying to get the patient to engage in action or to communicate with other persons around him. The neurologists and neurosurgeons talk about tracts, nuclei and other anatomical subdivisions of the brain when in effect they are trying to influence the perception, expression and decision-making of the patient.

In part, the lack of proper conceptualizations for operators and clinicians is due to the nature of their work. Cumbersome methods that take hours or days to evaluate are not suitable because situations change and knowledge gained must be acted upon. Thus what the social scientist has to offer frequently is too cumbersome and time-consuming, and what the engineer has to offer deals mostly with construction rather than with repair. What we need is a clinical methodology that delivers us practical ways of recording, condensing and analyzing actual communications and a theoretical science concerned with disturbances of communication. If we believe that deviant behavior is controlled by erroneous information, then we must see to it that correct information is always available wherever action occurs.

NOTES

1. Ackerknecht, E. H.: *A Short History of Psychiatry.* Hafner Publishing Co., New York, 1959.

2. Ackerman, N. W.: *The Psychodynamics of Family Life.* 379 pp. Basic Books, Inc., New York, 1958.

3. Ashby, W. R.: *An Introduction to Cybernetics.* John Wiley & Sons, Inc., New York, 1956.

4. Ashby, W. R.: "Cybernetics." In *Recent Progress in Psychiatry*, Vol. 3, pp. 94–117. Headley Brothers, London, 1958.

5. Ashby, W. R.: *Design for a Brain*, Ed. 2. John Wiley & Sons, Inc., New York, 1960.

6. Bateson, G., Jackson, D. D., Haley, J., and Weakland, J.: "Toward a theory of schizophrenia." *Behavioral Sci.*, *1:* 251–264, 1956.

7. Berelson, B.: *Content Analysis in Communications Research*. Free Press of Glencoe, New York, 1952.

8. Bertalanffy, L. von.: "The theory of open systems in physics and biology." *Science, 111:* 23–29, 1950.

9. Born, M.: *Natural Philosophy of Cause and Chance*. Oxford University Press, London, 1948.

10. Brillouin, L.: *Science and Information Theory*, Ed. 2. Academic Press, Inc., New York, 1962.

11. Broadbent, D. E.: *Perception and Communication*. Pergamon Press, London, 1958.

12. Cherry, C.: *On Human Communication*. John Wiley & Sons, Inc., New York, 1957.

13. Churchman, C. W.: *Prediction and Optimal Decision*. Prentice Hall, Inc., Englewood Cliffs, N. J., 1961.

14. Conference on Brain and Behavior: Brain and Behavior, Proceedings of the First Conference, 1961, edited by M. A. B. Brazier, Vol. 1. American Institute of Biological Science, Washington, 1961.

15. Feldman, S. S.: *Mannerisms of Speech and Gesture in Everyday Life*. International Universities Press, New York, 1959.

16. Foerster, H. von: "Communication amongst automata." *Am. J. Psychiat., 118:* 865–871, 1962.

17. Foerster, H. von, Mead, M., and Teuber, H.-L.: "A note by the editors." In *Cybernetics, Transactions of 8th Conference.* pp. xi–xx. Josiah Macy, Jr., Foundation, New York, 1952.

18. Frank, L. K.: *Nature and Human Nature*. Rutgers University Press, New Brunswick, N. J., 1951.

19. Garner, W. R.: *Uncertainty and Structure as Psychological Concepts*. John Wiley & Sons, Inc., New York, 1962.

20. George, F. H.: *The Brain as a Computer*. Pergamon Press, London, 1962.

21. Gombrich, E. H.: *Art and Illusion*, Ed. 2. Pantheon Books, Inc., New York, 1961.

22. Gorsline, D.: *What People Wore*. Viking Press, New York, 1952.

23. Grinker, R. R. (Editor): *Toward a Unified Theory of Human Behavior*. Basic Books, Inc., New York, 1956.

24. Group for the Advancement of Psychiatry, Committee on Research: Some Observations on Controls in Psychiatric Research. G.A.P. Report No. 42, pp. 533–618. Group for the Advancement of Psychiatry, New York, 1959.

25. Hall, E. T.: *The Silent Language*. Doubleday & Company, Inc., Garden City, N. Y., 1959.

26. Haney, W. V.: *Communication—Patterns and Incidents*. Richard D. Irwin, Homewood, Illinois, 1960.

27. Harlow, H. F., and Harlow, Margaret K.: "The effect of rearing conditions on behavior." Bull. Menninger Clin., *26:* 213–224, 1962.

28. Hartley, E. L., and Hartley, Ruth E.: *Fundamentals of Social Psychology*. Alfred A. Knopf, Inc., New York, 1951.

24. Hayakawa, S. I.: *Semantics*. ETC., *9:* 243–257, 1952.

30. Hess, E. H.: "Imprinting." *Science, 130:* 133–141, 1959.

31. Hinkle, L. E., Jr., and Wolff, H. G.: "Communist interrogation and indoctrination of 'enemies of the states.' " *A. M. A. Arch. Neurol. & Psychiat.*, *76:* 115–174, 1956.

32. Horowitz, I. L.: *Philosophy, Science and the Sociology of Knowledge*. Charles C. Thomas, Publisher, Springfield, Ill., 1961.

33. Hoselitz, B. F. (Editor): *A Reader's Guide to the Social Sciences*. Free Press of Glencoe, New York, 1959.

34. International Encyclopedia of Unified Science. *Foundations of the Unity of Science*, edited by O. Neurath and others, Vols. 1 and 2. University of Chicago Press, Chicago, 1938–.

35. Kalinowsky, L. B., and Hoch, P. H.: *Somatic Treatments in Psychiatry*. Grune & Stratton, Inc., New York, 1961.

36. Kety, S. S.: "A biologist examines the mind and behavior." *Science, 132:* 1861–1870, 1960.

37. Kilpatrick, F. P. (Editor): *Explorations in Transactional Psychology*. New York University Press, New York, 1961.

38. Klapper, J. T.: *The Effects of Mass Communication*. Free Press of Glencoe, New York, 1960.

39. Latil, P. de: *Thinking by Machine*. Houghton Mifflin Co., Boston, 1957.

40. Laver, J.: *Taste and Fashion*. Harrap, London, 1937.

41. Leighton, A. H.: *An Introduction to Social Psychiatry*. Charles C. Thomas, Publisher, Springfield, Ill., 1960.

42. Lifton, R. J.: *Thought Reform and the Psychology of Totalism*. W. W. Norton & Company, Inc., New York, 1961.

43. MacKay, D. M.: "Towards an information-flow model of human behavior." *Brit. J. Psychol.*, *47:* 30–43, 1956.

44. Meerloo, J. A. M.: *Conversation and Communication*. International Universities Press, New York, 1952.

45. Meyer, L. B.: *Emotion and Meaning in Music*. University of Chicago Press, Chicago, 1956.

46. Miller, G. A.: *Language and Communication*. McGraw-Hill Book Company, Inc., New York, 1951.

47. Miller, G. A., Galanter, E., and Pribram, K. H.: *Plans and Structure of Behavior*. Holt, Rinehart & Winston, New York, 1960.

48. Miller, J. G.: "Information input overload and psychopathology." *Am. J. Psychiat.*, *116:* 695–704, 1960.

49. Morris, C. W.: *Signs, Language, and Behavior*. Prentice-Hall, Inc., Englewood Cliffs, N. J., 1946.

50. Nagel, E.: "Automatic control." *Sci. Am., 187:* 3, 44–47, 1952.

51. Neiman, L. J., and Hughes, J. W.: "The problem of the concept of role—a re-survey of the literature." *Social Forces, 30:* 141–149, 1951.

52. Osgood, C. E., and Sebeok, T. A. (Editors): "Psycholinguistics: A Survey of Theory and Research Problems." *Int. J. Am. Linguist.*, Memoir 10. Indiana University Publications in Anthropology and Linguistics, Bloomington, Indiana, 1954.

53. Ostwald, P. F.: *Soundmaking: The Acoustic Communication of Emotion.* Charles C. Thomas, Publisher, Springfield, Illinois, 1963.

54. Packard, V.: *The Hidden Persuaders.* David McKay Co., Inc., New York, 1957.

55. Paillard, J.: "The patterning of skilled movements." In *Neurophysiology,* Vol. 3, pp. 1679–1708 (Handbook of Physiology, Section 1). American Physiological Society, Washington, 1960.

56. Pei, M.: *The Story of Language.* J. B. Lippincott Company, New York, 1949.

57. Pribram, K. H.: "The intrinsic systems of the forebrain." In *Neurophysiology,* (Handbook of Physiology, Section 1) Vol. 2, pp. 1323–1344. American Physiological Society, Washington, 1960.

58. Rapoport, A.: "Critiques of game theory." *Behavioral Sci., 4:* 49–66, 1959.

59. Redfield, C. E.: *Communication in Management.* (Rev. ed.) University of Chicago Press, Chicago, 1958.

60. Revesz, G.: *The Origins and Prehistory of Language.* Longmans, Green & Co., Inc., London, 1956.

61. Riley, J. W., and Riley, M. W.: "Mass communication and the social system." In *Sociology Today,* edited by R. K. Merton, L. Broom, and L. S. Cottrell, Jr., pp. 537–578. Basic Books, Inc., New York. 1959.

62. Ruesch, J.: "The observer and the observed," pp. 36–54: Table 5: "System of relationships relevant in a unified theory of behavior," pp. 303–304; and "Analysis of various types of boundaries," pp. 340–361. In *Toward a Unified Theory of Human Behavior,* edited by R. R. Grinker. Basic Books, Inc., New York, 1956.

63. Ruesch, J.: *Disturbed Communication.* W. W. Norton & Company, Inc., New York, 1957.

64. Ruesch, J.: *Therapeutic Communication.* W. W. Norton & Company, Inc., New York, 1961.

65. Ruesch, J.: "Declining clinical tradition." *J. A. M. A., 182:* 110–115, 1962.

66. Ruesch, J., and Bateson, G.: *Communication: The Social Matrix of Psychiatry.* W. W. Norton & Company, Inc., New York, 1951.

67. Ruesch, J., and Kees, W.: *Nonverbal Communication.* University of California Press, Berkeley, 1956.

68. Ruesch, J., and Prestwood, A. R.: "Interaction processes and personal codification." *J. Personality. 18:* 391–430, 1950.

69. Sachs, C.: *World History of the Dance.* W. W. Norton & Company, Inc., New York, 1937.

70. Sarbin, R. T.: "Role theory." In *Handbook of Social Psychology,* edited by G. Lindzey, Vol. 1, pp. 223–258. Addison-Wesley, Reading, Mass., 1954.

71. Scott, G.: *The Architecture of Humanism* (1914). Doubleday Anchor Books, Garden City, N. Y., 1954.

72. Scott, J. P.: *Animal Behavior.* University of Chicago Press, Chicago, 1958.

73. Sebeok, T. A.: "Coding in the evolution of signalling behavior." *Behavioral Sci., 7:* 430–442, 1962.

74. Shannon, C. A., and Weaver, W.: *The Mathematical Theory of Communication.* University of Illinois Press, Urbana, Ill., 1949.

75. Skinner, B. F.: *Verbal Behavior*. Appleton-Century-Crofts, Inc., New York, 1957.

76. Spiegel, J. P.: "The resolution of role conflict within the family." *Psychiatry, 20:* 1–16, 1957.

77. Spitz, R. A.: "Anaclitic depression." In *The Psychoanalytic Study of the Child*, Vol. 2, pp. 313–342. International Universities Press, New York, 1946.

78. Stanislavsky, K.: "Stanislavsky on the Art of the Stage." Faber & Faber, Ltd., London, 1950.

79. Stevens, S. S. (Editor): "Handbook of Experimental Psychology." John Wiley & Sons, Inc., New York, 1951.

80. Stolurow, L. M.: *Teaching by Machine*. United States Department of Health, Education, and Welfare, Washington, 1961.

81. Symposium on Principles of Sensory Communication, Endicott House, 1959; *Sensory Communication*, edited by W. A. Rosenblith. The M. I. T. Press, Cambridge, Mass., and John Wiley & Sons, Inc., New York, 1961.

82. Szasz, T. S.: *The Myth of Mental Illness*. Paul B. Hoeber, Inc., New York, 1961.

83. Teuber, H.-L.: "Perception." In *Neurophysiology* (Handbook of Physiology, Section 1), Vol. 3, pp. 1595–1668. American Physiological Society, Washington, 1960.

84. Train, A. K.: *The Story of Everyday Things*. Harper & Brothers, New York, 1941.

85. Walter, W. G.: *The Living Brain*. W. W. Norton & Company, Inc., New York, 1953.

86. Walter, W. G.: "Where vital things happen." *Am. J. Psychiat., 116:* 673–694, 1960.

87. Whorf, B. L.: *Language, Thought, and Reality*, edited by J. B. Carroll. The M. I. T. Press, Cambridge, Mass., and John Wiley & Sons, Inc., New York, 1956.

88. Wiener, N.: *Cybernetics, or Control and Communication in the Animal and the Machine*, Ed. 2. John Wiley & Sons, Inc., New York, 1961.

89. Wiener, N.: *The Human Use of Human Beings* (rev. ed.). Houghton Mifflin Co., Boston, 1954.

90. Williams, R. H. (Editor): *The Prevention of Disability in Mental Disorders*. Public Health Service Publication No. 924, Washington, 1962.

LOVE IN A MACHINE AGE*

Paul Weiss

*t*he participants in this symposium all suppose, without question or examination, that one never knows other minds—or, to put it better, other selves with their minds, wills, emotions, etc.—directly. They resolutely put aside the suggestion that there may be an immediate intuition, sympathy, love, or other way of penetrating beyond the outward forms men exhibit. They take it for granted that no one can even reach the edge of another's privacy, that one cannot possibly get below his surface. Most of them speak as if there were no "below"; they are phenomenalists, differing amongst themselves as to whether or not they want to stress language, behavior, perception, process, or some other horizontally-structured way of dealing with the world. One need remark only that there are other reputable philosophic positions besides phenomenalism—metaphysical theories which insist that there are substances, existentialisms with their acknowledgement of radical privacies, and the like—to know that the common position of these symposiasts is open to question. It is surely unwarranted. I think it is mistaken.

For the moment let us put that matter aside. The question then before us would seem to be fourfold:

1. Do or can machines act in ways which in principle duplicate all the acts of men?

2. If machines could not duplicate all men's actions, would such behavior testify to the presence in men of some inward nature or power?

3. If machines could duplicate all men's actions, would that testify to the presence in the machines of some inward nature or power?

4. Would the incapacity to distinguish the behavior of men from that of machines show that men were indistinguishable from machines?

* Reprinted from Sidney Hook, editor, *Dimensions of Mind*, 1960, by permission of New York University Press.

1. Behavior occurs in space and time. There is no path or rhythm which one can antecedently claim is closed to some machine or other. It seems clear, then, that the behavior of men can in principle be duplicated by machines.

2. Were a man to behave in ways machines could not, this would show only that he was more flexible, had a wider range, than those artifacts had. It would not necessarily show that he had a private nature, mind, or will, and that the machines did not.

3. Were a machine to behave just as men do, it would have to be credited with a mind, if minds are accredited to men; or the men must be denied to have minds, if this is denied to the machine.

4. When I see others I see them from the outside. If this is the only source of my knowledge of them I cannot know whether or not they have minds. Attending only to *other* men, and observing only their behaviors, I cannot find a way of distinguishing them in principle from all possible machines. But if there be another source of knowledge regarding at least one man, which is not grounded on observable public behavior, then men and machines can be distinguished, despite a lack of difference in their behaviors.

I know myself not only from the outside but from within. Others may not know that I have a mind. Since I can see in the mirror, and in other ways, that I behave somewhat like other men, I conclude that they have minds similar to mine, or that I, being alone in having a mind, am a distinct type of being. And if I cannot distinguish men from machines, I must go on to say that the machines too have minds, or that once again I am distinct in type from them.

To say that I am a distinct type of being is to make an ontological claim. To say that I am like others but have a source of information regarding myself which they do not have, is, in contrast, to make an epistemological claim. The former insists on a difference in natures despite all publicly available evidence that can be produced to the contrary. It goes beyond what the facts warrant. The fact that others are not sure that I have a mind does not make me conclude that I do not have one. Rather, I conclude that they are not privy to all my sources of information. The only warranted conclusion to be drawn is the epistemological one that though I am of the same type as they are, as evidenced by our behavior, I have a source of evidence they do not have regarding the existence of my own mind. Since behaviorally they are of the same type as I am, I must credit each of them with a mind as well, and with the capacity to draw on direct evidence showing that he has one.

When machines behave as men do, I ought to say of those artifacts what I now say of those men: that they too have minds. Furthermore, I ought to say that they have wills as well, that they have private selves, secret feelings, a damning conscience, foolish hopes, good and bad intentions, justified and unjustified beliefs. I ought to grant that they have aesthetic sensitivity, the power to speculate, and that they may even have a religious faith. I ought to say of them, as I say of myself, that they are responsible, they are guilty, they are human—all too human. In short, I ought to say that the kind of mind I know I have, must be attributed to all beings which behave as I do, no matter what their origin or appearance—providing behavior is the only criterion for determining whether or not beings are of the same type.

If we now withdraw the supposition shared by the symposiasts and affirm that through love and sympathy we can penetrate beneath the forms men exhibit in public, and can therefore directly reach their private beings, we will still be able to say that, on the basis of bodily behavior alone, we rightly can attribute minds, wills, feelings, etc., to machines, as well as to other men. But we will also be able to say that we cannot love those machines. There will perhaps be some men we will not love, and some machines to which we will become attached. If we find a being which looks and behaves like other men and is beyond our capacity ever to love, we must say of it that it is only a machine, to be placed outside the society where only men can be. Should we find a machine which we can love, we must say of it that it has a human nature and human powers. We will, in short, divide beings, all of whom behave in the same way, into two classes, calling "men" those which are in principle within our powers to love, and calling "machines" those which we cannot possibly love.

Alternatively, I may find that I am unable to love what other men or even machines may report that they can love. If I cannot show that they are in error, I must conclude that they are superior to me. If it is the case that I not only do not, but cannot possibly, love Nazis, or Israelis, or Japanese, or whatever, while others, whether they be machines or men, *can* love them, it is *I* who must be said not to be human. I preserve my humanity only so far as I am one who is intrinsically able to love whatever can be loved.

Both what cannot be loved by one who can love, and what cannot love what can be loved, are less than human, no matter how much they look like and behave like men. Machines fail on both counts. They are not on a footing with me. They are, in short, not human, and thus cannot be said to have selves or minds, rights or responsibilities. The conclusion is not surprising, for we all know that a machine is an artifact whose parts are united so as to enable them to act together, whereas a man is a unity in which the whole governs the behavior of the parts. Only such a unity has a self, with feelings, mind, will, and the rest.

Phenomenalism may reach the point where men and machines are indistinguishable. It must then conclude that machines, like men, have minds, or conversely, that men, like machines, have no minds. The results are equivalent. But love and pity, hate and contempt, will then show how limited phenomenalism is.

Phenomenalism may—indeed must—stop short with behavior. It may fail to see but cannot make nonexistent what love discerns. In a machine age, as in any other, it is love that marks the man.

SOME COMMUNICATION MACHINES*
AND THEIR FUTURE

Norbert Wiener

Up to the present, we have been discussing machines which as far as the general public is concerned seem either to share the characteristic detachment from immediate human concerns of theoretical science or to be definitely beneficent aids to the maimed. We now come to another class of machines which possess some very sinister possibilities. Curiously enough, this class contains the automatic chess-playing machine.

Sometime ago, I suggested a way in which one might use the modern computing machine to play at least a passable game of chess. In this work, I am following up a line of thought which has a considerable history behind it. Poe discussed a fraudulent chess-playing machine due to Maelzel, and exposed it; showing that it was worked by a legless cripple inside. However, the machine I have in mind is a genuine one, and takes advantage of recent progress in computing machines. It is easy to make a machine that will play merely legal chess of a very poor brand; it is hopeless to try to make a machine to play perfect chess for such a machine would require too many combinations. Professor John von Neumann of the Institute for Advanced Studies at Princeton has commented on this difficulty. However, it is neither easy nor hopeless to make a machine which we can guarantee to do the best that can be done for a limited number of moves ahead, say two; and which will then leave itself in the position that is the most favorable in accordance with some more or less easy method of evaluation.

The present ultra-rapid computing machines may be set up to act as chess-playing machines, though a better machine might be made at an exorbitant price if we chose to put the work into it. The speed of these modern computing machines is enough so that they can evaluate every possibility for two moves ahead in the legal playing-time of a single move.

The number of combinations increases roughly in geometrical progression. Thus the difference between playing out all possibilities for two moves and for three moves is enormous. To play out a game—something like fifty moves—is hopeless in any reasonable time. Yet for beings living long enough, as von Neumann has shown, it would be possible; and a game played perfectly on each side would lead, as a foregone conclusion, either always to a win for White, or always to a win for Black, or most probably always to a draw.

Mr. Claude Shannon of the Bell Telephone Laboratories has suggested a machine along the same lines as the two-move machine I had contemplated, but considerably improved. To begin with, his evaluation of the final position after two moves would make allowances for the control of the board, for the mutual protection of the pieces, etc., as well as the number of pieces, check, and checkmate. Then too, if at the end of two moves, the game should be unstable, by the existence of check, or of an important piece in a position to be taken, or of a fork, the mechanical player would automatically play a move or two ahead until stability should be reached. How much this would slow the game, lengthening each move beyond the legal limit, I do not know; although I am not convinced that we can go very far in this direction without getting into time trouble at our present speeds.

I am willing to accept Shannon's conjecture that such a machine would play chess of a high amateur level and even possibly of a master level. Its game would be stiff and rather uninteresting, but much safer than that of any human player. As Shannon points out, it is possible to put enough chance in its operation to prevent its constant defeat in a purely systematic way by a given rigid sequence of plays. This chance or uncertainty may be built into the evaluation of terminal positions after two moves.

The machine would play gambits and possibly end games like a human player from the store of standard gambits and end games. A better machine would store on a tape every game it had ever played and would supplement the processes which we have already indicated by a search through all past games to find something apropos: in short, by the power of learning. Though we have seen that machines can be built to learn, the technique of building and employing these machines is still very imperfect. The time is not yet ripe for the design of a chess-playing machine on learning principles, although it probably does not lie very far in the future.

A chess-playing machine which learns might show a great range of performance, dependent on the quality of the players against whom it had been pitted. The best way to make a master machine would probably be to pit it against a wide variety of good chess players. On the other hand, a well-contrived machine might be more or less ruined by the injudicious choice of its opponents. A horse is also ruined if the wrong riders are allowed to spoil it.

In the learning machine, it is well to distinguish what the machine can learn and what it cannot. A machine may be built either with a statistical preference for a certain sort of behavior, which nevertheless admits the possibility of other behavior; or else certain features of its behavior may be rigidly and unalterably determined. We shall call the first sort of determination *preference*, and the second sort of determination *constraint*. For example, if the rules of legal chess are not built into a chess-playing machine as constraints, and if the machine is given the power to learn, it may change without notice from a chess-playing machine into a machine doing a totally different task. On the other hand, a chess-playing machine with the rules built in as constraints may still be a learning machine as to tactics and policies.

The reader may wonder why we are interested in chess-playing machines at all. Are they not merely another harmless little vanity by which experts in design seek to show off their proficiency to a world which they hope will gasp and wonder at their accomplishments? As an honest man, I cannot deny that a certain element of ostentatious narcissism is present in me, at least. However, as you will soon see, it is not the only element active here, nor is it that which is of the greatest importance to the non-professional reader.

Mr. Shannon has presented some reasons why his researches may be of more importance than the mere design of a curiosity, interesting only to those who are playing a game. Among these possibilities, he suggests that such a machine may be the first step in the construction of a machine to evaluate military situations and to determine the best move at any specific stage. Let no man think that he is talking lightly. The great book of von Neumann and Morgenstern on the *Theory of Games* has made a profound impression on the world, and not least in Washington. When Mr. Shannon speaks of the development of military tactics, he is not talking moonshine, but is discussing a most imminent and dangerous contingency.

In the well-known Paris journal, *Le Monde*, for December 28, 1948, a certain Dominican friar, Père Dubarle, has written a very penetrating review of my book *Cybernetics*. I shall quote a suggestion of his which carries out some of the dire implications of the chess-playing machine grown up and encased in a suit of armor.

> One of the most fascinating prospects thus opened is that of the rational conduct of human affairs, and in particular of those which interest communities and seem to present a certain statistical regularity, such as the human phenomena of the development of opinion. Can't one imagine a machine to collect this or that type of information, as for example information on production and the market; and then to determine as a function of the average psychology of human beings, and of the quantities which it is possible to measure in a determined instance,

what the most probable development of the situation might be? Can't one even conceive a State apparatus covering all systems of political decisions, either under a regime of many states distributed over the earth, or under the apparently much more simple regime of a human government of this planet? At present nothing prevents our thinking of this. We may dream of the time when the *machine à gouverner* may come to supply—whether for good or evil—the present obvious inadequacy of the brain when the latter is concerned with the customary machinery of politics.

At all events, human realities do not admit a sharp and certain determination, as numerical data of computation do. They only admit the determination of their probable values. A machine to treat these processes, and the problems which they put, must therefore undertake the sort of probabilistic, rather than deterministic thought, such as is exhibited for example in modern computing machines. This makes its task more complicated, but does not render it impossible. The prediction machine which determines the efficacy of anti-aircraft fire is an example of this. Theoretically, time prediction is not impossible; neither is the determination of the most favorable decision, at least within certain limits. The possibility of playing machines such as the chess-playing machine is considered to establish this. For the human processes which constitute the object of government may be assimilated to games in the sense in which von Neumann has studied them mathematically. Even though these games have an incomplete set of rules, there are other games with a very large number of players, where the data are extremely complex. The *machines à gouverner* will define the State as the best-informed player at each particular level; and the State is the only supreme co-ordinator of all partial decisions. These are enormous privileges; if they are acquired scientifically, they will permit the State under all circumstances to beat every player of a human game other than itself by offering this dilemma: either immediate ruin, or planned co-operation. This will be the consequences of the game itself without violence. The lovers of the best of worlds have something indeed to dream of!

Despite all this, and perhaps fortunately, the *machine à gouverner* is not ready for a very near tomorrow. For outside of the very serious problems which the volume of information to be collected and to be treated rapidly still put, the problems of the stability of prediction remain beyond what we can seriously dream of controlling. For human processes are assimilable to games with incompletely defined rules, and above all, with the rules themselves functions of the time. The variation of the rules depends both on the effective detail of the situations engendered by the game itself, and on the system of psychological reactions of the players in the face of the results obtained at each instant.

It may even be more rapid than these. A very good example of this seems to be given by what happened to the Gallup Poll in the 1948 election. All this not only tends to complicate the degree of the factors which influence prediction, but perhaps to make radically sterile the mechanical manipulation of human situations. As far as one can judge, only two conditions here can guarantee stabilization in the mathematical sense of the term. These are, on the one hand, a sufficient ignorance on the part of the mass of the players exploited by a skilled player, who moreover may plan a method of paralyzing the consciousness of the masses; or on the other, sufficient good-will to allow one, for the sake of the stability of the game, to refer his decisions to one or a few players of the game who have arbitrary privileges. This is a hard lesson of cold mathematics, but it throws a certain light on the adventure of our century: hesitation between an indefinite turbulence of human affairs and the rise of a prodigious Leviathan. In comparison with this, Hobbes' *Leviathan* was nothing but a pleasant joke. We are running the risk nowadays of a great World State, where deliberate and conscious primitive injustice may be the only possible condition for the statistical happiness of the masses: a world worse than hell for every clear mind. Perhaps it would not be a bad idea for the teams at present creating cybernetics to add to their *cadre* of technicians, who have come from all horizons of science, some serious anthropologists, and perhaps a philosopher who has some curiosity as to world matters.

The *machine à gouverner* of Père Dubarle is not frightening because of any danger that it may achieve autonomous control over humanity. It is far too crude and imperfect to exhibit a one-thousandth part of the purposive independent behavior of the human being. Its real danger, however, is the quite different one that such machines, though helpless by themselves, may be used by a human being or a block of human beings to increase their control over the rest of the human race or that political leaders may attempt to control their populations by means not of machines themselves but through political techniques as narrow and indifferent to human possibility as if they had, in fact, been conceived mechanically. The great weakness of the machine—the weakness that saves us so far from being dominated by it—is that it cannot yet take into account the vast range of probability that characterizes the human situation. The dominance of the machine presupposes a society in the last stages of increasing entropy, where probability is negligible and where the statistical differences among individuals are nil. Fortunately we have not yet reached such a state.

But even without the state machine of Père Dubarle we are already developing new concepts of war, of economic conflict, and of propaganda on the basis of von Neumann's *Theory of Games*, which is itself a communicational theory, as the developments of the 1950s have already shown. This theory of games, as I have said in an earlier chapter, contributes to the theory of language, but there are in existence government agencies bent on applying it to military and quasi-military aggressive and defensive purposes.

The theory of games is, in its essence, based on an arrangement of players or coalitions of players each of whom is bent on developing a strategy for accomplishing its purposes, assuming that its antagonists, as well as itself, are each engaging in the best policy for victory. This great game is already being carried on mechanistically, and on a colossal scale. While the philosophy behind it is probably not acceptable to our present opponents, the Communists, there are strong signs that its possibilities are already being studied in Russia as well as here, and that the Russians, not content with accepting the theory as we have presented it, have conceivably refined it in certain important respects. In particular, much of the work, although not all, which we have done on the theory of games, is based on the assumption that both we and our opponents have unlimited capabilities and that the only restrictions within which we play depend on what we may call the cards dealt to us or the visible positions on the chess board. There is a considerable amount of evidence, rather in deed than in words, that the Russians have supplemented this attitude to the world game by considering the psychological limits of the players and especially their fatigability as part of the game itself. A sort of *machine à gouverner* is thus now essentially in operation on both sides of the world conflict, although it does not consist in either case of a single machine which makes policy, but rather of a mechanistic technique which is adapted to the exigencies of a machine-like group of men devoted to the formation of policy.

Père Dubarle has called the attention of the scientist to the growing military and political mechanization of the world as a great superhuman apparatus working on cybernetic principles. In order to avoid the manifold dangers of this, both external and internal, he is quite right in his emphasis on the need for the anthropologist and the philosopher. In other words, we must know as scientists what man's nature is and what his built-in purposes are, even when we must wield this knowledge as soldiers and as statesmen; and we must know why we wish to control him.

When I say that the machine's danger to society is not from the machine itself but from what man makes of it, I am really underlining the warning of Samuel Butler. In *Erewhon* he conceives machines otherwise unable to act, as conquering mankind, by the use of men as the subordinate organs. Nevertheless, we must not take Butler's foresight too seriously, as in fact at his time neither he nor anyone around him could understand the true nature of the behavior of automata, and his statements are rather incisive figures of speech than scientific remarks.

Our papers have been making a great deal of American "know-how" ever since we had the misfortune to discover the atomic bomb. There is one quality more important than "know-how" and we cannot accuse the United States of any undue amount of it. This is "know-what" by which we determine not only how to accomplish our purposes, but what our purposes are to be. I can distinguish between the two by an example. Some years ago, a prominent American engineer bought an expensive player-piano. It became clear after a week or two that this purchase did not correspond to any particular interest in the music played by the piano but rather to an overwhelming interest in the piano mechanism. For this gentleman, the player-piano was not a means of producing music, but a means of giving some inventor the chance of showing how skillful he was at overcoming certain difficulties in the production of music. This is an estimable attitude in a second-year high-school student. How estimable it is in one of those on whom the whole cultural future of the country depends, I leave to the reader.

In the myths and fairy tales that we read as children we learned a few of the simpler and more obvious truths of life, such as that when a djinnee is found in a bottle, it had better be left there; that the fisherman who craves a boon from heaven too many times on behalf of his wife will end up exactly where he started; that if you are given three wishes, you must be very careful what you wish for. These simple and obvious truths represent the childish equivalent of the tragic view of life, which the Greeks and many modern Europeans possess, and which is somehow missing in this land of plenty.

The Greeks regarded the act of discovering fire with very split emotions. On the one hand, fire was for them as for us a great benefit to all humanity. On the other, the carrying down of fire from heaven to earth was a defiance of the Gods of Olympus, and could not but be punished by them as a piece of insolence towards their prerogatives. Thus we see the great figure of Prometheus, the fire-bearer, the prototype of the scientist; a hero but a hero damned, chained on the Caucasus with vultures gnawing at his liver. We read the ringing lines of Aeschylus in which the bound god calls on the whole world under the sun to bear witness to what torments he suffers at the hands of the gods.

The sense of tragedy is that the world is not a pleasant little nest made for our protection, but a vast and largely hostile environment, in which we can achieve great things only by defying the gods; and that this defiance inevitably brings its own punishment. It is a dangerous world, in which there is no security, save the somewhat negative one of humility and restrained ambitions. It is a world in which there is a condign punishment, not only for him who sins in conscious arrogance, but for him whose sole crime is ignorance of the gods and the world around him.

If a man with this tragic sense approaches, not fire, but another manifestation of original power, like the splitting of the atom, he will do so with fear and trembling. He will not leap in where angels fear to tread, unless he is prepared to accept the punishment of the fallen angels. Neither will he calmly transfer to the machine made in his own image the responsibility for his choice of good and evil, without continuing to accept a full responsibility for that choice.

I have said that the modern man, and especially the modern American, however much "know-how" he may have, has very little "know-what." He will accept the superior dexterity of the machine-made decisions without too much inquiry as to the motives and principles behind these. In doing so, he will put himself sooner or later in the position of the father in W. W. Jacobs' *The Monkey's Paw*, who has wished for a hundred pounds, only to find at his door the agent of the company for which his son works, tendering him one hundred pounds as a consolation for his son's death at the factory. Or again, he may do it in the way of the Arab fisherman in the *One Thousand and One Nights*, when he broke the Seal of Solomon on the lid of the bottle which contained the angry djinnee.

Let us remember that there are game-playing machines both of the Monkey's Paw type and of the type of the Bottled Djinnee. Any machine constructed for the purpose of making decisions, if it does not possess the power of learning, will be completely literal-minded. Woe to us if we let it decide our conduct, unless we have previously examined the laws of its action, and know fully that its conduct will be carried out on principles acceptable to us! On the other hand, the machine like the djinnee, which can learn and can make decisions on the basis of its learning, will in no way be obliged to make such decisions as we should have made, or will be acceptable to us. For the man who is not aware of this, to throw the problem of his responsibility on the machine, whether it can learn or not, is to cast his responsibility to the winds, and to find it coming back seated on the whirlwind.

I have spoken of machines, but not only of machines having brains of brass and thews of iron. When human atoms are knit into an organization in which they are used, not in their full right as responsible human beings, but as cogs and levers and rods, it matters little that their raw material is flesh and blood. *What is used as an element in a machine, is in fact an element in the machine.* Whether we entrust our decisions to machines of metal, or to those machines of flesh and blood which are bureaus and vast laboratories and armies and corporations, we shall never receive the right answers to our questions unless we ask the right questions. The *Monkey's Paw* of skin and bone is quite as deadly as anything cast out of steel and iron. The djinnee which is a unifying figure of speech for a whole corporation is just as fearsome as if it were a glorified conjuring trick.

The hour is very late, and the choice of good and evil knocks at our door.

STRATEGY AND CONSCIENCE*

Anatol Rapoport

*b*y a dialogue I mean a verbal interchange in which positive as well as negative responses of the participating parties occur. This definition would exclude the exchanges of diatribes and invectives which characterize so much of political discourse (national and international). The definition also excludes many instances of formal debate, such as take place in courtrooms, legislative chambers, and forums. Although these encounters are often kept within bounds of politeness by certain rules of decorum, they nevertheless seldom amount to more than exchanges of verbal blows. At best, they consist of statements of opposing points of view "in parallel" as it were. The participants actually address their remarks not to each other, not even at each other (although at times they seem to do so) but rather past each other to third parties—the audience, the electorate, the jury, etc. In other words, the participants do not seriously try to change the views of their *opponents*. They merely compete for attention and for the sympathy of the by-standers.

In a dialogue the efforts of the participants are actually directed toward changing or at least modifying the opponent's point of view. Accordingly, if a participant in a dialogue is seriously concerned with this aim, he will be concerned with appropriately effective techniques. It may turn out that the usual forensic techniques, while effective in scoring points, influencing juries, "public," etc., are useless for the purpose of the dialogue itself, namely, for effecting a shift in the thinking of the opponent.

In an earlier book[1] I listed what I believe to be the essential features of a dialogue (ethical debate), namely:

1. The ability and willingness of each participant to state the position of the opponent to the opponent's satisfaction (exchange of roles)

2. The ability and willingness of each participant to state the conditions under which the opponent's position is valid or has merit (recognition that any position whatever has *some* region of validity)

3. The ability and willingness of each opponent to assume that in many respects the opponent is like himself; that is to say, that a common ground exists where the opponents share common values, and each is aware of this common ground and, perhaps, of the circumstances which have led the opponent to the position he holds (empathy)

The question I am now raising is whether a dialogue is possible in the United States on the basic issues related to international relations. The question is important to us Americans because we have always taken pride in living in an "open society," i.e., one characterized by earnest exchanges of views between unintimidated people.

It should be noted that I am not asking whether the critics of the present mode of foreign policy have a voice. They have. A voluminous "peace literature" freely produced and distributed attests to it. Nor am I asking to what extent this voice is heard or is listened to. I am asking whether a fruitful exchange is possible between groups committed to practically incompatible approaches to problems of war and peace.

WHO ARE THE STRATEGISTS?

The ills plaguing the world have frequently been blamed on identifiable groups of people, nations, minority groups, adherents of assorted creeds, professions, etc. In my references to "the strategists," I may have given the impression that I have singled out a group of people who are exerting a pernicious influence on United States foreign policy. My intent, however, was to examine a way of thinking, not a group of people.

When I say "strategist," I mean someone who at the moment conceives international problems in strategic terms. At other times, he may think about the same problems in other terms, and so the same person may at times be a "strategist" and at other times may not. Therefore, the fact that strategists are "like everybody else," i.e., share their psychological make-up with a broad spectrum of the population, are motivated or constrained by the same impulses and norms—this fact is irrelevant in the matter of identifying "the strategists." The strategists constitute not a sector of the population but a sector of social roles. They are strategists when they are playing out their roles, i.e., when they are thinking strategically.

Another misunderstanding which should be forestalled lurks in the temptation to link the strategists with certain political views. There are people in the United States who nurture deep hatreds against the Enemy. Such hatreds lead those people to advocate courses of action which can hardly be supported by "rational" considerations, however rationality is defined. These people call for immediate cessation of negotiations with the Enemy, a declaration that a state of war already exists, and similar histrionics. There are few, if any, strategists, among the "total victory" enthusiasts or among compulsive flag wavers. Indeed, many strategists express considerable contempt for these gentry.

THE ABSTRACTIONISTS

I believe there are two types of strategists in the United States. One type I shall call the abstractionists. The abstractionists have at times been called the "cool young men." Their habitat is the research factories which service the armed forces. Their mode of thought is largely apolitical. That is to say, in formulating strategic problems, the abstractionist would feel quite comfortable if the players were relabeled. In fact, he is used to labeling them "A" and "B" in the first place. It is among the abstractionists that the impact of game-theoretical formulations is most strongly felt, and it is to them that the motto is addressed which is said to adorn an office at the Rand Corporation: "Don't think—compute!"

The abstractionists' contribution to the present conduct of international conflict is largely in the fields of operations research and logistics. Military problems, given certain norms, have "optimal" answers. For example, on the basis of known effects of nuclear blasts and thermal effects, calculations can be made concerning the number of bombers which are able to wreak a given level of destruction. On the basis of attrition rates which can be reasonably expected, assuming a certain effectiveness of the enemy's defenses, one can calculate the number of bombers which should be sent in order for the required number to get through. In replacing bombers by missiles, one calculates what one is exchanging for what: to what extent the heavier development effort is compensated by cheaper production, to what extent the "capabilities" derived from missiles will be matched by the opponent's efforts, etc., etc.[2]

On the defense side, one must know what to expect from ground-to-air defenses and air-to-air defenses against bombers; what one can hope for in the way of antimissile missiles and, if one really wants to think ahead, in the way of anti-antimissile missiles. One must know how much concrete can withstand how must blast pressure and how much heat, and one must translate this knowledge into designs of "hardened" missile sites, or "shelters" for civilians. These are clearly the same old problems of war "economics." Only the content has changed. Where one hundred years ago it was necessary to think about how much hay a cavalry regiment would require, fifty years ago about how many railroad cars (40 *hommes*—8 *chevaux*) were optimal for an echelon, twenty-five years ago about the fire power of a Sherman tank, one has now graduated to the mathematics of missile guidance and overkill factors. The technical knowledge required for the really advanced problems of this sort is enormous. Specialization is, of course, mandatory, and the joints between the specialities must also be welded, which requires still another class of "integrating specialities."

Into this picture, the game-theoretical orientation fits most naturally. For the logistic efforts of one side are, of course, opposed at all times by corresponding efforts of the enemy. No doubt this feature has always been present in strategic formulation. But game theory seems to have given the formulations of logistic problems a new, exciting luster and a rigor comparable to that conferred by advanced methods of mathematics upon the physical sciences.

Game-theoretical models are not confined to military tactics and strategy. As an example consider the following situation. Assume that an agreement has been concluded between Country A and Country B on some method of arms control or a disarmament procedure or, perhaps, on a ban against testing nuclear weapons. Suppose the agreement provides for a maximum number of inspections per year by either party on the territory of the other. The timing and the places of inspections are to be at the discretion of the inspecting party. Here is an opportunity to formulate a genuine two-person game involving mixed strategies. For clearly, secrecy about when and where an inspection is to be made is of central importance if (1) the inspected party is to be discouraged from attempting evasions and (2) if the chances for discovering evasions are to be maximized. Accordingly, a game can be formulated between two parties, one called Inspectors, the other Evaders. The payoffs accruing to the Inspectors are of two kinds, namely: (1) negative payoffs associated with the extent of undiscovered violations perpetrated by the Evaders and (2) positive payoffs associated with the number of violations discovered. For the Evaders, naturally, these payoffs have the opposite sign: It is in their interest to get away with as many violations as possible.

The game calls for mixed stategies. For example, if a violation is the possession of mobile missile-firing installations, the idea is to keep moving them around to minimize the chances of their being discovered. (If the missile launchers stay in one place, then the Inspectors, having failed to find a launcher at one site, can safely choose a different site on their next inspection and eventually close in on their prize.) The Inspectors, on the other hand, must also randomize their inspections geographically and possibly in time so as to minimize the number of launchers which the Evaders can hope to get away with and/or to maximize their chances of discovering one.

The theory of the two-person zero-sum game states that there exists an optimum strategy for the Evaders, namely, a maximum number of illegal missile launchers (or nuclear test explosions or whatever) and a certain randomization pattern in space and, perhaps, in time. Also for the Inspectors there is an "optimal" mixed strategy of randomized inspections.*

The challenge offered by problems of this sort is formidable and understandably intriguing to the specialist. There is practically no limit to the complexities that can be introduced. For instance, in the case of mobile missile launchers, not all locations may be equally valuable as launching sites. Therefore, the payoffs necessary to the Evaders involve the number of undetected launchers weighted by the frequencies with which they can be placed in the tactically preferable locations. If the relative "values" of the locations are also known to the Inspectors, they must weight their inspections accordingly with frequencies.

One cannot hope to solve the problem in all of its complexity at once, but as in the case of any mathematicized science, one can begin with some drastically simplified models and work one's way up to more and more realistic ones. In doing so, one follows the tested methods of applied mathematics: One brings to bear the greatest intellectual prowess on man's most excellent mode of thought—problem solving. In this mode, it is irrelevant to ask who are the Evaders and who the Inspectors and why the ones are so anxious to cheat and the others to catch them at cheating. In fact, the "solution" of the game reveals an optimal strategy *both* to the ones and to the others. The services of the same mathematician are available to both sides (as once were the services of the Prussian military specialists). There is even no point to keeping research of this sort classified; for the same solution can be obtained independently by the other side.

In short, the abstractionist works in a context devoid of content. It is in this sense that the abstractionist is characteristically apolitical.

THE NEO-TRADITIONALISTS

Strategists of another type, whom I shall call the neo-traditionalists, think in somewhat more political terms. Unlike the abstractionists, who are likely to have received their training in mathematics or in the physical sciences, the neo-traditionalists are more likely to have a background in political science, occasionally in history or economics. To them the participants in the present conflict are not interchangeable players A and B, but specific nations, the great powers, their allies, and their satellites. The powers also play a game, but theirs is the real game of identifiable "interests" instead of hypothetical parries, thrusts, and "nuclear exchanges."

* A paper treating a similar problem was presented at the International Conference on Arms Control in Ann Arbor, Michigan, in December 1962 and again in January 1964.

I call these writers neo-traditionalists because the most conspicuous feature of their mode of thought is the revival of traditional views of international politics.

This trend is most clearly discernible in the writings of Henry A. Kissinger. It is epitomized in a tribute to Clausewitz.

> War, argued Clausewitz, can never be an act of pure violence because it grows out of the existing relations of states, their level of civilization, the nature of their alliances, and the objectives in dispute. War would reach its ultimate form only if it became an end in itself, a condition which is realized only among savages and probably not even among them. For war to rage with absolute violence and without interruption until the enemy is completely defenseless is to reduce an idea to absurdity.[3]

This paraphrase of Clausewitz occurs in the context of attributing Clausewitzian ideals to the Communists. In fact, in the immediately succeeding paragraph Kissinger quotes a Soviet military authority: "If war is a continuation of politics, only by other means, so also peace is a continuation of struggle, only by other means."[4] I came across this statement after I started to write this book and was startled with its striking similarity to my own opening sentence. However, as the reader must have gathered by now, this book is a polemic *against* the view that politics ought to be equated to a struggle for power, while the views of Kissinger, as those of Shaposhnikov (the Soviet strategist, whom he quotes) and of Clausewitz amount to an acceptance of the power-struggle definitions of both war and peace.

At this point some of the neo-traditionalists may well point out the distinction between what ought to be and what is. There may be some among them who will readily admit that the perpetual struggle among the powers is not a desirable state of affairs. But they will insist that it is an actual one, and that therefore a theory of international relations ought to be predicated on this actuality. This is the traditional position of *realpolitik*. Later we shall inquire into the nature of the difference between the two senses of the word "accept," the sense of recognition and that of approval. For the present we shall confine ourselves to the non-controversial meaning of "acceptance," with which the strategists will readily agree. They accept (in the sense of recognizing as real, perhaps as inevitable) the power struggle as a normal relation among sovereign states and see international political "reality" rooted essentially in the issues of that struggle.

Why, then, one might ask, if the reality of the power struggle is axiomatic, and if the "rational" use of force is an obvious desideratum, is it necessary to reiterate this with so much emphasis, as is done in the writings of the neo-traditionalists?

The answer to this question is quite clear in the writings of Kissinger.

Since World War I, we have been witnessing a *perversion* of the rational power principle, he says. War has ceased to be a tool by means of which rational participants in the power game pursue their "interests." A particularly vicious symptom of this degeneration of war as a rational pursuit, according to Kissinger, is found in American thought about war. There is a reason for this in our recent experience with war. He writes:

> The literalness of our notion of power made it impossible to conceive of an effective relationship between force and diplomacy. A war which started as a surprise attack on us had of necessity to be conducted in a fit of righteous indignation, and the proper strategy for waging it was one of maximum destructiveness. By the same token now that the risks of war had grown so fearsome, the task of diplomacy was to attempt to settle disputes by the process of negotiation, and this, in turn, was conceived as a legal process in which force played a small role, if any. The objective of war was conceived to be victory, that of diplomacy peace. Neither could reinforce the other, and each began where the other left off."[5]

Observe what is being said. Diplomacy and war have become separated. They ought to be reintegrated. This is exactly what Clausewitz was saying in his famous dictum. His magnum opus *On War* was written shortly after the Napoleonic Wars. These wars had departed from the accustomed patterns of the eighteenth century. The objectives of pre-Napoleonic wars were not "total." No state sought to deprive another state of its sovereignty. A war was simply one way of conducting disputes. For example, if the crowned heads had an argument as to who should succeed to the throne of Spain, they sent their armies on marches. After some maneuvers and perhaps a pitched battle or two, the monarchs would have a family reunion (most of them were cousins) and settle the business. This was *not* Napoleon's way. He was not anybody's cousin, and he played for keeps. An upstart corporal wearing an emperor's crown had no use for the niceties of the European "system."

The system was restored (or was thought to have been restored) in 1815, and for a century Europe reverted to the old game called the balance of power. It is of this game that the neo-traditionalists write with sometimes undisguised nostalgia. The rules of the balance-of-power game are spelled out by Morton Kaplan.[6]

1. Act to increase capabilities but negotiate rather than fight.
2. Fight rather than pass up an opportunity to increase capabilities.
3. Stop fighting rather than eliminate an essential national actor.*

> * Compare this principle with the "balance" described in G. Orwell, *Nineteen Eighty-Four* (New York: Harcourt, Brace & World, 1955), where war has become chronic and the alliances shift every time it looks as if one side is going to lose for good.

4. Act to oppose any coalitions or single actor which tends to assume a position of predominance with respect to the rest of the system.

5. Act to constrain actors who subscribe to supranational organizing principles.

6. Permit defeated or constrained essential national actors to re-enter the system as acceptable role partners or act to bring some previously inessential actor within the essential actor classification. Treat all essential actors as acceptable role partners.

The over-all objective of the balance-of-power game, then (the objective of all the players as distinguished from their individual objectives), was not the preservation of peace but the preservation of the system. The victor must make sure that the defeated participant is reintegrated into the system, so that he can fight another time; for, who knows, next time he may be an ally.

The strategists are seldom so naive as to believe that the European system can be restored in its entirety, and they note the features of our era which make this impossible.

First and foremost of these is the destructiveness of modern weapons. Nowadays, the decision to "fight" rather than allow this or that is a decision to stake "national survival" on the outcome. Indeed, as even many of the strategists admit, a decision to employ all the existing technical capacity in a war may be tantamount to a decision to commit national suicide *regardless* of the outcome.

Second, specifically with regard to the United States, the all-or-none conception of war and peace is incompatible with the rules of the balance-of-power game. The United States has never been a member of the system. Consequently, the Clausewitzian conception of war as a rational pursuit of national interest has never been internalized in our way of thinking. We still harbor the illusion (or so it appears to the strategists) that war is a dirty business and that the goal of diplomacy is peace.

Finally, there have appeared on the scene other powers to be reckoned with who have no use for the "system," namely, the U.S.S.R. and China. Kissinger calls them revolutionary powers (analogous to France of 1794). Kaufman calls them aggressive powers: "It has long been a basic assumption of American foreign policy that both the Soviet Union and Red China are aggressive powers, that they assign a very high priority to expansion in the hierarchy of their goals, and are likely to use any and all means, including violence, to attain their ends."[7]

In view of the acceptance of the power struggle principle by the neo-traditionalists, it seems strange that any power would be singled out as an "aggressive" power simply because it is likely to "use violence to attain its ends." What is meant here (it should be understood, in fairness to the author) is that there are no apparent limits to *how much* power the U.S.S.R.

and China will try to attain. In other words, they will not, according to this view, play the game according to the rules set up by the old established members of the club.

What, then, is to be done? Time was when the United States Secretary of State could announce that any encroachment by the revolutionary powers on the status quo would be likely to be countered with a nuclear attack on their homelands. But this did not work. For one thing, "public opinion" is to be reckoned with in a democracy. Kaufmann writes:

> . . . a policy of deterrence will seem credible only to the extent that important segments of public opinion in domestic [sic] and allied countries support it. . . . This consideration suggests a rather crucial and specific requirement that a policy of deterrence must fulfill. Its potential costs must seem worth incurring. In other words, there must be some relationship between the value of the objective sought and the costs involved in its attainment. A policy of deterrence which does not fulfill this requirement is likely to result only in deterring the deterrer.[8]

The central idea in the writings of the neo-traditionalists is the Gilbertian notion that the punishment ought to fit the crime. The trouble with the doctrine of massive retaliation is that the magnitude of the threat mitigates against our willingness to use it. A threat of massive retaliation which is not believed by the threatened party can have disastrous consequences for the would-be retaliator. For if the threat is not believed, the bluff can be called. And if the bluff is called, the fist-shaking party faces a choice between nasty alternatives—to unleash a nuclear war or to back down and so reduce the credibility of future threats. The massive retaliator appears, then, to be talking loudly and carrying a stick so big that he may not be able to lift it.

The prudent thing, according to the neo-traditionalist, is to have a range of both decibels and sticks at one's disposal and *to use* either or both as the situation warrants: small transgressions—small punishments; big transgressions—big punishments. And the important thing is to keep the *capability* of the biggest punishment which technology allows and also the determination to use it "if necessary."

This is the gist of the limited war theory, the neo-traditionalists' answer to the threat of mutual annihilation. To their credit, it must be stressed that both the "need" for the theory and its aim are spelled out in the clearest terms. The "need" arose from the bankruptcy of the massive retaliation doctrine. It was impractical to bomb Moscow every time a riot occurred in Caracas. The Communists, knowing this, could proceed to "nibble away at the edges of the Free World." The aim of the theory was to restore war to its rightful and honorable place in international affairs. ". . . the problem is this: How can the United States utilize its military power as a rational and effective instrument of national policy?"[9]

If limited war was to become a rational and respectable substitute for total war, its strategic theory ought to occupy more of the strategists' attention; consequently, all-out war became a topic to be avoided, and so it is, in most of the writings of the neo-traditionalists.

Herman Kahn played the part of the *enfant terrible* when he broke through the tacit taboos and plunged into the "extended" theory, into the oh, so evermore exciting challenges and potentialities of thermonuclear war.

The neo-traditionalists had stopped at the edge, because it seemed to them that "the pursuit of national policy by thermo-nuclear war" was a contradiction in terms. Kahn's greatest achievement was to show, at least to his own satisfaction, that this was not necessarily the case, first, because there were untapped potentialities in the art of blackmail against the background of thermonuclear annihilation; second, because if nuclear war were to be fought after all, the strategist should not shirk his duty—he should work out (well in advance) the best way of fighting such a war if only to "prevail" (since "victory" in the accepted sense was difficult to define); third, because there was a public relations job to be done: What sort of impression do we make if we keep sniveling about the horrors of war?

Kahn became the loudest and clearest spokesman of the "cool young men."

WHO ARE THE OTHERS?

I have now identified the strategists and have presented their framework of thought. As the reader may have gathered from the title of this book, I juxtapose to the mode of thinking in which strategy is central another mode in which conscience is central. My task is now to describe this other mode and the camp to which people who think in it belong.

I do not know what to call those people, and I will not bother. The designing of strategies is a profession; an appeal to conscience is not. At least the professionalization of this activity tends to degrade it, as the history of organized religions has shown. Therefore, one cannot always recognize members of the conscience camp by what they do publicly. To be sure, many of them engage in agitation and in organization of community and political action, just as the strategists are frequently found among consultants to military agencies. But just as the way of thinking of the strategist is spread far beyond the circle of professionals, so the other way of thinking is not confined to the "professional" peace worker. It will be useful, therefore, to mention some other divisions of views which are correlated with the division between the strategic thinkers and the others, but do not quite coincide with it.

In the press, the dichotomy "warhawks vs. peace doves" was coined. This dichotomy implies commitments to war and to peace respectively and is not useful, since the coldest blooded of the cold warriors can protest his devotion to peace. One cannot challenge this protestation without questioning its sincerity, and this will not be done in this book.

Another dichotomy, proposed by Singer,[10] is between the "armers" and the "disarmers." On this scale, positions are clearly discernible, and the distinction coincides more closely with the one we are concerned with. Also, the individuals who line up along the armers-disarmers axis line up pretty much the same way on the strategy-conscience axis. Yet the armers-disarmers division makes for a confrontation on matters of *policy*, not modes of thought. It is possible to arrive at a position favoring disarmament without leaving the strategic mode of reasoning. There are disarmers who write effectively on this issue entirely in the strategic mode.*

A dialogue on the level of a policy debate is certainly possible. Such a dialogue between, say, the armers and the disarmers might be fruitful if in its course the underlying assumptions made by both parties were brought out, provided some agreement could be reached at the outset about desirable goals. One such agreement appears plausible. Many of the armers are firmly convinced that their program is most likely to prevent the outbreak of a nuclear war (if not of "small" limited wars). Whatever the disarmers may feel about the feasibility or the morality of limited wars, most of them would agree that the prevention of nuclear war is a desirable goal under any circumstances. The two camps can thus agree on at least one goal. Since the disarmers are equally convinced that only disarmament can ultimately prevent nuclear war, the disagreement is seen to be about means. This sort of disagreement can be fruitfully discussed. It is, in fact, easy to take the next step, that is, to state the fundamental assumptions of both sides with regard to some proposed policy, say the policy of deterrence. The armers, it seems, believe:

1. That the capacity to destroy the opponent is *necessary* to prevent him from destroying you. (In other words, if it were not for our retaliatory capacity, we would have been destroyed by now);

2. That the capacity to destroy the opponent is *sufficient* to prevent him from destroying you. (In other words, deterrence is a workable safeguard).

Most disarmers deny both of these assumptions. The debate, therefore, is joined at the very base of the two positions.

If a debate crystallized around the choice of a policy (e.g., a "hard" versus a "soft" policy on a specific issue), the armers and the disarmers

---

* For typical examples of peace strategies see A. Etzioni, *The Hard Way to Peace, A New Strategy* (New York: Collier Books, 1962); A. Waskow, *The Limits of Defense* (New York: Doubleday, 1962); and A. Waskow, "Nonlethal equivalents of war," in *International Conflict and Behavioral Science*, "The Craigsville Papers." Edited by R. Fisher. New York: Basic Books, 1964.

could also formulate their respective positions in terms of possible out-comes, their estimated probabilities, and utilities assigned to them. They would then find that the disarmers assign greater probabilities and larger negative utilities to escalation and war; the armers, on the contrary, assign higher probabilities and greater utilities to the other side's backing down. In this sense both positions are seen to be based on "rational" considerations. Their differences are traceable to different subjective estimates and values which are unavoidable in decision problems.

It will thus be found that *up to a point* disagreements arising in the pur-suit of strategic analysis can, in principle, be resolved, not in the sense of effecting agreements but in the "optical" sense of being resolved into com-ponents, so that the analysis can proceed to the next stage. Ultimately, no further resolution will be possible, because the basic values will have been reached. Polite dialogue must stop at this point: One can only agree to disagree on subjective estimates of unique future events and on preferences. Beyond this point, attempts to continue the discussion in the same mode will either get nowhere or will explode into hostile exchanges.

But the dialogue could continue if the mode of discourse were changed. It could continue if one allowed introspection, insight, and conscience to guide the discussion. Therefore, whether a dialogue is possible beyond the point of the "irreducible" clash of values depends on whether the strategist is able and willing to talk in another language and to think in another mode.

What, then, is the way of thinking of those who are concerned primarily with conscience, and how does it differ from the strategic mode?

First, whereas the strategic thinker conceives of each choice of action primarily (perhaps exclusively) in terms of its effects on the environment, the conscience-driven thinker conceives actions primarily with regard to their effects on the actor.

Second, whereas the strategist can begin his work only when values (utilities) are given or assumed, the conscience-driven thinker considers the determination of these values to be the principal problem. He rejects the relativist notion that all values are matters of preference like brands of cigarettes. To be sure, one cannot "prove" the superiority of one set of values over another if one confines one's self to methods of proof appro-priate to other inquiries. Nor can one prove by rational analysis that *King Lear* is a more profound work than *Tarzan of the Apes*. The conscience-driven thinker will not relinquish the problem of discerning human values simply because the problem does not yield to rational analysis; nor will he divorce any important sphere of human activity from this problem.

Third, while the strategist frequently recognizes the importance of self-fulfilling assumptions, their role is hardly ever actually taken into account in strategic analysis. The strategist assumes not only that the values are given but also that the "state of the world" at a given moment (including the values and the thinking processes of the enemy) is an objective fact to be ascertained. The critic of strategic thinking, on the contrary, while admitting that the state of the non-human environment may be considered as an "objective fact" at a given time, denies that values and predispositions are "objective facts." What they "are," in his way of thinking, is to a significant degree determined by what we think of them. Therefore in this area the aphorism of Henry Margenau is especially appropriate: "All of man's facts have become acts."

It is extremely difficult for one who subscribes to this orientation to join in a dialogue with a strategist, even with the best intentions. The basic question in the strategist's mind is this: "In a conflict how can I gain an advantage over him?" The critic cannot disregard the question, "If I gain an advantage over him, what sort of person will I become?" For example, he might ask what kind of a nation the United States might become if we succeeded in crushing all revolutions as easily as in Guatemala. With regard to deterrence, the critic might ask not "What if deterrence fails?" (everyone worries about *that*) but, on the contrary, "What if deterrence works?" Erich Fromm asks just this question: He inquires into the kind of *reality* behind the strategist's prescriptions of security:

> . . . the biggest and most pervasive reality in any man's life if deterrence should "work" is the poised missile, the humming data processor connected to it, the waiting radiation counters and seismographs, the overall technocratic perfection (overlying the nagging but impotent fear of its imperfection) of the mechanism of holocaust.[11]

The critic is convinced of the corrupting effect of power, especially of unimpeded power. And this, for him, is not simply "something to think about" in our off moments, but a fundamental insight. Moreover, he is convinced that this insight is not a symptom of softheadedness. It stems from looking at the facts of history, not ignoring them. If Stalin's Russia is to be used as an example of pure despotism (as the rationalizers of the Cold War frequently insist), it ought to be an object lesson on the results of power unimpeded by conscience. Moreover, conscience is silent when the wielders of power are convinced that it is being used to achieve good ends.

The neo-traditionalists' acceptance of international relations as a power game seems self-defeating to one who questions the value of power. Here the strategist will, of course, argue that his "acceptance" of the power game is not predicated on approval, that he merely takes the world "as it is." But the strategists' conclusions are not mere descriptions. They are frankly recommendations, predominantly recommendations to try to get more power in the power struggle, and so are predicated on the tacit assumption that power is a "pure good." The conscience-driven thinker challenges this assumption.

In my grandmother's time, body weight was considered a "pure good." I remember a passage from one of her letters written long ago from the Old Country. "Your aunt Rose, glory be, has added to her health (knock on wood). She has gained 16 kilograms since the birth of her baby and now tips the scales at 102." Similarly, financial standing is considered a "pure good" in our society, certainly as it applies to firms and often to individuals. Yet it seems as reasonable to question this assumption and even to deny it, as it is to question the assumption that health is reflected in obesity. With regard to power, we also have weighty reasons to question its value and to inquire into the mentality that considers the power game among nations as a normal, civilized state of affairs. For that is what Clausewitz implied when he said that only savages fight wars for the sake of fighting. We may forgive Clausewitz, writing before Victoria's accession, this cavalier distinction between civilization and savagery. But after what the descendants of Clausewitz brought about in Europe, it seems odd that this distinction is still made by the new traditionalists, who seek to restore respectability to war by making it "an instrument of policy."

In spite of occasional protestations on the part of strategists that their job is rational analysis, not value judgments, value judgments are unavoidably included in their analyses, because the end results of these analyses are policy recommendations. For example, some strategists pride themselves on having broken through the inhibitions which delayed a strategic analysis of thermonuclear war. In assuming the posture of staring this eventuality in the face, they liken themselves to the surgeon who does not permit himself to be swayed either by the horror of what he sees or even by empathy with the patient (for he needs detachment to cut human flesh). This comparison may be valid if thermonuclear war is viewed as a disaster to be guarded against and coped with, if, in spite of precautions, it does occur. However, thermonuclear war is not a natural disaster. It is being carefully planned and prepared by the strategists themselves. It could not occur if the strategists of both sides did not put forward convincing arguments about the necessity of possessing "nuclear capabilities" and the "will to use them." In this context, the "detachment" of the strategist resembles not so much that of the surgeon as that of a butcher or still more that of all the other organizers of mass exterminations. Those technicians too were for the most part "detached" in the sense that their work was not charged with affect. German chemists were detached when they prepared the poison gas; German engineers were detached when they built the gas chambers; German transportation experts were detached and efficient as they kept the trains moving, carrying people to the slaughter sites; German bookkeepers were detached while keeping tallies of the dispatched, etc. Doubtless many of those responsible for this activity took a certain pride in having overcome any inhibitions they might have had in this matter. They might have been sincerely convinced that the "Jewish question" was a problem to be solved in a detached and definitive manner, possibly for the good of humanity. In other words, the charge of depravity, sadism, etc., can be made convincingly only against certain isolated individuals. It cannot be made against the entire corps of specialists who planned, designed, and carried out the exterminations of the 1940's. These people did not go berserk. They were carrying out their duties methodically and systematically. They were "normally functioning" human beings.

Our strategists are also exactly like other people of their social class, education, and background. They enjoy the same sort of personal relations as the rest of us, appreciate the same gifts that life bestows, suffer from the same griefs and misfortunes. The monstrosity of their work carries little or no emotional meaning for them, not because they are mentally ill, but because they share with the rest of us or perhaps are more richly endowed than the rest of us with the most creative of human faculties, which becomes also the most dangerous one when coupled with a lack of extensional imagination—the faculty of abstraction.

To the mathematicians among them equations on the blackboard are just equations. Mathematics is a great leveler. When a problem is mathematically formulated, its *content* has disappeared and only the form has remained. To the strategists "targets" are indeed only circles on maps; overkill is a coefficient; nuclear capacity a concept akin to heat capacity or electric potential or the credit standing of a concern. The logic of abstract reasoning applies in the same way to all problems which are logically isomorphic.

The logician, the mathematician, the statistician, and the strategist all derive their competence (and so their social status) from an ability to handle abstract chains of reasoning detached from content. This, rather than freedom from preconceived notions and from the bias of vested interest, is the true meaning of their detachment.

If a dialogue is to take place between strategy and conscience, these are the things that must be said.

Given the etiquette of civilized discussion, especially in the English-speaking world, it is difficult to bring such matters up without eliciting accusations of foul play. The strategists accuse the moralists of prudery, of refusing to face certain facts of life. But the moralists can claim with equal, I would say with much greater, conviction that it is the strategists and their supporting hosts of bureaucrats who refuse to look facts in the face.

At a recent trial of a group of British pacifists (who engaged in a sit-down protest at Wethersfield Air Base on December 1, 1961), one of the defendants, acting as his own counsel, was cross-examining a government witness, an air force officer. The following is an excerpt from the cross-examination.

> Q: So actually there is no order which you would not accept?
> A: It is my duty to carry out any order that is given to me.
> Q: Would you press the button that you know is going to annihilate millions of people?
> A: If the circumstances demanded it, I would.
> Q: Would you slit the throats of all the two-year-old children in this country, Air Commodore?
> Mr. Justice Havers: I think you must stop all that.[12]

This line of questioning was forbidden by the judge as irrelevant. But from the point of view of the defendants, the picture evoked by the questions was far more relevant to the issue tried (whether the war resisters acted against the interests of the United Kingdom) than are the concepts in which the military thinks. The military concepts of defense have only a "logical" relevance to the country's national interests. That is, they are connected to the conventional ideas of "national interest" by the force of our thinking habits, but by hardly anything else. On the other hand, the horrible deaths of a nation's two-year-olds has a *direct* relevance to the country's "national interest." These deaths are expected as *actual*, not merely logical, consequences of nuclear war. Nevertheless, the demand for "rational argument" is a demand that the moral aspect of genocide be dismissed as "irrelevant."

I heard this attitude stated quite frankly by an official of our Department of Defense, a man not only of superlative intelligence but also easy to talk to, in the sense that he listened carefully, got the central point of what was said, and replied directly to it.

"You keep worrying what is going to happen to the two-year-olds," he said, when I kept harping on the subject, following the example of the British defendant, "but what I want to know is who is going to get West Berlin, if we do what you propose."

And again, "No. I don't see them [the Communists] as fiends or criminals. To me the whole thing looks more like a basketball game between Pekin, Illinois, and Peoria, Illinois."

The moral issues are beyond the scope of military and political decisions. Moral convictions are private and so should not be injected into the formulation of public policy. But more effective than any explicit arguments against bringing in the moral issue is the functional deafness developed by the strategists to any discourse in other than the strategic mode. Consequently, if someone wants to *reach* the strategists, to induce them to listen seriously, he must either gloss over the moral issues or lay them aside altogether. Someone with a facile knowledge of weaponry and logistics has an excellent chance of catching the strategist's ear. Someone moved by a passionate concern for human values but with no understanding of the intricate strategic issues and their highly proliferated ramifications may as well be speaking a dead language.

The emphasis by the critic of strategic thinking on the vital importance of the self-predictive assumption is, perhaps, the crucial stumbling block to the dialogue.* For the strategist's deeply internalized conviction is that he takes the world "as it is." To the critic, however, the world looks somewhat as it does to the wisest of the three umpires. The first umpire, who was a "realist," remarked, "Some is strikes and some is balls, and I calls them as they is." Another, with less faith in the infallibility of the profession, countered with, "Some is strikes and some is balls, and I calls them as I sees them." But the wisest umpire said, "Some is strikes and some is balls, but they ain't nothing till I calls them."

A value is not a fact. The act of choosing a value, and the act of guessing the other's values, are facts. It is, therefore, by no means a matter of indifference what values one puts into one's own matrix and what values one will assign to the payoffs of the other. The game one will play depends vitally (sometimes irrevocably) on the values one has put in. But in real life it is the way the game is played that reveals the values. How "objective," then, are the strategists' estimates if there is good reason to suppose that the strategists themselves have made the game what it is? In no laboratory would the results of observations be taken seriously if there was reason to suspect that the methods of observation had influenced the results. Nevertheless it is precisely in their claims to "scientific objectivity" that the defenders of strategic analysis are most vociferous when confronted with questions of value. On the basis of their "objectivity" they accuse of muddleheadedness and naiveté anyone who asks embarrassing questions about whether their games are worth playing, or whether one ought to identify with actors whose moral code resembles that of Louis XIV, Frederick the Great, and Catherine II at its best and that of Attila, Genghis Khan, and Hitler at its worst.

If dialogue becomes impossible on these matters, it is because neither side can really listen to the other. In most cases, such blocks to communication are unfortunate. The improvement of communication is one of the crucial problems of our time, and brave efforts go into this enterprise. Books are written and courses taught on this subject; innumerable techniques are proposed, ranging from forensics to semantics. I often wonder

---

* The crucial role of self-fulfilling assumptions as a strategic factor is clearly recognized by both Kahn (*On Thermonuclear War*) and Schelling (*The Strategy of Conflict*). However, they treat this factor only as a serious difficulty in designing strategy, never as a ground for questioning the foundations of strategic thinking itself.

whether it is worthwhile to try to bridge the chasm between strategic and conscience-inspired thinking. It may be feasible and advisable to broaden the views of both management and labor: The industrial process must keep functioning, and both sides may stand to gain from increased mutual understanding. It is imperative to establish avenues of communication between Blacks and Whites and between East and West, because they all must either learn to live with each other or perish. In the case of strategy and conscience, I am not sure. Here, I believe, is essential incompatibility, not merely a result of misunderstanding. I do not believe one can bring both into focus. One cannot play chess if one becomes aware of the pieces as living souls and of the fact that the Whites and the Blacks have more in common with each other than with the players. Suddenly one loses all interest in who will be champion.

NOTES

1. A. Rapoport, *Fights, Games, and Debates* (Ann Arbor, Mich.: University of Michigan Press, 1960).

2. U. S. Senate, *Study of Airpower*. Hearings before the Subcommittee on the Air Force of the Committee on Armed Services, 84th Cong., 2d sess. Washington, D. C.: Government Printing Office, 1956.

3. H. A. Kissinger, *Nuclear Weapons and Foreign Policy* (abridged edition) (Garden City, N. Y.: Doubleday, 1958), p. 65.

4. B. M. Shaposhnikov, *Mozg Armii* (Moscow-Leningrad: Gosizdat, 1929), cited in Kissinger, above.

5. Kissinger, *Nuclear Weapons and Foreign Policy*, p. 29.

6. M. A. Kaplan, *System and Process in International Politics* (New York: John Wiley & Sons, 1957), p. 23.

7. W. W. Kaufmann (ed.), *Military Policy and National Security* (Princeton, N. J.: Princeton University Press, 1956), p. 1.

8. W. W. Kaufmann, "The Requirements of Deterrence," in Kaufmann, *Military Policy and National Security*, p. 20.

9. R. E. Osgood, *Limited War. The Challenge to American Strategy* (Chicago: University of Chicago Press, 1957), p. ix.

10. J. D. Singer and A. Rapoport, "The Armers and the Disarmers," *Nation*, March 2, 1963.

11. E. Fromm, "The Case for Unilateral Disarmament," *Daedalus*, 89 (Fall 1960), pp. 1015–1028.

12. J. D. Garst, "Conscience on Trial," *Nation*, March 24, 1962.

MISBEHAVIORAL SCIENCE*

Jacques Barzun

*L*anguage is the chief medium of the historical and misbehavioral; it is so if only because the nonliterary arts of painting, music, and the dance are themselves subject to verbal interpretation, history, criticism, and transmission. And this reminds us that the public mind, the "common air" I referred to, lives by language too. The lack or failure in the historical realm is thus at every point a defect in language. What has happened to language, the acknowledged falling-off of the past half century, is therefore instructive about our condition.

Anyone can see the external signs and obvious causes of change: the mixing of peoples, the spate of democratic and totalitarian harangues, the burst of inventions and new sciences, the freedom to play with language that literacy and advertising encourage—all has rendered virtually meaningless the phrase "mother tongue." The dictionary is no longer a list of words spoken by the people, but a semi-encyclopedia, in which a score of technical vocabularies lead an autonomous existence, together with initials, abbreviations, and trade names. In the holes and corners sulks the native tongue, heavily laced with slang, the jargon of war, and popular misconceptions of scientific terms. From these vocables[1]—nearly half a million in the latest Webster—it would be difficult to choose a central group of words and phrases whose uses and connotations form a public idiom.

This is a loss whose effects are felt as the "problem of communication" in political and business life. In private life, the tone and *interest* of conversation likewise suffer from the decreasing family likeness among the words that spring to the lips—the semi- and pseudo-technical mixed with the vaguely metaphorical. Flexibility may seem a convenience, but the user

* Pp. 201–214, *Science: The Glorious Entertainment*, by Jacques Barzun. Copyright © 1964 by Jacques Barzun. Reprinted by permission of Harper & Row, Publishers, and by permission of Martin Secker and Warburg Ltd.

pays for it in the choppiness of his stream of thought and the crudity of the fragments of feeling it carries. For whether he knows it or not, language is the keeper and shaper of his consciousness, and he cannot habitually cast his will and fears and hopes in broken or foolish patterns of words without becoming a foolish and discontinuous mind.

It would take a treatise to discuss the unstudied ways in which we record in the living languages the jerky motions of our spirit. Only a few that have relevance to scientific culture and some of its products need occupy us here.

The modern desire to be authoritative and complete in the manner of science takes the form of preferring the abstract and general to the concrete and particular. The businessman sees ahead of him a vague series of activities, meetings, paper work, and lumps them together as that which will "finalize" the deal. "Finish the business" is far too homely for his purpose. The contrast of these phrases defines a state of mind. We see it again in the classifying word, most often carelessly chosen, whose purpose is to show that the things denoted belong to the order of natural facts, capable of study. Thus one lawsuit might accidentally take a long time to settle, but when all long cases are known as "durable" they take on the air of a new product—"durable cases."

Again, a person's acts are peculiarly his own; if, therefore, we want to make them the property of the investigator they must be welded into a process or entity. Thus do desires, impulses, and temptations merge into *motivation*. Already as a child, the man showed a willingness or a reluctance to learn, which the school "handled" as "his motivation"; he had it or had it not, like the measles. The critic of a novel similarly looks, not at the ideas or actions of the hero, but at his "psychology." It would be a mistake to see in this tendency, which is common throughout the West, a mere wish to dignify the thing said. That wish is present, no doubt, but in a lesser degree than the determination to be comprehensive and detached.

Like the equation of science, the abstract noun takes its subject out of Time, where the verb would keep it: motives begin and end but motivation goes on forever. And once applied to a corner of the mind, the abstracting principle leaves no particulars alone. For example, business firms and other institutions no longer build a building, they put up a "facility."[2] This means that it will be fully equipped and serve several purposes. Then no one can object on the score of fact: "You *said* an office building, but I see it has a restaurant and a swimming pool." The two tendencies of naming completely and doing it by abstraction are not opposites: they both give "objectivity" to the parts of life which we isolate for endless analysis, and they submit the result to community inspection, as science does with its objects.

The result for language is that it approaches a system of interchangeable parts—a machine. With the right terms in -tion and the usual linking words, there is no need to choose and group words with a care for etymology, sound, rhythm, or tone. Gradually, idiomatic expressions fall apart and syntax becomes unnecessary. The cohesiveness of languages, so to speak, has been declining in all the western tongues, especially English. Foreign speakers have unintentionally helped to break the forms, but they have done less harm than such inventions as Basic English and structural linguistics. For both these systems view words as counters, to be assembled as if there were no constituted language behind them, no other speakers, but only an algebra of a + b in which terms are coupled to force a meaning by juxtaposition.[3] Basic is thus a typical artifact of techne and also a scientific abstraction that professes to convey the "essentials" by means of some nouns and a few weak verbs.

That by allowing this the method of Basic does not prepare the learner for the language—at least not until the language has wholly lost its set ways—is perhaps unimportant when the native speakers of English are busy getting rid of these ways from within. They make new words, at need or not; they telescope old ones meaninglessly, twist meanings, ignore, then forget, distinctions, confuse persons and things (as in the false possessive: "Florida's governor") and grow deaf to connotations and cacophony. Some of this fiddling is nervousness; it works off the irritability of people who are held by their needs and occupations to a very exact memory of numbers, technicalities, and trade names. Language is the one malleable stuff they have left to play with, and play is liberating and amusing: it is creativity.

Besides, the city dweller under techne has the excuse that the speech at his disposal for the experiences of daily life is impoverished as compared with, say, that of a sailor or an old-fashioned peasant. Their words are more numerous, they are sharp, varied, fit, and pleasing in themselves. Even for the humblest they color the web of life.[4] Drabness certainly accounts for the spastic efforts of certain weeklies to liven up their prose by antigrammar, pedantry, and other affectations. Most journals that are specialized in subject matter, yet must appeal to readers who are not professionals—for example, the excellent magazine *Trains*—develop their own "crisp" jargon, which is only to a small extent technical. The rest is contrived for color like the sports writer's prose; it helps make the readers feel knowing and apart. And besides, the impression is given that the writing is "efficient."

Efficiency is the modern-sounding ideal substituted by the linguists for correctness, and it is of course just as difficult to ascertain and apply. At one end, efficiency seems to mean giving the gist, the drift or minimum of information; at the other, it means the strong, striking, unusual way of putting things. Either extreme reflects the fact that language has become what the science-inspired linguists thought it was: a tool of communication. The possibility that language conveys meaning by intangible, nonmechanical means, by an inaudible surplus of meaning above the meaning of words, and which arises from their choice and arrangement—this is missing from the deliverances of linguists, as it is from the thoughts of a people schooled to think that a language is a piece of private, instead of public, property.

Lexicographers ratify the dogma that there is no right or wrong way to speak or write, but only speechways—speech facts—which are all equally acceptable so long as the speaker's meaning is communicated. How this is achieved and tested and why in another part of society other experts are agitated by the aforementioned problem of communication is not explained. But one result of the combined dogma and problem is that when disagreement occurs, in business or sociability, everybody is ready with the platitude that it is a "semantic problem"—two things for one word. For the semanticists have popularized the belief that words betray, that one should always define one's terms, and that language rich in overtones tyrannizes the mind through the emotions. This "conditioning" occurs, no doubt, but it need not. There is an art of words which gives exact meaning without defining and without tyranny. But who can rely on it when the linguistic powers are misled and misused? To consider language a "tool," that is, to regard words as lying outside consciousness, ready to be used like a pair of tongs for picking up meanings as needed, is of course in keeping with the "objective" view of behavior. To counteract this, professional writers proffer the remedy we have so often met in techne: when two things that belong together have been separated, someone makes good the loss by supplying an "additive" to the deprived. The empty clangor of abstraction in our speech leads to the journalist's slick phrase and clever neologism, which are imitated in talk from the prose they enliven; an unjust war is waged on harmless old clichés, and violence is practiced on idioms to refurbish them. Soon, playing with language becomes compulsive. The urge is to surprise and be creative in the manner of a poet. And hence the excess of metaphor indulged in, even at the cost of making one's meaning obscure or forgetting it in nonsense.[5] Metaphor affects vocabulary: *pinpoint, spearhead, highlight; bottleneck, framework, floor and ceiling;* and it inspires the repetitious imagery of the executive routine—"play it by ear" (which is a misnomer for "improvise"), "wear two hats," and other circumlocutions.

Metaphor has also become the standard medium of criticism, social philosophy, education, and political debate, and too often of legal opinions. Throughout, the hope is to recapture the unique life, the colorful misbehavior of each act.[6] It almost always turns out to be merely bad poetry: the author of the manual on organizing conferences spoke of them as offensives and he talked of tactics when he meant catering.

This figurative habit is endemic in the scientific culture, for it serves the double desire of avoiding abstraction and of showing to the eye, without whose witness reality nowadays seems dim. Yet these spurs to imagination destroy it by excess, while enfeebling the words thus abused. From the ease of putting abstractions end to end and letting images do the work of thought, the reader contracts the habit of never thinking what particulars properly fit under either and he grows more and more detached from experience. Formerly, good prose was that which struck a balance between abstract and concrete and reserved the effect of imagery for explanation or emphasis. The reader was not put to work visualizing strings of metaphors or thinking up instances to fill out abstractions. Prose could be exact without being either flowery or dull: it was not trying to be either poetry or science.

While this transformation of language was going on at large, poets and novelists also were experimenting (as they called it) in an effort to restore freshness and force to vocabulary and syntax. The writers of the past hundred years, from Rimbaud and Mallarmé to Joyce and Faulkner, have had to play with language in deadly earnest, struggling to keep meanings sharp and sensations uppermost, because the forces of literacy were making words smooth and empty.[7] But the liberties writers took in protest only removed another barrier and scruple. Everybody's urge to innovate, to be free and creative, seemed warranted by the work of Hopkins and Yeats and their progeny. By now the punning of Joyce, the alliteration of Hopkins, and the grammatical freedom of Gertrude Stein, Faulkner, and Proust are in the common domain of conversation, advertising, art criticism, and industrial technology. This was to be expected in a unified culture in which poets, advertising men, scholars, journalists, artists, critics, and politicians[8] all have a stake in working their will on the language, and are encouraged by the scientific linguists to believe that here is play that has no rules and tampering that is free of penalties.

The reader who knows that nine tenths of our old-established words are originally metaphors may wonder why I single out that verbal device as a chief evil in our speech, from which it spreads its infection to our minds. The answer is that there are metaphors and metaphors. Those embedded in the language possess varying degrees of energy, ranging from dead to live, and the dead metaphors form no part of the excess I observe. When one says *examine*, no one thinks of the pointer of a balance. But differently put, the same image (as in *weighing* an opinion) still has life and must be used with caution: one should not weigh an opinion to see if it will hold water and stand the acid test of public scrutiny.[9]

But this muddled metaphoric style, common as it is today, is less a condition than a by-product of the intent I see giving shape to our sensibility and, most lately, affecting science itself. The principle of metaphor is the joining of distinct ideas to show their likeness and suggest also their difference. Now, man's new power to transform matter and combine processes makes him relish above all else the idea of double natures and "two-way utility," of three-in-one substances and agents made up of miraculously fused incompatibles. The invented names for these things are in effect metaphors. They are also puns and portmanteaus in the manner of Lewis Carroll and James Joyce: *aqualung, transistor* (transfer+resistor). Even in the new words for a single idea there is often a duplicity in the echoing of others that possess dignity and force. This is so, for example, in *automation* and in *microbus* and all the neologisms in *-matic* and *-rama*. When a megaton bomb was being talked about, gas stations put up signs about their product's megatine power. The same urge to borrow and enhance moved the writer who proposed to replace *weightlessness* in space flight by *abweight*.[10]

To be sure, the mixing of Latin and Greek and of either with English to supply new names did not begin with our century, but the practice was bound to deteriorate when those playing with classical roots did not know the language they came from or care for the one which they were enlarging. In truth, there never was an age so poor at naming things. One has only to mention all the *-tron* hybrids which are the acme of meaninglessness.[11] But there is worse in the growing list of cases in which confusion seems to be deliberately courted. It is foolish to call projectiles Jupiter and Saturn when two of the planets already bear those names; it is downright stupid to choose *plasma* to mean an ionized gas at high temperature, when plasma already means the fluid part of blood and a kind of quartz. *Plastic*, which used to mean malleable, shapable, is now associated with hard grainless materials (and in Europe with portable bombs) so that *plasma* and *plastic* now evoke simultaneously the ideas of hard and soft, of blood and art and explosives, of solid and viscous and gaseous and fluid.[12] Until this triumph of nomenclature we knew that anything could mean anything; now we must wonder whether something can mean everything.

No doubt those who use modern ambiguities are specialists who will not cross the line where each word begins to mean something else, so that no physical danger is likely to result from the equivocal sounds. Yet the duplicity, at once careless and deliberate, is harmful in a way more pervasive and permanent than any material mistake. The contemporary world is hard enough to understand, its parts are sufficiently strange and its meanings cause enough fright, to make all possible clarity desirable. It would seem but elementary caution in a scientific culture to call things by their proper names. But the tendency is all the other way. One does not know where to turn to avoid misnomers. In the excitement of war, press and public speak of the *rape* of a small country when they mean its seizure by armed force. Afterwards they speak of material deprivation as *austerity*, when there is nothing austere about either those who grumble or those who keep cheerful. If prominent American families engage in public life, they are at once called "dynasties"—clearly with no heed to what a dynasty implies. This mania for false analogy is now so usual that the startling sobriquet no longer produces its intended effect. Yet it continues to blur mental images. When a swamp near New York was made fit for school children to go there and study living things, the newspapers felt compelled to call it a "classroom," though one would have thought a swamp was precisely *not* a classroom, but its opposite and counterpart.

If one passes from newspapers to scholarly prose, say, that of the behavioral scientists, one finds the misuse of terms no less frequent. The very word "behavior" is applied, again by a kind of metaphor, to entities that do not in fact behave. In economics, for instance, the phrase "cost behavior" means nothing more than variation. Nor are the humanists more sensitive to ambiguity. Philosophers of science speak of "lawful behavior" to distinguish the movements of physical objects from the actions of men, "lawful" being here a sort of pun like "durable" when applied to protracted lawsuits.

Indeed, punning, which has been barred from conversation and literature as contemptible (except when it is profound), has returned as the serious business of experts in communication.[13] Playing on words is of course a great device in advertising, where the prohibition of common words as trade names has engendered a second vocabulary of misspelled homonyms—*easy, rite, expaditer, nutrument*—and innumerable portmanteau creations (e.g., "leisuals" for informal footwear), which may not last long in current use, yet which make their mark upon the eye and mind. Children's difficulties with spelling and composition are surely not lessened by this propaganda for wrong vowels and substandard words.

All this suggests that a part at least of the continual slithering of meaning in modern tongues is attributable, not to ignorance or carelessness by themselves, but to a deep sense of the instability of things. This feeling finds vent in the hybrid words (e.g., *Stellerator*); it informs the cant metaphors (e.g., "population explosion"); it shifts precise technicalities to vague uses (e.g., "epidemic proportions" to mean "very large"); it looks restlessly for variants (*difference* becomes *differential; basic, basal; advice* from the weather bureau is given in *advisories—surmises* will no doubt be called *suppositories*); it reduces a whole range of words to the service of one old idea (e.g., *pecuniary* becomes *financial* which becomes *fiscal*, until one hears that Mr. X, who is short of cash, "is having fiscal troubles"); it feels the need to translate the simple and personal into the lofty and general, often with a confusing idea added (e.g., the *poor* are the *underprivileged*, which may be so, but why privilege, suddenly, in our democratic life?).

This instability that I detect explains also the desire to fix the fluid world by compounding terms in the manner of chemistry: the "power-order conceptual framework" is as near as you can get to "trinitrotoluene" in political science. Tumbling from idea to idea through fugitive association lends the appearance of knowledge and mastery, although underneath there is a culpable absent-mindedness. Thus the engineer directing the Venus Project is called "the present-day Jules Verne"; and when a cherished film star commits suicide, a television retrospect of her career is entitled "Who Killed Marilyn Monroe?" What Jules Verne actually did or why it is absurd to represent Miss Monroe's death as murder by society are questions beneath the notice of our sophisticated misusers of words.

Nevertheless, it is shortsighted to suppose that this large-scale garbling we permit and come to relish does not alter the strength and quality of the language.[14] Some vagaries disappear but their traces remain as forms of thought, and it is only the unperceiving linguists aping science who think that a belief in the aesthetic virtues of language is an illusion fostered by writers. "Words are the people's; yet there is a choice of them to be made," as Ben Jonson remarked.[15] When the principle of choice is destroyed by the combined efforts of ignorance, trade, science, Basic English, and machine "translation," the language will no more be recoverable from the fragments than the Taj Mahal would be if ground to powder. English has a fair chance of becoming a world language if something of its spirit keeps it a language, but the increasing use of it as an inelegant algebra must bring it to a condition of which the sympathetic observer can only say: "They have neither Speech nor Language but their voices are Heard."

If what I discern is in truth a powerful tendency, someone may object, "Why argue against a trend?" To which the answer is: "What difference between yielding to a trend and giving in to conformity?" Besides, a trend is variable and may be reversed; as history, which is the graveyard of trends and the birthplace of countertrends, amply shows. I go on therefore to discuss the inroads of metaphor and duplicity into science. The breach was made when, as we saw in Chapter V, contemporary science acknowledged that its work consisted of regarding phenomena as—some convenient entity or model or system. Regarding-as is the essence of metaphor and ambiguity, and when this discovery seizes hold of the mind, it can come to seem a key that will open all locks. In a suggestive book of essays entitled *On Knowing*, the Harvard psychologist Jerome Bruner has developed the idea of metaphor to the point where he himself seems scarcely willing to write a literal sentence. His thoughtful work is full of remarks such as: "The psychologist . . . searches widely and metaphorically for his hunches. . . . If he is lucky, or if he has subtle psychological intuition, he will from time to time come up with hunches, combinatorial products of his metaphoric activity . . . he will go so far as to tame the metaphors that have produced the hunches. . . . It is my impression . . . that the forging of metaphoric hunch into testable hypothesis goes on all the time."[16]

One suspects after many more uses of the word that "metaphor" itself is used metaphorically and that in some of the uses it stands merely for "conception" or perhaps only "statement." At any rate, the game is in full swing and not a day passes without some branch of science electing to express its hypotheses or conclusions in language appropriate to something else. The geneticists have gained the attention they deserved by ringing the changes on the idea of a code buried in the chromosome molecule. It does not *act* or *behave:* it issues instructions, information, and the like: "DNA gives the replicating cell all the necessary information for perpetuating its features." Similarly, the attempt to manipulate the factors of heredity is called "genetic surgery." Recently also, the spectroscopists have taken to speaking of the "fingerprint" that a substance—say an amino acid—discloses to their apparatus and by which it is identified. At first the metaphoric word is put in quotation marks, soon it becomes the accepted, the only word for the procedure or its result. There lurks in this a pedagogic intention, but it leaves every subject filled with alien notions of doubtful clarity.[17]

To the extent that the popularization of science reaches a widening public, all this bad poetry spreads the sense of total interchangeability among things, and thereby strengthens the mechanical principle.

Certainly, the most dehumanizing of the current metaphors is the now deeply rooted one which calls electronic computers brains, without quotation marks, and carries out this metaphor as far as it will go, which is to say from brain to mind. The machines are spoken of as learning and thinking and even "learning to make errors"; they are said to have memories, to simulate complex situations, to translate, and to teach. According to a circular from the Department of Commerce about translating Russian: "The machine is then asked to recognize the syntactical relations between the words." One waits for the day when it will return an ironic answer. Meanwhile it is not to their use but to the machines themselves as "collaborators" that results in textual study are ascribed; and for all I know they are thanked in prefaces. Some manufacturers, no longer content with successive models of such machines, refer to them officially as belonging to separate generations. Up to that point the public had merely been given the impression that computers afforded every kind of knowledge except carnal knowledge; now we are no longer sure.

Greater love of the machine cannot be conceived than that man should think his own mind inferior to the thing he has made. One hears it said in support of the brain analogy that "already the computer has outstripped the maker's own capabilities," as if this did not apply to a corkscrew or a pair of scissors. Man makes tools which work better for limited purposes than his own fingers. And he makes them by an activity of mind. It will be time to speak of computers as minds, or even brains, when they lay their heads or other parts together to make a man.[18]

But the machine, as sensible scientists have tried to point out, is not even a brain: "It is a remarkably fast and phenomenally accurate moron, rather than a 'giant brain.'" And again: "When an electronic engineer next tells you that a new electronic brain is as good as the brain of man, ask him when he expects to make a tube that will renew the metal of which it is made and not lose the specific 'memory' change [charge?] which it holds as a result of some specific past impulse."[19]

One would suppose that practiced metaphor-makers would be sensitive to the differences between what they join; that they would remember, on the one hand, the gap between brain structure and consciousness; and on the other, the danger that what we are totally ignorant of should appear to be understood by recourse to verbalism. Such a self-discipline would not preclude admiration for the electronics engineer or wonder at the magic of his circuits, which do such useful things at superhuman speeds. But these speeds, like the accuracy of the performance, are a clear proof that we are not dealing with human minds. The people's good sense might have jibbed at the bad poetry, if the older and sounder view of language had still prevailed when computers first became known. But the mystery by which minds are read through sounds and by which ideas are transfixed through marks on paper was by then forgotten. The "mechanism" was thought to be understood; so all care was abandoned and misnaming pursued its frivolous fancy. Thus it comes about that people with Ph.D.'s who observe the ritual accuracy of their clan say they have a "translating machine" when they have mechanized a narrow vocabulary, and a "teaching machine" when they have mechanized a drill book. Had they invented the printing press they would be calling it a reading machine.

NOTES

1. "Vocables" means able to be voiced and is thus ironic here: thousands of new "words" are unspeakable and are referred to by initials, like the well-known DNA, which stands for deoxyribonucleic acid.

2. The tendency to make a singular out of a plural collective noun—a tactic, a statistic, an ethic—looks at first like a reversal of the abstracting habit; the speaker wants a concrete particular. But this is not so; he wants the abstract umbrella still shading his particular. Otherwise he would say this move, this number, this code.

3. "Even if we dispensed with case and person altogether, our sentences would make perfect grammatical sense: 'I gave *she* the book . . . I *is* here . . . You *is* here . . .' Their meanings are completely clear." These encouragements to the young go well with the introductory remark: "From the standpoint of speech, therefore, a sentence could be scientifically defined as *any stretch of utterance between breath intakes*." Harold Whitehall, *Structural Essentials of English*, New York, 1956, 108, 29.

The counterpart of this is the "scientific" definition of reading: "a processing skill of symbolic reasoning sustained by the interfacilitation of an intricate hierarchy of substrata factors that have been mobilized as a psychological working system and pressed into service in accordance with the purpose of the reader." Quoted in *Council for Basic Education Bulletin*, September, 1960, 11.

4. In comparing this quality in different cultures, we must be aware that the difference between *Metrecal* and *Liebfraumilch* is not in the substances alone.

5. E.g., "This world-wide bottleneck must be reduced."

6. Kipling was a pioneer in this "effective" sort of description. His old steamers always "waddle" out of the harbor. The device becomes a systematic impropriety in terminology, as may be seen in almost any novel: ". . . the wind nudging the ship along, boosting it by the stern . . . cuffing the port side. . . ."

7. "The English language has, in fact, so contracted to our own littleness that it is no longer possible to make a good book out of words alone. A writer must concentrate on his vocabulary. . . . He must let his omissions suggest that which the language can no longer accomplish." Cyril Connolly, *The Unquiet Grave*, 1945, 98.

8. The politics of Marxism, which led to the renaming of familiar facts in a tendentious and pseudo-technical way (deviationism, agrarianism, bourgeois moralism, negativism, etc.) have greatly contributed to the decay.

9. *Acid test, crucial* (experiment), *psychological moment* and many other metaphorical uses of phrases that the public connects with techne and science began to enter common speech seventy-five years ago, yet few if any added precision to the workaday language. *Focus* was borrowed from photography by the educationists half a century ago and we have not had a clear statement from them since.

10. It may be too much to say that there is a germ of metaphor in the acronyms with which our minds are cluttered, but word-play and double meaning are present: the original title, which is made up of long abstract nouns, is designed to provide initials that spell a word such as SHAPE or SHAEF. It thus serves as the poor man's scientific symbolism.

11. These compounds are obviously made by persons who think that the second half of *electron* (Greek for *amber*) has some meaning of its own that can supplement the various roots to which it is soldered. This collective ignorance and tastelessness have given *cyclotron, cavitron* and *phytotron*, all created by scientists. *Accutron, Puritron, Insectron, Chemetron*, and *Post-tronic* (for posting books in a bank) doubtless came out of the sales conference and public relations laboratory.

12. There is the further complication that the study of the gas—plasma physics—divides into the study of stream plasma and discontinuous plasma.

13. What other than a professional excuse could there be for choosing "May Day" as the convenient phrase to speak out over the radio as the ship is about to sink? If the origin is m'aider, as is commonly thought, it is inefficient, for no French ear will recognize any native verb in the sounds of the English phrase, and conversely no other speakers will easily catch the closed vowels of the French pronunciation. As for the overtones of the word "May"—maypole, Queen of the May, the merry month—none of these, apparently, should cause the men of the merchant marine to resent as an irony the new signal for their last day of life.

14. If the reader has noticed my use of "ologies" as an independent word, he may be interested to know that I am not innovating. J. A.

Froude and perhaps others used it as early as the middle of the nineteenth century; for the word occurs in a letter by Thomas Hughes's father, dated Jan. 25, 1849: "Before steam and the 'ologies came in . . ." Thomas Hughes, *Memoir of a Son and Brother*, 1873, 106.

15. Ben Jonson, *Timber, or Discoveries*, ed. Ralph S. Walker, Syracuse, 1953, 41.

16. Jerome Bruner, *On Knowing: Essays for the Left Hand*, Cambridge (Massachusetts),1962, 4–5.

17. The humanists are not slow to catch the trick: to justify the open-stage production of plays, they feel bound to say that it is "the most appropriate spatial metaphor for the public and esthetic questions of the day." Editorial in *Tulane Drama Review*, Winter 1963–64.

18. The late John von Neumann, I am told, proved mathematically that a machine could be "programed" to engineer the construction of another machine. One need not question the proof in order to question both the feasibility and the implication of the proposal: so far, no machine will program itself.

19. John I. Griffin, *Statistics: Methods and Applications*. New York, 1962, 49; Leonard Carmichael, *The Making of Modern Mind*, Houston, 1956, 19.

CALCULATING MACHINE*

E. B. White

A publisher in Chicago has sent us a pocket calculating machine by which we may test our writing to see whether it is intelligible. The calculator was developed by General Motors, who, not satisfied with giving the world a Cadillac, now dream of bringing perfect understanding to men. The machine (it is simply a celluloid card with a dial) is called the Reading-Ease Calculator and shows four grades of "reading ease"—Very Easy, Easy, Hard, and Very Hard. You count your words and syllables, set the dial, and an indicator lets you know whether anybody is going to understand what you have written. An instruction book came with it, and after mastering the simple rules we lost no time in running a test on the instruction book itself, to see how *that* writer was doing. The poor fellow! His leading essay, the one on the front cover, tested Very Hard.

Our next step was to study the first phrase on the face of the calculator: "How to test Reading-Ease of written matter." There is, of course, no such thing as reading ease of written matter. There is the ease with which matter can be read, but that is a condition of the reader, not of the matter. Thus the inventors and distributors of this calculator get off to a poor start, with a Very Hard instruction book and a slovenly phrase. Already they have one foot caught in the brier patch of English usage.

Not only did the author of the instruction book score badly on the front cover, but inside the book he used the word "personalize" in an essay on how to improve one's writing. A man who likes the word "personalize" is entitled to his choice, but we wonder whether he should be in the business of giving advice to writers. "Whenever possible," he wrote, "personalize your writing by directing it to the reader." As for us, we would as lief Simoniz our grandmother as personalize our writing.

* From *The Second Tree from the Corner*, by E. B. White. Copyright 1951 by E. B. White. Originally appeared in *The New Yorker* and reprinted by permission of Harper & Row, Publishers, and by permission of Hamish Hamilton Ltd.

In the same envelope with the calculator, we received another training aid for writers—a booklet called "How to Write Better," by Rudolf Flesch. This, too, we studied, and it quickly demonstrated the broncolike ability of the English language to throw whoever leaps cocksurely into the saddle. The language not only can toss a rider but knows a thousand tricks for tossing him, each more gay than the last. Dr. Flesch stayed in the saddle only a moment or two. Under the heading "Think Before You Write," he wrote, "The main thing to consider is your *purpose* in writing. Why are you sitting down to write?" And Echo answered: Because, sir, it is more comfortable than standing up.

Communication by the written word is a subtler (and more beautiful) thing than Dr. Flesch and General Motors imagine. They contend that the "average reader" is capable of reading only what tests Easy, and that the writer should write at or below this level. This is a presumptuous and degrading idea. There is no average reader, and to reach down toward this mythical character is to deny that each of us is on the way up, is ascending. ("Ascending," by the way, is a word Dr. Flesch advises writers to stay away from. Too unusual.)

It is our belief that no writer can improve his work until he discards the dulcet notion that the reader is feeble-minded, for writing is an act of faith, not a trick of grammar. Ascent is at the heart of the matter. A country whose writers are following a calculating machine downstairs is not ascending—if you will pardon the expression—and a writer who questions the capacity of the person at the other end of the line is not a writer at all, merely a schemer. The movies long ago decided that a wider communication could be achieved by a deliberate descent to a lower level, and they walked proudly down until they reached the cellar. Now they are groping for the light switch, hoping to find the way out.

We have studied Dr. Flesch's instructions diligently, but we return for guidance in these matters to an earlier American, who wrote with more patience, more confidence. "I fear chiefly," he wrote, "that my expression may not be *extra-vagant* enough, may not wander far enough beyond the narrow limits of my daily experience, so as to be adequate to the truth of which I have been convinced. . . . Why level downward to our dullest perception always, and praise that as common sense? The commonest sense is the sense of men asleep, which they express by snoring."

Run that through your calculator! It may come out Hard, it may come out Easy. But it will come out whole, and it will last forever.

part two

COMMUNICATION AS DIALOGUE

A. Dimensions of Dialogue

B. The Works of Love

BETWEEN MAN AND MAN: THE REALMS*

Martin Buber

*t*he realms of the life of dialogue and the life of monologue do not coincide with the realms of dialogue and monologue even when forms without sound and even without gesture are included. There are not merely great spheres of the life of dialogue which in appearance are not dialogue, there is also dialogue which is not the dialogue of life, that is, it has the appearance but not the essence of dialogue. At times, indeed, it seems as though there were only this kind of dialogue.

I know three kinds. There is genuine dialogue—no matter whether spoken or silent—where each of the participants really has in mind the other or others in their present and particular being and turns to them with the intention of establishing a living mutual relation between himself and them. There is a technical dialogue, which is prompted solely by the need of objective understanding. And there is monologue disguised as dialogue, in which two or more men, meeting in space, speak each with himself in strangely tortuous and circuitous ways and yet imagine they have escaped the torment of being thrown back on their own resources. The first kind, as I have said, has become rare; where it arises, in no matter how "unspiritual" a form, witness is borne on behalf of the continuance of the organic substance of the human spirit. The second belongs to the inalienable sterling quality of "modern existence." But real dialogue is here continually hidden in all kinds of odd corners and, occasionally in an unseemly way, breaks surface surprisingly and inopportunely—certainly still oftener it is arrogantly tolerated than downright scandalizing—as in the tone of a railway guard's voice, in the glance of an old newspaper vendor, in the smile of the chimney-sweeper. And the third. . . .

A *debate* in which the thoughts are not expressed in the way in which

* Reprinted with permission of The Macmillan Company from *Between Man and Man*, by Martin Buber. First published 1947 by Routledge & Kegan Paul Ltd., and used with their permission.

they existed in the mind but in the speaking are so pointed that they may strike home in the sharpest way, and moreover without the men that are spoken to being regarded in any way present as persons; a *conversation* characterized by the need neither to communicate something, nor to learn something, nor to influence someone, nor to come into connexion with someone, but solely by the desire to have one's own self-reliance confirmed by marking the impression that is made, or if it has become unsteady to have it strengthened; a *friendly chat* in which each regards himself as absolute and legitimate and the other as relativized and questionable; a *lovers' talk* in which both partners alike enjoy their own glorious soul and their precious experience—what an underworld of faceless spectres of dialogue!

The life of dialogue is not one in which you have much to do with men, but one in which you really have to do with those with whom you have to do. It is not the solitary man who lives the life of monologue, but he who is incapable of making real in the context of being the community in which, in the context of his destiny, he moves. It is, in fact, solitude which is able to show the innermost nature of the contrast. He who is living the life of dialogue receives in the ordinary course of the hours something that is said and feels himself approached for an answer. But also in the vast blankness of, say, a companionless mountain wandering that which confronts him, rich in change, does not leave him. He who is living the life of monologue is never aware of the other as something that is absolutely not himself and at the same time something with which he nevertheless communicates. Solitude for him can mean mounting richness of visions and thoughts but never the deep intercourse, captured in a new depth, with the incomprehensibly real. Nature for him is either an *état d'âme*, hence a "living through" in himself, or it is a passive object of knowledge, either idealistically brought within the soul or realistically alienated. It does not become for him a word apprehended with senses of beholding and feeling.

Being, lived in dialogue, receives even in extreme dereliction a harsh and strengthening sense of reciprocity; being, lived in monologue, will not, even in the tenderest intimacy, grope out over the outlines of the self.

This must not be confused with the contrast between "egoism" and "altruism" conceived by some moralists. I know people who are absorbed in "social activity" and have never spoken from being to being with a fellow-man. I know others who have no personal relation except to their enemies, but stand in such a relation to them that it is the enemies' fault if the relation does not flourish into one of dialogue.

Nor is dialogic to be identified with love. I know no one in any time who has succeeded in loving every man he met. Even Jesus obviously loved of "sinners" only the loose, lovable sinners, sinners against the Law; not those who were settled and loyal to their inheritance and sinned against him and his message. Yet to the latter as to the former he stood in a direct relation.

Dialogic is not to be identified with love. But love without dialogic, without real outgoing to the other, reaching to the other, and companying with the other, the love remaining with itself—this is called Lucifer.

Certainly in order to be able to go out to the other you must have the starting place, you must have been, you must be, with yourself. Dialogue between mere individuals is only a sketch, only in dialogue between persons is the sketch filled in. But by what could a man from being an individual so really become a person as by the strict and sweet experiences of dialogue which teach him the boundless contents of the boundary?

What is said here is the real contrary of the cry, heard at times in twilight ages, for universal unreserve. He who can be unreserved with each passer-by has no substance to lose; but he who cannot stand in a direct relation to each one who meets him has a fullness which is futile. Luther is wrong to change the Hebrew "companion" (out of which the Seventy had already made one who is near, a neighbour) into "nearest." If everything concrete is equally near, equally nearest, life with the world ceases to have articulation and structure, it ceases to have human meaning. But nothing needs to mediate between me and one of my companions in the companionship of creation, whenever we come near one another, because we are bound up in relation to the same center.

THE BASIC MOVEMENTS

I term basic movement an essential action of man (it may be understood as an "inner" action, but it is not there unless it is there to the very tension of the eyes' muscles and the very action of the foot as it walks), round which an essential attitude is built up. I do not think of this happening in time, as though the single action preceded the lasting attitude; the latter rather has its truth in the accomplishing, over and over again, of the basic movement, without forethought but also without habit. Otherwise the attitude would have only aesthetic or perhaps also political significance, as a beautiful and as an effective lie. The familiar maxim, "An attitude must first be adopted, the rest follows of itself" ceases to be true in the circle of essential action and essential attitude—that is, where we are concerned with the wholeness of the person.

The basic movement of the life of dialogue is the turn towards the other. That, indeed, seems to happen every hour and quite trivially. If you look at someone and address him you turn to him, of course with the body, but also in the requisite measure with the soul, in that you direct your attention to him. But what of all this is an essential action, done with the essential being? In this way, that out of the incomprehensibility of what lies to hand this one person steps forth and becomes a presence. Now to our perception the world ceases to be an insignificant multiplicity of points to one of which we pay momentary attention. Rather it is a limitless tumult round a narrow breakwater, brightly outlined and able to bear heavy loads —limitless, but limited by the breakwater, so that, though not engirdled, it has become finite in itself, been given form, released from its own indifference. And yet none of the contacts of each hour is unworthy to take up from our essential being as much as it may. For no man is without strength for expression, and our turning towards him brings about a reply, however imperceptible, however quickly smothered, in a looking and sounding forth of the soul that are perhaps dissipating in mere inwardness and yet do exist. The notion of modern man that this turning to the other is sentimental and does not correspond to the compression of life today is a grotesque error, just as his affirmation that turning to the other is impractical in the bustle of this life today is only the masked confession of his weakness of initiative when confronted with the state of the time. He lets it dictate to him what is possible or permissible, instead of stipulating, as an unruffled partner, what is to be stipulated to the state of *every* time, namely, what space and what form it is bound to concede to creaturely existence.

The basic movement of the life of monologue is not turning away as opposed to turning towards; it is "reflexion."

When I was eleven years of age, spending the summer on my grand-parents' estate, I used, as often as I could do it unobserved, to steal into the stable and gently stroke the neck of my darling, a broad dapple-grey horse. It was not a casual delight but a great, certainly friendly, but also deeply stirring happening. If I am to explain it now, beginning from the still very fresh memory of my hand, I must say that what I experienced in touch with the animal was the Other, the immense otherness of the Other, which however, did not remain strange like the otherness of the ox and the ram, but rather let me draw near and touch it. When I stroked the mighty mane, sometimes marvellously smooth-combed, at other times just as astonishingly wild, and felt the life beneath my hand, it was as though the element of vitality itself bordered on my skin, something that was not I, was certainly not akin to me, palpably the other, not just another, really the Other itself; and yet it let me approach, confided itself to me, placed itself elementally in the relation of *Thou* and *Thou* with me. The horse, even when I had not begun by pouring oats for him into the manger, very gently raised his massive head, ears flicking, then snorted quietly, as a conspirator gives a signal meant to be recognizable only to his fellow-conspirator; and I was approved. But once—I do not know what came over the child, at any rate it was childlike enough—it struck me about the stroking, what fun it gave me, and suddenly I became conscious of my hand. The game went on as before, but something had changed, it was no longer the same thing. And the next day, after giving him a rich feed, when I stroked my friend's head he did not raise his head. A few years later, when I thought back to the incident, I no longer supposed that the animal had noticed my defection. But at the time I considered myself judged.

Reflexion is something different from egoism and even from "egotism." It is not that a man is concerned with himself, considers himself, fingers himself, enjoys, idolizes and bemoans himself; all that can be added, but it is not integral to reflexion. (Similarly, to the turning towards, completing it, there can be added the realizing of the other in his particular existence, even the encompassing of him, so that the situations common to him and oneself are experienced also from his, the other's end.) I term it reflexion when a man withdraws from accepting with his essential being another person in his particularity—a particularity which is by no means to be circumscribed by the circle of his own self, and though it substantially touches and moves his soul is in no way immanent in it—and lets the other exist only as his own experience, only as a "part of myself." For then dialogue becomes a fiction, the mysterious intercourse between two human worlds only a game, and in the rejection of the real life confronting him the essence of all reality begins to disintegrate.

INTERSUBJECTIVITY*

Gabriel Marcel

*D*uring the last two chapters, but particularly during the very last one, we have gradually come to acknowledge how impossible it is not only to give, on one's own account, an objective answer to the question, "Who am I?" but also even to imagine the valid giving of such an answer by anybody else who was considering one's life from the outside. Little by little, we have been forced to insist that my life is essentially ungraspable; that it eludes me and indeed eludes, in all directions, itself. Nevertheless, I can be called upon to sacrifice my life or, at the very least, to consecrate it. We should pause for a moment over this notion of consecration; self-sacrifice can be considered, of course, as merely the consummation of an act that consists of living for something, of dedicating oneself to what Josiah Royce called a cause, meaning an idea or a quest. But we should pause here again to ask ourselves what the secret link can be that binds my life to such an act of self-dedication. Can we consider the act as a sort of seal set, as it were, on my life from the outside? It is obvious that we cannot: the words "from the outside" are grossly inadequate, and in fact where exactly, when we talk of this act of dedication coming from the outside, do we imagine it as coming from? No, it is only from the very depths of my own life that this inner need for self-dedication can spring.

Moreover, we are here rediscovering, at a level of higher potency, the truth which we acknowledged in our third chapter when we recognized, as the phenomenology of Husserl recognizes, that every kind of awareness is essentially awareness of something other than itself; so human living, driven in this way to dedicate itself, seems also essentially the living of something other than itself. What can make our path difficult and uncertain at this moment is, however, that we are inclined to take it as an axiom that

* Reprinted from Gabriel Marcel, *The Mystery of Being*, Vol. 1, pp. 210–224, and used by permission of the publishers, The Harvill Press Ltd., London, and Henry Regnery Company, Chicago.

awareness and life are concepts different in kind. But the arguments of our last chapter in particular should enable us to grasp the fact that such a difference in kind can no longer be postulated when I am speaking, not of life as a mere phenomenon to be investigated, but of my own life. I cannot speak of my own life without asking myself what point it has, or even whether it points in any direction at all. . . . The pun there, by the way, may appear frivolous but it is necessary to convey the ambiguity of the French word "sens," which refers here not only to the *meaning*—in one of the multifarious senses of that slippery English word—but also the *bearing*, or *direction*, or *relevance*, or *orientation*, of my life. The verb "to mean," in English, has, of course, these two among its many other other senses: "I don't see what you mean" can be the equivalent of, "I don't follow the sense of what you are saying," but also of, "I follow the sense of what you are saying, but I don't see its bearing on our general argument." "Meaning," however, has far too many other senses, and is too vague and confused a word altogether in its popular usage to be suitable here. The Germans convey the two uses of "sens" neatly by the words "Bedeutung" and "Richtung" and they have an intermediate word "Sinn," though it does not strictly imply the notion of orientation.

After that little linguistic digression, let us repeat the proposition from which it arose. I cannot speak of my life without asking myself what point it has, or even whether it points in any direction at all; and even if I decide that it is in fact a pointless business, that it points nowhere, still the very fact that I have raised the question presupposes the assumption that life, in some cases at least, might have a point. If I could really uproot this assumption from my mind, at the same stroke my life would cease to be my own life. I mean that I would cease to apprehend it as my own; this would be that final estrangement from oneself that, in the ideal limiting case, can be reached only by a slave, and by a slave who has ceased to be aware of his own state of servitude. And in fact there is every reason to suppose that except in this abstract sense, as an ideal limiting case, such final self-estrangement is inconceivable. For I think that there can be no doubt that there does remain in every slave, fairly deep down, an obscure awareness of having been outraged, and with this awareness at least an indistinct, incipient protest, a feeling that one's life ought not to be a slave's life, that its proper growth has been thwarted.

When I ask whether my life has a point, it does seem that I am imagining a kind of significance, or relevance, which my life would go on having whether or not I wanted it to; I am, or so it seems to me, more or less explicitly relating my question to the idea of a play in which I have to take a part; I am asking myself about the possible theme of the performance in which I have been induced to participate. From this point of view I might compare my situation with that of an actor who has been given his own cues and lines, but who has not had the play as a whole read to him and has not even been told briefly what it is about. He has merely been told: at such and such a cue, you will make your entrance, you will speak the following lines, accompanying your lines by this piece of business, then you will make your exit. The actor has to suppose that his lines and his business, which in themselves seem to him almost pointless, have their point in relation to the total pattern of the play. Thus if life as a whole has a point—or as we would say here, not to break the metaphor, a plot or a theme—then in some sense my own life has a plot or a theme, too.

However, if we stick to our actual situation, it is obvious that the life I have to live is not quite on all fours with the sort of episode I have just been describing. Keeping to the theatrical comparisons, which seem almost to be imposed on us at this point, we might say that in fact I am not told in advance what my lines and business are to be; I have to go right out there and improvise. But where the actor in the old *commedia dell' arte* had to improvise on the rough outline of a story given to him in advance, I am given no such rough outline. It is just as if—or so it seems at a first glance —the producer of the play had carelessly omitted to provide me with just the information I needed to carry out the task that had been entrusted to me in a proper fashion. Given all this, might I not be led into calling the very existence of the producer into question? Or, to put the point more precisely, would I not have solid grounds for asserting that, whether or not there really is a producer, everything is run just as if there wasn't one? This comes down once more to saying that there is no rough outline, no plot, or, to go back to the phrase we started with, that my life has no point. From this perspective, I will naturally be led to ask whether I myself, against the grain as it were of this general pointlessness, can by my own efforts give my life a point; can I myself confer a kind of significance on it? This is, in its atheistic form, the position of contemporary existentialism. Of course, we have already seen quite a number of reasons for considering it to be an untenable position.

Did I not affirm at the beginning of this lecture that it seems impossible that the act by which I consecrate my life to some idea or quest could be regarded as external to my life, but that, on the contrary, the act rather resembles the bursting of my life into flower? But according to the hypothesis of atheistic existentialism, which I have just formulated, this act of consecration would be something external to my life. The hypothesis implies, apparently, something more or less of the following sort: that my life has come into my hands by accident, through the merest unforeseeable chance, like a notecase that one happens to find dropped on the pavement. If I am an honest person, I have no doubt tried to return the notecase to its owner; all my attempts to find him have proved vain, and here I am in possession of a considerable sum of money. What shall I do with it, to what use shall I put it? In this case, we should notice that our question has a definite scope and implies a range of possible definite answers; finding this money may give me a chance to satisfy some old wish—or to pay some old debt— or to help somebody who is not merely in a state of poverty but in a state of wretchedness. I must make a choice between such concrete possibilities. But such possibilities, it should be noted, have their roots in my own life, such as it was *before* I found the notecase. My life, itself, on the other hand, cannot really be compared to this lucky find. I do not *find myself alive*, in the sense in which I might find the owner of these stray coins or notes. My existence as a living being precedes this discovery of myself as a living being. One might even say that, by a fatal necessity, I pre-exist myself. But this forces us to take up a position diametrically opposed to that, for instance, of Sartre, in that sentence of his that has been so often quoted: "Man's motto is to be a maker and, as a maker, to make himself and to be nothing but the self he has made for himself." Everything that we have been saying up to this very moment forces us to take our stand against any such affirmation. "It would be impossible," I wrote, commenting on this sentence in my essay, *Techniques of Degradation*, "to deny in a more aggressive fashion the existence of any sort of natural world, of anything that is inherited by us, or, more profoundly, of reality itself, that reality which is conferred upon us or in which we participate, and which gives us a greater impetus, the deeper we penetrate into it."

The time has come when we should attempt to draw out all the implications of the notions of a situation, and of participation as we have attempted to elucidate them in our previous three chapters. It may be, however, that to reach our goal we may find it convenient to go back, in the first instance, to the problem of the relationships between myself and others, as that problem now stands, in the light of our previous observations, and particularly in the light of that criticism of the notion of a *state of consciousness* which I roughed out in chapter three. I think my best course will be to present you with a condensed version of my analysis in my essay, *Homo Viator*, an analysis which is a kind of nucleus of the possible phenomenology of the relationships between myself and others.

We should notice, to start with, that the ego, as such, shows up in an extraordinarily vivid and aggressive fashion in the mental world of the child; and one might add that this vividness and aggressiveness persist, in later years, to the degree to which that mental world survives in the adult. The child, let us say, runs up to his mother and offers her a flower. "Look," he says, "that was me, *I* picked it." His tone and his gestures are very significant; he is pointing himself out as somebody who deserves the admiration and gratitude of grown-ups. Look, it is I, I in person, I, all present and correct here, who have plucked this flower! Above all, don't believe for a minute that it was Jim or Lucy who picked it. The child's,

"*I* did it, " in fact, excludes in the most definite fashion the deplorable misunderstanding by which *my* exploit could be attributed to others. But we find adults standing up in the same way for the ego's rights. Let us take the example of the amateur composer who has just been singing, in a throaty voice, a song for which he has written the tune. Some artless listener asks, was that by Debussy? "Oh, no," says the composer, bridling and smirking, "that was a little thing of my own." Here again the ego is trying to attract to itself the praise, the surprised and admiring comments, of a something *other* than itself, that it uses as a sounding-board. In every case of this sort one may say that the ego is present in the flesh, appealing or protesting, in various tones of voice, that nobody should infringe on its rights, or, if you like, tread on its toes. Notice, too, that in all such cases one essential factor is what I shall call, a little pedantically, *ecceity*: that is, a hereness and a nowness, or rather a here-and-nowness; we can think of the ego in this sense, in fact, as a sort of personified here-and-now that has to defend itself actively against other personified heres-and-nows, the latter appearing to it essentially as just so many threats to what I have called its rights. These rights, however, have essentially a pre-juridical character, they are from the beginning inseparably linked to the very fact of existing and thus are exposed continually to all sorts of more or less mortifying infringements. In so far as I feel myself in danger of being passively overlooked or actively slighted in a hundred ways that all cut me to the quick, one might say, in fact, that I have no protective skin at all, that the quick is exposed already.

The obvious example to take at this point is, of course, that of the shy young man who is making his first appearance at some fashionable dance or cocktail party. Such a young man is, as you so admirably express it in English, to the highest degree *self-conscious*. He feels himself the cynosure, and the extremely vulnerable cynosure, of neighbouring eyes. It seems to him that all the other people at the party, none of whom he knows, are looking at him, and looking at him, too, with what meaning glances! Obviously they are making fun of him, perhaps of his new dinner jacket which does not fit him as well as it should, perhaps of his black bow tie, which was all right when he last looked in the mirror, but now, he feels quite sure, has gone lopsided. And then, of course, he cut himself when he was shaving. And everybody must have noticed how clumsily he held his glass just a moment ago, so that some of the sherry slopped over. And so on, and so on. . . . To such a young man it seems that he has been literally thrown (as Christians were thrown to the lions) to the malevolent lucidity of other people's glances. Thus he is at once preoccupied with himself to the highest possible degree and hypnotized at the same time to a quite supreme degree by others, by what he imagines other people may think of him. It is this paradoxical tension which your excellent word *self-consciousness* so compactly expresses.

But on the other hand this tension is quite at the opposite pole from what I have at various times called, and shall here call again, *intersubjectivity*. And the opposite nature of the two things cannot be too heavily underlined. Let us suppose that some unknown person comes up at our party to say a word or two to the shy young man and put him at his ease. The latter, to begin with, does not find himself entering into the direct relation with his new acquaintance that is expressed by the pronoun *you* but instead thinks of him as *him*. Why is *he* talking to me? What is *he* after? Is he trying to satisfy some sinister and mocking curiosity? Let us be on our guard anyway. Let us be extremely non-committal in our answers to his question. Thus, because he is on the defensive with this other guest, our young man has to the least possible degree what can be described as a genuine encounter or conversation *with* him. He is not really *with* the other any more than he can help being. But in a very general fashion, indeed, one might say that it is the relationship expressed by the preposition *with* that is eminently intersubjective. The relationship that *with* expresses, here, does not for instance really apply to the world of objects, which taken as a whole, is a world merely of juxtaposition. A chair is *alongside* a table, or *beside* it, or we put the chair *by* the table, but the chair is never really *with* the table in this sense.

But let us get back to our example and let us suppose that the ice is after all broken, and that the conversation takes on a more intimate character. "I am glad to meet you," says the stranger, "I once knew your parents," and all at once a bond is created and, what specially matters, there is a relaxation of tension. The attention of the young man ceases to be concentrated on himself, it is as if something gripped tight together inside him were able to loosen up. He is lifted out of that stifling here-and-nowness in which, if I may be allowed a homely comparison, his ego was sticking to him as an adhesive plaster sticks to a small cut. He is lifted right out of the here and now, and, what is very strange surely, this unknown person whom he has just met accompanies him on this sort of magic voyage. They are together in what we must call an elsewhere, an elsewhere, however, which has a mysteriously intimate character. Let us say, if you like, that they are linked to each other by a shared secret. I shall have to come back, no doubt, to the notion of the secret as a mainspring of intersubjectivity, but let us notice, before we leave our example, that ties of quite a different nature might have grown up between the stranger and the shy young man. A man whom I run into quite casually learns that I am very fond of coffee, coffee is desperately scarce in France at the time, so he gives me a hint about how to get some on the black market. One cannot say that this incident is enough in itself to create a bond between me and him; all we have in common is a *taste*, and that is not enough to draw us together at the ontological level, that is *qua* beings. And neither, on the other hand, is a taste for coffee, even combined with a certain broad-mindedness about means of getting hold of coffee, enough in itself to create the sense of complicity and freemasonry in vice that might arise from the avowal, to somebody who shared it, of some much more dubious inclination. But such a sense of complicity is not really what we have in mind, either; rather it is in the sort of case where I discover that a stranger has recognized the deep, individual quality of somebody whom I myself have tenderly loved and who retains a place in my heart, that true intersubjectivity arises.

We could also take examples of intersubjectivity from artistic and religious experience. But it is clear that there would be no absolute discontinuity between the examples taken from ordinary life and those from the higher reaches of the spirit; on the contrary there would be a kind of graduated scale, with something like the mystical communion of souls in worship at the top end, and with something like an *ad hoc* association for some strictly practical and rigidly defined purpose at the bottom. But it would be possible to show that a single human relationship can work its way all the way up and down this scale; this, for instance, is quite obviously true of marriage. There may be moments of drought in marriage when the wife becomes for her husband that "silly creature who should have been busy darning socks, but there she was clucking round the tea table with a lot of old hens," and there may be almost mystical moments when the wife is acknowledged and loved as the bearer of a unique value to which eternal bliss has been promised. One might therefore say that there is an hierarchy of choices, or rather of invocations, ranging from the call upon another which is like ringing a bell for a servant to the quite other sort of call which is really like a kind of prayer. But, as I tried to show in my first *Metaphysical Journal*, in invocations of the first sort—where we press a bell or make some other sort of signal to show that we want service—the Thou we are invoking is really a He or a She or even an It treated pragmatically as a Thou. When I stop somebody in the street to ask my way, I do say to him, it is true, "Can *you* tell me how to get to such-and-such a Square?," but all the same I am making a convenience of him, I am treating him as if he were a signpost. No doubt, even in this limiting case, a touch of genuine intersubjectivity can break through, thanks to the magical powers of the tone of voice and the glance. If I have really lost my bearings, if it is late, if I fear that I may have to grope my way for hours through some labyrinthine and perhaps even dangerous warren of streets, I may have a fleeting but irresistible impression that the stranger I am appealing to is a brother eager to come to my aid. What happens is, in a word, that the stranger has started off by putting himself, as it were, ideally in my shoes. He has come within my reach as a person. It is no longer a mere matter of his showing me the way as a guide-book or a map might, but of his really giving a helping hand to somebody who is alone and in a bewildered state. This is nothing more than a sort of spark of spirituality, out as soon as it is in; the stranger and I part almost certainly never to see each other again, yet for a few minutes, as I trudge homewards, this man's unexpected cordiality makes me feel as if I had stepped out of a wintry day into a warm room.

On an occasion of such a sort, we have lingered for a moment on the threshold of intersubjectivity, that is, of the realm of existence to which the preposition *with* properly applies, as it does not properly apply, let me repeat, to the purely objective world. Within the realm of intersubjectivity, naturally, a whole throng of different sorts of relationship must be distinguished from each other. Words like "ensemble" in French, "together" in English, "zusammen" in German, can be entirely deceptive, particularly in the cases where they refer to travelling or even to working together, to the togetherness of the bus or the factory. There are certainly cases in which what is called collective labour can be considered, at least from the point of view of how it looks on the surface, as the arithmetical sum of the various special tasks performed by each separate individual. And yet even in such cases as this there is certainly also something that arithmetic cannot account for. There is at least in the background a sense of a common fate, there is certainly an indistinct awareness of the conditions to which all the workers in such a factory as we have in mind must without distinction subject themselves, finding, perhaps in every case, that such self-subjection goes against the grain. This feeling of community in effort and struggle that such factory workers have is quite enough in itself to deprive us of any right to treat them as simple units of force that can be added to each other. But we should recognize all the same that the level of reality represented by the preposition *with* can be a rather low and barren level—and this is naturally even more true in the case of the togetherness of passengers in a public vehicle. The content of this sort of reality, the reality for so many people of work and the journey to work, enriches itself only in the degree they learn to know themselves and to know their companions of bus or bench both in the uniqueness of their diverse beings and in the single colour of their common fate. It is only on this condition that a true companionship can be created such as that, for example, which existed in the army during the late war between fighting soldiers, and perhaps in a greater degree still between prisoners-of-war and civilian deportees in various German camps. An ordeal endured in common is the cement of such companionships, it is what permits them to arise.

But when we talk of common sufferings cementing human *relationships*, let us notice that this word is likely to lead us into error, unless we take it in a much deeper sense than its usual one, for instance, in treatises on logic : we must think of the relationship between two terms as something that really does bind them, as something that causes them to negate themselves as simple, detached terms. We might make this point clearer if we said that relationships between things are external, relationships between people are internal. When I put the table *beside* the chair I do not make any difference to the table or the chair, and I can take one or the other away without making any difference; but my relationship *with* you makes a difference to both of us, and so does any interruption of the relationship make a difference. Between two people, in fact, who have an intimate relationship, a kind of unity tends to be created which makes a third person, who has not been initiated into the relationship, who does not participate in it, feel an intruder. Many women must have had this feeling—and it is a very painful feeling—when their husbands or their sons had reunions with old comrades of the army or of the prisoner-of-war or detention camps in their presence. We come up here, once more, against the notion of the shared secret (the secret, in our present example, *not* shared by the intrusive third party) which I mentioned at the beginning of this analysis; and we can see how important and also how ambiguous the notion is. What appears to the non-initiated person as a secret may be merely a few jokes, a few allusions, to which she has no clue, and which therefore inevitably irritate her. But the secret may also, and in a deeper sense, be a really incommunicable experience—generally a painful one—about which the initiated feel that others, who did not share it in the flesh, have no right to speak. It is just at this point that what we call in France pure sociology, and what you call anthropology, the study of customs and ceremonies, strikes on something deeper than itself, something that constitutes us in our very selfhood. I have only, for that matter, given very simple examples here; from my own dramatic works I could take more complicated ones, particularly from *Quartet in F Sharp*, of which the first version dates back to the first World War, but which anticipates in the most concrete fashion this whole philosophy of intersubjectivity.

In this play of mine, I present the extremely rich and in the end indefinable network of relationships that interweaves itself between a woman, her first husband (a musician whom she divorces) and the musician's brother, whom she marries after the divorce. The climax of the play is the woman's sudden awareness of a suprapersonal unity which in some sense subsumes under itself the two men she has successively loved; she is no longer able to distinguish whether what she has loved in the second husband is, or is not, a mere reflection of the first. But on the other hand the fondness of the brothers for each other resists this new test, and the movement of the play is towards the discovery, as it were, of a kind of musical order of relationships in comparison with which the individual's usual hasty judgments about himself, and about others, seem precarious and destructive.

The notion of intersubjectivity is obviously capable of multifarious developments. In the first place, it is not in any hesitant fashion that I suggest it is only this notion that can throw light on the more obscure and more important aspects of what is improperly called psychical but should, I think, be called metapsychical research. As Carrington has made perfectly clear, telepathy is an inconceivable process unless we are willing to acknowledge that there is a region where the words *I* and *You* cease to denote two nuclei quite distinct from each other between which objective relations can be established by the emission of signals. And if one thinks it over, one will also perceive that all human intercourse worthy of the name takes place in an atmosphere of real intimacy that cannot be compared to an exchange of signals between an emission post and a reception post; this, of course, is the same sort of point as was made in a previous chapter when we talked about sensation and the impossibility of considering it as the equivalent of the emission and reception of a message.

But there is no doubt at all that we ought to go further, and to acknowledge that intersubjectivity plays its part also within the life of the subject, even at moments when the latter's only intercourse is with itself. In its own intrinsic structure subjectivity is already, and in the most profound sense, genuinely intersubjective; and it is at this point that the whole development of our argument becomes organically connected with the earlier part of this lecture.

THE DIALOGUE (*Ecclesiam Suam, Part III*)

Pope Paul VI

*t*here is a third attitude which the Catholic should adopt at this period in the history of the world, an attitude characterized by study of the contacts which the church ought to maintain with humanity. If the church acquires an evergrowing awareness of itself, and if the church tries to model itself on the ideal which Christ proposes to it, the result is that the church becomes radically different from the human environment in which it, of course, lives or which it approaches. The Gospel makes us recognize such a distinction when it speaks to us of "the world," i.e., of humanity opposed both to the light of faith and to the gift of grace, of humanity which exalts itself in a naive optimism which believes that its own energies suffice to give man complete, lasting, and beneficent self-expression. Or, finally, of humanity, which plunges itself into a crude form of pessimism which declares its own vices, weaknesses, and moral ailments to be fatal, incurable, and perhaps even desirable as manifestations of freedom and of authenticity. The Gospel, which recognizes, denounces, pities, and cures human misfortunes with penetrating and sometimes with heart-rending sincerity, does not yield to any illusions about the natural goodness of man (as if he were sufficient unto himself and as if he needed nothing else than to be left free to express himself according to his whims) nor to any despairing resignation to the incurable corruption of human nature. The Gospel is light, it is newness, it is energy, it is rebirth, it is salvation. Hence it both creates and defines a type of new life about which the New Testament teaches us a continuous and remarkable lesson which is expressed in the warning of St. Paul: "You must not fall in with the manners of this world. There must be an inward change, a remaking of your minds, so that you can satisfy yourselves what is God's will, the good thing, the desirable thing, the perfect thing."

This distinction between the life of the Christian and the life of the worldling also derives from the reality and from the consequent recognition of the sanctification produced in us by our sharing in the Paschal mystery and, above all, in Holy Baptism, which, as was said above, is and ought to be considered a true rebirth. Again St. Paul reminds us of this truth: "We who were taken up into Christ by baptism have been taken up, all of us, into His death. In our baptism, we have been buried with Him, died like Him, that is, just as Christ was raised up by His father's power from the dead, we too might live and move in a new kind of existence."

It will not be amiss if the Christian of today keeps always in view His original and wondrous form of life which should not only sustain him with the happiness that results from his dignity but also protect him from an environment which threatens him with the contagion of human wretchedness and with the seduction of human glory.

See how St. Paul himself formed the Christians of the primitive church: "You must not consent to be yokefollowers with unbelievers. What has innocence to do with lawlessness? What is there in common between light and darkness? How can a believer throw in his lot with an infidel?" Christian education will always have to remind the student today of his privileged position and of his resultant duty to live in the world but not in the way of the world, according to the above-mentioned prayer of Jesus for his disciples: "I am not asking that thou shouldst keep them clear of what is evil, they do not belong to the world, as I, too, do not belong to the world." And the church adopts this prayer as its own.

But this distinction is not a separation. Neither is it indifference or fear or contempt. When the church distinguishes itself from human nature, it does not oppose itself to human nature, but rather unites itself to it. Just as the doctor who, realizing the danger inherent in a contagious disease, not only tries to protect himself and others from such infection, but also dedicates himself to curing those who have been stricken, so too the church does not make an exclusive privilege of the mercy which the divine goodness has shown it, nor does it distort its own good fortune into a reason for disinterest in those who have not shared it, but rather in its own salvation it finds an argument for interest in and for love for anyone who is either close to it and can at least be approached through universal effort to share its blessings.

If, as we said before, the church has a true realization of what the Lord wishes it to be, then within the church there arises a unique sense of fullness and a need for outpouring, together with the clear awareness of a mission which transcends the church, of a message to be spread. It is the duty of evangelization. It is the missionary mandate. It is the apostolic commission. An attitude of preservation of the faith is insufficient. Certainly we must preserve and also defend the treasure of truth and of grace which has come to us by way of inheritance from the Christian tradition. "Keep safe what has been entrusted to thee," warns St. Paul.

But neither the preservation nor the defense of the faith exhausts the duty of the church in regard to the gifts which it possesses. The duty consonant with the patrimony received from Christ is that of spreading, offering, announcing it to others. Well do we know that "go, therefore, make disciples of all nations" is the last command of Christ to His Apostles. By the very term "Apostles" these men define their inescapable mission. To this internal drive of charity which tends to become the external gift of charity we will give the name of dialogue, which has in these days come into common usage.

The church should enter into dialogue with the world in which it exists and labors. The church has something to say. The church has a message to deliver. The church has a communication to offer.

It is no secret that this important facet of the contemporary life of the church will be specially and fully studied by the Ecumenical Council, with full freedom in discussing them. We wish only to invite you, venerable brethren, to preface such study with certain considerations in order that we see more clearly the motives which impel the church toward the dialogue, the methods to be followed, and the goals to be achieved. We wish to give, not full treatment to topics, but proper dispositions to hearts.

Nor can we do otherwise in our conviction that the dialogue ought to characterize our apostolic office, heirs as we are of such a pastoral approach and method as has been handed down to us by our predecessors of the past century, beginning with the great, wise Leo XIII. Almost as a personification of the gospel character of the wise scribe, who, like the father of a family, "knows how to bring both new and old things out of his treasure-house." In a stately manner he assumed His function as teacher of the world making the object of His richest instruction the problems of our time considered in the light of the word of Christ. Thus, also did His successors, as you well know. Did not our predecessors, especially Pope Pius XI and Pope Pius XII, leave us a magnificently rich patrimony of teaching which was conceived in the loving and enlightened attempt to join divine to human wisdom, not considered in the abstract, but rather expressed in the concrete language of modern man?

And what is this apostolic endeavor if not a dialogue? And does it not place an even sharper emphasis on its teaching in the sense of approaching as close as possible to the experience and the understanding of the contemporary world? And was not the Council itself assigned—and justly so—a pastoral function which would be completely focused on the injection of the Christian message into the stream of the thought, of the speech, of the culture, of the customs, of the strivings of man as he lives today and acts in this life? Even before converting the world, nay, in order to convert it, we must meet the world and talk with it.

Concerning our lowly self, although we are reluctant to speak of it and would prefer not to attract to it the attention of others, we cannot pass over in silence, in this deliberate communication to the episcopal hierarchy and to the Christian people, our resolution to persevere, so far as our weak energies will permit and, above all, so far as the grace of God will grant us the necessary means, in the same direction and in the same effort to approach the world in which Providence has destined us to live, with all due reverence to be observed in this approach, and with all due solicitude and love, in order that we may understand it and offer it the gifts of truth and of grace of which Christ has made us custodians in order that we may communicate to the world our wonderful destiny of redemption and of hope. Deeply engraved on our heart are those words of Christ which we would humbly but resolutely make our own: "When God sent His son into the world, it was not to reject the world, but so that the world might find salvation through Him."

See, then, venerable brethren, the transcendent origin of the dialogue. It is found in the very plan of God. Religion, of its very nature, is a relationship between God and man. Prayer expresses such a relationship in dialogue. Revelation, i.e., the supernatural relationship which God Himself, on His own initiative, has established with the human race, can be represented as a dialogue in which the world of God is expressed in the incarnation and therefore in the Gospel. The fatherly and holy conversation between God and man, interrupted by original sin, has been marvelously resumed in the course of history.

The history of salvation narrates exactly this long and changing dialogue which begins with God and brings to man a many-splendored conversation. It is in this conversation of Christ among men that God allows us to understand something of Himself, the mystery of His life, unique in its essence, trinitarian in its persons. And He tells us finally how He wishes to be known. He is love. And how He wishes to be honored and served by us: Love is our supreme commandment.

The dialogue thus takes on full meaning and offers grounds for confidence. The child is invited to it. The mystic finds a full outlet in it.

We need to keep ever present this ineffable, yet real relationship of the dialogue, which God the Father, through Christ in the Holy Spirit, has offered to us and established with us, if we are to understand the relationship which we, i.e., the church, should strive to establish and to foster with the human race.

The dialogue of salvation was opened spontaneously on the initiative of God: "He [God] loved us first." It will be up to us to take the initiative in extending to men this same dialogue, without waiting to be summoned to it.

The dialogue of salvation began with charity, with the divine goodness: "God so loved the world as to give His only-begotten son." Nothing but fervent and unselfish love should motivate our dialogue.

The dialogue of salvation was not proportioned to the merits of those toward whom it was directed, nor to the results which it would achieve or fail to achieve: "Those who are healthy need no physician," so also our own dialogue ought to be without limits or ulterior motives.

The dialogue of salvation was made accessible to all. It was destined for all without distinction. In like manner our own dialogue should be potentially universal, i.e., all-embracing and capable of including all, excepting only one who would either absolutely reject it or insincerely pretend to accept it.

The dialogue of salvation normally experienced a gradual development, successive advances, humble beginnings before complete success. Ours, too, will take cognizance of the slowness of psychological and historical maturation and of the need to wait for the hour when God may make our dialogue effective. Not for this reason will our dialogue postpone till tomorrow what it can accomplish today. It ought to be eager for the opportune moment. It ought to sense the preciousness of time. Today, i.e., every day, our dialogue should begin again. We, rather than those toward whom it is directed, should take the initiative.

The dialogue of salvation did not physically force anyone to accept it. It was a tremendous appeal of love which, although placing a vast responsibility on those toward whom it was directed, nevertheless left them free to respond to it or to reject it. Even the number of miracles and their remonstrative power were adapted to the spiritual needs and dispositions of the recipients, in order that their free consent to the divine revelation might be facilitated, without, however, their losing the merit involved in such a consent.

So, too, although our own mission is the announcement of the truth which is both indisputable and necessary for salvation, that mission will not be introduced in the armor of external force, but simply through the legitimate means of human education, of interior persuasion of ordinary conversation, and it will offer its gift of salvation with full respect for personal and civic freedom.

As is clear, the relationships between the church and the world can assume many mutually different aspects. Theoretically speaking, the church could set its mind on reducing such relationships to a minimum, endeavoring to isolate itself from dealings with secular society, just as it could set itself the task of pointing out the evils that can be found in secular society, condemning them and declaring crusades against them, as also it could approach so close to secular society as to strive to exert a preponderant influence on it or even to exercise a theocratic power over it, and so on.

But it seems to us that the relationship of the church to the world, without precluding other legitimate forms of expression, can be represented better in a dialogue, not, of course, a dialogue in a univocal sense, but rather a dialogue adapted to the nature of the interlocutor and to factual circumstances (the dialogue with a child differs from that with an adult, that with a believer from that with an unbeliever). This has been suggested by the custom, which has by now become widespread, of conceiving the relationships between the sacred and the secular in terms of the transforming dynamism of modern society, in terms of the pluralism of its manifestations, likewise in terms of the maturity of man, be he religious or not, enabled through secular education to think, to speak, and to act through the dignity of dialogue.

This type of relationship indicates a proposal of courteous esteem, of understanding, and of goodness on the part of the one who inaugurates the dialogue. It excludes the prior condemnation, the offensive and time-worn polemic, the emptiness of useless conversation. If this approach does not aim at effecting the immediate conversion of the interlocutor, inasmuch as it respects both his dignity and his freedom, nevertheless it does aim at helping him, and tries to dispose him for a fuller sharing of sentiments and convictions.

Hence, the dialogue supposes that we possess a state of mind which we intend to communicate to others and to foster in all our neighbors: the state of mind of one who feels within himself the burden of the apostolic mandate, of one who realizes that he can no longer separate his own salvation from the endeavor to save others, of one who strives constantly to put the message of which he is custodian into the mainstream of human discourse.

The dialogue is, then, a method of accomplishing the apostolic mission, it is an example of the art of spiritual communication. Its characteristics are the following:

1. Clearness above all. The dialogue supposes and demands comprehensibility. It is an outpouring of thought. It is an invitation to the exercise of the highest powers that man possesses. This very claim would be enough to classify the dialogue among the best manifestations of human activity and culture. This fundamental requirement is enough to enlist our apostolic care to review every angle of our language to guarantee that it be understandable, acceptable, and well-chosen.

2. A second characteristic of the dialogue is its meekness, the virtue that Christ sets before us to be learned from Him:

"Learn of me, because I am meek and humble of heart." The dialogue is not proud, it is not bitter, it is not offensive. It communicates to the example it proposes. It is not a command, it is not an imposition. It is peaceful, it avoids violent methods. It is patient. It is generous.

3. Finally, pedagogical prudence, which esteems highly the psychological and moral circumstances of the listener whether he be a child,

uneducated, unprepared, diffident, hostile. Prudence strives to learn the sensitivities of the hearer and requires that we adapt ourselves and the manner of our presentation in a reasonable way lest we be displeasing and incomprehensible to him.

In the dialogue, conducted in this manner, the union of truth and charity, of understanding and love is achieved.

In the dialogue one discovers how different are the ways that lead to the light of faith, and how it is possible to make them converge on the same goal. Even if these ways are divergent, they can become complementary by forcing our reasoning process out of the worn paths and by obliging it to deepen its research, to find fresh expressions.

The dialectic of this exercise of thought and of patience will make us discover elements of truth also in the opinions of others, it will force us to express our teaching with great fairness, and it will reward us for the work of having explained it in accordance with the objections of another or despite his slow assimilation of our teaching. The dialogue will make us wise. It will make us teachers.

And how is the dialogue to be carried on?

Many, indeed, are the forms that the dialogue of salvation can take. It adapts itself to the needs of a concrete situation, it chooses the appropriate means, it does not bind itself to ineffectual theories and does not cling to hard and fast forms when these have lost their power to speak to men and move them.

The question is of great importance, for it concerns the relation of the church's mission to the lives of men in a given time and place, in a given culture and social setting.

To what extent should the Church adapt itself to the historic and local circumstances in which its mission is exercised? How should it guard against the danger of a relativism that would falsify its moral and dogmatic truth?

And yet, at the same time, how can it fit itself to approach all men so as to save all, according to the example of the apostle:

"I became all things to all men that I might save all."

The world cannot be saved from the outside. As the word of God became man, so must a man to a certain degree identify himself with the forms of life of those to whom he wishes to bring the message of Christ. Without invoking privileges that would but widen the separation, without employing unintelligible terminology, he must share the common way of life—provided that it is human and honorable—especially of the most humble, if he wishes to be listened to and under man's voice, but to his heart. A man must first be understood, and, where he merits it, agreed with. In the very act of trying to make ourselves pastors, fathers and teachers of men, we must make ourselves their brothers. The spirit of dialogue is friendship and, even more, is service. All this we must remember and strive to put into practice according to the example and commandment that Christ left to us.

But the danger remains. The apostle's art is a risky one. The desire to come together as brothers must not lead to a watering-down or subtracting from the truth. Our dialogue must not weaken our attachment to our faith. In our apostolate we cannot make vague compromises about the principles of faith and action on which our profession of Christianity is based. An immoderate desire to make peace and sink differences at all costs is, fundamentally, a kind of scepticism about the power and content of the word of God which we desire to preach. Only the man who is completely faithful to the teaching of Christ can be an apostle. And only he who lives his Christian life to the full can remain uncontaminated by the errors with which he comes into contact.

We believe that the Council, when it comes to deal with questions on the church's activity in the modern world, will indicate a number of theoretical and practical norms for the guidance of our dialogue with men of the present-day. We believe, too, that in matters concerning the apostolic mission of the church, on the one hand, and on the other the diverse and changing circumstances in which that mission is exercised, it will be for the wise, attentive government of the church to determine from time to time the limits and forms and paths to be followed in maintaining and furthering a living and fruitful dialogue.

Accordingly, let us leave this aspect of the subject and confine ourselves to stressing once again the supreme importance which Christian preaching maintains, an importance which grows greater daily, for the Catholic Apostolate and specifically for the dialogue. No other form of communication can take its place. Not even the enormously powerful technical means of press, radio and television. In a sense, the apostolate and preaching are the same. Preaching is the primary apostolate.

Our apostolate, venerable brothers, is above all the ministry of the word. We know this very well, but it seems good to remind ourselves of it now, so as to direct our pastoral activities aright. We must go back to the study, not of human eloquence or empty rhetoric, but of the genuine art of the sacred word.

We must search for the laws of its simplicity and clarity, for its power and authority, so as to overcome our natural lack of skill in the use of the great and mysterious spiritual instrument of speech and to enable us worthily to compete with those who today exert so much influence through their words by having access to the organs of public opinion. We must beg the Lord for the great and uplifting gift of speech, to be able to confer on faith its practical and efficacious principle, and to enable our words to reach out to the ends of the earth. May we carry out the prescriptions of the Council's constitution on sacred liturgy with zeal and ability. And may the catechetical teaching of the faith to the Christian people, and to as many others as possible, be marked by the aptness of its language, the wisdom of its method, the zeal of its exercise supported by the evidence of real virtues, and may it strive ardently to lead its hearers to the security of the faith, to a realization of the intimate connection between the divine word and life, and to the illumination of the living God.

We must, finally, refer to those to whom our dialogue is directed. But even on this point we do not intend to forestall the Council, which, please God, will soon make its voice heard.

Speaking in general on the role of partner in dialogue, a role which the Catholic Church must take up with renewed fervor today, we should like merely to observe that the church must be ever ready to carry on the dialogue with all men of good will, within and without its own sphere. There is no one in whom its ministry has no interest. It has no enemies, except those who wish to be such. Its name of Catholic is not an idle title. Not in vain has it received the commission to foster in the world unity, love and peace.

The church is not unaware of the formidable dimensions of such a mission. It knows the limitation of its power. It knows, likewise, its own human weaknesses and failing.

It recognizes, too, that the acceptance of the Gospel depends, ultimately, not upon any apostolic efforts of its own nor upon any favorable temporal conditions, for faith is a gift of God and God alone defines in the world the times and limits of salvation. But the church knows that it is the seed, the leaven, the salt and light of the world.

It sees clearly enough the astounding newness of modern times, but with frank confidence it stands upon the paths of history and says to men: "I have that for which you search, that which you lack."

It does not thereby promise early felicity, but it does offer something— its light and grace, which makes the attainment as easy as possible.

And then it speaks to men of their transcendent destiny. In doing this it speaks to them of truth, justice, freedom, progress, concord, peace and civilization. These are words whose secret is known to the church, for Christ has entrusted the secret to its keeping.

And so the church has a message for every category of humanity: for children, for youth, for men of science and learning, for the world of labor and for every social class, for artists, for statesmen and for rulers. Most of all, the church has words for the poor, the outcasts, the suffering and the dying, for all men.

In speaking in this way, we may seem to be allowing ourselves to be carried away in the contemplation of our mission and to be out of touch with reality as regards the actual relations of mankind with the Catholic Church. But that is not so. We see the concrete situation quite clearly. To give a brief idea of it, we think it can be described as consisting of circles around the central point in which God has placed us.

The first of these circles is immense. Its limits stretch beyond our sight and merge with the horizon. It is that of mankind as such, the world. We gauge the distance that lies between us and the world, yet we do not consider the world a stranger.

All things human are our concern. We share with the whole of mankind a common nature, human life with all its gifts and problems. In this primary, universal reality we are ready to play our part, to acknowledge the deep-seated claims of its fundamental needs, to applaud the new, and sometimes sublime, expressions of its genius.

We possess, too, vital moral truths, to be brought to men's notice and to be corroborated by their conscience, to the benefit of all. Wherever men are trying to understand themselves and the world, we can communicate with them.

Wherever the councils of nations come together to establish the rights and duties of man, we are honored when they allow us to take our seat among them. If there exists in men "a soul naturally Christian," we desire to show it our respect and to enter into conversation with it.

Our attitude in this, as we remind ourselves and every one else, is, on the one hand, entirely disinterested: We have no temporal or political aim whatever, and, on the other hand, its purpose is to raise up and elevate to a supernatural and Christian level every good human value in the world. We are not civilization, but we promote it.

We realize, however, that in this limitless circle there are many, very many unfortunately, who profess no religion. And we are aware also that there are many who profess themselves, in various ways, to be atheists. We know that some of these proclaim their godlessness openly and uphold it as a program of human education and political conduct, in the ingenuous but fatal belief that they are setting men free from false and outworn notions about life and the world and are, they claim, putting in their place a scientific conception that is in conformity with the needs of modern progress.

This is the most serious problem of our time. We are firmly convinced that the theory on which the denial of God is based is utterly erroneous. This theory is not in keeping with basic, undeniable requirements of thought. It deprives the reasonable order of the world of its genuine foundation. This theory does not provide human life with a liberating formula but with a blind dogma which degrades and saddens it. This theory destroys, at the root, any social system which attempts to base itself upon it. It does not bring freedom. It is a sham, attempting to quench the light of the living God.

We shall, therefore, resist with all our strength the assaults of this denial. This we do in the supreme cause of truth and in virtue of our sacred duty to profess Christ and His gospel, moved by deep, unshakable love for men and in the invincible hope that modern man will come again to discover, in the religious ideals that Catholicism sets before him, his vocation to the civilization that does not die, but ever tends to the natural and supernatural perfection of the human spirit, and in which the grace of God enables man to possess his temporal goods in peace and honor, and to live in hope of attaining eternal goods.

These are the reasons which compel us, as they compelled our predecessors and, with them, everyone who has religious values at heart, to condemn the ideological systems which deny God and oppress the church, systems which are often identified with economic, social and political regimes, amongst which atheistic Communism is the chief. It could be said that it is not so much that we condemn these systems and regimes as that they express their radical opposition to us in thought and deed. Our regret is, in reality, more sorrow for a victim than the sentence of a judge.

Dialogue in such conditions is very difficult, not to say impossible although, even today, we have no preconceived intention of excluding the persons who profess these systems and belong to these regimes. For the lover of truth, discussion is always possible. The difficulties are enormously increased by obstacles of the moral order: by the absence of sufficient freedom of thought and action and by the perversion of discussion so that the latter is not made use of to seek and express objective truth but to serve predetermined utilitarian ends.

This is what puts an end to dialogue. The church of silence, for example, speaks only by her sufferings, and with her speaks also the suffering of an oppressed and degraded society, in which the rights of the spirit are crushed by those who control its fate. If we begin to speak in such a state of affairs, how can we offer dialogue, when we cannot be anything more than a "voice crying in the wilderness"? Patience and always love, in such conditions are the witnesses that the church can still offer, and not even death can silence it.

But though we must speak firmly and clearly in declaring and defending religion and the human values that it proclaims and upholds, we are moved by our pastoral office to seek in the heart of the modern atheist the motives of his turmoil and denial.

His motives are many and complex, so that we must examine them with care if we are to answer them effectively. Some of them arise from the demand that divine things be presented in a worthier and purer way than is, perhaps, the case in certain imperfect forms of language and worship, which we ought to try to purify so that they express as perfectly and clearly as possible the sacred reality of which they are the sign.

We see these men full of yearning, prompted sometimes by passion and desire for the unattainable, but often also by great-hearted dreams of justice and progress.

In such dreams, noble social aims are set up in the place of the absolute and necessary God, testifying thereby to the ineradicable need for the divine source and end of all things, whose transcendence and immanence it is the task of our teaching office to reveal with patience and wisdom.

Again, we see them, sometimes with ingenuous enthusiasm, having recourse to human reason, with the intention of arriving at a scientific explanation of the universe. This procedure is all the less reprehensible in that it is often based upon laws of logical thought not unlike those of our classical school.

It is a procedure that leads in a direction quite contrary to the will of those who use it, thinking to find in it an unanswerable proof of their atheism and its own intrinsic validity, for it leads them onward towards the new and final metaphysical and logical assertion of the existence of the Supreme God.

In this cogent process of reasoning the atheistic politico-scientist stops short willfully at a certain point and so extinguishes the sovereign light of the intelligibility of the universe.

Is there no one among us who could help him to reason on to a realization of the objective reality of the cosmic universe, a realization that restores to man the sense of the divine presence, and brings to his lips the humble, halting words of a consoling prayer?

Sometimes, too, the atheist is spurred on by noble sentiments and by impatience with the mediocrity and self-seeking of so many contemporary social settings. He knows well how to borrow from our gospel modes and expressions of solidarity and human compassion. Shall we not be able to lead him back one day to the Christian source of such manifestations of moral worth?

Accordingly, bearing in mind the words of our predecessor of venerable memory, Pope John XXIII, in his encyclical "Pacem in Terris" to the effect that the doctrines of such movements, once elaborated and defined, remain always the same, whereas the movements themselves cannot help but evolve and undergo changes, even of a profound nature, we do not despair that they may one day be able to enter into a more positive dialogue with the church than the present one that we now of necessity deplore and lament.

But we cannot turn our gaze away from the contemporary world without expressing a cherished desire, namely that our intention of developing and perfecting our dialogue in the varied and changing facets that it presents, may assist the cause of peace between men, by providing a method that seeks to order human relationships in the sublime light of the language of reason and sincerity and by making a contribution of experience and wisdom that can stir up all men to the consideration of the supreme values.

The opening of a dialogue such as ours would be, disinterested, objective and sincere, is in itself a decision in favor of a free and honorable peace.

CONVERSATION AND COMMUNICATION*

Joost A. M. Meerloo

Things that have nothing in common with each other cannot be understood by each other mutually; the conception of the one does not include the conception of the other.

—Spinoza

*b*etween two beings there is always the barrier of words. Man has so many ears and he speaks so many languages. Should it nevertheless be possible to understand one another? Is real communication possible if word and language betray us every time? Shall, in the end, only the language of guns and tanks prevail and not human reason and understanding?

Such is the dilemma of modern man. There is an urge to talk and understand, but other impulses break through instead. As soon as people meet they long for communication, but word and precedent keep them at a distance.

I meet a school friend after many years. We smile over common memories of the past. "Do you remember Joe?" "What happened to Dick?" Soon we realize that life has aligned us in opposing political camps. Silences become more painful, but our wish for the old community of boyhood is still there.

Words and language represent, first of all, personal melodies. Many people seek an individualizing form of expression; a distantiation from their companions. Even the most exact physical scientist tries to express his individuality in his dryly written publications, even though his work deals with general phenomena. We all wish to exhibit our personal findings and opinions—so great is the urge for both self-esteem and esteem from others.

The individualizing artist who searches our particular expressions and distinctiveness conflicts with the social search for standardization and uniformity. Word and communication bear the marks of this conflict. Sometimes we reproduce catchwords; still other times, individual expression prevails.

Understanding, insight, empathy, comprehension—all are attempts to know what happens in another human being. These are more or less conscious modes of identification which derive from the first distantiation from purely biological impulses. As we have said earlier, the small child places itself opposite objects and tries to get a conception of them. Early empathy and identification ask for a rebellious attitude, self-exploration in a world of magic thinking. Our intellectual training, however, inhibits the process of feeling *with* and *in* things. It teaches children to observe facts and events in a cold and sober way; to walk around them but never to creep *into* them with their imagination. Feeling about things is regarded as inferior to formal consideration of them.

Can man step away from his intellectual island and attempt more effective communication? Deep communication, "feeling in" and "listening surrender" to another must be learned first in the family circle. It is here that the first understanding through mutual identification is trained. Only if this mutual relationship is good can the individual integrate himself into other social formations. Many who do not succeed at home search for love and understanding in the outside world, but before they can understand others they must conquer the neurotic tendencies formed in their uncongenial home environments.

Often we give in to the terrible pretense of understanding because we don't want contact and communication. We say "yes" when there is no understanding at all, or even when there is fear of being understood, fear of losing oneself. Sometimes we try to understand by hearing, reading, and ruminating, finally giving way to mythical confusion. Instead of understanding, we learn to submit to a magic juggler of words.

Deep understanding and communication begin between two people. If this has been experienced, the way to the world lies open. Understanding is pausing momentarily, stepping outside the continual stream of occurrences to observe the passing scene. He who always runs through life never learns to understand anyone else.

What is the impulse for understanding each other? It is not only a loving interest, not only putting oneself in another's place to achieve more peaceful co-operation, it is also the wish to control the secrets of the other person, to obtain power over him by understanding him. Understanding gives self-assurance, but understanding is a vital component of our social compulsions. We must live together, we are involved in the same social pressures, and processes, we must learn how to react and how to respond to each other's behavior. Hence, we must know how the other person will react. Without mutual understanding community life is impossible. Every animal learns to adjust himself to the jungle community, but man learns more; he learns to deal with his fellow beings. For man there is mutual interaction through which both parties change. There is mutual redemption and mutual self-clarification in human communication. Human understanding means identification with the behavior of others, getting acquainted with it in order to be able to anticipate behavior. The thinking man is an anticipating man.

However, understanding our fellow beings does not always help us defend ourselves against our private drives. The better we understand and the better we can communicate, the more successful we may become in our aggressive strategy. Thus, a cynical attitude toward our own instinctual drives may develop—its purpose to protect ourselves against being understood. We accept our drives without any attempt at correction. Through better understanding of others our power of self-deceit may increase. We analyze the partner but may lose all self-knowledge.

How many sleepless nights I have had in my attempts at understanding the many events in our chaotic world. . . . Man is so intelligent, yet mankind acts so stupidly. How did our good human sense become so isolated?

There were historical periods in which good general mental relationships were possible, partly because there was an international language (Latin in the Middle Ages) and common goals between the governing layers of the various communities. After the Renaissance, however, the new economy with its advanced techniques standardized much of human behavior, but alienated humans from each other mentally.

National isolationism is reflected in our emphasis on the mother tongue. There are still dreamers who advocate an international language in the service of international understanding. Happy dreams must be kept alive and propagated; nevertheless, it will be very difficult to find a common language for all men. The unconscious patterns of thinking and identification are very different in different countries. In the same words, the souls speak different tongues.

In the future international language—when it does come—many different dialects will be spoken. Monolinguistic pacts will be drawn up and violated, because words and pacts tend to disintegrate. Primitive and cultured interpretations of words will remain alongside idealistic and hypocritical explanations. People behind the Iron Curtain are conditioned differently for the words *liberty* and *democracy* than we are. When we use these words, their conception will be different unless a common basis of education, indoctrination and conditioning is possible.

Speaking the same thought language is not dependent on the word language per se, but on the will to understand and co-operate. For one person "fair play" is the highest ethic in human relations; another denies all principles and is swayed by the continual shift in political opportunities. Much of our common understanding is based on our pre-verbal understanding—on what was received and conquered in the cradle.

Mutual understanding is the result of maximal communication through mutual empathy. It can approximately be reached through means of manifold tools of communication, of which semantic language is only one.

Only people of similar mental and cultural structure are able to have deep contact with each other. The more primitive and simple structure will never understand the more civilized and differentiated one. The lower form cannot comprehend the higher one and for the higher structure it is very different to imagine itself in the more primitive situation.

Every world of thoughts is limited by its own language and patterns of thinking. The more developed form, even when it can imagine the simpler form, is limited by its own rigidity and habit formation, as a result of which the stammering of others cannot be reached or understood. We are all bound to the formalities and compulsions included in a certain language. In this country our speech patterns are conditioned quite differently from those of the Chinese or Russians. Truth can be accepted only when we are ready for it; otherwise our minds make venom of it.

Different cultural patterns act as a limitation for mutual understanding between individuals and groups. Let us not forget that there is a natural hostility toward the more differentiated mentality. People hate difficulties; they hate things they cannot understand. As one of Hitler's friends expressed it: "When I hear the word 'civilization' I reach for my gun."

Only the mature wish for mutual identification, for psychological understanding, and a loving approach toward others, can surpass such limitations. This attitude makes it possible to understand the lower or the different form, and to estimate the more differentiated capacities. Good conversation is only possible with people who love and value each other. They understand one another because they mutually supply and complement the imperfections of the word.

Good understanding means freeing oneself of word and language and of one's personal limitations of thinking. Let us call it intuitive understanding. There is harmony, a correlation of rhythm and intention, of mood and word sounds. The dilemma of every communication is the choice between verbal communication and silence.

Understanding is possible without words.

CONVERSATION AND WISDOM

Every speaker, teacher or philosopher attracts a circle of listeners, a conversational audience. He adjusts to the circle and it to him, and each helps to mold the other. Our most profound impressions can only be transferred by direct human contact, from man to man. Libraries cannot replace the sphere of personal impact and influence.

In conversation a common thinking develops with ties beyond word and speech. Common thinking includes far more than language. He who is privileged to listen in this way to a wiser man is drawn upward into higher spheres of wisdom, though he may later be incapable of repeating what he has learned. There is wisdom among people that cannot be printed. Many students are shocked when their teacher appears in print—they find that his oral wisdom, his appeal, has not yet yielded to transmission into written symbols.

All conversations exert a formal influence. Consider whom you choose for company; unwittingly you take over their language, their gestures and their habits of thought. People need to receive and differentiate all varieties and amounts of words, to form new adjustments and modifications—and this is only possible in direct contact with diverse companions. Lacking training and exercise, our language fails to develop. Full acculturation presupposes the introjection of new word pictures and new ways of expression.

True, we do not always wish to be edified by conversation! Most people love relaxation and wish to be lazy sometimes. But as soon as an emotionally charged subject comes to the fore the words begin to fly and a dialectic fight takes place, even among people who do not intend it.

Pity those logic-loving persons who always evoke discussion in order to learn. They want conversation, hoping to increase their wisdom or their knowledge of facts. From a feeling of inferiority they develop a talmudistic attitude. Every new acquaintance is accepted as a virtual teacher, every conversation is viewed as an opportunity to glean pearls of wisdom. Once the initial feeling of flattery subsides one grows very weary of such people. Like infants at the breast, they hang on your lips, long after your fountain of words has run dry.

You will meet, too, the mysterious pseudo magician, who purports to spread hidden wisdom in every expression he uses. He wants to fascinate and hypnotize his audience; he talks in oblique, cryptic terms and expects response to his sphinx language. Some scientists and theologians support this attitude.

Usually, however, one's initial attitude subsides during conversation, common thoughts begin to prevail, and intercommunication dominates over individual peculiarities. There is alternate speaking and listening, opinions are mixed and verified and the atmosphere of intellectual play is born. This volatile conversation of minds that meet and understand one another changes continually in tone and mood, and even the wine is forgotten.

Socrates regarded conversation as an avenue toward clearer ideas.

Kant, the quiet, lonely man from Königsberg, was suspicious of conversation and dialectics; he called them the art of hiding your lack of knowledge. But without conversation no mental development could take place.

Every conversation, in order to become a mutual exchange of value, must reflect the enriched experience of man. In this way, word and response, seen against their human background, grow to a joyous conversational play.

THE PLAY OF CONVERSATION

Indeed, conversation is a play through which we touch the spheres of art. We even consciously play at theater and show off, according to our different degrees of refinement. Sometimes it is a very earnest play, sometimes a gay musical. The prima donna is pushed out of the group. Too learned and scientific deliberations during the conversation make people laugh. "Please," the hostess begs, partly amused and partly annoyed, "pay some attention to your food, too." And, full of pity, she watches the good food grow cold before the inattentive student. He, eager beaver, forgets to enjoy the more material pleasures because he plays too much with words. It's far nicer to talk about more general, everyday subjects—music, the theater, the latest rumor.

The beautiful glow persists; the mood of satisfied laziness and not personal prestige. The subject as such matters little. When the engineer in love explains his newest engine to his darling, all his love and feeling may be transferred to his scientific explanations; he finishes, nevertheless, with self-laughter.

"Shall I burn you?" asks the silent peasant, who can find no other words, to his beloved. His pipe glows in the twilight and both lean against the meadow fence. But there is no need to say more. . . .

Conversation is not merely arguing and demonstrating, convincing and insisting. Commercially-minded people wish it were. They seek the direct effect; it must be aimed at something. But conversation is play and enjoyment—for the eyes, the ears, and the spirit. It is the source of wisdom we cannot get from books.

For some, only words convey meaning. These people overemphasize the semantic aspect. They stick to words when they should be silent, they orate when they have to wash the dishes. And the talking youngsters, who forget all spontaneity in their preoccupation with verbal accuracy! They talk about love and marriage, but gain not a grain of tenderness thereby. If their sweetheart bursts into tears they start a fresh conversation on the pros and cons of sorrow.

A person may speak the most beautiful words, yet gain no contact with his audience. His moments of silence grow especially awkward. Speech may be as deceiving as writing, but no speaker cares to know it himself. He must believe in his own show.

I cannot converse with my authoritarian-minded friend. His looks are too serious and he dictates the subject matter at dinner. The play of conversation must be a collective action; it must be speaking in such a way that the listener is able to receive the words and to know how to deal with them. It must remain a mutual experience, for only so is it real communication.

CONVERSATION, THE TOOL OF MUTUAL UNDERSTANDING

People need conversation to help check the mechanical trend of civilization. Tired of official wordiness, tired of politics and politicians, surfeited with slogans and catchwords, they have lost faith in good conversation as well. They do not believe in their unconscious drives toward more sincere human relationships.

The problem of loneliness and mental isolation is acute in our era. The more tyranny and suppression are imposed from outside, the more lonely the mature person feels.

Through lack of sincere conversation and communication the sound minds among us are dishonored in their own house. Hypocrisy and showmanship rule the day. We devote ourselves to the mechanistic quiz, the glorified fact, the I.Q., the multiple-choice examination—but not to creative expression and character. We glorify the tools of production, but devaluate the tools of human contact—sociability and the purer reality of conversation.

Let us believe again in conversation, in the veracity of unspoken relationships behind words. Let us laugh together about something. Let us discharge our mutual aggression in puns and jokes. Let us sneer and spit on what we do not understand, but let us be conscious of it! Let us talk—yes, let us speak aggressively—it does not matter, for sympathy speaks in our eyes.

If there is no free conversation human aggression accumulates. A man who listens only to his radio or is caught by the hypnotism of the movies must discharge his aggression somewhere else. But the civilizing sublimation of conversation does not reach him, so he cannot get rid of his aggression.

People have learned to be silent listeners. Dictatorship asks only for silent citizens. If man cannot redeem himself of his everyday tensions through words, the archaic primitive demands within him grow more and more awake. The world falls prey to his accumulated obsessions, and in the end collective madness breaks through. Let us talk now, so that we do not become mad animals!

Conversation gives deeper information about mankind because it gives it involuntarily. It tells about the unconscious. The group in conversation incites us to reveal more of ourselves than we can possibly intend—and this is good! We try to by-pass our deeper feelings, but gradually we drop our resistance. We are shy and ashamed, but we grow into the open atmosphere of friendship. We give our secrets away and hear another's secrets. We are curious, and our curiosity is satisfied. We want to exceed human frontiers, we want to know what is behind social taboos. What happened? What happened in you? How did you react? Conversation answers the greedy, questioning child in us, for the early childhood questions ever resound in us. Man is a peeping, prying discoverer of secrets. Formal talk will never ferret out the answers.

It does not matter if he talks nonsense. The verbal contact as such makes sense. It is the atmosphere and companionship which please us. We are warmed and delighted because we are together in a play without rules. A feeling of comfort and well-being steals over us, a notion of being safe and well defended. We are caught up in the ecstasy of life that became word.

I have the loveliest memories of evenings spent in a flower-scented garden, with tea and the sweet smells of approaching night. Nature was full of conversation with us and we, in the end, hushed and listened to her voice. We listened together, and grew aware of a world full of abundant gifts . . .

THE MIRACLE OF DIALOGUE

Reuel L. Howe

$\mathcal{E}$very man is a potential adversary, even those whom we love. Only through dialogue are we saved from this enmity toward one another. Dialogue is to love, what blood is to the body. When the flow of blood stops, the body dies. When dialogue stops, love dies and resentment and hate are born. But dialogue can restore a dead relationship. Indeed, this is the miracle of dialogue: it can bring relationship into being, and it can bring into being once again a relationship that has died.

There is only one qualification to these claims for dialogue: it must be mutual and proceed from both sides, and the parties to it must persist relentlessly. The word of dialogue may be spoken by one side but evaded or ignored by the other, in which case the promise may not be fulfilled. There is risk in speaking the dialogical word—that is, in entering into dialogue—but when two persons undertake it and accept their fear of doing so, the miracle-working power of dialogue may be released.

If the claims we are making here for dialogue are a cause for surprise to the reader, the reason may be that dialogue has been equated too exclusively with the conversational parts of a play. We think of it differently—as the serious address and response between two or more persons, in which the being and truth of each is confronted by the being and truth of the other. Dialogue, therefore, is not easy and comfortable to achieve, a fact which may explain why it occurs so rarely. And its rare occurrence accounts for the frequent absence of its benefits in our communication with one another.

To say that communication is important to human life is to be trite, but that bit of triteness witnesses to an invariable truth: communication means life or death to persons. A study of the nature of communication is needed in this day of mass communication. On a colossal scale never known before

Reprinted from Reuel L. Howe, *The Miracle of Dialogue*, by permission of The Seabury Press, Inc., publishers.

and with technical aids that surpass the wildest imaginings of yesterday's science fiction, man can bombard his fellow man's mind, feelings, and will with a subtleness and effectiveness that is frightening. Books like *The Hidden Persuaders* by Vance Packard describe how man becomes the victim of communication rather than communication being a means by which he finds himself in his relation with other men in a community of mutual criticism and helpfulness.

Both the individual and society derive their basic meaning from the relations that exist between man and man. At the moment of birth the individual comes into personal being in response to his being met by his mother and father and all the others who care for him in all the concreteness of his need. And out of that same meeting the family community is born. Many people think that the individual as a social being derives from a "given" social nature of man; others hold that society and interpersonal relations are the sum of individual lives. Neither of these views recognizes that upon which both depend, namely, the interaction between the individual and his personal environment. Recently a group of ministers was told that until the Church becomes a community, it will not be able to communicate adequately. Left unanswered was the question: How does the Church or any other group of people become a community? And the answer is simple: it becomes a community when as persons the members enter into dialogue with one another and assume responsibility for their common life. Without this dialogue individuals and society are abstractions. It is through dialogue that man accomplishes the miracle of personhood and community.

There are many illustrations of the importance of dialogue. Earlier, reference was made to the infant's becoming a person in response to the meeting between him and his family. From the very beginning of the individual's life it is communication that guarantees its continuation. While dependent on food and care, the newborn infant also needs the communication that is implicit in them and conveyed in the way they are given. Mother feeds and bathes, cuddles and sings to her baby, and through this activity the infant receives the message that she loves him and wants him. This message also means to him that he is loved and therefore lovable, accepted and therefore acceptable. Or, if his mother is hostile and irritable and expresses her resentment in neglect and roughness, he receives the contrary message that she regards him as a nuisance, which conveys to him that he is unloved and unlovable, unaccepted and unacceptable. In the first instance, the message of love and care is lifegiving and nurturing; in the second, the message is alienating and destructive. And this is true for mother as well as for child, because in loving and serving her child the mother is giving herself, making herself available as a person to him. For the act of loving another gives life to the lover as well as to the one loved, and to speak the word of love is to be loved as well as to love.

The infant participates in this dialogue, too. He cries, waves his arms, kicks his legs, and in other non-verbal ways asks his questions and makes his positive and negative comments about his life. The response of his world, made to him by his mother and those around him, influences quite decisively his future capacity for communication. If his initial communications are accepted, not necessarily approved, he will grow in his capacity to speak; if they are not, he will become inhibited, resentful, and defensive, which in turn may only increase his mother's destructive communication. Sometimes the communication between them makes both sad and listless, and at other times glad and alive.

The relation between a man and a woman also can reveal how indispensable is the life of dialogue. In addition to their differences as man and woman, there are other multi-faceted differences between them. Some event in which each has participated has brought them together, such as a meeting of eyes or the recognition in a discussion that they share the same opinion or attitude. In this kind of event the dialogue begins. Each then undertakes to seek and explore the other. It is important to know who the other truly is, and through dialogue that employs both the language of relationship and the language of words to seek to know life through the other. Love is born out of this dialogue in which there is both the intimacy of what these two people share in common and the distance of the unplumbed mystery of each. The emergence of this mutual awareness in the relationship reveals an important distinction between monological and dialogical love. Monological love enjoys only self-centeredly the feelings of a relationship. The lover exploits the beloved for the sake of the emotional dividend to be had. In contrast, dialogical love is outgoing. The lover turns to the beloved not to enjoy her selfishly but to serve her, to know her, and through her to be. Correspondingly, the beloved seeks the lover not to enjoy him for herself but to serve him, to know him, and in knowing him and being known by him to find her own being. In dialogical love there is enjoyment of love, but since it is not exploitive, the enjoyment increases rather than diminishes the power to love.

Marriage is an ultimate commitment to this kind of human relationship, expressing the realization that to become a person one has to share in the being of another, and that one has to offer oneself as a person, in relation with whom the other may participate in the realization of his own being. The dialogue is in earnest. And every aspect of the relationship becomes a vehicle for it: verbal activity, living together, the assumption of responsibilities, sexual relations, and recreation. And this relationship will continue to be a living one so long as each keeps in communication with the other. Each must try to speak honestly out of his own conviction, discipline his subjective feelings, seek patiently to keep aware of the partner as another person, and try to keep open to the meaning of everything that happens in the relationship. Whenever either party begins to be more concerned for himself than for the other, when he uses the other as a thing for any purpose whatever, when he hides in defensive behavior, the marriage has become monological and broken. When this happens either or both of the partners may indignantly demand that the other repent and reform in the interest of a mended relationship. Healing of a marriage or any other relationship cannot occur when the partners see themselves as separate individuals with a right to demand services of each other. Healing can come only when one or the other is able to turn toward his partner, to accept the risk of giving himself in love, and to search himself for whatever reform may be necessary. A wife, for example, may be able to make this kind of gift, and yet have it fail to heal because her husband cannot accept her gift and give himself in return. But if he can, then the miracle will occur and the dead relationship will be called again into life.

The relationship between parents and children also calls for a practice of the principle of dialogue. How hard it is for parents to respect and trust the uniqueness and powers of their children! While there are those aspects of life in which parents must decide and act for them until such time as they are able to decide and act for themselves, children should always have the experience of being met as free persons in a trusting and responsible relationship. The need for this trust increases as the children grow older, and it becomes acute at adolescence when the transition from childhood to adulthood is taking place. Then it is imperative that young persons be allowed their freedoms, but equally imperative that they also have encounter with persons of conviction who, at the same time, respect their freedoms. Without this kind of relationship the individual simply flees from life, becomes passive and locked up within himself; or he may become a fighting person whose creativity is lost in the wastelands of his aggression. The importance of dialogue for this juncture of growth lies in the fact that it expresses mutual respect so that youth need neither repress creativity nor throw it away, and age need neither seek to dominate nor turn away from youth in frustration. In those instances where the young person has withdrawn from life or is in hostile combat with it, as in delinquency, dialogue may accomplish the miracle of bringing the young person back into a creative relation to life.

Dialogue is indispensable also in the search for truth and here, too, it is a worker of miracles. Unfortunately, many people hold and proclaim what they believe to be true in either an opinionated or defensive way. Religious people, for example, sometimes speak the truth they profess monologically, that is, they hold it exclusively and inwardly as if there was no possible relation between what they believe and what others believe, in spite of every indication that separately held truths are often complementary. The monological thinker runs the danger of being prejudiced, intolerant, bigoted, and a persecutor of those who differ from him. The dialogical thinker, on the other hand, is willing to speak out of his convictions to the holders of other convictions with genuine interest in them and with a sense of the possibilities between them.

Let us take, for example, a man who, as a student of human relations, is interested in the functioning of groups. At the moment he believes that the dynamics of a group are best understood by studying the individual and what happens to him as a member of the group. This student could hold this view of group process aggressively and defensively against all other theories; but in that case his view would remain unaffirmed, uncorrected, and without complement of or completion by other views. Instead, he turns from his "individual-centered" view of group process to the "group-centered" interpretation, with the honest desire to discover what group life looks like from that point of view. He thus brings his own theory into dialogue with another, and when he discovers that the two are complementary, his earlier understanding is broadened and deepened. He may also discover that he contributed something to the theory he examined. Then he learns of still another view, the "reality-centered" concept of group life, to which he now turns dialogically. Each of these views, when held separately and uncriticized or unmodified by the views of others, is inadequate for a complete interpretation of group life. In dialogue, however, these views mutually qualify and supplement each other and thus provide a comprehensive view that is more completely the truth than is any one of them by itself. When this comprehensive concept of group relations is now brought into dialogue with different theological insights into human relations, a yet more profound and inclusive view of group relations will emerge. Dialogue, therefore, produces miracles of discovery, opening to us the mysteries of life.

Another area in desperate need of dialogical spirit and action is that of politics. National parties are often pitted against each other solely in the interest of their own success and sometimes to the cost of the country they are professing to serve; and nations look toward themselves and not toward each other, thus threatening the welfare of the planet. Indeed, the human race stands in danger of being destroyed because of the deliberate effort of parties and nations to advance their own cause by falsifying the aims and character of their opponents. With this frequently goes an ignoring of one's own sin and responsibility, a representation of the self as being better than it is, and a sense of injury at the hands of the other, as if the fiction created about them was true. The abuse of dialogue has gone on so long that politicians find it difficult to break out of their monological fantasies and move toward a dialogical meeting. What is needed is the coming together of men of conviction from their respective camps who are willing to talk honestly with one another in the face of mutual criticism and loyalty to their own views. If these men would speak with one another not as pawns on a chessboard but as themselves in the sanctuary of truth, the sphere of public life would be transformed by the miracle of dialogue.

LOVE AS ENERGY*

Pierre Teilhard de Chardin

We are accustomed to consider (and with what a refinement of analysis!) only the sentimental face of love, the joy and miseries it causes us. It is in its natural dynamism and its evolutionary significance that I shall be dealing with it here, with a view to determining the ultimate phases of the phenomenon of man.

Considered in its full biological reality, love—that is to say the affinity of being with being—is not peculiar to man. It is a general property of all life and as such it embraces, in its varieties and degrees, all the forms successively adopted by organised matter. In the mammals, so close to ourselves, it is easily recognized in its different modalities: sexual passion, parental instinct, social solidarity, etc. Farther off, that is to say lower down on the tree of life, analogies are more obscure until they become so faint as to be imperceptible. But this is the place to repeat what I said earlier when we were discussing the "*within* of things." If there were no internal propensity to unite, even at a prodigiously rudimentary level—indeed in the molecule itself—it would be physically impossible for love to appear higher up, with us, in "hominised" form. By rights, to be certain of its presence in ourselves, we should assume its presence, at least in an inchoate form, in everything that is. And in fact if we look around us at the confluent ascent of consciousness, we see it is not lacking anywhere. Plato felt this and has immortalised the idea in his *Dialogues*. Later, with thinkers like Nicolas of Cusa, mediaeval philosophy returned technically to the same notion. Driven by the forces of love, the fragments of the world seek each other so that the world may come to being. This is no metaphor; and it is much more than poetry. Whether as a force or a curvature, the universal gravity of bodies, so striking to us, is merely the reverse or shadow of that which really moves nature. To perceive cosmic energy "at the fount" we must, if there is a *within* of things, go down into the internal or radial zone of spiritual attractions.

Love in all its subtleties is nothing more, and nothing less, than the more or less direct trace marked on the heart of the element by the psychical convergence of the universe upon itself.

This, if I am not mistaken, is the ray of light which will help us to see more clearly around us.

We are distressed and pained when we see modern attempts at human collectivisation ending up, contrary to our expectations and theoretical predictions, in a lowering and an enslavement of consciousness. But so far how have we gone about the business of unification? A material situation to be preserved; a new industrial field to be opened up, better conditions for a social class of less favoured nations—those are the only and very mediocre grounds on which we have so far tried to get together. There is no cause to be surprised if, in the footsteps of animal societies, we become mechanised in the very play of association. Even in the supremely intellectual act of science (at any rate as long as it remains purely speculative and abstract) the impact of our souls only operates obliquely and indirectly. Contact is still superficial, involving the danger of yet another servitude. Love alone is capable of uniting living beings in such a way as to complete and fulfill them, for it alone takes them and joins them by what is deepest in themselves. This is a fact of daily experience. At what moment do lovers come into the most complete possession of themselves if not when they say they are lost in each other? In truth, does not love every instant achieve all around us, in the couple or the team, the magic feat, the feat reputed to be contradictory, of "personalising" by totalising? And if that is what it can achieve daily on a small scale, why should it not repeat this one day on world-wide dimensions?

Mankind, the spirit of the earth, the synthesis of individuals and peoples, the paradoxical conciliation of the element with the whole, and of unity with multitude—all these are called Utopian and yet they are biologically necessary. And for them to be incarnated in the world all we may well need is to imagine our power of loving developing until it embraces the total of men and of the earth.

It may be said that this is the precise point at which we are invoking the impossible. Man's capacity, it may seem, is confined to giving his affection to one human being or to very few. Beyond that radius the heart does not carry, and there is only room for cold justice and cold reason. To love all and everyone is a contradictory and false gesture which only leads in the end to loving no one.

To that I would answer that if, as you claim, a universal love is impossible, how can we account for that irresistible instinct in our hearts which leads us towards unity whenever and in whatever direction our passions are stirred? A sense of the universe, a sense of the *all*, the nostalgia which seizes us when confronted by nature, beauty, music—these seem to be an expectation and awareness of a Great Presence. The "mystics" and their commentators apart, how has psychology been able consistently to ignore this fundamental vibration whose ring can be heard by every practised ear at the basis, or rather at the summit, of every great emotion? Resonance to the All—the keynote of pure poetry and pure religion. Once again : what does this phenomenon, which is born with thought and grows with it, reveal if not a deep accord between two realities which seek each other; the severed particle which trembles at the approach of "the rest"?

We are often inclined to think that we have exhausted the various natural forms of love with a man's love for his wife, his children, his friends and to a certain extent for his country. Yet precisely the most fundamental form of passion is missing from this list, the one which, under the pressure of an involuting universe, precipitates the elements one upon the other in the Whole—cosmic affinity and hence cosmic direction. A universal love is not only psychologically possible; it is the only complete and final way in which we are able to love.

But, with this point made, how are we to explain the appearance all around us of mounting repulsion and hatred? If such a strong potentiality is besieging us from within and urging us to union, what is it waiting for to pass from potentiality to action? Just this, no doubt; that we should overcome the "anti-personalist" complex which paralyses us, and make up our minds to accept the possibility, indeed the reality, of some *source* of love and *object* of love at the summit of the world above our heads. So long as it absorbs or appears to absorb the person, the collectivity kills the love that is trying to come to birth. As such the collectivity is essentially unlovable. That is where philanthropic systems break down. Common sense is right. It is impossible to give oneself to anonymous number. But if the universe ahead of us assumes a face and a heart, and so to speak personifies itself,[1] then in the atmosphere created by this focus the elementary attraction will immediately blossom. Then, no doubt, under the heightened pressure of an infolding world, the formidable energies of attraction, still dormant between human molecules, will burst forth.

The discoveries of the last hundred years, with their unitary perspectives, have brought a new and decisive impetus to our sense of the world, to our sense of the earth, and to our human sense. Hence the rise of modern pantheism. But this impetus will only end by plunging us back into super-matter unless it leads us towards someone.

For the failure that threatens us to be turned into success, for the concurrence of human monads to come about, it is necessary and sufficient for us that we should extend our science to its farthest limits and recognise and accept (as being necessary to close and balance space-time) not only some vague future existence, but also, as I must now stress, the radiation as a present reality of that mysterious centre of our centres which I have called Omega.

NOTES

1. Not, of course, by becoming a person, but by charging itself at the very heart of its development with the dominating and unifying influence of a focus of personal energies and attractions.

THE THEORY OF LOVE*

Erich Fromm

*A*ny theory of love must begin with a theory of man, of human existence. While we find love, or rather, the equivalent of love, in animals, their attachments are mainly a part of their instinctual equipment; only remnants of this instinctual equipment can be seen operating in man. What is essential in the existence of man is the fact that he has emerged from the animal kingdom, from instinctive adaptation, that he has transcended nature—although he never leaves it; he is a part of it—and yet once torn away from nature, he cannot return to it; once thrown out of paradise—a state of original oneness with nature—cherubim with flaming swords block his way, if he should try to return. Man can only go forward by developing his reason, by finding a new harmony, a human one, instead of the pre-human harmony which is irretrievably lost.

When man is born, the human race as well as the individual, he is thrown out of a situation which was definite, as definite as the instincts, into a situation which is indefinite, uncertain and open. There is certainty only about the past—and about the future only as far as that it is death.

Man is gifted with reason; he is *life being aware of itself*; he has awareness of himself, of his fellow man, of his past, and of the possibilities of his future. This awareness of himself as a separate entity, the awareness of his own short life span, of the fact that without his will he is born and against his will he dies, that he will die before those whom he loves, or they before him, the awareness of his aloneness and separateness, of his helplessness before the forces of nature and of society, all this makes his separate, disunited existence an unbearable prison. He would become insane could he not liberate himself from this prison and reach out, unite himself in some form or other with men, with the world outside.

* Pp. 7–32, "The Theory of Love," from *The Art of Loving*, by Erich Fromm. Copyright © 1956 by Erich Fromm. Reprinted by permission of Harper & Row, Publishers, and of George Allen and Unwin, Ltd.

The experience of separateness arouses anxiety; it is, indeed, the source of all anxiety. Being separate means being cut off, without any capacity to use my human powers. Hence to be separate means to be helpless, unable to grasp the world—things and people—actively; it means that the world can invade me without my ability to react. Thus, separateness is the source of intense anxiety. Beyond that, it arouses shame and the feeling of guilt. The experience of guilt and shame in separateness is expressed in the Biblical story of Adam and Eve. After Adam and Eve have eaten of the "tree of knowledge of good and evil," after they have disobeyed (there is no good and evil unless there is freedom to disobey), after they have become human by having emancipated themselves from the original animal harmony with nature, i.e., after their birth as human beings—they saw "that they were naked—and they were ashamed." Should we assume that a myth as old and elementary as this has the prudish morals of the nineteenth-century outlook, and that the important point the story wants to convey to us is the embarrassment that their genitals were visible? This can hardly be so, and by understanding the story in a Victorian spirit, we miss the main point, which seems to be the following: after man and woman have become aware of themselves and of each other, they are aware of their separateness, and of their difference, inasmuch as they belong to different sexes. But while recognizing their separateness they remain strangers, because they have not yet learned to love each other (as is also made very clear by the fact that Adam defends himself by blaming Eve, rather than trying to defend her). *The awareness of human separation, without reunion by love—is the source of shame. It is at the same time the source of guilt and anxiety.*

The deepest need of man, then, is the need to overcome his separateness, to leave the prison of his aloneness. The *absolute* failure to achieve this aim means insanity, because the panic of complete isolation can be overcome only by such a radical withdrawal from the world outside that the feeling of separation disappears—because the world outside, from which one is separated, has disappeared.

Man—of all ages and cultures—is confronted with the solution of one and the same question: the question of how to overcome separateness, how to achieve union, how to transcend one's own individual life and find at-onement. The question is the same for primitive man living in caves, for nomadic man taking care of his flocks, for the peasant in Egypt, the Phoenician trader, the Roman soldier, the medieval monk, the Japanese samurai, the modern clerk and factory hand. The question is the same, for it springs from the same ground: the human situation, the conditions of human existence. The answer varies. The question can be answered by animal worship, by human sacrifice or military conquest, by indulgence in luxury, by ascetic creation, by the love of God, and by the love of Man.

While there are many answers—the record of which is human history—
they are nevertheless not innumerable. On the contrary, as soon as one
ignores smaller differences which belong more to the periphery than to
the center, one discovers that there is only a limited number of answers
which have been given, and only could have been given by man in the
various cultures in which he has lived. The history of religion and philosophy is the history of these answers, of their diversity, as well as of their
limitation in number.

The answers depend, to some extent, on the degree of individuation
which an individual has reached. In the infant I-ness has developed but
little yet; he still feels one with mother, has no feeling of separateness as
long as mother is present. Its sense of aloneness is cured by the physical
presence of the mother, her breasts, her skin. Only to the degree that the
child develops his sense of separateness and individuality is the physical
presence of the mother not sufficient any more, and does the need to overcome separateness in other ways arise.

Similarly, the human race in its infancy still feels one with nature. The
soil, the animals, the plants are still man's world. He identifies himself
with animals, and this is expressed by the wearing of animal masks, by the
worshipping of a totem animal or animal gods. But the more the human
race emerges from these primary bonds, the more it separates itself from
the natural world, the more intense becomes the need to find new ways of
escaping separateness.

One way of achieving this aim lies in all kinds of *orgiastic* states. These
may have the form of an auto-induced trance, sometimes with the help of
drugs. Many rituals of primitive tribes offer a vivid picture of this type of
solution. In a transitory state of exaltation the world outside disappears,
and with it the feeling of separateness from it. Inasmuch as these rituals are
practiced in common, an experience of fusion with the group is added
which makes this solution all the more effective. Closely related to, and
often blended with this orgiastic solution, is the sexual experience. The
sexual orgasm can produce a state similar to the one produced by a trance,
or to the effects of certain drugs. Rites of communal sexual orgies were a
part of many primitive rituals. It seems that after the orgiastic experience,
man can go on for a time without suffering too much from his separateness.
Slowly the tension of anxiety mounts, and then is reduced again by the
repeated performance of the ritual.

As long as these orgiastic states are a matter of common practice in a
tribe, they do not produce anxiety or guilt. To act in this way is right, and
even virtuous, because it is a way shared by all, approved and demanded by
the medicine men or priests; hence there is no reason to feel guilty or
ashamed. It is quite different when the same solution is chosen by an
individual in a culture which has left behind these common practices.

Alcoholism and drug addiction are the forms which the individual chooses in a non-orgiastic culture. In contrast to those participating in the socially patterned solution, such individuals suffer from guilt feelings and remorse. While they try to escape from separateness by taking refuge in alcohol or drugs, they feel all the more separate after the orgiastic experience is over, and thus are driven to take recourse to it with increasing frequency and intensity. Slightly different from this is the recourse to a sexual orgiastic solution. To some extent it is a natural and normal form of overcoming separateness, and a partial answer to the problem of isolation. But in many individuals in whom separateness is not relieved in other ways, the search for the sexual orgasm assumes a function which makes it not very different from alcoholism and drug addiction. It becomes a desperate attempt to escape the anxiety engendered by separateness, and it results in an ever-increasing sense of separateness, since the sexual act without love never bridges the gap between two human beings, except momentarily.

All forms of orgiastic union have three characteristics: they are intense, even violent; they occur in the total personality, mind *and* body; they are transitory and periodical. Exactly the opposite holds true for that form of union which is by far the most frequent solution chosen by man in the past and in the present: the union based on *conformity* with the group, its customs, practices and beliefs. Here again we find a considerable development.

In a primitive society the group is small; it consists of those with whom one shares blood and soil. With the growing development of culture, the group enlarges; it becomes the citizenry of a *polis*, the citizenry of a large state, the members of a church. Even the poor Roman felt pride because he could say *"civis romanus sum"*; Rome and the Empire were his family, his home, his world. Also in contemporary Western society the union with the group is the prevalent way of overcoming separateness. It is a union in which the individual self disappears to a large extent, and where the aim is to belong to the herd. If I am like everybody else, if I have no feelings or thoughts which make me different, if I conform in custom, dress, ideas, to the pattern of the group, I am saved; saved from the frightening experience of aloneness. The dictatorial systems use threats and terror to induce this conformity; the democratic countries, suggestion and propaganda. There is, indeed, one great difference between the two systems. In the democracies non-conformity is possible and, in fact, by no means entirely absent; in the totalitarian systems, only a few unusual heroes and martyrs can be expected to refuse obedience. But in spite of this difference the democratic societies show an overwhelming degree of conformity. The reason lies in the fact that there *has* to be an answer to the quest for union, and if there is no other or better way, then the union of herd conformity becomes the predominant one. One can only understand the power of the fear to be different, the fear to be only a few steps away from the herd, if one understands the depths of the need not to be separated. Sometimes this fear of non-conformity is rationalized as fear of practical dangers which could threaten the non-conformist. But actually, people *want* to conform to a much higher degree than they are *forced* to conform, at least in the Western democracies.

Most people are not even aware of their need to conform. They live under the illusion that they follow their own ideas and inclinations, that they are individualists, that they have arrived at their opinions as the result of their own thinking—and that it just happens that their ideas are the same as those of the majority. The consensus of all serves as a proof for the correctness of "their" ideas. Since there is still a need to feel some individuality, such need is satisfied with regard to minor differences; the initials on the handbag or the sweater, the name plate of the bank teller, the belonging to the Democratic as against the Republican party, to the Elks instead of to the Shriners become the expression of individual differences. The advertising slogan of "it is different" shows up this pathetic need for difference, when in reality there is hardly any left.

This increasing tendency for the elimination of differences is closely related to the concept and the experience of equality, as it is developing in the most advanced industrial societies. Equality had meant, in a religious context, that we are all God's children, that we all share in the same human-divine substance, that we are all one. It meant also that the very differences between individuals must be respected, that while it is true that we are all one, it is also true that each one of us is a unique entity, is a cosmos by itself. Such conviction of the uniqueness of the individual is expressed for instance in the Talmudic statement: "Whosoever saves a single life is as if he had saved the whole world; whosoever destroys a single life is as if he had destroyed the whole world." Equality as a condition for the development of individuality was also the meaning of the concept in the philosophy of the Western Enlightenment. It meant (most clearly formulated by Kant) that no man must be the means for the ends of another man. That all men are equal inasmuch as they are ends, and only ends, and never means to each other. Following the ideas of the Enlightenment, Socialist thinkers of various schools defined equality as abolition of exploitation, of the use of man by man, regardless of whether this use were cruel or "human."

In contemporary capitalistic society the meaning of equality has been transformed. By equality one refers to the equality of automatons; of men who have lost their individuality. *Equality today means* "sameness," *rather than "oneness."* It is the sameness of abstractions, of the men who work in the same jobs, who have the same amusements, who read the same newspapers, who have the same feelings and the same ideas. In this respect one must also look with some skepticism at some achievements which are usually praised as signs of our progress, such as the equality of women.

Needless to say I am not speaking against the equality of women; but the positive aspects of this tendency for equality must not deceive one. It is part of the trend toward the elimination of differences. Equality is bought at this very price: women are equal because they are not different any more. The proposition of Enlightenment philosophy, *L'âme n'a pas de sexe*, the soul has no sex, has become the general practice. The polarity of the sexes is disappearing, and with it erotic love, which is based on this polarity. Men and women become the *same*, not *equals* at opposite poles. Contemporary society preaches this ideal of unindividualized equality because it needs human atoms, each one the same, to make them function in a mass aggregation, smoothly, without friction; all obeying the same commands, yet everybody being convinced that he is following his own desires. Just as modern mass production requires the standardization of commodities, so the social process requires standardization of man, and this standardization is called "equality."

Union by conformity is not intense and violent; it is calm, dictated by routine, and for this very reason often is insufficient to pacify the anxiety of separateness. The incidence of alcoholism, drug addiction, compulsive sexualism, and suicide in contemporary Western society are symptoms of this relative failure of herd conformity. Furthermore, this solution concerns mainly the mind and not the body, and for this reason too is lacking in comparison with the orgiastic solutions. Herd conformity has only one advantage: it is permanent, and not spasmodic. The individual is introduced into the conformity pattern at the age of three or four, and subsequently never loses his contact with the herd. Even his funeral, which he anticipates as his last great social affair, is in strict conformance with the pattern.

In addition to conformity as a way to relieve the anxiety springing from separateness, another factor of contemporary life must be considered: the role of the work routine and of the pleasure routine. Man becomes a "nine to fiver," he is part of the labor force, or the bureaucratic force of clerks and managers. He has little initiative, his tasks are prescribed by the organization of the work; there is even little difference between those high up on the ladder and those on the bottom. They all perform tasks prescribed by the whole structure of the organization, at a prescribed speed, and in a prescribed manner. Even the feelings are prescribed: cheerfulness, tolerance, reliability, ambition, and an ability to get along with everybody without friction. Fun is routinized in similar, although not quite as drastic ways. Books are selected by the book clubs, movies by the film and theater owners and the advertising slogans paid for by them; the rest is also uniform: the Sunday ride in the car, the television session, the card game, the social parties. From birth to death, from Monday to Monday, from morning to evening—all activities are routinized, and prefabricated. How should a man caught in this net of routine not forget that he is a man, a unique individual, one who is given only this one chance of living, with hopes and disappointments, with sorrow and fear, with the longing for love and the dread of the nothing and of separateness?

A third way of attaining union lies in *creative activity*, be it that of the artist, or of the artisan. In any kind of creative work the creating person unites himself with his material, which represents the world outside of himself. Whether a carpenter makes a table, or a goldsmith a piece of jewelry, whether the peasant grows his corn or the painter paints a picture, in all types of creative work the worker and his object become one, man unites himself with the world in the process of creation. This, however, holds true only for productive work, for work in which *I* plan, produce, see the result of my own work. In the modern work process of a clerk, the worker on the endless belt, little is left of this uniting quality of work. The worker becomes an appendix to the machine or to the bureaucratic organization. He has ceased to be he—hence no union takes place beyond that of conformity.

The unity achieved in productive work is not interpersonal; the unity achieved in orgiastic fusion is transitory; the unity achieved by conformity is only pseudo-unity. Hence, they are only partial answers to the problem of existence. The full answer lies in the achievement of interpersonal union, of fusion with another person, *in love*.

This desire for interpersonal fusion is the most powerful striving in man. It is the most fundamental passion, it is the force which keeps the human race together, the clan, the family, society. The failure to achieve it means insanity or destruction—self-destruction or destruction of others. Without love, humanity could not exist for a day. Yet, if we call the achievement of interpersonal union "love," we find ourselves in a serious difficulty. Fusion can be achieved in different ways—and the differences are not less significant than what is common to the various forms of love. Should they all be called love? Or should we reserve the word "love" only for a specific kind of union, one which has been the ideal virtue in all great humanistic religions and philosophical systems of the last four thousand years of Western and Eastern history?

As with all semantic difficulties, the answer can only be arbitrary. What matters is that we know what kind of union we are talking about when we speak of love. Do we refer to love as the mature answer to the problem of existence, or do we speak of those immature forms of love which may be called *symbiotic union*? In the following pages I shall call love only the former. I shall begin the discussion of "love" with the latter.

Symbiotic union has its biological pattern in the relationship between the pregnant mother and the foetus. They are two, and yet one. They live "together" (*symbiosis*), they need each other. The foetus is a part of the mother, it receives everything it needs from her; mother is its world, as it were; she feeds it, she protects it, but also her own life is enhanced by it. In the *psychic* symbiotic union, the two bodies are independent, but the same kind of attachment exists psychologically.

The *passive* form of the symbiotic union is that of submission, or if we use a clinical term, of *masochism*. The masochistic person escapes from the unbearable feeling of isolation and separateness by making himself part and parcel of another person who directs him, guides him, protects him; who is his life and his oxygen, as it were. The power of the one to whom one submits is inflated, may he be a person or a god; he is everything, I am nothing, except inasmuch as I am part of him. As a part, I am part of greatness, of power, of certainty. The masochistic person does not have to make decisions, does not have to take any risks; he is never alone—but he is not independent; he has no integrity; he is not yet fully born. In a religious context the object of worship is called an idol; in a secular context of a masochistic love relationship the essential mechanism, that of idolatry, is the same. The masochistic relationship can be blended with physical, sexual desire; in this case it is not only a submission in which one's mind participates, but also one's whole body. There can be masochistic submission to fate, to sickness, to rhythmic music, to the orgiastic state produced by drugs or under hypnotic trance—in all these instances the person renounces his integrity, makes himself the instrument of somebody or something outside of himself; he need not solve the problem of living by productive activity.

The *active* form of symbiotic fusion is domination or, to use the psychological term corresponding to masochism, *sadism*. The sadistic person wants to escape from his aloneness and his sense of imprisonment by making another person part and parcel of himself. He inflates and enhances himself by incorporating another person, who worships him.

The sadistic person is as dependent on the submissive person as the latter is on the former; neither can live without the other. The difference is only that the sadistic person commands, exploits, hurts, humiliates, and that the masochistic person is commanded, exploited, hurt, humiliated. This is a considerable difference in a realistic sense; in a deeper emotional sense, the difference is not so great as that which they both have in common: fusion without integrity. If one understands this, it is also not surprising to find that usually a person reacts in both the sadistic and the masochistic manner, usually toward different objects. Hitler reacted primarily in a sadistic fashion toward people, but masochistically toward fate, history, the "higher power" of nature. His end—suicide among general destruction—is as characteristic as was his dream of success—total domination.[1]

In contrast to symbiotic union, mature *love* is *union under the condition of preserving one's integrity*, one's individuality. *Love is an active power in man*; a power which breaks through the walls which separate man from his fellow men, which unites him with others; love makes him overcome the sense of isolation and separateness, yet it permits him to be himself, to retain his integrity. In love the paradox occurs that two beings become one and yet remain two.

If we say love is an activity, we face a difficulty which lies in the ambiguous meaning of the word "activity." By "activity," in the modern usage of the word, is usually meant an action which brings about a change in an existing situation by means of an expenditure of energy. Thus a man is considered active if he does business, studies medicine, works on an endless belt, builds a table, or is engaged in sports. Common to all these activities is that they are directed toward an outside goal to be achieved. What is *not* taken into account is the *motivation* of activity. Take for instance a man driven to incessant work by a sense of deep insecurity and loneliness; or another one driven by ambition, or greed for money. In all these cases the person is the slave of a passion, and his activity is in reality a "passivity" because he is driven; he is the sufferer, not the "actor." On the other hand, a man sitting quiet and contemplating, with no purpose or aim except that of experiencing himself and his oneness with the world, is considered to be "passive," because he is not "doing" anything. In reality, this attitude of concentrated meditation is the highest activity there is, an activity of the soul, which is possible only under the condition of inner freedom and independence. One concept of activity, the modern one, refers to the use of energy for the achievement of external aims; the other concept of activity refers to the use of man's inherent powers, regardless of whether any external change is brought about. The latter concept of activity has been formulated most clearly by Spinoza. He differentiates among the affects between active and passive affects, "actions" and "passions." In the exercise of an active affect, man is free, he is the master of his affect; in the exercise of a passive affect, man is driven, the object of motivations of which he himself is not aware. Thus Spinoza arrives at the statement that virtue and power are one and the same.[2] Envy, jealousy, ambition, any kind of greed are passions; love is an action, the practice of a human power, which can be practiced only in freedom and never as the result of a compulsion.

Love is an activity, not a passive affect; it is a "standing in," not a "falling for." In the most general way, the active character of love can be described by stating that love is primarily *giving*, not receiving.

What is giving? Simple as the answer to this question seems to be, it is actually full of ambiguities and complexities. The most widespread misunderstanding is that which assumes that giving is "giving up" something, being deprived of, sacrificing. The person whose character has not developed beyond the stage of the receptive, exploitative, or hoarding orientation, experiences the act of giving in this way. The marketing character is willing to give, but only in exchange for receiving; giving without receiving for him is being cheated.[3] People whose main orientation is a non-productive one feel giving as an impoverishment. Most individuals of this type therefore refuse to give. Some make a virtue out of giving in the sense of a sacrifice. They feel that just because it is painful to give, one *should* give; the virtue of giving to them lies in the very act of acceptance of the sacrifice. For them, the norm that it is better to give than to receive means that it is better to suffer deprivation than to experience joy.

For the productive character, giving has an entirely different meaning. Giving is the highest expression of potency. In the very act of giving, I experience my strength, my wealth, my power. This experience of heightened vitality and potency fills me with joy. I experience myself as overflowing, spending, alive, hence as joyous.[4] Giving is more joyous than receiving, not because it is a deprivation, but because in the act of giving lies the expression of my aliveness.

It is not difficult to recognize the validity of this principle by applying it to various specific phenomena. The most elementary example lies in the sphere of sex. The culmination of the male sexual function lies in the act of giving; the man gives himself, his sexual organ, to the woman. At the moment of orgasm he gives his semen to her. He cannot help giving it if he is potent. If he cannot give, he is impotent. For the woman the process is not different, although somewhat more complex. She gives herself too; she opens the gates to her feminine center; in the act of receiving, she gives. If she is incapable of this act of giving, if she can only receive, she is frigid. With her the act of giving occurs again, not in her function as a lover, but in that as a mother. She gives of herself to the growing child within her, she gives her milk to the infant, she gives her bodily warmth. Not to give would be painful.

In the sphere of material things giving means being rich. Not he who *has* much is rich, but he who *gives* much. The hoarder who is anxiously worried about losing something is, psychologically speaking, the poor, impoverished man, regardless of how much he has. Whoever is capable of giving of himself is rich. He experiences himself as one who can confer of himself to others. Only one who is deprived of all that goes beyond the barest necessities for subsistence would be incapable of enjoying the act of giving material things. But daily experience shows that what a person considers the minimal necessities depends as much on his character as it depends on his actual possessions. It is well known that the poor are more willing to give than the rich. Nevertheless, poverty beyond a certain point may make it impossible to give, and so is degrading, not only because of the suffering it causes directly, but because of the fact that it deprives the poor of the joy of giving.

The most important sphere of giving, however, is not that of material things, but lies in the specifically human realm. What does one person give to another? He gives of himself, of the most precious thing he has, he gives of his life. This does not necessarily mean that he sacrifices his life for the other— but that he gives him of that which is alive in him; he gives him of his joy, of his interest, of his understanding, of his knowledge, of his humor, of his sadness—of all expressions and manifestations of that which is alive in him. In thus giving of his life, he enriches the other person, he enhances the other's sense of aliveness by enhancing his own sense of aliveness. He does not give in order to receive; giving is in itself exquisite joy. But in giving he cannot help bringing something to life in the other person, and this which is brought to life reflects back to him; in truly giving, he cannot help receiving that which is given back to him. Giving implies to make the other person a giver also and they both share in the joy of what they have brought to life. In the act of giving something is born, and both persons involved are grateful for the life that is born for both of them. Specifically with regard to love this means: love is a power which produces love; impotence is the inability to produce love. This thought has been beautifully expressed by Marx: "Assume," he says, "*man* as *man*, and his relation to the world as a human one, and you can exchange love only for love, confidence for confidence, etc. If you wish to enjoy art, you must be an artistically trained person; if you wish to have influence on other people, you must be a person who has a really stimulating and furthering influence on other people. Every one of your relationships to man and to nature must be a definite expression of your *real, individual* life corresponding to the object of your will. If you love without calling forth love, that is, if your love as such does not produce love, if by means of an *expression of life* as a loving person you do not make of yourself a *loved person*, then your love is impotent, a misfortune."[5] But not only in love does giving mean receiving. The teacher is taught by his students, the actor is stimulated by his audience, the psychoanalyst is cured by his patient—provided they do not treat each other as objects, but are related to each other genuinely and productively.

It is hardly necessary to stress the fact that the ability to love as an act of giving depends on the character development of the person. It presupposes the attainment of a predominately productive orientation; in this orientation the person has overcome dependency, narcissistic omnipotence, the wish to exploit others, or to hoard, and has acquired faith in his own human powers, courage to rely on his powers in the attainment of his goals. To the degree that these qualities are lacking, he is afraid of giving himself —hence of loving.

Beyond the element of giving, the active character of love becomes evident in the fact that it always implies certain basic elements, common to all forms of love. These are *care, responsibility, respect,* and *knowledge.*

That love implies *care* is most evident in a mother's love for her child. No assurance of her love would strike us as sincere if we saw her lacking in care for the infant, if she neglected to feed it, to bathe it, to give it physical comfort; and we are impressed by her love if we see her caring for the child. It is not different even with the love for animals or flowers. If a woman told us that she loved flowers, and we saw that she forgot to water them, we would not believe in her "love" for flowers. *Love is the active concern for the life and the growth of that which we love*. Where this active concern is lacking, there is no love. This element of love has been beautifully described in the book of Jonah. God has told Jonah to go to Nineveh to warn its inhabitants that they will be punished unless they mend their evil ways. Jonah runs away from his mission because he is afraid that the people of Nineveh will repent and that God will forgive them. He is a man with a strong sense of order and law, but without love. However, in his attempt to escape, he finds himself in the belly of a whale, symbolizing the state of isolation and imprisonment which his lack of love and solidarity has brought upon him. God saves him, and Jonah goes to Nineveh. He preaches to the inhabitants as God has told him, and the very thing he was afraid of happens. The men of Nineveh repent their sins, mend their ways, and God forgives them and decides not to destroy the city. Jonah is intensely angry and disappointed; he wanted "justice" to be done, not mercy. At last he finds some comfort in the shade of a tree which God has made to grow for him to protect him from the sun. But when God makes the tree wilt, Jonah is depressed and angrily complains to God. God answers: "Thou hast had pity on the gourd for the which thou hast not labored neither madest it grow; which came up in a night, and perished in a night. And should I not spare Nineveh, that great city, wherein are more than sixscore thousand people that cannot discern between their right hand and their left hand; and also much cattle?" God's answer to Jonah is to be understood symbolically. God explains to Jonah that the essence of love is to "labor" for something and "to make something grow," that love and labor are inseparable. One loves that for which one labors, and one labors for that which one loves.

Care and concern imply another aspect of love; that of *responsibility*. Today responsibility is often meant to denote duty, something imposed upon one from the outside. But responsibility, in its true sense, is an entirely voluntary act; it is my response to the needs, expressed or unexpressed, of another human being. To be "responsible" means to be able and ready to "respond." Jonah did not feel responsible to the inhabitants of Nineveh. He, like Cain, could ask: "Am I my brother's keeper?" The loving person responds. The life of his brother is not his brother's business alone, but his own. He feels responsible for his fellow men, as he feels responsible for himself. This responsibility, in the case of the mother and her infant, refers mainly to the care for physical needs. In the love between adults it refers mainly to the psychic needs of the other person.

Responsibility could easily deteriorate into domination and possessiveness, were it not for a third component of love, *respect*. Respect is not fear and awe; it denotes, in accordance with the root of the word (*respicere*=to look at), the ability to see a person as he is, to be aware of his unique individuality. Respect means the concern that the other person should grow and unfold as he is. Respect, thus, implies the absence of exploitation. I want the loved person to grow and unfold for his own sake, and in his own ways, and not for the purpose of serving me. If I love the other person, I feel one with him or her, but with him *as he is*, not as I need him to be as an object for my use. It is clear that respect is possible only if *I* have achieved independence; if I can stand and walk without needing crutches, without having to dominate and exploit anyone else. Respect exists only on the basis of freedom: "*l'amour est l'enfant de la liberté*," as an old French song says; love is the child of freedom, never that of domination.

To respect a person is not possible without *knowing* him; care and responsibility would be blind if they were not guided by knowledge; the knowledge which is an aspect of love is one which does not stay at the periphery, but penetrates to the core. It is possible only when I can transcend the concern for myself and see the other person in his own terms. I may know, for instance, that a person is angry even if he does not show it overtly; but I may know him more deeply than that; then I know that he is anxious and worried; that he feels lonely, that he feels guilty. Then I know that his anger is only the manifestation of something deeper, and I see him as anxious and embarrassed, that is, as the suffering person, rather than as the angry one.

Knowledge has one more, and a more fundamental, relation to the problem of love. The basic need to fuse with another person so as to transcend the prison of one's separateness is closely related to another specifically human desire, that to know the "secret of man." While life in its merely biological aspects is a miracle and a secret, man in his human aspects is an unfathomable secret to himself—and to his fellow man. We know ourselves, and yet even with all the efforts we may make we do not know ourselves. We know our fellow man, and yet we do not know him, because we are not a thing, and our fellow man is not a thing. The further we reach into the depth of our being, of someone else's being, the more the goal of knowledge eludes us. Yet we cannot help desiring to penetrate into the secret of man's soul, into the innermost nucleus which is "he."

There is one way, a desperate one, to know the secret: it is that of complete power over another person; the power which makes him do what we want, feel what we want, think what we want; which transforms him into a thing, our thing, our possession. The ultimate degree of this attempt to know lies in the extremes of sadism, the desire and ability to make a human being suffer; to torture him, to force him to betray his secret in his suffering. In this craving for penetrating man's secret, his and hence our own, lies an essential motivation for the depth and intensity of cruelty and destructiveness. In a very succinct way this idea has been expressed by Isaac Babel. He quotes a fellow officer in the Russian civil war, who has just stamped his former master to death, as saying: "With shooting—I'll put it this way—with shooting you only get rid of a chap. . . . With shooting you'll never get at the soul, to where it is in a fellow and how it shows itself. But I don't spare myself, and I've more than once trampled an enemy for over an hour. You see, I want to get to know what life really is, what life's like down our way."[6]

In children we often see this path to knowledge quite overtly. The child takes something apart, breaks it up in order to know it; or it takes an animal apart; cruelly tears off the wings of a butterfly in order to know it, to force its secret. The cruelty itself is motivated by something deeper: the wish to know the secret of things and of life.

The other path to knowing "the secret" is love. Love is active penetration of the other person, in which my desire to know is stilled by union. In the act of fusion I know you, I know myself, I know everybody—and I "know" nothing. I know in the only way knowledge of that which is alive is possible for man—by experience of union—not by any knowledge our thought can give. Sadism is motivated by the wish to know the secret, yet I remain as ignorant as I was before. I have torn the other being apart limb from limb, yet all I have done is to destroy him. Love is the only way of knowledge, which in the act of union answers my quest. In the act of loving, of giving myself, in the act of penetrating the other person, I find myself, I discover myself, I discover us both, I discover man.

The longing to know ourselves and to know our fellowman has been expressed in the Delphic motto "Know thyself." It is the mainspring of all psychology. But inasmuch as the desire is to know all of man, his innermost secret, the desire can never be fulfilled in knowledge of the ordinary kind, in knowledge only by thought. Even if we knew a thousand times more of ourselves, we would never reach bottom. We would still remain an enigma to ourselves, as our fellow man would remain an enigma to us. The only way of full knowledge lies in the *act* of love: this act transcends thought, it transcends words. It is the daring plunge into the experience of union. However, knowledge in thought, that is psychological knowledge, is a necessary condition for full knowledge in the act of love. I have to know the other person and myself objectively, in order to be able to see his reality, or rather to overcome the illusions, the irrationally distorted picture I have of him. Only if I know a human being objectively, can I know him in his ultimate essence, in the act of love.[7]

The problem of knowing man is parallel to the religious problem of knowing God. In conventional Western theology the attempt is made to know God by thought, to make statements *about* God. It is assumed that I can know God in my thought. In mysticism, which is the consequent outcome of monotheism (as I shall try to show later on), the attempt is given up to know God by thought, and it is replaced by the experience of union with God in which there is no more room—and no need—for knowledge *about God*.

The experience of union, with man, or religiously speaking, with God, is by no means irrational. On the contrary, it is as Albert Schweitzer has pointed out, the consequence of rationalism, its most daring and radical consequence. It is based on our knowledge of the fundamental, and not accidental, limitations of our knowledge. It is the knowledge that we shall never "grasp" the secret of man and of the universe, but that we can know, nevertheless, in the act of love. Psychology as a science has its limitations, and, as the logical consequence of theology is mysticism, so the ultimate consequence of psychology is love.

Care, responsibility, respect and knowledge are mutually interdependent. They are a syndrome of attitudes which are to be found in the mature person; that is, in the person who develops his own powers productively, who only wants to have that which he has worked for, who has given up narcissistic dreams of omniscience and omnipotence, who has acquired humility based on the inner strength which only genuine productive activity can give.

Thus far I have spoken of love as the overcoming of human separateness, as the fulfillment of the longing for union. But above the universal, existential need for union rises a more specific, biological one: the desire for union between the masculine and feminine poles. The idea of this polarization is most strikingly expressed in the myth that originally man and woman were one, that they were cut in half, and from then on each male has been seeking for the lost female part of himself in order to unite again with her. (The same idea of the original unity of the sexes is also contained in the Biblical story of Eve being made from Adam's rib, even though in this story, in the spirit of patriarchalism, woman is considered secondary to man.) The meaning of the myth is clear enough. Sexual polarization leads man to seek union in a specific way, that of union with the other sex. The polarity between the male and female principles exists also *within* each man and each woman. Just as physiologically man and woman each have hormones of the opposite sex, they are bisexual also in the psychological sense. They carry in themselves the principle of receiving and of penetrating, of matter and of spirit. Man—and woman—finds union within himself only in the union of his female and his male polarity. This polarity is the basis for all creativity.

The male-female polarity is also the basis for interpersonal creativity. This is obvious biologically in the fact that the union of sperm and ovum is the basis for the birth of a child. But in the purely psychic realm it is not different; in the love between man and woman, each of them is reborn. (The homosexual deviation is a failure to attain this polarized union, and thus the homosexual suffers from the pain of never-resolved separateness, a failure, however, which he shares with the average heterosexual who cannot love.)

The same polarity of the male and female principle exists in nature; not only, as is obvious in animals and plants, but in the polarity of the two fundamental functions, that of receiving and that of penetrating. It is the polarity of the earth and rain, of the river and the ocean, of night and day, of darkness and light, of matter and spirit. This idea is beautifully expressed by the great Muslim poet and mystic, Rumi:

> Never, in sooth, does the lover seek without being sought by his beloved.
> When the lightning of love has shot into *this* heart, know that there is love in *that* heart.
> When love of God waxes in thy heart, beyond any doubt God hath love for thee.
> No sound of clapping comes from one hand without the other hand.
> Divine Wisdom is destiny and decree made us lovers of one another.
> Because of that fore-ordainment every part of the world is paired with its mate.
> In the view of the wise, Heaven is man and Earth woman: Earth fosters what Heaven lets fall.
> When Earth lacks Heat, Heaven sends it; when she has lost her freshness and moisture, Heaven restores it.
> Heaven goes on his rounds, like a husband foraging for the wife's sake;
> And Earth is busy with housewiferies: she attend to births and suckling that which she bears.
> Regard Earth and Heaven as endowed with intelligence, since they do the work of intelligent beings.
> Unless these twain taste pleasure from one another, why are they creeping together like sweethearts?
> Without the Earth, how should flower and tree blossom? What, then, would Heaven's water and heat produce?
> As God put desire in man and woman to the end that the world should be preserved by their union,
> So hath He implanted in every part of existence the desire for another part.

Day and Night are enemies outwardly; yet both serve one purpose,
Each in love with the other for the sake of perfecting their mutual work;
Without Night, the nature of Man would receive no income, so there
   would be nothing for Day to spend.[8]

The problem of the male-female polarity leads to some further discussion of the subject matter of love and sex. I have spoken before of Freud's error in seeing in love exclusively the expression—or a sublimation—of the sexual instinct, rather than recognizing that the sexual desire is one manifestation of the need for love and union. But Freud's error goes deeper. In line with his physiological materialism, he sees in the sexual instinct the result of a chemically produced tension in the body which is painful and seeks for relief. The aim of the sexual desire is the removal of this painful tension; sexual satisfaction lies in the accomplishment of this removal. This view has its validity to the extent that the sexual desire operates in the same fashion as hunger or thirst do when the organism is undernourished. Sexual desire, in this concept, is an itch, sexual satisfaction the removal of the itch. In fact, as far as this concept of sexuality is concerned, masturbation would be the ideal sexual satisfaction. What Freud, paradoxically enough, ignores, is the psycho-biological aspect of sexuality, the masculine-feminine polarity, and the desire to bridge this polarity by union. This curious error was probably facilitated by Freud's extreme patriarchalism, which led him to the assumption that sexuality per se is masculine, and thus made him ignore the specific female sexuality. He expressed this idea in the *Three Contributions to the Theory of Sex*, saying that the libido has regularly "a masculine nature," regardless of whether it is the libido in a man or in a woman. The same idea is also expressed in a rationalized form in Freud's theory that the little boy experiences the woman as a castrated man, and that she herself seeks for various compensations for the loss of the male genital. But woman is not a castrated man, and her sexuality is specifically feminine and not of "a masculine nature."

Sexual attraction between the sexes is only partly motivated by the need for removal of tension; it is mainly the need for union with the other sexual pole. In fact, erotic attraction is by no means only expressed in sexual attraction. There is masculinity and femininity in *character* as well as in *sexual function*. The masculine character can be defined as having the qualities of penetration, guidance, activity, discipline and adventurousness; the feminine character by the qualities of productive receptiveness, protection, realism, endurance, motherliness. (It must always be kept in mind that in each individual both characteristics are blended, but with the preponderance of those appertaining to "his" or "her" sex.) Very often if the masculine *character* traits of a man are weakened because emotionally he has remained a child, he will try to compensate for this lack by the exclusive emphasis on his male role in *sex*. The result is the Don Juan, who needs to prove his male prowess in sex because he is unsure of his masculinity in a characterological sense. When the paralysis of masculinity is more extreme, sadism (the use of force) becomes the main—a perverted—substitute for masculinity. If the feminine sexuality is weakened or perverted, it is transformed into masochism, or possessiveness.

Freud has been criticized for his overevaluation of sex. This criticism was often prompted by the wish to remove an element from Freud's system which aroused criticism and hostility among conventionally minded people. Freud keenly sensed this motivation and for this very reason fought every attempt to change his theory of sex. Indeed, in his time, Freud's theory had a challenging and revolutionary character. But what was true around 1900 is not true any more fifty years later. The sexual mores have changed so much that Freud's theories are not any longer shocking to the Western middle classes, and it is a quixotic kind of radicalism when orthodox analysts today still think they are courageous and radical in defending Freud's sexual theory. In fact, their brand of psychoanalysis is conformist, and does not try to raise psychological questions which would lead to a criticism of contemporary society.

My criticism of Freud's theory is not that he overemphasized sex, but his failure to understand sex deeply enough. He took the first step in discovering the significance of interpersonal passions; in accordance with his philosophic premises he explained them physiologically. In the further development of psychoanalysis it is necessary to correct and deepen Freud's concept by translating Freud's insights from the physiological into the biological and existential dimension.[9]

NOTES

1. Cf. a more detailed study of sadism and masochism in E. Fromm, *Escape from Freedom*, Rinehart & Company, New York, 1941.

2. Spinoza, Ethics IV, Def. 8.

3. Cf. a detailed discussion of these character orientations in E. Fromm, *Man for Himself*, Rinehart & Company, New York, 1947, Chap. III, pp. 54–117.

4. Compare the definition of joy given by Spinoza.

5. "Nationalökonomie und Philosophie," 1844, published in Karl Marx' *Die Frühschriften*, Alfred Krämer, Verlag, Stuttgart, 1953, pp. 300, 301. (My translation, E.F.)

6. I. Babel, *The Collected Stories*, Criterion Books, New York, 1955.

7. The above statement has an important implication for the role of psychology in contemporary Western culture. While the great popularity of psychology certainly indicates an interest in the knowledge of man, it also betrays the fundamental lack of love in human relations today. Psychological knowledge thus becomes a substitute for full knowledge in the act of love, instead of being a step toward it.

8. R. A. Nicholson, *Rumi*, George Allen and Unwin, Ltd., London, 1950, pp. 112–3.

9. Freud himself made a first step in this direction in his later concept of the life and death instincts. His concept of the former (*eros*) as a principle of synthesis and unification is on an entirely different plane from that of his libido concept. But in spite of the fact that the theory of life and death instincts was accepted by orthodox analysts, this acceptance did not lead to a fundamental revision of the libido concept, especially as far as clinical work is concerned.

part three

PERSON TO PERSON: PSYCHOLOGICAL APPROACHES

A. The Theory of Communication

B. Therapeutic Communication

TOWARD A PSYCHOLOGICAL THEORY OF HUMAN COMMUNICATION*

Franklin Fearing

*t*he tremendous significance of communication in human affairs is briefly and arrestingly characterized by a nonpsychologist, Kenneth Burke, when at the end of a penetrating discussion of these problems (9) he says ". . . there is no place for purely human boasts of grandeur, or for forgetting that men build their cultures by huddling together, nervously loquacious, at the edge of an abyss."

It is the purpose of the present paper to present a broad conceptual framework within which the how and why of human loquacity (and related processes) may be considered. The increasing amount of published research on human communicative behavior has made the lack of theoretical integration noticeable. In recent volumes (8, 19, 36) this deficiency has been noted or implied, especially by Hovland (17) and Bryson (8).†

In the present discussion communicative behavior is placed in the context of the current formulations‡ regarding cognitive-perceptual processes conceived as dynamically related to the need-value systems of individuals. Broadly stated, these conceptualizations assert that these systems, which are central in the personality structure of the individual, interacting with the environment, result in instabilities and disequilibriums which are co-ordinated with an increase in tension in the individual, and that cognitive-perceptual processes structure the environment in a specific manner so as to reduce tension.

---

* Reprinted from the *Journal of Personality*, Vol. XXII (1953), pp. 71–78. Used by permission of Duke University Press.

† This is not to say that there have been no attempts to formulate communications theory. In addition to the important formulations of Lasswell (25), Mead (29), and Burke (9, 10), the recent papers by Hovland (18), Pronko (34), and Smith (38, 39) contain theoretical discussions.

‡For example, Bruner and Postman (6, 33), Frenkel-Brunswick (15), and many others.

Communicative behavior is a specific form of molar behavior which occurs in a situation or field possessing specified properties, the parts of which are in interdependent relationship with each other. A theory of such behavior is concerned with forces, psychological, social, and physical, which determine the course of this behavior and its outcomes in relation to the culture in which it occurs. Such a theory should formulate hypothetical constructs and present a terminology with appropriate definitions in the following four interrelated areas: (a) the forces which determine the *effects* of communication, that is, constructs regarding individuals designated *interpreters*; (b) the forces which determine the *production* of communications, that is, constructs about *communicators*; (c) the nature of communications *content* considered as a stimulus field; (d) the characteristics of the *situation* or *field* in which communication occurs.

All the practical and theoretical problems of communications research lie in these four areas. It is essential to the formulations in the present paper that the behavior events in these areas be regarded as *dynamically interrelated*. An important implication of this assumption is that any change occurring in any subregion will have effects in all other regions.

DEFINITIONS OF BASIC TERMS

Certain terms referring to regions of the communications field are used throughout the present discussion. Their definitions follow.

COMMUNICATOR. A communicator is a person (or persons) who produces or controls the production of a body of sign-symbol material with the intent (this term is discussed later) of cognitively structuring the field (or fields) of specific interpreters who are assumed by the communicator to have specific needs and demands. They may or may not be physically present, but are always part of the psychological field of the communicator. The communicator reacts or is capable of reacting to the body of produced material in the same manner in which he anticipates the interpreters will react. There is a special category of communicators who do not originally produce the sign-symbol material, but who, within certain limits, are able to control or manipulate its subsequent presentation. These we shall call pseudo-communicators.

INTERPRETER. An interpreter is one who perceives (cognitively structures) a specific body of sign-symbol material produced by specific communicators as a stimulus field in terms of his existing patterns of needs, expectancies, and demands. In perceiving this stimulus field the interpreter implicitly or explicitly identifies its artifactual character and structures its source. The definitions of this structurization vary from a vague "they say" to a definitive identification of the communicator. In any event, part of the stimulus field for the interpreter is the personal agency in its production. The objective truth of these assumptions by the interpreters is not involved.*

COMMUNICATIONS CONTENT. Communications content is an organized stimulus field consisting primarily of signs and symbols produced by a communicator and perceived through single or multisensory channels. It must be susceptible to similar structurizations by both communicator and interpreter. Structurization of the stimulus field may be either simple or complex and in the spatial or temporal dimensions or both. Temporal structurization is usually more highly differentiated, and also permits greater perceptual freedom on the part of interpreters. Plays, novels, scientific papers are structurally complex as contrasted with a road sign or a single, attention-attracting signal, e.g., Hey there! Communications content may be distinguished from the context in which it appears. The "timing" of an official announcement, the setting of a scene in a play, the psychological properties of a particular communications medium, or the status and personality of a speaker are examples of context. These contextual aspects of the stimulus are sometimes referred to as independent extraneous factors designated by such terms as "suggestion" or "prestige." Asch (3) has recently discussed this and pointed out that content of a statement may not be separated from its context, and that content is psychologically changed by context. Considered as a stimulus field to which interpreters respond, however, content and context are a unified whole or gestalt.

The communicator or his surrogate is a part of the context in every communication. In responding to content the interpreter, vaguely or clearly, structures its source. In some cases the communicator's characteristics, real or imagined, play a major role in so far as the effects on the interpreter are concerned.

COMMUNICATIONS SITUATION. Communication occurs in a situation possessing quasi-physical, quasi-social and quasi-psychological properties which induce and determine the course of behavior of communicators and interpreters. A primary characteristic of this field as perceived by either the communicator or interpreter or both is its lack of a clear and stable organization. Correlated with the perceived instability is an increase in tension

---

* Much current communications research is concerned with interpreter responses to communications content either during exposure (called *response analysis* [35] or subsequent to exposure (called *effects analysis*, [14, 19, 23]). The last, of course, is subject to intervening experiences of the interpreter and, strictly speaking, is not part of the communicative situation. Especially significant from the point of view of the conceptualizations proposed are the studies of how particular interpreters utilize communications content. Merton's study of the Kate Smith broadcasts (30), and the studies of daytime radio serials by Arnheim (2), Herzog (16) and Warner and Henry (43) contribute relevant data.

on the part of the potential communicators and interpreters. This is the "need to communicate" and the "need to be communicated to."* The situation is cognitively restructured by the produced content, and the communication may be said to occur when the perception of such content brings communicators and interpreters into dynamic relationships. Existing tensions may be either increased or reduced depending on the perceptual-need systems of the individuals involved, and the specific character of the communications content. The central importance of sign-symbol material in bringing about these effects for man is related to his unique capacity as a symbol-producing and symbol-manipulating organism.

The dynamics of the interrelated parts of the communication situation may be summarized as follows: (a) the existence of specific tensional states related to perceived instabilities, disturbances, or needs in the psychological fields of the individuals involved; (b) the production of a structured stimulus field (communications content) consisting of signs and symbols; and (c) the achievement of a more stable organization through cognitive restructuring of the fields induced by such content. The relationships in the communication situation have a strategic character in that they involve a variety of manipulatory activities through which individuals strive to achieve an understanding of each other and their environments. This is the meaning of communication in human society.

It is necessary to distinguish the interactions between individuals in the communication situation from other forms of social interaction. Recent papers by Maslow (28) and Arnheim (1) discuss a form of interaction between organisms which closely resembles communication. *Expression* or *expressive behavior* refers to postural, gestural (including vocalizations), and other bodily changes which are perceived and cognized by others. Arnheim notes that the general appearance and all the overt activities of the body may be "expressive." The flushed face, the upraised fist, the sagging shoulders are stimulus patterns which may be perceived and cognized in various ways by another organism. But these interactions are *not* communication, although they may easily be confused with it.

Maslow differentiates instrumental behavior, or "coping" behavior, as he terms it, from expressive behavior. Coping behavior is "essentially an interaction of the character with the world, adjusting each to the other with mutual effect." Noninstrumental or expressive behavior, on the other hand, "is essentially an epiphenomenon of the nature of character structure." Coping behavior is characteristically motivated, determined by

---

* A wide range of "needs" may be served in communication situations. The studies of Herzog (16), Warner and Henry (43) and Arnheim (2) show how particular interpreters seek specific satisfactions from communications content.

environmental and cultural variables, easily controlled, designed to cause changes in the environment, concerned with need-gratification and threat-reduction, and highly conscious.* The act of producing content in the communications situation may be regarded as a special case of coping behavior. The borderline case between a communicative interaction would be the smile which is "expressive"—presumably of some bodily affective state—and the smile that is produced with intent to affect the behavior of another. It may be difficult to establish criteria to differentiate between expressive behavior and communication, but the reality and importance of the distinction must be accepted.

In addition to its instrumental or homeostatic role, communication is essentially creative. This is partly the result of the central role and unique potentialities of signs and symbols. The structuring processes resulting in the produced content may represent new (emergent) insights for both the producer of the content and the interpreters, and are essentially creative acts, perhaps the prototype of all creative activity in the arts and sciences. "Creative" as used here means that the resultant of the structuring process —the "structure"—is not merely a summation of existing elements, but a gestalt possessing properties different from those of the component elements. The structuring process is creative also in the sense that it does not necessarily depend on antecedent experience (learning) or innate factors in the individual. In this connection the comments of Chein (13) seem applicable to the communications situation when he says, "The important dynamic fact is *how the person perceives the situation and what he wants in it* rather than the fact that learning had previously taken place." (Italics added.) Chein believes there is an "intellectual trap" in the assumption that a psychological process must be accounted for as either learned or innate. "We believe that new insights do arise, and we see no good reason why novel features of current situations should not be perceived or why previously unnoticed features of repeatedly experienced situations may not be perceived for the first time."

COMMUNICATIONS CONTENT AND THE CONCEPT "INTENT." The special, almost unique, characteristic of the communication situation is the production of a stimulus field possessing special characteristics which differentiate it from other stimuli to which organisms respond. These are: (a) it is *produced* by one or more individuals in the communication situation with the *intent* of structuring the fields of both its producers and interpreters; (b) it utilizes sign-symbol materials which have common significations for both the producer and interpreters; and (c) it implicates specific interpreters and communicators who are assumed to possess certain need

---

* Similar distinctions have been made by others. Lewis (26), for example, distinguishes between the "declarative" and "manipulative" use of language by the child.

patterns and perceptual capacities for which the produced content is relevant.*

The construct intent in (a) above refers to the fact that the act of producing content is *directed* rather than random or aimless, and implicitly or explicitly assumes future effects. We have noted that the production of communications content appears to be a special case of coping behavior as defined by Maslow, especially as it reflects the perception of a concrete social situation, and the need-value structure of the communicator. In this sense intent is very similar to Cantril's (12) "expectancy," which he defines as "our present reaction to the future in terms of what will happen to us if we do (or don't) do certain things now." As Cantril points out, what really concerns us "now" are possible future effects—effects which we may be able to modify. Intent is correlated with a tension system, and may be generalized as a need to communicate.

The intent of the communicator in producing specific content is not only concerned with expected effects on interpreters, but assumes they possess particular need patterns and perceptual capacities. In other words, *in the act of producing content, the interpreters are always in the psychological field of the communicator.* The communicator's perceptions of the interpreters may determine the character of the content he produces. The degree of specificity with which these presumed effects are defined by the communicator may vary widely from one communication situation to another, but clearly or vaguely they are dynamically a part of the communication situation.

It does not follow from this, however, that the communicator always produces content which is directly responsive to interpreter needs or reactions. In face-to-face communications, for example, where communicator and interpreter physically are in each other's presence, the produced content is more likely to be adjusted to the immediate responses of the interpreter. In a large proportion of human communications the communicator and interpreter are separated spatially or temporally. Here the communicator produces content on the basis of assumptions about interpreters which he may or may not be ready or able to modify in terms of interpreter response. In the limiting case, either because the communicator conceives the communication in strictly linear terms and hence is psychologically incapable of modifying content, or because of technological

---

* Schneirla has recently (37) emphasized the same point of view in his discussion of the distinctions between subhuman and human "communication." He notes that social interchange in insects resembles human communication only superficially. In human communication, according to Schneirla, the following criteria are met: (a) symbols are used intentionally with respect to anticipated consequences; (b) they have meaningful connections with objects and situations; (c) they influence both the user and the interpreter in characteristic ways; and (d) they are patterned according to the motivations and perceptions of the communicator.

limitations of the medium used which make modification of content difficult or impossible, communication may break down completely.

In producing communications, the intent-pattern of the communicator may bear a significant relation to his role in the power-structure of the groups, subcultures, or class in which he has membership. This has important theoretical and practical implications, since it asserts a possible relationship between all communication and the power-structures in the culture. "Control" and "power," as those terms are used here, refer to the fact that communications content is the primary agency in human society through which individuals have social relationships with each other and with their physical environments. For example, the amount and quality of information available at any given time regarding any human problem are functions of the activities of specific communicators with specific intents. Such information may furnish the frame of reference for human action, and in this sense controls. However, since the relationship between communicator and interpreter is not a simple linear one in which certain content is produced and transmitted intact to recipients, control is not necessarily communicator-centered. Rather, it is complex and interdependent, involving feed-back mechanisms of the type recently described by Norbert Wiener (45). In so far as the communicator recognizes and adjusts to the need structure and perceptual capacities of the interpreter, he shares control with him.

CONTENT ANALYSIS. The stimulus material produced by the communicator under the organizing forces just described is defined operationally as an organization of sign-symbols which may be subject to *content analysis*. Content analysis refers to a specific set of procedures the object of which is to make available quantitative and qualitative statements regarding communications content.* One effect of this requirement is that communications content must be capable of being reproduced in permanent form.

The characteristics of this stimulus must be established by procedures applied independently of particular communicators and interpreters. Such an analysis establishes a set of reference points with respect to which other aspects of the communications field—for example, the intent of communicators, including their emotional and personality dynamics, or effects on interpreters—may be validly and reliably appraised. Content analysis may be carried out in accordance with a highly rigorous design, or be relatively impressionistic—the professional critic's review of a novel is a form of

---

* The technique and problems of content analysis are discussed in Lasswell and Leites (25), Berelson and Lazarsfeld (4), and Spiegelman, Terwilliger, and Fearing (42). Examples of the application of these techniques to particular contents are White (44), and Spiegelman, Terwilliger, and Fearing (40, 41). The use of less rigorous techniques are illustrated in Kracauer (24) and Wolfenstein and Leites (48).

content analysis—but it is essential to any systematic study of communication situations.

If the analysis is to claim any degree of scientific rigor it must meet reliability and validity tests, the analysts must be trained in the use of the procedures, and the categories used must be based on objective criteria.*

SIGN-SYMBOL MATERIAL. A second characteristic of communications content is its utilization of signs and symbols. The definitions proposed by Charles Morris (32), and the general theoretical orientation of George Mead (29) are used in the present discussion. Morris's definition of a symbol as a sign produced by its interpreter that acts as a substitute for some other sign with which it is synonymous is adopted here.

Mead has recognized the enormous implications for society of the symbol-using processes. For him symbols are not merely sense stimuli to which mental states—"meanings," "concepts," "ideas," etc.—have become attached. They are gestures, and are "significant" because the communicator who produces the gesture incipiently responds to it in the same way as the individual to be affected by it—in Mead's terminology, "the other." This, for Mead, is the essence of the social process. Communication "is not simply a matter of abstract ideas, but is a process of putting one's self in the place of the other person's attitude, communicating through significant symbols" (p. 327).

Morris points out that although "spoken-heard" signs (language) play a central role in the life of man these are not the only types of symbolic material. An important type of nonlinguistic symbolic material is that which Morris terms "iconic." An iconic sign is any sign which is similar in some respect to that which it denotes. Both auditory and visual signs may be iconic. Morris notes that ". . . photographs, portraits, maps, road-markers, models are iconic to a high degree; dreams, paintings, pageants, the dance, dress, play, and architecture are iconic in varying degrees" (p. 190). A form of communications content involving what Morris calls the "iconic performance of actions" is of particular importance in current communications research. Examples include ritual, film and stage performances, story telling, comic strips, and many others.

SOME DIMENSIONS OF COMMUNICATIONS

In terms of the theory here presented the communicator, content, and interpreter are "in" every communications situation and are dynamically related. It would be useful to conceptualize these relationships in terms of hypothetical properties or dimensions which are dependent on specific

---

* The techniques for determining validity and reliability are discussed by Janis (20), Kaplan and Goldsen (21), and Spiegelman, Terwilliger, and Fearing (42).

variables in the communications situation. It should be possible to define a given communication situation by its position on a variety of such dimensions. Several problems present themselves. In the first place, it is necessary to establish the equivocality of each dimension and the objective criteria to be used in fixing any position or series of positions on it. Second, there is the problem of describing, and, for experimental purposes, controlling, the variables which underlie each continuum and determine the positions thereon. Ultimately, of course, it would be necessary to determine the kind of relationships existing between the various continua. The suggested dimensions which follow are to be regarded as highly tentative. The possibilities are not exhausted and it is possible that those proposed will not survive experimental analysis.

SPECIFICITY OF INTENT. This dimension defines the definiteness with which the communicator envisages the effects of the content he produces. Intent is a manifestation of the need-tensional variables in the personality structure of the communicator; it acts as a selector and organizer of material. It has already been pointed out that the interpreter is always part of the psychological field of the communicator in the act of producing content. The specificity dimension defines the potency of the interpreter image on content. It expresses itself in the degree to which the communication is *planned*.

Highly specific or "planned" communications are usually interpreter centered. The communicators are (a) explicit regarding the effects to be achieved on particular interpreters, and (b) consciously manipulating content in the light of these assumptions. A propaganda campaign, for example, is directed toward particular "publics" who are assumed by the communicator to have certain wants, to be alert or apathetic, stupid or intelligent.

Communications which are relatively unspecific, on the other hand, are to a greater degree communicator centered. That is, in general, the communicator is more concerned with expressing himself than with possible effects on others. In the limiting case at the unplanned end of the continuum, we do not have communicative behavior, but expressive behavior, in the sense of Maslow. At this end of the continuum we should expect to find material produced which in a larger degree reflects the personality structure and emotional dynamics of the communicator and is very slightly concerned with potential interpreters. Examples of relatively unplanned communications are face-to-face conversations, some, but not all, personal letters, rumors (except those which are "planted" for specific effects), diaries, and certain types of autobiographical material.*

* These types of communications content are typically produced in the clinical situation and are analyzed for the information they yield regarding the personality structures of the subjects.

A group of factors which are significantly correlated with high specificity of intent are those relating to the communicator's social role, especially his power role in the groups of which he is a member. Broadly speaking, all highly planned communications are power communications in the sense that specific behavioral effects are expected to follow specific content. The control of content assumes the control of these effects, and hence is closely connected with the power structures of the society. Lasswell (25) has discussed the concern of ruling elites, as he terms them, with communication as a means of preserving power. He notes that in the instance of conflicts between ruling elites there develops a struggle for the control of channels of communication.

Highly planned communications of this type are frequently produced by various types of professional communicators. These include public relations specialists, advertising copy writers, professional propagandists, publicity specialists, psychological warfare specialists, and others.* These communicators have a degree of professional competence in the use of symbols, particularly those required for a particular communications medium.

The assignment of a particular communication to a position on the specificity continuum may be based on data from two sources : (a) statements by or information about communicators; and (b) content analyses made for the purpose of inferring the character of the communicator's intent.† Information regarding the first might be based on the use of clinical techniques or from a variety of secondary as well as primary sources. These will, in themselves, be communications, and their analysis will have to take into account all the factors which are involved in the communicative process.

REALITY. This dimension refers to the degree to which a communications content reflects or is identifiable with psychological or physical reality. Operationally, the degree of reality as here defined *is a function of the manipulatory activities of the communicator in producing content.* These include selecting, isolating, or otherwise ordering content and contextual variables. The degree of freedom which the communicator permits himself in arranging communications content determines the position of the content on the real-irreal dimension. A newsreel, "on the spot" radio broadcast, TV broadcast of an event, a map, a road sign occupy positions toward the "real" end of the continuum; that is, they are examples of content which has been subject to a minimal amount of arrangement or selection

---

* The specific character of the intent of these specialists, their research techniques, selection of content, and strategies of presentation have been described by a professional public relations counsellor, Edward L. Bernays, in a recent article (5) which bears the significant title "The Engineering of Consent." See also Merton (30).

† White's analysis (44) of *Black Boy* for the purpose of understanding the author's value system is an example.

by the communicator. The perceptual responses of the interpreters to these cues may be ordered to a closely related authenticity dimension.

AUTHENTICITY. This dimension refers to the degree to which communications content contains cues which the interpreter accepts as congruent with "reality" as he knows it. Such cues are in the content or provided by its context, and they are perceived by the interpreter as an indication that the content has been manipulated by the communicator. The objective reality of such manipulation is not involved. The newsreel, documentary, and fictional film are perceived by most interpreters as differing with regard to authenticity.

The cues which carry the signification of authenticity for the interpreter are, at least in part, the result of cultural conditioning. The label "newsreel" is in itself such a cue—and is part of the context in the presentation of the film; the use of nonprofessional actors in a documentary and the use of natural settings are cues of authenticity. "Objective" reporting is accepted as authentic as contrasted with "interpretive" reporting, because of numerous cues signifying "objectivity" in the former. These cues may be simulated with intent. An example of the results of such simulation was the famous broadcast *War of the Worlds*, which had high irreality, but, we may assume, was unintentionally authentic for many interpreters. In this case the cues for authenticity were psychologically more potent than the specific indications of irreality.

AMBIGUITY. This dimension is concerned with properties of communications content which makes it susceptible to variant structurizations by interpreters. A content may be said to be *relatively unambiguous when it is maximally resistant to such variant structurizations.* In the limiting case it would be susceptible to only one structurization. This definition of ambiguity is consistent with that discussed in the recent paper by Luchins (27). Luchins suggests that an "ambiguous stimulus field is one which allows various structurizations." Luchins notes that ambiguity and structural clarity of the stimulus are not in a simple dependent relationship. Rather, the question is the extent to which a given content permits variant interpretations. *All communications contents are in some degree ambiguous.* This may be termed the Principle of Necessary Ambiguity, and is basic to the understanding of all communications effects. Examples of ambiguous content are those found in the analyses of the deviant responses to the Mr. Biggott cartoons (22), and to the *War of the Worlds* broadcast (11). The study of Wiese and Cole (46) on children's responses to the film *Tomorrow the World* shows the extent to which apparently unambiguous thematic material is subject to variant meanings.

The important variables are in the content (including context). These include structural simplicity or complexity, amount of detail, etc. It is probable that content which is structurally simple, for example, a road sign, will be less ambiguous than content which is complex, for example, a scene in a play.

CONGRUENCY. This dimension refers to the degree to which the presented content is relevant to the need-value-demand systems of the interpreter. The relevant variables are those in his need-value structure and symbol-manipulating habits, conceived as acting on content of specific structure. For example, interpreters with specific and persisting goal integrations, strong value orientations and stereotypes, specific prior experience in or involvement with particular content, or any other form of persistent set will either reject (in the limiting case) or markedly modify presented content in the direction of greater congruity with their predispositions. Their perceptions of specific content will be deviant as compared with the perceptions of interpreters whose need-value system is less rigid, or to a greater degree is congruent with the presented content. In other situations the intensity and specificity of need for a structured field—that is, need for information, guidance, direction, or "meaning"—will determine the degree of congruence of presented content. The familiarity with the symbols used in particular content, and the degree to which they have common significations for communicators and interpreters are, of course, fundamentally important variables.

The relation between the congruity and ambiguity dimensions is close but not a simple dependent one. Current discussions (15, 31, 33) of the personality variables in perception contain data relevant to the dynamics of these relationships. The effects of predispositions or sets (also called "hypotheses") of great strength on the perception of stimulus material that is relatively ambiguous is discussed by Miller (31). He notes that personality and motivational factors will have maximum effects on the emergence of perception in situations where information is ambiguous. Bruner (7) also notes that "the less ambiguous the information, the less the effect of past experience in confirming hypotheses and the greater the use of input information."

By definition, an ambiguous communications content is permissive of a large number of structurizations. Such content would presumably be congruent with a wide variety of interpreter predispositions.* Each would be able to perceive what he wished to perceive. On the other hand, a highly unambiguous content might be either congruent or highly incongruent with particular interpreter predispositions. If congruent, the result would be acceptance with minimal modifications. If incongruent, the result might be rejection in the limiting case, or intense conflict. The study by Wilner (47) previously referred to on the perceptual processes of highly

---

* The Wiese-Cole study (46) is a case in point. Children from differing socio-economic classes perceived quite different meanings in the anti-Nazi themes in the film *Tomorrow the World.*

prejudiced and relatively unprejudiced persons of a motion picture film *Home of the Brave* contains relevant data. Certain characters in the film are presented relatively unambiguously as regards their attitudes toward Negroes. Such unambiguous characterizations were highly incongruent with rigid attitude-value orientations of some of the subjects. The unambiguity of the characterizations makes it difficult for these subjects to misperceive ("distort") them, with the result that the subjects are thrown into conflict. Communications content of this type is, of course, structurally complex, that is, has many themes and subthemes other than those that are congruent or incongruent with particular need-value systems of interpreters. This may enable them to avoid the conflict by perceiving other aspects of the content—in the case of the film mentioned above, other traits of the character.

It is possible to postulate the outcomes (effects on interpreters) of certain hypothetical limiting cases in which congruency and ambiguity vary with respect to each other.

CASE 1: High intensity (rigidity) of interpreter sets of "hypotheses" plus highly ambiguous content. Result: Interpreter readily *projects* with the result that the content is given a firmer structure or restructured in the direction of interpreter's hypotheses.

CASE 2: High intensity of "hypotheses" plus unambiguous content. Result: Interpreter readily *identifies* if content is congruent with hypotheses. If content is not congruent conflict results in various patterns of evasion and rejection, or interpreter may "leave the field" entirely.

CASE 3: Low intensity of "hypotheses" plus ambiguous content. Result: Interpreter may seek more firm structurization utilizing whatever cues are available, or he may be indifferent and relatively unaffected.

CASE 4: Low intensity of "hypotheses" plus unambiguous content. Result: Interpreter may identify with content.

In the foregoing hypothetical cases it is assumed that a specific communications field exists in which all other parameters are constant. The constructs "identification" and "projection" are employed to indicate the direction of the relationship between interpreter and content. In general, "identification" refers to the situation in which conditions are optimal for the acceptance by the interpreter of the structurizations offered by all or part of the content. "Projection" refers to the situation in which the interpreter is able wholly or partially to restructure the content in a manner consistent with his dominant hypotheses. The terms are not mutually exclusive. Rather, they may be conceived as "pulls," in which the direction of structurization in the communications situation is determined by the relative strengths of the need-demand system of the interpreter and the clarity of the content itself. This can be determined only by analyses based on relevant data regarding the need-demand systems (hypotheses) of interpreters and content analyses in a specific communications situation.

SUMMARY

A conceptual frame of reference for human communicative behavior has been proposed which places it in the context of current personality-perceptual theory. Specific dynamic relationships between communicators and interpreters are hypothesized. These are distinguished from other forms of social interaction by (a) their instrumental-creative character and (b) the production of a stimulus field possessing particular properties. Both the production and response to this field are determined by perceived instabilities in the environment as related to the need-value systems of communicators and interpreters. In responding both communicators and interpreters cognitively restructure the situation in the direction of a greater understanding of each other and of their environments. Some of the dynamical processes in the communications situation are expressed genotypically in the form of hypothetical dimensions.

NOTES

1. Arnheim, R. The gestalt theory of expression. *Psychol. Rev.*, 1949 56, 156–171.

2. ———. The world of the daytime serial. In P. F. Lazarsfeld and F. N. Stanton (Eds.), *Radio research. 1942–1943.* New York: Duell, Sloan and Pearce, 1944.

3. Asch, S. E. "The doctrine of suggestion, prestige and limitation in social psychology." *Psychol. Rev.*, 1948, 55, 250–276.

4. Berelson, B., and Lazarsfeld, P. "The analysis of communications content." Mimeographed manuscript circulated by authors.

5. Bernays, E. "The engineering of consent." *Ann. Amer. Acad. pol. soc. Sci.*, 1947, 250, 113–120.

6. Bruner, J. S. "Symbolic value as an organizing factor in perception." *J. soc. Psychol.*, 1948, 27, 203–208.

7. ———. "Personality dynamics and the process of perceiving." In Robert R. Blake and Glenn V. Ramsey (Eds.), *Perception: an approach to personality.* New York: Ronald Press, 1951. Pp. 121–148.

8. Bryson, Lyman (Ed.) *The communication of ideas.* New York: Harper and Brothers, 1948.

9. Burke, Kenneth. *Permanence and change.* New York: New Republic, Inc., 1935.

10. ———. *A rhetoric of motives.* New York: Prentice-Hall, Inc., 1950.

11. Cantril, H. *Invasion from Mars.* Princeton, N.J.: Princeton University Press, 1940.

12. ————. *Understanding man's social behavior; preliminary notes.* Princeton, N.J.: Office of Public Opinion Research, 1948.

13. Chein, I. "Behavior theory and the behavior of attitudes: some critical comments." *Psychol. Rev.*, 1948, 55, 175–188.

14. Fearing, Franklin. "Motion pictures as a medium of instruction and communication: an experimental analysis of the effects of two films." *University Calif. Publ. Culture Soc.*, 1950, Vol. 2, No. 3.

15. Frenkel-Brunswick, Else. "Personality theory and perception." In Robert R. Blake and Glenn V. Ramsey (Eds.), *Perception: an approach to personality.* New York: Ronald Press, 1951.

16. Herzog, Herta. "Psychological gratifications in daytime radio listening." In T. M. Newcomb and E. L. Hartley (Eds.), *Readings in social psychology.* New York: Henry Holt and Co., 1947.

17. Hovland, Carl I. "Social communication." *Proc. Amer. phil. Society*, 1948, 92, 371–375

18. ————. "Psychology of the communication process." In Wilbur Schramm (Ed.), *Communications in modern society.* Urbana, Ill: University of Illinois Press, 1948.

19. Hovland, Carl I., Lumsdaine, A. A., and Sheffield, F. D. *Experiments on mass communication.* Princeton, N.J.: Princeton University Press, 1949.

20. Janis, Irving L. "The problem of validating content analysis." In H. D. Lasswell, *et al.*, *Language of politics.* New York: G. W. Stewart, 1949.

21. Kaplan, A., and Goldsen, J. M. "The reliability of content analysis categories." In H. D. Lasswell, *et al.*, *Language of politics.* New York: G. W. Stewart, 1949. Pp. 83–112.

22. Kendall, P. L., and Wolf, K. M. "The analysis of deviant cases in communications research." In P. F. Lazarsfeld and F. N. Stanton (Eds.), *Communications research: 1948–1949.* New York: Harper and Brothers, 1949.

23. Klapper, J. T. *The effects of the mass media.* New York: Bureau of Applied Social Research, Columbia University, 1949.

24. Kracauer, Siegfried. *From Caligari to Hitler: a psychological history of the German film.* Princeton, N.J.: Princeton University Press, 1947.

25. Lasswell, H. D., Leites, N., *et al. Language of politics; studies in quantitative semantics.* New York: G. W. Stewart, 1949.

26. Lewis, M. M. *Language in society: the linguistic revolution and social change.* New York: Social Science Publishers, 1948.

27. Luchins, A. S. "The stimulus field in social psychology." *Psychol. Rev.*, 1950, 57, 27–30.

28. Maslow, A. H. "The expressive component in behavior." *Psychol. Rev.*, 56, 261–272.

29. Mead, George H. *Mind, self, and society.* Chicago: University of Chicago Press, 1934.

30. Merton, Robert K. *Mass persuasion: the social psychology of a war bond drive.* New York: Harper and Brothers, 1946.

31. Miller, James G. "Unconscious processes in perception." In Robert R. Blake and Glenn V. Ramsey (Eds.), *Perception: an approach to personality.* New York: Ronald Press, 1951. Pp. 258–283.

32. Morris, Charles. *Signs, language and behavior*. New York: Prentice-Hall, Inc., 1946.

33. Postman, L., and Bruner, J. S. "Perception under stress." *Psychol. Rev.*, 1948, 55, 314–324.

34. Pronko, N. H. "Language and psycholinguistics: a review." *Psychol. Bull.*, 1946, 43, 189–239.

35. Rose, Nicholas. "A psychological study of motion picture audience behavior." Unpublished doctoral dissertation, University of California, 1951.

36. Schramm, Wilbur (Ed.), *Communications in modern society*. Urbana, Ill.: University of Illinois Press, 1948.

37. Schneirla, T. C. "The concept of levels in the study of social phenomena." In M. Sherif and C. W. Sherif (Eds.), *Groups in harmony and tension*. New York: Harper and Brothers, 1953. Pp. 54–75.

38. Smith, M. "Communicative behavior." *Psychol. Rev.*, 1946, 53, 294–301.

39. ———. "The communicative act." *J. soc. Psychol.*, 1950, 31. 271–281.

40. Spiegelman, M., Terwilliger, C., and Fearing, F. "The content of comic strips: a study of a mass medium of communication." *J. soc. Psychol.* 1954, 38.

41. ———. "The content of comics: goals and means of comic strip characters." *J. soc. Psychol.*, 1953, 189–204.

42. ———. "The reliability of agreement in content analysis." *J. soc. Psychol.*, 1953, 37, 175–188.

43. Warner, W. L., and Henry, W. E. "The radio day-time serial; a symbolic analysis." *Genet. psychol. Monogr.*, 1948, 37, 3–72.

44. White, R. R. "Black boy: a value analysis." *J. abnorm. soc. Psychol.*, 1947, 42, 440–462.

45. Wiener, N. *The human use of human beings: cybernetics and society*. Boston: Houghton Mifflin, 1950.

46. Wiese, M., and Cole, S. "A study of children's attitudes and the influence of a commercial motion picture." *J. Psychol.*, 1946, 21, 151–171.

47. Wilner, Daniel. "Attitude as a determinant of perception in the mass media of communication: reactions to the motion picture, *Home of the Brave*." Unpublished doctoral dissertation, University of California, 1950.

48. Wolfenstein, M. and Leites, N. *Movies: a psychological study*. Glencoe, Ill.: Free Press, 1950.

ISOMORPHIC INTERRELATIONSHIPS
BETWEEN KNOWER AND KNOWN*

Abraham H. Maslow

*m*y general thesis is that many of the communication difficulties between persons are the byproduct of communication barriers *within* the person; and that communication between the person and the world, to and fro, depends largely on their isomorphism (or similarity of structure or form); that the world can communicate to a person only that of which he is worthy, that which he deserves or is "up to"; that to a large extent, he can receive from the world, and give to the world, only that which he himself is. As Kierkegaard said of a certain book, "Such works are like mirrors; if an ape peeps in, no apostle will look out." Goethe's contention was that we can fully understand only what we really love.

For this reason, the study of the "innards" of the personality is one necessary base for the understanding of what he can communicate to the world, and what the world is able to communicate to him. This truth is intuitively known to every therapist, every artist, every teacher, but it should be made more explicit.

Of course I take communication here in the very broadest sense. I include all the processes of perception and of learning, and all the forms of art and of creation. And I include primary process cognition (archaic, metaphorical, poetic, mythological cognition) as well as verbal, rational, secondary process communication. I want to speak of what we are blind and deaf to as well as what gets through to us; of what we express dumbly and unconsciously as well as what we can verbalize or structure clearly.

A main consequence of this general thesis—that difficulties with the outer parallel difficulties within the inner—is that we should expect communication with the outer world to improve along with improvement in the development of the personality, along with its integration and wholeness,

* Reprinted from *Sign, Image, Symbol*, ed. G. Kepes. Copyright © 1966 by George Braziller, Inc. Reprinted by permission.

and along with freedom from civil war among the various portions of the personality, i.e., perception of reality should improve. One then becomes more perceptive in the sense that Nietzsche says that one must have earned for oneself the distinction necessary to understand him.

SPLITS WITHIN

First of all, what do I mean by failure of internal communication? Ultimately the simplest example is that of dissociation of the personality, of which the most dramatic and most usually known form is the multiple personality. The recent book and movie *Three Faces of Eve* is an excellent example. I have examined as many of these cases as I could find in the literature, and a few I had access to myself, along with the less dramatic fugues and amnesias. They seem to me to fall into a general pattern which I can express as a tentative general theory, which will be of use to us in our present task because it tells something about the splits in *all* of us.

In all the cases I know about, the "normal" or presenting personality has been a shy or quiet or reserved person, most often a female, rather conventional and controlled, rather submissive and even self-abnegating, unaggressive and "good," tending to be mousy, and easily exploited. In all cases, the "personality" that broke through into consciousness and into control of the person was the very opposite, impulsive rather than controlled, self-indulgent rather than self-abnegating, bold and brassy rather than shy, flouting the conventions, eager for a good time, aggressive and demanding, immature.

But this is a split that we can see in *all* of us in a less extreme form. This is the inward battle between impulse and control, between individual demands and the demands of society, between maturity and immaturity, between irresponsible pleasure and responsibility. Most of us manage to make better compromises or integrations between these opposites and so we don't split as dramatically as did Eve. To the extent that we succeed in being *simultaneously* the mischievous, childish rascal *and* the sober, responsible, impulse-controlling citizen, to that extent are we less split and more integrated. This, by the way, is the ideal therapeutic goal for multiple personalities, that is, to retain both or all three personalities, but in a graceful fusion or integration under conscious or preconscious control.

Each of these multiple personalities communicates with the world, to and fro, in a different way. Each talks differently, writes differently, indulges itself differently, makes love differently, selects different friends. "The willful child" personality in one case I had contact with had a big, sprawling child's handwriting and vocabulary and misspelling. The "self-abnegating, exploitable" personality had a mousy, conventional, good-schoolgirl handwriting. One "personality" read and studied books. The other couldn't, being too impatient and uninterested. How different would have been their art productions had we thought to get them.

In the rest of us too those portions of our selves which are rejected and relegated to unconscious existence can and inevitably *do* break through into open effects upon our communication, both intake and output, affecting our perceptions as well as our actions. This is easily enough demonstrated by projective tests on one side and art expression on the other.

The projective test shows how the world looks to us, or better said, it shows how we organize the world, what we can take out of it, what we can let it tell us, what we choose to see and what we choose *not* to listen to or see.

Something similar is true on our expressive side. We express what we are (3). To the extent that we are split, our expressions and communications are split, partial, onesided. To the extent that we are integrated, whole, unified, spontaneous and fully functioning, to that extent are our expressions and communications complete, unique and idiosyncratic, alive and creative, rather than inhibited, conventionalized, and artificial, honest rather than phony. Clinical experience shows this for pictorial and verbal art expressions, and for expressive movements in general, and probably also for dance, athletic and other total bodily expressions. This is true not only for the communicative effects that we *mean* to have upon other people; it also seems to be true for the effects we don't mean to have.

Those portions of ourselves that we reject and repress (out of fear or shame) do not go out of existence. They do not die, but rather go underground. Whatever effects these underground portions of our human nature may thereafter have upon our communications tend either to be unnoticed by ourselves or else to be felt as if they were not part of us, e.g., "I don't know what made me say such a thing." "I don't know what came over me."*

OTHER SPLITS WITHIN THE PERSONALITY

Pursuing this same theme, of the ways in which splits within the personality contaminate our communications to the world and from the world,

---

* To me this phenomenon means that expression is not alone a cultural thing; it is also a biological phenomenon. We *must* talk about the instinctoid elements in human nature, those intrinsic aspects of human nature which culture cannot kill but only repress, and which continue to affect our expression—even though in a sneaky way—in spite of all the culture can do. Culture is only a necessary cause of human nature, not a sufficient cause. But so also is our biology only a necessary cause and not a sufficient cause of human nature. It is true that only in a culture can we learn a spoken language. But it is just as true that in that same cultural environment a chimpanzee will *not* learn to speak.

I say this because it is my vague impression that communication is studied too exclusively at the sociological level and not enough at the biological level.

I turn to several well-known pathological examples. I cite them also because they seem to be exceptions to the general rule that the healthy and integrated person tends to be a superior perceiver and expresser. There is both clinical and experimental evidence in large quantity for this generalization; for instance, the work of Eysenck and his colleagues. And yet, there are exceptions that force us to be cautious.

The schizophrenic is one in whom the controls and defenses are collapsing or have collapsed. The person then tends to slip into his private inner world, and his contact with other people and with the natural world tends to be destroyed. But this involves also some destruction of the communications to and from the world. Fear of the world cuts communication with it. So also can inner impulses and voices become so loud as to confuse reality testing. But it is also true that the schizophrenic patient sometimes shows a selective superiority. Because he is so involved with forbidden impulses and with primary process cognition (or archaic thinking), he is reported occasionally to be extraordinarily acute in interpreting the dreams of others or in ferreting out the buried impulses of others; for instance, concealed homosexual impulses.

It can work the other way about too. Some of the best therapists with schizophrenics were themselves "schizzy." And here and there we see a report that former patients can make exceptionally good and understanding ward attendants. This works on about the same principle as Alcoholics Anonymous. Some of my psychiatrist friends are now seeking this participant understanding by having an experience of being transiently psychotic with LSD or mescalin. One way of improving communication with a Y is to be a Y (4).

In this area we can learn much also from the psychopathic personalities, especially the "charming" type. They can be described briefly as having no conscience, no guilt, no shame, no love for other people, no inhibitions, and few controls, so that they pretty well do what they want to do. They tend to become forgers, swindlers, prostitutes, polygamists, and to make their living by their wits rather than by hard work. These people because of their own lacks are generally unable to understand in others the pangs of conscience, regret, unselfish love, compassion, pity, guilt, shame, embarrassment. What you are not, you cannot perceive or understand. It cannot communicate itself to you. And since what you are does sooner or later communicate itself, eventually the psychopath is seen as a cold, horrible, and frightening person, even though at first he seems so delightfully carefree, unneurotic, gay, and free.

But again we have an instance in which sickness, though it involves a *general* cutting of communications, also involves in specialized areas, a greater acuteness and skill. The psychopath is extraordinarily acute at discovering the psychopathic element in *us*, however carefully we conceal it.

He can spot and play upon the swindler in us, the forger, the thief, the liar, the faker, the phony, and can ordinarily make a living out of this skill. They say, "You can't con an honest man," and seem very confident of their ability to detect any "larceny in the soul." (Of course, this implies that they can detect the *absence* of larceny, which means in turn that the character becomes visible in mien and demeanor, at least to the intensely interested observer, i.e., it communicates itself to those who can understand it and identify with it. Or as I have seen it said, "Time wounds all heels." The heels, thus visibly marked, are then able to know each other.)

MASCULINITY AND FEMININITY

The close relationship between intra- and interpersonal communication is seen with especial clarity in the relations between masculinity and femininity. Notice that I do not say "between the sexes," because my point is that the relations *between* the sexes are very largely determined by the relation between masculinity and femininity *within* each person, male or female.

The most extreme example I can think of is the male paranoid who very frequently has passive homosexual yearnings, in a word, a wish to be raped and injured by the strong man. This impulse is totally horrifying and unacceptable to him, and he struggles to repress it. A main technique that he uses (projection) helps him to deny his yearning and to split it off from himself, and at the same time permits him to think about and talk about and be preoccupied with the fascinating subject. It is the *other* man who wants to rape him, not he who wishes to be raped. And so we get a suspiciousness in such a patient that can express itself in the most pathetically obvious ways, e.g., he won't let anyone get behind him, he'll keep his back to the wall, etc.

This is not so crazy as it sounds. Men throughout history have regarded women as temptresses, because they—the men—have been tempted by them. Men tend to become soft and tender, unselfish and gentle when they love women. If they happen to live in a culture in which these are non-masculine traits, then they get angry at women for weakening them (castrating them), and they invent Samson and Delilah myths to show how horrible women are. They project malevolent intentions. They blame the mirror for what it reflects.

Women, especially "advanced" and educated women in the United States, are frequently fighting against their own very deep tendencies to dependency, passivity, and submissiveness (because this unconsciously and foolishly means to them a giving up of selfhood or personhood). It is then easy for such a woman to see men as would-be dominators and rapists and to treat them as such, frequently by dominating *them*.

For such reasons and others too, men and women in most cultures and in most eras have misunderstood each other, have not been truly friendly with each other. It can be said in our present context that their intercommunications have been and are still bad. Usually one sex has dominated the other. Sometimes they manage to get along by cutting off the women's world from the men's and making a complete division of labor, with concepts of masculine and feminine character that are very wide apart, with no overlapping. This makes for peace of a certain sort but certainly not for friendship and mutual understanding. What do the psychologists have to suggest about the improvement of understanding between the sexes? The psychological solution stated with especial clarity by the Jungians but also generally agreed upon is as follows: The antagonism between the sexes is largely a projection of the unconscious struggle *within* the person, between his or her masculine and feminine components. To make peace between the sexes, make peace within the person.

The man who is fighting within himself all the qualities he and his culture define as feminine will fight these same qualities in the external world, especially if his culture values maleness more than femaleness, as is so often the case. If it be emotionality, or illogic, or dependency, or love for colors, or tenderness with babies, he will be afraid of these in himself and fight them and try to be the opposite. And he will tend to fight them in the external world too by rejecting them, by relegating them to women entirely, etc. Homosexual men who solicit or accost are very frequently brutally beaten up by the men they approach, most likely because of the fears they arouse by being tempting. And it certainly fortifies this conclusion when we learn that the beating up often comes *after* the homosexual act.

What we see here is an extreme dichotomizing, either-or, Aristotelian thinking of the sort that Korzybski considered so dangerous. My psychologist's way of saying the same thing is "Dichotomizing means pathologizing; and pathology means dichotomizing." The man who thinks you can be *either* a man, *all* man, *or* a woman, and *nothing but* a woman, is doomed to struggle with himself, and to eternal estrangement from women. To the extent that he learns the facts of psychological "bisexuality," and becomes aware of the arbitrariness of either-or definitions and the pathogenic nature of the process of dichotomizing, to the degree that he discovers that differences can fuse and be structured with each other, and that they needn't be exclusive and mutually antagonistic, to that extent will he be a more integrated person, able to accept and enjoy the feminine within himself (the "Anima," Jung calls it). If he can make peace with his female inside, he can make peace with the females outside, understand them better, be less ambivalent toward them, and even admire them more as he realizes how superior their femaleness is to his own much weaker version. You can certainly communicate better with a friend who is appreciated and understood than you can with a feared, resented, and mysterious enemy. To make friends with some portion of the outside world, it is well to make friends with that part of it which is within yourself.

(I do not wish to imply that one process necessarily comes before the other. They are parallel and it can start the other way about, i.e., accepting x in the outside world can help achieve acceptance of that same x in the inside world.)

PRIMARY- AND SECONDARY-PROCESS COGNITION

My final example of intrapersonal split which parallels split with the world is the dichotomizing of conscious and unconscious cognitive processes or, to use Freud's later terminology, of primary process and secondary process. Unconscious thinking, perceiving, communication are archaic (in Jung's sense), mythological, poetic, metaphorical, proverbial, often concrete rather than conceptualized. It is characteristic of our night and day dreams, of our imagination, of revery, of an essential aspect of all art, of the first stages of creative production, of free association, etc.

It is generally stigmatized by most well-adjusted, sane, sober adults in the West as childish, crazy, senseless, wild. It is therefore threatening to their adult adjustment to the outer world, is regarded as incompatible with it and is therefore often repudiated. This means it can't be communicated with, and can't be used.

This repudiation of the inner psychic world in favor of the external world of common sense "reality" is stronger in those who *must* deal successfully with the outer world primarily. Also, the tougher the environment is, the stronger the repudiation of the inner world must be, and the more dangerous it is to a "successful" adjustment. Thus the fear of poetic feeling, of fantasy, of dreaminess, of emotional thinking, is stronger in men than in women, in adults than in children, in engineers than in artists.

Observe also that we have here another example of the profound Western tendency, or perhaps general human tendency to dichotomize, to think that between alternatives or differences one must choose *either* one or the other, and that this involves repudiation of the not-chosen, as if one couldn't have both (a sort of two-party system).

And again we have an instance of the generalization that what we are blind and deaf to within ourselves, we are also blind and deaf to in the outer world, whether it be playfulness, poetic feeling, aesthetic sensitivity, primary creativity, or the like.

This example is especially important for another reason, namely that it seems to me that reconciling this dichotomy may be *the* best place for educators to begin in the task of resolving *all* dichotomies. That is, it may be a good and practicable starting point for teaching humanity to stop thinking in a dichotomous way in favor of thinking in an integrative way.

This is one aspect of the great frontal attack upon an overconfident and isolated rationalism, verbalism, and scientism that is gathering force. The general semanticists, the existentialists, the phenomenologists, the Freudians, the Zen Buddhists, the mystics, the Gestalt therapists, the humanistic psychologists, the Jungians, the self-actualization psychologists, the Rogerians, the Bergsonians, the art educators, the "creative" educationists, and many others, are all helping to point out the limits of language, of abstract thought, and of orthodox science. These have been conceived as controllers of the dark, dirty, dangerous, and evil human depths. But now as we learn steadily that these depths are the wellsprings not only of neuroses but also of health, of joy, of creativeness, we begin to speak of the *healthy* unconscious, of healthy regression, of healthy instincts, of healthy nonrationality, of healthy intuition. And we begin to desire to salvage these capacities for ourselves.

The general theoretical answer seems to lie in the direction of integration and away from splitting and repressing. (I warn you that all these movements I've mentioned can too easily become themselves splitting forces. Antirationalism, anti-abstractionism, antiscience, anti-intellectualism are also splits. Properly defined and conceived, intellect is one of our greatest and most powerful integrating forces.)

AUTONOMY AND HOMONOMY

Another paradox that faces us as we try to understand the relations between inner and outer, between self and world, is the very complex interrelation between autonomy and homonomy. We can easily agree with Angyal (1) that there are within us these two general directions or needs, one toward selfishness, we may say crudely, and one toward unselfishness. The trend toward autonomy, taken by itself, leads us toward self-sufficiency, toward strength over against the world, toward fuller and fuller development of our own inner unique self out of its laws, its own inner dynamics, autochthonous laws of the psyche rather than of the environment. These psychic laws are different from, separate from, and even opposed to the laws of the nonpsychic world of the external reality. This quest for identity or search for self (individuation, self-actualization) has certainly been made familiar to us by the growth and self-actualization psychologists, not to mention the existentialists, and the theologians of many schools.

But we are also aware of the equally strong tendency, seemingly contradictory, toward giving up the self, toward submerging ourselves in the not-self, toward giving up will, freedom, self-sufficiency, self-control, autonomy. In its sick forms this results in authoritarianism, in the wild romanticism of blood, earth and instinct, in masochism, in contempt for the human being, in the search for values either *outside* the human being altogether or else in his lowest animal nature, both of which rest on contempt for the human being (5).

In another place (4) I have made the differentiation between the high homonomy and the low homonomy (high and low Nirvana). Now I should like to differentiate the high autonomy from the low autonomy and then show how these differentiations can help us to understand the isomorphism between inner and outer and thereby to lay a theoretical base for improvement of communication between the personality and the world.

The autonomy and strength that are found in emotionally secure people are different from the autonomy and strength of insecure people (3, Chapter 3). Very broadly, and without too much inaccuracy, we can say that insecure autonomy and strength are a strengthening of the personality *over against* the world, in an either-or dichotomy in which personality and world are not only quite separate but also mutually exclusive, as if they were *enemies*. We might also call this selfish autonomy and strength. In a world in which one is either hammer or anvil, these are the hammers. In the monkeys in which I first studied the different qualities of strength, this was called autocratic or Fascistic dominance. In the college students who were later studied it was called insecure high dominance (3, Chapter 3).

Secure high dominance was another matter altogether. Here there was affection for the world and for others, an Adlerian type of big-brotherly responsibility, and a feeling of trust in and identification with the world rather than antagonism and fear toward it. The superior strength of these individuals was therefore used for enjoyment, for love, and for helping others.

On various grounds we can now find it possible to speak of these differentiations as between psychologically healthy and unhealthy autonomy and between psychologically healthy and unhealthy homonomy. And we find that this differentiation enables us to see that they are interrelated rather than opposed to each other; for as the person grows healthier and more authentic, we find that the high autonomy and the high homonomy grow together, appear together and tend finally to fuse and to become structured into a higher unity that includes them both. The dichotomy between autonomy and homonomy, between selfishness and unselfishness, between the self and the not-self, between the pure psyche and outer reality tends to disappear and can be seen as a byproduct of immaturity and of incomplete development.

Although this transcendence of dichotomy can be seen as a usual thing in self-actualizing persons, it can *also* be seen in most of the rest of us in our most acute moments of integration within the self and between self and the world. In the highest love between man and woman or parent and child, as the person reaches the ultimates of strength, of self-esteem, of individuality, so also does he simultaneously merge with the other, lose self-consciousness, and more or less transcend the self and selfishness. The same can happen in the creative moment, in the profound aesthetic experience, in the insight experience, in giving birth to a child, in dancing, in athletic experiences, and in others that I have generalized as peak experiences (4). In all these peak experiences it becomes impossible to differentiate sharply between the self and the not-self. As the person becomes integrated so does his world simultaneously grow integrated. As he feels good, so does the world look good. And so on.

Observe that this is an empirical statement and not a philosophical or theological one. Anyone can repeat these findings. I am definitely speaking of human experiences and not of supernatural ones.

Secondly, observe that this implies a disagreement with various theological statements which imply that transcending the limits of self means spurning or repudiating or *losing* the self or the individuality. In the peak experiences of ordinary people and in self-actualizing people as well, these are end-products of the development of greater and greater autonomy, of the achievement of identity; and are the products of self-transcendence, not of self-obliteration.

Thirdly, observe that they are transient experiences, and not permanent ones. If this is a going into another world, then there is always a coming back to the ordinary world.

B-COGNITION, FULL FUNCTIONING, SPONTANEITY

We begin to know something in a scientific way about the more integrated personality as it affects receiving and emitting communications. For instance, the many studies of Carl Rogers (7) and his collaborators indicate that, as the person improves in psychotherapy, he becomes more integrated in various ways, and that he becomes more "open to experience" (more efficient perceiving) and more "fully functioning" (more honestly expressive). This is our main body of experimental research, but there are also many clinical and theoretical writers who parallel and support these general conclusions at every point.

My own pilot explorations (not exact enough to be called researches in the contemporary sense) come to the same conclusions from another angle, i.e., the direct exploration of the relatively healthy personality. First of all, they support the finding that integration is one defining aspect of psychological health. Secondly, they support the conclusion that healthy people are more spontaneous and more expressive, that they emit behavior more easily, more totally, more honestly.

Thirdly, they support the conclusion that healthy people perceive better (themselves, other people, all of reality), although, as I have indicated, this is not a *uniform* superiority. A current story has the psychotic saying, "2 plus 2 equal 5," while the neurotic says, "2 plus 2 equal 4, but I can't *stand* it!" I might add that the valueless person—suffering from a new kind of illness—says, "2 plus 2 equal 4. So what!" And the healthier person says in effect, "2 plus 2 equal 4. How perfect!"

Or to put it in another way, Joseph Bossom and I have recently published an experiment (2) in which we found that secure people tended to see photographed faces as more warm than did insecure perceivers. The question remains for future research, however, as to whether this is a projection of kindness, of naivete, or of more efficient perception. What is called for is an experiment in which the faces perceived have *known* levels of warmth or coolness. Then, we may ask, are the secure perceivers who perceive or attribute more warmth right or wrong? Or are they right for warm faces and wrong for cool faces? Do they see what they want to see? Do they want to like what they see?

BEING WORTHY OF THE EXPERIENCE

A last word about what I have called B-cognition (cognition of Being). This seems to me to be the purest and most efficient kind of perception of reality (although this remains to be tested experimentally). It is the truer and more veridical perception of the percept because most detached, more objective, least contaminated by the wishes, fears and needs of the perceiver. It is noninterfering, nondemanding, most accepting. In B-cognition, dichotomies tend to fuse, categorizing tends to disappear, and the percept is seen as unique.

Self-actualizing people tend more to this kind of perceiving. But I have been able to get reports of this kind of perception in practically *all* the people I have questioned, in the highest, happiest, most perfect moments of their lives (peak experiences). Now, my point is this. Careful questioning shows that, as the percept grows more individual, more unified and integrated, more enjoyable, more rich, so also does the perceiving individual grow more alive, more integrated, more unified, more rich, more healthy for the moment. They happen simultaneously and can be set off on either side, i.e., the more whole the percept (the world) becomes, the more whole the person becomes. And also, the more whole the person becomes, the more whole becomes the world. It is a dynamic interrelation. The meaning of a message clearly depends not alone on its content but also on the extent to which the personality is able to respond to it. The "higher" meaning is perceptible only to the "higher" person.

As Emerson said, "What we are, that only can we see." Only we must now add that what we see tends in turn to make us what it is and what we are. The communication relationship between the person and the world is a dynamic one of mutual forming and lifting-lowering of each other, a process that we may call "reciprocal isomorphism." A higher order of persons can understand a higher order of knowledge; but also a higher order of environment tends to lift the level of the person, just as a lower order of environment tends to lower it.

NOTES

1. Angyal, A., *Foundations for a Science of Personality.*

2. Bossom, J., and Maslow, A. H., "Security of judges as a factor in impressions of warmth in others," *J. Abnorm. and Social Psychol.*, 1957, 55, 147–8.

3. Maslow, A. H., *Motivation and Personality.* Harper, 1954.

4. Maslow, A. H., *Toward a Psychology of Being.* Van Nostrand, 1962.

5. Maslow, A. H., *Religions, Values and Peak-Experiences.* Ohio State University Press, 1964.

6. Murphy, G., *Human Potentialities.* Basic Books, 1950.

7. Rogers, C., *On Becoming A Person.* Houghton Mifflin, 1961.

PERCEPTION: A TRANSACTIONAL APPROACH*†

William H. Ittelson and Hadley Cantril

*e*very one of us every minute of our waking lives is constantly and continuously perceiving, with the possible exception of brief moments of
intense concentration. Whatever else we may be doing—whether thinking
or talking, reading or writing, going to the movies or taking a walk, working
or playing—we are also perceiving. We are constantly perceiving simply
because it is an inseparable and necessary part of everything we do.

The dictionary defines perception as "the awareness of objects." While
this definition is by no means entirely adequate from the standpoint of
scientific psychology, it nevertheless provides our first clue as to why perceiving plays such an important and central role in all our living and why
the study of perception is one of the oldest, as well as most recent, activities
of mankind. For it is through perception that we come in contact with the
world.

All organisms can be said to perceive. Even unicellular micro-organ-
isms demonstrate differential sensitivity to environmental conditions. But
from the evolutionary standpoint, the most interesting development is
the appearance in all higher animals of so-called *distance receptors*, primarily eyes and ears, which in a sense liberate the organism from complete
dependence on the state of things directly adjacent to its bodily surfaces,
enabling it to deal with environmental happenings quite distant from
itself. The familiar five senses of the Greeks—sight and sound, touch, taste

* The approach to perception sketched here is the result of informal work
together with Adelbert Ames, Jr., F. P. Kilpatrick, A. H. Hastorf, Andie
Knutson, Earl Kelly, Ross Mooney, Hoyt Sherman, Merle Lawrence, Charles
Bumstead and Charles Slack. We have also benefited from discussion with
Horace Kallen, Dr. Norman Kelman and Dr. Alfred Stanton. But none of these
individuals should be held accountable for what is contained in this paper.

and smell—although still as nicely descriptive as ever, have lost scientific status with the discovery in some animals of special sensitivities, for example, thermal sensitivity; with the recognition of sensitivity to internal bodily conditions, for example, hunger and muscular states; and with the extension of perception in man to include complex psychological activities, such as the perception of emotions in others.

While there is no sharp distinction evident between the perceptual physiology of man and that of other animals, there is, nevertheless, good evidence for believing that in many ways perception in man is quite different from that in other animals. By analogy we can point out that there is no clear-cut, qualitative difference between the brain of man and that of lower animals. Yet many capacities, such as abstract thought and communication, which appear in other animals in only a most primitive way, are in man qualitatively quite different. With this reminder that some conclusions about perception in man may not apply to any other organisms, we will confine the remainder of our discussion to the process of perceiving in man.

THE MAJOR CHARACTERISTICS OF PERCEPTION

There are three features of perception which deserve special attention with respect to human perception. First, the facts of perception always present themselves through concrete individuals dealing with concrete situations. They can be studied only in terms of the *transactions* in which they can be observed. Second, within such transactions, perceiving is always done by a particular person from his own unique position in space and time and with his own combination of experiences and needs. Perception always enters into the transaction from the unique *personal behavioral center* of the perceiving individual. And, third, within the particular transaction and operating from his own personal behavioral center, each of us, through perceiving, creates for himself his own psychological environment by attributing certain aspects of his experience to an environment which he believes exists independent of the experience. This characteristic of perception we can label *externalization*.

PERCEPTION AS TRANSACTION

In man, perceiving is not only an inseparable part of all waking activity, but even more important, perceiving never occurs independent of some other activity. We cannot somehow isolate a perception in its "pure" state, as a chemist might isolate a pure chemical or a biologist a pure strain, and then proceed to study it in isolation. Such an approach sounds seductively simple but in practice is plain nonsense. Perceiving never takes place "by itself." It can only be studied as part of the situation in which it operates.

Of course, the abstraction of some very simple act of perceiving from the rest of an ongoing situation for purposes of experimentation is frequently necessary. But this is always done at the risk of seriously distorting the subject matter. The starting point for perceptual studies must always be perceiving as it is encountered in concrete real-life situations. The student of perception is frequently forced to obtain data under conditions remote from those in which perception normally operates, but he must always be sensitive to the limitations of attempting to treat such data as if they had relevance to real-life situations.

Neither a perception nor an object-as-perceived exists independent of the total life situation of which both perception and object are a part. It is meaningless to speak of either as existing apart from the situation in which it is encountered. The word *transaction* is used to label such a situation. For the word *transaction* carries the double implication (1) that all parts of the situation enter into it as active participants, and (2) that they owe their very existence as encountered in the situation to this fact of active participation and do not appear as already existing entities merely interacting with each other without affecting their own identity. The term *transaction* was first used in this general context by Dewey and Bentley,[1] for whom it took on far-reaching philosophical significance. Speaking more specifically of visual perception, Bentley has said, "We do not, however, take the organism and environment as if we could know about them separately in advance in our special inquiry, but we take their interaction itself as subject-matter of study. We name this *transaction* to differentiate it from interaction. We inspect the thing seen not as the operation of an organism upon an environment, nor of the environment on an organism but as itself an event."[2]

This point of view is in many ways foreign to our common-sense view of things. We tend to look at the objects and people around us as entities existing in their own right and quite independent of our transactions with them. As we shall see, this common-sense view is necessary for us if we are to carry on our daily activities and is itself one of the products of the process of perception. But a simple analogy will show that this common-sense view is not adequate for scientific understanding. Consider our problem as that of understanding a baseball batter fully and in all his complexity. It is immediately apparent that the baseball batter does not exist independent of the pitcher. We cannot have a batter without a pitcher. It is true that someone can throw a ball up in the air and hit it with a bat, but his relationship to the batter in the baseball game is very slight. Similarly, there is no pitcher without a batter. The pitcher in the bull-pen is by no means the same as the pitcher in the game. But providing a pitcher for a batter is still not enough for us to be able to define and study our batter. The batter we are interested in does not exist outside of a baseball game, so that in order to study him completely we need not only pitcher, but catcher, fielders, teammates, officials, fans, and the rules of the games. Our batter, as we see him in this complex transaction, simply does not exist anywhere else independent of the transaction. The batter is what he is because of the baseball game in which he participates and, in turn, the baseball game itself is what it is because of the batter. Each one owes its existence to the fact of active participation with and through the other. If we change either one, we change the other.

PERCEPTION AS UNIQUE

Just as no single aspect of the transaction can be said to exist in its own right apart from the transaction, so not even the transaction itself can be treated as existing in its own right. Even the scientist studying the transaction enters into it as a participant. He does not somehow stand outside the transaction and observe it from some remote and inaccessible height. There are as many possible points from which the transaction can be entered into as there are participants. Each participant observes and acts from his own *personal behavioral center*. Perceiving is always an activity by a unique participant from his unique position, providing him with his own unique world of experience. To the extent that two persons' positions overlap, including not only their orientations in time and space but also their interests and purposes, they will tend to have common perceptions and common experiences. And it is these common aspects which make social activity possible.

PERCEPTION AS EXTERNALIZATION

Probably the most obvious aspect of the experience of perception is that it is externally oriented—that is, the things we see and hear and taste and touch are experienced as existing outside of ourselves and as possessing for themselves the characteristics which we see in them. But it is also clear that perception is part of the experience of the individual. One essential feature of perception, then, is the external orientation of certain aspects of experience. In perceiving, parts of our own experience are attributed to events external to ourselves in whose independent existence we firmly believe. "The act of perceiving in itself so implies the act of considering-it-real that the latter can be called an attribute of the act of perceiving."[3] When we perceive, we externalize certain aspects of our experience and thereby create for ourselves our own world of things and people, of sights and sounds, of tastes and touches. Without taking any metaphysical position regarding the existence of a real world, independent of experience, we can nevertheless assert that the world-as-experienced has no meaning and cannot be defined independent of the experience. The world *as we experience it* is the product of perception, not the cause of it.

It should be pointed out that this view is quite recent historically. The early study of perception was concerned with the question of what is done *by* the environment *to* the organism while perceiving. This view, that something in some sense goes "into" the organism, has persisted from the time of the Greeks, who spoke of objects emitting small replicas of themselves which were received by the perceiver, right up to much present-day psychology, with its interest in "stimulus determination" of perception. Only recently has this question been rephrased so that now we are concerned with what is done *by* the organism. What does the organism actually *do* when it perceives? To say that the organism externalizes certain aspects of its experience is not to answer this question, but merely to point out one characteristic of the process. It does serve to emphasize that the study of perception takes the active perceiving individual as its proper point of departure.

These three major characteristics of perception can be summarized by saying that perceiving is that part of the process of living by which each one of us, from his own particular point of view, creates for himself the world within which he has his life's experiences and through which he strives to gain his satisfactions. Before discussing in the next section ways in which this process has been experimentally studied, it is important to point out that each feature of this process carries with it its own special difficulties and obstacles in the way of understanding.

SOME DIFFICULTIES IN THE STUDY OF PERCEPTION

We have already indicated that perceiving is an integral part of every transaction of living. Indeed, it is difficult for any of us to think of ourselves as living without perceiving. To perceive is as natural and necessary as to sleep. Yet its very naturalness and all-pervasiveness make perception a difficult subject-matter to grasp. Most of us would probably be willing to say, "I perceive the way I do because that's the way I am. I see things the way I do because that's the way they are." But while this statement may have a certain superficial validity, it blinds us to important questions as to the function and development of the perceptual process. Many of the findings of the scientific study of perception go quite contrary to this common-sense view. And their acceptance is made difficult by the very naturalness of perceiving.

The fact of externalization presents an even more serious barrier to the study of perception. We tend to believe that things as we see them exist "out there" apart from us and independent of the experience of seeing. This belief is strong in all of us, and as we shall see later, it must be strong if we are to be able to act at all effectively. But the danger of this belief when studying perception lies in the fact that it provides us, in a sense, with the answer to our problem in advance of our study. If the objects of perception exist in their own right as perceived, then all we have to do is fit the perception to an already existing object. The error of this naive view was nicely expressed by Whitehead when he said, "We must not slip into the fallacy of assuming that we are comparing a given world with given perceptions of it. The physical world is in some general sense of the term, a deduced concept."[4] While Whitehead was referring to the physical sciences, what he says applies even more forcibly to our consideration of the world as perceived.

Another serious difficulty in the study of perception is presented by the fact that perceiving is a personal experience, that it can be accounted for adequately only from the point of view of the perceiving individual's personal behavioral center. This necessitates an approach to the study of perception which differs in important ways from that used in most scientific studies. When one scientist reports his work to another, he makes statements which, while they refer to natural phenomena, are actually reducible to statements about what the other scientist will experience if he does certain things. This is essentially the operational view which has in recent years gained widespread acceptance. Operational statements of this sort are an important part of the science of psychology. They are essentially statements in which one psychologist tells another what he will experience if he performs certain operations. They say nothing about the experience of the subject on whom these operations are performed. Such statements are indispensable to psychology, but they are not enough. You, as a person, are not usually interested in how well two other people who happen to call themselves psychologists can predict to each other what behavior of yours they will observe under certain circumstances. You are interested ordinarily in your own personal experiences. Psychology, therefore, in addition to operational statements made from the standpoint of an outside observer, also employs statements made from the standpoint of the individual's *personal behavioral center*. Without such statements we have a psychology of zombies or, to use a more popular engineering term, of "black boxes."

But there is an even more important reason why the study of perception in particular has to be undertaken from the point of view of the perceiver. The scientist himself is also and always a perceiver. When he makes operational statements he is abstracting from his own personal experience certain aspects which he believes are, or can be, shared by another person. Any scientist who makes statements about perception as if he were not himself a perceiver is doing more than committing a logical fallacy; he is talking nonsense. A scientist may be a *student of* any other subject-matter. He is always a *participant in* perception.

THE CENTRAL PROBLEM OF PERCEPTION

Perhaps because of these difficulties, an understanding of perception is one of the most fascinating and central problems a psychologist faces. Our perceptions give each of us the only world we know. It is this world in which we act. And we act in terms of our perceptions. Our perceptions provide us with predictions as to what will probably happen if we act in a particular way. Our actions will be effective only in so far as the predictions derived from our perceptions correspond to what we actually experience when we act. This, then, is the central problem of perception: to study the degree of correspondence between the significances which we *externalize* and those which we *encounter* and to understand the process by which this correspondence is achieved.

While it is implicit in all we have said so far, it should be emphasized that the study of perceptual correspondence from this point of view also requires a consideration of the *purposes* of the perceiver. For the significances we encounter in the course of acting can only be evaluated in terms of what we intend to do. There is no *at*tention without *in*tention.

As a simple example, let us consider a man playing tennis who, as we watch him, consistently swings at and misses the ball. Our evaluation of his performance will be quite different if he is playing a championship match than if he is playing with his young son. Both he and we will feel quite different about his perceptions if he wants to hit and misses than if he wants to miss and misses. A statement about perceptual correspondence necessarily implies a statement about purposes. Thus it becomes clear why accurate perceptions of the behaviour of other people are so difficult to achieve. For other people, like ourselves, have *their* own purposes. And it is by no means a simple matter to acquire a correspondence between the purposes we attribute to other people and the purposes they may actually be pursuing. We must always bear in mind that the purposes we attribute to other people we are dealing with are just as "real" as the characteristics we attribute to objects.

NOTES

1. Dewey, John, and Arthur F. Bentley: *Knowing and the Known*, Boston, Beacon Press, 1949.

2. Bentley, Arthur F.: "The fiction of 'retinal image,' " Chapter 15 in *Inquiry into Inquiries: Essays in Social Theory* (Ed. with Introduction by Sidney Ratner), Boston, Beacon Press, 1954.

3. Schilder, Paul: *Medical Psychology* (Trans. by David Rapaport), New York, International Universities Press, 1953, p. 40.

4. Whitehead, A. N.: *The Aims of Education*, New York, Mentor Books, 1949, p. 166.

PSYCHOLOGICAL MODELS FOR GUIDANCE*

Gordon W. Allport

*H*owever excellent his natural eyesight may be, a counselor always looks at his client through professional spectacles. It could not be otherwise. After all, he has invested time and money in his psychological training. Of what use is it unless it adds special prisms to his own unaided eyesight?

The lenses we wear are ground to the prescription of our textbooks and teachers. Even while we are undergraduates a certain image of the nature of man is fitted to our eyes. We grow accustomed to the image and when we become practitioners or teachers we may still take it for granted.

But every so often comes a time for optical re-examination. Perhaps the image we have is still the best fit we can get; perhaps it is not. We can tell only by examining alternative lenses. In particular I believe that three are worthy of special scrutiny:

> 1. *Man seen as a reactive being.* Under this rubric I would include outlooks known as naturalism, positivism, behaviorism, operationism, physicalism; these are also sometimes called—mistakenly, I think—"scientific psychology."
>
> 2. *Man seen as a reactive being in depth.* Here I include what is variously called psychoanalysis, psychodynamics, depth psychology.
>
> 3. *Man seen as a being-in-process-of-becoming.* This label covers recent trends known as holism, orthopsychology, personalistics, existential psychology.

These three images provide a focus not only for guidance practices, but for all other professional psychological activity whether it be teaching, research, counseling or therapy.

* Gordon W. Allport, "Psychological Models for Guidance," *Harvard Educational Review*, XXXII (1962), 373–381. Reprinted by permission.

214

MAN: A REACTIVE BEING

One hundred years ago in his *Beiträge* Wilhelm Wundt mapped a program for the newly conceived science of psychology. His own view of the proper development of this science was broad and permissive, especially in the field of social psychology. But what has taken hold in the Anglo-American tradition is the experimental outlook of his *Physiologische Psychologie*. Fusing with Darwinism, Machian positivism, the quantitative outlook of Galton and his successors, as well as with techniques invented by Binet, Pavlov, Hull and others—this experimental outlook prevailed and has ground the lens that is fitted to the eyes of almost all undergraduate students of psychology. Many of us who continue in the profession feel no need for further correction in this image of man.

Seen through this lens man is no different in kind from any other living reactor; and therefore, like the paramecium or pigeon, may be studied biologically, behaviorally, mathematically. To be sure, a few special concepts need to be devised to take care of the vast complexity of human behavior, but all these concepts—among them habit hierarchy, secondary reinforcement, input and output of information, and the like—are consistent with the postulates of physicalism and naturalism.

If we ask, "What does it mean to be a human being?" this school of thought replies, "Man is one more creature of nature; his behavior though complex is predictable in principle. His present state is determined by his past state. A man's consciousness is unreliable and must be distrusted, preferably disregarded altogether. We seek the general laws of nature, not personal uniqueness. We study man, not men; objective reality, not subjective."

In principle this broad positive tradition, which we all know so well, puts a desirable end to psychological naïveté. It cautions us not to believe every verbal report that comes to our ears; it warns us to be skeptical of our own naked eyesight; and from it we learn to check ourselves for observer reliability. It teaches us to use precise and repeatable methods. Because of its stress on reliable methods this favored tradition in psychology has become known as "scientific psychology." Its methods are indeed scientific; but its primary postulate—that man is simply a reactive organism—is no more scientific than any other postulate.

It is here that the counselor encounters his first difficulty. Trained in tests, statistics, and experimental design, he may think, quite mistakenly, that to employ these useful aids he must also view his client as a reactive being—an exclusive product of stimulus impact, homeostasis, drive-reduction and reinforcement learning. The term "scientific" has spread like a grease spot from method to theory. Just because most of our methods evolved through the positivistic tradition does not mean that the postulates of this tradition concerning the nature of man are the only acceptable postulates for scientific psychology.

A counselor whose theoretical spectacles disclose a merely reactive being is likely to think of his client in terms of past conditioning and potential re-conditioning; in terms of reinforcements, in terms of environmental determinism. He will assume that his client's basic motives are drive-reduction or second-order conditionings which in some shadowy way are supposed to account for all his adult interests and vocational ambitions.

The vocabulary emanating from this type of postulate is replete with terms like *reaction, response, reinforcement, reflex, respondent, reintegration*—all sorts of *re*-compounds. The reference is backward. What *has* been is more important than what *will* be. Terms such as *proaction, progress, program, production, problem-solving*, or *propriate* are characteristically lacking. One would think that the client seated opposite would *pro*test, for the language of response negates the subject's immediate certainty that his life lies in the future.

The positivistic view of man as a reactor has performed a good service, shaking us out of common sense naïveté, endowing us with useful methods, and correctly informing us that man is, in *some* aspects of his being, a simple respondent to simple pressures. Its postulates are, however, questionable. It sees reality as ordered but not as personal; it sees consciousness as a nuisance; it looks at man as reactive, not proactive.

It is probably true that no counselor fully follows this creed in his daily practice. Indeed he could not do so. It is too impoverished a view of real life. When a convinced positivist attempts to fit his image of man to concrete human situations, as B. F. Skinner has done in *Walden Two*, the result strikes many of us as threadbare, even pitiable.

Probably for this reason many behaviorists (starting even as far back as E. B. Holt in *The Freudian Wish and its Place in Ethics*) attempt to combine stimulus-response with psychoanalysis. Neal Miller and John Dollard in their *Personality and Psychotherapy* offer a good example. Man as a reactive being is combined with man as a reactive being in depth.

MAN: A REACTIVE BEING IN DEPTH

So influential is this image of man that we find it everywhere: dominant in literature, in social work, in guidance, in therapeutic practice, and in the market place. There is no need today to describe this image to any educated, or even semi-educated, American adult. Freudianism, like positivism, is our daily dish.

What I should like to do is to make clear that Freudianism (in spite of its less reliable methods) is a close kin of traditional positivism. The only change in the image of man lies in adding the depth dimension. To the long psychological vocabularly of *re*-compounds, depth psychology adds *repression, regression, resistance, abreaction, reaction formation,* and many others.

Like other simple naturalistic views of man, psychoanalaysis put its chief weight upon the press of pleasure and pain. This pressure produces in the organism a tendency to seek an equilibrium between the force of his drives and the circumstances of reality. The fact that Freud maximizes the role of sex and locates the whole constellation of reactive forces chiefly in the unconscious does not alter the essential similarity.

For Freud causation lies in the past history of the individual just as it does for the conditioned-response theorist. Both have a dismaying disregard for the person's phenomenology of the future, for his sense of personhood and sense of freedom. The ego is a reactive agent, having no energy of its own, but borrowing from the unsocialized Id.

Central to depth psychology, and important for guidance, is the doctrine of *recall* and *recovery* (two more *re*-compounds). Therapy, and presumably guidance, proceeds by disclosing to the client some buried motive, or a troublesome and repressed psychic trauma. The client's salvation, if indeed he has any, lies in this vital recall. A troublesome memory is brought to cognizable form. Presumably the result is helpful to the individual in solving his conflicts. The theory, however, does not allow for any interaction between the person and the recovered memory. Simple re-instatement is itself, as Freud says, the "pure gold" of psychoanalysis. What values a client should live by when once the re-instatement has taken place is not the "pure gold" of psychoanalysis. That all adult values are simply sublimated aim-inhibited wishes, is the central doctrine. Freud never allows for the individual's capacity to disregard his past or to reshape it freely. Indeed, since the structure of the Id never changes, the future can at best be a redirection, never a transformation, of one's purposes. What one becomes is essentially what one is, and what one was.

Among the valid portions of psychoanalysis of special use to all counselors is the brilliant account given us by Freud, and by his daughter Anna, of the defensive mechanisms of the ego. In dealing with our client we do well to follow the advice of psychoanalysis and watch for rationalizations, denials of reality through repression, and displacements of aggression. All these, and other, ego-defenses belong to the nature of man, and therefore must find a place in any theory of human personality.

But what perplexes me is why so many of the ego-processes described by psychoanalysis should be merely protective strategies. Are there no ego-processes that lead to a transformation of what is recovered? To a creative cognition? To a revised sense of personhood and a new phenomenology of the future? To Freud the person seems never to be truly proactive, seldom even active. Almost always he is seen as reactive to early fixations—perhaps to some castration threat that occurred years ago, or to some other un-socialized infant complex, especially to Oedipal fantasies. My difficulty with this image of man is summed up most tersely by the late satirist, Max Beerbohm, who said, "They were a tense and peculiar family—those Oedipuses."

There is, I am well aware, a large group of theories that derive from the psychodynamic tradition but at the same time deviate considerably from the orthodox view of reactivity-in-depth. All these theories, in my judgment, move in a desirable direction. Here I shall mention only some of the relevant authors: Adler, Jung, Hartmann, Horney, Erikson, Fromm. Still more deviant from Freud are Goldstein, Maslow, Rogers, and Robert White. These and other writers offer a type of theory that views man as a being in the process of becoming. Many of them ask the pivotal question differently from the reactivist schools of thought. And it makes a good deal of difference just how a question is asked.

> A story is told about two priests. They were arguing whether it was proper to smoke and to pray at the same time. One said "Yes," the other "No." To settle the matter they decided that both should write to the Holy Father for his opinion. Sometime later they met and compared notes. Each claimed that the Holy Father had supported his view. They were perplexed. Finally one asked, "How did you phrase your question?" The other replied: "I asked whether it was proper to smoke while one is praying; and the Pope answered, 'Certainly not, praying is serious business and permits no distractions.' And how did you phrase your question?" "Well," said the other, "I asked if it were proper to pray while smoking, and the Pope answered, 'Certainly, prayer is always in order.' "

Instead of asking Aristotle's question, "What is the place of man in Nature?" many authors today are asking St. Augustine's question, "Who am I?" This question, rephrased in the 20th Century, has opened the floodgates to a new theorizing of the broad type often labeled *existentialist*.

MAN: BEING IN THE PROCESS OF BECOMING

Seelye Bixler, former president of Colby College, tells of a student who recently remarked, "I can't tell you how much satisfaction I take in my existential despair." In some student circles despair has always been popular. To label it "existentialist" makes it doubly attractive, in fact irresistible.

But overlooking the fashionable flavor of existentialism it is surely necessary for the modern counselor to take seriously the present-day anxieties of the younger generation. No longer can youth contemplate its future under the protection of the great social stabilizers of the past. No longer can one counsel within the framework of Victorian decorum, theological certainties, or the Pax Britannica. It is obvious to us all that some sort of shattering transformation is under way. The comfortable stabilities of culture, caste, the gold standard, and military supremacy are no longer ours.

Nor are the comfortable stabilities of traditional psychology adequate. Of what use is it to invoke an impersonal theory of learning, a biological theory of motivation, and a late Victorian formula for the unconscious, when youth's problems today are acutely conscious, intensely personal, and propelling him like an unguided astronaut into an unknown future? A counselor is not equipped for his job unless he can share in some degree the apprehensions of modern youth, and sense the swampy underpinning on which youth treads. Over his desk the counselor might well tack the wisdom of the Spanish writer Unamuno, "Suffering is the life blood that runs through us all and binds us together." While not every youth who comes to the counselor is at that moment a sufferer, it is a safe assumption that he comes for guidance that will fortify him for the inevitable suffering that he will encounter in his course of life.

TENTATIVENESS AND COMMITMENT

From the existential point of view the ideal counselor will strive to develop two attitudes in his client. Taken separately they seem antithetical: but fused into a world-view they provide strength for the future. One attitude is *tentativeness* of outlook. Since certainties are no longer certain, let all dogmas be fearlessly examined, especially those cultural idols that engender a false sense of security: dogmas of race supremacy, of naïve scientism, of unilinear evolutionary progress. Let one face the worst in oneself and in the world around him, so that one may correctly estimate the hazards.

Taken by itself such tentativeness, such insightfulness, might well lead to ontological despair. Yet acceptance of the worst does not prevent us from making the best of the worst. Up to now psychologists have not dealt with the remarkable ability of human beings to blend a tentative outlook with firm commitment to chosen values. The poet Tennyson perceived the point.

> There lives more faith in honest doubt,
> Believe me, than in half the creeds.

A commitment is, as Pascal has said, a wager. One may lose it, but one may win. Cardinal Newman warned us that our religion can never be a matter of certainty. It is at best a subjective condition of certitude which he defined as "probability supported by faith and love." Yet a mature religion, thus defined, can be infinitely sustaining and heroically motivating. Existentialism, whether theistic or atheistic, makes the same point. We have the freedom to commit ourselves to great causes with courage, even though we lack certainty. We can be at one and the same time half-sure and whole-hearted.

William James, probably America's greatest thinker, tried to teach us this lesson, but fifty years ago we were not ready for it. It is surely note-worthy that, writing as he did in a period of social stability, James saw clearly how ultimately uncertain are our foundations of value. Wealth, he saw, was a false god, leading us into a national disease that has recently been called "galloping consumption." The more we build up our material resources, the more we fear poverty. In religion, James knew, there was no certainty; yet, like Cardinal Newman, he recognized the constructive power of a mature religious commitment. Whatever ideal leads to long-range constructive consequences is psychologically sound. It is also pragmatically true. And who is to say that we have a test for truth more absolute than our own commitment in so far as it is validated by fruitful consequences?

Neither positivistic nor psychodynamic schools of thought allow for the fact that our psychological constitution permits both total tentativeness and total commitment. Such a paradox reminds us of the electron that is able to go in two opposite directions at the same time. Taken by itself tentativeness is disintegrative; commitment is integrative. Yet the blend seems to occur in personalities that we admire for their soundness and perspective. Presumably through teaching and guidance we may develop both attitudes in our youth.

Whenever the two attitudes coexist in a life we find important desirable by-products from the fusion. One is a deep sense of compassion for the lot of the human race in general and in each separate social encounter that marks our daily life. The other by-product is likewise graceful; it is the sense of humor. Humor requires the perspective of tentativeness, but also an underlying system of values that prevents laughter from souring into cynicism. As Meredith said, humor is a capacity to laugh at the things you love and still to love them.

RATIONALISM VS. IRRATIONALISM

The chief criticism made of existentialism is that it leads away from reason and exalts irrationalism. While this charge may apply to certain literary and theological trends in the existential movement I doubt that it jeopardizes the future of scientific psychology. The attitudes of tentative-ness and commitment of which I speak are perfectly sound concepts—call them "intervening variables" if you wish. Indeed in so far as they reflect important states in human personality, and thus lead to improvement in understanding, prediction, and direction of human behavior, they are sounder scientific concepts than many of those we have been using.

And just what is rationalism? We venerate the ancient Greeks for their exaltation of human reason; and as psychologists we venerate Aristotle for asking the question, "What is man's place in nature?" But Greek rationalism was broader than the limited, method-centered, scientism into which it has degenerated. The Greeks themselves saw a place for tentativeness and commitment within the scope of reason. The case is beautifully stated in an ancient inscription found somewhere on the coast of Greece:

> A shipwrecked sailor buried on this coast
> Bids you set sail.
> Full many a bark, when we were lost,
> Weathered the gale.

The dead sailor urges us to make the wager, take the risk, although we cannot be sure of coming through to our destination.

IMPLICATIONS FOR THEORY

What does all this mean in terms of psychological theory, and in terms of guidance? First of all it means that in order to achieve a more realistic image of man and his potentialities, we need to revise our current theories of learning and growth, of motivation and personality structure. Elsewhere (in *Pattern and Growth in Personality*, 1961) I have discussed some of the needed changes in detail, and so shall say only a few words about each.

The trouble with our current theories of learning is not so much that they are wrong, but that they are partial. They fit best the learning of animals and young children. The concepts of conditioning, reinforcement, indentification, seem a bit hollow when the counselor tries to apply them to his work. They are not very helpful, for example, in explaining how a youth may learn both tentativeness of outlook and firmness of commitment. Supplementary theories in terms of organizational, biographical, and propriate learning are needed.

Except in the sense of physical maturation the concept of *growth* scarcely exists in psychology at all. Nor will it have its proper place until we have agreed upon normative standards for the maturity of personality. Up to now normative problems, except in the sense of statistical norms, are much neglected.

As for motivation and personality structure, psychologists are in a state of turmoil and disagreement. That the past stages of a life do not fully explain the motivational "go" of the present, I for one am firmly convinced. Therefore we need a concept (*functional autonomy*, I think, will do) to represent that portion of a life that is oriented toward the future and not toward the past. Also we need a theory of personal structure (of *personal dispositions*) to represent the important cleavages and foci of a given, concrete personality. Such a theory will, I am convinced, carry us much further than a conception of uniform variables to which every client is forcibly ordered, whether we call these variables factors, needs, dimensions, or common traits.

Most of all we need to surrender the models that would compress human personality into the routine homeostatic situation that we find in quasi-closed systems. Human personality is a wide-open system, responsive to tangible and intangible culture, on the look-out for new ideas, and capable of asking an altogether new type of question—asked by no other creature in nature, viz., "Who am I?"

There are, I am glad to say, many psychologists who feel as strongly as I that these various types of improvement need to be made before the counselor will have a fully fashioned science of psychology to undergird his practice.

IMPLICATIONS FOR GUIDANCE

Guidance is not a matter of gimmicks, nor of rules of thumb. A guide, like a philosopher and friend, is a person who loves wisdom and loves his fellow men. True, he has skills to mark him off from the professional philosopher or the untrained friend. To some extent the counselor's present-day skills are useful. Standard tests and measurements are helpful; so too achievement records and focused interviews. Most of our devices come from researches conducted under the positivistic outlook, or (in the case of projective techniques) under the psychodynamic. While many of them are serviceable I look forward to the invention of new instruments still better suited to the study of the central or propriate aspects of single personalities.

Most important, of course, are the spectacles the counselor wears. The image should no longer be borrowed from the tradition of simple naïve reactivism. Just as centimeters, grams, seconds are outmoded in modern physics so too are simple stimulus-response connections in modern psychology. In psychology, even more than in physics, we need theory capable of dealing with fluid becoming.

The plain fact is that man is more than a reactive being, more even than a reactive being in depth. If he were comfortably fixed at these levels we could with confidence apply a uniform stencil in studying his nature. But the life process is no less paradoxical than the processes of modern physics. How can one deal with space that is both finite and unbounded, with light that is both wave and particle, with electrons that pass from orbit to orbit without traversing the space between? Similarly, a human person is both structure and process, a being both biological and noetic, a being who changes his identity even while he retains it. Small wonder that at the end of his life, the famous physicist, P. W. Bridgman, said, "The structure of nature may eventually be such that our processes of thought do not correspond to it sufficiently to permit us to think about it at all."

We need not, I think, be quite so pessimistic. Our first duty is to affirm a new and wider rationalism; that is to say, to redouble our efforts to find a more adequate image of man to guide us in fashioning a more suitable science of personality.

And what about our personal attitudes as guidance specialists or teachers? Should we not cultivate the same twin virtues that we recommend to client and student: tentativeness and commitment? We can hold our own present image of man on trial, reviewing our own past psychological training in critical perspective. At the same time we can embrace courageously our task of interpreting the wisdom of the past in such a way as to make it most available to the youthful personality who is facing an uncertain, but not uninviting, future. Tentativeness and commitment are twin ideals for both counselor and client. To my mind they lie at the heart and center of guidance, of teaching, and of living.

THE MIND-BODY PROBLEM: A NEW VIEW*

Ludwig von Bertalanffy

i begin this paper with considerable apprehension. Even before commencing I note that the title itself is open to criticism: "The mind-body problem"—isn't that a question belonging to another department, that of philosophy in the faculty of arts? Also vulnerable is the fact that I have promised to discuss the problem from "a new point of view"; but this is one of the oldest problems in philosophy, tossed around for centuries and disputed by the most illustrious minds in vain. What is there that is "new" that can be presented here—especially when I cannot promise any novel and still unknown facts?

Thus I am well aware of the difficulties of the task, and would not have chosen it without cogent reasons. Discussions in recent years—such as an extensive symposium published by Hook (12), or the detailed dissertation by Feigl (10), to mention but two—follow the well-trodden path and result in little more than a reshuffling of old ideas.

A novel approach appears to be overdue, owing to the fact that the problem, far from being academic, is of immediate concern to the modern psychologist and psychiatrist. There are three reasons for this. The first is the high incidence of psychosomatic disorders. Psychosomatic disease is, of course, no new discovery; it was familiar to Hippocrates. However, without attempting to decide whether there is a true numerical increase due to the stress of modern life, or whether we have only become more aware of the problem, there is no question that psychosomatic disease is a medical problem of the first order. "Psychosomatic" is, of course, the mind-body problem expressed in medical terms. That business worries may cause ulcers is a clinical fact just as is the viral basis of pneumonia, but we have no simple way to reduce this to somatic medicine.

* Ludwig von Bertalanffy, "The Mind-Body Problem: A New View," *Psychosomatic Medicine*, XXIV (1964), pp. 29–45, reprinted by permission.

A second point is what may be called the *methodological helplessness of psychiatry*. We know only too well the limitations of modern medicine—from the cancer problem to trivial complaints like arthritis, but no other medical specialty is as insecure in its therapeutic approach. Within a lifetime, or less, we have seen radically different approaches come and go, from psychosurgery to electroshock to the soft talk of the psychotherapist to drug therapy and other measures. It is hardly an exaggeration to say that some therapy had a rationale but no success, as in the case of lobotomy; while others—-ECT and to a large extent, psychotherapeutic drugs—were moderately successful but have no rationale, having a purely trial-and-error basis. This state of affairs is not only unsatisfactory but implies considerable danger. It is true not only in a trivial way, as in the case of fractures which may occur with the use of ECT, but in a more alarming way, as in reserpine depression—a side effect of the purely empirical administration of the drug which, before it was recognized, led to therapeutic failures, including suicide. That psychiatry wavers between such extremes as drilling a hole in the skull, with insult to the most important system in the body, and the mere pep talk of some forms of psychotherapy is an expression of the deep-seated insecurity prevailing in this field. This is not a question of ignorance which may be overcome by some new discovery tomorrow—say, some new insight into the role of RNA in memory or some reformulation of the theory of instincts; rather, it seems as if our ways of thinking, our basic concepts and categories, are inadequate. A reconsideration of fundamentals is thus imperative—and an important part of this is the old problem of body and mind.

A third consideration may be called the *"Erewhon problem"* in modern society. I am not thinking of the more trivial aspect of Butler's utopia (8): that machines, instead of being servants to man, tend to become his masters. Rather, there is a more sophisticated part of the story. As you will remember, in *Erewhon*, organic disease, as a punishable offense, must be concealed at all costs. In contrast, social and moral dysfunction, such as "a mild case of embezzlement," is respectable and to be cured by practitioners called "straighteners." Isn't this largely what happens in our society? Being physically ill or merely getting old constitute a sort of punishable behavior; you will do well not to speak about it, lest you are fired from your job. In contrast, mental disturbance and moral offense tend to become respectable and are referred to the psychiatrist. From murder to divorce and failure in school, we are inclined to consider all unsocial or ineffective behavior not in relation to a badly shaken value system or to problems arising in a complex society, but as interesting psychiatric cases, preferably of wrong toilet training or brain mechanisms gone astray.

I submit—and shall try to show—that these and other inconsistencies and paradoxes in modern psychiatry are largely due to the fact that psychological theory is based on an obsolete belief in the dualism of body and mind.

THE CARTESIAN DUALISM

As mentioned, the problem of body and mind was up till now in the domain of philosophy, a playground for more-or-less skillful conceptual acrobatics. However, the development of modern science tells a different story—one important for our purposes. What were once considered philosophical problems of epistemology and metaphysics have become empirical questions to be investigated by scientific methods. This is true of the fundamental concepts in physics—space, time, matter, causality—and to an extent is also true for biology, which nowadays explores such problems as wholeness, teleology, and goal-directedness, which not long ago were the domain of a vitalistic demonology.

I believe a similar re-examination is also due for the problem which concerns us. We have to apply whatever the fields of science—such as biology, psychology, psychiatry, cultural anthropology, and comparative linguistics—can provide. In this way, we shall not arrive at "final solutions" dear to the heart of philosophers, but we may make some progress relevant to psychological theory and psychiatric practice.

It is well to present the problem in its traditional form, even at the risk of being trivial. There are two connected problems, which we may call the matter-mind and the brain-consciousness relations.

In our direct experience, we find two categories of things, which we call material and mental. Experience of material things is "public"; that is, every suitably located observer will have a similar experience of physical things such as chairs, houses, rivers, and the rest. In contrast, mental experience is "private": my toothache is not shared by the dentist or anybody else; only I am aware of it.

We know further that all awareness is in some way dependent on states of our body and especially the brain. Thus, the problem of the material and mental realms changes into the problem of the relations between brain and consciousness. Note that the viewpoint is essentially shifted. The distinction between material things and mental events is one of everyday observation. In contrast, the relations between brain and mind are highly sophisticated; when we speak of brain processes, we imply all relevant knowledge of physics, chemistry, neurophysiology, etc. That is, the universe of which science is speaking—molecules, chemical reactions, electrical currents, and what not—is not apprehended by direct experience, but is only connected with it by more-or-less elaborate chains of reasoning.

The problem, then, is briefly this: Matter exists in space and sends out certain physical effects—say, electromagnetic waves. These eventually reach a physicochemical system of fantastic complexity—my body with its sense organs and brain. Light causes chemical reactions in the retina; they are propagated through the optic nerve and eventually arrive at the visual cortex. Now, something fundamentally different from physicochemical processes, the sensation of red or green, occurs. Conversely, there are mental events such as emotion, volition, motivation. These mental events are mysteriously transformed into physiological processes in the motor area of the brain. These are propagated through the pyramidal tract and eventually reach the muscles; a voluntary action takes place.

This is the dualism as it was first stated by Descartes in the 17th Century. Descartes distinguished the *res extensa*—matter extended in space—and the *res cogitans*—the conscious mind. We may apply somewhat different terms, but the Cartesian dualism remains essentially the same.

Do not say that the Cartesian dualism is a dead horse or a straw man erected to be knocked down, as nowadays we have "unitary concepts" and conceive of man as a "psychophysical whole." These are nice ways of speaking, but as a matter of fact, the Cartesian dualism is still with us and is at the basis of our thinking in neurophysiology, psychology, psychiatry, and related fields.

I shall not enter into any detailed discussion of the traditional conceptions of the relation of body and mind and the shortcomings of such views. As is well known, the main traditional answers are the theories of psychophysical parallelism, of interaction, and of identity.

According to the doctrine of *psychophysical parallelism*, the chains of physical and of mental events run side by side, in some way corresponding to each other, but without mutual interference. But then the series of physical events is self-contained; it is fully determined, by the laws of neurophysiology and, ultimately, of physics. What actually happens would occur in exactly the same way if mental events were absent; hence mind appears as an unnecessary and inefficient epiphenomenon in the physical world. But ideas *do* move matter—in the individual, in society and in history. Observation, both introspective and behavioral, appears to show that behavior is determined by symbols, values, intentions, anticipation of the future—and these are something radically different from neurophysiological events, electric potentials, chemical reactions, and physicochemical processes in general.

The theory of *interaction* postulates an interference of mental in physical events and vice versa. This certainly corresponds to the unsophisticated impression, but remains unintelligible. How can an entity which, by definition, is nonphysical interact with physical and chemical processes? This contradicts the very principles of physiology and physics. Conversely, physical processes should always lead to other physical processes; it is baffling that (and how) some of them produce something different in principle, namely, sensations, feelings, etc.

Finally, the theory of *identity* assumes that it is some ultimate reality that appears under the different aspects of physical and mental experience. But what, then, is this reality? The only way to conceive of it is along the lines of the only reality immediately experienced by us—that is, the specimen of our own consciousness, self, or psyche. But then we come to a panpsychism which is hardly acceptable and does not conform to fact. Out of the vastness of physical processes taking place in the universe, only a tiny slice have their mental counterparts—namely, those occurring in a living brain; and again, of the multitude of behavioral responses and of physiological events taking place in the brain, only an extremely small fraction is accompanied by consciousness. We have no indication of any difference between brain-physiological processes—electric potentials, synaptic phenomena, chemical and hormonal transmission of impulses, etc.—that are accompanied by conscious events and those that are not.

All these theories, including recent discussions of the problem, take the Cartesian dualism for granted. We, however, shall come to an essential revision if we follow our program and try to apply the testimony provided by various branches of modern science.

We may anticipate the result in a few sentences. The Cartesian dualism between material things and conscious ego is not a primordial or elementary datum, but results from a long evolution and development. Other sorts of awareness exist and cannot be simply dismissed as illusory. On the other hand, the dualism between material brain and immaterial mind is a conceptualization that has historically developed, and is not the only one possible or necessarily the best one. As a matter of fact, the classic conceptualization of matter and mind, *res extensa* and *res cogitans*, no longer corresponds to available knowledge. We should not discuss the mind-body problem in terms of 17th-Century physics, but must reconsider it in the light of contemporary physics, biology, and behavioral and other sciences.

These are revolutionary or even paradoxical statements. Let us try to substantiate them.

THE TESTIMONY OF BIOLOGY

We may start with the testimony of biology. To avoid introducing another Cartesian dualism—namely that of animals as soulless machines and man only endowed with a soul—we shall have to concede that a monkey or dog sees, feels pain, has certain desires and antipathies. If we do, there is no break somewhere lower on the evolutionary ladder; descending to ever more simple types of animals, nervous systems, and behavior, we have no indication where precisely psyche leaves off, and only reflexes and neuro-physiological events remain.

On the other hand, we have good reason to believe that the universes apprehended by subhuman beings are very different from ours. To an extent, we are able to reconstruct them. This is the domain of von Uexküll's (21, 22) classic and colorful descriptions of the *Umwelt* or ambient world experienced by a dog, a fly, a starfish, a tick, a paramecium, and other animals. Without going into details, two fundamental principles of ethology should be emphasized; the *Umwelt* of a given species is determined by the latter's organization—in particular, the structure of its receptor and effector organs; and the human *Umwelt*—the world as *we* experience it—is only one of countless universes of living beings.

So far as we are able to tell, it appears that a principle of differentiation obtains. That is, what to us are exterior objects on the one hand, and our conscious ego on the other, slowly differentiate or crystallize out of an originally undifferentiated singleness of exteroceptive and proprioceptive experience. It is easy to see that the universe of objects around us is especially connected with sensation at a distance, particularly vision. Two factors are involved in the separation of physical objects and individual consciousness: first, suitable receptor organs, as just mentioned; second, the higher level of human awareness, symbolic factors, language, and thought, entering into perception and helping to establish the two worlds of objects around us and of conscious ego.

THE TESTIMONY OF DEVELOPMENTAL PSYCHOLOGY

This object-subject differentiation becomes much clearer when we come to social and child psychology. For the sake of brevity, we may consider both simultaneously although we should always keep in mind that the individual development of the child is not simply a recapitulation of the evolution of the human race.

Anthropology teaches us that peoples in other cultures have world outlooks and conceptualizations different from ours. According to developmental psychology, the dualism between external world and ego, self-evident as it may appear, is in fact the outcome of a long development (cf. the excellent discussion in Meerloo (16), pp. 196 ff.).

The most primitive stage apparently is one where a difference between outside world and ego is not yet experienced. A psychiatric term is very useful in this respect. This is the notion of *ego boundary*. As is well known, psychiatry speaks of the breaking-down of ego boundary in schizophrenia. where the border line between objects outside and what is merely hallu-cinated—between the "public" and "private" worlds—becomes vague or disappears. This, indeed, is part of the definition of schizophrenia; but a similar state of indefinite ego barrier obtains in normal development. The baby does not yet distinguish between himself and things outside; only slowly does he learn to do so—mainly owing to the obstacles and hindrances imposed by outside objects upon his activities.

In the next stage, the ego barrier develops but is not fixed in the sense of inanimate things outside and a feeling and volitional ego inside. Rather this is the stage of animism: Outside things—not only humans, but animals, plants, and even inorganic objects—are endowed with emotions and volitions, benevolent or, more often, malevolent and similar to those of the experiencing individual—the child or primitive human. Remnants of this animistic experience are still present in the adult personality. To cite a trivial example, we get "mad" at some object for which we are searching and which seems to behave like a malevolent hobgoblin, intentionally hiding itself. The same still applies to rather sophisticated ways of scientific thought. The animistic view is still in force in Aristotelian science. As Aristotle has it, each thing seeks its "natural place" and is endowed with a psychoid entelechy.

Meanwhile, the specific human faculty of speech, and symbolic activities in general (3), have developed. Here we come to a magical phase, where the animistic experience still persists, but with an important addition: the human being has gained the power of language and other symbols. However, no clear distinction is yet made between the symbol and the thing designated. Hence, in some way the symbol (e.g., the name or other image) *is* the thing, and manipulation of the symbolic image—such as uttering the name of a thing with appropriate ceremony, depicting the beasts to be hunted, and the like—gives power over the objects concerned. The savage, the infant, and the regressed neurotic have no end of rituals for exerting such magic control.

Only in the last stage is the neat separation of external reality, ego, and symbols fully achieved. The ego boundary is established. Parts of experience—one's own body and mental processes—can be controlled immediately, while another part—the world outside—is only amenable to indirect and limited control, either by physical action or by a mental interpolation of symbolic processes. It has been said that inanimate matter is an invention of the physicists of the Renaissance. Even then, it took a long time to de-anthropomorphize physics. We need only remember the long struggle about the physical concept of "force" which was at first conceived as an anthropomorphic principle and only lately de-personalized into energy as a purely mathematical concept.

This development may be formulated in somewhat different terms, but I think we can agree that it is essentially correct and can serve as a basis for further discussion.

I believe that the basic question in the mind-body problem is whether we should take the world outlook of the Western adult for granted, and dismiss all others as primitive superstition, or whether we should probe the bases of both everyday experience and the universe of science. I believe we have good reasons for pursuing the latter course.

THE TESTIMONY OF INTROSPECTIVE PSYCHOLOGY

Philosophers have always begun by taking the duality of the physical and mental worlds as an unquestionable datum. However, any amount of psychological evidence shows that things are not that simple. Perception of the most trivial objects—tables, chairs, houses, people—is not a mere sum of sensations or of the "sense data" positivist philosophers are fond of describing; perception is comprised of *Gestalten* of sense data plus memory, concept formation, verbal and other symbolic elements, conditioning to suitable use of objects, and many other factors. Experiment shows that even in perception made intentionally simple in the laboratory, motivation and expected gratification modify what is perceived. Considering the amount of individual learning, conditioning, and motivation that enters perception, it is extremely hard to say what proportion of the world as we see it is actually "public" in the sense of the positivistic definition. Even illusions participate in normal perception. Essential prerequisites for experiencing of the world around us as a well-organized entity are the constancy phenomena of psychology: constancy of size, shape, color, etc., of perceived objects. But the constancy phenomena are based upon discrepancies between sensation and perception—that is, upon mechanisms which, in psychological experiment, appear as illusions. It is not by intuitive experience but only by more-or-less elaborate functions of testing that we can tell what "really" belongs to perceived objects and what is illusion and delusion.*

Furthermore, we do not find a simple antithesis between physical objects

---

* It should be noted in passing that many so-called "private," mental data are as amenable to objective test as are physiological or physical data. This is shown by any psychological experiment. Whether an animal or human subject has the allegedly "private" experience of seeing green (or is color blind, or has another visible spectrum) can be tested by independent observers in the same way as physiological processes are tested—i.e., by observation of suitably chosen reactions to stimuli. Instruments like the polygraph permit extensive (although by no means infallible) insight into the subject's "private" mental life. Thus the commonly accepted antithesis is problematic. Experience of material things is largely "private" because it depends upon individual learning, motivation, etc.; and mental experience is largely "public" because it is verifiable by independent observers.

outside and myself inside, but all sorts of intergradations. In the visual and tactual fields, our experience is not one of perceptions or simple sensations —which latter are a product of the laboratory—but variously shaped, colored, etc., objects. In auditory experience, it is already less clear what is outside or inside. Is the *Art of the Fugue* an object in space, or does it belong to inner experience? Equally unclear are the distinction and spatial localization of olfactory and gustatorial sensation. Thus, in introspection, the ego boundary again appears fluid.

Conversely, the experience of my ego is not that of an immaterial entity, but is the universe of experience (proprioceptive in the widest sense of the word) that reports about a certain "material" thing which in physical language is called my body—just as exteroceptive experience is the universe of experience reporting about "material" things around me. I experience my feeling ego not as an immaterial soul, but as certain sensations of my body; my thinking ego not as pure mind, but as subvocal speech (tension of certain parts of my musculature, etc.), my willing ego not as pure will, but as certain sensations of "pulling myself together," etc. Take this proprioceptive experience away and no consciousness of myself is left, in the same way as outside things disappear when I close my eyes. I believe William James, one of the most acute introspectionists, was quite right in emphasizing this observation, but this does not imply uncritical acceptance of the so-called James-Lange theory as a physiological hypothesis.

Here, too, are all intermediates between sharp spatial localization and indefinite feelings. Pain is experienced in a well-circumscribed area of my body, the tooth or finger, in much the same way as a chair or tree is localized in the outside space of visual experience. But feeling well or sick, elated or depressed, is experienced by my body as a whole, rather like hearing a sound which is localizable only with difficulty. At the end of the scale is seemingly pure mental experience when, for example, in solving an arithmetical problem we nearly forget ourselves although some tension of certain muscles, subvocal speech, etc., still may be observed.

For this reason, it is not to be conceded that, as Kant has had it, experience of the outside world is spatial, and inner or ego experience only temporal. The complex of proprioceptive experience that constitutes my ego is localized in space just as is the universe of exteroceptive experience. It is less sharply localized, it is true, but then in outside experience there are all shades from definite localization (vision, touch) to increasingly indefinite ones (hearing, the chemical senses).

And, of course, in pathological states, the ego boundary becomes blurred or disappears. A few micrograms of LSD will suffice to produce this effect. The voices hallucinated by a schizophrenic and those heard in normal discourse have equal reality value for the individuals concerned. But even with those who claim to be more or less normal, the borders between conscious ego, the unconscious, the physiological body, and outside objects are not rigid.* Every neurotic shows that vegetative functions that are purely physiological in the "normal" are psychological in him and vice versa. Yoga practice shows that physiological functions, otherwise involuntary and so supposedly concerning the body only, can be brought under conscious control. Or take the example of the phantom limb, whose presence after amputation a patient may still feel and experience. Conversely, a tool or machine may become a part of the experienced ego, a sort of extension or expansion of it. A good driver feels with the whole automobile. A good microscopist feels not with the tips of his fingers, but rather with the screws of his instruments.

* The unconscious never fitted the Cartesian dualism for the excellent reason that Descartes never thought of it. Physical entities on the one hand, the conscious mind on the other—this *was* the Cartesian dualism; and the neat scheme was upset the moment the unconscious was discovered.

The original definition equated "mental events" with consciousness or awareness. This would make the concept of a mental unconscious selfcontradictory. It is, of course, not at all difficult to say that the unconscious ultimately reduces to neurophysiological events, mnemonic traces, reverberating circuits, effects of early conditioning, coded programming, etc. But then the Cartesian problem only reappears at a deeper level. Suppose the unconscious is composed of neurophysiological memory traces; then its conversion into conscious mental processes (e.g., in the psychoanalytic interview) is just as unintelligible as is the conversion of neurophysiological events in the visual cortex into colors seen.

Modern computers show "ratiomorphic" behavior: they make calculations, have a memory, may be goal-seeking, etc., and in general behave in ways which in former times have been considered the privilege of rational and conscious mind. We have, however, no reason to assume that a machine that we have constructed has "consciousness." Exactly the same applies to the overwhelming majority of biological regulations: they are "ratiomorphic," but we empirically know by introspection that they are unconscious. This being so, we are back at the epiphenomenalistic riddle: Why has consciousness evolved at all, if the job is done anyway by mechanisms lacking consciousness? As a rule, evolution does not produce characteristics that are useless; and to count consciousness among such "useless" characteristics as do occasionally occur (the colors of butterfly wings, the elaborate antlers in various species of deer, may belong to this category) implies that the evolution of man was a particularly meaningless incident in evolution. The question looks different only when we give consciousness its due, if it is regarded not as an inconsequential epiphenomenon but as one which has functions not performed by ratiomorphically working mechanisms; that is, when man with his consciousness is the creator of a new world beyond physiological mechanisms and mere feelings of what is going on in the machine. Man as creator of his own universe—that of symbols and culture—justifies himself as a conscious being. As a merely adaptive mechanism, conscious action, as compared with the elegance of organic regulations, is a bungler and has, by 1963, made a mess of things such as has not occurred in 2 billion years of evolution.

CATEGORIES OF EXPERIENCE

In order to build from sensations and perceptions an experienced universe, mental operations are needed which Kant has subsumed under the concept of *categories*. But, contrary to Kant's view, the categories of space, time, number, causality, ego, etc., are not given once and for all as *a priori* concepts valid for every rational being; they are the product of a long and tortuous development. They are preconditioned by biological organization. As Lorenz (13) has emphasized, neither man nor any other living being would have long survived if its perceptions did not mirror—in whatever distorted way—those features of the universe upon which the life of the species depends. But this implies only some sort of isomorphism, not an exact replication of reality. So far as human beings are concerned, the categories of experience further crystallize out in close interaction with social and cultural factors. Within the present framework we have to refrain from a detailed analysis, which has been given elsewhere (2). To give just a hint in what direction these processes may be sought, however, we refer to Piaget's (18) investigations of how categories are established in the mental development of the child by interaction of organizational and behavioral factors: and to Cassirer's (9) work on how categories develop in cultural evolution, as studied by comparison of primitive and civilized peoples. It further seems that the formation of categories interacts with linguistic factors: The structure of language is both a conditioning factor and an expression of how the universe is organized. Here the so-called Whorfian hypothesis (23) regarding the relation of the experienced universe with the structure of language would deserve further discussion.*

> * This is one reason why any hope of "solving" the mind-body problem by considering it as arising from "conceptual confusion" and by linguistic analysis of "the way in which we use mental and physical terms in ordinary language" (Feigl [10]) is misplaced. We start from the antithesis: mind-body as it has developed within Western science. But our ordinary language and conceptual analysis would be drastically different if we were to start with Plato's *logistikón*, *thymoeidés* and *epithymetikón*, with Aristotle's *anima rationalis*, *sensitiva* and *vegetativa*, with the *pneûma* and *psyché* of the Gnostics, with the Indian *âtman* and *karma*, or any other outlandish psychology—that is, with other conceptualizations which are not necessarily inferior to Western psychology, and may be superior. The latter for the reason (2, 4) that our Indogermanic languages, as well as the models we apply in scientific psychology, can express the "mental" only by physicalistic similes. This is a grave handicap. Other categorizations within a different linguistic framework are quite conceivable, and may permit a much more genuine and therefore realistic psychology than ours. The hope of arriving at a "solution" of the mind-body problem by way of "common sense" and "analysis of ordinary language" (as was proposed by some positivists) is of a fantastic naïveté. If this advice had been followed in science, the sun would still revolve around the earth, as both common sense and ordinary language unmistakably tell us that he rises in the East and sets in the West.

What this all amounts to is that the mind-body problem needs a much more intensive, scientific study than has ever been undertaken. Before we can even discuss mind and body in terms of the Cartesian dualism, we have to study the history, prehistory, and biology of these concepts. Taking them for granted and then trying to find some logical trick to coordinate them is, to use a famous simile, like observing the visible part of an iceberg and forgetting the much larger mass of ice below the waves of the sea.

EMPATHY AND THE PROBLEM OF OTHER MINDS

We have still to look at the universe of science, and possible consequences—theoretical and practical—of what has been said. Before doing this, I will glance at a further problem, that called in psychology, empathy, and in philosophy, cognition of other minds.

In some mysterious way we know that fellow beings experience anger, pain, pleasure, that they are endowed with mental experiences similar to ours. The behavioristic explanation is well known. It is that other minds are approached by a process of inference: If I feel pain or another emotion, I make a face or show other behavioral symptoms. Hence if I see you making a face of the type concerned I infer from these behavioral clues that you feel corresponding pain or other emotion, and the possibility of making such inferences is acquired by a learning process.

In our opinion, the phenomenon of empathy and the experience of other minds is not a complex inference, and even less something verbally taught by the human mother to her infant, as some behaviorists have hypothesized. Rather, it is something very primitive or primeval; and empathy in civilized man is a pale remnant of a faculty of intuitive understanding which was much more highly developed in primitive man and even in animals. As a matter of fact, a pet dog or a budgie appear empathically to understand my humors and intentions, sometimes to a degree surpassing the empathic understanding by the human partner. And this is the more remarkable because facial anatomies and expressive movements are so extremely unlike. The dog knows whether he is wanted or not; the budgie knows the location of my mouth, which he may kiss, or my eyes which he must not, and does not, peck. Where does this knowledge come from? It can hardly be an innate schema bred by selection in evolution; budgies in the South American forest and humans were widely separated until budgies, not long ago, were imported as pets. The faculty does not appear to be learned—the dog has no opportunity to make comparative studies of human and canine expressions. Even the scientist who is eager to exclude all metaphysics can hardly avoid the impression that empathy (and related phenomena of mass psychology*) are a remnant of a collective unconscious out of which individualized egos grew, but which still persists in traces. Of course, "collective unconscious" is a reification, a hypostatization into substance of what actually are only dynamic happenings; but so are "force," "energy," and other respectable concepts of science. Using such models, we must only be careful to keep this in mind and not to make such concepts into metaphysical (and, as is often the case, divine or demonic) entities.

The connections of art, morals, religion, etc., with empathy need no emphasis, although they should be discussed in detail. Art and poetry presuppose empathy, cognition of other minds, animistic experience, the *tat tvam asi*—whatever term you choose to label this sort of awareness. In a way, the "world experience" of the child and the primitive is carried over into the most exalted manifestations of culture. However, one has to be a dry-as-dust positivist to consider the worlds of the artist and poet as merely an archaic relic. One will rather say that there are other, and perhaps higher, forms of awareness than those of ordinary life and of science; that the world of science is only one perspective of reality, highly useful and successful in its way, but not the exclusive one.

This has certainly been the claim of the mystics over the millennia. The unitive knowledge of which mysticism speaks is a form of experience said to be beyond ego and world, mind and body. That it is a genuine experience is confirmed by the fact of a *philosophia perennis*, of the independent appearance of the same mystical experience among humans of different creeds, cultures, and times.

Maslow (14, 15) has, I believe, well characterized in scientific terms what he calls "being cognition" in contrast to ordinary cognition. As is well known, Maslow distinguishes between the normal "deficiency cognition" which was the sole one taken into consideration by traditional Western psychology—that is, experience oriented toward coping with reality by means of adaptive perception and within an accepted symbolic framework —and "being cognition" attained in the peak of love, mystic, esthetic, etc., experience. Peak experience is nonutilitarian; it transcends the boundary

---

* One can, of course, say that a mob is a sum of individuals, that they all feel and act the same way because of exposure to the same stimuli and conditioning. However, one wonders whether this elementaristic explanation is the whole truth. Both in its sublime and bestial deeds, mass-mind seems to transcend the individuals. If, for example, the mob is excited to actions of selfsacrifice, how is even an overwhelming emotion to overcome the basic instinct of self-preservation? It is seductive to refer to terms previously introduced: In the mob, the ego barrier becomes blurred, as is also the case in pathologic states of schizophrenia or drug-induced "model psychoses." The criterion of "privacy" of mental experience (cf. footnote, p. 231) would require reconsideration if emotions were indeed "infectious."

between ego and nonego; it renounces "rubricizing," that is, bringing things into the framework of symbolic categories; and it is detached from personal goals and anxieties.

We shall do well to adopt a *perspectivistic viewpoint* (2). The world-view of science is admirable so far as it goes, that is, as a way of conceptual and technological control of nature. However, it is only one perspective of reality. The perspective of the artist and, in the last resort, of the mystic, is another, and this also is justified pragmatically: not in the way of controlling the world by technical marvels, but in the way of a self-realization of the human personality.

THE TESTIMONY OF PHYSICS

When we finally come to science, it is not new to say that it is not essentially different from ordinary experience, but rather is its expansion, refinement, and further conceptualization. Again it has to be said that our Western science—essentially oriented by theoretical physics—is not the only possible one. A leading mathematician (Gödel, quoted by Oppenheimer [17]) has stated that it was purely an historical accident that our mathematics has developed along quantitative lines. Other, nonmetrical forms of mathematics and corresponding models are quite possible and are, in fact, found in recent developments (e.g. game and decision theory [7]). Historically, there have been very different forms of science, that is, theoretical conceptualizations and models of what is experienced (2, 20).

The Cartesian dualism, the antithesis between soulless matter outside and immaterial soul inside, arises as a conceptualization characteristic of a well-defined state of Western science—the *res extensa*, the famous billiard balls, the atoms, moving in space according to the laws of classical mechanics,* and *res cogitans*, the working of the rational mind, the philosopher

---

* Even modern positivistic writing does not get away from this naïve metaphysics as is shown, e.g., by a paper by Smith (19) (approvingly quoted by Feigl [10], p. 35). As in the time of Moleschott and Karl Vogt, the "living object is a swarm of particles in space"; "consciousness is a physical process or event within the living object"; and although "the exact nature of this process or event will no doubt remain obscure for a long time," "there can be little reasonable doubt of the basic fact." It is amazing how little "naturalistic" philosophers have been influenced by what has transpired in science during the past 50 years: for example, that according to quantum physics, not even so-called "elementary" physical events are elementary in a "swarm of particles" but show holistic characteristics of interaction; that, besides "particles," physics always contained nonmaterial entities such as energy; that Einstein's basic formula $E = mc^2$ (one very *concrete* consequence of which are atomic bombs) has eradicated the popular visual model of "particles," etc. One is hard put to understand what is meant by "consciousness being a physical process" if one does not agree with Karl Vogt that the brain secretes thought just as the kidney secretes urine.

meditating on a comfortable chair in his studio, playing with highly abstract symbols. It is not a primeval datum, but rather the last outgrowth and flowering of an immense development occurring in the maturation of the human individual, in the evolution of man from lower animals, and in the history of culture from savage tribes to the rationalist philosopher of the 17th century.

Turning to modern science, what is left of these entities? Modern physics has destroyed the concept of matter except as a manner of speaking. The ultimate components of physical reality are not small bodies any more, but rather dynamic events, of which we can only say that certain aspects of their behavior can be described by certain mathematical laws.

Present psychological theory cannot of course be compared in sophistication with physics. Nevertheless, the general trend in physical and psychological science is similar.

Physics expands the range of the observable by inventing instruments— microscopes, electronmicroscopes, and Wilson chambers—and so discovers entities beyond unaided sensory experience: cells, molecules, atomic particles, and so forth. Similarly, psychology expands the range of the observable by inventing suitable techniques. Psychoanalysis, for example, uncovers a realm of the unconscious which is not observed in naïve experience. In order to explain what is observed, both physics and psychology construct models and theoretical systems which greatly surpass immediate experience and are linked with the latter only by long chains of deductive reasoning. In this way, what is eventually left in physics is a conceptual system permitting a more-or-less exact description of relationships among entities which, in their ultimate being, remain unknown. Psychology does the same. Constructs like id, ego, superego, drives, repression, and all sorts of other psychological hypothetical constructs or models are invented to describe and bring into a rational system certain relationships in experience. What these entities "are," metaphysically, remains undefined, and (as Freud sometimes has) they may just as well be represented by mere letter symbols.

Thus, in the world picture of modern science, no ultimate reality is claimed for the little billiard balls and an immaterial mind to play with or be affected by them or, to use more modern terms, to interfere in the gaps of microphysical causality as left by the Heisenberg relation. Rather there is a reality which in exteroceptive experience is observed as a world of things, and in proprioceptive experience as the ego. In science, this is described, with respect to certain structural aspects, by physical and psychological theories.

ISOMORPHISM AND GENERAL THEORY

I, for one, would not care to add another discussion of the mind-body problem to the many existing ones if it were not for a working hypothesis that may lead to new approaches in both theoretical and practical areas. I submit that this is precisely the outcome of our considerations.

We have agreed, I presume, that physics and psychology (both taken in a wide sense) are conceptual constructs representing certain aspects of reality. The first consequence is that we have to relinquish so-called reductionism. The concepts of psychology cannot be reduced to those of neurophysiology, as should have been clear from the start. Neither is the mental world an epiphenomenon to the physical world of atoms, chemical reactions, electric currents, etc., which is completely determined in itself by the laws of physics, so that the mental series would represent an inconsequential and unintelligible duplication. Both the worlds of physics and of psychology are constructs to bring certain aspects of the experienced universe under the rule of law.

Nevertheless, excluding reduction of psychology to neurophysiology, we can indicate what their relation is and how unification of both fields may be sought.

We must postulate an *isomorphism* between the constructs of psychology and neurophysiology in order to relate them. This is both the minimum hypothesis required and the maximum hypothesis permitted by science : the minimum hypothesis, because neurophysiology would make no sense without correspondence to mental processes; the maximum hypothesis, because this is the most we can say without metaphysics. However, one must be careful not to take this isomorphism in a simple and naïve way. It does not imply any simple similarity between psychological and brain-physiological processes, say, between visual gestalten and corresponding electric fields in the brain. Here the simile of modern "thinking machines" is illustrative. For example, we can well imagine—and I think this would even be technologically feasible—a machine that builds automobiles in a fully automated way. This would imply a program running through a computer and a series of allied machines. But the program—perhaps in the form of a punched tape—has no apparent resemblance to the automobile produced, although in the way of a code, it is isomorphic with the latter. Incidentally, something similar is actually the case in biology, namely with respect to the genetic code of protein synthesis contained in the nucleic acids of the chromosomes. If, as seems probable at present, the memory function is connected with the RNA (ribonucleic acid) of neurons, this also would pre-suppose a presently unknown manner of coding. Hence, isomorphism between psychological and neurophysiologic happenings need not presuppose any simple resemblance between both series.

Now, in what way can neurophysiological and psychological theory further be unified? I believe we can give quite a definite answer to this question, also. As has been stated, the unification will not be along the lines of taking the constructs of physics as absolutes and reducing to them psychological constructs. Rather I see the unification of physiological and psychological theory in constructs which are generalized with respect to both, and in this sense are neutral with respect to physics and psychology. We have a fair idea what such generalized theory may look like (7). Recent theory construction in cybernetics, information theory, general system theory, game and decision theory, etc., elaborates constructs precisely of this kind—that is, constructs that are neither physical nor psychological, but are applicable to both fields. Admittedly, this is only a beginning, but I believe the problem is rather clearly posed: the formulation of a generalized theory within which both psychical and neurophysiological constructs appear as specifications.

A NEW CONCEPT OF THE PSYCHOPHYSICAL ORGANISM

Such theory, even in the vague outline which we can give it at present, can have very definite practical consequences.

The dichotomy in psychiatric therapy between physical and psychological methods is a consequence of the philosophical antithesis of body and mind. The conventional model of brain function was physicalistic, that is, adopted from traditional physics without regard to biology. This model conceives of the organism as an essentially inert system which is activated only by external factors. This is the way ordinary physical systems behave; from it, follows what may be called the "automaton model" of the living and behaving organism. It can easily be shown that this automaton model predominated until now in psychology (7), in terms of the S-R and other schemes. The concept of psychological and social homeostasis; Freud's principle of stability according to which the tendency of the organism is to release tensions and come to rest in an equilibrium state; the consideration of mental illness as disturbance of such equilibrium, and the consequent ideal of man as a robot to be maintained in optimal psychological and social homeostasis and adjustment to given conditions—all this and much more are consequences or different expressions of the automaton model.

However, this model is unsatisfactory in theory and dangerous in its practical consequences. Modern biology teaches us that the organism is not an ordinary physical system, that is, one corresponding to conventional (or rather, obsolete) physical theory. It is a so-called open system, and among the characteristics of open systems is that they not only respond to stimuli but show what may be called inner or autonomous activity (5). This, of course, corresponds to the experience of both classical (1) and recent neurophysiology (11). It will suffice here to mention arousal systems, such as the reticular activating system, to illustrate the importance of autonomous activity.

And, of course, what has been said also corresponds to experience in psychiatry and mental health. If, according to the S-R scheme, the supreme tendency of the psychophysical organism is to satisfy biological needs, why is it that, in our so-called affluent society where the biological needs of hunger and sex and daily life in general *are* satisfied as never before, we have an unprecedented increase in mental cases? I think the fact that 50% or so of hospital populations is psychiatric patients is the most dramatic illustration that something is fundamentally wrong with conventional principles. And I believe it is possible to define what is wrong rather clearly, and to draw the practical conclusions.

The overcoming of physicalism leads us to replace the S-R scheme and automaton model by a more realistic one which approaches the psychophysical organism as an internally active system. This implies a re-evaluation of both psychological theory and practice. As a matter of fact, with notions such as emphasis on activity and creativity, selfrealization, and the like, psychology has already escaped the fetters of the S-R model and is tending toward new concepts of the kind I tried to indicate.

CULTURE AND VALUES

Finally, the uncritical acceptance of the Cartesian dualism has led us to forget that matter and mind by no means cover the entire field of reality. There are many realities which are neither physical nor mental, but which are beyond and outside the Cartesian antithesis. We cannot enter into a detailed discussion or definition, but obviously, beside responding to biological needs, human behavior is fundamentally determined by realities which, in a loose way, we may call cultural, symbolic, spiritual values and the like. It is easy to see that they fall into neither of the Cartesian categories—they are neither physical, like rocks and animals, atoms and chemical reactions; nor are they mental, like feelings and thoughts, motivations and other psychological constructs. I suggest that if one is to think this through, he start with trivial facts in our society—say, the Bureau of Internal Revenue as a very real entity which nevertheless is neither a physical thing nor, unfortunately, a mental hallucination—and go on up to the sublime achievements of culture called science, works of art, religious values, and so forth. One should think over whether a Beethoven symphony, a Rembrandt painting, or the system of physics can be defined in terms of the categories of "physical" and "mental." It will easily be found that they cannot be.* But it is just such realities on the higher or symbolic level which determine the most important part of human behavior (3).

Again, this is not metaphysical speculation, but reflects on psychiatry. I have said that hitherto psychiatry was determined by the Cartesian antithesis—being either physical (like psychosurgery, shock, drugs, etc.) or psychological (in terms of attempting to treat the individual mind). It is a consequence of this that it could not deal with broad fields of mental health and disturbance. Much is said, for example, of existential neurosis arising not from frustration of biological needs or from particular conflicts, but from the meaninglessness of life in modern society, a world in which values, purposes, and goals have collapsed. What has this to do with electrical potentials in the brain or unsatisfied drives? Nevertheless, the affliction may be sufficient to provoke suicide. Or, in the problem of delinquency (assuming, for the sake of argument, that it is a psychiatric problem, which could well be disputed), it has been said that a new style of crime has appeared —crime not because of need, for material gain, or out of passion, but crime for "thrills," or for establishing a reputation as a "tough guy." But what can be done about it with tranquilizing drugs or conventional psychotherapy? There is no disturbed brain physiology, nor do phenomena like existential anxiety and new-fashioned crime fit into the usual psychological or Freudian categories. The only thing that can be said is that these are disturbances which originate in a breakdown of the value system, loss of goals of life and of spiritual orientation (6)—that is, they come from that third realm, other than matter and mind.

I believe I have succeeded in showing that our topic is not a purely academic one, a playground for abstract philosophies, but one intimately connected with great problems of our time and society—and especially with psychiatric questions. Much more could and should be said; I have done hardly more than hint at problems and further developments.

----

* What, for example, is "Science?" It certainly is, so to speak, a selfpropelling entity, that is, a system organized and developing according to its immanent laws. It is a "reality" in the only operational and nonmetaphysical sense of the word, that is, something deeply influencing human behavior, society, life, and even survival. But it certainly is not "material," the sum of textbooks, professors, and laboratories in existence. Nor is it "mental," the aggregate of the psychologies of persons engaged in research, teaching, and administration. Also it is not a mere collective noun for certain human behavior because, as we have said, it has its own laws of systemic construction which are neither laws of physics nor of psychology. The answer, of course, is that science, like art, music, ethics, religion, and other cultural entities, is a symbolic system transcending both material things to which it may apply, and individual psychologies. It is the vice of the Cartesian dualism that it leaves no place for such entities, which are precisely those that distinguish human from animal behavior.

SUMMARY AND CONCLUSION

A modern reconsideration of the mind-body problem must consider, first, recent developments in biology, developmental psychology, cultural anthropology, linguistics, psychopathology, theoretical physics, etc. Second to be taken into account are developments in modern physics and biology that show that problems formerly considered to be epistemological, philosophical or metaphysical (e.g., those of space, time, causality, wholeness, directedness, etc.) have become increasingly subject to empirical research. The same will apply to the mind-body problem.

The problem encompasses two levels, namely, those of direct experience and of the concepts of science. In direct experience (introspection) the antithesis between ego and nonego ("material things") is a result of a long developmental process, biological as to the evolution of man, psychological as regards child psychology, and cultural as to human history. It is not a self-evident category nor is it *a priori* for every human or rational being. Other forms of consciousness, such as peak experience in emotional climax, art, mysticism, etc., cannot be disregarded as mere primitive precursors of the so-called objective world view of the average westerner in the 20th century. They are different forms of cognition in their own right.

In science, the antithesis of "matter" and "mind" is a conceptualization characteristic of the mechanistic model and world-view of physics. "Mind" and "matter" are reifying conceptualizations that become increasingly inadequate in modern science. The concept of "matter" in the classical sense is abandoned in modern physics. Similarly, the concept of "mind" is a reification of what actually is a dynamic process. This concept no longer holds in present science, as is shown, for example, by the concept of the unconscious, which does not fit into the Cartesian dualism.

Both physics, including neurophysiology, and psychology, including unconscious processes, are theoretical constructs aimed at explaining, predicting, and controlling observable events; they are connected with the latter only by extensive chains of reasoning. Both are progressively deanthropomorphized, that is, the properties characteristic of human experience and *Umwelt* are progressively eliminated. What eventually remains are conceptual models and relations serving the purposes of explanation, prediction, and control. This process is far advanced in physics and beginning in psychology.

The new approach to the mind-body problem constitutes a working hypothesis that should lead to new insight, to useful consequences in both theoretical psychology and psychiatry. A unification of both conceptual systems—those of neurophysiology and of psychology—appears to be possible by use of models that are neutral and superordinated to both. The beginnings of such a development can already be noted.

It is a necessary postulate for neurophysiology and psychology that their constructs are in some way isomorphic. Such isomorphism need not involve similarity of neurophysiological and psychological events; the concept of coding gives an indication of isomorphism without any direct similarity or resemblance.

The new approach in the mind-body problem leads to a more realistic model of the psychophysical organism; it amends the conventional S-R and automaton model of neurophysiology and psychology.

The classical dualism omitted precisely that realm which is specific to human, as compared to animal behavior and psychology: the field of culture, symbols, values, etc., which are neither "physical" nor "mental," but have their own autonomous laws. Basic as well as clinical psychology must recognize this realm because it is precisely the sphere of specifically human behavior, and new developments in both fields may be expected from a proper acknowledgement of this fact.

NOTES

1. Von Bertalanffy, L. *Problems of Life, An Evaluation of Modern Biological Thought*. Wiley, New York, 1952. Torchbook edition, Harper, New York, 1960, pp. 114–122.

2. Von Bertalanffy, L. An essay on the relativity of categories. *Philosophy of Science, 22:* 243, 1955.

3. Von Bertalanffy, L. A biologist looks at human nature. *Scient. Month. 82:* 33, 1956. Reprinted in: *Contemporary Readings in Psychology*, Daniel, R. S., Ed. Houghton Mifflin, Boston, 1959; *Reflexes to Intelligence. A Reader in Clinical Psychology*, Beck, S. L. and Molish, H. B., Eds. Free Press, Glencoe, 1959, p. 280.

4. Von Bertalanffy, L. Modern concepts on biological adaptation. In *The Historical Development of Physiological Thought*, Brooks, C. M., and Cranefield, P. F., Eds. Hafner, New York, 1959.

5. Von Bertalanffy, L. Some biological considerations on the problem of mental illness. *Bull. Menninger Clin. 23:* 41, 1959. Also in *Chronic Schizophrenia*, Appleby, L., Scher, J. M., and Cumming, J., Eds. Free Press, Glencoe, 1960.

6. Von Bertalanffy, L. Human values in a changing world. In *New Knowledge in Human Values*, Maslow, A. H., Ed. Harper, New York, 1959.

7. Von Bertalanffy, L. General system theory—A critical review. *General Systems, Yrbk. Soc. General Systems Res. 7:* 1, 1962.

8. Butler, S. *Erewhon*. Modern Library, New York, 1927.

9. Cassirer, E. *The Philosophy of Symbolic Forms*. 3 vols. Yale University Press, New Haven, 1953–57.

10. Feigl, H. The "mental" and the "physical." In *Minnesota Studies in the Philosophy of Science*, Vol. II: Concepts, Theories, and the Mind-Body Problem. Feigl, H., Scriven, M., and Maxwell, G., Eds. Univ. Minn. Press, Minneapolis, 1958.

11. Hebb, D. O. Drives and the C.N.S. (conceptual nervous system). *Psychol. Rev. 62:* 243, 1955.

12. Hook, S. (Ed.) *Dimensions of Mind.* N. Y. Univ. Press, New York, 1960.

13. Lorenz, K. Die angeborenen Formen möglicher Erfahrung. *Z. Tierpsychologie 5:* 235, 1943.

14. Maslow, A. H. Cognition of being in the peak-experiences. *J. Genetic Psychol. 94:* 43, 1959.

15. Maslow, A. The creative attitude. *The Structuralist, 3:* 4, 1963.

16. Meerloo, J. A. M. *The Rape of the Mind.* World, Cleveland, 1956.

17. Oppenheimer, R. Analogy in science. *Am. Psychologist. 11:* 127, 1956.

18. Piaget, J. *The Construction of Reality in the Child.* (Trans. by M. Cook). Basic Books, New York, 1954.

19. Smith, K. The naturalistic conception of life. *Am. Scientist. 46:* 413, 1958.

20. Spengler, O. *Der Untergang des Abendlandes.* 2 vols. (ed. 82). C. H. Beck, Munich, 1923.

21. Von Uexküll, J. *Umwelt und Innenwelt der Tiere.* Ed. 2. Springer, Berlin, 1929.

22. Von Uexküll, J., and Kriszat, G. *Streifzüge durch die Umwelten von Tieren und Menschen.* Springer, Berlin, 1934.

23. Whorf, B. L. *Collected Papers on Metalinguistics.* Foreign Service Institute, Department of State, Washington, D.C., 1952.

THE THERAPEUTIC RELATIONSHIP: RECENT THEORY AND RESEARCH*

Carl R. Rogers

i have long been interested in the elements that account for change in personality and behavior. I have tried to seek out and discover some of the lawful order that exists in this complex and subtle realm. A number of years ago I became interested in the conditions that foster constructive psychological change, psychological development, or growth toward maturity. I wanted to find the commonalities—if any exist—between different ways of helping people, different orientations to psychotherapy. I tried to abstract from my experience in therapy, from my observations of others who were carrying on therapy, from recordings of therapists with quite divergent views, and from the meager research available the conditions that facilitate psychological growth.

As I worked on and pondered this problem, I gradually developed a decidedly unorthodox cluster of hypotheses. It seemed to me that the only way of explaining the divergent modes of helping individuals was to say that the helpers or therapists had certain basic attitudes in common. I shall try to describe shortly the way these attitudes seem to me. After I had formulated these ideas for myself, I decided to try to obtain the reactions of others with the hopeful thought that some research on this issue might be stimulated. So in 1957 I published an article, "The Necessary and Sufficient Conditions of Therapeutic Personality Change" (4). The response convinced me that many people were eagerly looking for some answer to the perplexing question of what it is that facilitates psychological change. The formulation aroused considerable interest, and, even more important, it has stimulated a number of research investigations.

I should like to say at the outset that the radical nature of the formulation I proposed was primarily in what it omitted. I hypothesized that

---

* Carl R. Rogers, "The Therapeutic Relationship: Recent Theory and Research," *Australian Journal of Psychology*, XVII (1965), 95–108, reprinted by permission.

personality change in the client or patient in psychotherapy came about not because of the professional qualifications and training of the therapist, not because of his special knowledge (medical or psychological), not because of his ideological orientation to psychotherapy (psychoanalytic, Jungian, client-centered, Adlerian, Gestalt, and so forth), not because of his techniques in the interview, not because of his skill in making interpretations, but primarily or solely because of certain attitudinal characteristics in the relationship. It is these characteristics that I should like to describe.

Individuals come to psychotherapy with a bewildering diversity of problems and an enormous range of personal characteristics. They are met by therapists who show an almost equally wide range of views on what will be helpful in therapy, and these therapists exhibit also very diverse personality characteristics in meeting their clients. Yet underneath all this diversity, it seemed to me that I could discern an underlying process that might even be cast in terms of some sort of psychological equation. It could be phrased in this fashion: If certain definable conditions exist in the psychological relationship between client and therapist, then constructive or therapeutic personality change will occur in the client.

Perhaps first I should indicate very briefly what I mean by "constructive" or "therapeutic" personality change. I am using here a very simple and common-sense definition. I mean any change in the personality structure and in the behavior of the individual that clinicians would agree implies greater integration, less internal conflict, more energy utilizable for effective living. I mean a change in behaviors away from those generally regarded as immature and toward behaviors regarded as mature, responsible, and socialized.

THE THREE ESSENTIAL CONDITIONS IN THE THERAPIST

It is my hypothesis that such changes will come about if there exist in the therapist three attitudinal patterns. In addition, there is one condition that must exist in the client if change is to come about.

In the first place, it is hypothesized that personal growth is facilitated when the psychotherapist is what he *is*, when in the relationship with his client he is genuine and "without front" or facade, openly showing the feelings and attitudes that at any moment are flowing in him. We have coined the term "congruence" to try to describe this condition. By this we mean that the feelings the therapist is experiencing are available to him, available to his awareness, that he is able to live these feelings, to "be" them, and to communicate them if appropriate. It means that he comes into a direct personal encounter with his client, meeting him on a person-to-person basis. It means that he is *being* himself, not denying himself. No one

fully achieves this condition, yet the more the therapist is able to listen accep-
tantly to what is going on within himself and the more he is able to *be* the complexity of his feelings without fear, the higher the degree of his congruence.

I think that we readily sense this quality in our everyday life. We could
each of us name persons whom we know who always seem to be operating
from behind fronts, who are playing roles, who tend to say things they do
not feel. They are exhibiting incongruence. We do not reveal ourselves too
fully to such people. On the other hand, each of us knows individuals whom
we somehow trust because we sense that they are being what they *are*, that
we are dealing with the persons themselves and not with polite or professional facades. This quality is the one of which we are speaking, and it is
hypothesized that the more genuine and congruent the therapist in the
relationship, the more probability there is that personality change in the
client will occur.

I have received much clinical and research confirmation for this hypothesis in our work in recent years with randomly selected hospitalized
schizophrenic patients. The individual therapists in our research program
who seemed to be most successful in dealing with these unmotivated,
poorly educated, resistant, chronically hospitalized individuals were those
who were first of all *real*, who reacted in genuine, human ways as persons,
who exhibited their genuineness in therapeutic relationships, and who
were perceived as real by the patients. Being congruent may mean at times
expressing real annoyance or concern or frustration in the relationship. It
always means expressing these feelings as something existing in the
therapist, not as an accusation about the client.

It is this aspect of my hypothesis that seems to explain why people of
such divergent treatment philosophies as Dr. John Rosen, Dr. Carl
Whitaker, Dr. Albert Ellis, and myself can each in his own way be effective
with clients. Rosen challenges, Whitaker indulges in mutual fantasy, Ellis
shakes a didactic finger, I try to understand. To the extent that each of us is
a real person and able to let the realness show through he tends I believe to
reach his clients, even though in very different ways.

Now the second condition: I hypothesize that when the therapist is
experiencing a warm, positive, and acceptant attitude toward what *is* in the
client, this facilitates change. It involves the therapist's genuine willingness
for the client to be whatever feeling is going on in him at that moment—
fear, confusion, pain, pride, anger, hatred, love, or courage. It means that
the therapist cares for the client in a nonpossessive way, as a person with
human potentialities. It means that he prizes the client in a total, rather than
a conditional way. I mean that he does not simply accept the client when he
is behaving in certain ways and disapprove of him when he behaves in
other ways. He experiences an outgoing, positive feeling, without reserva-
tions, without *evaluations*. The term we have come to use for this attitude

is "unconditional positive regard," and we believe that, the more this attitude is experienced by the therapist and perceived by his client, the more likelihood there is that therapy will be successful and that change and development will take place.

It is clear that one does not have to be a professional to experience this attitude. In a therapy group I conducted at one hospital, a woman who had been hospitalized for many years, but who had shown much improvement during the preceding two years and who has now left the hospital, gave a moving account of what had helped her. I had been much impressed by her improvement, which clearly began before she entered group therapy, and one day when she said, "This is the first year I have *felt* like leaving the hospital," I said, "Gladys, why is this? What has made the difference?" She said, "Well, what changed it was when the Morses began taking me home— the ones I call Mom and Dad, although they are not. I want to get out mostly to show my appreciation to them for what they have done."

And then she told how, by chance, through their daughter, a nurse at the hospital, this middle-aged couple had become interested in her. They brought a picnic lunch for their daughter and included Gladys. They took her home. "I just sat. Wouldn't move. I was real scared." But they continued to take her to their home. Gladys said: "They've stood an awful lot. Even when I was unruly and snotty to them, they stood by me, they didn't let me down." Little by little this educationally retarded girl who could not even read, who had always been unstable, who had been psychotic, hallucinated, and for years a difficult patient, began to respond. She said, "They helped me more than any doctor," and then added, "'Course, doctors help too. But they stood by me even when I was disgusting an' that, and saying things I shouldn't.'"

In one sense this story is not unusual. Probably each of us could report some similar incident. But I want to point out its significance. Little by little the Morses' nonpossessive love for this young woman, their caring, got through to her and transformed her from a hallucinated psychotic to a positive and realistic person who now has a good chance of success outside the hospital walls. This older couple made it clear to the patient that they cared for her no matter how bizarre her behavior, no matter how much she rejected them. It was an unconditional positive regard, and it gradually changed her life and her personality. It is this kind of attitude, I believe, that also exists in the therapist when he is effective. It produces results. Gladys said: "Now when I go home they can't tell me from their other children. If Mom has a washing to do, I don't ask her. I just go ahead and do it."*

---

* A very clear example of the way in which nonpossessive caring can get through to a hospitalized schizophrenic patient is provided in the tape recording of two interviews with Mr. Vac. This tape is available (with transcript) from the Tape Library of the American Academy of Psychotherapists, 6420 City Line Avenue, Philadelphia 51, Pennsylvania.

The third essential condition of change is that the therapist be experiencing an accurate empathic understanding of the client's private world. To sense the client's inner world of private personal meanings as if it were his own, but without ever losing the "as if" quality, is empathy, and it seems essential to therapeutic change. To sense the client's anger or his fear or his feeling of being persecuted as if it were the therapist's own, yet without letting his own anger, fear, or suspicion be bound up in it, is the condition we are endeavoring to describe. When the client's world is clear to the therapist and when he can move about in it freely, then he can both communicate his understanding of what is already known to the client, and he can also voice meanings in the client's experience of which the client is scarcely aware. It is this kind of highly sensitive empathy that seems essential to therapeutic change.

I suspect that each of us has discovered that this kind of understanding is extremely rare. We neither receive it nor offer it with any great frequency. Instead we offer another type of understanding, which is very different, for example, "I understand what is wrong with you" or "I understand what makes you act that way." These types of understanding are those that we usually offer and receive—evaluative understanding from the outside. But when someone understands how it feels and seems to be me, without wanting to analyze me or judge me, then I can blossom and grow. I am sure I am not alone in that feeling. I believe that when the therapist can grasp the moment-to-moment experiencing occurring in the inner world of the client, as the client sees it and feels it, without losing the separateness of his own identity in this empathic process, then change is likely to occur.

A FOURTH CONDITION IN THE CLIENT

Unless some communication of the sort of attitude I have been describing has been achieved, it does not exist in the world of the client and thus cannot be effective. Consequently, it is necessary to add one more condition to our equation. When the client perceives to a minimal degree the genuineness of the therapist and the acceptance and empathy that the therapist experiences for him, then change in personality and behavior is predicted. It is necessary that the therapist's behaviors and words be perceived by the client as meaning that, to some degree, the therapist is real, that the therapist does care, that the therapist does seem to understand something of his inner feelings and personal world.

THE ESSENTIAL HYPOTHESIS

Let me restate very briefly the essentially simple but somewhat radical hypothesis I have set forth. I have said that constructive personality change comes about only when the client perceives and experiences a certain psychological climate in the relationship. The elements of this climate do not consist of knowledge, intellectual training, intellectual orientation in psychotherapy, or techniques. They are feelings or attitudes that must be experienced by the therapist and perceived by the client if they are to be effective. The three I have singled out as essential are: the realness, genuineness, or congruence of the therapist; a warm, acceptant prizing of the client, an unconditional positive regard; and a sensitive, empathic understanding of the client's feelings that is communicated to the client.

Another aspect of the hypothesis is that it has been stated in such a way that it is testable. Operational definitions of these qualities can be formulated and indeed have been formulated, and thus we can begin to discover empirically whether or not such qualities in the relationship are indeed causal factors in bringing about change in psychotherapy.

EMPIRICAL STUDIES OF THE HYPOTHESIS

I should like to digress for a moment, to say how personally rewarding the consequences have been when I have been able and willing to set forth a testable hypothesis. In regard to the conditions I have been describing, for example, I can well remember how uneasy and insecure I felt in making the first presentation of the unorthodox hypothesis I have formulated to a group at The University of Michigan. I not only felt that I was sticking my neck out; I also felt that I was sticking it out a long way. The discussion that followed made it very clear that other people felt the same way. But when a hypothesis is set forth in terms that can be made operational, then the situation does not need to end in argument or difference of opinion. It can be settled by a recourse to the facts. And the most exciting thing about the hypothesis of the therapeutic relationship that I have briefly sketched is not its newness—for in many ways it is not entirely new—but in the fact that it has led to a very considerable amount of empirical investigation to test whether it is true, partly true, or false. I should like to summarize some of these researches and what they seem to mean.

The Hypothesis as Tested by Observer Judgments

The first study I wish to report is one completed by Halkides (3). Her study was based on twenty recorded cases, ten of which could be classed by several objective criteria as more successful and ten as less successful. She took an earlier and a later recorded interview from each of these

cases. On a random basis she picked nine client-counselor interaction units
—that is, client statements and counselor responses—from each of these
interviews. She thus had nine early interaction units and nine later
interaction units from each case. These interview samples were then placed in
random order for judging. Three judges worked together during a training
period in which they tried to become sensitive to the attitudinal qualities of
the therapist by listening to interview recordings and making ratings of
them. They then were ready to turn to the interview samples for this study.
Working independently and with no knowledge of the cases or the degrees
of success or the sources of any given unit, the judges listened to these
counselor-client interactions and rated each unit on a seven-point scale
for the counselor's empathy. When they had completed this work, they
went through the samples again, rating the degree of the counselor's unconditional positive regard for the client and of the counselor's genuineness. Finally they went through the samples once more to rate the degree to
which the counselor's response matched the emotional intensity of the
client's expression—a condition that Halkides hypothesized to be as
important as the three conditions I had formulated.

There seemed a very remote possibility of any positive findings considering all the sources of unreliability in the study and the smallness of
the interview samples. Yet the reliability of the judges' ratings was high—
in the neighborhood of .90. It was also found that a high degree of each of
these attitudinal conditions—empathy, unconditional positive regard, and
congruence—was associated with the more successful cases, and this association was highly significant at the .001 level. The data thus tended strongly
to confirm the hypothesis. The matching of the client's affective intensity
by the therapist did not correlate significantly with the other conditions or
with the degree of success.

The Hypothesis Tested by Client and Therapist Perceptions

A series of investigations of the hypothesis regarding the therapeutic
relationship has been completed by Barrett-Lennard (1, 2). Rather than
using objective observers and interview material, he proposed to study the
essential qualities in the relationship by measuring the manner in which the
relationship was perceived by the client and the therapist. He developed a
Relationship Inventory that has different forms for client and therapist and
is designed to study five dimensions of the relationship. To give the flavor
of this instrument, I shall list a few items from his inventory.

For example, in trying to measure the extent to which the client was
empathically understood, he included items like the following to be
evaluated by the client on a six-point scale from "strongly true" to "definitely untrue."

He generally senses or realizes how I am feeling.

When I do not say what I mean at all clearly he still understands me.

He understands my words, but does not realize how I feel.

For the therapist's form, these items were changed to:

I generally sense or realize how he is feeling.

When he does not say what he means at all clearly, I still understand him.

I understand his words, but not how he feels.

Barrett-Lennard divided the dimension of unconditional positive regard into two aspects. First he wished to measure the level of regard, the degree of liking for the client by the therapist. For this purpose, there were items like the following, each one again to be rated by the client from "strongly true" to "strongly not true":

He likes seeing me.

He cares about me.

He is indifferent to me.

To measure the unconditionality of the regard, the extent to which there were "no strings attached" to the counselor's liking, items of this sort were included:

Sometimes he responds to me in a more positive or friendly way than he does at other times.

He likes me better when I behave in some ways than he does when I behave in other ways.

In order to measure the genuineness, or congruence, of the therapist in the relationship, there were items of this sort:

He does not try to mislead me about his own thoughts or feelings.

He behaves just the way that he is in our relationship.

He pretends that he likes me or understands me more than he really does.

Barrett-Lennard also wished to measure a fifth variable that he regarded as important—the therapist's psychological availability or willingness to be known. For this purpose, he included items of this kind:

He will freely tell me his own thoughts and feelings when I want to know them.

He is unwilling to tell me how he feels about me.

He is uncomfortable when I ask him something about himself.

Using this Relationship Inventory, Barrett-Lennard studied first a series of forty-two clients dealt with by twenty-one therapists, in which he had several objective measures of the degree of change in the client. He administered the Relationship Inventory to each client and therapist after the fifth interview and again at the termination of therapy.

I find the results of his study to be of real interest. Let me try to summarize them.

1. Those clients who eventually showed more therapeutic change perceived more of the four hypothesized attitudinal conditions in their relationships with their therapists at the time of the early interviews than did those who eventually showed less change. The fifth condition—the willingness of the therapist to be known—was not significantly associated with later success. The meaning of this finding is that, when the client perceived these qualities in the relationship early in therapy, the prognosis was good. It was a clear confirmation of the hypothesis that, if the client perceives the therapist as experiencing liking and understanding of him and if he perceives the therapist as a real and genuine person, then change is facilitated.

2. The correlation between the *client* perception of these attitudinal conditions and the degree of changes was higher than the correlation between therapist perception and degree of change. This finding too was in accord with the theory. If the therapist was experiencing these attitudes in himself toward the client early in therapy, it was a reasonably good indication that constructive change would occur. But if the client *perceived* the therapist as holding these attitudes, it was an even better predictor of constructive change. It is not enough that the therapist hold these attitudes; they must also be perceived by the client.

3. There are two additional findings in this study that deserve consideration, though they are a little more complicated. Those clients who at the time they began therapy were better adjusted, as measured by different psychological tests, tended to perceive more of the hypothesized therapeutic conditions in the relationship than did those clients who were less well adjusted. This finding was unexpected. On first thought it might seem to indicate that these perceived conditions were not a *cause* of movement toward better adjustment but an *effect* of better adjustment. Perhaps only those individuals who are already well adjusted can be nondefensive enough to perceive such attitudes on the part of the therapist.

To pursue this issue further, Barrett-Lennard divided the twenty-one therapists into a more experienced and a less experienced group. That this division was meaningful seems indicated by the fact that the clients of the more experienced therapists showed more personality change. When he compared the clients in these groups he found that the clients of the more experienced therapists perceived more of the therapeutic conditions than did the clients of the less experienced therapists. It seems reasonable to conclude that the behaviors of the more experienced therapists communicated more of these attitudinal qualities than did the behaviors of the less experienced therapists. But it is also true that the ability to perceive these qualities was in part a function of the client's openness or adjustment. These findings seem to point up the fact that, in an interactional situation, as therapists grow more skillful, they are more able to experience and provide the conditions that make for therapy. On the other hand, these conditions can only be effective in the relationship to the extent that the client perceives them, and to some degree his ability to perceive them depends on his own adjustment.

Testing the Hypothesis in Psychotherapy with Schizophrenics

I should like to introduce one other line of evidence from our current and just-completed investigation of the therapeutic relationship with schizophrenics (5). We were dealing largely with unmotivated schizophrenics, mostly of lower socioeducational status and more or less chronic in their conditions. Though this investigation has not yet been published, we already have findings that bear on the hypothesis I have advanced. Drawing on the work of Gendlin, Kiesler, Van der Veen, and others, I shall mention a few of our findings very briefly.

First of all, schizophrenic patients perceive much lower levels of these attitudes in their therapists than do neurotic clients, though there is good reason to believe that the therapists are experiencing much the same attitudes with each group. This observation confirms Barrett-Lennard's finding that the more disturbed person can less easily perceive and trust the positive attitudes of the therapist.

In the second place, the more the schizophrenic patient perceives of these attitudes in the relationship and especially the more he sees his therapist as real, the more evidence he gives of therapeutic movement as measured by our process scales. He shows a greater degree of self-experiencing and self-exploration, a greater openness to what is going on within himself, greater evidence of being involved in a process of change.

A third finding is that the greater the degree of the therapist's empathy and congruence, the higher the level of process indices in the patient's interactions with a *third* person, in this case the sampling interviewer, who saw the patient every three months. In other words, the more satisfactory the relationship in therapy, the more likely it is that the client will show an openness to his own experience, less rigidity, more spontaneity, more capacity for communicating himself in a relationship with another person.

Finally there are a number of findings that indicate that patients involved in relationships high in these growth-promoting qualities show the greatest degree of constructive personality change. For example, the most striking of these findings is that those patients who received the highest degree of sensitively empathic understanding in their therapeutic relationships, as judged by unbiased rates, show the greatest decrease in schizophrenic pathology, as measured by the Minnesota Multiphasic Inventory. On the other hand (and this finding is disturbing), those patients in relationships low in empathic understanding show actual worsening in their schizophrenic pathology. At the conclusion of our tests, they were worse off than were the matched control individuals who had had no individual therapy.

Without trying to go further into this very complex research, I shall simply say that it indicates that the attitudinal qualities I have described are provided largely by the therapist but elicited partly by certain characteristics in the patient. They are interactional events. When, however, the relationship exhibits these qualities to a high degree, indices of movement or change are evident in the patient, and an improved inner integration, a reduction in pathological behavior, and an improvement in social adjustment follow.

SIGNIFICANCE OF THESE STUDIES

As I mull over the various studies that I have briefly summarized, they seem to me to have a number of rather deeply significant meanings. In the first place they indicate that it is possible to study cause and effect in psychotherapy. These studies are actually, so far as I know, the first to endeavor to isolate and measure the primary change-producing influences in psychotherapy. Whether they are still further confirmed or are contradicted or modified by future studies, they represent pioneering investigations of the question, "What really makes the difference in psychotherapy?" And the answer they give is that the attitudes provided by the therapist, the psychological climate that he is largely responsible for creating, *really* make the difference, really induce change. In the second place, the findings do tend to support in general the theory advanced about the equation of psychotherapy. We can now say with some assurance and factual support that a relationship perceived by the client as characterized by a high degree of congruence or genuineness in the therapist; by sensitive and accurate empathy on the part of the therapist; by a high degree of regard, respect, and liking for the client by the therapist; and by an absence of conditionality in this regard has a high probability of being therapeutically effective. This statement holds, whether we are speaking of neurotic individuals who come of their own initiative seeking help or of chronically schizophrenic persons with no conscious desire to seek help. This statement also holds whether these attitudinal elements are rated by impartial observers who listen to samples of the recorded interviews or are measured in terms of the client's perception of the relationship. To me it seems quite a forward stride to be able to make such statements in an area as complex and subtle as the field of psychotherapy.

Another significant element of these studies is that they have shown that the individual's perception of a relationship, the relationship as it exists phenomenologically, has a meaningful association with objective measures of change. In view of some of the trends in psychological thought and research today, this association is an important instance of movement toward "a science of inner experience," as Bergin has called it. Research in psychotherapy is bringing back into the world of psychology the subjective experiences of the individual by learning how to measure objectively the cues that point toward such subjective experience. To measure reliably such an inner, subjective experience as the degree of the therapists' liking for his client or the degree to which the therapist is genuine in his feelings may thus in the long run be very important for psychology in general.

There is another highly practical significance to these studies. They each indicate quite clearly that, by assessing a relationship early in its existence, we can to some degree predict the probability of its stimulating growth.

There is another and broader significance of these studies. They would, if further confirmed, seem to have profound implications for the training of therapists and counselors. If we wish workers to be effective in their helping relationships, we should focus less on courses in abnormal psychology and psychopathology, different therapeutic orientations, theories of personality, training in psychiatric and psychological diagnosis, and should concentrate more on two other elements. We should endeavor to select for such training individuals who already possess high degrees of the qualities I have described in their ordinary relationships with other people. We should want people who were warm, spontaneous, real, and understanding. We should also endeavour to plan the educational program so that these individuals would, in their training courses, come increasingly to experience empathy and liking from others and for others and that they would find it increasingly easier to be themselves, to be real, to be spontaneous and expressive. When I ask myself whether or not the training programs I know, either in psychology or psychiatry, approach this goal, I come up with a strong negative. It seems to me that most of our professional training programs make it *more* difficult for the individual to be himself and more likely that he will play a professional role. Often he becomes so burdened with theoretical and diagnostic baggage that he becomes *less* able to understand the inner world of another person as it seems to that person. Also, as his professional training continues, it all too often occurs that his initial warm liking for other persons is submerged in a sea of psychiatric and psychological evaluation and hidden under an all-enveloping professional role.

SPECULATION

I should like to speculate for a moment, going well beyond the specific findings of these studies. I am sure that the hypothesis proposed about the attitudes that facilitate psychological growth and development will, in the course of time, be modified. I am sure that the studies thus far completed will be qualified by the findings of further studies. Yet it does seem to be quite within the range of possibility that, in the not too distant future, we shall acquire an increasingly accurate knowledge of the elements that make for constructive psychological development, just as we have in the realm of nutrition acquired an increasingly accurate knowledge of the elements that promote physical growth. As this knowledge accumulates and as our instruments grow sharper, then there is the exciting possibility that we may be able, relatively early in the game, to predict whether or not a given relationship will actually promote individual psychological growth and development, just as we can assess the diet of a child in India or the Congo and predict the extent to which it will promote or inhibit physical growth. This possibility opens some astonishing vistas. Suppose we could measure a given parent-child relationship and could not only predict whether it was likely to promote growth but also assess the deficiencies that would keep it from being as helpful as it could be. Suppose that, in like manner we could assess a given teacher-pupil relationship in the classroom or the relationship between an executive and the men who report to him or the relationship between a doctor and his patients. In short, I suggest that we may have the beginning here of a significant flowering of psychological knowledge to a point at which we can encourage those relationships in which individual development toward psychological maturity is most probable and at which we can help to remedy those relationships in which psychological growth seems less likely. Enough pilot work has been done with the Relationship Inventory in teacher-pupil situations and in some parent-child relationships to make this goal seem not a far-off dream but a real possibility.

In concluding I cannot resist quoting a paragraph from a letter from a psychotherapist friend in which he states very well a point of view that I deeply share:

> I do not believe that even therapists are fully aware of how novel and unique is the relationship in which they are engaged. In all the long history of man, in the centuries and centuries that he has existed, for the first time in this long stretch of time, there are human beings who have made a profession and calling of listening to other human beings with sympathy, with understanding, with acceptance; and in many instances making no effort to alter these other human beings, to change them, push them around, persuade them. There has never been a relationship even remotely resembling this, a relationship in which a person makes no

demands for himself. For hostile, judgmental, egotistical, self-loving and self-seeking man, this is indeed a radical and revolutionary relationship. And it represents, also, probably the hardest and strangest role for man to provide.

What I have been saying in this paper is that we are making progress in understanding the nature of this unique therapeutic relationship. I have been saying that the essential elements appear to be not technical knowledge or ideological sophistication but personal human qualities—something the therapist *experiences*, not something he *knows*. And I have said that the empirical knowledge we have gained thus far confirms this view. In a variety of clients, normal, neurotic, and psychotic, with many different therapists and studying the relationship from the vantage point of the client, the therapist, or the uninvolved observer, the answer tends to come out the same: attitudes of realness, genuine liking, and sensitive empathy help to create a climate that produces constructive personal growth and change. And the ramifying implications of these findings are great indeed.

NOTES

1. Barrett-Lennard, G. T. Dimensions of therapist response as causal factors in therapeutic change. *Psychol. Monogr.*, 1962, 76, (43, Whole No. 562).

2. Barrett-Lennard, G. T. Personal communication to the author, describing further analysis of data in preceding reference.

3. Halkides, G. An experimental study of four conditions necessary for therapeutic change. Unpublished doctoral dissertation, University of Chicago, 1958.

4. Rogers, C. R. The necessary and sufficient conditions of therapeutic personality change. *Jour. Cons. Psych.*, 21, 1957. 95–103.

5. Rogers, C. R., Gendlin, E. T., Kiesler, D. J., & Truax, C. B. *The therapeutic relationship and its impact: A study of psychotherapy with schizophrenics.* (In press.) Univer. of Wisconsin Press.

THE ROLE OF COMMUNICATION IN THERAPEUTIC TRANSACTIONS*

Jurgen Ruesch

*P*eople influence one another by means of communication. The psychosocial therapies—particularly psychotherapy, psychoanalysis, group therapy, hypnosis and various forms of counseling—all have as their central therapeutic tool the human function of communication. The therapeutically effective events, therefore, must be embedded in the processes of communication. The exploration of these events is only beginning, but as more becomes known it is hoped that therapeutic methods will become more effective.

COMMUNICATION AND THE GOALS OF THERAPY

Any communicative encounter begins with the establishment of areas of mutual agreement that may serve as points of reference in the future. The patient's desire to improve, the fact that he has been ill or the fact that he grants the doctor the privilege of exploring his life history may provide a convenient point of departure in psychotherapy.

After a common frame of reference has been established, the doctor begins to explore the patient's image of himself and of the world. If gross discrepancies exist between this image and the realities as seen by others, the doctor will strive to make the patient understand these differences.

The next problem involves the patient's acceptance of his own established behavior, certain features of which he frequently will tend to ignore. Among the unalterable realities are age, sex, sometimes occupation, past events and the historical period in which we live. Then comes the recognition of the somewhat alterable features of behavior. If the patient is inclined to incur debts, to get drunk or to be precise and methodical in his work, all

* Jurgen Ruesch, "The Role of Communication in Therapeutic Transactions," *Journal of Communication*, XIII (1963), 132–139, reprinted by permission.

of this has to be reviewed and recognized. Rarely does the therapist change a behavioral tendency that has been established over decades. Instead his task frequently consists of supporting the patient in the direction he will take anyway, but helping him to proceed in a more productive manner. The exhibitionist may improve his performance and participate in theatrical activities; the suspicious person may become a detective, a pest controller or a customs inspector; the deviant person may be integrated by helping other deviants; the self-centered individual may gradually develop a sense of humor and learn to acknowledge openly his vanity and his need for success, support and group membership. If a person strives for status, open admission of his concern will make it possible for him to engineer his task more effectively. If the patient gets to know himself and the world in which he lives, he is in a position to steer his existence more effectively.

A further aim of therapy is the correction of defective processes of communication (7). The assumption can be made that when the patient has learned to communicate effectively, his opinions about scientific, esthetic, political and moral issues will be corrected through interchange with his peers. Successful communication leads to self-correction. The therapist therefore functions both as a teacher and as an engineer who, like a trouble-shooter, helps his patient to repair his broken-down system of communication. To implement this task he discusses only those opinions, values and habits which interfere with the patient's proper communication, in the hope that conscious inspection and correct use, first in the therapeutic hour and later at large, will exert a corrective effect.

Correction of the patient's faulty ways of communication may involve any of the following:

> The patient's views pertaining to physical and social reality—that is, the context in which a communicative exchange takes place.
>
> His habits of reception.
>
> His ways of decision-making, scanning of memories, combining of newly received information with old information and abstraction.
>
> His skill of expression in word and gesture; his ability to engage in action and test out his conclusions.
>
> The appropriacy of his knowledge with regard to the topic he is communicating about.
>
> The appropriacy of his language and symbolization systems relative to the task he wishes to pursue.
>
> His skill in handling metacommunicative processes—that is, messages which, both in perception and in transmission, serve the purpose of instructing, interpreting or classifying.
>
> His awareness of the effects his behavior produces in others.

The driving force that makes any correction of communicative behavior possible is the sensation of pleasure experienced in successful communication. The human being is a herd animal whose relations with others in the group are implemented by the processes of communication. To be acknowledged is pleasurable; to be understood is even more pleasurable and to reach an agreement is perhaps most exciting. People therefore engage in communication because successful communication provides pleasure and failure of communication brings tension. Once the patient has discovered this he will make every effort to communicate effectively in order to secure this pleasure for himself. To this end, he has to relinquish his symptoms, put himself into a state of well-being and seek the company of others. And to maintain pleasurable communication he will have to look out also for the well-being of others

Still another goal of therapy is to impart to the patient the sense of freedom and pleasure associated with symbolic mastery. The restrictions upon action which are experienced in daily life can be compensated for by freedom in symbolic expression (3). Most patients suffer from the magic belief that thinking and feeling are equivalent to action. They believe that if they imagine something it will occur. When they realize that censorship comes at the action level rather than at the symbolic level, they experience relief and gain a feeling of freedom which is expressed in more independent thinking and action. Self-expression therefore becomes possible because it it recognized to occur through words or gestures and not to have physical consequences (4). While the patient acquires this symbolic freedom, he continually has to test out whether his thoughts and wishes really do not exert a powerful influence upon others. If the therapist can bring him to express his destructive thoughts in words, the patient improves. Apparently the causal linking of private thoughts with outer events can only be maintained as long as the thoughts remain secret. Public knowledge seems to destroy the magic.

When the patient has learned to distinguish fact from fantasy and has acquired a view of the world which in essential points coincides with that of others, he also has to reconcile what exists today with what existed yesterday and what will exist tomorrow. Successful integration of both the simultaneously existing realities at the present and the successive realities believed to have existed in the past or expected to exist in the future is essential to mature functioning.

THE IMPLEMENTATION OF THERAPEUTIC GOALS

The therapeutic attitude of the doctor is characterized by his acceptance of the patient's experiences without reproach for distortions of reality, by an eagerness to understand, by empathy for the patient's anxiety and by a readiness to act if necessary. Many patients test whether the doctor underestimates their judgment, whether he can correct himself and whether he is capable of evaluating their secret attitudes towards themselves. It is important for the patient to discover that the therapist can tolerate tension and even abuse, that he does not pretend to be omnipotent and that he is ruthlessly honest. If the doctor admits that there are things he cannot understand, the patient is likely to gain confidence in him. Above all, the therapist must regard behavior and action as baselines of reality and must consider words—including his own—as secondary. If discrepancies arise between talking and doing, action always speaks louder than words. Once the patient has learned to observe action and to base his conclusions upon action rather than words he has a basis on which to function.

The tactics of psychotherapy revolve around three communicative processes: understanding, acknowledgment and agreement. Understanding is a prerequisite of successful communication; it involves the meaningful integration of newly acquired information into a body of already existing knowledge. Understanding between two people occurs if correspondence of information can be established (6). Understanding, however, does not imply agreement. Agreement involves decision-making and commitment; acknowledgment and understanding do not. To reach an agreement, the participants must isolate one aspect of communication and confine the transaction to this aspect. In therapy, then, the first task is to achieve understanding—that is, the therapist must establish in his head a model of what is going on in and around the patient without judging, agreeing or committing himself to future action. Second, the therapist acknowledges that he has understood the patient. Finally, doctor and patient attempt to reach agreements on limited subjects or to state their disagreements. This last step can be taken only when the patient is strong enough to tolerate disagreement with his therapist. Once he has mastered these three basic processes the patient is ready to learn more complicated functions of communication.

Once the processes of understanding, acknowledging and agreeing are being used successfully by both doctor and patient they can be employed to tackle the nature of the patient's thoughts, fantasies and preoccupations. The result of such endeavors is known as insight, which is a combined affective-intellectual phenomenon. Richness of experience depends upon synchronization of perception with expression, of past memories with present events, of emotions with intellect, of subjective views with objective evidence. If this "putting together" is undertaken by another person—the therapist—it is called interpretation. At first the therapist adds two and two together; but as the patient acquires insight he learns to do this himself and he gradually finds that his thoughts, feelings and actions occur more in unison. He focuses less on part functions, he gets along without perpetually analyzing his behavior and he ceases to anticipate unrealistically. This functioning in unison, in turn, produces more insight, and this may be regarded as a sign that improvement has taken place. Insight—the connection of previously unrelated events—occurs because feelings and thoughts which heretofore had to be isolated and separated now can be brought together without anxiety.

The pleasure that the patient has found in successful communication can be utilized to promote further change. If he can achieve pleasurable exchange with the therapist, the patient is willing to acquire new information and to alter some of his views. Correction of old information occurs essentially through two kinds of feedback; an intraorganismic system focusing upon unconscious or repressed experiences that have not been considered previously, and an interpersonal system whereby the therapist, through his comments, forces the patient to integrate new information with older views. The therapist thus uses two procedures: one is commonly employed in any communication—namely, the transmission of information; the other is a method new to the patient—the mobilization of information inside himself. Juxtaposition of the information derived from the therapist with that derived from within the patient brings about tension which the patient has to resolve; and in order to resolve it he turns to established facts, tries to reach agreements with the therapist and adjusts his views accordingly.

The mobilization of information inside the patient is achieved through uncovering, discovering and recovering—the three royal roads to the unconscious (5). The orthodox method is to uncover by means of dream analysis and free association the unconscious motivations of the patient. This requires only continuous contact with one and the same person and the abandonment of conscious control. Psychoanalysts specialize in uncovering, although the method is not entirely specific for the analytic situation. We must assume that some uncovering was practiced in certain monks' orders in the middle ages (1, 8), and it has been used in recent brainwashing procedures as well (2).

The second method is to observe the manner in which unconscious forces are expressed in overt behavior. The skilled therapist then may respond in such a way that the patient will discover some of his unconscious concerns. Discovering is familiar to all people who have experienced suddenly coming face to face with an error they have made or remembering a name that they could not recall a moment before. Many educational procedures use the method of discovering to help the individual cope with self and his surroundings.

The third method is to react in such a way that the impact upon the patient will change some of his unconscious constellations without his being aware of it. In this process the patient becomes aware of his unconscious for a brief moment and then quickly covers it over again. The changes that occur in the unconscious are read from the temporarily altered external behavior of the patient.

In communication between people the unconscious forces operative inside the individual often contradict the overt actions or statements. To eliminate these contradictions and to establish communication that is synchronous at all levels are the goals of the communication therapies. But in reality there often exist contradictions that cannot be resolved, and here the process of repression becomes helpful. Although one can hardly speak of the "amount" of repression, it would appear that the frequency of repression—too often or not often enough—as well as the time duration of such a repression is of the utmost importance. While excessive repression is to blame for the pathology of hysterical characters, we find that in schizophrenic conditions insufficient repression is the source of the trouble.

As uncovering, discovering and recovering are the roads to the unconscious, so are covering up, taking for granted and forgetting the roads to logical, conscious thought and goal-directed action. The opposite of uncovering is covering up, whereby the patient succeeds in repressing conscious preoccupations. Taking for granted is the opposite of discovering; here the patient eliminates conscious concern by acting unself-consciously. Forgetting is the counterpart of recovering; it applies to the loss of a conscious thought sequence so that its impelling truth does not interfere with other thoughts of the individual. It appears that for healthy functioning each individual must possess flexible means of dealing with experience; at times he must be able to immerse details in the vast pool of the unconscious and at other times he must be able to recapture them for conscious inspection.

SUMMARY

The core of all psychiatric therapies is the improvements of the communicative behavior of the patient. This endeavor is based upon the following rationale:

1. An appropriate view of self and of the world is the prerequisite for intelligent and adaptive action and interaction with others.

2. Appropriate views can be acquired only if the functions of communication are intact and correction and self-correction operate properly.

3. If the patient never acquired mastery of certain aspects of communication, an attempt is made to teach these in therapy; and if his functions of communication are faulty, an attempt is made to correct these by somatic, psychological and social means.

NOTES

1. A. L. Huxley, *Devils of Loudun* (New York: Harper and Brothers, 1952).

2. R. J. Lifton, *Thought Reform and the Psychology of Totalism* (New York: W. W. Norton and Co., 1961).

3. J. A. M. Meerloo, *Conversation and Communication* (New York: International Universities Press, 1952).

4. R. T. Oliver and D. A. Barbara, *The Healthy Mind in Communion and Communication* (Springfield: Charles C. Thomas, 1962).

5. S. Rado, *Psychoanalysis and Behavior* (New York: W. W. Norton and Co., 1957).

6. J. Ruesch, *Disturbed Communication* (New York: Grune and Stratton, 1956).

7. J. Ruesch, *Therapeutic Communication* (New York: W. W. Norton and Co., 1961).

8. W. Sargant, *Battle for the Mind* (New York: Doubleday and Co., 1957).

HEALING AS PARTICIPATION: TILLICH'S "THERAPEUTIC THEOLOGY"*†

Hanna Colm

*P*aul Tillich's Systematic Theology has brought him the reputation of being "the most enlightening and therapeutic theologian of our time."[1] His new book, *The Courage To Be*, makes a significant contribution not only to theology and philosophy but also to the interpretation of psychotherapy, especially psychoanalysis. In this paper, I will not deal with the theological and philosophical aspects of Tillich's work per se but only with their bearing on psychoanalysis. I would like, however, to state briefly some of Tillich's basic concepts, particularly his doctrine of man, as developed in his *The Courage To Be*.

COURAGE AND EXISTENTIAL ANXIETIES

Courage, according to Tillich, is the self-affirmation of man's essential nature; it is being oneself and this means to follow one's inner aim. In being oneself man belongs to the "world"—other people from whom he is separated as an individual at the same time that he belongs to them. Since Tillich correlates self and world, he also correlates individualization and participation. Courage is always twofold in that it is self-affirmation in terms of both self-realization and of participation. Out of this twofold affirmation

* Hanna Colm, "Healing as Participation: Comments Based on Paul Tillich's Existential Philosophy," *Psychiatry*, XVI (1953), 99–111. Copyright 1953 by The William Hanson White Psychiatric Foundation, Inc. Reprinted by special permission of The William Alanson White Psychiatric Foundation, Inc.

† The consideration of Tillich's philosophy in this paper is confined to his latest book, *The Courage To Be*; New Haven, Yale Univ. Press, 1952.

For assistance in the preparation of this paper, I wish to make grateful acknowledgment to Claire Bloomberg.

grows the supreme courage "in which man accepts himself though he is not acceptable and accepts acceptance of himself wherever he participates, though he is not acceptable." In this supreme courage man experiences participation in the "ground of being" and comes to an acceptance of the structure of all being—which is basically a religious experience.

There are, in human existence, elements which conflict with man's essential self-affirmation. Therefore courage is always characterized by "self-affirmation in-spite-of. . . ." Courage involves the unavoidable sacrifice of elements which, although they belong to one's being, would prevent us from reaching our actual fulfillment were they not sacrificed. In this way the most essential part of our being prevails against the less essential.

What then are these elements which conflict with man's essential self-affirmation? Tillich thinks of these elements in terms of three existential anxieties which courage does not deny or evade but "takes upon itself":

> I suggest that we distinguish three types of anxiety according to the three directions in which nonbeing threatens being. Nonbeing threatens man's ontic self-affirmation, relatively in terms of fate, absolutely in terms of death. It threatens man's spiritual self-affirmation, relatively in terms of emptiness, absolutely in terms of meaninglessness. It threatens man's moral self-affirmation, relatively in terms of guilt, absolutely in terms of condemnation. . . . In all three forms anxiety is existential in the sense that it belongs to existence as such and not to an abnormal state of mind as in neurotic (and psychotic) anxiety.

Courage is the capacity of man to deal affirmatively with these anxieties.

In different cultures and in different periods of history, varying manifestations of these three basic anxieties have been predominant. But in one form or another, these anxieties are always there. Man is not himself, he is not creative, without them. It follows, then, that neither religion nor therapy can act to free man from these anxieties—they can only help him deal with these anxieties affirmatively.

PATHOLOGICAL ANXIETIES

Although Tillich makes a distinction between pathological and existential anxieties, he emphasizes that there is often no clear-cut boundary line between the anxiety of the healthy and the anxiety of the sick. In a period of history in which there is rapid change in reality, "a fanatical defender of the established order" may be as compulsive as the neurotic who defends his imaginary world. Or again, religion even if it "does not lead to or does not directly support pathological self-reduction, . . . can reduce the openness of man to reality, above all to the reality which is himself."

Tillich's distinction between existential and pathological anxieties is of great interest to the therapist or analyst in that it can be useful in elucidating the direction in which therapy or analysis should move.

"Pathological anxiety," Tillich says, "is a state of existential anxiety under special conditions." What then are these special conditions? Tillich sees man's experience of meaninglessness, radical doubt, despair, and loneliness in our time as the cause of this neurotic development. The Enlightenment took from man the absoluteness of God and created a feeling that all values in life are relative—"God is dead," as Nietzsche and the Existentialists have put it. The concentration of the Enlightenment on technical conquest of the world has fostered greater urbanization and mechanization of those activities of living which had previously been meaningful. Thus life has lost its previous meaning. The neurotic is the person in our time who is most sensitive to this dehumanization. Because he is, more than the average person, sensitive and threatened by the negative of life, of being, and of himself, he withdraws to a limited area of living to avoid the negative and its risk. Neurosis is a method through which the human being tries to escape from anxiety by escaping from being himself: "Neurosis is the way of avoiding nonbeing by avoiding being." In the neurotic state, some of the potentialities of the self "are not admitted to actualization, because actualization of being implies the acceptance of nonbeing and its anxiety." The neurotic "surrenders part of his potentialities in order to save what is left." He has "settled down to a fixed, though limited and unrealistic, self-affirmation. This is, so to speak, the castle to which he has retired and which he defends with all means of psychological resistance against attack." The neurotic in his anxious withdrawal separates himself from the whole of life —he is "a separated part from unity with the whole and disintegrates in his isolation." This sickness is a more or less total negation of his essential need for "being a part"—of experiencing communion with other human beings—and a negation of his basic relation to other men as partners. He closes himself off from significant areas of life because his trust and confidence are undermined by his doubts about life—because the polar tension in life between the positive and the negative, the individual and the whole, threatens him. He is a captive of his anxieties.

> [The healthy, average person also] keeps himself away from the extreme situations, [but he does it] by dealing courageously with concrete objects of fear. He is usually not aware of nonbeing and anxiety in the depth of his personality.... His anxiety does not drive him to the construction of imaginary worlds. . . . The neurotic is sick and needs healing because of the conflict in which he finds himself with reality. . . . Pathological anxiety, in spite of its creative potentialities, is illness and danger and must be healed by "nonbeing taken into a courage" which enables man to deal with anxieties affirmatively and realistically. The intensity of the neurotic can make him creative though he is less "extensive"—expansive—than the normal.

This distinction between existential and pathological anxieties suggests a division between the ministerial and the therapeutic functions.[2] However, since neurotic anxiety is "the inability to take one's existential anxiety upon oneself," the ministerial function comprehends both itself and the medical function. Conversely, "the psychotherapist can implicitly communicate courage-to-be and the power of taking existential anxiety upon oneself. He does not become a minister in doing so and he never should try to replace the minister, but he can become a helper to ultimate self-affirmation, thus performing a ministerial function." We must recognize that the healer often has to fulfill a ministerial function in a time in which a great many people have no access to institutional religion and professional ministers.

THE AIM OF PSYCHOANALYSIS

In a recent lecture on "The Goals of Psychoanalysis,"[3] Erich Fromm described the way in which the goals of present-day practice have changed from those formulated by Freud. Freud, according to Fromm, helped man to emancipate himself from the conflict between his instinctive drives and the moral prejudices of nineteenth-century society. This emancipation was an essential part of man's gaining the courage to be himself. Fromm contrasted this achievement of Freud's with much of present-day practice which is concerned with adjustment of the patient to the necessities of his personal or office life. Yet I think that this kind of adjustment should not be belittled. In a time of mass neurosis and limited psychotherapeutic resources, some superficial help can make life more livable. Since such help does not go to the roots of the neurosis, many patients are of course not satisfied with symptom treatment. Character neurosis, as Fromm points out, requires a transformation of the person. Fromm says the patient ultimately must learn to love; Tillich says he must gain courage to take upon himself the anxieties inherent in human existence. The two concepts are not inconsistent with each other.

As I have noted, Tillich's concept of self-affirmation is not an individualistic concept. It is affirmation by self-realization *and* by participation in the whole to which man belongs, in which process love and trust will naturally be freed. Virtue, according to Tillich—"and love is the highest virtue"—is the highest form of self-assertion of which a person is capable. The analytic aim, according to Tillich, is to free the withdrawn human being so that he can find the deep-reaching courage to affirm himself. Out of the person's own restoration and affirmation of his essential being will grow his own individual form of love. This courage to affirm oneself presupposes a lack of defenses against the negative in one's being. Out of the experience of the acceptability of the negative in oneself will grow an acceptance of the ontological structure of life which, in turn, enables one to trust the negative aspects of life—accepting the fact that the negative and the positive in life are in dynamic and ultimately constructive tension. This courage accepts as meaningful the negative in oneself, in one's fellow man, and in all life; such courage naturally creates respect, tolerance, and love for the other person, who also is a participant in life. It involves the acceptance of the "demonic" in oneself and in life as a potentially constructive element of being, which is actually a religious experience.

This exalted concept of the aims of psychoanalysis is not a mere invention of the philosopher. It is, I believe, a reality with which every psychotherapist is familiar. Many times a patient who comes to analysis because of troublesome symptoms, finds out in the course of analysis that his trouble stems from his feeling that he is just a ball kicked around by strange forces inside himself. Since he cannot control these forces, he becomes depressed, hates himself, and is tempted to throw life away. In short, life is meaningless to him because he cannot find his way to self-affirmation.

The following case clearly illustrates the change in a patient from merely pathological anxiety about symptoms to existential concern:

> A woman who came to me for help for her child saw very soon that the child was a second edition of herself, and that it was she herself who wanted help. Like her daughter, she suffered from chronic diarrhea, which was a continuing source of embarrassment to her in her work; she felt that this was her main problem. But by the time the symptom had disappeared—which was actually very early in her analytic work—she had reached the point where she saw very clearly what lay behind her symptom; she had forgotten that the symptom itself was her original complaint. Actually she was afraid that she was "missing" life; this feeling stemmed from her self-hate, which she projected onto her child.
>
> Once the symptom had disappeared, existential anxiety of death, guilt, and meaninglessness became evident. Her hidden pathological death wishes for her child were connected with a feeling of the worthlessness and the unacceptability of her own life, and of its utter meaninglessness. Her feelings of worthlessness and unacceptability arose from the fact that she had hated her own mother who had been overambitious. The patient's mother had had to be the "queen" in every situation, with no place next to her for her daughter. The patient's intense hatred of her mother, who had blocked her attempts at self-affirmation, produced feelings of guilt in the patient and the need for self-punishment. In the course of her work with me, it became clear that the death wishes for her child carried with them the fear of her own death—the fear that she would not be able to affirm her life and give it meaning and value. Here the originally pathological anxiety became existential concern.

THE PSYCHOANALYST'S ROLE

What help can then be given to a patient who suffers from his pathological defenses against existential anxiety? Tillich again makes certain suggestions which, I believe, closely correspond to much of what is going on in psychoanalytic practice today. For instance, Tillich says "that the courage-to-be is the courage to accept oneself as accepted in spite of being unacceptable. . . . Accepting acceptance though being unacceptable is the basis for the courage of confidence."[4]

There are three essential elements in this experience of confidence—the patient's experience (1) of being unacceptable, (2) of being accepted by somebody else, and (3) of accepting the acceptance. The following sentence states in the most concise form Tillich's interpretation of what is going on in an analysis as it comes to grips with the patient's ultimate concern: "In the communion of healing, for example the psychoanalytical situation, the patient participates in the healing power of the helper by whom he is accepted although he feels unacceptable." This will ultimately also result in the patient's active acceptance of the analyst in *his* humanness and of the finite structure of life in all of its aspects.

In terms of the existential aim of psychoanalysis, Tillich questions the idea which has developed in psychoanalytic theory that the analyst should not judge. This idea of avoiding judgments has grown out of Freud's recognition that the therapist can help the patient only if the patient helps himself; that is, he can only help the patient to verbalize and clarify his subconscious conflict and to break the barrier of moral judgment. According to Freud, the main function of the healer is to listen. Even facts that are "shocking" in terms of the moral code of society are accepted by the therapist as natural events without judging them as being either good or bad.

Tillich feels that the patient cannot have the experience of being accepted if the therapist remains a silent or "neutral" wall as the patient reveals his troubles. Freud's idea that the analyst should be a blank screen on which the patient projects his difficulties and conflicts no longer makes sense once the assumption is made that the patient's primary problem is not his symptom, but is his difficulties in relationships with his fellow man. Then the problem of acceptability moves into the center of the conflict.

RECENT DEVELOPMENTS IN EUROPE

In recent European literature,[5] the role of the analyst has been reexamined in the light of the existential interpretation of neurotic conflict. This examination of a scientific discipline by what is essentially philosophy represents an interesting and important development in European thinking. The existentialist's and the analyst's approach had entirely different origins.

Freud's emphasis on the individual as a prey to his impulses and drives found little response in the thinking of existentialism. Jung's criticism of Freud, however, served as a bridge between the two modes of thinking. Jung, who enjoyed much wider acceptance in Europe than in America, showed a genuine concern about the individual as a whole and his relation to the "collective unconscious." Although existentialism as a philosophy and psychoanalysis as a method of treatment basically moved in different directions, some existentialists became deeply interested in the philosophical basis of analysis and some analysts became interested in the practical implications of existential thinking. Out of this twofold interest arose the European existentialist analyst. The existentialist analyst went beyond Freud and Jung in that he felt that man could not become himself merely through an inner integration with himself, but must experience an integration between the self and the other.[6] This integration takes place when there is a mutual realization of the self and the other with acceptance and confirmation. Buber says, "Man wants to be accepted in his being by man and wants to mean something to the being of the other person. An animal does not need this acceptance but it belongs to the essence of the human being."[7] Trueb also points out that "in his self as the ground of his being man is essentially made to affirm himself in encounter with and responding to the other person."[8] Only out of the "synthesis of the individual with the situation of his world can human spiritual inner life grow."[9] Neurosis is the outcome of the refusal of a self-centered self to meet another self.

The aim of the therapeutic process is therefore the recovery of the willingness of the patient to encounter the world in which he is placed; and the recovery of this willingness constitutes in itself the "healing" of the person. As Trueb says, "Only genuine partnership can save the sick person who has withdrawn from dynamic encounter with the world into isolation."[10] Here the therapist is not merely a figure on whom the patient projects his ideas and conflicts, but is also genuinely and necessarily his partner. The patient must make contact with the therapist as a representative of the world, for it is the world's finiteness and limitations toward the patient which have made him untrusting and thus sick.[11]

To sum up the approach of the European existentialist therapist in contrast to Freud and Jung: A neurotic person cannot be changed or transformed merely by going through a monologic process by which he gains knowledge of himself or of the collective unconscious in himself. The goal can be approached only through two diametrically opposed processes, one being as essential as the other: (1) the elimination of the patient's unconscious defensive processes, enabling the patient gradually to face his inner being—the positive and the negative in himself; and (2) the gradual reopening of contact with the world through the encounter with the therapist. The weight in this approach is on the dialogic study in which the patient tries to understand *with* the analyst his own inner processes. It is in this encounter that his trust in himself and his acceptance of himself grow, since he learns to see himself not as exceptionally different from other persons, but as one who, like them, needs and depends on other human beings. Thus he will gradually learn to understand and accept the tragic finiteness of the world by which he was hurt, and to re-evaluate his own failure and guilt in withdrawing from its imperfections. This re-evaluation can only be experienced in the encounter with another person—"healing through contact and encounter with another person," as Trueb says. "This participation—encounter—potentially grows into a we-experience of closeness and friendship."

"PARTNERSHIP" IN THE MEANING OF SULLIVAN AND TILLICH

In this country, Harry Stack Sullivan was one of the first to see analysis as an interpersonal experience; this is basically the same approach as that of the European existentialists, though with a different rationale.[12] Therapy, according to Sullivan, is observant participation. In order to heal a neurotic person who has withdrawn defensively from contact with people and has isolated himself from real living, Sullivan describes as *essential* the experiencing of the interrelation of the patient and the therapist and the intensive study of it. Only in this partnership can the patient learn to know his own difficulties in relation to another person, and to sort out those parts of his relationship which are real in terms of his partner, and those in which he reacts defensively and parataxically—that is, in terms of his past. Sullivan was aware that the patient could not accept this as participation resulting in acceptance as long as the therapist considered it as merely an objective experience. He encouraged his students to show some irritation or anger to their patients when they were in the later stages of analysis if it came up in the participating relationship—although this anger would have to be gauged in terms of the patient's vulnerability. At the same time, he demanded that the student rigorously and objectively observe the feeling evoked in himself by the analysand in order to understand the interpersonal process.

This approach of participant interaction is actually very close to Tillich's feeling that the analyst who acts only as a mute catalyzer will not be able to achieve the ultimate aim of analysis. For Tillich, the analysis cannot be a one-way street but must be a real encounter. From the existential point of view, he asserts that the therapeutic experience can become alive and transforming only if it is a genuine partnership, offered in the spirit of understanding and acceptance: "You must participate in a self in order to know what it *is*. By participation you change it." This acceptance is in contrast to the patient's usual experience with his fellow man in that the society has previously rejected him hostilely because of its inability to understand his unrealistic involvement with the past. For the patient, this means that only through continuing encounters with other persons does he become and remain a person. This partnership experience, for Tillich, is the core of the healing experience; without it the patient cannot find his way to the courage to affirm himself through participation.

TILLICH'S CONCEPT OF JUDGING

A new and essential part of Tillich's concept of participation is the idea that the patient must have the experience of being judged, which Tillich believes is a precondition of feeling "accepted in-spite-of." The patient must have the experience of encountering another person who accepts him "in-spite-of," which implies judging *and* accepting. This point seems to be implied in the thinking of the European existentialists since they place stress on mutual encounter and acceptance. It is also vaguely suggested by Sullivan in his formulation of the importance of a genuine response of irritation or anger on the part of the analyst as a necessary precondition for the patient's understanding of his "sick" or "unrealistic" behavior and of the response it evokes in others. In neither case, however, is this point brought to focus and discussion as in Tillich.

For Tillich, judging is one of the most essential factors in the healing process. This judging is not in terms of any accepted moral code, but in terms of the patient's own being.[13] Does the patient act in genuine self-affirmation or with defensiveness? If acting in self-affirmation, the patient shows a genuine response to the situation in which he acts. If acting with defensiveness, he hides and protects his genuine feeling, carrying over responses which originated in the past as a protective measure and do not fit into the present situation. When a person acts with defensiveness in a real-life situation, the other person is usually hurt—he becomes the victim of the parataxic involvement of the first person. In the encounter with the analyst, who stands for the other, the patient learns to understand the difference between his genuine responses and his defensive, parataxic responses. It is here that the importance of "being judged" is apparent. In his existential concern about his lack of courage to accept himself "in-spite-of" the patient needs a realistic experience of facing his full being—his negative as well as his positive aspects—with another person who judges the patient with standards of his own inner being and *accepts* both the negative and the positive.

Without the experience of judgment, acceptance loses its depth. Tillich asserts that, even if the analyst follows Freudian theory by attempting to avoid making judgments, the patient actually may regard the analyst as a judge whose acceptance has significance to the patient only because he respects the analyst's judgment. If the analyst's acceptance is too easy, it loses its healing power. Such acceptance cannot be accepted by the patient and the patient thinks of the acceptance as a "condoning" unless the experience of being nonacceptable is deep and genuine. The analyst who, by his detachment, gives the impression that nothing really matters and brushes aside all guilt because it can all be understood in the light of what happened to one's parents or to oneself in infancy, can be of only limited help. The patient can accept the acceptance only if the analyst has shared the patient's experience of guilt and doubt, and has taken them seriously as they have manifested themselves in the patient's social life. Without this judgment, the analyst would prevent his patient from "taking guilt into his self-affirmation"; he would be standing in the way of the patient's "acceptance in-spite-of." The experience of acceptance in spite of oneself can reach such a redeeming depth only when the analysis has pierced through the superficial acceptability and into the judging and transforming communion with another person, who—according to Tillich's theological concept—represents "God and God's acceptance." God is the "ground of being," and it is the "ground of being" as manifested in man which contains the potential power of acceptance of that which is separated—the self and the world; in religious terms this power is grace. In other words, grace, creativity, new beginning, healing—call it what you will—is a factor in the "ground of being" and can be felt in man through an experience of acceptance and forgiving between men. It is useless for the analyst, in an attempt to be unjudgmental, to teach the patient to merely substitute the words "constructive" or "unconstructive" for "good" and "bad." Anxiety cannot be eliminated by semantics. Only if the patient accepts the judgment of himself and the analyst as valid, can the patient's experience of self-acceptance and of being accepted by the analyst "in-spite-of" obtain the depth that is salvation.

"Self-affirmation in spite of anxiety of guilt and condemnation presupposes participation in something that transcends the self," Tillich says. It cannot grow merely through an inner psychic process of knowing oneself and one's inner processes. In the communion of healing as found in the analytic situation, the patient participates in the healing power of the helper —as Tillich puts it—by whom he is judged and accepted although he feels himself unacceptable. The healer in this relationship does not stand for himself as an individual, but represents the objective power of the "ground of being" for acceptance and self-affirmation. This objective power works in the patient through the healer. *Of course* it must be embodied in a person who can realize guilt, who can judge, and who can accept in spite of judgment. The analyst can judge because he is a human being and because he genuinely has the social standards of judgment of his time and his culture. But his understanding does not permit him to condemn; *because* he understands, he forgives. Tillich's assumption leads him to the conclusion that analytic theoretical methods will presently have to come to terms with this existential point of view.

PARTNERSHIP AND JUDGING IN THE FRAME-WORK OF ANALYTIC WORK

Since Freud, the effort of psychoanalysis to avoid any moralistic judging in terms of the social code of the time has driven it into a nonjudging attitude, which is an outgrowth of the rationalism of Freud's time. I believe that at the present time the existentialist approach has something to offer to psychoanalytic theory in that it points out the necessary role which a nonmoralistic judging can play in the psychoanalytic process.

In this country, Sullivan's approach, as I have mentioned before, represents a partial step in the same general direction. He has thought of analysis as a partnership experience in which genuine emotional responses on the part of the analyst act as a therapeutic agent in the relationship.

These responses are naturally more guarded in the initial phases of therapy because of the intense vulnerability of the patient. Gradually, as the patient's vulnerability decreases, as he becomes more trusting and gains the strength to face his own inner reality in relation to others, the analyst dares to be less guarded and begins to share some of his emotional reactions with the patient, in an attempt to elucidate with the patient his parataxic ways of living and the response these evoke in others. To couch Sullivan's thinking in Tillich's terms, one might say that the analyst's reaction—irritation or anger—certainly often reflects judgment, while the immediate attempt of both analyst and analysand to understand how the analyst evoked these emotions offers a very realistic experience of uninterrupted, continuing acceptance on a deeper, more essential level.

In the course of an analysis, the patient is usually very deeply concerned for fear he will be judged and condemned by the analyst. He fears that he will lose the analyst's love as he reveals himself with all his negative feelings —his envy and his hate. The analyst who responds by making the patient see that he is more concerned with getting love than with loving often misses the point. What is really at stake is the patient's overwhelmingly anxious concern with his own self-judgment and his fear lest the analyst judge and condemn him. Both analyst and patient know that they react, at least somewhat, to the patient's confessed envy and hate, in terms of the social standards of the culture in which both participate. It would not be honest for the analyst to try to help the analysand forget about these standards, in order to help him out of self-condemnation. This would be helping him to live less responsibly. What is needed is the warmth of understanding and sympathy—a we-feeling between the participants—which makes it possible for both to look at the patient's self-condemnation, to judge, and to accept in spite of the judgment. It would not help for the analyst to ask, "Why do you keep on judging yourself?" In our culture, such a question is unrealistic and would appear phony to the analysand. It is much more honest for the analyst to say—and it is essential for the patient to hear— "Your feeling is indeed negative here. Why can you not accept something negative in yourself?" Or, "Why do you think I cannot accept the negative in you?" This brings the experience of being judged *and* accepted into clearer focus for the patient. The analyst needs to understand with the patient in what ways the negative is in productive tension to the positive, and in what ways the negative is unproductive because it has been kept out of awareness—to distinguish between the areas in which the patient can still grow and those in which he has to accept his limits.

If one considers analysis as an "encounter" rather than merely an impersonal projection of the patient's feelings on the screen of the analyst, then it seems logical to question the theory that the analyst's approach at the beginning of analysis should be basically different from that used at the end. The present intense attempt of some analysts to keep their own human reactions out of the picture in the beginning of analysis seems questionable to Tillich and also to me, although of course the analyst must recognize the patient's vulnerability in the beginning and be somewhat more guarded, as Sullivan points out. When the patient is overwhelmed with facing his hate or envy or competitive violence, a "we" response, such as "We tend to be hateful if we are frightened or frustrated," can be more helpful than merely a detached, unjudging "This is your defense," which only adds to the patient's agony and loneliness and self-condemnation. The "we" response gives the patient a feeling of communion in human finiteness. The analyst who says "we," facing with his patient the hate he condemns, conveys without words his acceptance of his own and the patient's humanness. This is evident in group analysis, in which the "we" approach is implicit and the patient sees that the other participants struggle with the same difficulties and reactions that he does. The analyst who says "we tend to" also counteracts an unnecessary and unrealistic build-up of himself as perfect in the eyes of the patient. This response conveys to the patient that the analyst accepts his own humanness : it is probably the most convincing way of showing the patient that he is accepted in spite of his hate. Both Trueb and Binswanger say in effect that this response conveys the feeling, "We meet as partners in our human shortcomings and inadequacies"—an experience which the patient will have fully only at the end of analysis when the analyst allows his own emotional human reactions to come more freely into the open.

PSYCHOANALYSIS AS A MUTUAL ENCOUNTER

In recent literature, countertransference has been discussed in such a way as to bring into pronounced focus the necessity for an alive feeling in the psychoanalytic situation, including *mutual* judging and acceptance.[14] In the end phase of analysis, a fully realistic partnership experience necessarily comes into being and therefore into the full awareness of both analyst and analysand. In terms of an analysis which reaches an existential depth, the culmination of the interpersonal experience sets in when being accepted as a real person becomes of mutual concern, and is at stake for both.

For the analyst, this means that he can now allow his countertransference reactions to show openly and without guard—irritation, anger, competition, or even hate, as well as friendly and admiring feelings. This happens when the analyst begins to feel—often unconsciously at first—that the patient is healed and is potentially an *equal* partner. He dares to trust that the analysand will not lose the newly gained "we" feeling in a realistic experience with the fully human person of the analyst. In the course of this phase, the analyst himself enters an existential experience in which his courage to affirm himself and feel accepted "in-spite-of" is at stake for him also. Now he has passed beyond the mere verbal use of "we"—he dares to affirm his humanness and to live with his patient the concept of the potential creativeness of human finiteness in all its aspects. It is at this point that the analyst will have to go through the experience of anxiety. Will he be accepted or condemned by his patient? The analyst has to assert his own courage—the courage of trust and confidence that another human being will accept him, and the risk of possible failure. As the patient struggles with this challenge, the analyst will still have to help him. Yet this is the necessary culmination of the existential encounter of two human beings who struggle for *mutual* trust in each other which is no longer based on the patient's expectation of perfectness, but on his newly gained realistic concept of the finiteness of every human being. Here, finally, the acceptance of the bipolar structure of all life is lived out in a "we" experience.

For the patient, the fact that the analyst has dared to trust and has opened up to the patient as a fully equal partner, with the courage that is needed to expose himself in his human finiteness—to expose the nonbeing elements in himself—means that the analyst has ceased to consider him as a patient. It means that the patient has risen to the "courage of accepting the acceptance of another person" and is able to accept the analyst on realistic terms "in-spite-of." Now the analysis has become a mutual existential experience of trust and acceptance; the patient and the analyst are partners in a relationship which is potentially open for the mutuality of love. This is the most threatening phase for the analyst.[15] To cite Heidegger and Binswanger, "While in the first part of an analysis the encounter is necessarily in the mode of 'care,' this last phase is a real person-to-person encounter with the potentiality of failure as well as of mutuality and love."[16] If an analysis reaches this depth, both participants come out of this final struggle changed and enriched.

The most important factor in the existential healing process is not merely the skill of the analyst; it lies in the fact that he dares to be a real person who lives out with his patient the areas that he has opened up for the patient. He must be aware of the existential importance of his own courage and honesty. In the course of discussing countertransference and its role in analysis, many analysts are coming to think that participation is a necessary ingredient of analysis, though we are still trying to formulate this concept and have not yet fully come to terms with the problem involved. Weigert, in a recent talk on "Limits to Therapeutic Expectations in Psychoanalysis Due to Countertransference,"[17] sees the analyst's participation in terms of a dynamic inner process in which there is a polar swing from identification to detachment. For Tillich this is not enough. He sees participation in the sense of relatedness, as an encounter between two persons. In his sense, healing cannot occur merely in the course of the objective and detached elucidation of the patient's behavior, important as this is in the understanding of his defenses. The weight for Tillich is on participation—not merely on one (the analyst) identifying with the other—as it involves *two* persons who take part as two different human beings, who meet with different feeling values and judgments, and whose very difference provides a factor essential for the healing process. In other words, it is necessary that another person understand objectively, react with true feeling, judge, and accept. The patient must have the experience of the "other person" in the analyst as one who can accept "in-spite-of." Only in this way can the patient come to terms with "taking guilt into his self-affirmation." "No self-acceptance is possible if one is not accepted in a person-to-person relation," as Tillich says.

As Buber[18] says, "The patient in distress does not actually call for merely the dependable skill of the therapist, but he calls up the analyst's own 'ground': that is, the self of the therapist, who is—beyond methods and experience—familiar with the demonic in himself and is also blessed with the humble power of struggling with it and surmounting it—again and again willing to struggle and surmount the demonic." The analyst has to be most of all a person who is aware of the existential importance (in order to be able to help others) of his own courage and his own honesty in never-ceasing willingness to struggle and surmount his own conflicts and the negative of his own being. I agree with Tillich that analytic practice today does not recognize to the fullest extent the fact that the person of the analyst as a partner to the patient actually plays at least as great a role as his technical skill.

In Tillich's terms, the healing power of mutual acceptance and love is a religious experience: "The source of the courage which affirms itself 'in-spite-of' is the ground of life—God." And man's courage is the key to the ground of life—to the creativeness of being—which we call in religious terms "grace." Tillich would call the final experience between analyst and analysand an experience of mutual forgiveness, which is again religious: "God's forgiveness can be experienced only in the forgiveness among men."

In Tillich's terms, the analysis is also religious in that it tries to integrate and affirm the being as well as the nonbeing of the analysand who has heretofore tried to escape the nonbeing in himself: "Nonbeing drives being out of its seclusion. . . . The demonic is experienced not as unambiguously negative but as a part of the creative power of being." For Tillich, the self-affirmation "in-spite-of" that reveals the power of being in every act of courage is equivalent to "Faith," again a religious term. This Faith "bridges the infinite gap between the infinite and the finite by accepting that in spite of it the power of being is present, that he who is separated is accepted." Such Faith is a state of being which transends everything that exists and in which everything that exists participates; it is a state of being which is grasped by the power of being. He who is grasped by this power is able to affirm himself because he knows that he is affirmed by the very power of being. For the sick and neurotic person, the analytic working through of his defensive and life-evading anxieties becomes, in Tillich's view, a religious experience. He feels that a clear-cut distinction between the minister's function and that of the analyst is not possible. This does not mean that each takes the role of the other, but rather an attitude of humility and co-operation on both sides, since by necessity each is trespassing beyond his field of competence.

In concluding this paper, it has occurred to me that the following case of a psychotic child whom I treated illustrates the existential role that acceptance plays in therapy and will perhaps best serve to communicate the way in which I feel Tillich's approach represents an adjunct to therapy.

Peter's psychosis was grounded in the feeling that he was condemned by himself, his family, and God. His mother had grown up in a severely condemning and punishing religious atmosphere. Religion had become identical to her with guilt and condemnation, feelings which she had conveyed to the child despite her earnest belief that she had overcome them in herself. Peter's father had been away during the war. The mother, being a very dependent woman, had longed for his return, and she had made a sort of little husband of the child during her husband's absence. When the father did return and the little boy was suddenly shut off from the cozy relationship he had had with his mother, he was full of hatred for the interloper. Because of the mother's unconscious condemnation of hatred, she could not help the child to forgive himself by recognizing and understanding his feelings. Instead she allowed herself to be fooled by his frantic attempts to love his father. This left Peter alone with his secret hatred, and he was prey to feelings of guilt and self-condemnation because of it. As a result he felt an outcast and punished himself by excluding himself from human relationships to such an extent that he was unable to talk sense; his communications consisted of a sort of mumbling gibberish interspersed with actual words.

For over a year he played out his crime in many versions, but he never allowed me to really reach him. Since he feared my condemnation, there was no real communication between us—merely talk from him or from me. He assumed that I would not accept him any more than he did himself. His only way of getting into contact with me was to shoot at me with a toy pistol, showing a degree of horror and despair I have never before seen in a child. This was his defense against what he felt was my nonacceptance to which his own lack of self-acceptance had condemned him. Gradually, I did come to feel rejected and unacceptable because of my inability to evoke his trust.

Although I felt unhappy, I did not want to give up trying. Then he began to change his pattern—instead of shooting at me he shot in intense anxiety at the sky through the window. It seemed to me that he was shooting in despair at God; but at the same time he was revealing some trust in me when he allowed himself to do this. When I asked him what made him shoot at God, he responded by wrapping himself up in the curtains and hiding. This meant to me that I had finally understood him and had reached him for the first time. In addition, I understood this response to mean, "I am unbelievably bad." Again he was unapproachable for a long time, although he continued to shoot at God. At times he stopped this shooting and sang, "Jesus loves me." But I felt that the despair with which he sang said in effect, "He loves all the others—not me."

Some hours later, as Peter was shooting at God, a little girl who had come too early for her hour stormed into the playroom. Peter could not stand to have her come into the room with us, and he beat at me with his gun with full force. When I took the gun out of his hand, he went on beating at me with his fists. As I warded him off, I suddenly felt that this child was fighting himself physically closer and closer to me. I took him into my arms, saying "Peter, this is what you really want." His fury stopped. He put his head on my shoulder and stayed that way for the rest of his hour.

From that time on he could talk to me and communicate in a meaningful way. In his reliving of his first experience of intense jealousy and envy toward his father, which was so condemned by himself, he could show me his anguish and hatred. He felt understood and accepted. To me this meant that he had gained some self-acceptance through the mere fact that I had gone on trying to help him throughout the long, frustrating months when I had actually despaired of gaining his trust. His first step into the state of being acceptable "in-spite-of" was apparently taken on the day when I understood without horror that he was shooting at God. Some hours later, he felt my judgment when I said, "No, you can't beat me"; at the same time, he had the feeling of being understood and forgiven when I took him in my arms, saying "this is what you really want." In this moment of his utter despair as he was reliving the situation which caused his self-condemnation, the feeling of being acceptable won out over the self-rejection. At this moment he had also actually forgiven me: he "accepted" me in spite of the many wrong attempts to help him—he opened up to me "in-spite-of."

NOTES

1. Theodore M. Greene, "Paul Tillich and our secular Culture"; in *The Theology of Paul Tillich*, edited by Charles W. Kegley and R. W. Breball; New York, Library of Living Theology, Vol. I, 1952.

2. Tillich does not limit either the ministerial or the medical function to the narrow professional definition.

3. This lecture was given at the Washington School of Psychiatry, January 18, 1953.

4. Tillich remarks in this context: "One must remind theologians and ministers that in the fight against the anxiety of guilt by psychotherapy the idea of acceptance has received the attention and gained the significance which in the Reformation period was to be seen in phrases like 'forgiveness of sins' or 'justification through faith.' "

5. Martin Heidegger, *Sein und Zelt*; Halle, Max Niemeyer, 1927.

Karl Jaspers, *Von der Wahrheit*; München, R. Piper, 1947.

Ludwig Binswanger, "Uber Psychotherapie" and "Uber die daseinsanalytische Forschungsrichtung in der Psychiatrie," *Zur phaenomenologischen Anthropologie*; Bern, A. Francke, A. G. Verlag, 1947.

Ludwig Binswanger, *Die Bedcutung der Dasinsanalytik Martin Heideggers für das Selbstverständnis der Psychiatrie*; Bern, A. Francke A. G. Verlag, 1947.

Hans Trueb, *Heilung aus der Begegnung*; Stuttgart, Ernst Klett, 1951.

Martin Buber, *Urdistanz und Beziehung*; Heidelberg, Verlag Lampert, Schneider, 1951

Martin Buber, *Das Problem des Menschen*; Heidelberg, Verlag Lampert Schneider, 1948.

Romano Guardini, *Die Macht*; Würzburg, Werkbund Verlag, 1951.

Romano Guardini, *Das Ende der Neuzeit*; Würzburg, Werkbund Verlag, 1951.

Ernst Michel, *Der Partner Gottes*; Heidelberg, Verlag Lampert Schneider, 1946.

Ernst Blum, "Grundsätzliches zur Psychotherapeutischen Situation," *Psyche* (1950) 4:537-556.

Edith Weigert, "Existentialism and Its Relations to Psychotherapy," *Psychiatry* (1949) 12:399-412.

6. This development has found its fullest expression in Tillich and Fromm, and, more recently, in Rollo May.

7. Martin Buber, *Urdistanz und Bezichung*, reference footnote 5.

8. Trueb, reference footnote 5; p. 39.

9. Trueb, reference footnote, 5; p. 39.

10. Trueb, reference footnote, 5; p. 48.

11. See Felix Schottlaender, "Das Problem der Begegnung in der Psychotherapie," *Psyche* (1946) 2: 494–507.

12. Harry Stack Sullivan, *Conceptions of Modern Psychiatry*; Washington, D.C., William Alanson White Psychiatric Foundation, 1947, See also Edith Weigert, reference footnote 5.

13. See Edith Weigert, "Die Entwicklung der Psychoanalytischen Ausbildung in U.S.A." *Psyche* (1950) 4: 632–640: "Classical psychoanalysis has taken justified pride in its objectivity toward human value systems, for it has undertaken the task of examining the dynamic factors that account for the values and ideals that a person has. It is, however, a widespread error if the psychoanalyst is considered to be a value-free researcher. The endeavor to promote mental health is a value to which the psychoanalyst is obligated. Other values valid for the analyst are the patient's growth, maturation, inner independence (which must be brought into accord with social adjustment), as well as freedom from excessive anxiety and the ability productively to bear anxiety and denial. The psychoanalyst obligated to these general human values keeps separate his personal, religious, or political valuations from his professional work in the service of the higher value of scientific objectivity" (p. 638).

See also Erich Fromm's *Man for Himself: An Inquiry into the Psychology of Ethics*; New York, Rinehart, 1947.

14. See, for example, Edith Weigert, "Contribution to the Problem of Terminating Psychoanalysis," *Psychoanalytic Quart.* (1952) 21: 465–480.

15. Edith Weigert, reference footnote 13: "The analyst himself also experiences his analysand as his judge, as parents often experience their children as the next generation, which will survive them."

16. Ludwig Binswanger, *Die Bedeutung der Daseinsanalytik Martin Heideggers*, reference footnote 5.

17. This talk was given before the Washington Psychoanalytic Society on February 21, 1953, as part of a panel discussion on "Contraindications and Limits to Therapeutic Expectations in Psychoanalysis."

18. Preface by Martin Buber, to Hans Trueb, reference footnote 5; p. 10.

A PSYCHIATRIST LOOKS AT HIS PROFESSION*

Robert Coles

*r*ecently, in the emergency ward of the Children's Hospital in Boston, an eight-year-old girl walked in and asked to talk to a psychiatrist about her "worries." I was called to the ward, and when we ended our conversation I was awake with sorrow and hope for this young girl, but also astonished at her coming. As a child psychiatrist, I was certainly accustomed to the troubled mother who brings her child to a hospital for any one of a wide variety of emotional problems. It was the child's initiative in coming which surprised me. I recalled a story my wife had told me. She was teaching a ninth-grade English class, and they were starting to read the Sophoclean tragedy of Oedipus. A worldly thirteen-year-old asked the first question: "What is an Oedipus complex?" Somehow, in our time, psychiatrists have become the heirs of those who hear the worried and see the curious. I wondered, then, what other children in other times did with their troubles and how they talked of the Greeks. I wondered, too, about my own profession, its position and its problems, and about the answers we might have for ourselves as psychiatrists.

We appear in cartoons, on television serials, and in the movies. We are "applied" by Madison Avenue, and we "influence" writers. Acting techniques, even schools of painting are supposed to be derived from our insights, and Freud has become what Auden calls "a whole climate of opinion." Since children respond so fully to what is most at hand in the adult world, there should have been no reason for my surprise in that emergency ward. But this quick acceptance of us by children and adults alike is ironic, tells us something about this world, and is dangerous.

The irony is that we no longer resemble the small band of outcasts upon whom epithets were hurled for years. One forgets today just how rebellious

* Reprinted from Robert Coles, "A Young Psychiatrist Looks at His Profession," *The Atlantic Monthly* (1961), by permission of the author.

Freud and his contemporaries were. They studied archaeology and myth-
ology, were versed in the ancient languages, wrote well, and were a bit
fiery, a bit eccentric, a bit troublesome, even for one another. Opinionated,
determined, oblivious of easy welcome, they were fighters for their beliefs,
and their ideas fought much of what the world then thought.

This is a different world. People today are frightened by the memory
of concentration camps, by the possibility of atomic war, by the breakdown
of old empires and old ways of living and believing. Each person shares
the hopes and terrors peculiar to this age, not an age of reason or of enlightenment, but an age of fear and trembling. Every year brings problems
undreamed of only a decade ago in New York or Vienna. Cultures change
radically, values are different, even diseases change. For instance, cases of
hysteria, so beautifully described by Freud, are rarely found today. A kind
of innocence is lost; people now are less suggestible, less naive, more
devious. They look for help from many sources, and chief among them,
psychiatrists. Erich Fromm, in honor of Paul Tillich's seventy-fifth birth-
day, remarked: "Modern man is lonely, frightened, and hardly capable of
love. He wants to be close to his neighbor, and yet he is too unrelated and
distant to be able to be close. . . . In search for closeness he craves knowledge; and in search for knowledge he finds psychology. Psychology becomes a substitute for love, for intimacy. . . ."

Now Freud and his knights are dead. Their long fight has won acclaim
and increasing protection from a once reluctant society, and perhaps we
should expect this ebb tide. Our very acclaim makes us more rigid and
querulous. We are rent by rivalries, and early angers or stubborn idiosyncrasies have hardened into a variety of schools with conflicting ideas.
We use proper names of early psychiatrists—Jung, Rank, Horney—to describe the slightest differences of emphasis or theory. The public is interested, but understandably confused. If it is any comfort to the public,
so are psychiatrists, at times. Most of us can recall our moments of arrogance, only thinly disguised by words which daily become more like shib-
boleths, sound hollow, and are almost cant.

Ideas need the backing of institutions and firm social approval if they
are to result in practical application. Yet I see pharisaic temples being built
everywhere in psychiatry; pick up our journals and you will see meetings
listed almost every week of the year and pages filled with the abstracts of
papers presented at them. These demand precious time in attendance and
reading, and such time is squandered all too readily these days. Who of us,
even scanting sleep, can keep up with this monthly tidal wave of minute or
repetitive studies? And who among us doesn't smile or shrug, as he skims
the pages, and suddenly leap with hunger at the lonely monograph that
really says something? As psychiatrists we need to be in touch not only
with our patients but with the entire range of human activity. We need

time to see a play or read a poem, yet daily we sit tied to our chairs, listening and talking for hours on end. While this is surely a problem for all professions, it is particularly deadening for one which deals so intimately with people and which requires that its members themselves be alive and alert.

It seems to me that psychiatric institutions and societies too soon become bureaucracies, emphasizing form, detail, and compliance. They also breed the idea that legislation or grants of money for expansion of laboratories and buildings will provide answers where true knowledge is lacking. Whereas we desperately need more money for facilities and training for treatment programs, there can be a vicious circle of more dollars for more specialized projects producing more articles about less and less, and it may be that some projects are contrived to attract money and expand institutions rather than to form any spontaneous intellectual drive. We argue longer and harder about incidentals, such as whether our patients should sit up or lie down; whether we should accept or reject their gifts or answer their letters; how we should talk to patients when they arrive or leave. We debate for hours about the difference between psychoanalysis and psychotherapy; about the advantages of seeing a person twice a week or three times a week; about whether we should give medications to people, and if so, in what way. For the plain fact is that, as we draw near the bureaucratic and the institutionalized, we draw near quibbling. Maybe it is too late, and much of this cannot be stopped. But it may be pleasantly nostalgic, if not instructive, to recall Darwin sailing on the *Beagle*, or Freud writing spirited letters of discovery to a close friend, or Sir Alexander Fleming stumbling upon a mold of penicillin in his laboratory—all in so simple and creative a fashion, and all with so little red tape and money.

If some of psychiatry's problems come home from its position in the kind of society we have, other troubles are rooted in the very nature of our job. We labor with people who have troubled thoughts and feelings, who go awry in bed or in the office or with friends. Though we talk a great deal about our scientific interests, man's thoughts and feelings cannot be as easily understood or manipulated as atoms. The brain is where we think and receive impressions of the world, and it is in some ultimate sense an aggregate of atoms and molecules. In time we will know more about how to control and transform all cellular life, and at some point the cells of the brain will be known in all their intricate functions. What we now call "ego" or "unconscious" will be understood in terms of cellular action or biochemical and biophysical activity. The logic of the nature of all matter predicts that someday we will be able to arrange and rearrange ideas and feelings. Among the greatest mysteries before us are the unmarked pathways running from the peripheral nervous system to the thinking areas in the brain. The future is even now heralded by machines which think and by drugs which stimulate emotional states or affect specific moods, like depressions. Until these roads are thoroughly surveyed and the brain is completely understood, psychiatry will be as pragmatic or empirical as medicine.

Social scientists have taught us a great deal about how men think and how they get along with one another and develop from infancy to full age. We have learned ways of reaching people with certain problems and can offer much help to some of them. Often we can understand illnesses that we cannot so readily treat. With medicines, we can soften the lacerations of nervousness and fear, producing no solutions, but affording some peace and allowing the mind to seek further aid. Some hospitals now offer carefully planned communities where new friendships can arise, refuges where the unhappy receive individual medical and psychiatric attention. Clinics, though harried by small staffs and increasing requests, offer daily help for a variety of mental illnesses. Children come to centers devoted to the study and treatment of early emotional difficulties. If the etiologies are still elusive, the results of treatment are often considerable. Failures are glaring, but the thousands of desperate people who are helped are sometimes overlooked because of their very recovery. Indeed, it is possible that our present problems may give way to worse ones as we get to know more. The enormous difficulties of finding out about the neurophysiology of emotional life may ultimately yield to the Orwellian dilemma of a society in which physicists of the mind can change thoughts and control feelings at their will.

However, right now I think our most pressing concern is less the matter of our work than the matter of ourselves. For the individual psychiatrist, the institutional rigidities affect his thoughts and attitudes, taint his words and feelings, and thereby his ability to treat patients. We become victims of what we most dread; our sensibilities die, and we no longer care or notice. We dread death of the heart—any heart under any moon. Yet I see Organization Men in psychiatry, with all the problems of deathlike conformity. Independent thinking by the adventurous has declined; psychiatric training has become more formal, more preoccupied with certificates and diplomas, more hierarchical. Some of the finest people in early dynamic psychiatry were artists, like Erik Erikson, schoolteachers, like August Aichhorn, or those, like Anna Freud, who had no formal training or occupation but motivations as personal as those of a brilliant and loyal daughter. Today we are obsessed with accreditation, recognition, levels of training, with status as scientists. These are the preoccupations of young psychiatrists. There are more lectures, more supervision, more examinations for specialty status, and thus the profession soon attracts people who take to these practices. Once there were the curious and bold; now there are the carefully well-adjusted and certified.

When the heart dies, we slip into wordy and doctrinaire caricatures of life. Our journals, our habits of talk become cluttered with jargon or the trivial. There are negative cathects, libido quanta, "pre-symbiotic, normal-autistic phases of mother-infant unity," and "a hierarchically stratified, firmly cathected organization of self-representations." Such dross is excused as a short cut to understanding a complicated message by those versed in the trade; its practitioners call on the authority of symbolic communication in the sciences. But the real test is whether we best understand by this strange proliferation of language the worries, fears, or loves in individual people. As the words grow longer and the concepts more intricate and tedious, human sorrows and temptations disappear, loves move away, envies and jealousies, revenge and terror dissolve. Gone are strong, sensible words with good meaning and the flavor of the real. Freud called Dostoevsky the greatest psychologist of all time, and long ago Euripides described in *Medea* the hurt of the mentally ill. Perhaps we cannot expect to describe our patients with the touching accuracy and poetry used for Lady Macbeth or Hamlet or King Lear, but surely there are sparks to be kindled, cries to be heard, from people who are individuals.

If we become cold, and our language frosty, then our estrangement is complete. Living in an unreliable world, often lonely, and for this reason, attracted to psychiatry as a job with human contacts, we embrace icy reasoning and abstractions, a desperate shadow of the real friendships which we once desired. Estrangement may, indeed, thread through the entire fabric of our professional lives in America. Cartoons show us pre-empted by the wealthy. A recent study from Yale by Doctor Redlich shows how few people are reached by psychiatrists, how much a part of the class and caste system in America we are. Separated from us are all the troubled people in villages and farms from Winesburg to Yoknapatawpha. Away from us are the wretched drunks and the youthful gangs in the wilderness of our cities. Removed from us are most of the poor, the criminal, the drug addicts. Though there are some low-cost clinics, their waiting lists are long, and we are all too easily and too often available to the select few of certain streets and certain neighborhoods.

Whereas in Europe the theologian or artist shares intimately with psychiatrists, we stand apart from them afraid to recognize our common heritage. European psychiatry mingles with philosophers; produces Karl Jaspers, a psychiatrist who is a theologian, or Sartre, a novelist and philosopher who writes freely and profoundly about psychiatry. After four years of psychiatric training in a not uncultured city, I begin to wonder whether young psychiatrists in America are becoming isolated by an arbitrary definition of what is, in fact, our work. Our work is the human condition, and we might do well to talk with Reinhold Niebuhr about the "nature and destiny of man," or with J. D. Salinger about our Holden Caulfields.

Perhaps we are too frightened and too insecure to recognize our very brothers. This is a symptom of the estranged.

In some way our hearts must live. If we truly live, we will talk clearly and avoid the solitary trek. In some way we must manage to blend poetic insight with a craft and unite intimately the rational and the intuitive, the aloof stance of the scholar with the passion and affection of the friend who cares and is moved. It seems to me that this is the oldest summons in the history of Western civilization. We can answer this request only with some capacity for risk, dare, and whim. Thwarting us at every turn of life is the ageless fear of uncertainty; it is hard to risk the unknown. If we see a patient who puzzles us, we can avoid the mystery and challenge of the unique through readily available diagnostic categories. There is no end to classifications and terminologies, but the real end for us may be the soul of man, lost in these words: "Name it and it's so, or call it and it's real." This is the language of children faced with a confusion of the real and unreal, and it is ironic, if human, to see so much of this same habit still among psychiatrists.

Perhaps, if we dared to be free, more would be revealed than we care to admit. I sometimes wonder why we do not have a journal in our profession which publishes anonymous contributions. We might then hear and feel more of the real give-and-take in all those closed offices, get a fuller flavor of the encounter between the two people, patient and psychiatrist, who are in and of themselves what we call psychotherapy. The answer to the skeptic who questions the worth of psychotherapy is neither the withdrawn posture of the adherent of a closed system who dismisses all inquiry as suspect nor an eruption of pseudo-scientific verbal pyrotechnics. Problems will not be solved by professional arrogance or more guilds and rituals. For it is more by being than by doing that the meaningful and deeply felt communion between us and our patients will emerge. This demands as much honesty and freedom from us as it does from our patients, and as much trust on our part as we would someday hope to receive from them.

If the patient brings problems that may be understood as similar to those in many others, that may be conceptualized and abstracted, he is still in the midst of a life which is in some ways different from all others. We bring only ourselves; and so each meeting in our long working day is different, and our methods of treatment will differ in many subtle ways from those of all our colleagues. When so much of the world faces the ant-hill of totalitarian living, it is important for us to affirm proudly the preciously individual in each human being and in ourselves as doctors. When we see patients, the knowledge and wisdom of many intellectual ancestors are in our brains, and hopefully, some life and affection in our hearts. The heart must carry the reasoning across those inches or feet of office room. The psychiatrist, too, has his life and loves, his sorrows and angers. We know that we receive from our patients much of the irrational, misplaced, distorted thoughts and feelings once directed at parents, teachers, brothers, and sisters. We also know that our patients attempt to elicit from us many of the attitudes and responses of these earlier figures. But we must strive for some neutrality, particularly in the beginning of treatment, so that our patients may be offered, through us and their already charged feelings toward us, some idea of past passions presently lived. Yet, so often this neutrality becomes our signal for complete anonymity. We try to hide behind our couches, hide ourselves from our patients. In so doing we prolong the very isolation often responsible for our patients' troubles, and if we persist, they will derive from the experience many interpretations, but little warmth and trust.

I think that our own lives and problems are part of the therapeutic process. Our feelings, our own disorders and early sorrows are for us in some fashion what the surgeon's skilled hands are for his work. His hands are the trained instruments of knowledge, lectures, traditions. Yet they are, even in surgery, responsive to the artistry, the creative and sensitive intuition of the surgeon as a man. The psychiatrist's hands are himself, his life. We are educated and prepared, able to see and interpret. But we see, talk, and listen through our minds, our memories, our persons. It is through our emotions that the hands of our healing flex and function, reach out, and finally touch.

We cannot solve many problems, and there are the world and the stars to dwarf us and give us some humor about ourselves. But we can hope that, with some of the feeling of what Martin Buber calls "I-Thou" quietly and lovingly nurtured in some of our patients, there may be more friendliness about us. This would be no small happening, and it is for this that we must work. Alert against dryness and the stale, smiling with others and occasionally at ourselves, we can read and study; but maybe wince, shout, cry, and love, too. Really, there is much less to say than to affirm by living. I would hope that we would dare to accept ourselves fully and offer ourselves freely to a quizzical and apprehensive time and to uneasy and restless people.

part four

DEMOCRATIC DIALOGUE:
THE POLITICS OF COMMUNICATION

FREE TRADE IN IDEAS

Oliver Wendell Holmes, Jr.

Abrams *et al.* v. United States
No. 316. Argued October 21, 22, 1919.
Decided November 10, 1919.
Mr. Justice Holmes dissenting.

*t*his indictment is founded wholly upon the publication of two leaflets which I shall describe in a moment. The first count charges a conspiracy pending the war with Germany to publish abusive language about the form of government of the United States, laying the preparation and publishing of the first leaflet as overt acts. The second count charges a conspiracy pending the war to publish language intended to bring the form of government into contempt, laying the preparation and publishing of the two leaflets as overt acts. The third count alleges a conspiracy to encourage resistance to the United States in the same war and to attempt to effectuate the purpose by publishing the same leaflets. The fourth count lays a conspiracy to incite curtailment of production of things necessary to prosecution of the war and to attempt to accomplish it by publishing the second leaflet to which I have referred.

The first of these leaflets says that the President's cowardly silence about the intervention in Russia reveals the hypocrisy of the plutocratic gang in Washington. It intimates that "German militarism combined with allied capitalism to crush the Russian revolution"—goes on that the tyrants of the world fight each other until they see a common enemy—working class enlightenment, when they combine to crush it; and that now militarism and capitalism combined, though not openly, to crush the Russian revolution. It says that there is only one enemy of the workers of the world and that is capitalism; that it is a crime for workers of America, etc., to fight the workers' republic of Russia, and ends "Awake! Awake, you Workers of the World! Revolutionists." A note adds "It is absurd to call us pro-German.

We hate and despise German militarism more than do you hypocritical tyrants. We have more reasons for denouncing German militarism than has the coward of the White House."

The other leaflet, headed "Workers—Wake Up," with abusive language, says that America together with the Allies will march for Russia to help the Czecho-Slovaks in their struggle against the Bolsheviki, and that this time the hypocrites shall not fool the Russian emigrants and friends of Russia in America. It tells the Russian emigrants that they now must spit in the face of the false military propaganda by which their sympathy and help to the prosecution of the war have been called forth and says that with the money they have lent or are going to lend "they will make bullets not only for the Germans but also for the Workers Soviets of Russia," and further, "Workers in the ammunition factories, you are producing bullets, bayonets, cannon, to murder not only the Germans, but also your dearest, best, who are in Russia and are fighting for freedom." It then appeals to the same Russian emigrants at some length not to consent to the "inquisitionary expedition to Russia," and says that the destruction of the Russian revolution is "the politics of the march to Russia." The leaflet winds up by saying, "Workers, our reply to this barbaric intervention has to be a general strike!" and after a few words on the spirit of revolution, exhortations not to be afraid, and some usual tall talk ends "Woe unto those who will be in the way of progress. Let solidarity live! The Rebels."

No argument seems to me necessary to show that these pronunciamentos in no way attack the form of government of the United States, or that they do not support either of the first two counts. What little I have to say about the third count may be postponed until I have considered the fourth. With regard to that it seems too plain to be denied that the suggestion to workers in the ammunition factories that they are producing bullets to murder their dearest, and the further advocacy of a general strike, both in the second leaflet, do urge curtailment of production of things necessary to the prosecution of the war within the meaning of the Act of May 16, 1918, c. 75, 40 State. 553, amending Sec. 3 of the earlier Act of 1917. But to make the conduct criminal that statute requires that it should be "with intent by such curtailment to cripple or hinder the United States in the prosecution of the war." It seems to me that no such intent is proved.

I am aware of course that the word intent as vaguely used in ordinary legal discussion means no more than knowledge at the time of the act that the consequences said to be intended will ensue. Even less than that will satisfy the general principle and civil of criminal liability. A man may have to pay damages, may be sent to prison, at common law might be hanged, if at the time of his act he knew facts from which common experience showed that the consequences would follow, whether he individually could foresee them or not. But, when words are used exactly, a deed is not done with intent to produce a consequence unless that consequence is the aim of the deed. It may be obvious, and obvious to the actor, that the consequence will follow, and he may be liable for it even if he regrets it, but he does not do the act with intent to produce it unless the aim to produce it is the proximate motive of the specific act, although there may be some deeper motive behind.

It seems to me that this statute must be taken to use its words in a strict and accurate sense. They would be absurd in any other. A patriot might think that we were wasting money on aeroplanes, or making more cannon of a certain kind than we needed, and might advocate curtailment with success, yet even if it turned out that the curtailment hindered and was thought by other minds to have been obviously likely to hinder the United States in the prosecution of the war, no one would hold such conduct a crime. I admit that my illustration does not answer all that might be said but it is enough to show what I think and to let me pass to a more important aspect of the case. I refer to the First Amendment to the Constitution that Congress shall make no law abridging the freedom of speech.

I never have seen any reason to doubt that the questions of law that alone were before this Court in the cases of Schenck, Frohwerk and Debs, 249 U.S. 47, 204, 211, were rightly decided. I do not doubt for a moment that by the same reasoning that would justify punishing persuasion to murder, the United States constitutionally may punish speech that produces or is intended to produce a clear and imminent danger that it will bring about forthwith certain substantive evils that the United States constitutionally may seek to prevent. The power undoubtedly is greater in time of war than in time of peace because war opens dangers that do not exist at other times.

But as against dangers peculiar to war, as against others, the principle of the right to free speech is always the same. It is only the present danger of immediate evil or an intent to bring it about that warrants Congress in setting a limit to the expression of opinion where private rights are not concerned. Congress certainly cannot forbid all effort to change the mind of the country. Now nobody can suppose that the surreptitious publishing of a silly leaflet by an unknown man, without more, would present any immediate danger that its opinions would hinder the success of the government arms or have any appreciable tendency to do so. Publishing those opinions for the very purpose of obstructing, however, might indicate a greater danger and at any rate would have the quality of an attempt. So I assume that the second leaflet if published for the purposes alleged in the fourth count might be punishable. But it seems pretty clear to me that nothing less than that would bring these papers within the scope of this law. An actual intent in the sense that I have explained is necessary to constitute an attempt, where a further act of the same individual is required to complete the substantive crime, for reasons given in Swift & Co. v. United States, 196 U.S. 375, 396. It is necessary where the success of the attempt depends upon others because if that intent is not present the actor's aim may be accomplished without bringing about the evils sought to be checked. An intent to prevent interference with the revolution in Russia might have been satisfied without any hindrance to carrying on the war in which we were engaged.

I do not see how anyone can find the intent required by the statute in any of the defendant's words. The second leaflet is the only one that affords even a foundation for the charge, and there, without invoking the hatred of German militarism expressed in the former one, it is evident from the beginning to the end that the only object of the paper is to help Russia and stop American intervention there against the popular government—not to impede the United States in the war that it was carrying on. To say that two phrases taken literally might import a suggestion of conduct that would have interference with the war as an indirect and probably undesired effect seems to me by no means enough to show an attempt to produce that effect.

I return for a moment to the third count. That charges an intent to provoke resistance to the United States in its war with Germany. Taking the clause in the statute that deals with that in connection with the other elaborate provisions of the act, I think that resistance to the United States means some forcible act of opposition to some proceeding of the United States in pursuance of the war. I think the intent must be the specific intent that I have described and for the reasons that I have given I think that no such intent was proved or existed in fact. I also think that there is no hint at resistance to the United States as I construe the phrase.

In this case sentences of twenty years imprisonment have been imposed for the publishing of two leaflets that I believe the defendants had as much right to publish as the Government has to publish the Constitution of the United States now vainly invoked by them. Even if I am technically wrong and enough can be squeezed from these poor and puny anonymities to turn the color of legal litmus paper; I will add, even if what I think the necessary intent were shown; the most nominal punishment seems to me all that possibly could be inflicted, unless the defendants are to be made to suffer not for what the indictment alleges but for the creed that they avow—a creed that I believe to be the creed of ignorance and immaturity when honestly held, as I see no reason to doubt that it was held here, but which, although made the subject of examination at the trial, no one has a right even to consider in dealing with the charges before the Court.

Persecution for the expression of opinions seems to me perfectly illogical. If you have no doubt of your premises or your power and want a certain result with all your heart you naturally express your wishes in law and sweep away all opposition. To allow opposition by speech seems to indicate that you think the speech impotent, as when a man says that he had squared the circle, or that you do not care whole-heartedly for the result, or that you doubt either your power or your premises. But when men have realized that time has upset many fighting faiths, they may come to believe even more than they believe the very foundations of their own conduct that the ultimate good desired is better reached by free trade in ideas—that the best test of truth is the power of the thought to get itself accepted in the competition of the market, and that truth is the only ground upon which their wishes safely can be carried out. That at any rate is the theory of our Constitution. It is an experiment, as all life is an experiment. Every year if not every day we have to wager our salvation upon some prophecy based upon imperfect knowledge. While that experiment is part of our system I think that we should be eternally vigilant against attempts to check the expression of opinions that we loathe and believe to be fraught with death, unless they so imminently threaten immediate interference with the lawful and pressing purposes of the law that an immediate check is required to save the country. I wholly disagree with the argument of the Government that the First Amendment left the common law as to seditious libel in force. History seems to me against the notion. I had conceived that the United States through many years had shown its repentance for the Sedition Act of 1798, by repaying fines that it imposed. Only the emergency that makes it immediately dangerous to leave the correction of evil counsels to time warrants making any exception to the sweeping commands, "Congress shall make no law . . . abridging the freedom of speech." Of course, I am speaking only of expressions of opinion and exhortations, which were all that were uttered here, but I regret that I cannot put into more impressive words my belief that in their conviction upon this indictment the defendants were deprived of their rights under the Constitution of the United States.

Mr. Justice Brandeis concurs with the foregoing opinion.

NEITHER VICTIMS NOR EXECUTIONERS*

Albert Camus

THE CENTURY OF FEAR

*t*he 17th century was the century of mathematics, the 18th that of the physical sciences, and the 19th that of biology. Our 20th century is the century of fear. I will be told that fear is not a science. But science must be somewhat involved since its latest theoretical advances have brought it to the point of negating itself while its perfected technology threatens the globe itself with destruction. Moreover, although fear itself cannot be considered a science, it is certainly technique.

The most striking feature of the world we live in is that most of its inhabitants—with the exception of pietists of various kinds—are cut off from the future. Life has no validity unless it can project itself toward the future, can ripen and progress. Living against a wall is a dog's life. True—and the men of my generation, those who are going into the factories and the colleges, have lived and are living more and more like dogs.

This is not the first time, of course, that men have confronted a future materially closed to them. But hitherto they have been able to transcend the dilemma by words, by protests, by appealing to other values which lent them hope. Today no one speaks any more (except those who repeat themselves) because history seems to be in the grip of blind and deaf forces which will heed neither cries of warning, nor advice, nor entreaties. The years we have just gone through have killed something in us. And that something is simply the old confidence man had in himself, which led him to believe that he could always elicit human reactions from another man if

* George Braziller, Inc. Selections from the article "Neither Victims nor Executioners" by Albert Camus, from *Seeds of Liberation*, edited by Paul Goodman, reprinted with the permission of the publishers. Copyright © 1964 by *Liberation*.

he spoke to him in the language of a common humanity. We have seen men lie, degrade, kill, deport, torture—and each time it was not possible to persuade them not to do these things because they were sure of themselves and because one cannot appeal to an abstraction, i.e., the representative of an ideology.

Mankind's long dialogue has just come to an end. And naturally a man with whom one cannot reason is a man to be feared. The result is that—besides those who have not spoken out because they thought it useless—a vast conspiracy of silence has spread all about us, a conspiracy accepted by those who are frightened and who rationalize their fears in order to hide them from themselves, a conspiracy fostered by those whose interest it is to do so. "You shouldn't talk about the Russian culture purge—it helps reaction." "Don't mention the Anglo-American support of Franco—it encourages communism." Fear is certainly a technique.

What with the general fear of a war now being prepared by all nations and the specific fear of murderous ideologies, who can deny that we live in a state of terror? We live in terror because persuasion is no longer possible; because man has been wholly submerged in History; because he can no longer tap that part of his nature, as real as the historical part, which he recaptures in contemplating the beauty of nature of human faces; because we live in a world of abstractions, of bureaus and machines, of absolute ideas and of crude messianism. We suffocate among people who think they are absolutely right, whether in their machines or in their ideas. And for all who can live only in an atmosphere of human dialogue and sociability, this silence is the end of the world.

To emerge from this terror, we must be able to reflect and to act accordingly. But an atmosphere of terror hardly encourages reflection. I believe, however, that instead of simply blaming everything on this fear, we should consider it as one of the basic factors in the situation, and try to do something about it. No task is more important. For it involves the fate of a considerable number of Europeans who, fed up with the lies and violence, deceived in their dearest hopes and repelled by the idea of killing their fellow men in order to convince them, likewise repudiate the idea of themselves being convinced that way. And yet such is the alternative that at present confronts so many of us in Europe who are not of any party—or ill at ease in the party we have chosen—who doubt socialism has been realized in Russia or liberalism in America, who grant to each side the right to affirm its truth but refuse it the right to impose it by murder, individual or collective. Among the powerful of today, these are the men without a kingdom. Their viewpoint will not be recognized (and I say "recognized," not "triumph"), nor will they recover their kingdom until they come to know precisely what they want and proclaim it directly and boldly enough to make their words a stimulus to action. And if an atmosphere of fear does not encourage accurate thinking, then they must first of all come to terms with fear.

To come to terms, one must understand what fear means: what it implies and what it rejects. It implies and rejects the same fact: a world where murder is legitimate, and where human life is considered trifling. This is the great political question of our times, and before dealing with other issues, one must take a position on it. Before anything can be done, two questions must be put: "Do you or do you not, directly or indirectly, want to be killed or assaulted? Do you or do you not, directly or indirectly, want to kill or assault?" All who say No to both these questions are automatically committed to a series of consequences which must modify their way of posing the problem. My aim here is to clarify two or three of these consequences. . . .

A NEW SOCIAL CONTRACT

All contemporary political thinking which refuses to justify lies and murder is led to the following conclusions: (1) domestic policy is in itself a secondary matter; (2) the only problem is the creation of a world order which will bring about those lasting reforms which are the distinguishing mark of a revolution; (3) within any given nation there exist now only administrative problems, to be solved provisionally after a fashion, until a solution is worked out which will be more effective because more general.

For example, the French Constitution can only be evaluated in terms of the support it gives or fails to give to a world order based on justice and the free exchange of ideas. From this viewpoint, we must criticize the indifference of our Constitution to the simplest human liberties. And we must also recognize that the problem of restoring the food supply is ten times more important than such issues as nationalization or election figures. And although the food supply cannot be assured even within a single country, it is a more pressing problem and calls for expedients, provisional though they may be.

And so this viewpoint gives us a hitherto lacking criterion by which to judge domestic policy. Thirty editorials in *Aube* may range themselves every month against thirty in *Humanité*, but they will not cause us to forget that both newspapers, together with the parties they represent, have acquiesced in the annexation without a referendum of Briga and Tenda, and that they are thus accomplices in the destruction of international democracy. Regardless of their good or bad intentions, Mr. Bidault and Mr. Thorez are both in favor of international dictatorship. From this aspect, whatever other opinion one may have of them, they represent in our politics not realism but the most disastrous kind of Utopianism.

Yes, we must minimize domestic politics. A crisis which tears the whole world apart must be met on a world scale. A social system for everybody which will somewhat allay each one's misery and fear is today our logical objective. But that calls for action and for sacrifices, that is, for men. And if there are many today who, in their secret hearts, detest violence and killing, there are not many who care to recognize that this forces them to reconsider their actions and thoughts. Those who want to make such an effort, however, will find in such a social system a rational hope and a guide to action.

They will admit that little is to be expected from present-day governments, since these live and act according to a murderous code. Hope remains only in the most difficult task of all: to reconsider everything from the ground up, so as to shape a living society inside a dying society. Men must therefore, as individuals, draw up among themselves, within frontiers and across them, a new social contract which will unite them according to more reasonable principles.

The peace movement I speak of could base itself, inside nations, on work communities and, internationally, on intellectual communities; the former, organized cooperatively, would help as many individuals as possible to solve their material problems, while the latter would try to define the values by which this international community would live, and would also plead its cause on every occasion.

More precisely, the latter's task would be to speak out clearly against the confusions of the Terror and at the same time to define the values by which a peaceful world may live. The first objectives might be the drawing up of an international code of justice whose Article No. 1 would be the abolition of the death penalty, and an exposition of the basic principles of a sociable culture ("civilisation du dialogue"). Such an undertaking would answer the needs of an era which has found no philosophical justification for that thirst for fraternity which today burns in Western man. There is no idea, naturally, of constructing a new ideology, but rather of discovering a style of life.

Let us suppose that certain individuals resolve that they will consistently oppose to power the force of example; to authority, exhortation; to insult, friendly reasoning; to trickery, simple honor. Let us suppose they refuse all the advantages of present-day society and accept only the duties and obligations which bind them to other men. Let us suppose they devote themselves to orienting education, the press and public opinion toward the principles outlined here. Then I say that such men would be acting not as Utopians but as honest realists. They would be preparing the future and at the same time knocking down a few of the walls which imprison us today. If realism be the art of taking into account both the present and the future, of gaining the most while sacrificing the least, then who can fail to see the positively dazzling realism of such behavior?

Whether these men will arise or not I do not know. It is probable that most of them are even now thinking things over, and that is good. But one thing is sure: their efforts will be effective only to the degree that they have the courage to give up, for the present, some of their dreams, so as to grasp the more firmly the essential point on which our very lives depend. Once there, it will perhaps turn out to be necessary, before they are done, to raise their voices.

TOWARDS SOCIABILITY

Yes, we must raise our voices. Up to this point, I have refrained from appealing to emotion. We are being torn apart by a logic of History which we have elaborated in every detail—a net which threatens to strangle us. It is not emotion which can cut through the web of a logic which has gone to irrational lengths, but only reason which can meet logic on its own ground. But I should not want to leave the impression, in concluding, that any program for the future can get along without our powers of love and indignation. I am well aware that it takes a powerful prime mover to get men into motion and that it is hard to throw one's self into a struggle whose objectives are so modest and where hope has only a rational basis—and hardly even that. But the problem is not how to carry men away; it is essential, on the contrary, that they not be carried away but rather that they be made to understand clearly what they are doing.

To save what can be saved so as to open up some kind of future—that is the prime mover, the passion and the sacrifice that is required. It demands only that we reflect and then decide, clearly, whether humanity's lot must be made still more miserable in order to achieve far-off and shadowy ends, whether we should accept a world bristling with arms where brother kills brother; or whether, on the contrary, we should avoid bloodshed and misery as much as possible so that we give a chance for survival to later generations better equipped than we are.

For my part, I am fairly sure that I have made the choice. And, having chosen, I think that I must speak out, that I must state that I will never again be one of those, whoever they be, who compromise with murder, and that I must take the consequences of such a decision. The thing is done, and that is as far as I can go at present. Before concluding, however, I want to make clear the spirit in which this article is written.

We are asked to love or to hate such and such a country and such and such a people. But some of us feel too strongly our common humanity to make such a choice. Those who really love the Russian people, in gratitude for what they have never ceased to be—that world leaven which Tolstoy and Gorky speak of—do not wish for them success in power-politics, but rather want to spare them, after the ordeals of the past, a new and even more terrible bloodletting. So, too, with the American people, and with the peoples of unhappy Europe. This is the kind of elementary truth we are liable to forget amidst the furious passions of our time.

Yes, it is fear and silence and the spiritual isolation they cause that must be fought today. And it is sociability ("le dialogue") and the universal inter-communication of men that must be defended. Slavery, injustice and lies destroy this intercourse and forbid this sociability; and so we must reject them. But these evils are today the very stuff of History, so that many consider them necessary evils. It is true that we cannot "escape History," since we are in it up to our necks. But one may propose to fight within History to preserve from History that part of man which is not its proper province. That is all I have to say here. The "point" of this article may be summed up as follows:

Modern nations are driven by powerful forces along the roads of power and domination. I will not say that these forces should be furthered or that they should be obstructed. They hardly need our help and, for the moment, they laugh at attempts to hinder them. They will, then, continue. But I will ask only this simple question: what if these forces wind up in a dead end, what if that logic of History on which so many now rely turns out to be a will o' the wisp? What if, despite two or three world wars, despite the sacrifice of several generations and a whole system of values, our grand children—supposing they survive—find themselves no closer to a world society? It may well be that the survivors of such an experience will be too weak to understand their own sufferings. Since these forces are working themselves out and since it is inevitable that they continue to do so, there is no reason why some of us should not take on the job of keeping alive through the apocalyptic historical vista that stretches before us, a modest thoughtfulness which, without pretending to solve everything, will constantly be prepared to give some human meaning to everyday life. The essential thing is that people should carefully weigh the price they must pay.

To conclude: all I ask is that, in the midst of a murderous world, we agree to reflect on murder and to make a choice. After that, we can distinguish those who accept the consequences of being murderers themselves or the accomplices of murderers, and those who refuse to do so with all their force and being. Since this terrible dividing line does actually exist, it will be a gain if it be clearly marked. Over the expanse of five continents throughout the coming years an endless struggle is going to be pursued between violence and friendly persuasion, a struggle in which, granted, the former has a thousand times the chances of success than has the latter. But I have always held that, if he who bases his hopes on human nature is a fool, he who gives up in the face of circumstances is a coward. And henceforth, the only honorable course will be to stake everything on a formidable gamble: that words are more powerful than munitions.

HOPE FOR THIS HOUR*

Martin Buber

We ask about hope for this hour. This implies that we who ask experience this hour not only as one of the heaviest affliction but also as one that appears to give no essentially different outlook for the future, no prospect of a time of radiant and full living. Yet it is such an outlook for a better hour that we mean when we speak of hope.

Only by the great need of this hour being really felt in common can our question have a common significance, and only then may we expect an answer which will show us a way. A hundred or a thousand men might come together and each bring with him the daily need of his own life, his wholly personal world- and life-anxiety. Yet even though each laid his need together with the needs of the others, this would not produce a common need from which a genuinely common question could arise. Only if the personal need of each reveals the great need of man in this hour can the rivulets of need, united into a single stream, sweep the storming question upward.

What is of essential importance, however, is that we recognize not only the external manifestations of that common need perceptible to us, but also its origin and its depth. As important as it is that we suffer in common the human anguish of today, it is still more important to trace in common where it comes from. Only from there, from the source, can the true hope of healing be given us.

The human world is today, as never before, split into two camps, each of which understands the other as the embodiment of falsehood and itself as the embodiment of truth. Often in history, to be sure, national groups and religious associations have stood in so radical an opposition that the one side denied and condemned the other in its innermost existence. Now, however, it is the human population of our planet generally that is so

* "Hope for This Hour" from *Pointing the Way*, by Martin Buber. Copyright © 1957 by Martin Buber. Reprinted by permission of Harper & Row, Publishers, and of Routledge & Kegan Paul, Ltd.

divided, and with rare exceptions this division is everywhere seen as a necessity of existence in this world hour. He who makes himself an exception is suspected or ridiculed by both sides. Each side has assumed monopoly of the sunlight and has plunged its antagonist into night, and each side demands that you decide between day and night.

We can comprehend the origin of this cruel and grotesque condition in its simplest lines if we realize how the three principles of the French Revolution have broken asunder. The abstractions freedom and equality were held together there through the more concrete fraternity, for only if men feel themselves to be brothers can they partake of a genuine freedom from one another and a genuine equality with one another. But fraternity has been deprived of its original meaning, the relationship between children of God, and consequently of any real content. As a result, each of the two remaining watchwords was able to establish itself against the other and, by so doing, to wander farther and farther from its truth. Arrogant and presumptuous, each sucked into itself, ever more thoroughly, elements foreign to it, elements of passion for power and greed for possession.

In such a situation man is more than ever inclined to see his own principle in its original purity and the opposing one in its present deterioration, especially if the forces of propaganda confirm his instincts in order to make better use of them. Man is no longer, as in earlier epochs, content to take his own principle for the single true one and that which opposes it as false through and through. He is convinced that his side is in order, the other side fundamentally out of order, that he is concerned with the recognition and realization of the right, his opponent with the masking of his selfish interest. Expressed in modern terminology, he believes that he has ideas, his opponent only ideologies. This obsession feeds the mistrust that incites the two camps.

During the First World War it became clear to me that a process was going on which before then I had only surmised. This was the growing difficulty of genuine dialogue, and most especially of genuine dialogue between men of different kinds and convictions. Direct, frank dialogue is becoming ever more difficult and more rare; the abysses between man and man threaten ever more pitilessly to become unbridgeable. I began to understand at that time, more than thirty years ago, that this is the central question for the fate of mankind. Since then I have continually pointed out that the future of man as man depends upon a rebirth of dialogue.

I experienced a great satisfaction, therefore, when I read a short while ago the words in which a not just ordinarily competent man, Robert Hutchins, formulated the importance and possibility of a Civilization of the Dialogue. "The essence of the Civilization of the Dialogue presupposses mutual respect and understanding, it does not presuppose agreement." And further: "It is no good saying that the Civilization of the Dialogue cannot arise when the other party will not talk. We have to find the way to induce him to talk." As the means to this, Hutchins recommends showing interest and understanding for what the other has to say.

But there is an essential presupposition for all this: it is necessary to overcome the massive mistrust in others and also that in ourselves. I do not mean thereby the primal mistrust, such as that directed against those with strange ways, those who are unsettled, and those without traditions—the mistrust that the farmer in his isolated farmstead feels for the tramp who suddenly appears before him—I mean the universal mistrust of our age. Nothing stands so much in the way of the rise of a Civilization of Dialogue as the demonic power which rules our world, the demonry of basic mistrust. What does it avail to induce the other to speak if basically one puts no faith in what he says? The meeting with him already takes place under the perspective of his untrustworthiness. And this perspective is not incorrect, for his meeting with me takes place under a corresponding perspective. The basic mistrust, coming to light, produces ground for mistrust, and so forth and so forth.

It is important to perceive clearly how the specifically modern mistrust differs from the ancient mistrust, which is apparently inherent in the human being and which has left its mark in all cultures. There have always been countless situations in which a man in intercourse with a fellow-man is seized with the doubt whether he may trust him; that is, whether the other really means what he says and whether he will do what he says. There have always been countless situations in which a man believes his life-interest demands that he suspect the other of making it his object to appear otherwise than he is. The first man must then be on his guard to protect himself against this threatening false appearance.

In our time something basically different has been added that is capable of undermining more powerfully the foundations of existence between men. One no longer merely fears that the other will voluntarily dissemble, but one simply takes it for granted that he cannot do otherwise. The presumed difference between his opinion and his statement, between his statement and his action, is here no longer understood as his intention, but as essential necessity. The other communicates to me the perspective that he has acquired on a certain subject, but I do not really take cognizance of his communication as knowledge. I do not take it seriously as a contribution to the information about this subject, but rather I listen for what drives the other to say what he says, for an unconscious motive, say, or a "complex." He expresses a thought about a problem of life that concerns me, but I do not ask myself about the truth of what he says. I only pay attention to the question of which interest of his group has clothed itself in this apparently so objective judgment. Since it is the idea of the other, it is for me only an "ideology." My main task in my intercourse with my fellow-man becomes more and more, whether in terms of individual psychology or of sociology, to see through and unmask him. In the classical case this in no wise means a mask he has put on to deceive me, but a mask that has, without his knowing it, been put on him, indeed positively imprinted on him, so that what is really deceived is his own consciousness. There are, of course, innumerable transitional forms.

With this changed basic attitude, which has found scientific rationalization in the teachings of Marx and Freud, the mistrust between man and man has become existential. This is so indeed in a double sense: It is, first of all, no longer only the uprightness, the honesty of the other which is in question, but the inner integrity of his existence itself. Secondly, this mistrust not only destroys trustworthy talk between opponents, but also the immediacy of togetherness of man and man generally. Seeing-through and unmasking is now becoming the great sport between men, and those who practise it do not know whither it entices them. Nietzsche knew what he was doing when he praised the "art of mistrust," and yet he did not know. For this game naturally only becomes complete as it becomes reciprocal, in the same measure as the unmasker himself becomes the object of unmasking. Hence one may foresee in the future a degree of reciprocity in existential mistrust where speech will turn into dumbness and sense into madness.

One is still inclined to spare the other in order that one may oneself be spared. If he is ready at times to put himself in question he is generally able to stop in time. But the demonry is not to be trifled with. The existential mistrust is indeed basically no longer, like the old kind, a mistrust of my fellow-man. It is rather the destruction of confidence in existence in general. That we can no longer carry on a genuine dialogue from one camp to the other is the severest symptom of the sickness of present-day man. Existential mistrust is this sickness itself. But the destruction of trust in human existence is the inner poisoning of the total human organism from which this sickness stems.

All great civilization has been in a certain measure a Civilization of the Dialogue. The life substance of them all was not, as one customarily thinks, the presence of significant individuals, but their genuine intercourse with one another. Individuation was only the presupposition for the unfolding of dialogical life. What one calls the creative spirit of men has never been anything other than the address, the cogitative or artistic address, of those called to speak to those really able and prepared to hear. That which had concentrated here was the universal dynamism of dialogue.

There interposed in all times, of course, severe checks and disturbances; there was closedness and unapproachableness, dissembling and seduction. But where the human wonder bloomed time and again, these checks and disturbances were always overcome through the elemental power of men's mutual confirmation. The one turned to the other as to a unique personal being, undamaged by all error and trouble, and received the other's turning to him. The one traced the other in his being, in that in him which survived all illusions, and even if they fought each other, they confirmed each other as what they were. Man wishes to be confirmed by man as he who he is, and there is genuine confirmation only in mutuality.

Despite the progressive decline of dialogue and the corresponding growth of universal mistrust which characterize our time, the need of men to be confirmed still continues. But for the most part it no longer finds any natural satisfaction. As a result, man sets out on one of two false ways: he seeks to be confirmed either by himself or by a collective to which he belongs. Both undertakings must fail. The self-confirmation of him whom no fellow-man confirms cannot stand. With ever more convulsive exertions, he must endeavour to restore it, and finally he knows himself as inevitably abandoned. Confirmation through the collective, on the other hand, is pure fiction. It belongs to the nature of the collective, to be sure that it accepts and employs each of its members as this particular individual, constituted and endowed in this particular way. But it cannot recognize anyone in his own being, and therefore independently of his usefulness for the collective. Modern man, in so far as he has surrendered direct and personal mutuality with his fellows, can only exchange an illusory confirmation for the one mutuality that is lost. There is no salvation save through the renewal of the dialogical relation, and this means, above all, through the overcoming of existential mistrust.

Where must the will to this overcoming begin? More exactly, from what spiritual position is the man for whom existential mistrust has already become the self-understood gateway into intercourse with his fellow-man to be brought to self-criticism in this matter of decisive import? This is a position which can be described as the criticism of criticism. It is a matter of showing up a fundamental and enormously influential error of all the theories of seeing-through and unmasking. The gist of the error is this: when an element in the physical and spiritual existence of man which formerly was not or was too little noticed is now uncovered or clarified, one identifies it with man's total structure instead of inserting it in this structure. A leading methodological postulate of all anthropological knowledge in the broadest sense of the term must be that each newly uncovered and newly clarified element should be investigated in terms of its importance in relation to the other elements, which are already in some measure known and elucidated, and in terms of its reciprocal interaction with them. The decisive questions must be: what proportion exists between this element and the others, in what measure and in what way does it limit them and is it limited by them; in what dynamism of different historical and individual genetic moments of human existence is it to be included?

The first task of science at any given time must be, accordingly, to draw demarcation lines for the validity of theses which may be posited about the newly uncovered or newly clarified element; that is, to determine within which spheres it may claim validity. The theories of seeing-through and unmasking, both the psychological and the sociological, have neglected to draw these lines, and have time and again reduced man to the elements that have been uncovered. Let us consider, as an example, the theory of ideologies, according to which the views and judgments of a man belonging to a particular social class are to be examined essentially as products of his class position; that is, in connection with the action of his class for the promotion of its interests. Were the problem of class position and its influence stated with all clarity, the first scientific question would have to be: Since man is set in his world as in a manifold connection of influencing spheres, from the cosmic to the erotic, one of which spheres is the social level, what is the weight of the ideological class influence in relation to the non-ideological constitution of the person and what is their effect on each other? (In this connection it should be noticed that the influence of social levels, as we know, is in no way a simply positive one, for the rebellion against the class to which one belongs not seldom proves stronger than the tendency to conformity, and thus the idea stronger than the ideology.) For the time being, of course, the answer to such questions can only be set as a goal for scientific thought. But the setting of this goal is an essential precondition for the rightness of this thought.

Instead of this, the theories of ideology have reduced the man who holds opinions and formulates judgments to the ideological. This boundless simplification has contributed decisively to the development of existential mistrust. If we wish to overcome this mistrust, we cannot go back into an uncritical acceptance of men's statements. We must go beyond our present position by setting ever more exact measure and limits to the ideological critique. What I mean is not a vague idealism, but a more comprehending, more penetrating realism, a greater realism, the realism of a greater reality! Man is not to be seen through, but to be perceived ever more completely in his openness and his hiddenness and in the relation of the two to each other. We wish to trust him, not blindly indeed but clear-sightedly. We wish to perceive his manifoldness and his wholeness, his proper character, without any preconceptions about this or that background, and with the intention of accepting, accrediting and confirming him to the extent that this perception will allow.

Only if this happens and in so far as it happens can a genuine dialogue begin between the two camps into which mankind today is split. They who begin it must have overcome in themselves the basic mistrust and be capable of recognizing in their partner in dialogue the reality of his being. It is self-understood that these men will not speak merely in their own names. Behind them will be divined the unorganized mass of those who feel themselves represented through these spokesmen. This is an entirely different kind of representation and representative body from the political. These men will not be bound by the aims of the hour, they are gifted with the free far-sightedness of those called by the unborn; they will be independent persons with no authority save that of the spirit. Today, as we know, the spirit has less authority than ever, but there are world hours in which, despite all obstacles, the authority of the spirit suffices to undertake the rescue of man. Such an hour appears to me to draw near.

The representatives of whom I speak will each be acquainted with the true needs of his own people, and on these needs will be willing to stake themselves. But they will also turn understandingly to the true needs of other peoples, and will know in both cases how to extract the true needs from the exaggerations. Just for that reason they will unrelentingly distinguish between truth and propaganda within what is called the opposition of interests. Only when out of the alleged amount of antagonisms just the real conflicts between genuine needs remain can the consideration of the necessary and possible settlements between them begin. The question one must proceed from will be this, apparently the simplest of all questions, yet inviting many difficulties: What does man need, every man, in order to live as a man? For if the globe is not to burst asunder, every man must be given what he needs for a really human life. Coming together out of hostile camps, those who stand in the authority of the spirit will dare to think with one another in terms of the whole planet.

Which will prove stronger in the final accounting, man's common trust of existence or his mutual mistrust? Even if the representatives I hope for be found, their success will depend on those represented, on their unreserved honesty, their goodwill with its scorn of empty phrases, their courageous personal engagement. From this source alone can the power that the representatives need stream towards them. The hope for this hour depends upon the hopers themselves, upon ourselves. I mean by this: upon those among us who feel most deeply the sickness of present-day man and who speak in his name the word without which no healing takes place: I will live.

The hope for this hour depends upon the renewal of dialogical immediacy between men. But let us look beyond the pressing need, the anxiety and care of this hour. Let us see this need in connection with the great human way. Then we shall recognize that immediacy is injured not only between man and man, but also between the being called man and the source of his existence. At its core the conflict between mistrust and trust of man conceals the conflict between the mistrust and trust of eternity. If our mouths succeed in genuinely saying "thou," then, after long silence and stammering, we shall have addressed our eternal "Thou" anew. Reconciliation leads towards reconciliation.

IN DEFENSE OF POLITICAL COMPROMISE*

Floyd W. Matson

*I*n his celebrated essay "On Compromise," written in 1874, the English author and statesman John Morley developed a set of definitions which have had a lasting, if controversial, effect upon the language of politics. The book makes its intention plain in the opening sentence: "The design of the following essay is to consider . . . some of the limits that are set by sound reason to the practice of the various arts of accommodation, economy, management, conformity, or compromise."

Here are several senses of the word *compromise*, the least ambiguous and most significant of which are those suggested by *accommodation* and *conformity*. If it is not at once apparent it soon becomes abundantly clear that compromise for Lord Morley is a threat to principle, and principle is what must be preserved at all costs. There are qualifying phrases here and there, but the dominant impression left with the reader is that which is conveyed by these final sentences:

> A principle, if it be sound, represents one of the larger expediencies. To abandon that for the sake of some seeming expediency of the hour, is to sacrifice the greater good for the less, on no more creditable ground than that the less is nearer. It is better to wait, and to defer the realization of our ideas until we can realize them fully, than to defraud the future by truncating them, if truncate them we must, in order to secure a partial triumph for them in the immediate present. . . . What is the sense, and what is the morality, of postponing the wider utility to the narrower? Nothing is so sure to impoverish an epoch, to deprive conduct of nobleness, and character of elevation.

In fairness to the author, it should be said that this pompous peroration was intended to apply not so much to group conduct of social and political

* Reprinted by permission from the *Pacific Spectator*.

affairs as to individual conduct in thought and action; more precisely, to the conduct of individual Englishmen. It is important to an understanding of Morley to remember that he was addressing Englishmen in the glacial period of Victoria, when they appeared (to critics both foreign and domestic) more than ever a nation of shopkeepers. That there should be among the English people "a profound distrust of general principles" Morley accepted as "an inveterate national characteristic," but what he especially regretted was the tendency of his own age toward "a growing predominance of material, temporary, and selfish aims, over those which are generous, far-reaching, and spiritual; a deadly weakening of intellectual conclusiveness, and clear-shining moral illumination, and lastly, of a certain stoutness of self-respect for which England was once especially famous."

Morley's essay, then, was a manifesto spurring Englishmen to the defense of principle and the protection of morality, and an end to compromise with evil. On the personal level, as spiritual or psychological advice, these are good words for any time; but extrapolated to the social and political level they only confuse the issue and mistake the reality. "Those who would treat politics and morality apart," said Morley in another work, "will never understand the one or the other."

To this it may be answered that those who would treat politics and morality as inseparable are unlikely to be successful at either. For politics, as the art of the possible, is most successful—and even most respectable—when it has achieved a *modus vivendi* among the diversity of competing principles and interests. Moreover, while there may be no place for compromise in morality there is definitely a place for morality in compromise. The whole meaning of conciliation, as Edward Crankshaw has seen, is that of interaction between two or more firm points of view. It requires self-understanding as well as knowledge of the other side; and it calls for the wisdom to know when to give ground and when to stand firm. Compromise, let it be plainly stated, is not the sacrifice of principle but the recognition of principles other than one's own; it is a denial of omniscience and infallibility, and a reflection of the spirit of toleration. Compromise in fact is only toleration doing its work; and its dangers are the common dangers of toleration. If toleration in the area of thought and expression always carries with it what Laski described as "a certain penumbra of contingent anarchy," toleration in the field of political action carries with it the risk of being outmaneuvered. It follows that whenever, as in our own time, men's attention becomes fastened on the risk, rather than on the end for which the risk is taken, both freedom of speech and freedom of negotiation are imperiled.

The purpose of the present essay is to argue that for democratic society a politics without the spirit of compromise—an uncompromising politics—is neither desirable nor in fact possible. The case would need little pleading if there were a general acceptance of the necessary role of compromise in political life; but, at least in our own country and at the present time, the contrary is more nearly true. On the level of international politics especially, the time-honored methods of arbitration, conciliation, and mutual concession—even the cardinal principle of negotiation itself—are currently threatened by a jealous and parochial intolerance which condemns all efforts at conciliation as "appeasement" and summarizes its case in the hypocritical pronouncement "You can't do business with (those) dictators." We shall come back to the question of appeasement later on; here it may be sufficient to underline the observation of Crankshaw that "this horrible word, a dubious label for cowardice in face of a bully, now shows every sign of driving from our language and our thought one of its finest and most sturdy flowers: the word conciliation."

The sturdy flowers of *conciliation* and *compromise*, however, have been badly stained by ambiguity and could stand semantic pruning. *Compromise* especially has taken on some strange mutations. To Webster it suggests both a peaceable settlement of differences and an exposure to danger and scandal; Roget finds it synonymous with such dissimilar words as *endanger, taint, pacify,* and *atone.* These conflicting connotations are, of course, not so incompatible as they seem. Whatever else it may imply, compromise means giving up something, and there is always reluctance and frequently danger in that. As the *Britannica* crisply observes: "From the element of danger involved has arisen an invidious sense of the word, imputing discredit, so that being 'compromised' commonly means injured in reputation." The inference would seem to be plain that the invidious meaning is secondary and residual, if not downright illegitimate, while the proper meaning is that of mutual concession and agreement.

No lengthy argument should be necessary to demonstrate the intimate relationship of compromise to democratic government. It is no less true today than in the time of Burke that "all government,—indeed every human benefit and enjoyment, every virtue and every prudent act,—is founded on compromise and barter. We balance inconveniences; we give and take, we remit some rights, that we may enjoy others." Even in the most despotic regime a variety of concessions must be made by the ruler to the needs and interests of his subjects. But it is in democratic politics that the function of compromise, as the daily and deliberate adjustment of competing demands, is most significant.

In our own country its operations are especially apparent in the field of parliamentary action, where the passage of a law almost invariably represents a compromise between the various demands of interest groups and power blocs; there is no room, as Roland Young has said of Congress, for any group which holds out for the whole hog or none, which insists that it must define the rules or it won't play. In a broader sense American party politics may be regarded as a continuous exercise in compromise; compromise has been institutionalized in the party convention, mythicized in the image of the smoke-filled room, and stereotyped in the campaign speech.

The improvisation and frequent disorderliness of a political process based on compromise is not always, of course, a happy spectacle, and demands for the organization of our parties on a more coherent basis are often heard. "There is admittedly something nerve-racking," commented the editor of *Harper's* a few years ago, "about an Administration which plays by ear, shifting from one key to the other in an effort to harmonize with the theme songs of conflicting interests within its own party." But, as he went on to point out, "the alternatives might prove to be either the multi-party system which is so cacophonously exemplified by French politics or the one-party system which is so harmoniously achieved in Russia. Neither is particularly attractive."

Despite our domestic cultivation of the art of compromise, it is not surprising that among the Western partners in the cold war it should be America which is most uncompromising, and Britain which is most conciliatory; nor is this fact to be explained simply in terms of British weakness and American strength. At the high noon of the empire, when there was scarcely any foreign field without some corner forever England, Lord Morley was to be heard complaining of that "English feeling for compromise" which had led his countrymen to muddle through so ungracefully, and to gain their empire in a fit of absence of mind; and he quoted the observation of a foreigner that "it is not easy, humanly speaking, to wind an Englishman up to the level of dogma." (He might equally have appreciated the comment of another foreigner, Wilhelm Dibelius, that "the English state rests on two specifically English assumptions, common sense and the transformation of the antagonist into a privileged colleague.")

The spirit of compromise, by contrast, has never been a notable component of American diplomacy. While the nation was adolescent, we feared to be hoodwinked or bulldozed in our dealings with stronger powers; since we have come of age we have largely preferred to bulldoze on our own. While we have consented to arbitrate disputes of minor importance, as Thomas A. Bailey has seen, we have repeatedly declined to arbitrate important cases where the issue of war or peace hung in the balance. "One can scarcely point to a single instance," observes Professor Bailey, "when, if we had lost, we would have been seriously discommoded."

The traditional American distrust of diplomacy is closely associated with what Charles Burton Marshall has called "the notion that perfection was for the asking and that anything less than perfection was failure in international dealings." The singular good luck of the American nation through its first hundred years, when its universal ideals coincided almost fortuitously with both its national interest and the interest of the foremost world power, tended to obscure for many Americans the hard realities of international politics in which perfection, or even one's own way, is rarely to be had completely. Thus a foreign policy conceived, as Marshall puts it, "in terms of good principles destined for inevitable triumph over evil" has had more appeal for Americans than one "expressed in terms of interests susceptible of compromise with the interests of others."

Recent years have witnessed the growing ascendancy of this moralizing temper, which carries over into the affairs of states the absolute standards of right and wrong. It has come more and more to be accepted that in diplomacy as in war "there is no substitute for victory": a victory which must be total, entailing a surrender which is unconditional. What was once a conventional transaction between states comes to be viewed in terms of "ideological warfare," in which truth and justice are the exclusive province of one's own side, and concessions of whatever kind are tantamount to appeasement if not to open treason. Burke warned us long ago of "the delusive plausibilities of moral politicians"; more recently George F. Kennan has said of the modern concept of total victory that "there is no more dangerous delusion, none that has done us a greater disservice in the past or that threatens to do us a greater disservice in the future."

This intransigent philosophy has reached its climax in the diplomatic freeze of the cold war. The familiar specter of appeasement is once again invoked (by much the same groups, ironically, which ardently supported the policy that first gave meaning to the term), and it walks abroad in the land, striking fear in the hearts of loyal Americans and driving from their thought the old-fashioned concept of conciliation. As Max Lerner noted in the first stages of the cold war, the sense in which the term *appeasement* has come to be used covers any sort of concession or conciliation between the polarized powers of the US and the USSR. But, he went on to say, horseswapping is not appeasement; when major concessions are made by both parties to a dispute, "what you have is a form of conciliation or compromise, and compromise has always been considered a basic element of the democratic process and of international peace."

Compromise is indeed a basic element of the democratic process; and in this age of mass communications it is well to remember that its success has traditionally depended upon the preservation of an essential privacy. It is a truism of government that compromise cannot be pressed in public; the open forum of the parliamentary floor is well designed for ideology and rhetoric, but the real areas of agreement are more often to be found in committees, corridors, and cloakrooms. This fact has a special significance for international relations, where prior to 1918 the locus of decision was the comparatively closed and confidential conference of ministers and diplomatic staffs. The importance of privacy has been well emphasized by Sir Harold Nicolson, who points out that in state affairs "a negotiation is the subject of concession and counterconcession: if the concession offered is divulged before the public are aware of the corresponding concession to be received, extreme agitation may follow and the negotiation may have to be abandoned." Sir Harold echoes the injunction of the French diplomatist Jules Cambon: "The day secrecy is abolished, negotiation of any kind will become impossible."

The high principles of Woodrow Wilson, however otherwise inspiring, did the cause of international agreement no good by insisting that diplomacy "proceed always frankly and in the public view" toward "open covenants openly arrived at." At the time of its pronouncement as one of the Fourteen Points, this dictum was a justified reaction to the excesses of the secret treaties; but its long-range effect has been to throw the spotlight of publicity upon the most intimate and involved negotiations of governments, and to transform the quiet conference room into an auditorium. The tremendous acceleration of the mass media over subsequent years has greatly assisted this transformation, and diplomats in modern conference are compelled to address themselves, not to the other side of the table, but to the world in general and their own national publics in particular. In the interest of propaganda advantage, common values are minimized and differences exaggerated. More and more it happens that the conflicting parties find that they have gone so far in pushing their demands that they cannot compromise for fear of "losing face." Whenever a nation's leaders become "bidders at an auction of popularity," advised Burke, they will be turned into "flatterers instead of legislators. . . . Moderation will be stigmatized as the virtue of cowards; and compromise as the prudence of traitors."

These remarks serve to point up the crisis which arises from the contemporary distrust of compromise: i.e., the paralysis of communications between East and West, symbolized in the iron and silken and bamboo curtains which have been successively rung down between the opposing camps. It may be that already ideological differences on both sides have been too sharply drawn, and considerations of prestige become too powerful, to permit any repairing of communications and restoration of understanding. But if the failure is one of understanding, surely its solution short of hot war is possible only through renewed efforts at cultural and political contact: efforts which imply a spirit of toleration and a willingness to compromise. It is possible that all such attempts will be summarily rejected by an uncompromising East; but to those who say that understanding must be mutual at the outset it is enough to answer with Crankshaw that "there is no must about it. It would be very nice if it could be mutual, because then there would be no more problems of this kind. But although it takes two to make a quarrel, only one is necessary to avoid a quarrel." And in defense of compromise, finally, there is still no sounder argument than Burke's reminder to a very young gentleman at Paris that it is

> action and counter-action which, in the natural and in the political world, from the reciprocal struggle of discordant powers, draws out the harmony of the universe. These opposed and conflicting interests . . . interpose a salutary check to all precipitate resolutions. They render deliberation not a matter of choice, but of necessity; they make all change a subject of compromise, which naturally begets moderation . . . [and renders] all the headlong exertions of arbitrary power, in the few or in the many, for ever impracticable.

EDUCATION AND THE SOCRATIC DIALOGUE*

Robert M. Hutchins

*t*he obvious failures of the educational doctrines of adaptation, immediate needs, social reform, and of the doctrine that we need no doctrine at all may suggest to us that we require a better definition of education. Let us concede that every society must have some system that attempts to adapt the young to their social and political environment. If the society is bad, in the sense, for example, in which the Nazi state was bad, the system will aim at the same bad ends. To the extent that it makes men bad in order that they may be tractable subjects of a bad state, the system may help to achieve the social ideals of the society. It may be what the society wants; it may even be what the society needs, if it is to perpetuate its form and accomplish its aims. In pragmatic terms, in terms of success in the society, it may be a "good" system.

But it seems to me clearer to say that, though it may be a system of training, or instruction, or adaptation, or meeting immediate needs, it is not a system of education. It seems clearer to say that the purpose of education is to improve men. Any system that tries to make them bad is not education, but something else. If, for example, democracy is the best form of society, a system that adapts the young to it will be an educational system. If despotism is a bad form of society, a system that adapts the young to it will not be an educational system, and the better it succeeds in adapting them the less educational it will be.

Every man has a function as a man. The function of a citizen or a subject may vary from society to society, and the system of training, or adaptation, or instruction, or meeting immediate needs may vary with it. But the function of a man as man is the same in every age and in every society, since it results from his nature as a man. The aim of an educational system is the same in every age and in every society where such a system can exist: it is to improve man as man.

If we are going to talk about improving men and societies, we have to believe that there is some difference between good and bad. This difference must not be, as the positivists think it is, merely conventional. We cannot tell this difference by any examination of the effectiveness of a given program as the pragmatists propose; the time required to estimate these effects is usually too long and the complexity of society is always too great for us to say that the consequences of a given program are altogether clear. We cannot discover the difference between good and bad by going to the laboratory, for men and societies are not laboratory animals. If we believe that there is no truth, there is no knowledge, and there are no values except those which are validated by laboratory experiment, we cannot talk about the improvement of men and societies, for we can have no standard of promoting or judging anything that takes place among men or in societies.

Society is to be improved, not by forcing a program of social reform down its throat, through the schools or otherwise, but by the improvement of the individuals who compose it. As Plato said, "Governments reflect human nature. States are not made out of stone or wood, but out of the characters of their citizens: these turn the scale and draw everything after them." The individual is the heart of society.

To talk about making men better we must have some idea of what men are, because if we have none, we can have no idea of what is good or bad for them. If men are brutes like other animals, there is no reason why they should not be trained as brutes are trained. A sound philosophy in general suggests that men are rational, moral, and spiritual beings and that the improvement of men means the fullest development of their rational, moral, and spiritual powers. All men have these powers, and all men should develop them to the fullest extent.

Man is by nature free, and he is by nature social. To use his freedom rightly he needs discipline. To live in society he needs the moral virtues. Good moral and intellectual habits are required for the fullest development of the nature of man.

To develop fully as a social, political animal man needs participation in his own government. A benevolent despotism will not do. You cannot expect the slave to show the virtues of the free man unless you first set him free. Only democracy, in which all men rule and are ruled in turn for the good of life of the whole community, can be an absolutely good form of government.

The community rests on the social nature of men. Civilization is the deliberate pursuit of a common ideal. The good society is not just a society we happen to like or to be used to, as the positivists say. It is a community of good men.

Education deals with the development of the intellectual powers of men. Their moral and spiritual powers are the sphere of the family and the church. All three agencies must work in harmony; for, though a man has three aspects, he is still one man. But the schools cannot take over the role of the family and the church without promoting the atrophy of those institutions and failing in the task that is proper to the schools.

We cannot talk about the intellectual powers of men, though we can talk about training them, or amusing them, or adapting them, and meeting their immediate needs, unless our philosophy in general tells us that there is knowledge and that there is a difference between true and false. We must believe, too, that there are other means of obtaining knowledge than scientific experimentation. If valid knowledge can be sought only in the laboratory, many fields in which we thought we had knowledge will offer us nothing but opinion or superstition, and we shall be forced to conclude that we cannot know anything about the most important aspects of man and society. If we are to set about developing the intellectual powers of men through having them acquire knowledge of the most important subjects, we have to begin with the proposition that experimentation and empirical data will be of only limited use to us, contrary to the convictions of many American social scientists, and that philosophy, history, literature, and art give us knowledge, and significant knowledge, on the most significant issues.

If the object of education is the improvement of men, then any system of education that is without values is a contradiction in terms. A system that seeks bad values is bad. A system that denies the existence of values denies the possibility of education. Relativism, scientism, skepticism, and anti-intellectualism, the four horsemen of the philosophical apocalypse, have produced that chaos in education which will end in the disintegration of the West.

The prime object of education is to know what is good for man. It is to know the goods in their order. There is a hierarchy of values. The task of education is to help us understand it, establish it, and live by it. This Aristotle had in mind when he said: "It is not the possessions but the desires of men that must be equalized, and this is impossible unless they have a sufficient education according to the nature of things."

Such an education is far removed from the triviality of that produced by the doctrines of adaptation, of immediate needs, of social reform, or of the doctrine of no doctrine at all. Such an education will not adapt the young to a bad environment, but it will encourage them to make it good. It will not overlook immediate needs, but it will place these needs in their proper relationship to more distant, less tangible, and more important goods. It will be the only effective means of reforming society.

This is the education appropriate to free men. It is liberal education. If all men are to be free, all men must have this education. It makes no difference how they are to earn their living or what their special interests or aptitudes may be. They can learn to make a living, and they can develop their special interests and aptitudes, after they have laid the foundation of free and responsible manhood through liberal education. It will not do to say that they are incapable of such education. This claim is made by those who are too indolent or unconvinced to make the effort to give such education to the masses.

Nor will it do to say that there is not enough time to give everybody a liberal education before he becomes a specialist. In America, at least, the waste and frivolity of the educational system are so great that it would be possible through getting rid of them to give every citizen a liberal education and make him a qualified specialist, too, in less time than is now consumed in turning out uneducated specialists.

A liberal education aims to develop the powers of understanding and judgment. It is impossible that too many people can be educated in this sense, because there cannot be too many people with understanding and judgment. We hear a great deal today about the dangers that will come upon us through the frustration of educated people who have got educated in the expectation that education will get them a better job, and who then fail to get it. But surely this depends on the representations that are made to the young about what education is. If we allow them to believe that education will get them better jobs and encourage them to get educated with this end in view, they are entitled to a sense of frustration if, when they have got the education, they do not get the jobs. But, if we say that they should be educated in order to be men, and that everybody, whether he is a ditch-digger or a bank president, should have this education because he is a man, then the ditch-digger may still feel frustrated, but not because of his education.

Nor is it possible for a person to have too much liberal education, because it is impossible to have too much understanding and judgment. But it is possible to undertake too much in the name of liberal education in youth. The object of liberal education in youth is not to teach the young all they will ever need to know. It is to give them the habits, ideas, and techniques that they need to continue to educate themselves. Thus the object of formal institutional liberal education in youth is to prepare the young to educate themselves throughout their lives.

I would remind you of the impossibility of learning to understand and judge many of the most important things in youth. The judgment and understanding of practical affairs can amount to little in the absence of experience with practical affairs. Subjects that cannot be understood without experience should not be taught to those who are without experience. Or, if these subjects are taught to those who are without experience, it should be clear that these subjects can be taught only by way of introduction and that their value to the student depends on his continuing to study them as he acquires experience. The tragedy in America is that economics, ethics, politics, history, and literature are studied in youth, and never studied again. Therefore the graduates of American universities never understand them.

This pedagogical principle, that subjects requiring experience can be learned only by the experienced, leads to the conclusion that the most important branch of education is the education of adults. We sometimes seem to think of education as something like the mumps, measles, whooping-cough, or chicken-pox. If a person has had education in childhood, he need not, in fact he cannot, have it again. But the pedagogical principle that the most important things can be learned only in mature life is supported by a sound philosophy in general. Men are rational animals. They achieve their terrestrial felicity by the use of reason. And this means that they have to use it for their entire lives. To say that they should learn only in childhood would mean that they were human only in childhood.

And it would mean that they were unfit to be citizens of a republic. A republic, a true *res publica*, can maintain justice, peace, freedom, and order only by the exercise of intelligence. When we speak of the consent of the governed, we mean, since men are not angels, who see the truth intuitively and do not have to learn it, that every act of assent on the part of the governed is a product of learning. A republic is really a common educational life in process. So Montesquieu said that, whereas the principle of a monarchy was honor, and the principle of a tyranny was fear, the principle of a republic was education.

Hence the ideal republic is the republic of learning. It is the utopia by which all actual political republics are measured. The goal toward which we started with the Athenians twenty-five centuries ago is an unlimited republic of learning and a world-wide political republic mutually supporting each other.

All men are capable of learning. Learning does not stop as long as a man lives, unless his learning power atrophies because he does not use it. Political freedom cannot endure unless it is accompanied by provision for the unlimited acquisition of knowledge. Truth is not long retained in human affairs without continual learning and relearning. Peace is unlikely unless there are continuous, unlimited opportunities for learning and unless men continuously avail themselves of them. The world of law and justice for which we yearn, the world-wide political republic, cannot be realized without the world-wide republic of learning. The civilization we seek will be achieved when all men are citizens of the world republic of law and justice and of the republic of learning all their lives long.

This continuous lifelong liberal education that makes a man a citizen of the world republic of learning and that is indispensable if he is to do his part to bring about the world republic of law and justice is an intellectual discipline that fits a man to solve new problems as they arise, to grasp new facts as they appear, to meet new needs as they present themselves, and to remould the environment to make it conform to the aspirations of the human spirit.

The pedagogical content of this education may be simply stated. The liberally educated man must know how to read, write, and figure. He must know and understand the ideas that have animated mankind. He must comprehend the tradition in which he lives. He must be able to communicate with his fellow-men. Through familiarity with the best models he must have constantly before him that habitual vision of greatness without which, Whitehead said, any true education is impossible.

The process of such an education should be dialectical. The liberally educated man should be able to continue the Great Conversation that began in the dawn of history, that goes on at the present day, and that is best exemplified by the Socratic dialogue.

Socrates collected opinions, asked questions, clarified terms and ideas, and indicated commitments. That is all he did. All that was required of those who took part with him was that they should try to think and to understand one another. They did not have to agree with Socrates, before or after. They did not have to agree among themselves. If they came to conviction, they did so by their own free will. The only constraint upon them was the law of contradiction. They could not answer Yes and No to the same question at the same time.

As a sound philosophy in general teaches us that men are rational beings, so the educational philosophy dependent on it tells us that though men can be assisted to learn, they can learn only by themselves. They cannot be indoctrinated without violation of the laws of their nature. Criticism, discussion, question, debate—these are the truly human methods of instruction. Teaching, like midwifery, is a cooperative art. The great truth that Plato presented, somewhat romantically, in the dialogue called the *Meno*, as the doctrine of reminiscence, is that intellectual progress does not take place when the teacher is laying down the law and the pupil is memorizing it, but when teacher and pupil are working together to bring the pupil to the rational answer to the question before him. The Socratic dialogue is the great mirror of pedagogy, whether the student is a child or an adult.

The Socratic dialogue, too, may provide us with a model for the university, the institution that stands at the apex of the educational system and that eventually determines the character of all the rest of it.

In a paper written for the tercentenary of Harvard, Alfred North Whitehead said that the task of the universities is intellectual leadership and proposed that Harvard should fashion the mind of the twentieth century as the University of Paris fashioned that of the Middle Ages.

When I read Mr. Whitehead's article, I asked myself whether the universities had ever exerted intellectual leadership or had ever fashioned the mind of any epoch except the Middle Ages. Since the universities were not established till the Middle Ages, they could not have fashioned the mind of the ages before. As to the ages afterward, their minds were fashioned by individual men, or by small groups of men, most of whom were not associated with universities. One of the most striking things about the works that have made the minds of various ages is that almost none of them were written by professors. And where they were written by men who were sheltered by universities, the men and not the universities were responsible. That Newton worked at Cambridge should not blind us to the fact that in his day the British universities were sinking into a deep torpor, probably brought on by port, from which they were not to awaken for more than a hundred and fifty years. The influences that have been most effective on a world scale in fashioning the mind of the twentieth century up to now are Marx, Darwin, and Freud, not Heidelberg, Oxford, or the Sorbonne.

Ever since Mr. Whitehead's article appeared I have been trying to figure out how it was that the universities fashioned the mind of the Middle Ages when they have not been able to do so since. In order to discover whether the universities can exert intellectual leadership again, we have to find out how they did so once. Mr. Whitehead's answer was *suggestiveness*. They did it by suggestiveness, and suggestiveness comes from action. So Mr. Whitehead said that the way Harvard could do for modern times what the University of Paris did for the Middle Ages was to absorb into itself those schools of vocational training for which systematized understanding has importance.

This answer seemed inadequate to me thirteen years ago and has grown more so with every passing day. If this is all there is to it, the American universities should long since have fashioned the mind of this age, for they have absorbed into themselves not only all those vocational schools for which systematized understanding has importance, but also every other vocational school, so that the ordinary American university presents an array of vocational schools of incredible variety and insignificance.

What is important for us is not the fact that the medieval universities entered into the life of their time, but the way in which they did it. In the Middle Ages the whole university was both speculative and practical. The insight that produced this organization was that everything speculative has significance in the practical dimension, and everything practical, to be worth study, must have a speculative basis. The purpose for which any action was studied or taught was to increase the understanding of that action and what it implied. Not every occupation was a profession in the Middle Ages. A profession was a body of men trained in a subject matter that had intellectual content in its own right. The aim of the group was the common good. The universities of the Middle Ages did not enter into the life of their time through having schools that actually or ostensibly prepared men for vocations, but through a combination of the speculative and the practical that made the two indistinguishable as subjects of study and teaching.

The disciplines of the Middle Ages were studied together because they were lived together, and must be. Professors and students had a common heritage in the tradition of learning. They had a common training in the methods and techniques appropriate to each discipline. They did not necessarily agree on what ideas were basic, but they did have a common acquaintance with the ideas that could seriously claim to be basic and a commensurate ability, derived from a common training, to appraise and understand those ideas. The characteristic intellectual apparatus of the medieval university, as Mill nostalgically points out in his essay *On Liberty*, was the disputation, which has now disappeared from the Anglo-Saxon world.

If it is these features of the medieval university, rather than its specific-ally vocational interests, that helped the University of Paris to fashion the mind of the Middle Ages, we can understand why no universities since the Middle Ages have been able to duplicate the accomplishments of those which existed then.

In the essay that he wrote for the Harvard tercentenary, Etienne Gilson pointed out that the scholars of the Middle Ages wanted to universalize the faith. They had a strong belief in the universal character of rational truth. "Since faith could not possibly be proved by reason," Mr. Gilson says, "the only hope of universalizing it was to make it acceptable to reason." The method of seeking to make faith acceptable to reason was endless argumentation. Mr. Gilson concludes: "Thus did it come to pass that, viewing themselves as members of the same spiritual family, using a com-mon language to impart to others the same fundamental truth, those medieval scholars succeeded in living and working together for about three centuries, and so long as they did, there was in the world, together with a vivid feeling for the universal character of truth, some sort of Occidental unity."

The end of the Middle Ages brought with it great gains in every field of knowledge, except possibly philosophy and theology. The medieval period had been an age of debate. What followed was age upon age of dis-covery. Inquiry was promoted by specialization and the experimental method. In the Middle Ages the members of the University of Paris thought together. The subjects that were studied were studied together. Teachers and students tried to see everything in relation to everything else. They had to—their object was understanding through discussion. The discoverer or the experimenter, on the other hand, had to be a specialist as

soon as possible; his demands gradually broke down the common training
of the medieval period. Since his object was to open new fields, he did not
care for the tradition of learning. Descartes, for examples, began by repudiating all previous thinkers.

As the specialties multiplied, specialists could not think together. The
specialties were too numerous and diverse to be studied together. The discussion that was the principal activity of the medieval university had to
stop. The standard by which the medieval university determined what
should be studied had to go. Anything that any specialist wanted to study
had to be included. Who could say that one vocational school was any more
appropriate to a university than any other?

The processes of the last eight hundred years have been favorable to the
formal emancipation and education of the people. But in a period of discovery, a period of specialization and esoteric experiment, what can their
education be? Almost by definition nobody can know anything except a
specialist, and he can know nothing outside his specialty. At the same time
all the wonderful things that are happening in science can be made exciting
to the people, and a profit is to be garnered by writing them up in a cheerful
and inaccurate way for popular consumption.

So Hermann Hesse, in his novel *Magister Ludi*, calls this the "Age of
the Digest." This is the period of the fragmentary, the topical, the diverting
—the period of the uncomprehended trifle. It is a period of propaganda and
publicity.

The most remarkable paradox of our time is that, in proportion as the
instruments of communication have increased in number and power, communication has steadily declined. Mutual intelligibility is probably a rarer
phenomenon now than at any time in history.

The task of intellectual leadership now is to bring about a genuine communion of minds. But this is still the age of discovery. It is, therefore, still
the age of the individual thinker, of the specialist. And, as a consequence,
it is the age of the digest, with all the incoherence and triviality that must
characterize such an age. If there is to be a new cultural epoch and not
simply a further cultural collapse, the distinguishing feature of the new
epoch must be this: it must combine discovery and discussion. The object
must be, while retaining and encouraging the drive toward discovery, to
restore the conditions of conversation.

If then we ask how the university can repeat the brilliant leadership of
the University of Paris, and if the task of that leadership is to bring about a
genuine communion of minds through the restoration of the conditions of
conversation, we run at once against the fact that in the speculative realm
the modern university is chaotic, that in the practical realm it is silent, and
that the two realms are sharply divided from each other. The chaos
in the speculative realm means that ideas are unclear, unrelated, and

uncomprehended. The silence in the practical realm means that on matters of life or death to our society no disinterested voice reaches the public. The division of the speculative and the practical impoverishes both. The conditions of conversation do not exist within the university. In the academic world there is no genuine communion of minds.

One of the things most often proposed as a step toward communion of minds is international co-operation in science, art, and scholarship. Although such co-operation should be promoted, it would not do much to establish a community within a university, or within a country, or throughout the world. A scholar in one country can now communicate with another scholar in the same field anywhere in the West. He is usually incapable of communicating with a scholar in another field on his own campus. If the university as such, the university as distinguished from its individual members, is to exert intellectual leadership toward creating a genuine communion of minds, it must first have such communion within itself.

The task of bringing about communion within a modern university can be performed, if it can be performed at all, only through a common training, a common appreciation of the different kinds of knowledge and of the different methods and techniques appropriate to each, and a common, continuous discussion on the Socratic model of those ideas which can pretend to be important, together with the consideration of the practical implications of those ideas.

In such a community, men, even if they disagree, should be able to relate what they are thinking to what others are thinking or have thought on the same point and on all points connected with it. The individual should be able to locate himself in a universe of discourse. Ideally, enough unity should prevail in the world of thought so that no idea, no theory, doctrine, or general view of things could exist in isolation from the rest.

A university should be an intellectual community in which specialists, discoverers, and experimenters, in addition to their obligation to their specialties, recognize an obligation to talk with and understand one another. If they can restore the conditions of conversation among themselves, they can become a university, a corporate body of thinkers, that can exert intellectual leadership and hope to make some modest efforts to fashion the mind of its time. They could hope to achieve a *Summa Dialectica*, a summation of the possibilities of thought, of the methods of analyzing, relating, and understanding ideas, with an indication of real agreements and disagreements. It may not be possible to reconcile the ideologies that now divide the world. But we cannot tell whether or not they can be reconciled until we have first tried to get them clear.

The problem, then, is to retain the values of the age of discovery, to regain those of the age of debate, and to put an end to the age of the digest. And the problem is to do this through the university as a whole, not through individuals who happen to reside in it. To do this it would have to think as a university, and think both speculatively and practically. The intelligence of the university as such would have to be focused on great speculative and practical issues.

If, then, some modern sage, like Mr. Whitehead, were to ask once more how a university might exert intellectual leadership and fashion the mind of the twentieth century, he might create for himself a sort of myth or dream of the higher learning. In this myth he might fancy that the university, in addition to making the most sensational discoveries in all fields of knowledge, asked itself what were the crucial problems of contemporary civilization upon which the intelligence of the university might shed some light. He might see the university studying such questions as the crisis in our culture, the conflict between East and West, the relations of church and state, or the responsibility of the public for the health of the community, and giving its impartial advice to a people distracted by propaganda. He might imagine that even the specialized, theoretical thought of the university would be enriched and a genuine communion of minds advanced by this effort to focus the intellect of the university upon the continuing problems of human society.

Of course the sage would be enough of a sage to realize that the ideas that were brought to bear upon practical problems could not originate in or be validated by any official creed, dogma, or authority. In his dream the university would be aiming at restoring the conditions of conversation and reinterpreting basic ideas. Thus he would see the university taking up one such idea after another and discussing, clarifying, and modifying it in the light of modern discoveries. This would be the creation of a *Summa Dialectica*. He would see the university as a whole, the university as such, moving in both the speculative and the practical orders toward communion, unity, understanding, and the enlightenment of the world.

This is, of course, merely a myth, or a dream. And I fear that it will always remain so. I fear that the university, in Europe as well as in America, is so far sunk in empiricism, specialism, and positivism that we cannot look to it to repeat in our time the brilliant leadership of the University of Paris. What, then, is the world to do for intellectual leadership, which it needs more today than at any time in the past five hundred years?

I suggest that we may require another institution, which would leave the university to go on as it is doing now, which would not supplant the university, but which would take up the burden the university has laid down.

Such an institution would be composed of men who were prepared to conduct a continuous Socratic dialogue on the basic issues of human life. They would be specialists, but they would have passed beyond specialism. They would bring their specialized training and points of view to bear upon the common task of clarification and understanding. They would be prepared to think, both speculatively and practically; they would be able to communicate with one another and with the public. They would retain the advantages of the Age of Discovery and regain those of the Age of Debate.

They would establish a genuine communion of minds. They would know no limitations of national boundaries; for they could be assembled from all parts of the world. They could therefore at once advance and symbolize that world community, that world republic of learning, without which the world republic of law and justice is impossible.

They might give light to the nations now wandering in darkness. They might fashion the mind of the 20th century and make it equal to the dreadful obligations that Providence has laid upon it.

part five

THE MODERN PERSUASION:
THE RHETORICS OF MASS SOCIETY

COMMUNICATION AND HUMANITAS

Leo Lowenthal

*i*f one speaks today about communication, one is almost forced into a controversy over the mass media. The media are, of course, merely the instruments of possible communication—they are the tools our technology has developed and whose right application is in question. Technology has extended our access to the world as never before. Yet despite telephones, radios, television, increased literacy, expanded circulation of books, newspapers, and periodicals we are lonelier than ever before—and certainly our common human need for world peace seems further removed than ever. Deterioration of our intellectual and moral heritage has not only accompanied the quantitative growth of mass media in modern society but has been a result as well. It is my contention that an awareness of these problems is essential to the preservation of the dignity and growth of the individual.

We have learned very little from the social sciences about how communication has affected man's humanity. In fact, the discussion of communications, precisely because it is mainly a discussion of mass media of communication, has seriously jeopardized productive discourse between social scientists and humanists. Yet stereotypes of the humanities to the contrary, there are now some social scientists who believe that to get at the meaning of communication in our time we had better turn toward the realm of symbolic expression—to the arts and religion. The humanists, sometimes quite rightly, suspect that all the social scientists care about are quantifiable aggregates of people and facts or rather people as facts. A temperamental

335

illustration of the humanist's attitude we owe to W. H. Auden. To quote
from his poem "Under Which Lyre":

> Thou shalt not answer questionaires
> Or quizzes upon World-Affairs
> Nor with compliance
> Take any test.
> Thou shalt not sit
> With statisticians nor commit
> A social science.*

In prose, the poet is echoed by a worthy professor of English who wrote in
College English several years ago:

"Little did I know, and my colleagues less: the social sciences have
these many years been studying the popular arts as mass media of communication. In some vague way we had all heard of it, but what man of sensibility reading the words mass media and communication would attach any
meaning to them: he would shudder at the vulgar jargon and turn away.
I have since spent many a long hour over sociological monographs, many
of them as empty as they are execrably written. If I may say so without
reflecting on any one—least of all myself—the study of mass communications does not attract the best minds."

Communication has been almost completely divested of its human content, a content suggested by the word itself. For true communication
entails a communion, a sharing of innermost experience. The dehumanization of communication has resulted from its annexation by the media of
modern culture—by the newspapers first, and then by radio and television.

That this dehumanization should have been brought so near perfection
in a society that professes an ultimate commitment to the sanctity and autonomy of the individual is one of the grotesque ironies of history. When an
individual appears in the media of communication he is insidiously separated from his humanity. Mass communication relies upon the ideological
sanction of individual autonomy in the very process of exploiting individuality to serve mass culture. Note how, in the following advertisement of
Young Readers of America, a branch of the Book-of-the-Month Club,
Inc., Dr. Gallup's private achievement, his particularity, is annulled by his
being made into an instrument of persuasion:

"As Dr. George Gallup, a former psychology professor himself, points
out in a recent article in the *Ladies' Home Journal*, if a child can acquire the
habit of book reading, it will be invaluable in helping him to cope successfully with all his later experiences in life."

---

* "Under Which Lyre," copyright 1946 by W. H. Auden. Reprinted from
Nones, by W. H. Auden, by permission of Random House, Inc., and of Faber
and Faber, Ltd.

The passage borrows the halo of mass culture as reflected in public opinion surveys to make palatable the intake of high culture. In citing Gallup as an authority on the value of culture pursuits one relies for the "finer" things in life on the master mass diagnostician who knows what is in the mind of the "public" and, by implication, what is best for it. To identify him as a former psychology professor implies that he has a good educational background and a respectable professional career but invokes simultaneously the sanctions of the intellectual and the successful businessman.

There is a new venture named "Time Books." This enterprise promises a "Time Reading Program." The cost? Only $3.95 for each package of three or four books and for this monthly charge you will partake in "a planned approach," which guarantees that "though your time may be limited you will be reading widely and profitably. . . . books which are truly timeless in style and significance." The reliability of the selection is beyond any doubt: "This plan draws its strength from the fact that the editors spent thousands of hours finding the answers to questions that you too must have asked yourself many times. . . . it is part of their job to single out the few books that tower over all others." Meaning, quality, and importance of these publications are assured: "In each case the editors will write special introductions to underline what is unique in the book, what impact it has had or will have, what place it has earned in literature and contemporary thought." In addition, a kind of religious sanction attaches to the wrappings of the enterprise: "The books will be bound in durable, flexible covers similar to those used for binding fine Bibles and Missals." This circular, which must have come out in millions of copies, claims that "this letter" was "written only to people whom we know to be thoughtful readers." The circular is called a "letter," the most personal genre of individual communication in writing—an example within an example of the perversion of communication in mass communications.

The social scientists of the last two generations have evaded moral commitment by pretending to engage in value-free research—something that exists neither in logic nor in history. In an era of increasing positivistic infatuation (which includes a large share of the teachers in humanistic fields, who should know better), the inalienable birthright of the intellectual as a critic, trivial as it may sound, must be energetically asserted. Plainly the communications setup of the modern world has corrupted human communication, and its images have penetrated perniciously and painfully the private realms of individuals in their most intimate spheres of discourse. Conversation becomes "a waste of time." The coffee house, since Queen Anne's time the refuge of the most delicate or indelicate personal dialogue, has been observed to be on its way out in Europe and ironically to be on its way into the American scene—yet as an only slightly veiled version of the desolate Third Avenue bar, home of the homeless isolates who make up a significant part of the populace. And it would be parochial snobbery to characterize the decay of language as genuine experience, including the downgrading of unplanned conversation, as merely a phenomenon of American civilization.

Here is a response cited in a survey recently made in Japan: "For example it is night and you are sitting alone at your desk with a textbook open. . . . So you switch on the radio, and without seeming to listen you begin to hear the late-late jazz program. And then the rhythm of the music appropriately puts a part of yourself to sleep and banishes excessive worry and longing; and riding to its pace as though mounted on a belt-conveyor, your studies begin to advance a little as though they were automates. . . ."

But memorizing one's homework is not cultivating one's memory. Memory is man's receptacle of living language and language lived by him and his fellow man through human history. Modern man, however, suffers a shrinkage of memory. It often seems limited to the news of yesterday's, if not today's, newspaper or television shows. Not only automobiles and washing machines but also language itself suffers today the fate of planned, or at least factual, obsolescence. What is remembered and what is forgotten seem almost indistinguishable, left to chance without any significance.

Toward the end of the dialogue *Phaedrus*, Socrates tells the story of the inventor-god Theuth, who boasts to Thamus, the king-god of Egypt, about his innovations. They sound almost like the enumeration of the basic features of our modern life style—an obsession with technology as well as with organized leisure time. "He it was who invented numbers and arithmetic and geometry and astronomy, also the game of checkers and dice" —laying the groundwork as it were for the radiation laboratories and the gambling casinos. What Theuth is most proud of is the invention of the alphabet: "This invention will make the Egyptians wiser and will improve their memories; for it is an elixir of memory and wisdom that I have discovered." The wise king, however, spots in the invention of writing the dismal seeds of rote, repetition, and renunciation of self-reliance. Plato's genius discovers in the achievements of civilization its very threat to culture. Not the spoken word but its written coagulation contains the germ for scholarship and the literary arts, as well as for the derivative products of mass communications—from newspapers to comic books, from Time Reader leaflets to billboards (those frozen highwaymen of our time). Thamus throws back at Theuth the concept of the written alphabet as elixir (the *pharmakon*, as it is called in Greek) and instead of accepting it as a medication predicts its potential deadly powers: "For this invention will produce forgetfulness in the minds of those who learn to use it, because they will not practice their memory. Their trust in writing, produced by external characters which are no part of themselves, will discourage the use of their own memory within them. You have invented an elixir not of memory but of reminding and you offer your pupils the *appearance* of wisdom, not true wisdom, for they will read many things without instruction and will therefore seem to know many things, when they are for the most part ignorant and hard to get along with, since they are not wise, but only appear wise." As if Plato had wished to tell us with emphasis that communication only exists as shared experience, shared with one's own self and the selves of others, he applies the technique of the dialogue within the dialogue: Socrates speaks to Phaedrus about Theuth and Thamus speaking to each other. This technique is an emblem of con-versation—turning to each other and striving for the common. It is the emblem of the open heart, the open mind, the very opposite of the prejudice and stereotype that are forever present in mass communications and their precipitations on modern man and his life style of borrowed experience. Memory is a bench mark for human, or better, humanistic behavior, as opposed to the quasi-biological, day-by-day, futile-moment-by-futile-moment existence to which modern man seems to have committed himself. The continuity of scholarship, the timelessness of the symbolic mementos of the arts, the tradition-laden connotations of religions, the faithful and solidary behavior of an individual—all these elements are variations on the theme of memory, which I am inclined to equate with communication truly understood, as Plato equated it with philosophy. All these concepts—memory, communication, philosophy—refer to genuine experience. After 2000 years John Smith, the Cambridge Platonist, restated in 1660 this Platonic credo:

"As an organizing argument I suggest the need for the scrupulous education of man. There is no easy road. For our words must refer to our experiences if we are to know whereof we speak and they must evoke the experiences of our peers if we are to be understood."

I am tempted to say that the Platonic dialogue embraces the idea of the divine coffeehouse; in any case, Plato's insistence on the cultivation of memory as the touchstone of individuality and creative participation in human communication does not appear by chance in a dialogue whose essential theme is the philosophy of the beautiful.

True, the humanistic meaning of communication is not entirely forgotten and interred. Ezra Pound (who, in spite of his aberrations, retains the stature of the poet and humanist) writes:

". . . As language becomes the most powerful instrument of perfidy, so language alone can riddle and cut through the meshes. Used to conceal meaning, used to blur meaning, used to produce the complete and utter inferno of the past century [and I may add the present as well] . . . against which, SOLELY a care for language, for accurate registration by language avails."

A story yet to be written is a social history of the intellectual debate on the style of modern life and more specifically on the fate and vicissitudes of the standards of culture, taste, and morality under the impact of urbanization and industrialization. This debate comes to a head in the critical analysis of the role and substance of the arts and their degraded counterparts or, to use these vague contemporary terms, on the relationship of high culture and popular culture. At least since Montaigne and Pascal and most articulately in individual works, in the magazines of the professional writers in England in the eighteenth and nineteenth centuries and also in Continental Europe, a lively discussion arose around the very same issue that Plato so provocatively put before Western man : What is going to happen to us when the very ego, this precious invention of idealistic philosophy, romantic poetry, and the spirit of capitalist enterprise, becomes increasingly enmeshed in the mechanisms of conformity—the whole network of institutional and psychological controls ? It would reflect a painful misunderstanding of the significance of this widely ramified discourse and debate if we filed it away under the rubric "problems of leisure time." The very fact that the concern of these eighteenth- and nineteenth-century writers again and again turns toward the social supplies of leisure time—the novels, the theaters, the magazines, the newspapers, sports and games, and what have you—means that the worried and troubled intellectuals examine critically that space of life within which man is supposedly free, his "free time." Although, of course, the supporters of conformity who sell their talents to the highest bidders are not absent among the intellectuals, the emphasis remains on the open wound, the wound of imitation—not the imitation of Christ but the almost mimetic imitation of what one is supposed to imitate. Whether or not the discussants consider a solution of the crisis of man and society possible, whether improvement of education or return to romanticized forms of agricultural society or withdrawal to the ivory tower or "No Exit" is the powerless recommendation of the critics—the essential verdict (long before Ezra Pound) is directed toward the decay of language, the limbo of human communication. This theme was as essential for Goethe as for Flaubert, for Wordsworth as for Eliot, for Coleridge as for Nietzsche— or for that matter for a large list of contributors to *The Edinburgh Review* as well as to other journals of sophisticated opinion.

This truly humanistic critique turns against instrumentalist language (as means to an end) and advocates the autonomous character of the human word as an end in itself. But as a human end indeed! Language *qua* language must retain the sacred dignity of the human condition. This paradoxical statement is made with intent. Language is indeed ideally the definitive logos. There is nothing else available to us for ultimate expression and true manifestation of the individual than language. In this view, I agree with Jakob Burckhardt, whom one cannot reproach for being insensible to nonverbal creative artifacts, who once said: "If it were possible to express in words the quintessence, the idea of a work of art, art itself would become superfluous, and all buildings, statues, and pictures could as well have been unbuilt, unsculpted, unpainted." The symbolic language of Judaeo-Christian religion has continuously emphasized the noninstrumental essence of language by endowing it with divine origin. Whether you look at Psalm 139 ("For there is not a word in my tongue, but, lo, O God, thou knowest it altogether") or at Sermon 79 of John Donne ("The Holy Ghost is an eloquent author, a vehement and an abundant author but yet not luxuriant; he is far from a penurious but as far from a superfluous style too"), man is viewed as created in the image of God because it is language that allows him to partake in the divine. There is a Biblical passage that conveys archetypically the humanistic meaning of language. It is found in the First Book of Kings, Chapter 19: "And, behold, God passed by, and a great and strong wind rent the mountains, and brake in pieces the rocks before God; but God was not in the wind. And after the wind an earthquake; but God was not in the earthquake; and after the earthquake a fire; but God was not in the fire; and after the fire a still small voice," the voice of the Lord. When we talk about communication today, we are inclined to mean the strong wind and the earthquake and the fire of the mass media of communication, of manipulation, of advertisements, of propaganda, mass circulation, and so forth. Yet human communication is truly the "still, small voice."

The meaning of the sacred in language is paradoxical. The instrumentalist concept of language (so frequently practiced in mass communications but, alas, in the scholar's world as well) conceives of language as a tool, and as such it must be as near perfect as any sophisticated technological product. Its ideal would be speed reading and writing, the teaching machine, the computer. But these ideals are—to turn a theological phrase—the ideals of the devil because language as the expression of the creative individual must also be the witness of his ever present incompletion. Mortal as we are, our language must reflect our limitations as well as the ever present tasks, possibilities, and potentialities before us. This function is exactly what is betrayed or at least denied in the products of popular culture. When the motion picture is finished or *The Reader's Digest* is read or the crooner's songs are heard, there is nothing to be said or seen or heard any more. Creative imagination has become muted. The patterned communications mechanism has as its logical and psychological end the switching off of the projector, the radio set, and the television box or the final mute grimace of the singer. But the true meaning of communication, which is upheld by the literary artists and above all by the poets, insists on productive imagination, on ambiguity, even on silence. Today the communications conscience of man is kept alive by the artist who communicates the very breakdown of communication: James Joyce, for instance, when he explores the archaic secrets of word and syntax, or the dramatists of the Theater of the Absurd when they explore the radical gulf that separates word and meaning.

There is no need, however, to take recourse to the messages of the avant-garde. The scene is as of old, and the witnesses are available in more familiar places.

One hundred and fifty years ago Coleridge wrote a letter to his friend Southey aiming at a harmless act of manipulation. He requested Southey to write a letter to his magazine *The Friend* in a "humorous manner" so that he, Coleridge, would be able to reply and explain his attitude toward style in the same periodical. What Coleridge wanted to achieve by this planted interchange of letters was "in the answer [to Southey] to state my own convictions in full on the nature of obscurity." Needless to say, "obscurity" is used here in an ironical manner. Coleridge's intent was to stress the commitment of the true writer, the genuine communicator, toward the connotative character or, to speak in aesthetic terms, the ambiguity of language. This letter of Coleridge, written October 20, 1809, is a classic and valid statement on the theme to which this paper addresses itself. Here are the main elements: the absence of a responsible cultural elite that would serve as the guardian and taskmaster of intellectual creativity; the decreasing intellectual demands made on the reading public at large; and finally the all-embracing emergence of a one-dimensional, non-connotative, unambiguous language of efficiency and predigested derivative thought, which (as Plato stated) leaves no room for the unique and idiosyncratic, for productive imagination and the dissenting voice:

"No real information can be conveyed, no important errors radically extracted, without demanding an effort of thought on the part of the reader; but the obstinate, and now contemptuous, aversion to all energy of thinking is the mother evil, the cause of all the evils in politics, morals, and literature, which it is my object to wage war against; . . . Now, what I wish you to do for me . . . is . . . to write a letter to *The Friend* in a lively style, chiefly urging, in a humorous manner, my Don Quixotism in expecting that the public will ever pretend to understand my lucubrations, or feel any interest in subjects of such sad and unkempt antiquity, and contrasting my style with the cementless periods of the modern Anglo-Gallican style, which not only are understood *beforehand*, but, being free from all connections of logic, all the hooks and eyes of intellectual memory, never oppress the mind by any after recollections, but, like civil visitors, stay a few moments, and leave the room quite free and open for the next comers. Something of this kind, I mean, that I may be able to answer it so as, in the answer, to state my own convictions at full on the nature of obscurity. . . ." It is with consummate irony that Coleridge calls his philosophy of communication an act of Don Quixotism; he hardly could have found a more convincing metaphor to stress the productive ambiguity of artistic symbols than the reference to the noble knight who stands for the condemnation of banality and triviality and the unshakable commitment to the idea of men by artistically manipulating a world of trivial objects and persons—very much the archetype and pioneer of the modern absurdists. As if he had to answer the spurious arguments of the managers of the motion-picture industry and their confreres in other fields of mass entertainment who try to convince themselves that they have to follow the cues of the masses, Coleridge clearly indicts the manufacturers of information and entertainment for not "demanding an effort of thought on the part of the reader" and thus points the finger at the absence of a responsible cultural elite—an issue as much with us today as it was in the time of Coleridge or of Goethe and Stendhal, to name two of his comrades-in-arms.

It is predominantly the poet who in our time has remained the committed spokesman for language as the ever given realm of human fulfillment and the ever present realm of human frustration, creating higher levels of aspiration and attainment. Earlier Ezra Pound and Eliot were mentioned. Eliot created definitive lines for "demanding an effort of thought on the part of the reader," as well as of the writer himself. In "East Coker" he reports "trying to learn to use words":

> "....every attempt
> Is a wholly new start, and a different kind of failure
> Because one has only learned to get the better of words
> For the thing one no longer has to say, or the way in which
> One is no longer disposed to say it. And so each venture
> Is a new beginning, a raid on the inarticulate..."*

What comes to the fore in this generalized autobiography of the poet is the infinite care man owes to his most specific human endowment. It is important that we attempt to "raid" the inarticulate—that vast part of the self in which (it so often seems) the self most truly *is* and that is denied altogether by the pat, mechanical, and soporific oversimplifications of "mass communications." It is the "spiritual" dimension of life, the mystery at the very heart of being, that we betray by the hideous impoverishment of the vocabularies and instruments of our thought and feeling implicit in the mass enterprise of mass communications (to which we are all party in some measure).

Two thinkers as different as John Stuart Mill and Friedrich Nietzsche have voiced their sorrows over the style of modern life aided and abetted by literary mass production, which seems to leave the public no choice but an almost neurotic gobbling-up of an endless stream of sounds and sights and

---

* This portion of "East Coker" reprinted from *Four Quartets*, by T. S. Eliot, by permission of Harcourt, Brace & World, Inc., and of Faber and Faber, Ltd.

words—not to be remembered, not to be translated into productive enrichment, and not to be translated into "dreams," that "stuff" of which,
according to Shakespeare, our world is made. In an article "Civilization,"
which appeared in the *London and Westminster Review*, of April, 1836, John
Stuart Mill wrote: "The world . . . gorges itself with intellectual food, and
in order to swallow the more, *bolts it*. Nothing is now read slowly, or twice
over . . . He . . . who should and would write a book, and write it in the
proper manner of writing a book, now dashes down his first hasty thoughts,
or what he mistakes for thoughts, in a periodical. And the public is in the
predicament of an indolent man, who cannot bring himself to apply his
mind vigorously to his own affairs, and over whom, therefore, not he who
speaks most wisely, but he who speaks most frequently, obtains the
influence."

And in a similar vein, though in a most different style, Nietzsche wrote
in the preface of *The Dawn of Day*:

"I have not been a philologist in vain; perhaps I am one yet: a teacher of
slow reading. I even come to write slowly. At present it is not only my habit,
but even my taste, a perverted taste, maybe—to write nothing but what will
drive to despair every one who is in a hurry . . . philology is now more desirable than ever before; . . . it is the highest attraction and incitement in
an age of 'work': that is to say, of haste, of unseemly and immoderate
hurry-scurry, which is intent upon 'getting things done' at once, even every
book, whether old or new. Philology itself, perhaps, will not 'get things done'
so hurriedly: it teaches how to read *well*: i.e. slowly, profoundly, attentively,
prudently, with inner thoughts, with the mental doors ajar, with delicate
fingers and eyes . . ."

To sum up what has happened in our day and age: Communication has
become part of·a consumers' culture in which those who produce and those
who receive are hardly distinguishable from each other because they are
both the serfs of a life style of conformity and regulation. It is the basic
tragedy and paradox of modern civilization and particularly of our own
phase that the sermon of individualism has turned into the practice of conformity, that the ideology of education and persuasion through the spoken
and printed word has become the reality of insensibility and numbness to
meaning, and that the professed belief of the powers that be in all spheres
of public life—political or cultural or economic—in the persuasive influence
of the worded message is answered by increasing skepticism if not outright
disbelief in the word itself.

I don't have any prescriptions or utopias to offer, but I have summoned
some of the witnesses who, although rather weak as social powers, are yet
with us as the everpresent conscience of true human consciousness. If in
the beginning I have intimated my pessimism in regard to the communications research we social scientists have been conducting, I should like in the

end to regain at least some of the territory I have voluntarily ceded. None less than the great John Dewey, philosopher and social scientist as well, in his brilliant essay "Democracy and Education" presented us with a definition of communication that I predict will still live when many of the data of mass media communications research have collected dust:

"Society not only continues to exist *by* transmission, *by* communication. There is more than a verbal tie between the words common, community, and communication. Men live in a community in virtue of the things which they have in common; and communication is the way in which they come to possess things in common. . . . To be a recipient of a communication is to have an enlarged . . . experience. One shares in what another has thought and felt, and in so far, meagerly or amply, has his own attitude modified. Nor is the one who communicates left unaffected. . . . Except in dealing with commonplaces and catch phrases one has to assimilate, imaginatively, something of another's experience in order to tell him intelligently of one's own experience. All communication is like art."

SOCIETY AND CULTURE*

Hannah Arendt

*M*ass culture and mass society (the very terms were still a sign of repro-
bation a few years ago, implying that mass society was a depraved form of
society and mass culture a contradiction in terms) are considered by almost
everybody today as something with which we must come to terms, and in
which we must discover some "positive" aspects—if only because mass
culture is the culture of a mass society. And mass society, whether we like
it or not, is going to stay with us into the foreseeable future. No doubt mass
society and mass culture are interrelated phenomena. Mass society comes
about when "the mass of the population has become incorporated into
society."[1] Since society originally comprehended those parts of the population which disposed of leisure time and the wealth which goes with it,
mass society does indeed indicate a new order in which the masses have
been liberated "from the burden of physically exhausting labor."[2] Historically as well as conceptually, therefore, mass society has been preceded by
society, and society is no more a generic term than is mass society; it too can
be dated and described historically. It is older, to be sure, than mass society,
but not older than the modern age. In fact, all the traits that crowd psychology has meanwhile discovered in mass man: his loneliness (and loneliness
is neither isolation nor solitude) regardless of his adaptability; his excit-
ability and lack of standards; his capacity for consumption, accompanied
by inability to judge or even to distinguish; above all, his egocentricity and
that fateful alienation from the world which, since Rousseau, he mistakes
for self-alienation—all these traits first appeared in "good society," where
there was no question of masses, numerically speaking. The first mass
men, we are tempted to say, quantitatively so little constituted a mass
that they could even imagine they constituted an elite, the elite of good
society.

* Reprinted from Norman Jacobs, editor, *Culture for the Millions?* by permission of D. Van Nostrand Company, Inc.

Let me therefore first say a few words on the older phenomena of society and its relation to culture: say them not primarily for historical reasons, but because they relate facts that seem to me little known in this country. It may be this lack of knowledge that leads Mr. Shils to say "individuality has flowered in mass society," whereas actually the modern individual was defined and, indeed, discovered by those who—like Rousseau in the eighteenth or John Stuart Mill in the nineteenth century—found themselves in open rebellion against society. Individualism and the "sensibility and privacy" which go with it—the discovery of intimacy as the atmosphere the individual needs for his full development—came about at a time when society was not yet a mass phenomenon but still thought of itself in terms of "good society" or (especially in Central Europe) of "educated and cultured society." And it is against this background that we must understand the modern (and no longer so modern) individual who, as we all know from nineteenth- and twentieth-century novels, can only be understood as part of the society against which he tried to assert himself and which always got the better of him.

The chances of this individual's survival lay in the simultaneous presence within the population of other nonsociety strata into which the rebellious individual could escape; one reason why rebellious individuals so frequently ended by becoming revolutionaries as well was that they discovered in those who were not admitted to society certain traits of humanity which had become extinct in society. We need only read the record of the French Revolution, and recall to what an extent the very concept of *le peuple* received its connotations from a rebellion against the corruption and hypocrisy of the salons, to realize what the true role of society was throughout the nineteenth century. A good part of the despair of individuals under the conditions of mass society is due to the fact that these avenues of escape are, of course, closed as soon as society has incorporated all the strata of the population.

Generally speaking, I think it has been the great good fortune of this country to have this intermediary stage of good and cultured society play a relatively minor role in its development; but the disadvantage of this good fortune today is that those few who will still make a stand against mass culture as an unavoidable consequence of mass society are tempted to look upon these earlier phenomena of society and culture as a kind of golden age and lost paradise, precisely because they know so little of it. America has been only too well acquainted with the barbarian philistinism of the *nouveau riche*, but it has only a nodding acquaintance with the equally annoying cultural and educated philistinism of a society where culture actually has what Mr. Shils calls "snob-value," and where it is a matter of status to be educated.

This cultural philistinism is today in Europe rather a matter of the past, for the simple reason that the whole development of modern art started from and remained committed to a profound mistrust not only of cultural philistinism but also of the word culture itself. It is still an open question whether it is more difficult to discover the great authors of the past without the help of any tradition than it is to rescue them from the rubbish of educated philistinism. And this task of preserving the past without the help of tradition, and often even against traditional standards and interpretations, is the same for the whole of Western civilization. Intellectually, though not socially, America and Europe are in the same situation: the thread of tradition is broken, and we must discover the past for ourselves—that is, read its authors as though nobody had ever read them before. In this task, mass society is much less in our way than good and educated society, and I suspect that this kind of reading was not uncommon in nineteenth-century America precisely because this country was still that "unstoried wilderness" from which so many American writers and artists tried to escape. That American fiction and poetry have so suddenly and richly come into their own, ever since Whitman and Melville, may have something to do with this.

It would be unfortunate indeed if out of the dilemmas and distractions of mass culture and mass society there should arise an altogether unwarranted and idle yearning for a state of affairs which is not better but only a bit more old-fashioned. And the eager and uncritical acceptance of such obviously snobbish and philistine terms as highbrow, middlebrow, and lowbrow is a rather ominous sign. For the only nonsocial and authentic criterion for works of culture is, of course, their relative permanence and even their ultimate immortality. The point of the matter is that as soon as the immortal works of the past became the object of "refinement" and acquired the status which went with it, they lost their most important and elemental quality, which is to grasp and move the reader or spectator, throughout the centuries. The very word "culture" became suspect precisely because it indicated that "pursuit of perfection" which to Matthew Arnold was identical with the "pursuit of sweetness and light." It was not Plato, but a reading of Plato, prompted by the ulterior motive of self-perfection, that became suspect; and the "pursuit of sweetness and light," with all its overtones of good society, was held in contempt because of its rather obvious effort to keep reality out of one's life by looking at everything through a veil of sweetness and light. The astounding recovery of the creative arts in the twentieth century, and a less apparent but perhaps no less real recovery of the greatness of the past, began when good society lost its monopolizing grip on culture, together with its dominant position in society as a whole.

Here we are not concerned with society, however, but with culture—or rather with what happens to culture under the different conditions of society and of mass society. In society, culture, even more than other realities, had become what only then began to be called a "value," that is, a social commodity which could be circulated and cashed in on as social coinage for the purpose of acquiring social status. Cultural objects were transformed into values when the cultural philistine seized upon them as a currency by which he bought a higher position in society—higher, that is, than in his own opinion he deserved either by nature or by birth. Cultural values, therefore, were what values have always been, exchange values; in passing from hand to hand, they were worn down like an old coin. They lost the faculty which is originally peculiar to all cultural things, the faculty of arresting our attention and moving us. This process of transformation was called the devaluation of values, and its end came with the "bargain-sale of values" (*Ausverkauf der Werte*) during the 'twenties and 'thirties, when cultural values were "sold out" altogether.

Perhaps the chief difference between society and mass society is that society wanted culture, evaluated and devaluated cultural things into social commodities, used and abused them for its own selfish purposes, but did not "consume" them. Even in their most worn-out shapes, these things remained things, they were not "consumed" and swallowed up but retained their worldly objectivity. Mass society, on the contrary, wants not culture but entertainment, and the wares offered by the entertainment industry are indeed consumed by society just as are any other consumer goods. The products needed for entertainment serve the life process of society, even though they may not be as necessary for this life as bread and meat. They serve, as the phrase is, to while away time, and the vacant time which is whiled away is not leisure time, strictly speaking, that is, time in which we are truly liberated from all cares and activities necessitated by the life process, and therefore free for the world and its "culture"; it is rather leftover time, which still is biological in nature, leftover after labor and sleep have received their due. Vacant time which entertainment is supposed to fill is a hiatus in the biologically conditioned cycle of labor, in the "metabolism of man with nature," as Marx used to say.

Under modern conditions, this hiatus is constantly growing; there is more and more time freed that must be filled with entertainment, but this enormous increase in vacant time does not change the nature of the time. Entertainment, like labor and sleep, is irrevocably part of the biological life process. And biological life is always, whether one is laboring or at rest, engaged in consumption or in the passive reception of amusement, a metabolism feeding on things by devouring them. The commodities the entertainment industry offers are not "things"—cultural objects whose excellence is measured by their ability to withstand the life process and to become permanent appurtenances of the world—and they should not be judged according to these standards; nor are they values which exist to be used and exchanged; they are rather consumer goods destined to be used up, as are any other consumer goods.

Panis et circenses truly belong together; both are necessary for life, for its preservation and recuperation, and both vanish in the course of the life process—that is, both must constantly be produced anew and offered anew, lest this process cease entirely. The standards by which both should be judged are indeed freshness and novelty—standards by which we today (and, I think, quite mistakenly) judge cultural and artistic objects as well, things which are supposed to remain in the world even after we have left it.

As long as the entertainment industry produces its own consumer goods, all is well, and we can no more reproach it for the nondurability of its articles than we can reproach a bakery because it produces goods which, if they are not to spoil, must be consumed as soon as they are made. It has always been the mark of educated philistinism to despise entertainment and amusement because no "value" could be derived from them. In so far as we are all subject to life's great cycle, we all stand in need of entertainment and amusement in some form or other, and it is sheer hypocrisy or social snobbery to deny that we can be amused and entertained by exactly the same things which amuse and entertain the masses of our fellow men. As far as the survival of culture is concerned, it certainly is less threatened by those who fill vacant time with amusement and entertainment than by those who fill it with some haphazard educational gadget in order to improve their social standing.

If mass culture and the entertainment industry were the same, I should not worry much, even though it is true that, in Mr. Shils' words, "the immense advance in audibility and visibility" of this whole sector of life, which formerly had been "relatively silent and unseen by the intellectuals," creates a serious problem for the artist and intellectual. It is as though the futility inherent in entertainment had been permitted to permeate the whole social atmosphere, and the often described malaise of the artists and intellectuals is of course partly due to their inability to make themselves heard and seen in the tumultuous uproar of mass society, or to penetrate its noisy futility. But this protest of the artist against society is as old as society, though not older; the great revival of nearly all the arts in our century (which perhaps one day will seem one of the great artistic—and of course scientific—periods of Western civilization) began with the malaise of the artist in society, with his decision to turn his back upon it and its "values," to leave the dead to bury the dead. As far as artistic productivity is concerned, it should not be more difficult to withstand the massive temptations of mass culture, or to keep from being thrown out of gear by the noise and humbug of mass society, than it was to avoid the more sophisticated temptations and the more insidious noises of the cultural snobs in refined society.

Unhappily, the case is not that simple. The entertainment industry is confronted with gargantuan appetites, and since its wares disappear in consumption, it must constantly offer new commodities. In this predicament, those who produce for the mass media ransack the entire range of past and present culture in the hope of finding suitable material. This material, however, cannot be offered as it is; it must be prepared and altered in order to become entertaining; it cannot be consumed as it is.

Mass culture comes into being when mass society seizes upon cultural objects, and its danger is that the life process of society (which like all biological processes insatiably draws everything available into the cycle of its metabolism) will literally consume the cultural objects, eat them up and destroy them. I am not referring to the phenomenon of mass distribution. When cultural objects, books, or pictures in reproduction, are thrown on the market cheaply and attain huge sales, this does not affect the nature of the goods in question. But their nature is affected when these objects themselves are changed (rewritten, condensed, digested, reduced to *Kitsch* in the course of reproduction or preparation for the movies) in order to be put into usable form for a mass sale which they otherwise could not attain.

Neither the entertainment industry itself nor mass sales as such are signs of, not what we call mass culture, but what we ought more accurately to call the decay of culture in mass society. This decay sets in when liberties are taken with these cultural objects in order that they may be distributed among masses of people. Those who actively promote this decay are not the Tin Pan Alley composers but a special kind of intellectuals, often well read and well informed, whose sole function is to organize, disseminate, and change cultural objects in order to make them palatable to those who want to be entertained or—and this is worse—to be "educated," that is, to acquire as cheaply as possible some kind of cultural knowledge to improve their social status.

Richard Blackmur (in a recent article on the "Role of the Intellectual," in the *Kenyon Review*) has brilliantly shown that the present malaise of the intellectual springs from the fact that he finds himself surrounded not by the masses, from whom on the contrary, he is carefully shielded, but by these digesters, re-writers, and changers of culture whom we find in every publishing house in the United States, and in the editorial offices of nearly every magazine. And these "professionals" are ably assisted by those who no longer write books but fabricate them, who manufacture a "new" textbook out of four or five already on the market, and who then have, as Blackmur shows, only one worry—how to avoid plagiarism. (Meanwhile the editor does his best to substitute cliches for sheer illiteracy.) Here the criterion of novelty, quite legitimate in the entertainment industry, becomes a simple fake and, indeed, a threat: it is only too likely that the "new" textbook will crowd out the older ones, which usually are better, not because they are older, but because they were still written in response to authentic needs.

This state of affairs, which indeed is equalled nowhere else in the world, can properly be called mass culture; its promoters are neither the masses nor their entertainers, but are those who try to entertain the masses with what once was an authentic object of culture, or to persuade them that *Hamlet* can be as entertaining as *My Fair Lady*, and educational as well. The danger of mass education is precisely that it may become very entertaining indeed; there are many great authors of the past who have survived centuries of oblivion and neglect, but it is still an open question whether they will be able to survive an entertaining version of what they have to say.

The malaise of the intellectual in the atmosphere of mass culture is much more legitimate than his malaise in mass society; it is caused socially by the presence of these other intellectuals, the manufacturers of mass culture, from whom he finds it difficult to distinguish himself and who, moreover, always outnumber him, and therefore acquire that kind of power which is generated whenever people band together and act more or less in concert. The power of the many (legitimate only in the realm of politics and the field of action) has always been a threat to the strength of the few; it is a threat under the most favorable circumstances, and it has always been felt to be more dangerous when it arises from within a group's own ranks. Culturally, the malaise is caused, I think, not so much by the massive temptations and the high rewards which await those who are willing to alter their products to make them acceptable for a mass market, as by the constant irritating care each of us has to exert in order to protect his product against the demands and the ingenuity of those who think they know how to "improve" it.

Culture relates to objects and is a phenomenon of the world; entertainment relates to people and is a phenomenon of life. If life is no longer content with the pleasure which is always coexistent with the toil and labor inherent in the metabolism of man with nature, if vital energy is no longer fully used up in this cycle, then life may reach out for the things of the world, may violate and consume them. It will prepare these things of the world until they are fit for consumption; it will treat them as if they were articles of nature, articles which must also be prepared before they can enter into man's metabolism.

Consumption of the things of nature does no harm to them; they are constantly renewed because man, in so far as he lives and labors, toils and recuperates, is also a creature of nature, a part of the great cycle in which all nature wheels. But the things of the world which are made by man (in so far as he is a worldly and not merely a natural being), these things are not renewed of their own accord. When life seizes upon them and consumes them at its pleasure, for entertainment, they simply disappear. And this disappearance, which first begins in mass culture—that is, the "culture" of a society posed between the alternatives of laboring and consuming—is something different from the wear and tear culture suffered when its things were made into exchange values, and circulated in society until their original stamp and meaning were scarcely recognizable.

If we wish to classify these two anticultural processes in historical and sociological terms, we may say that the devaluation of culture in good society through the cultural philistines was the characteristic peril of commercial society, whose primary public area was the exchange market for goods and ideas. The disappearance of culture in a mass society, on the other hand, comes about when we have a consumers' society which, in so far as it produces only for consumption, does not need a public worldly space whose existence is independent of and outside the sphere of its life process. In other words, a consumers' society does not know how to take care of the world and the things which belong to it: the society's own chief attitude toward objects, the attitude of consumption, spells ruin to everything it touches. If we understand by culture what it originally meant (the Roman *cultura*—derived from *colere*, to take care of and preserve and cultivate) then we can say without any exaggeration that a society obsessed with consumption cannot at the same time be cultured or produce a culture.

For all their differences, however, one thing is common to both these anticultural processes: they arise when all the worldly objects produced by the present or the past have become "social," are related to society, and are seen in their merely functional aspect. In the one case, society uses and exchanges, evaluates and devaluates them; in the other, it devours and consumes them. This functionalization or "societization" of the world is by no means a matter of course; the notion that every object must be functional, fulfilling some needs of society or of the individual—the church a religious need, the painting the need for self-expression in the painter and the need of self-perfection in the onlooker, and so on—is historically so new that one is tempted to speak of a modern prejudice. The cathedrals were built *ad majorem gloriam Dei*; while they as buildings certainly served the needs of the community, their elaborate beauty can never be explained by these needs, which could have been served quite as well by any nondescript building.

An object is cultural to the extent that it can endure; this durability is the very opposite of its functionality, which is the quality which makes it disappear again from the phenomenal world by being used and used up. The "thingness" of an object appears in its shape and appearance, the proper criterion of which is beauty. If we wanted to judge an object by its use value alone, and not also by its appearance (that is, by whether it is beautiful or ugly or something in between), we would first have to pluck out our eyes. Thus, the functionalization of the world which occurs in both society and mass society deprives the world of culture as well as beauty. Culture can be safe only with those who love the world for its own sake, who know that without the beauty of man-made, worldly things which we call works of art, without the radiant glory in which potential imperishability is made manifest to the world and in the world, all human life would be futile and no greatness could endure.

NOTES

1. Edward Shils, "Mass Society and Its Culture," *Daedalus*, Spring, 1960, page 288.
2. *Ibid.*, page 289.

TELEVISION AND THE NEW IMAGE OF MAN*

Ashley Montagu

$t$he first major step taken by the order of mammals that eventually led to the emergence of man was the adoption of a way of life which placed a high premium upon the experience of the world through vision. Assisted by the sense of hearing, vision has been man's principal means of perception, of endowing the raw sensation with meaning, and of apprehending the dimensions of space and its content. This has constituted the experience of man's primate ancestors for a period extending over 70 million years, culminating in that most complex development—the visual brain in man.

It is, perhaps, not surprising that the vast world of experience that television presents to the sedentary viewer should have the unprecedented appeal and immediate impact it does. That one picture is worth a thousand words was already fully understood by prehistoric man of the Old Stone Age, for he spent a great deal of his time manipulating the natural and supernatural powers through the agency of his invocational cave paintings and similar devices. Prayer and incantation undoubtedly accompanied the graphic acts of communication, but these were private ritualistic acts. Television is a public communication, in which the pictures are living events brought to the viewer either as they are occurring, or as they have occurred, with words and sounds that are the living realities, and not merely the counterparts, of those who have uttered or created them. As such, television has conquered and controls both time and space. The whole world of experience is now brought to the viewer seated in his own home before his television set. On the television screen he may observe the living scroll of history unroll before his eyes at the very time it is being written thousands of miles distant in regions otherwise quite inaccessible to him. Persons and places, events and ideas, are brought to him to see and hear and contemplate that he would otherwise never have experienced.

* Reprinted from *The Eighth Art*, New York, 1963, by permission of Holt, Rinehart and Winston and of the Columbia Broadcasting System.

Television is the "Magic Lantern" of our grandparents, with the difference that while the "Magic Lantern" projected a static, soundless, motionless image, television brings to the viewer the simultaneous dynamic stimulations of sight, sound, and motion. Indeed, television represents the most vital of all living miracles. And as with most miracles, the theoretical and technical development of television began in the minds of men, in Clerk Maxwell's equations, in Hertz's waves, Nipkow's disc, and in Zworykin's iconoscope, and it is in the minds of men that this great victory of mind over matter can achieve even more consequential miracles; for television has it in its power to be the instrument of far greater good than any other device born of man's ingenuity, not excluding the invention of printing.

Commercial television was authorized in July 1941. At the end of World War II there were 7,000 television sets in the United States. At the present time (1965) there are, in the United States, some 60 million television sets in active use, and almost everyone capable of watching television does. This means, in fact, that in less than a single generation television has become the most important means of communication in the country. Not only is the extent of its reach without precedent or parallel, but what is even more to the point so is its influence. Television is capable of moving men to thought and action as no other medium is, and no other medium is more fully capable of reifying the maxim that the meaning of a word is the action it produces.

It is generally agreed that were it not for television John F. Kennedy would not have been elected President of the United States. The television debates between the candidates for the Presidency, placed not only the issues, the skills, and the knowledge of the principals before the public, but also their personalities. It is believed that a large number of individuals who might otherwise have voted for Mr. Nixon switched their vote to Mr. Kennedy not only because of the better total showing that they believed Mr. Kennedy to have made, but also because Mr. Nixon's personality did not impress them as favorably as did Mr. Kennedy's.

Another example of the powerful influence of television is represented by the McCarthy-Army Hearings. No one who saw those revolting proceedings on television will ever forget the impact they made, and, above all, at that heroically dramatic moment when Mr. Welch administered the ringing rebuke which it is generally agreed delivered the *coup-de-grâce* to the career of the late Senator Joseph McCarthy. If it had not been for television much of the impact of those hearings would have been lost, for the conduct and personalities of the principals could not have been communicated anywhere nearly as well by any other medium. It was one thing for his colleagues to experience Mr. McCarthy on the floor of the Senate, but quite another for those selfsame Senators to experience their colleague through the pressure of public opinion that television made possible. Without this pressure there would have been no Senate vote of censure on Mr. McCarthy, and the latter would impenitently have proceeded on his reckless way. No court of law has ever held the scales of justice more fairly balanced than television did for the judge and jury represented by the viewing public of the McCarthy-Army hearings. Those televised hearings were the beginning of the end of Senator Joseph McCarthy.

The difference that television has made in national elections, by bringing virtually the full proceedings into the home, is incalculable. Participation in the inauguration ceremonies is now possible for every American by way of television. The President and other members of the government now address the people directly, so that for the first time in the history of nations the representatives of the people can communicate with them immediately, and receive their response almost as immediately. The fact that this is possible draws attention to an extremely important change which television has brought about. Just as the automobile has produced vast social changes, and the airplane has contracted space, television has accelerated the rate of communication at many very different levels of discourse. There can be not the least doubt that television has it within its power to become the most important of all agencies of social change. And this brings us squarely to the question which this chapter is designed to ask, and to answer, namely: What are the uses of television?

No critical examination of the uses of television should, however, leave the question structured in that form. A more realistic form of the question is: What are the uses and abuses of television? Just as the morbid, the pathological, helps us to understand better the meaning of healthy functioning, so a brief consideration of the abuses of television may help us to understand better what the impediments are to the development of the healthy uses of television.

The principal fault of the networks and the planners of programs has been the underestimation of the needs of the great varieties of viewers, actual and potential, of television. Too often the television audience has been treated as if it were some conglomerate mass, of low intelligence and of even lower taste, incapable of appreciating the best that is being said, done, and performed in the world. We are told that the average mental age in America is about 13 years. During the greater part of its history television has looked as if it were deliberately appealing to an audience of that mental age. After all, the sponsor would pay most for the program that reached the greatest number of potential purchasing units, and television is in business, and to stay in business it has to make a profit. Television has never exclusively catered to what it has considered to be the needs of the mass audience, and television can always claim that it gives the public what it wants.

Without putting too fine a point upon it, those who will guide the future development of television require to understand that it is not so much what the public wants as what the people need that should be considered, and that what the people want is not incompatible with what the people need. The advertising world has long understood that it is not difficult to persuade people to want what they do not need. It would balance things in the right direction if the mandarins of television would help people to want the things they need. In recent years some progress has been made in this direction, but, alas, too often, the viewer seated before his television screen cannot, after a while, help exclaiming:

> But, soft! what light through yonder window breaks?
> It speaks, and yet says nothing.

And often, worse than nothing. There can be no possible excuse for many of the most popular television programs of the present and past. Take, for example, the westerns. These, for the most part, are not only degrading and debasing, but they also serve to falsify and perpetuate the myth of the savage American Indian. Apart from the anthropological absurdities that are invariably committed, the American Indian is still mostly presented as a savage, inferior, unfeeling barbarian. Although, here too, there has been some improvement in recent years, and some American Indians are presented as relatively acceptable human beings, the James Fenimore Cooper wooden Indian still holds the stage. In these same programs the quanta of evil, treachery, rapine, and murder (not to mention the murder of the language) that are set out for the delectation of the viewer, are utterly loathsome and abominable. There can be very little doubt that such programs habituate those who are exposed to them to an easy valuation of life, a not uncongenial view of the place of violence in human relations, and the cultivation of an opportunistic morality. Television can no longer be regarded as a merely passive viewing. It is an experience in which the viewer usually participates and identifies with one or other of the characters or the values he represents. The viewer is influenced, and television cannot evade its responsibility for the consequences by disclaiming any other than a business interest in what it is doing.

But enough on the obvious abuses of television, the principal and worst of which seems to me to be the commercially motivated servitude to erroneous ideas concerning the needs of the masses, and the consequent debasement of the image of man to which this leads. The bright speciousness and mindless vulgarity of some of the most popular television programs—programs in which the human experience is neither extended nor enlarged, but impoverished and corrupted—constitute living testimony to the depths to which television can descend. Let us now consider some of the better uses to which television can be put.

Using the word education in its original non-formal sense, *educare*, to nourish and to cause to grow, television potentially constitutes the greatest educational medium of all time. By its very nature television enjoys an unprecedented opportunity to be a power for good in this world, for the enrichment of the lives of men and the enlargement of the conception of mankind, such as no other medium has ever enjoyed. I am using the term "education" in its broadest sense, but strictly within the limits defined above, as meaning the nourishing and causing to grow of man's potentialities for humanity, for humaneness, for love, and not merely instruction in the three "R's." I also use the term in its practical meaning, not in its formal classroom sense, as meaning that anything which is learned contributes either positively or negatively, for better or for worse, to one's education.

Without in the least undervaluing the important future which television has before it in the classroom, it is outside the classroom, in the informal setting of the home, for all the members of the family but especially for adults, that television can make a major creative contribution in education and re-education. Man is a myth-making animal, and the myth-making faculty assists him to "explain" whatever is in need of explanation. One of the functions of myth is to enable the individual to live comfortably with his beliefs in a fidelity so satisfyingly ritualistic that he eventually comes to identify his prejudices with the laws of nature or the canons of received religion. It is at just this juncture that television can enter as the creative solvent and educate by re-educating.

It is not the function of television to hold up a mirror for man to see himself merely as he is and to maintain himself in that image. On the contrary, it should be the function of television to exhibit the image of man as he can and should be, for man is a growing creature and his birthright is development. For development he requires the stimulation of new experience and new ideas, and not the vacuous kind of entertainment he is so often offered. Television is in an unrivalled position to bridge the gap for man between the world of what *is* and the world of *what ought to be*, or rather the gap between what man has made of the world and what man can make of it, what he *ought* to make of it. Every society to a large degree creates itself through the image it holds up for itself to see. Culture, that is, the man-made part of the environment, is never a static thing but always a dynamic process. Television, therefore, will contribute to the individual and the social good to the extent that it projects "good" images. To the extent that it projects the trivial, the meretricious, and the stereotyped, television will contribute to cultural and social shallowness.

Television, then, is an institution of major social importance. It is, therefore, time that television took a good dispassionate look at itself, and arrived at some common agreement as to what its aims and purposes should be. For too long television has appeared to resemble the young man in the Italian proverb who having taken every road that he saw eventually got nowhere. The concentration on staying in business has been equated with making money, and it is this that has led to the general lack of purpose and directiveness, and to the subordination of desirable ends to undesirable means. Expediency appears to be a governing principle of what under healthier conditions one would prefer to think of as a "service" rather than as an "industry."

In spite of itself television has become one of the most widely influential institutions of all time. Perhaps the meaning of an institution should be defined. An institution is an organization designed to regulate behavior with respect to the values considered essential to group welfare and survival. As *the* most widely influential institution in the land, television has become the god of the common man's idolatry, his oracle, and the principal source of his news and entertainment. By no more than the turn of a knob he can tune in on men and events with an immediacy and impact which he could never otherwise experience. In the face of the viewer's hunger to have the vast spaces of his mind filled, it is a kind of treason, a failure of the viewer in his need, to fill those vacant spaces with the kind of vacuities with which he is too often presented.

As an institution of unprecedented reach and power television has not yet taken itself seriously enough. Now and again there are signs that those who preside over the destinies of television would like to make an earnest attempt to define its role in contributing to the welfare of the people, but somehow or other the attempt gets lost in the next "spectacular." The responsibility which should accompany the power seems to get dissipated in the fragmentation of the power and the demands of a constantly changing panorama of the slight and the ephemeral. There is an atmosphere of insecurity, of capriciousness, and of opportunism in the television world which appears to grow out of the lack of any clearly defined codification of its own role and significance, and even any clear recognition of the nature of its own power. Hence, without recognition of the responsibility that power entails, the corrupting effect of power inevitably follows, and is seen in the contaminated programs that supervene so perfunctorily one upon the other with an odious disregard for the standards of excellence of which we hear so much.

Television must become alive to its institutional powers and responsibilities, and invest itself with a form and a being rather more elevating and in keeping with the functions it should perform than those to which it has seemed to aspire in the past. Emancipation from the sterile puerilities which find so congenial a home in the television world, is not incompatible with the provision of every variety of entertainment, which will amuse and divert and have no other purpose but to do so. But in the name of nothing more nor less than good taste let us abate the noisome vulgarity of so much that passes for entertainment today. Vulgarity is *not* what the viewer wants, in spite of what the pundits and pollsters may say, for the simple reason that there is not one kind of television viewer but many different kinds, with different tastes and different standards, but all characterized by the common trait of being able to learn to accept what is good, especially when the bad is not offered.

If television will responsibly use the power with which it is endowed, it will not permit itself to have its tastes formed for it by the pressures exerted by majority opinion. The strength of a democracy lies in the possibilities for increasing its orders of freedom without yielding to the pressure of any group, no matter how massive. And as Lord Acton pointed out many years ago, freedom does not consist in the liberty to do what one likes, but in the right to be able to do what one ought. And doing what one ought is not incompatible with liking what one ought to do. Right and wrong, good and bad, are not values that can be determined by a show of hands, but by the measure of universal criteria, which television might well adopt as the standards by which to direct its own activities.

What *ought* to be done is what is *good*, and the good is simply defined as any act or acts which confer survival benefits upon others in a creatively enlarging manner. And this, as the institution it has become, television is so eminently well equipped to do, efficiently and unsanctimoniously.

There is a new image of man emerging in the world, and to that transformation television has made a major contribution. Television has done so by bringing the peoples of every part of the world, in their native habitats and out of them, into the living room of the viewer. Representatives of many of these peoples have been seen in interviews, at the United Nations, on panels, and elsewhere. The personalities of these individuals, the charm, high intelligence, and warm humanity which they frequently exhibit, as they have projected from the television screen, have had the most extraordinary effects upon millions of viewers who, it is important to note, would have remained largely unaffected by exposure to any other means of communication. The repeated shock of recognition experienced in this way has led to the revelation of the fact that the whole world of mankind is, indeed, kin, and that so-called "inferior races" are only technologically inferior to us, and that given adequate opportunities they are *obviously* capable of producing men and women of high intellectual caliber, and of a humanity which can at least compare favorably with our own. The very expression "inferior race" is one that would be considered in bad taste by more people today than would have been thought possible only a few years ago. To this, without any awareness of the fact that it was doing so, and without the least propagandistic motivation, television has made a very substantial contribution. While much has been achieved in this enlargement of the image of man, it is as nothing compared with what yet remains to be achieved.

It is not merely the image of mankind that is undergoing a renovation. Equally significant is the revision of the individual's self-image which television is capable of working. The potentialities of man are infinitely varied and exciting. But the image of man and of human potentialities handed down to us by tradition and traditional ways of setting limits to individual development often constrict and imprison what is best in man. Today more than ever he stands in need of the stimulation and direction which will release the "imprison'd splendour" that is within him.

What man stands so critically in need of today are the models, the images, that will be to him the standards upon which he can form himself, and by means of which he can learn to work upon himself, to free himself from the errors in which he has been conditioned, and the incapacities for thinking in which he has been trained. These are, of course, functions that should be performed in the home and in our educational institutions. The hope is that this will become increasingly possible. Toward such an end television can make and continue to make a major contribution, not by offering viewers programs that will divert them from the main business of life, but by giving them the programs that will help them to live as humanely, richly, and effectively as possible. It is to the achievement of such humanistic ends that television should be primarily dedicated—not so much by giving people what they want as by giving them the best one has to give.

To the extent that television contributes to the enhancement of man's understanding, the deepening of his sensibilities, involvement in the welfare of others, and the ability to weigh the evidence critically for himself—to that extent will television not only assist man to fulfill himself, but in this manner, and in this manner alone, will television serve to fulfill itself.

THE GILDED BOUGH: MAGIC AND ADVERTISING*

Howard Luck Gossage

*M*agic is mankind's oldest continuous belief. It antedates either religion or science, and although both appear to have sprung from it, neither has supplanted it entirely, or is soon likely to.

By magic I don't mean pulling a rabbit out of the hat or sawing a woman in half or other such edifying spectacles, but magical thinking as it has been thought by man for a million years and still is. To be sure we do not subscribe to the total and literal beliefs of either our remote ancestors or the Australian aborigines. And the higher one goes in the intellectual order the less susceptibility to magical thinking one will encounter.

But even where faith has faded, the imagery of magic remains. For so broad and basic are its points of reference that it is difficult to avoid them in human intercourse. The language of magic is truly the universal tongue.

Magic, moreover, is the most adaptable of creatures; it moves in, makes itself at home, and fades into the wallpaper. It so thoroughly identifies with its surroundings as to be unnoticed by the inhabitants. This is to say that magic is never an isolated phenomenon, it is invariably germane to its period. Which is why such now obvious performances of magical thinking as the Inquisition, the Dutch tulip craze of the seventeenth century, the stock-market boom of the late 'twenties, Couéism, McCarthyism, and chain letters escaped recognition at the time. It is possibly too early to pass final judgment on farm surpluses, credit cards, filter tips, and the theory of an ever-expanding economy.†

† But not too early to observe that the 1965 administrative crisis at the University of California was touched off by a four-letter cabalistic symbol high on the taboo list. Although its meaning had little to do with the issues at hand, its mere utterance at a student rally prompted a reaction which caused both the President and the Chancellor to resign. It is hard to imagine that "Abracadabra," though much longer, would have been more effective.

Magical stewardship in every age resides at the heart of the era's chief concerns: hunting, agriculture, religion, politics, commerce, nationalism, or whatever. (James Webb Young, the dean of American advertising men, tells me that the magical authority of the Egyptian priesthood was founded on their knowledge of the rise and fall tables of the Nile. This amounted to more than a paltry prediction trick to amaze the fellahin, for the river's timely flooding was the source of Egypt's wealth.) The chief concern of our era is the consumption of goods and services. It is a big job, but to assist we have the biggest propaganda force the world has ever seen, advertising.

One of the characters in Christopher Fry's play of the Middle Ages, "The Lady's Not for Burning," says, "Religion has made an honest woman of the supernatural." Someone is always ready to make an honest woman of her. Today advertising is her most ardent—or most affluent—suitor.

Advertising is a brand-new instrument, unique to our age, but at the same time it plays mankind's oldest themes. The reason is this: In an advertisement's effort to persuade people of the justice of its cause, whatever it may be, it invariably seeks a common denominator. The more people it attempts to persuade, the more common the denominator, the more basic the appeal will be. When, in addition, the product advertised is virtually identical with its competitors, or when the product's value to its user is largely subjective, the appeals become so basic that they slide away from fact as we know it. They go beyond reason into something even more basic, the most common denominator of all, magic.

Sir James Frazer in his classic on the subject of anthropological magic, *The Golden Bough*, divided the field into two general parts: theoretical magic and practical magic. Theoretical magic has to do with natural law, the rules which govern the sequence of events throughout the world: the rising of the Sun, the changing of the seasons, the moving of the heavens, the surging of the tides. Only recently in human history have we discarded theoretical magic as an explanation of these phenomena. If we wonder why it took so long, it is well to remember that there are still people who believe the world is flat; and that to this day our senses testify that the Sun circles the Earth rather than the other way round.

Practical magic, our chief concern here, is a body of rules for human beings to follow in order to achieve desired ends. Its techniques are still very much with us, and advertising—itself devoted to satisfaction of human desires—has availed itself of them.

Frazer separates practical magic loosely into what he calls imitative magic and contagious magic. Imitative magic assumes that objects which have been in contact will continue to act on each other at a distance after the physical contact has been severed. An example of imitative magic might be the sticking of needles through wax figures or hanging in effigy.

The underlying rationale is probably the same as that of the rejected swain who tears up his girl's picture. The objective mind might detect an application of imitative magic in an airline advertisement of a few years ago which consisted of a picture of the sea with a strip torn off it and the words, "Starting Dec. 23 the Atlantic Ocean will be 20% smaller."

Another example of imitative magic—in that it is based on the assumption that effect will resemble cause—is the use of powdered rhinoceros horn, which I understand is highly prized in the Far East as an adjunct to virility; look how powerful the rhino is! I don't know what powdered rhinoceros horn costs but its users probably find it worth the price. Analogous to this was the recent rage for queen bee jelly. One supposes that it served to satisfy a womanly urge to extreme, uncompetitive femininity; to be the only queen in the hive. Or could it be that women have some deep, unconscious impulse to mate in mid-air?

Closely akin to imitative magic but somewhat different in its application is contagious magic. The idea here is that an object which has been associated with one person will continue to be associated with that person. His fingernail parings, hair, etc., will thus do nicely in preparing a love philter to be used on him. But it works another way too: a thing can also carry with it whatever qualities the person who owned it, or touched it, or used it had. Thus, relics sanctified by a witch doctor, or a lock of Elvis' hair, or autographs, or Miss Rheingold, and all testimonial advertising are examples of belief in contagious magic. For instance, I can buy Gillette Razor Blades just like the ones used by that star athlete on television the other night . . . although I am always a little fearful the whole thing might backfire and, instead of acquiring his physical powers, I might end up with his vocal prowess.

All toiletry advertising draws heavily on practical magic for its substance. Like the love philter, it promises that you will be irresistible. If you use most hair preparations or aftershave lotions you are taking your chastity in your hands. If a girl uses virtually any advertised facial soap she is triumphantly assured of a glorious marriage to a pimple-free, vibrant youth, six feet four inches tall with gleaming teeth and perfect elimination: their respective toiletries have brought them together.

Also implied in the above examples is the suggestion that whatever benefits the product may bestow will be denied you if you don't use it. If you do not use Brylcream all the girls may not pursue you. More explicit is the threat contained in mouthwash advertising: Not only will the girls not pursue you, but you will drive them away unless you gargle. This is even more magical than the other threat because while you can see by looking in a mirror that your hair looks wretched, it is very difficult for you to smell your own breath. You have no real way of knowing whether you are ruining your love life or blasting your career. The mouth wash thus becomes a charm by which you may avoid *possibly* dire consequences; and the beauty of it is that you will never know whether it worked or not since even your best friend won't tell you.

This brings us to another aspect of magic: taboo. Here we see advertising actually creating and naming taboos. The most famous, B.O. and Halitosis, are archaeological specimens from an age which we might fix as either Late Iron Tonic or Early Soap. It is doubtful whether such epidemics are really catchy today; the Gray Sickness has never achieved plague proportions despite best efforts. Bad breath and body odor have always existed, of course, but as individual matters. To transfer them from personal idiosyncrasies into tribal taboos is a magicianly trick indeed.

But we are frittering around in very trivial taboo territory; let's get into the deep stuff. Cosmetic advertising. According to Freud, "the basis of taboo is a forbidden action for which there exists a strong inclination in the unconscious." That is to say we have a deep-seated desire to violate taboo and put ourselves above it, beyond the reach of its strictures. The cosmetic industry plays this line for all it is worth. Consider the names of perfumes: Forbidden Fruit, My Sin, Shocking, Sortilege, Black Magic, and even Tabu; and many others which I am too frightened to remember.

Revlon must keep a staff witch if we are to judge from certain of their advertisements. I don't know which taboos Miss Fire-and-Ice wished to violate, but they must have been honeys. Ravishment seemed to be the very least she had on her mind.

Miss Pango Peach, on the other hand, seemed to take a more tempered view of the subject. Her voluptuous demands, though probably excessive, did not appear to include either whips or cannibalism. You will recall my mentioning, in connection with queen bee jelly, the mating habits of bees. You know, of course, that the successful bee suitor explodes immediately following the happy event; the latitude or something. I predict that some day someone will make a fortune by marketing praying mantis marmalade. Some brassière advertising also obviously exploits the desire to violate taboo. However, fashion advertising as a whole seems to dwell in another magical area.

Have you ever wondered why fashion models look the way they do? A couple of years ago, Stan Freberg, the humorist, swept by compassion, proposed that a fund be established to send the girls to camp to fatten them up a little and put the roses back in their cheeks. If you ask a woman why models look like that she will say that skinny girls show off clothes better. I find this next to no answer at all; for the real essence of their unearthly appearance is simply that: they are unearthly. Their attitudes are trance-like, as though they were frozen in those bizarre poses by a spell. They are supernatural representations and I defy you to account for them in any other fashion.

Nor are these the only supernatural figures in advertising. I should point out here that the heart and soul of the magician's power has always been his command of what we might call the "nearby supernatural" as opposed to the "remote supernatural." The magician does not pray or implore these approachable supernatural forces to aid him; he dominates them through his superior knowledge and power. He is their master and they perform at his direction. Advertising invokes supernatural entities in many forms and some of them are pretty obvious. Mr. Clean, for example; he materializes at man's—or in this case, woman's—bidding, and works like magic. Think of the number of times you have seen the words "like magic" in advertisements. These devices are effective because command of the supernatural is one of mankind's oldest dreams—and the basis of literature from man's earliest myths to the *Arabian Nights*, *Faust*, *Superman*, and *Damn Yankees*.

Some of these supernatural manifestations are, of course, far more subtle than Mr. Clean, Elsie the Cow, or Mr. Coffee Nerves. Some of our most stimulating advertising summons what I can only regard as Mephistopheles-like figures. Mephistopheles, you will recall, is suave, imperturbable, of-the-world-worldly but not really a part of it. His presence is not to be accounted for by ordinary standards, he is simply there; he has materialized. And he usually bears the sign by which we know him: a mark that sets him apart from mere mortals, whether it be a cloven hoof, beard, tattoo, or a black eye-patch. He is a fascinating chap and you can say this for him, he likes people. Mephistopheles grants a boon: eternal life, youth, prowess, togetherness, unfulfilled dreams. His price is always something. When it is such a small thing as a pack of cigarettes, or a soft drink, or a lipstick, why should not one take the chance?

As distinguished from our accessibility to the nearby, workaday supernatural is our helplessness in the face of the remote supernatural. The remote supernatural is those forces quite beyond our control: death, disaster, the vagaries of fortune. The remote supernatural is nobody's plaything; it cannot be evoked at will or used as a tool. There is nothing man can do about it and yet he must do *something*. So he performs rituals, makes sacrifices, builds monuments, fathers many children, keeps his fingers crossed, saves his money for a rainy day, and buys life insurance. Surely, it is reasonable to save and have life insurance, but the reasons for doing so are likely far beyond reason.

First off, saving for a rainy day is quite a different matter from saving for a purpose like buying a house or taking a trip. People save for a rainy day without, in most cases, any certainty when the rainy day will arrive or even whether it will arrive. And we all have known people who would not touch their savings even when the rainy day *did* arrive. This, it seems to me, is an act in appeasement of the remote supernatural, a bribe to fortune; an act beyond mere prudence.

Similarly, the buying of insurance is in part an act to propitiate Providence and rests solidly on primitive instincts and emotions way at the back of the mind. The first of these is pure anguish in the face of the unknowable; the second is a belief in luck. An insurance policy is more than a highly sophisticated bet against odds, it also assumes the properties of a talisman to counteract disaster or stall off death.

It may be easier to see this when we apply it to, let us say, fire insurance or accident insurance. I think there is no arguing that a definite feeling of courting disaster exists when one is uninsured; it is positively unlucky; you are just asking for it. This magical instinct may influence the buying of *any* insurance, whether it be life, plate-glass, or the coverage you get when you stuff quarters in the machine at the airport. This last, while apparently life insurance, is not the same thing, really. One buys life insurance because one knows one is going to die—the only question is when. One does not expect to be wiped out in an airplane accident—the odds are enormously against it. The quarters buy a cheap charm to carry you through to the end of the journey.

Incidentally, in the field of credit we see financial institutions venturing into magic in more pointed ways. Installment credit buying is surely a tacit invitation to think magically about money. The English term for such buying is revealing: the Never-never. The most flagrant example is seen in the recent rise of the credit card. According to one motivational researcher quoted in Vance Packard's *The Waste Makers*, "Credit cards are magic since they serve as money when one temporarily has no money. They thus become symbols of power and inexhaustible potency." And, may I add, with the rainy day built in.

By now I hope it is apparent that there is a broad field of human susceptibility to magic. Advertising, abhorring a vacuum, has rushed in to fill it. In doing so it produces some magic on its own.

Through advertising, a product will acquire what Martin Mayer, in *Madison Avenue, U.S.A.*, called "the added ingredient" and what I must regard as a magical property, beyond natural and ordinary logic. This property is frequently so pervasive that all of the product's being and authority reside in the advertising; the product *is* its advertising. And what do we call an object that carries magical properties? A charm. A product will tend to be a charm to the extent that its authority exceeds bare fact.

Let me give you a parallel. A red traffic light is a piece of colored glass with a bulb behind it. It means stop. But, as S. I. Hayakawa, the semanticist, points out, in practice it often *is* stop. Recall how guilty you feel when you run an obviously stuck light, even late at night with no one in sight for thirty miles in either direction. Another example: If you were to take a piece of cloth and jump up and down on it in public you would be mobbed or at the very least arrested—provided the cloth in question were the

American flag. The flag in this instance not only symbolizes the United States, it *is* the United States, and as such is a charm.

Similarly, such humble items as toothpaste, soaps, and cigarettes are charms. Advertising has imbued them with prowess quite beyond any reasonable assessment of their plain-Jane natures. Now, to do this sort of charm-school job—and have it take—is not as easy as you might think. Usually there is nowhere to go but up: to the supernatural. Their slogans, therefore, will be supra-factual ("Contains New XK-140"), supra-logical ("You'll wonder where the yellow went"), or merely supra-dooper. More- over, with repetition any slogan will lose whatever sense it had to begin with and only the magical litany will remain; it will become an incantation pure and simple. Given enough exposure it may attain the ultimate symbol meaningful/less/ness of L.S./M.F.T. Even a slogan containing such sound —for a cigarette—reasons as "Filter, flavor, flip-top box" will assume, after the first few hearings, the properties of an incantation. This is true of all jingles, if they are any good.

Speaking of Marlboro, I understand that they introduced the original tattooed man because they wished to change the "product image" to a masculine one. That sounds logical except that as it turned out his hex- signed presence was an argument beyond any logic I know of. It is magic— a seemingly pertinent but logically irrelevant association of ideas. We may see a different application of this principle in a recent series of Shell gasoline advertisements. They feature famous works of craftsmanship in the shape of shells. These ads are done with great dignity and point out that they, Shell, do good work, too. Here we note imitative magic; their Shell and Cellini's shell; and also contagious magic: his craftsmanship bestowed by association on their craftsmanship.

By extension it could be argued that Texaco's admirable sponsorship of the Metropolitan Opera broadcasts—or any sponsorship for that matter —has a contagious magic aspect. The same might be said of Container Corporation's magnificent series on "Great Ideas of Western Man." If guilt by association is a magical technique (and it is) then so is quality by association.

This is not to say that the facts behind these associative devices are magical or illusory; they are real, they are supportable in practice. But no Indian tribe in performing a corn dance ever omitted to plant the seed either.

Now it is reasonable to ask whether all advertising is likely to employ magic of one sort or another. I suppose so, in the sense that every person alive—even one who makes all his purchases on the basis of Consumers Union recommendations—employs magical symbolism in some fashion. If it is more apparent in advertising, it is because advertising itself is more apparent. However, we should distinguish between advertising's white magic and black magic. The difference depends chiefly on whether the technique is used as a means of illustrating a point (Chase Manhattan Bank's nest egg) or constitutes a point itself ("9 out of 10 Witch Doctors Approve"). The former we could call magical imagery; the latter, magical thinking. If some advertising is more blatantly guilty of magical thinking than others, it is because some audiences are more simple-minded.

But, whatever its form, advertising's magic is relatively lucid in that it never confuses the main issue, what it has to sell. The same cannot be said for the economy advertising represents. Perhaps it is just the way it is explained, but the stability of our economic system apparently rests squarely on a magical device, the pyramid club. This is not, I regret to say, a private, crotchety view of my own; both of the candidates in the recent election seemed to embrace it vigorously. Both parties swore fealty to ever-expanding production; this presumably based on ever-expanding population and ever-expanding consumption. Not only are all of these terms plainly impossible, but unnerving as well. Put like that, our economy sounds like nothing so much as the granddaddy of all chain letters. All you can do is hope to get your name to the top of the list—or die—before something happens (like peace) and the whole thing collapses.

Is our economy really so magically conceived? I don't know and I'll wager you don't either. But there must be some sounder prospect than that of endlessly consuming more and more; force-fed, like so many Strasbourg geese. An explanation of the economic system to its people (and what strange abracadabra turned us into consumers anyway?) in sensible terms might be a fitting project for advertising and its clients to undertake as a public, and private, service.

THE FOLKLORE OF MASS PERSUASION

Floyd W. Matson

*t*he assault upon the rationality and responsibility of man is as old, at least, as Mephistopheles. But it requires no very deep sense of history to recognize that there are moments when the attacking spirit is in the ascendant and others when it is visibly under a cloud. During much of our national history, for example, the reality of the frontier combined with the theory of the Enlightenment to render Americans impatient of any aspersions upon their manifest perfectibility. "Aristocratic nations," as Tocqueville reminded us, "are naturally too liable to narrow the scope of human perfectibility; democratic nations, to expand it beyond reason."

On the other hand, there are probably few Americans today who would deny that the irrationalist philosophy—the doctrine that human behavior is governed by forces beneath or beyond the level of conscious control—is once again rampant among us. The various behavioral sciences engaged in the study of man appear almost to vie with one another in determining which can paint the darkest picture of the futility of man's hope and the inexorability of man's fate. A few years ago one dissenting sociologist, writing on "Social Science and the Distrust of Reason," defined this bleak perspective in terms worth retrieving:

> The eighteenth century philosophers believed in reason and perfectibility. But the belief in the potentiality of the individual was threatened, together with the belief in reason, once the Idols and prejudices of the mind were felt to be more than mere impediments to the free pursuit of truth. If the quest for knowledge is thought to be obstructed by the nature and the social existence of man, then this quest will be undertaken in a spirit of basic pessimism. How can men hope to profit from the use of knowledge in society if the belief in the basic orderliness of society has declined and if the belief has increased that man's social relations are a breeding ground of error and prejudice? How can we expect the individual to benefit from education, when it is believed that he

always acts as a member of his group and that his every action is but a repercussion of emotional patterns established through the experience of early childhood ? The basic pessimism which inspires these questions is characteristic of the social sciences today. Faith in the scientific method has increased, but the belief in reason and human perfectibility has declined.[1]

If, despite this trend of fashion, there are still some yea-sayers among us, some die-hard celebrants of the open mind and the free will, they are likely to be dismissed with gentle condescension as mere humanists—as museum pieces—who may possibly be permitted to retain their sinecures as archaic reminders of the prescientific past but must not be allowed to meddle in the serious scholarly business of mathematically computing, empirically validating, and rigorously testing the precise degree of *Homo's* lack of sapience.

Even the humanists, however, have in the main permitted themselves to be browbeaten into a fatal degree of submission by the measuring rods of their scientific colleagues and have come very close to accepting the behaviorist assumption of man's indefinite manipulability—if not also the value-neutral posture of detachment that elsewhere accompanies it. The most eloquent and inspired of recent protests against the "hidden persuaders" and all the subliminal subverters of the mind—such protests as those of George Orwell and Aldous Huxley—do not seriously challenge the validity or effectiveness of the demonic devices they describe; on the contrary, they are clearly prompted by the suspicion that the scientific premises of the propagandists and persuaders are all too correct. What they protest, for the most part, is not the truth-claim of the irrationalist thesis but only the prospect of its aggressive enforcement against a defenseless and acquiescent humanity.

Is this the way the Enlightenment world view ends: not with a bang but a whimper ?

Nowhere is the frustration and perplexity of men of good will—combining theoretical acceptance of the irrationalist doctrine with moral repudiation of its consequences—more poignantly on display than in the study of persuasion, both "pure" and applied. The typical textbook on the subject—whether it is entitled *The Process of Persuasion*, *The Art of Persuasion*, *How to Win the Conference*, or *The Technique of Handling People*—devotes nine-tenths of its pages to a recitation of the overwhelming clinical evidence of man's subhuman propensities and the final tenth to exhorting its readers not to take advantage of them.

This ambivalence is still more acutely felt in that expanding literature of protest, both academic and popular, that has accompanied the advent of what might be called "commercial psy-war" (psychological warfare against the consumer) and that is dedicated to unmasking and exposing the hidden persuaders. We have even been treated to a new variety of social-science fiction in which the villains wear gray flannel and talk in the shorthand symbolism of "PR" and "MR"—but otherwise are transparent reincarnations of the sorcerers and witches of earlier folklore, not least of all in their possession of magical powers against which human reason can offer no defense.

The term "social-science fiction" has, indeed, a dual reference. First, of course, a great deal of actual fiction (from *Brave New World* to *The Golden Kazoo*) has been composed upon this theme. But what is more important, the "social science" upon which the new techniques of persuasion and manipulation are allegedly based is itself, I believe, more fictional than real—or, to be precise, it is an unexamined body of fallacy and folklore that has been flagrantly misconceived, misunderstood, and misapplied.

In large part this misconception is calculated and opportunistic. The cult of irrationality has always had its vested interests, as Dostoevsky's Grand Inquisitor long ago made plain. It has them still today—not only in Moscow and Peking, but on Madison Avenue, in Detroit, and in political party headquarters across the land.

For an example, that is admittedly a caricature, let us observe Dr. Ernest Dichter, director of the Institute for Motivational Research and possibly the most successful practitioner of this new occult science. "His headquarters," according to the bemused author of *The Hidden Persuaders*, "which can be reached only by going up a rough winding road, are atop a mountain overlooking the Hudson River, near Croton-on-the-Hudson. It is a thirty-room field-stone mansion where you are apt to see children watching TV sets. The TV room has concealed screens behind which unseen observers sometimes crouch [Orwell's two-way television?], and tape recorders are planted about to pick up the children's happy or scornful comments."[2]

From this awesome sketch the inference is unavoidable that Dr. Dichter is practicing very expertly what he preaches—practicing, that is, upon his own clients in commerce and industry what he counsels them in turn to practice upon *their* clients. Surely all this melodrama of castles on the Hudson, winding mountain roads, unseen observers, and the rest is not so much functional as it is psychological. It is the penumbra of mystery that any good boiler-plate manufacturer might hopefully expect to see surrounding the modern witch doctor and mind reader. It goes with this fashionable clairvoyance as it used to go with seances and tea leaves.

The analogy is suggestive. For the new gospel of professional persuasion bears much the same relation to social and psychological science as alchemy once bore to chemistry and astrology to astrophysics. The hucksters have donned the raiment of the research lab and adopted its jargon; in their own terms, they have projected a respectable scientific "image," like the actor-doctors of the aspirin commercials. But in the end it is only show business—or, more accurately, it is a show for business.

The dubious character of the "behavioral science" that underlies the work of the professional persuaders is demonstrable in what passes among them for a basic conceptual scheme. In the effort to appropriate whatever may serve their purposes and confirm their claims, they have fastened in particular upon two celebrated systems of psychological theory; stimulus-response behaviorism and Freudian psychoanalysis. These two distinctive approaches to human conduct are exploited interchangeably, and even simultaneously, on the evident assumption that they are congenial companions—merely two sides of the same coin. At first glance this practice may seem only a healthy eclecticism; in fact, however, it is the wildest confusion—the product either of folly or of knavery.

In the entire history of the study of psychology, it would be difficult to point to any more profound and irreconcilable conflict than the one that has endured for more than a generation between behaviorism and psychoanalysis. The behaviorists, from Watson to Skinner, have defined human behavior as a neurological process substantially identical with the conduct of animals and have generally regarded the notion of "mind" or consciousness as the vestigial superstition of a prescientific era.

Thus Watson could declare, with the candor that endeared him to a generation of merchants (he left the academic laboratory, one recalls, for the presidency of the nation's largest advertising agency): "[The behaviorist has] dropped from his scientific vocabulary all subjective terms such as sensation, perception, image, desire, purpose, and even thinking and emotion as they were subjectively defined."[3]

On the other hand, as every schoolboy knows, classical psychoanalysis has defined behavior strictly in psychogenetic terms, as the overt expression of covert conflicts and unconscious strivings. The familiar assumptions of Freudian theory need no elaboration here; it is sufficient to point out that each of the two psychological schools—psychoanalysis and behaviorism—has persistently recognized in the other its antithesis if not its chief antagonist. (As early as the Twenties Watson maintained that "Much of the confusion we have today dates back to Freud . . . I venture to predict that twenty years from now an analyst using Freudian concepts and Freudian terminology will be placed upon the same plane as a phrenologist.")[4]

Nevertheless, the mass persuaders have either failed to perceive or (what is more likely) have chosen to ignore the fundamental discrepancies between the behaviorist and psychoanalytic schools and have blithely shuffled them together as equal and interchangeable components of the official doctrine. As, however, to accept the premises of either theory is virtually to reject the premises of the other, the most generous view of this forced marriage must regard it as a model of incompatibility.

But if on logical or scientific grounds such reckless procedure appears a form of madness, there is definitely method to it. Although the conceptual schemes of behaviorism and psychoanalysis are in crucial respects mutually exclusive, they do share in common one vital assumption regarding human behavior: the assumption that it is fundamentally irrational and irresponsible. Both theories regard the individual as an essentially passive agent, a merely reactive mechanism, through whom and upon whom inexorable forces (whether of external or of internal origin) work their will and have their way. For Watson, there is simply no conscious mind at all—no purpose, no will, no subjective striving whatever. For Freud, the thin red line of ego, although it does maintain a precarious existence, is all but erased by the moving fingers of Eros and Thanatos—the instincts of life and death—which having writ move on, leaving their indelible imprints behind. On the reckoning of either theory we are all (as someone has said of the heroes of Hemingway) merely men to whom things are done, and our behavior is accordingly irrational, predictable, and manipulable.

Given this unique convergence of points of view, it becomes less difficult to understand why two otherwise clashing psychologies should be equally congenial to the professional persuaders. Both give the appearance of scientific support (although at least one must do so for the wrong reasons) to the premise of irrationality that sustains the new industry of consent engineers. It is instructive to note that other and no less lively psychological theories that give emphasis to rational and volitional factors in behavior—like those of ego psychology, neo-Freudianism, and transactionalism—find slight favor among the mass persuaders. The reason for this avoidance is not far to seek. There would be little call and less reward for these mass-motivation researchers if human conduct were indeed substantially the product of conscious purpose—if, that is, it should turn out that people often do things for the reasons they think they do. In order to protect their vested interest, the commercial persuaders are compelled to become both the prophets and the high priests of the new cult of irrationality.

Furthermore, it must be admitted that they are not without an impressive following of true believers, drawn primarily from the ranks of industry and commerce. It is virtually a truism today that in our "affluent society" the stability of the economy depends upon ever rising levels of production and that this dependence in turn presupposes a rate of consumption that borders on the compulsive and is undeterred by considerations of rationality or utility. Witness that modern marvel of Yankee ingenuity known as "psychological obsolescence," by which consumers are encouraged to become ashamed of their chromy possessions, from tractors to tract homes, even before they are freely and clearly possessed. Add to it the dilemma of producers who are well aware that their soaps and soporifics are only "marginally" distinguishable, if at all, from those of their competitors.

"Brand distinction" and "brand loyalty" can therefore be attained, in the generality of cases, only through artifice and sleight-of-mind—that is, through the devices of hidden persuasion. Under such conditions it is hardly surprising that numbers of merchants and manufacturers should be eager to join the irrationalist cult and contribute to the cause.

It cannot, of course, be expected that the mass persuaders and their clients will admit that their faith is grounded upon a foundation so crassly expedient and self-serving. They advance their claim to authority, rather, on the basis of the supposed scientific evidence of human behavior, as well as of their own presumptive competence in altering and controlling it.

The folklore character of much of that evidence may be indicated by a single illustration. Probably no term is more central to the vocabulary of the motivation researchers, or more monotonously reiterated, than the familiar "conditioned reflex." The concept derives originally from the famous experiment by Pavlov in which the salivary reflex of dogs, stimulated by the appearance of food, was "conditioned" to respond to various "substitute stimuli" that were first associated with the food and then presented independently. The animals were made to salivate by the sound of a bell, the sight of an electric light, and so forth. In sum, the conditioned-reflex experiments (subsequently elaborated by a generation of behaviorists) demonstrated that the *same* response could be produced by a variety of stimuli; the crucial point was that, although the stimulus might be changed, the response remained invariable.

But as the concept of "conditioned response" or "conditioning" has come to be applied to propaganda and persuasion, it has undergone a subtle and remarkable change. In the broader context, it refers to changing and varying the responses themselves: to the process of altering conduct and modifying opinions, of instilling new beliefs and transforming behavior. According to one textbook, we are all "creatures of conditioned reflex"— from which the author concludes that skilled persuaders should be able to evoke whatever responses they desire and to change them at will.[5] In short, the term has taken on exactly the opposite of its original meaning: it is now the *response* that is supposedly altered, while the stimulus may or may not remain the same. To be sure, behaviorists have exerted themselves to seek ways of relating "conditioned response" to the process of learning but with conspicuously barren results. In the end it remains undeniable that, as Robert E. L. Faris has pointed out, "no new response is acquired in the process of conditioning. There is no new learning at all . . . The conditioned response is the same old response, evoked by a new signal."[6] To speak, then, of "conditioning" as the process of deliberately changing human behavior and of teaching new responses is to employ a jargon without scientific support—whatever prestige it may enjoy in the developing folklore of persuasion.

Much else that is taken as established in the gospel of the motivation researchers is subject to similar criticism. For one thing, the underlying premise of human malleability and irrationality, once accepted, tends to become a selfconfirming hypothesis by virtue of the resort to experimental depth-probing devices that are capable of recording only the unconscious and involuntary responses of subjects—however insignificant or secondary those factors may in fact be. For instance, the widespread use of the Rorschach and other projective tests as means of exploring hidden motivations has been called critically into question by the discovery that normal, well-adjusted persons frequently give no evidence whatever of their dominant motives through such methods.[7] At best, it is pointed out, these psycho-diagnostic instruments elicit no more information from normal individuals than might be obtained more easily by straightforward questioning of the subjects in direct interview. "At no point," writes Gordon W. Allport, "do these methods ask the subject what his interests are, what he wants to do, or what he is trying to do . . . Has the subject no right to be believed?"[8] And his own answer, on the basis of evidence drawn from recent research in motivation theory, is that the normal person has not only the right but the competence to speak for himself, to be heard, and to be believed.

These highly significant findings appear to fulfill almost to the letter the prophecy voiced with some bitterness not long ago by the author of *The Organization Man*: "Some day someone is going to create a stir by proposing a radical new tool for the study of people. It will be called the face-value technique. It will be based on the premise that people often do what they do for the reasons they think they do."[9]

I do not mean to suggest, of course, that every interpretation of human nature and conduct that lends encouragement to the cynical enterprise of the mass-motivation researchers has been eliminated from the behavioral sciences. On the contrary, as suggested earlier, there can be little doubt that the irrationalist thesis is still the dominant and fashionable one within these disciplines. But, what is more significant because much less well known, there can be equally little doubt that a legitimate and formidable "resistance movement" (which at least one social scientist has labeled the "Humanist Underground") is vigorously contesting the field with the irrationalists and challenging the validity of their ruling myth.

I can do no more than mention a few notable examples of dissent and new departure among the social sciences. In social psychology, the work of the gestaltists generally—and of such leaders as Solomon Asch and the late Max Wertheimer in particular—has done much to restore dignity and responsibility to the psychological image of man.[10] In psychoanalysis, the neo-Freudians generally (and such spokesmen as Erich Fromm and Karen Horney in particular) have performed an equivalent service in countering the classical division of "man against himself" with a systematic affirmation of "man for himself."[11] In the applied sciences of social casework and counseling, the liberating principles developed especially by Carl R. Rogers and by the "functionalists" under the late Kenneth L. M. Pray have served to offset the authoritarian tendencies of the Freudian-based "diagnostic" school of casework theory.[12] In sociology, the diverse but not divergent contributions of such scholars as David Riesman, C. Wright Mills, Louis Wirth, Herbert Blumer, and Reinhard Bendix have defied the trend toward positivism and pessimism by giving deliberate emphasis both to the normative responsibilities of social science and to the active energies and creative capacities of human beings.[13]

Finally, and perhaps most significantly of all, in the psychological study of perception—the field most directly pertinent to an analysis of persuasion and propaganda—the rigid structure of the stimulus-response school has been severely shaken if not overturned by the "new look" theory of perception as a selective and dynamic function, an organized and purposeful "transaction" through which the individual actively relates himself to his world. In the sharpest possible contrast to the traditional account of perception as "that which is done by the environment to the organism," the functional approach (as described by Cantril and Ittelson) "takes the active perceiving individual as its proper point of departure" and defines the act of perceiving as "that part of the process of living by which each one of us, from his own particular point of view, creates for himself the world within which he has his life's experiences and through which he strives to gain his satisfactions."[14]

The inference to be drawn from these auspicious developments in the systematic study of man is not one, surely, of any encouragement to the professional manipulators of symbols and persons. Despite the advertised inroads of the MR technicians and their various big brothers, despite the awe-inspiring devices of tyranny over the mind and of infiltration beneath it, despite the commercial conspiracies of social science and private interest —despite all these elements, man is still at some time the master of his fate : and the fault, dear humanists, is not in our stars (nor in our childhoods, nor our instincts, nor our conditioning) but in our conscious selves that we are . . . what we are. If, on the provisional evidence of the clinic and the laboratory, there remains some question of the capacity of man to make his way on earth and if there is not yet occasion for rejoicing in his final triumph, neither is there certain and compelling cause for alarm. It was a prominent perceptual psychologist who wrote that "Every perception is an act of creation ; every action is an act of faith."[15] And it was a prominent perceptive humanist who declared, upon receiving the Nobel Prize :

> It is easy enough to say that man is immortal simply because he will endure ; that when the last ding-dong of doom has clanged and faded from the last red and dying evening, that even then there will still be one

more sound: that of his puny inexhaustible voice, still talking. I refuse to accept this. I believe that man will not merely endure, he will prevail. He is immortal, not because he alone among creatures has an inexhaustible voice, but because he has a soul, a spirit, capable of compassion, and sacrifice, and endurance. . . .[16]

And capable also, we may add, of *resistance*—to the persuasive appeals of his own inexhaustible voice.

NOTES

1. Reinhard Bendix, *Social Science and the Distrust of Reason* (University of California Publications in Sociology and Social Institutions, Vol. 1, No. 1 [1951], p. 21.

2. Vance Packard, *The Hidden Persuaders* (New York: David McKay Company, Inc., 1957), p. 31.

3. John B. Watson, *Behaviorism* (Chicago: University of Chicago Press, 1958), pp. 6–7.

4. *Ibid.*, p. 297.

5. Clyde Miller, *The Process of Persuasion*, quoted in Packard, *op. cit.*, p. 24.

6. Robert E. L. Faris, *Social Psychology* (New York: The Ronald Press Company, 1952), p. 79.

7. See Gordon W. Allport, "The Trend in Motivational Theory," in Clark E. Moustakas, ed., *The Self: Explorations in Personal Growth* (New York: Harper & Row, Publishers, 1956).

8. *Ibid.*, pp. 27–28.

9. William H. Whyte, Jr., *The Organization Man* (New York: Simon & Schuster, 1956), p. 40.

10. See Solomon E. Asch, *Social Psychology* (New York: Prentice-Hall, Inc., 1952); and Max Wertheimer, *Productive Thinking* (New York: Harper & Row, publishers, 1945).

11. See Erich Fromm, *Man for Himself: An Inquiry into the Psychology of Ethics* (New York: Holt & Rinehart, & Winston, Inc., 1947); and Karen Horney, *Neurosis and Human Growth: The Struggle Toward Self-Realization* (New York: W. W. Norton & Company, Inc., 1950).

12. See Carl R. Rogers, *Counseling and Psychotherapy* (New York: Houghton Mifflin & Company, 1942); and Kenneth L. M. Pray, *Social Work in a Revolutionary Age* (Philadelphia: University of Pennsylvania Press, 1949).

13. An older American tradition in social science, which has nurtured Blumer and others, should be mentioned here. It is the tradition that may be said to have begun with William James and reached its culmination in the social psychology of George Herbert Mead and John Dewey. An excellent discussion of the current revival of this tradition may be found in Ernest Becker, *The Revolution in Psychiatry* (New York: Free Press, 1964), *passim*.

14. William H. Ittelson and Hadley Cantril, *Perception: A Transactional Approach* (New York: Doubleday & Company, Inc. 1954), p. 5.

15. *Ibid.*, p. 30. The words appear to be those of Cantril.

16. William Faulkner, Nobel Prize award speech, 1949.

part six

SYMBOLIC INTERACTION:
THE SOCIOLOGY OF COMMUNICATION

COMMUNICATION AND SOCIAL ORDER*

Hugh Dalziel Duncan

*t*he best we have done thus far in communication theory in sociology is to make vague statements about the reciprocal relationship between society and communication. We have also elaborated biological, physical, mechanical, and, more recently, electronic analogies of communication into models, or "designs," for exercises in research technique. These analogical models are spun out in great detail through elaborate research techniques, which are often not so much a statement of relationship between a hypothesis and data, as an attempt to rephrase old propositions in the new jargon, or to describe how techniques were applied to data selected to fit the technique.

Social acts are now described as events that order themselves through a "tendency to self-maintenance." Social systems are likened to solar systems, and social roles are said to "bring out" possibilities of behavior which fit the "needs and tolerances of the particular patterned structure." In this model of society, attitudes "gear" and "mesh" because "patterned structure" and "integrative patterns . . . bring it about that all the statuses of the society intermesh like a series of interlocking wheels." Communication of expressive symbols is not studied as an enactment of social order, but as a process of cathexis in which meanings are "attached" to objects and persons.

In other analogies, men are likened to dogs, rats, chickens, or pigeons, and we are told that what is true of pigeons in cages is also true of men in society, or, among the more sophisticated technicians, that if men were held like pigeons in a cage then what is true of the behavior of pigeons would be true of men. Such wild analogical leaps from animals and machines to men are often justified on the basis of technique alone. For if (so the argument runs) a certain technique for ordering data about pigeons is

* Hugh D. Duncan, *Communication and Social Order*, The Bedminster Press, New York, 1962, pp. XV–XXX. Copyright © 1962 by The Bedminster Press. Reprinted by permission.

"scientific," then the same technique applied to men in society will yield studies of similar "scientific" value. *How* a study is done, not what questions were asked, and the kind of data used, determine its "scientific" value in this kind of thinking.

In the many hundreds of pages of recent sociological theory there is scarcely any indication that communication of significant symbols is anything more than some kind of epiphenomenon of a reality "beyond" symbols. Attitudes do not arise in symbolic acts, or in symbolic phases of action (in which, as heroes, villains, and clowns to each other, we play our parts in a great social drama of social order) but in "expressive reference" contexts, in which attitudes become a "symbolic generalization of cathexis" which functions to maintain "the pattern integrity" of the symbolic system.[1]

And while there is much greater concern with the social function of symbols in Dilthey, Simmel, and Mannheim, and other European students of society, there is a singular lack of congruence between structure and function in their models and images of society. Even Mannheim, who talks at great length about "thought styles"—a concept which he borrows from the history of art—never makes clear just how the structure of "existential" thought functions in communication. The Freudian libido, like the actor in Parsons' system, cathects, but does not communicate. Simmel's forms of sociation emerge, and continue to exist, in social processes that are not determined by the use of symbols in communication, but by social forces that are "like atoms."

Other sociologists find their sociological "facts" in "historical and political reality." Just how one gets at this without symbolic theory and method, or the use of sociological models based on communication, is seldom discussed. Sentences like "What dramatic vision of hell can compete with the events of twentieth-century war ?"[2] assume that the "events" of war can be known by means other than a dramatic construction of them, or that they become events in some nonsymbolic realm which does not depend on how they are dramatized by artists in the press, radio, television, literature, cinema, and other arts. What is the source of C. Wright Mills' knowledge of events ? How can "events" of war in the past or the present make themselves known to us as social and historical facts, if not through some kind of symbolic construction ? How can sociologists, to say nothing of historians, think at all about societal events unless they use models, images, structures—or whatever the forms of our thought are called—of how men *communicate* as they act together in society?

Symbols are the directly observable data of sociation, and, since it is impossible to use symbols without using them in some kind of structure or form, we cannot discourse about society with any degree of precision unless we discourse about the forms social relationships assume in communication. There may be some reality underlying symbols, but all we know about what people do is the meaning of what they say[3] they do. Even Mills admonishes his social scientist: "Always keep your eyes open to the image of man." But where does one find an "image of man ?" All we see of man, certainly all we can report of his social activities, are various forms of expression. We no longer need to be told that men exist in history, or society, but to be shown *how* such existence can be studied in some sociological frame of reference.

It will be argued throughout this book that a sociological theory of social action can be created only if we show how *forms*, as well as contents, of symbolic expression are used to create and sustain social order. Following Simmel, we argue that the study of society is the study of forms of sociation. But we argue further—and here our clue is supplied by Mead and Burke— that the data of sociation exist in the various kinds of symbolic expressions men use to enact their social roles in communication with one another. It is not enough to invoke ritual play, ceremony, festivals, games, or drama as analogies for society unless we make clear *how* these become, and continue to be, *social* forms.

Nor is it of much help to the development of sociological theory to invoke social contexts as "referents" to symbols unless we show just how these referents exist in the symbols. That is, if we say that struggle to attain social order determines social relations, we must show how various significations of social order can be studied as they are used in the communication of such order. As we shall stress in our remarks on social transcendence, authorities use many kinds of symbols to justify their rule. In our view, these justifications ought to be studied in concrete symbolic acts, or in symbolic phases of action. Power always involves persuasion, and whether we persuade under principles of sovereignty, ruling myths, dominant ideas, ideologies, or whether we study ruling ideas of social order as folklore, legitimations, or collective representation, we must study what *kind* of order they involve and above all how this order is expressed in communication.

We must show how social order is expressed, for all we really can observe about order is how it is communicated. We talk, sometimes very grandly, about public sentiments, the people's will, the voice of the people, the leadership principle, the divine right of kings, or the kingdom of God. But when we are asked to point out how these great transcendent images of social order operate, we turn to the various ways in which they are expressed in communication. And social order, we note, always involves people who communicate as superiors, inferiors, and equals, and pass from one position to another. Such communication is always a form of address, a kind of hierarchical rhetoric, in which, as superiors, inferiors, and equals, in passage from one position to another, we justify our rank to ourselves and to others by enacting in various kinds of community dramas the value to some great transcendent principle of social order of the roles we play.

As matters now stand in American social thought, the study of forms of communication is suspect, or tolerated only until social scientists achieve an "intellectual clarity" which science, and usually science based on quantification, is supposed to produce. Men of letters also warn us that using literature or other art works as cultural case histories is false, because art exists "in its own right" and cannot be explained by the culture of an age or country. There is no question about our need for intellectual clarity, and certainly it is true that art cannot be explained by social referents alone. All critics admit that *War and Peace* becomes singularly unclear about the nature of peace (if not of war), and that Tolstoy "distorts" the Russian class struggle in 1800 to produce an art work, not to write social history, just as Freud "distorted" the Oedipus legend and drama to create a model of family interaction, not to write a history of Greek drama.

But when we turn to the sociologist or the aesthete for help in freeing ourselves from the "distortions" of the artist, we find ourselves in the same situation as Freud when he tried to understand why men act as they do from what they said about what they did—or as sociologists do when they must interpret symbolic material in case histories, interviews, or life histories. As anthropologists, psychologists, or sociologists, we join with historians, philosophers, and artists in the realization that our knowledge of human motives is limited by our knowledge of the systems of expressions in which motives are communicated. Even Freud, who hoped all his life to create a mechanical model of mentation, said in 1909: "Dream symbols that do not find support in myths, fairy tales, popular usages, etc., should be regarded as doubtful." Later, in 1917, in his lecture, "Symbolism in Dreams," he is even more explicit.

> How do we profess to arrive at the meaning of these dream-symbols, about which the dreamer himself can give us little or no information. . . . My answer is that we derive our knowledge from widely different sources: from fairy tales and myths, jokes and witticisms, from folklore, i.e., from what we know of the manners and customs, sayings and songs, of different people, and from poetic and colloquial usage of language.[4]

Freud is not alone in his belief that understanding society depends on our understanding of symbols. Dilthey argued that speech is the most complete, exhaustive, and objectively intelligible expression of man. He pointed out many times that the exegesis, or interpretation of the remains of human existence which are contained in writing, is central to every method of understanding used in the human sciences. Simmel's forms of sociation are based on many analogies, but he often returns to art form to illustrate his general idea of social form.[5] Kenneth Burke stresses that social interaction is not a process, but a dramatic expression, an enactment of roles by individuals who seek to identify with each other in their search to create social order. George Herbert Mead, too, described such enactments as forms similar to those in play, games, and drama. Our need to stress form in terms of expression and emotion, as well as mechanics and motion, has been pointed out by Talcott Parsons, whose model of man in society is certainly far different from that of Dewey, Mead, or Burke. He says: "Expressive symbolism is that part of the cultural tradition most directly integrated with the cathectic interests of the actor. . . . [Expressive symbols] organize the interaction process through normative regulation, through imposing standards on it."[6]

Dewey, like Mead, Cooley, and Burke, searched for models of society in art, because he believed that art experience is the most characteristically human of all experiences. Dewey and Mead selected the moment of consummation, as found in the experience of art, as the decisive phase of the act. In his own "Rejoinder" to the various essays on his own work collected and edited by Paul A. Schilpp in *The Philosophy of John Dewey*,[7] Dewey is careful to point out that making his theory of instrumentalism synonymous with knowledge reached through science based on quantification is foreign to his whole philosophy.[8] In his summary of Dewey's work, Ratner (who edited much of Dewey's work with his approval) says: ". . . one finds Dewey's best and profoundest exposition of his integral conception of Philosophy, or the nature of intelligence, in his *Art as Experience*."[9]

For Mead, the moment of consummation as found in aesthetic experience was of crucial importance to the study of nature as well as man in society. In the consummatory moment in art, the future (or end) of the act, as well as the past (or tradition), is objectified in expressive forms which bring the end of the act into consciousness. These forms are real because they are public; they are social because they exist in communication. Dewey says: "Literature conveys the meaning of the past that is significant in present experience and is prophetic of the larger movements of the future. . . . The first stirrings of dissatisfaction and the first intimations of a better future are always found in works of art. . . . Factual science may collect statistics and make charts. But its predictions are . . . but past history reversed. Change in the . . . imagination is the precursor of the changes that affect more than the details of life."[10]

Mead argued that art experience must be studied because it tells us much about "the goals toward which our efforts run." Movement into a future, Mead continues, always brings novelty into action. As we press toward our goals we must deal with aspects of the situation that are simply unpredictable. Thus, all action is problematic, and all imagined ends and recalled traditions are hypothetical at best. But this does not mean that the imagined futures, or goals, of human action embodied in art are mere subjective fantasies. They are objective because they are public forms of expression, and instrumental because they are means by which we organize action in a present. For if we do not have clearly expressed goals, either in public symbols of an imagined future or a recalled past which we are striving to recapture, we have no guides and cannot act at all. In short, art *orders* social experience through creating forms which all, artist and public alike, use to communicate so that they *can* act together.

In more recent works in sociology, the search for ways to use art to understand society has shifted from general assertions on the interdependency of society and art, to attempts to create specific descriptions of institutional and community roles. Thus W. Lloyd Warner, in his *The Living and the Dead, a Study of the Symbolic Life of Americans*, says:

> The community in which his [Biggy Muldoon, the political leader of Yankee City] rise and fall took place was more than a setting for the drama. The forces acting within it helped to create his personality; they were the all-powerful feelings and beliefs that functioned in his career like Fate in the lives of Greek tragic heroes. Indeed, a good case could be made demonstrating that the flaws in the characters of Greek tragedy and the fates they suffered were no more than the basic precepts and principles of their society, its social logics, operating in the dramas and in the beliefs and values of the audience who watched them. Since Greek dramas are still powerful—for Oedipus Rex can bring tears to the eyes of modern audiences—it seems probable that these same fates and flaws operate in the lives of contemporary men.[11]

The problem now is no longer one of asserting that there is a reciprocal relation between art and society, but of showing *how* this relationship exists. This does not mean there is no more need for theory. There is great need, for until we have a series of *sociological* propositions on the function of art and communication in society, we cannot create hypotheses for dealing with the concrete data of communication in society. Behaviorists are right in their attack on "symbolic interactionists" who keep repeating that symbolic interaction is the characteristic human interaction, yet fail to show *how* symbolic interaction can be studied as a social fact. If we cannot show *how* it affects human conduct, then we must leave the field to those who, within clearly specified limits, are saying some things about conduct that can be verified by other students of society.

We do not answer the behaviorists, or the new school of social mechanists led by Parsons, by criticizing them for the limited range of their observations, their neglect of significant symbols, their naive analogical thinking, or by branding them immoral because they reduce men to machines or animals. That is, we do not answer them as sociologists concerned with rigorous discourse. The only proper answer to behaviorists (of whatever school) is to show how what we say ought to be done in symbolic analysis can be done. For, if we know how symbols ought not to be studied, we must know how they ought to be studied. We ought to be able to communicate clearly just what we mean by saying that sociation takes place in specific forms of communication, and that these forms are created in various expressive systems. And if we argue that the study of one of these expressive systems, art, becomes the study of society, we must indicate what kind of art we are talking about.

The use of symbolic forms of expression to develop theory and method in the human studies is not new. The works of Fustel de Coulanges,[12] W. Robertson Smith,[13] Emile Durkheim,[14] Bronislaw Malinowski,[15] and A. R. Radcliffe-Brown,[16] as well as the work of Weber, Troeltsch, and Tawney, indicate how much social thought owes to the study of symbolic expression in society. But these studies, and, indeed, almost the whole body of sociological thought on the nature of the social bond, are based on religious expression. Art is often used, but only to illustrate "sentiments of attachment" in the expression of the social bond. It is accepted as a kind of conductor (message track in modern jargon) of the underlying reality of religious sentiment as exemplified in the religious rite. Such rites are accepted, in turn, as paradigms for the social bond because it is believed, following Bacon, that religion is the most substantial bond of humanity.

Social mechanists assure us they have escaped the subjectivism of social theory based on symbols by creating "objective" models of sociation that do not depend on individual consciousness. Yet even in the midst of their mechanical images of "geared" motives and moving equilibrium, there are constant references to communication as something more than a kind of cathexis. There is an admission, if not an elaboration, of the fact that men use symbols to "condition" or "motivate" themselves and others. In such views, the symbols men use to motivate themselves serve as triggers to release "forces" whose power is derived from non-symbolic sources in nature, the body, or socio-political laws. And since these "forces" are "beyond" symbols, they can be studied as "processes" in much the same way processes are studied in nature.

But, as Lotze pointed out, *even* in a physical field (mechanical or electronic) interaction cannot be conceived of without reference to points or agents which are internally modified by, and in turn modifiers of, the process which affects them. When we describe mechanical causation we say that the impact of one element on another "communicates" motion, so that the element struck passes from a state of rest (or from one phase) to one of motion (or to another), while the striking element has experienced a change of an opposite character. But even as a description of a physical field, this explains nothing. For, if all that happens in communication is the communication of motion, why does it not pass through the striken element and leave its state unchanged ? Or, in sociological terms, if social forces "affect" the actor, but are not in turn affected by him, then how do we explain the individual, or the creation of symbols used in role enactment by individuals in social interaction? This is *not* simply a "metaphysical problem" which we can thrust aside "to get down to business" as rugged empiricists. The same dilemma haunts Parsons' work. If statuses and roles are "analogous to the particle of mechanics, not to mass or velocity, but are not, in general, attributes of the actor,"[17] what are the observable data of role enactment?

Park and Burgess, following the tradition of Cooley, Dewey, and Mead, stated that sociology must deal with communication as the prime medium of interaction. But their model of communication was only another variant of mechanism. For, despite all talk about society existing in communication, the symbols which we use to communicate, and the function of art in society receive small notice. Symbols are but an expression of a reality beyond symbols. This reality is some kind of process in which competition, conflict, accommodation, and assimilation are conceived of as "a constellation of social forces." Thus, while communication is named as the medium of social interaction, the medium itself (the forms of expression we use in communication) is not studied,[18] and we are locked again in the dismal circle in social thought which tells us that social forces determine society because society determines social forces.

Thus the student who seeks to understand society in terms of communication as role enactment must enter a debate whose terms have been set by anthropologists who find their models of sociation in the expression of religious symbols, or by sociologists who find their model in the functioning of a machine. Mechanists are old foes; many battles have been fought with them, and the arsenal of weapons for taking the field against them is well stocked. But sociologists who believe that art, as well as religion, is a constituent social act, have few weapons and certainly few allies—in the arts or in sociology. They must be content for the moment to lead a kind of purgatorial existence in which they are damned by humanists for perverting art, and by sociologists for abandoning science.

To say that what is true of machines is true of men, or that a rational act must be likened to a mechanical act, or that emotion is but another name for motion—this is useful so long as we limit our conclusions to the data used. But when we become "mystics of the machine" and reify our mechanical concepts by treating them as a substance, or a quality of social action, we confuse metaphor and fiction with hypotheses. Even the dedicated behaviorist must admit that he cannot, as a behaviorist, equate quantity and quality in any scientific way.[19] That is, the quantity of somatic discharge cannot be related to the quality of satisfaction or dissatisfaction experienced by the organism in the process of discharge.

But to say that what is true of men in religious worship is also true of men in society also creates many difficulties. We know how easily religious rites, and especially those based on the tragic scapegoat, can be torn out of context and used by the state, or by the church itself, to uphold secular powers whose capacity for corruption is vast indeed. So long as we confuse all authority with supernatural authority, reason in society cannot exist. Too often in the religious rite, those who oppose the gods must suffer and die. Social theory based on such models of the act cannot admit ambiguity, doubt, competition, disagreement, conflict, or opposition, for when society is dominated by religion, those who do not accept authority as they accept God are heretics who must recant or be punished. And, if we follow Durkheim, when men do not accept the god-like authority of superiors they end by living apart from their fellows in a state of anomie whose burden of loneliness and alienation is too great to endure. Such men, in refusing to accept the commandments of their authorities, excommunicate themselves.

It is for such reasons, and others which the text will make clear, that we turn to art, and particularly to comic art, for help in constructing a social theory of communication, and indicating sociological ways of thinking about society in terms of role enactment as a communicative act. We argue that until we can think of ambiguity, doubt, tension, estrangement, and all the ways in which we differ, as well as agree with one another, we cannot think well about democratic, or indeed, *any* society. As we hope to make clear, social order is always defined in terms of disorder, and in the present sad state of affairs in human society, order is at best merely a resolution of struggle between authorities of widely different views who seek to convince us, often by terrible as well as benign means, that their principles alone are the principles of order. Art, we shall argue, is the realm where the expression of doubt, ambiguity, and difference is normal. We shall argue, too, that art gives us forms which make it possible for us to *confront* our differences and thus bring them into consciousness so we can communicate with each other, as well as with our gods.

We do not argue that human society is characterized by communication alone. Animals communicate, machines signal through built-in message tracks, matter readjusts to changes in conditions, organisms respond to stimuli; but whether we call such responses "signals," "signs," "cathexis," or "stimulus and response," we are not talking about communication in the sense of the term as developed in this book. Nor do we argue that art is determined by communication alone. Artists create symbols to express themselves, to name or designate things and events, as they also struggle to make their forms consistent within themselves. And while these are all related to communication, they are by no means subordinated to it. All that we say here is that *from a sociological view* communication is the category of art with which we should be concerned. We argue here that human communication in society is an attempt to create symbols whose use is believed to uphold social order.

Social order is considered here in some detail as a drama of social hierarchy in which we *enact* roles as superiors, inferiors, and equals. We enact roles through communication, and when we enter a group to begin communication, we enter hierarchical relationships which are determined by the consensually validated symbols of the group in which we seek to play our part. No individual is always inferior, superior, or equal. Differential status is common to all societies, and passage from one position to another must be provided if the society is to function well. Thus the study of differential status, so common to democratic society, is necessary to an understanding of any kind of hierarchy, as well as to the satisfaction of our own moral needs as citizens of a democratic commonwealth. For among kings, as among common people, status is won by successful appeals to others who, like the audience of a great drama, determine our success and failure as we play our many roles in society. Status enactment is always a *plea*, a petition, for status is *given*, never taken.

Social order, we argue further, is always a resolution of struggle between superiors, inferiors, and equals. This struggle takes the form of a great community drama in which, through comedy as well as tragedy, the community seeks to ward off threats to the majesty of its transcendent symbols of social integration. Skill in playing hierarchical roles is determined by skill in hierarchical address. The actor in the social drama of hierarchy must please his superiors, inspire his inferiors, and convince his equals. Yet even at best the actor in this drama is never quite successful, and sometimes he fails completely. Thus, no society can survive unless symbolic resources are available for expiating guilt arising out of failures by superiors, inferiors, and equals, to uphold principles of hierarchy believed necessary to the survival of the group.

The failure of our civilization, the pride of men who conquered space but who could not conquer themselves, will someday be subjects for great tragedy and great comedy—if anyone is left to enjoy either. For the next bombs which fall will destroy the world, and all the fair hopes of men will vanish in the dust. Men have lived under terror of annihilation before. The early Christians were convinced too, that the world was coming to an end. But beyond the dark horror of nothingness there stood the vision of a paradise, a world of beauty and goodness beyond the world of suffering and evil that men knew. What vision do we have as we stand in horror before an impending doom from the skies, haunted by the terrible cries of the victims of Stalin and Hitler?

Our world died in the concentration camps of Hitler and the slave labor camps of Stalin. The hapless Jews of Europe who shuffled in endless lines to torture and death, so that our "pure Aryan blood" could be purified, were the last victims of the "Master Race." But their doom sealed the doom of their masters. For who can ever believe again in the justice of an Aryan

civilization? And now that the same civilization which permitted enslavement, torture, and slaughter has greater power to do evil, the terror of life
increases. We see now how fortunate were the early Christians whose last
visions in the suffering and pain of torture and death were visions of a
paradise beyond the world. We have no paradise. The terrestrial heavens
promised us by science and technology have not arrived, and few believe
they ever will.

But times of despair can also be times of greatness. For if we can summon up courage to *confront* our evil, to look into the terrible abyss of the
human spirit, and to record what we see there, we may yet survive. Or, if we
do not, we can at least leave a record which might be of help to others.
Men like Hitler and Stalin ruled through social mystification. To argue that
economic or political causes made possible their great conspiracies against
humanity, would tell us little about why such causes took the form of black
tyranny in one nation and of social welfare in another. Hitler never pre-
tended that he was offering his people full bellies and comfortable shelter.
On the contrary, he offered them sacrifice and death in struggle against
enemies at home and abroad. He created a kind of social drama that we
must learn to understand if we are to survive the next "savior" who arises
among us—if we are to survive at all.

Authority is always legitimized through reference to social order, but
authority must not be confused with superiority or inferiority alone, as it
has been so often by those who use tragic ritual or tragic ritual drama for
their models of the enactment of social order. Equality, the expression of
the will of equals in rules and law, is as universal a form of authority as that
based on supernatural legitimation in religion and politics. Without
equality, no social order—not even the worst tyranny—can exist. And when
there is little equality, reason in society soon withers and dies, the social
relationship of friendship cannot come into being, and all relations depending on equality among peers cannot exist. Reason in society depends on
free and informed discussion among equals, just as friendship depends on
free interchange among equals. Equality is necessary to all institutions and
situations where men must agree to bind themselves under rules of their
own creation. Without equality, rules cannot function, and without rules,
society, and particularly democratic society, cannot exist, because free,
open, and informed discussion can take place only between equals. Gods
do not discuss; they command.

No social order exists without disorder. In tragic communal rites disorder is exercised through punishment, torture, and death. But there is
another kind of communal rite which we use to face disorder. This is
comedy, which is a kind of sanctioned disrespect, where we are allowed to
express doubt and question over the transcendent principles that those in
power uphold in the name of social order. Just as we turn to tragic rites for

help in creating models of sociation, so can we turn to comic forms of expression. For in comedy we *uncover* the ambiguities and contradictions which beset us as we seek to act together. And since we are permitted in comedy to discuss openly what we cannot even mention in tragic ritual, comedy offers many clues to the difficulties men find in playing their social roles. The study, then, of art, and particularly comic art, is the proper study of man in society, because it is study of the resolution between order and disorder in society.

This book ends in exhortation. The steps leading to the concluding homily may be summarized as follows: Man as a social being exists in and through communication; communication is as basic to man's nature as food and sex; sociation inescapably involves hierarchy; hierarchy involves incongruities which society solves well or ill (as in war, genocide, or sadism and masochism); until society masters the dynamics of hierarchy as a set of relationships between superiors, inferiors, and equals, all sociation is in a parlous state; art works offer our best clues for the analysis of these dynamics; and finally, students of society must learn how to proceed with such analysis if we are to create a science of human conduct that tells us something about motivation.

NOTES

1. Talcott Parsons, Robert F. Bales, and Edward A. Shils, *Working Papers in the Theory of Action* (Glencoe, Ill.: The Free Press, 1953), esp. Chapter 2, "The Theory of Symbolism in Relation to Action," by Talcott Parsons.

2. C. Wright Mills, *The Sociological Imagination* (New York: Oxford Univ. Press, 1959), p. 17. Mills argues that the study of alienating methods of production, enveloping techniques of political domination, international anarchy, the pervasive transformations of the nature of man, and the conditions and aims of his life, is the proper sociological study of man. He rules out the study of symbols in art and communication because art, unlike the social sciences, lacks "intellectual clarity" and "does not and cannot formulate" private troubles and public issues in contemporary society. He assigns no weight to symbols as causal factors in motivation, and shows small concern with the effect of symbolic form on the social content of what form expresses.

3. "Saying" is not limited to words alone. All the arts of expression are involved in even the most simple acts of communication.

4. Sigmund Freud, *A General Introduction to Psychoanalysis*, authorized translation by Joan Riviere (Garden City, N.Y.: Garden City Publishing Co., Inc., 1943). This passage occurs near the beginning of Lecture 10, "Symbolism in Dreams."

5. I have discussed this in some detail in my article "Simmel's Image of Society," which appears in *Georg Simmel, 1858–1918, A Collection of Essays, with Translations and a Bibliography*, edited by Kurt H. Wolff (Columbus: Ohio State Univ. Press, 1959).

6. Talcott Parsons, *The Social System* (Glencoe, Ill.: The Free Press, 1951), p. 386. Just how expressive symbols *impose* standards is never made clear by Parsons. His statements on the weakness of sociological theory in dealing with expressive symbols would be much more helpful if he would tell us more about *why* social theory has not been able to deal with expressive symbols.

7. Paul Arthur Schilpp, ed., *The Philosophy of John Dewey* (New York: Tudor Publishing Co., 1939).

8. *Ibid.*, pp. 520–521.

9. Ratner discusses this point in his article on Dewey in Schilpp. In his article on "The Nature of Aesthetic Experience" (which is discussed in Chapter 6 of this book), where he expounds his social theory of art, Mead says in a footnote to the title: "I have not made specific acknowledgements in this article to Professor Dewey, but the reader who is familiar with his *Experience and Nature* will realize that it was written under the influence of that treatise."

10. John Dewey, *Art as Experience* (New York: Minton Balch & Co., 1934).

11. W. Lloyd Warner, *The Living and the Dead: A Study of the Symbolic Life of Americans* (New Haven: Yale Univ. Press, 1959), p. 24. Part V, "Theory and Method for the Study of Symbolic Life" (pp. 445–506) is a discussion of modifications of the theories of Freud, Mead, and Durkheim in terms of Warner's struggle to create working hypotheses from Durkheim's theory of collective representations. Durkheim's collective representations are not derived from art, but from religious rites. I have indicated what I believe to be the fallacies and, for a democratic society, the dangers of confusing the social bond with the religious bond in my article "The Development of Durkheim's Concept of Ritual and the Problem of Social Disrelationships," which appears in *Emile Durkheim: 1858–1917, A Collection of Essays, with Translations and a Bibliography*, edited by Kurt H. Wolff (Columbus: Ohio State Univ. Press, 1959), pp. 97–117.

12. Numa Denis Fustel de Coulanges, *La cité antique* (Paris: Hachette, 1864).

13. William Robertson Smith, *Lectures on the Religion of the Semites* (Edinburgh: Black, 1889).

14. Emile Durkheim, *Les formes elémentaires de la vie religieuse* (Paris: Alcan, 1912).

15. Bronislaw Malinowski, *Magic, Science, and Religion*, and Other Essays, Selected and with an Introduction by Robert Redfield (Glencoe, Ill.: The Free Press: 1948).

16. Alfred Reginald Radcliffe-Brown, *The Andaman Islanders* (Cambridge: The University Press, 1922).

17. Talcott Parsons, *The Social System* (Glencoe, Ill.: The Free Press, 1951), p. 25. The components of interaction are discussed on pp. 3–22 and 24–26.

18. Basically this was because neither Park nor Burgess believed that symbolic forms *determined* social forms. Society "caused" expression, but *how* we express ourselves, and the resources in various expressive systems for such expression, did not "cause" society. The paradox of deriving our knowledge of society from symbolic expressions which in themselves had

nothing to do with determining society did not escape Professors Redfield, Blumer, and Wirth. Mead's "significant symbol" always haunted the Chicago School. It was obvious that art had something to do with society, for art was the domain of the significant symbols, as Dewey and Mead used the term. But the question of how to state *social* categories of art was never resolved. The problem, however, was kept alive. The Chicago School never capitulated to mechanism, as the work of Warner shows, and as this book, by a student of Burgess, Wirth, Blumer, Redfield, Warner, and Burke, should make clear.

19. But what the behaviorist does not admit is that if we regard men as dogs (which we have learned to control through hunger), it is very easy to reduce men to the level of dogs so that we can control them in like fashion. The German concentration camps and the Russian labor camps are terrible witness to what can be done to men by reducing them to animals. *How* we study men has *moral*, as well as "purely scientific" consequences. If we *regard* men as machines, we are but a step away from *treating* them as machines.

THOUGHT, COMMUNICATION, AND THE SIGNIFICANT SYMBOL

George Herbert Mead

We have contended that there is no particular faculty of imitation in the sense that the sound or the sight of another's response is itself a stimulus to carry out the same reaction, but rather that if there is already present in the individual an action like the action of another, then there is a situation which makes imitation possible. What is necessary now to carry through that imitation is that the conduct and the gesture of the individual which calls out a response in the other should also tend to call out the same response in himself. In the dog-fight this is not present: the attitude in the one dog does not tend to call out the same attitude in the other. In some respects that actually may occur in the case of two boxers. The man who makes a feint is calling out a certain blow from his opponent, and that act of his own does have that meaning to him, that is, he has in some sense initiated the same act in himself. It does not go clear through, but he has stirred up the centers in his central nervous system which would lead to his making the same blow that his opponent is led to make, so that he calls out in himself, or tends to call out, the same response which he calls out in the other. There you have the basis for so-called imitation. Such is the process which is so widely recognized at present in manners of speech, of dress, and of attitudes.

We are more or less unconsciously seeing ourselves as others see us. We are unconsciously addressing ourselves as others address us: in the same way as the sparrow takes up the note of the canary we pick up the dialects about us. Of course, there must be these particular responses in our own mechanism. We are calling out in the other person something we are calling out in ourselves, so that unconsciously we take over these attitudes. We are unconsciously putting ourselves in the place of others and acting as others act. I want simply to isolate the general mechanism here, because it is of very fundamental importance in the development of what we call self-consciousness and the appearance of the self. We are, especially through the use of the vocal gestures, continually arousing in ourselves those responses which we call out in other persons, so that we are taking the attitudes of the other persons into our own conduct. The critical importance of language in the development of human experience lies in this fact that the stimulus is one that can react upon the speaking individual as it reacts upon the other.

A behaviorist, such as Watson, holds that all of our thinking is vocalization. In thinking we are simply starting to use certain words. That is in a sense true. However, Watson does not take into account all that is involved here, namely, that these stimuli are the essential elements in elaborate social processes and carry with them the value of those social processes. The vocal process as such has this great importance, and it is fair to assume that the vocal process, together with the intelligence and thought that go with it, is not simply a playing of particular vocal elements against each other. Such a view neglects the social context of language.[1]

The importance, then, of the vocal stimulus lies in this fact that the individual can hear what he says and in hearing what he says is tending to respond as the other person responds. When we speak now of this response on the art of the individual to the others we come back to the situation of asking some person to do something. We ordinarily express that by saying that one knows what he is asking you to do. Take the illustration of asking someone to do something, and then doing it oneself. Perhaps the person addressed does not hear you or acts slowly, and then you carry the action out yourself. You find in yourself, in this way, the same tendency which you are asking the other individual to carry out. Your request stirred up in you that same response which you stirred up in the other individual. How difficult it is to show someone else how to do something which you know how to do yourself! The slowness of the response makes it hard to restrain yourself from doing what you are teaching. You have aroused the same response in yourself as you arouse in the other individual.

In seeking for an explanation of this, we ordinarily assume a certain group of centers in the nervous system which are connected with each other, and which express themselves in the action. If we try to find in a central nervous system something that answers to our word "chair," what we should find would be presumably simply an organization of a whole group of possible reactions so connected that if one starts in one direction one will carry out one process, if in another direction one will carry out another process. The chair is primarily what one sits down in. It is a physical object at a distance. One may move toward an object at a distance and then enter upon the process of sitting down when one reaches it. There is a stimulus which excites certain paths which cause the individual to go toward that object and to sit down. Those centers are in some degree physical. There is, it is to be noted, an influence of the later act on the earlier act. The later process which is to go on has already been initiated and that later process has its influence on the earlier process (the one that takes place before this process, already initiated, can be completed). Now, such an organization of a great group of nervous elements as will lead to conduct with reference to the objects about us is what one would find in the central nervous system answering to what we call an object. The complications are very great, but the central nervous system has an almost infinite number of elements in it, and they can be organized not only in spatial connection with each other, but also from a temporal standpoint. In virtue of this last fact, our conduct is made up of a series of steps which follow each other, and the later steps may be already started and influence the earlier ones. The thing we are going to do is playing back on what we are doing now. That organization in the neural elements in reference to what we call a physical object would be what we call a conceptual object stated in terms of the central nervous system.

In rough fashion it is the initiation of such a set of organized sets of responses that answers to what we call the idea or concept of a thing. If one asked what the idea of a dog is, and tried to find that idea in the central nervous system, one would find a whole group of responses which are more or less connected together by definite paths so that when one uses the term "dog" he does tend to call out this group of responses. A dog is a possible playmate, a possible enemy, one's own property or somebody else's. There is a whole series of possible responses. There are certain types of these responses which are in all of us, and there are others which vary with the individuals, but there is always an organization of the responses which can be called out by the term "dog." So if one is speaking of a dog to another person he is arousing in himself this set of responses which he is arousing in the other individual.

It is, of course, the relationship of this symbol, this vocal gesture, to such a set of responses in the individual himself as well as in the other that makes of that vocal gesture what I call a significant symbol. A symbol does tend to call out in the individual a group of reactions such as it calls out in the other, but there is something further that is involved in its being a significant symbol: this response within one's self to such a word as "chair," or "dog," is one which is a stimulus to the individual as well as a response. This is what, of course, is involved in what we term the meaning of a thing, or its significance.[2] We often act with reference to objects in what we call an intelligent fashion, although we can act without the meaning of the object being present in our experience. One can start to dress for dinner, as they tell of the absent-minded college professor, and find himself in his pajamas in bed. A certain process of undressing was started and carried out mechanically; he did not recognize the meaning of what he was doing. He intended to go to dinner and found he had gone to bed. The meaning involved in his action was not present. The steps in this case were all intelligent steps which controlled his conduct with reference to later action, but he did not think about what he was doing. The later action was not a stimulus to his response, but just carried itself out when it was once started.

When we speak of the meaning of what we are doing we are making the response itself that we are on the point of carrying out a stimulus to our action. It becomes a stimulus to a later stage of action which is to take place from the point of view of this particular response. In the case of the boxer the blow that he is starting to direct toward his opponent is to call out a certain response which will open up the guard of his opponent so that he can strike. The meaning is a stimulus for the preparation of the real blow he expects to deliver. The response which he calls out in himself (the guarding reaction) is the stimulus to him to strike where an opening is given. This action which he has initiated already in himself thus becomes a stimulus for his later response. He knows what his opponent is going to do, since the guarding movement is one which is already aroused, and becomes a stimulus to strike where the opening is given. The meaning would not have been present in his conduct unless it became a stimulus to strike where the favorable opening appears.

Such is the difference between intelligent conduct on the part of animals and what we call a reflective individual.[3] We say the animal does not think. He does not put himself in a position for which he is responsible; he does not put himself in the place of the other person and say, in effect, "He will act in such a way and I will act in this way." If the individual can act in this way, and the attitude which he calls out in himself can become a stimulus to him for another act, we have meaningful conduct. Where the response of the other person is called out and becomes a stimulus to control his action, then he has the meaning of the other person's act in his own experience. That is the general mechanism of what we term "thought," for in order that thought may exist there must be symbols, vocal gestures generally, which arouse in the individual himself the response which he is calling out in the other, and such that from the point of view of that response he is able to direct his later conduct. It involves not only communication in the sense in which birds and animals communicate with each other, but also an arousal in the individual himself of the response which he is calling out in the other individual, a taking of the role of the other, a tendency to act as the other person acts. One participates in the same process the other person is carrying out and controls his action with reference to that participation. It is that which constitutes the meaning of an object, namely, the common response in one's self as well as in the other person, which becomes, in turn, a stimulus to one's self.

If you conceive of the mind as just a sort of conscious substance in which there are certain impressions and states, and hold that one of those states is a universal, then a word becomes purely arbitrary—it is just a symbol.[4] You can then take words and pronounce them backwards, as children do; there seems to be absolute freedom of arrangement and language seems to be an entirely mechanical thing that lies outside of the process of intelligence. If you recognize that language is, however, just a part of a co-öperative process, that part which does lead to an adjustment to the response of the other so that the whole activity can go on, then language has only a limited range of arbitrariness. If you are talking to another person you are, perhaps, able to scent the change in his attitude by something that would not strike a third person at all. You may know his mannerism, and that becomes a gesture to you, a part of the response of the individual. There is a certain range possible within the gesture as to what is to serve as the symbol. We may say that a whole set of separate symbols with one meaning are acceptable; but they always are gestures, that is, they are always parts of the act of the individual which reveal what he is going to do to the other person so that when the person utilizes the clue he calls out in himself the attitude of the other. Language is not ever arbitrary in the sense of simply denoting a bare state of consciousness by a word. What particular part of one's act will serve to direct co-operative activity is more or less arbitrary. Different phases of the act may do it. What seems unimportant in itself may be highly important in revealing what the attitude is. In that sense one can speak of the gesture itself as unimportant, but it is of great importance as to what the gesture is going to reveal. This is seen in the difference between the purely intellectual character of the symbol and its emotional character. A poet depends upon the latter; for him the language is rich and full of values which we, perhaps, utterly ignore. In trying to express a message in something less than ten words, we merely want to convey a certain meaning, while the poet is dealing with what is really living tissue, the emotional throb in the expression itself. There is, then, a great range in our use of language; but whatever phase of this range is used is a part of a social process, and it is always that part by means of which we affect ourselves as we affect others and mediate the social situation through this understanding of what we are saying. That is fundamental for any language; if it is going to be language one has to understand what he is saying, has to affect himself as he affects others.

NOTES

1. Gestures, if carried back to the matrix from which they spring, are always found to inhere in or involve a larger social act of which they are phases. In dealing with communication we have first to recognize its earliest origins in the unconscious conversation of gestures. Conscious communication—conscious conversation of gestures—arises when gestures become signs, that is, when they come to carry for the individuals making them and the individuals responding to them, definite meanings or significations in terms of the subsequent behavior of the individuals making them; so that, by serving as prior indications, to the individuals responding to them, of the subsequent behavior of the individuals making them, they make possible the mutual adjustment of the various individual components of the social act to one another, and also, by calling forth in the individuals making them the same responses implicitly that they call forth explicitly in the individuals to whom they are made, they render possible the rise of self-consciousness in connection with this mutual adjustment.

2. The inclusion of the matrix or complex of attitudes and responses constituting any given social situation or act, within the experience of any one of the individuals implicated in that situation or act (the inclusion within his experience of his attitudes toward other individuals, of their responses to his attitudes toward them, of their attitudes toward him, and of his responses to these attitudes) is all that an *idea* amounts to; or at any rate is the only basis for its occurrence or existence "in the mind" of the given individual.

In the case of the unconscious conversation of gestures, or in the case of the process of communication carried on by means of it, none of the individuals participating in it is conscious of the meaning of the conversation—that meaning does not appear in the experience of any one of the separate individuals involved in the conversation or carrying it on; whereas, in the case of the conscious conversation of gestures, or in the case of the process of communication carried on by means of it, each of the individuals participating in it is conscious of the meaning of the conversation, precisely because that meaning does appear in his experience, and because such appearance is what consciousness of that meaning implies.

3. For the nature of animal conduct see "Concerning Animal Perception," *Psychological Review*, XIV (1907), 383 ff.

4. Muller attempts to put the values of thought into language; but this attempt is fallacious, because language has those values only as the most effective mechanism of thought merely because it carries the conscious or significant conversation of gestures to its highest and most perfect development. There must be some sort of an implicit attitude (that is, a response which is initiated without being fully carried out) in the organism making the gesture—an attitude which answers to the overt response to the gesture on the part of another individual, and which corresponds to the attitude called forth or aroused in this other organism by the gesture—if thought is to develop in the organism making the gesture. And it is the central nervous system which provides the mechanism for such implicit attitudes or responses.

The identification of language with reason is in one sense an absurdity, but in another sense it is valid. It is valid, namely, in the sense that the process of language brings the total social act into the experience of the given individual as himself involved in the act, and thus makes the process of reason possible. But though the process of reason is and must be carried on in terms of the process of language—in terms, that is, of words—it is not simply constituted by the latter.

SYMBOL SPHERES IN SOCIETY*

Hans H. Gerth and C. Wright Mills

*L*anguage is central to the concerns of social psychology because it has to do with the functioning of institutions as well as with the socialization of the individual. By considering the social and the personal functions of language we can relate intimate details about the person and the psychic structure to broader conceptions of institutional organization. To understand how any given person strives, feels, and thinks we have to pay attention to the symbols he has internalized; but to understand these symbols we have to grasp the way in which they co-ordinate institutional actions.[1] Symbols mediate entire institutional arrangements as well as the conduct and roles of persons.

In the psychic structure, language articulates and patterns the objects and noises which we see and hear; we come to know many of our feelings and wishes in terms of specific vocabularies. By singling out targets for action, language helps turn impulses into defined purposes, inchoate sensations into perceptions, vague feelings into known emotions.

In the person, symbols lend motives to conduct, and signal the expectations of others. Symbols provide the person with a frame of reference for his experience, and this frame of reference is not only "social" in general, it may be definitely related to the operations of specific institutions.

If we examine the content and functions of communication within institutions, or within the various institutional orders of a social structure, we notice that certain symbols tend to recur more frequently than others in given contexts. This universe of discourse—the vocabularies, pronunciations, emblems, formulas, and types of conversation which are typical of an institutional order—makes up "the symbol sphere" of this order.

* From *Character and Social Structure*, by Hans Gerth and C. Wright Mills, copyright 1953 by Harcourt, Brace & World, Inc., and reprinted with their permission and that of Routledge & Kegan Paul, Ltd.

404

Such symbols may be acoustic—as in music or in speech—or they may be visual—as in written and printed imagery and signs. The distinctions and symbols of a symbol sphere of a given institutional order are related to the preoccupations and practices of persons in that order. For since language helps us to co-ordinate social activities, it reflects the objects with which persons of the order deal and the conduct patterns with which they do so.

Thus the myths of religion, the incantations of magic, the technical jargon of an occupation, the high-brow pronunciations and slang of status groups, the tête-à-tête of lovers, and the table-talk of families—all these represent modes of speech which reflect different institutional contexts. We become more aware of this when we examine foreign languages. Arabic, for example, "contains about 6,000 names for 'camel,' " or derived from camel—for breeding-camels and running-camels and for female camels in all the various stages of pregnancy.[2] The practices and objects involved in a society of camel breeders are reflected in the content and distinctions which make up the symbol sphere of their society. The Teutonic languages have terms for horse, steed, mare, stallion, all of which to the Greek were simply hippos.

Religious institutions develop their own rhetoric and liturgy—the hymn, the prayer, the sermon, the benediction. Similarly in the political economic orders we find genres of talk and of writing—the sales talk, low- and high-pressure; the election speech, stump or fireside. And, of course, the bulk of our modern fiction is a symbolic elaboration of love and kinship relations. Not all societies, of course, develop identical symbols for the same pursuit; the increasingly precise notation, and hence the symbolic recording, of musical sound patterns is peculiar to occidental civilization. In like manner, not all institutions of the same order have identical symbols. Puritanism, for example, suppressed instrumental music as well as opera and the dance. Catholicism, however, has made rich use of all the arts, with the exception of dancing, as symbolic means of religious worship.

Certain emblems and modes of language not only recur in given social contexts but seem to be more important to the maintenance of certain institutions, to their chains of authority and to the authoritative distribution of their roles. The contexts in which these symbols appear may seem to be "staged"; they are dramatic, solemn, weird. They carry more "weight." These symbols may be repeated every day by everyone; or they may be used only on extraordinary occasions and by specifically authorized persons. As we have seen, the symbols which thus justify a social structure or an institutional order are called symbols of "legitimation," or "master symbols," or "symbols of justification."

By lending meaning to the enactment of given roles, these master symbols sanction the person in re-acting the roles. When internalized they form unquestioned categories which channel and delimit new experiences; they promote and constrain activities. When public justifications are privately internalized, they make up the stuff of self-justification, operating as reasons and motives leading persons into roles and sanctioning their enactment of them. Indeed, no self-justification is likely to be entirely private; unless it is accepted by others it does not secure the private self in feeling that all is well. If, for example, "individualistic" institutions are publicly justified, then reference to self-interest may be acceptable as justification for individual conduct. Personal reasons are thus related to public legitimations.

While the symbols typically found in any order comprise the symbol sphere of that order, those symbols that justify the institutional arrangement of the order are its master symbols. To the social scientist such master symbols are of special interest in that they allow us to understand the cohesion of role configurations, their permanence and change, and their function in the intrapsychic life of persons.

The more refined symbol elaborations of the philosopher, theologian, publicity director, scientist, or artist may not be so immediately important for the understanding of a period and society as are the doctrines which do not seem to be "doctrines" at all, but rather facts. In the experience of men enacting the roles of their time, they seem "inevitable categories of the human mind. Men do not look on them merely as correct opinion, for they have become so much a part of the mind, and lie so far back, that they are never really conscious of them at all. They do not see them, but other things *through* them. It is these abstract ideas at the center, the things which they take for granted that characterize a period."[3]

Those in authority within institutions and social structures attempt to justify their rule by linking it, as if it were a necessary consequence, with moral symbols, sacred emblems, or legal formulae which are widely believed and deeply internalized. These central conceptions may refer to a god or gods, the "votes of the majority," the "will of the people," the "aristocracy of talents or wealth," to the "divine right of kings," or to the allegedly extraordinary endowment of the person of the ruler himself.

Various thinkers have used different terms to refer to this phenomenon: Mosca's "political formula" or "great superstitions,"[4] Locke's "principle of sovereignty,"[5] Sorel's "ruling myth,"[6] Thurman Arnold's "folklore,"[7] Weber's "legitimations,"[8] Durkheim's "collective representations,"[9] Marx's "dominant ideas,"[10] Rousseau's "general will,"[11] Lasswell's "symbols of authority," or "symbols of justification,"[12] Mannheim's "ideology,"[13] Herbert Spencer's "public sentiments"[14]—all testify to the central place of master symbols in social analysis. . . .

COMMUNICATION

Out of the total range of symbols socially available, each person picks up certain symbols which he passes on to others. Each person who faces the total volume of symbols transmits a selected number and a selectively arranged portion of the total. Generally, we speak of manipulation or management of symbols when this channeling and rearranging of selected symbols is done consciously and in an organized way. Competition among symbols referring to given objects or legitimating different institutional roles may lead to the purposive manipulation or management of the spheres of symbols by symbol experts.

In a stratified society it is possible to debunk or to build up a given stratum by selecting the symbols which are used to represent it. To devaluate a religious, political, or ethnic group, one selects the lowest representative of the group—of the Jewish community, e.g.—and generalizes him as "*the* Jew." To build up a group or stratum one focuses upon the "best" representative, selecting those traits that are most approved of by those to whom one would build up the group, and generalizes him as "*the* Jew." Such images are known as stereotypes. They are symbols built out of a selection of alleged traits yet represented as the whole truth. Stereotypes which debunk or build up a group may not be set forth in their totality at any one time. A newspaper, for instance, may use the symbol "Negro" every time a Negro commits a petty crime, but avoid mentioning "Negro" when a Negro performs some meritorious act. The stereotype of "Negro" is thus built from an accumulation of incidents with which the symbol is associated.

When a small-town youngster goes to a big city and does well, the town's newspaper may carry the story: Podunk boy makes good. But if he gets lost in the anonymity of the city and wanders into crime, the local newspaper may not play the fact up. By selecting from the totality of world, national, and local affairs, the story of the local youngster who grew up to make $50,000 a year, the glory of his success is reflected on the symbol, Podunk. His success is shared; ascribed in part to the community. His failures are ignored, or ascribed to him alone. The stereotyped image of Podunk is built up to the accumulation of such stories and by the omission of other types of fact. At the same time, a generally optimistic tone of individual success is maintained in the sphere of symbols.

We may distinguish several ways in which conduct is positively or negatively stereotyped, and ascribed to the individual alone or to groups to which he belongs by virtue of actual or past membership:

I. Meritorious conduct may be strictly ascribed to the individual, as in the case of Homer's build-up of Achilles, or as in the modern cult of genius. In legend, the family of descent is often entirely eradicated by means of an ascription of divine origin, or by "foundling" sagas. II. Liabilities of conduct may be ascribed strictly to the individual, as in contemporary democratic court proceedings. III. Meritorious conduct may be ascribed to the individual as a representative of a group whose members are eager to share in the prestige accretion of their outstanding members. This occurs in the construction of self-images by groups and collectivities, as when Americans see themselves as in the "land of the free and the brave," or nineteenth-century Germans saw themselves as a "nation of poets and thinkers." IV. Conduct liabilities may be typically ascribed by dominant groups to the individual as a representative of despised lower or hostile out-groups. In the Soviet Union and its orbit, "bourgeois" descent—for the failure—is never an accident," just as in Nazi Germany "Jewish descent" was the reference point for alleged criminal dispositions, despite all statistical evidence to the contrary.

In the selecting and editing of symbols referring to nations, all these processes may be observed. Nations compete for prestige with other nations in terms of symbols and events which are associated by symbol manipulations, with stereotyped images of the whole. To an inhabitant of nineteenth-century India, "the British" may be an irate man with battleships, troops, and whipping canes; a beef-eating barbarian who consumes alcohol on so supreme a religious occasion as The Lord's Supper. But in the edited sphere of symbols, "British" may appear to Englishmen as a rotund gentleman surrounded by "tricky natives," or a nation of small shopkeepers trying honestly to get along in the world. During wartime, "Uncle Sam" gets a fierce compelling look in his cartooned eyes as he points his finger at *you*. The superegos of some members of the public may be stimulated by such compulsive figures. The guilt feelings thus engendered may increase the participation of fortune, time, and life in the war effort.

A nation becomes "one and indivisible" through a continual process of communalization. This communalization is directed by those strata that successfully address their political expectations to the rest of the population in the name of the "nation." To the extent to which this process is successful, "a nation one and indivisible" exists. The most effective symbols implementing the process are those of common historical fate, of common triumphs of the past; national history bespeaking of grandeur; a national mission; assurance of the nation's worth for mankind. The emphases, as between the past or the future, may shift. When the "American dream" is no longer stressed, or does not seem unilinear and unambiguous, the press may demand greater emphasis on instruction in the nation's history as beneficent to civic morale and patriotism. History teaching is, of course, subject to selective emphases and stylizations stemming from patriotic loyalties rather than scientific detachment.[15] Much of the national historiography of the nineteenth century falls under the same heading: Germany had her

Treitschke, Great Britain her Seeley. The American Mahan, as the philosopher and historian of "seapower," could hardly have emerged on Prussian soil, and neither could a Delbruck, the German historian of warfare, arise in a great maritime power. "History," it is often said, is concerned with the past that is "dead," but as an ongoing enterprise it is of vital concern to the living in an age of nations with rival claims to disputed areas, new boundaries, and opportunities seized and justified in terms of "historical rights."

In a world where primary experience has been replaced by secondary communications—the printed page, the radio, and the picture screen—the chances for those in control of these media to select, associate, manipulate, and diffuse symbols are increased. In the twentieth century, a unified symbol sphere, one monopolized by certain master symbols, is more likely to be the result of a monopoly of the channels of communications, and of a forceful tabooing of countersymbols, than the result of any harmonious institutional basis. It is more likely to be imposed than to grow. But the symbols which are thus made masterful are not likely to be so deeply and unquestioningly internalized as those arising as adequate and meaningful expressions of a harmony of institutionalized roles. Where there are deep antagonisms in the institutional structure, men seeking to transform power into authority may grasp all the more compulsively for the channels of mass communication, but their monopolization of these media does not necessarily mean that the symbols they diffuse will be master symbols.

NOTES

1. See Gerth and Mills, *Character and Social Structure*, Chap. IV and V.

2. See W. I. Thomas, *Primitive Behavior* (New York: McGraw-Hill, 1937), p. 68.

3. T. E. Hulme, *Speculations* (London: Routledge, 1936), p. 50.

4. G. Mosca, *The Ruling Class*, H. D. Kahn, tr. (New York: McGraw-Hill, 1939), pp. 70–71.

5. John Locke, *Two Treatises Concerning Government* (London, 1924).

6. Georges Sorel, *Reflections on Violence*, T. E. Hulme, tr. (New York: Viking, 1914.

7. Thurman W. Arnold, *The Folklore of Capitalism* (New Haven: Yale Univ. Press, 1937).

8. Max Weber, *The Theory of Social and Economic Organization*, Talcott Parsons and A. M. Henderson, trs. (New York: Oxford, 1948), Chapters I and III.

9. Emile Durkheim, *The Elementary Forms of the Religious Life* (New York: Macmillan, 1915).

10. K. Marx and F. Engels, *The German Ideology* (New York: International Publications, 1939).

11. Jean-Jacques Rousseau, *The Social Contract* (New York: Hafner, 1947).

12. H. D. Lasswell, *World Politics and Personal Insecurity* (New York: McGraw-Hill, 1935), and *Politics: Who Gets What, When, How* (New York: McGraw-Hill, 1936). See also Kenneth Burke, *Attitudes Towards History* (New York: New Republic, 1937), Vol. II, pp. 232ff.

13. Karl Mannheim, *Ideology and Utopia*, Louis Wirth and Edward Shils, trs. (New York: Harcourt, Brace, 1936).

14. Herbert Spencer, *Principles of Sociology* (London, 1882–1896), Vol. II, Book 1, pp. 319 ff.

15. See B. Pierce, *Civic Attitudes in American School Textbooks* (Chicago: Univ. of Chicago Press, 1930).

INFORMAL SOCIAL COMMUNICATION*

Leon Festinger

*t*he importance of strict theory in developing and guiding programs of
research is becoming more and more recognized today. Yet there is considerable disagreement about exactly how strict and precise a theoretical
formulation must be at various stages in the development of a body of
knowledge. Certainly there are many who feel that some "theorizing" is too
vague and indefinite to be of much use. It is also argued that such vague and
broad "theorizing" may actually hinder the empirical development of an
area of knowledge.

On the other hand there are many who express dissatisfaction with instances of very precise theories which do exist here and there, for somehow
or other a precise and specific theory seems to them to leave out the "real"
psychological problem. These persons seem to be more concerned with
those aspects of the problem which the precise theory has not yet touched.
From this point of view it is argued that too precise and too strict theorizing
may also hinder the empirical development of an area of knowledge.

It is probably correct that if a theory becomes too precise too early it can
have tendencies to become sterile. It is also probably correct that if a theory
stays too vague and ambiguous for too long it can be harmful in that nothing can be done to disprove or change it. This probably means that
theories, when vague, should at least be stated in a form which makes the
adding of precision possible as knowledge increases. It also probably means
that theory should run ahead, but not too far ahead, of the data so that the
trap of premature precision can be avoided. It certainly means that theories,
whether vague or precise, must be in such a form that empirical data can
influence them.

This article is a statement of the theoretical formulations which have
been developed in the process of conducting a program of empirical and

* Reprinted from *Psychological Review*, LVII (1953), 271–92, by permission.

411

experimental research in informal social communication. It has grown out of our findings thus far and is in turn guiding the future course of the research program.* This program of research concerns itself with finding and explaining the facts concerning informal, spontaneous communication among persons and the consequences of the process of communication. It would seem that a better understanding of the dynamics of such communication would in turn lead to a better understanding of various kinds of group functioning. The theories and hypotheses presented below vary considerably in precision, specificity and the degree to which corroborating data exist. Whatever the state of precision, however, the theories are empirically oriented and capable of being tested.

Since we are concerned with the spontaneous process of communication which goes on during the functioning of groups we must first differentiate the variety of types of communication which occur according to the theoretical conditions which give rise to tendencies to communicate. It is plausible to assume that separating the sources or origins of pressures to communicate that may act on a member of a group will give us fruitful areas to study. This type of differentiation or classification is, of course, adequate only if it leads to the separation of conceptually clear areas of investigation within which communication can be organized into statable theoretical and empirical laws.

We shall here deal with those few of the many possible sources of pressures to communicate in which we have thus far been able to make theoretical and empirical progress. We shall elaborate on the theory for regarding them as giving rise to pressures to communicate and on specific hypotheses concerning the laws of communication which stem from these sources.

I. PRESSURES TOWARD UNIFORMITY
IN A GROUP

One major source of forces to communicate is the pressure toward uniformity which may exist within a group. These are pressures which, for one reason or another, act toward making members of a group agree concerning some issue or conform with respect to some behavior pattern. It is stating the obvious, of course, to say that these pressures must be exerted by means of a process of communication among the members of the group. One must also specify the conditions under which such pressures toward uniformity arise, both on a conceptual and an operation level so that in any specific situation it is possible to say whether or not such pressures exist.

* This research program consists of a number of coördinated and integrated studies, both in the laboratory and in the field. It is being carried out by the Research Center for Group Dynamics under contract N6onr-23212 NR 151–698 with the Office of Naval Research.

We shall, in the following discussion, elaborate on two major sources of pressures toward uniformity among people, namely, social reality and group locomotion.

1. *Social Reality*

Opinions, attitudes, and beliefs which people hold must have some basis upon which they rest for their validity. Let us as a start abstract from the many kinds of bases for the subjective validity of such opinions, attitudes, and beliefs one continuum along which they may be said to lie. This continuum we may call a scale of degree of physical reality. At one end of this continuum, namely, complete dependence upon physical reality, we might have an example such as this : A person looking at a surface might think that the surface is fragile or he might think that the surface is unbreakable. He can very easily take a hammer, hit the surface, and quickly be convinced as to whether the opinion he holds is correct or incorrect. After he has broken the surface with a hammer it will probably make little dent upon his opinion if another person should tell him that the surface is unbreakable. It would thus seem that where there is a high degree of dependence upon physical reality for the subjective validity of one's beliefs or opinions the dependence upon other people for the confidence one has in these opinions or beliefs is very low.

At the other end of the continuum where the dependence upon physical reality is low or zero, we might have an example such as this : A person looking at the results of a national election feels that if the loser had won, things would be in some ways much better than they are. Upon what does the subjective validity of this belief depend? It depends to a large degree on whether or not other people share his opinion and feel the same way he does. If there are other people around him who believe the same thing, then his opinion, is, to him, valid. If there are not others who believe the same thing, then his opinion is, in the same sense, not valid. Thus where the dependence upon physical reality is low the dependence upon social reality is correspondingly high. An opinion, a belief, an attitude is "correct," "valid," and "proper" to the extent that it is anchored in a group of people with similar beliefs, opinions, and attitudes.

This statement, however, cannot be generalized completely. It is clearly not necessary for the validity of someone's opinion that everyone else in the world think the way he does. It is only necessary that the members of that group to which he refers this opinion or attitude think the way he does. It is not necesary for a Ku Klux Klanner that some northern liberal agree with him in his attitude toward Negroes, but it is eminently necessary that there be other people who also are Ku Klux Klanners and who do agree with him. The person who does not agree with him is seen as different from him and not an adequate referent for his opinion. The problem of independently defining which groups are and which groups are not appropriate reference groups for a particular individual and for a particular opinion or attitude is a difficult one. It is to some extent inherently circular since an appropriate reference group tends to be a group which does share a person's opinions and attitudes, and people tend to locomote *into* such groups and *out of* groups which do not agree with them.

From the preceding discussion it would seem that if a discrepancy in opinion, attitude, or belief exists among persons who are members of an appropriate reference group, forces to communicate will arise. It also follows that the less "physical reality" there is to validate the opinion or belief, the greater will be the importance of the social referent, the group, and the greater will be the forces to communicate.

2. *Group Locomotion*

Pressures toward uniformity among members of a group may arise because such uniformity is desirable or necessary in order for the group to move toward some goal. Under such circumstances there are a number of things one can say about the magnitude of pressures toward uniformity.

(a) They will be greater to the extent that the members perceive that group movement would be facilitated by uniformity.

(b) The pressures toward uniformity will also be greater, the more dependent the various members are on the group in order to reach their goals. The degree to which other groups are substitutable as a means toward individual or group goals would be one of the determinants of the dependence of the member on the group.

We have elaborated on two sources of pressure toward uniformity among members of groups. The same empirical laws should apply to communications which result from pressures toward uniformity irrespective of the particular reasons for the existence of the pressures. We shall now proceed to enumerate a set of hypotheses concerning communication which results from pressures toward uniformity.

II. HYPOTHESES ABOUT COMMUNICATION RESULTING FROM PRESSURES TOWARD UNIFORMITY

Communications which arise from pressures toward uniformity in a group may be seen as "instrumental" communications. That is, the communication is not an end in itself but rather is a means by which the communicator hopes to influence the person he addresses in such a way as to reduce the discrepancy that exists between them. Thus we should examine the determinants of : (1) when a member communicates, (2) to whom he communicates and (3) the reactions of the recipient of the communication.

(1) Determinants of the magnitude of pressure to communicate:

Hypothesis 1a: *The pressure on members to communicate to others in the group concerning "item x" increases monotonically with increase in the perceived discrepancy in opinion concerning "item x" among members of the group.*

Remembering that we are considering only communication that results from pressures toward uniformity, it is clear that if there are no discrepancies in opinion, that is, uniformity already exists in the group, there will be no forces to communicate. It would be plausible to expect the force to communicate to increase rapidly from zero as the state of affairs departs from uniformity.

Hypothesis 1b: *The pressure on a member to communicate to others in the group concerning "item x" increases monotonically with increase in the degree of relevance of "item x" to the functioning of the group.*

If "item x" is unimportant to the group in the sense of not being associated with any of the values or activities which are the basis for the existence of the group, or if it is more or less inconsequential for group locomotion, then there should be few or no forces to communicate even when there are perceived discrepancies in opinion. As "item x" becomes more important for the group (more relevant), the forces to communicate when any given magnitude of perceived discrepancy exists, should increase.

Corroborative evidence for this hypothesis is found in an experiment by Schachter (8) where discussion of the same issue was experimentally made relevant for some groups and largely irrelevant for others. It is clear from the data that where the discussion was relevant to the functioning of the group there existed stronger forces to communicate and to influence the other members. Where the issue is a relevant one the members make longer individual contributions to the discussion and there are many fewer prolonged pauses in the discussion.

Hypothesis 1c: *The pressure on members to communicate to others in the group concerning "item x" increases monotonically with increase in the cohesiveness of the group.*

Cohesiveness of a group is here defined as the resultant of all the forces acting on the members to remain in the group. These forces may depend on the attractiveness or unattractiveness of either the prestige of the group, members in the group, or the activities in which the group engages. If the total attraction toward the group is zero, no forces to communicate should arise; the members may as easily leave the group as stay in it. As the forces to remain in the group increase (given perceived discrepancies in opinion and given a certain relevance of the item to the functioning of the group) the pressures to communicate will increase.

Data from an experiment by Back (1) support this hypothesis. In this experiment groups of high and low cohesiveness were experimentally created using three different sources of attraction to the group, namely, liking the members, prestige attached to belonging, and possibility of getting a reward for performance in the group activity. For each of the three types of attraction to the group the more cohesive groups were rated as proceeding at a more intense rate in the discussion than the corresponding less cohesive groups. In addition, except for the groups where the attraction was the possibility of reward (perhaps due to wanting to finish and get the reward) there was more total amount of attempted exertion of influence in the highly cohesive groups than in the less cohesive groups. In short, highly cohesive groups, having stronger pressures to communicate, discussed the issue at a more rapid pace and attempted to exert more influence.

(2) Determinants of choice of recipient for communications:

Hypothesis 2a: *The force to communicate about "item x" to* A PARTICU-LAR MEMBER *of the group will increase as the discrepancy in opinion between that member and the communicator increases.*

We have already stated in Hypothesis 1a that the pressure to communicate in general will increase as the perceived non-uniformity in the group increases. In addition the force to communicate will be strongest toward those whose opinions are most different from one's own and will, of course, be zero towards those in the group who at the time hold the same opinion as the communicator. In other words, people will tend to communicate to those within the group whose opinions are most different from their own.

There is a clear corroboration of this hypothesis from a number of studies. In the previously mentioned experiment by Schachter (8) the distribution of opinions expressed in the group was always as follows: Most of the members' opinions clustered within a narrow range of each other while one member, the deviate, held and maintained an extremely divergent point of view. About five times as many communications were addressed to the holder of the divergent point of view as were addressed to the others.

In an experiment by Festinger and Thibaut (5) the discussion situation was set up so that members' opinions on the issue spread over a considerable range. Invariably 70 to 90 per cent of the communications were addressed to those who held opinions at the extremes of the distribution. The curve of number of communications received falls off very rapidly as the opinion of the recipient moves away from the extreme of the distribution. The hypothesis would seem to be well substantiated.

Hypothesis 2b: *The force to communicate about "item x" to* A PARTICU-LAR PERSON *will decrease to the extent that he is perceived as not a member of the group or to the extent that he is not wanted as a member of the group.*

From the previous hypothesis it follows that communications will tend to be addressed mainly toward those with extreme opinions within the group. This does not hold, however, for any arbitrarily defined group. The present hypothesis, in effect, states that such relationships will apply only within *psychological* groups, that is, collections of people that exist as groups psychologically for the members. Communications will tend not to be addressed towards those who are not members of the group.

The study by Schachter (8) and the study by Festinger and Thibaut (5) both substantiate this hypothesis. In Schachter's experiment those group members who do not want the person holding the extremely divergent point of view to remain in the group tend to stop communicating to him towards the end of the discussion. In the experiment by Festinger and Thibaut, when the subjects have the perception that the persons present include different kinds of people with a great variety of interests, there tends to be less communication toward the extremes in the last half of the discussion after the rejection process has had time to develop. In short, communication towards those with different opinions decreases if they are seen as not members of the *psychological* group.

Hypothesis 2c : *The force to communicate "item x" to a particular member will increase the more it is perceived that the communication will change that member's opinion in the desired direction.*

A communication which arises because of the existence of pressures toward uniformity is made in order to exert a force on the recipient in a particular direction, that is, to push him to change his opinion so that he will agree more closely with the communicator. If a member is perceived as very resistant to changing his opinion, the force to communicate to him decreases. If it seems that a particular member will be changed as the result of a communication so as to increase the discrepancy between him and the communicator, there will exist a force not to communicate to him. Thus under such conditions there will be tendencies *not* to communicate this particular item to that member.

There is some corroboration for this hypothesis. In a face to face verbal discussion where a range of opinion exists, the factors which this hypothesis points to would be particularly important for those members whose opinions were near the middle of the range. A communication which might influence the member at one extreme to come closer to the middle might at the same time influence the member at the other extreme to move farther away from the middle. We might then expect from this hypothesis that those holding opinions in the middle of the existing range would communicate less (because of the conflict) and would address fewer communications to the whole group (attempting to influence only one person at a time).

A number of observations were conducted to check these derivations. Existing groups of clinical psychologists who were engaging in discussions to reconcile their differences in ratings of applicants were observed. Altogether, 147 such discussions were observed in which at least one member's opinion was in the middle of the existing range. While those with extreme opinions made an average of 3.16 units of communication (number of communications weighted by length of the communication), those with middle opinions made an average of only 2.6 units of communication. While those with extreme opinions addressed 38 per cent of their communications to the whole group, those with middle opinions addressed only 29 per cent of their communications to everyone.

(3) Determinants of change in the recipient of a communication:

Hypothesis 3a: *The amount of change in opinion resulting from receiving a communication will increase as the pressure towards uniformity in the group increases.*

There are two separate factors which contribute to the effect stated in the hypothesis. The greater the pressure towards uniformity, the greater will be the amount of influence exerted by the communications and, consequently, the greater the magnitude of change that may be expected. But the existence of pressures toward uniformity will not only show itself in increased attempts to change the opinions of others. Pressures toward uniformity will also produce greater readiness to change in the members of the group. In other words, uniformity may be achieved by changing the opinions of others and/or by changing one's own opinions. Thus we may expect that with increasing pressure towards uniformity there will be less resistance to change on the part of the members. Both of these factors will contribute to produce greater change in opinion when the pressure toward uniformity is greater.

There is evidence corroborating this hypothesis from the experiment by Festinger and Thibaut (5). In this experiment three degrees of pressure towards uniformity were experimentally induced in different groups. Irrespective of which of two problems were discussed by the group and irrespective of whether they perceived the group to be homogeneously or heterogeneously composed, the results consistently show that high pressure groups change most, medium pressure groups change next most, and low pressure groups change least in the direction of uniformity. While the two factors which contribute to this effect cannot be separated in the data, their joint effect is clear and unmistakable.

Hypothesis 3b: *The amount of change in opinion resulting from receiving a communication will increase as the strength of the resultant force to remain in the group increases for the recipient.*

To the extent that a member wishes to remain in the group, the group has power over that member. By power we mean here the ability to produce real change in opinions and attitudes and not simply change in overt behavior which can also be produced by means of overt threat. If a person is unable to leave a group because of restraints from the outside, the group can then use threats to change overt behavior. Covert changes in opinions and attitudes, however, can only be produced by a group by virtue of force acting on the member to remain in the group. Clearly the maximum force which the group can successfully induce on a member counter to his own forces can not be greater than the sum of the forces acting on that member to remain in the group. The greater the resultant force to remain in the group, the more effective will be the attempts to influence the member.

This hypothesis is corroborated by two separate studies. Festinger, Schachter and Back (4) investigated the relationship between the cohesiveness of social groups in a housing project (how attractive the group was for its members) and how effectively a group standard relevant to the functioning of the group was maintained. A correlation of .72 was obtained between these two variables. In other words, the greater the attractiveness of the group for the members, the greater was the amount of influence which the group could successfully exert on its members with the result that there existed greater conformity in attitudes and behavior in the more cohesive groups.

Back (1) did a laboratory experiment specifically designed to test this hypothesis. By means of plausible instructions to the subjects he experimentally created groups of high and low cohesiveness, that is, conditions in which the members were strongly attracted to the group and those in which the attraction to the group was relatively weak. The subjects, starting with different interpretations of the same material, were given an opportunity to discuss the matter. Irrespective of the source of the attraction to the group (Back used three different types of attraction in both high and low cohesive conditions) the subjects in the high cohesive groups influenced each other's opinions more than the subjects in the low cohesive groups. In short, the greater the degree of attraction to the group, the greater the amount of influence actually accomplished.

Hypothesis 3c: *The amount of change in opinion resulting from receiving a communication concerning "item x" will decrease with increase in the degree to which the opinions and attitudes involved are anchored in other group memberships or serve improvement need satisfying functions for the person.*

If the opinion that a person has formed on some issue is supported in some other group than the one which is at present attempting to influence him, he will be more resistant to the attempted influence. Other sources of resistance to being influenced undoubtedly come from personality factors, ego needs and the like.

Specific evidence supporting this hypothesis is rather fragmentary. In the study of social groups in a housing project by Festinger, Schachter and Back (4), the residents were asked whether their social life was mainly outside the project or not. Of those who conformed to the standards of their social groups within the project about 85 per cent reported that their social life was centered mainly within the project. Less than 50 per cent of those who did not conform to the standards of the project social group, however, reported that their social life was centered mainly in the project. It is likely that they were able to resist the influences from within the project when their opinions and attitudes were supported in outside groups.

The experiments by Schachter (8) and by Festinger and Thibaut (5) used the same discussion problem in slightly different situations. In the former experiment subjects identified themselves and verbally supported their opinions in face-to-face discussion. In the latter experiment the subjects were anonymous, communicating only by written messages on which the sender of the message was not identified. Under these latter conditions many more changes in opinion were observed than under the open verbal discussion situation even though less time was spent in discussion when they wrote notes. This difference in amount of change in opinion is probably due to the ego defensive reactions aroused by openly committing oneself and supporting one's opinions in a face-to-face group.

(4) Determinants of change in relationship among members:

Hypothesis 4a: *The tendency to change the composition of the psychological group (pushing members out of the group) increases as the perceived discrepancy in opinion increases.*

We have already discussed two of the responses which members of groups make to pressures toward uniformity, namely, attempting to influence others and being more ready to be influenced. There is still a third response which serves to move toward uniformity. By rejecting those whose opinions diverge from the group and thus redefining who is and who is not in the psychological group, uniformity can be accomplished. The greater the discrepancy between a person's opinion and the opinion of another, the stronger are the tendencies to exclude the other person from the psychological group.

There is evidence that members of groups do tend to reject those whose opinions are divergent. In the study of social groups within a housing project Festinger, Schachter and Back (4) found that those who did not conform to the standards of their social group were underchosen on a sociometric test, that is, they mentioned more persons as friends of theirs than they received in return. Schachter (8) did an experiment specifically to test whether or not members of groups would be rejected simply for disagreeing on an issue. Paid participants in the groups voiced divergent or agreeing opinions as instructed. In all groups the paid participant who voiced divergent opinion on an issue was rejected on a postmeeting questionnaire concerning whom they wanted to have remain in the group. The same paid participants, when voicing conforming opinions in other groups, were not rejected.

Hypothesis 4b: *When non-conformity exists, the tendency to change the composition of the psychological group increases as the cohesiveness of the group increases and as the relevance of the issue to the group increases.*

We have previously discussed the increase in forces to communicate with increase in cohesiveness and relevance of issue. Similarly, these two variables affect the tendency to reject persons from the group for non-conformity. Theoretically we should expect any variable which affected the force to communicate (which stems from pressures toward uniformity) to affect also the tendency to reject non-conformers in a similar manner. In other words, increases in the force to communicate concerning an item will go along with increased tendency to reject persons who disagree concerning that item.

The previously mentioned experiment by Schachter (8) was designed to test this hypothesis by experimentally varying cohesiveness and relevance in club groups. In this experiment the more cohesive groups do reject the non-conformer more than the less cohesive groups and the groups where the issue is relevant reject the non-conformer more than groups where the issue is not very relevant to the group functioning. Those groups where cohesiveness was low and the issue was not very relevant show little, if any, tendency to reject the deviate.

III. FORCES TO CHANGE ONE'S POSITION IN A GROUP

Another important source of forces to communicate are the forces which act on members of groups to locomote (change their position) in the group, or to move from one group to another. Such forces to locomote may stem from the attractiveness of activities associated with a different position in the group or from the status of that position or the like. Thus a new member of a group may wish to become more central in the group, a member of an organization may wish to rise in the status hierarchy, a member of a business firm may want to be promoted or a member of a minority group may desire acceptance by the majority group. These are all instances of forces to locomote in a social structure.

It is plausible that the existence of a force acting on a person in a specific direction produces behavior in that direction. Where locomotion in the desired direction is not possible, at least temporarily, there will exist a force to communicate in that direction. The existence of a force in a specific direction will produce behavior in that direction. One such kind of behavior is communication. This hypothesis is not very different from the hypothesis advanced by Lewin (6) to account for the superior recall of interrupted activities.

An experiment by Thibaut (9) tends to corroborate this theoretical analysis. In his experiment he created two groups, one of high status and privileged, the other of low status and under-privileged. These two groups, equated in other respects, functioned together so that the members of the high status group could play an attractive game. The low status group functioned merely as servants. It was clear that forces were acting on the members of the low status group to move into the other group. As the privilege position of the high status group became clearer and clearer the amount of communication from the low status team to the high status group increased. The number of communications from members of the high status group to the low status group correspondingly decreased. When, in some groups, the status and privilege relationship between the two teams was reversed toward the end of the experimental session, thus reducing the forces to locomote into the other group, the number of communications to that other group correspondingly decreased.

Further corroboration is found in a preliminary experiment, mainly methodologically oriented, conducted by Back et al. (2). In this experiment new items of information were planted with persons at various levels in the hierarchy of a functioning organization. Data on transmission of each of the items of information were obtained through cooperators within the organization who were chosen so as to give adequate coverage of all levels and all sections within it. These cooperators recorded all instances of communication that came to their attention. Of seventeen acts of communication recorded in this manner, eleven were directed upwards in the hierarchy, four toward someone on the same level and only two were directed downwards. The existence of forces to move upward in such a hierarchical organization may be taken for granted. The great bulk of the communications recorded went in the same direction as these forces to locomote.

In considering communication among members of differentiated social structures it is important also to take into account restraints against communication.

Infrequent contact in the ordinary course of events tends to erect restraints against communication. It is undoubtedly easier to communicate a given item to a person whom one sees frequently or to a person to whom one has communicated similar items in the past. The structuring of groups into hierarchies, social clusters, or the like, undoubtedly tends to restrict the amount and type of contact between members of certain different parts or levels of the group and also undoubtedly restricts the content of the communication that goes on between such levels in the ordinary course of events. These restrictions erect restraints against certain types of communication.

There are some data which tend to specify some of the restraints against communication which exist. In the study of the communication of a spontaneous rumor in a community by Festinger, Cartwright et al. (3) it was found that intimacy of friendship tended to increase ease of communication. Persons with more friends in the project heard the rumor more often than those with only acquaintances. Those who had few friends or acquaintances heard the rumor least often. At the same time this factor of intimacy of friendship was not related to how frequently they relayed the rumor to others. In other words, it was not related to forces to communicate but seemed to function only as a restraint against communicating where friendship did not exist.

There is also some evidence that the mere perception of the existence of a hierarchy sets up restraints against communication between levels. Kelley (7) experimentally created a two-level hierarchy engaging in a problem-solving task during which they could and did communicate within levels and between levels. Control groups were also run with the same task situation but with no status differential involved between the two subgroups. There was more communication between subgroups under these control conditions than where there was a status differential involved.

It seems that, in a hierarchy, there are also restraints against communicating hostility upwards when the hostility is about those on upper levels. In the same experiment by Kelley there was much criticism of the *other group* expressed by both high status and low status members. The proportion of these critical expressions which are directed upward by the low status group is much less, however, than the proportion directed downward by the high status groups.

IV. EMOTIONAL EXPRESSION

An important variety of communications undoubtedly results from the existence of an emotional state in the communicator. The existence of joy, anger, hostility and the like seems to produce forces to communicate. It seems that communications resulting from the existence of an emotional state are consummatory rather than instrumental.

By an instrumental communication we mean one in which the reduction of the force to communicate depends upon the effect of the communication on the recipient. Thus in communication resulting from pressures toward uniformity in a group, the mere fact that a communication is made does not affect the force to communicate. If the effect has been to change the recipient so that he now agrees more closely with the communicator, the force to communicate will be reduced. If the recipient changes in the opposite direction, the force to communicate to him will be increased.

By a consummatory communication we mean one in which the reduction of the force to communicate occurs as a result of the expression and does not depend upon the effect it has on the recipient. Certainly in the case of such communications the reaction of the recipient may introduce new elements into the situation which will affect the force to communicate, but the essence of a consummatory communication is that the simple expression does reduce the force.

Specifically with regard to the communication of hostility and aggression, much has been said regarding its consummatory nature. The psycho-analytic theories of catharsis, in particular, develop the notion that the expression of hostility reduces the emotional state of the person. There has, however, been very little experimental work done on the problem. The previously mentioned experiment by Thibaut in which he created a "privileged-underprivileged" relationship between two equated groups has some data on the point. There is evidence that those members of the "underprivileged" groups who expressed their hostility toward the "privileged" groups showed less residual hostility toward them in post-experimental questionnaires. There is, however, no control over the reactions of the recipients of the hostile communications nor over the perceptions of the communicators of what these reactions were. An experiment is now in progress which will attempt to clarify some of these relationships with both negative and positive emotional states.

V. SUMMARY

A series of interrelated hypotheses has been presented to account for data on informal social communication collected in the course of a number of studies. The data come from field studies and from laboratory experiments specifically designed to test the hypotheses.

Three sources of pressures to communicate have been considered:

1. Communication arising from pressures toward uniformity in a group. Here we considered determinants of magnitude of the force to communicate, choice of recipient for the communication, magnitude of change in recipient and magnitude of tendencies to reject non-conformers.

2. Communications arising from forces to locomote in a social structure. Here we considered communications in the direction of a blocked locomotion and restraints against communication arising in differentiated social structures.

3. Communications arising from the existence of emotional states. In this area data are almost completely lacking. Some theoretical distinctions were made and an experiment which is now in progress in this area was outlined.

NOTES

1. Back, K. The exertion of influence through social communication. *J. abn. soc. Psychol.*, 1950.

2. ———, Festinger, L., Hymovitch, B., Kelley, H. H., Schachter, S., and Thibaut, J. The methodological problems of studying rumor transmission. *Human Relations*, 1950.

3. Festinger, L., Cartwright, D., *et al*. A study of a rumor: its origin and spread. *Human Relations*, 1948, 1, 464–486.

4. ———, Schachter, S., and Back, K. *Social pressures in informal groups: a study of a housing project*. New York: Harper & Bros., 1950.

5. ———, and Thibaut, J. Interpersonal communication in small groups, *J. abn. soc. Psychol.*, 1950.

6. Lewin, K. Formalization and progress in psychology. In *Studies in Topological and Vector Psychology I., Univ. Ia. Stud. Child Welf.*, 1940, 16, No. 3.

7. Kelley, H. H. Communication in experimentally created hierarchies. *Human Relations*, 1950.

8. Schachter, S. Deviation, rejection, and communication. *J. abn. soc., Psychol.* (1950).

9. Thibaut, J. An experimental study of the cohesiveness of underprivileged groups. *Human Relations*, 1950, 3.

THE COMMUNICATION OF WELFARE: CLIENT AND CASEWORKER

Floyd W. Matson

*O*ver the last generation a new and closer interaction has grown up between the American citizen and the agencies of his government, as society has come to assume definite responsibility for maintaining standards of health, subsistence, and welfare. For increasing numbers this association is peculiarly intimate. As one writer has pointed out, ". . . literally millions of people have been brought into a new relationship with officials of their local, state, and national governments—namely, the relationship of client and social caseworker. Governmental social casework today affects the lives of more than five and a half million recipients of public assistance, a quarter of a million children receiving public child welfare casework services, some 300,000 juvenile delinquents, and an uncounted number of veterans and other persons 'receiving services'—a total not far from, and possibly, greater than, five percent of our population. Moreover, the trend has been consistently upwards."[1]

A study of the client-caseworker relationship has importance beyond its application to the needs and problems of the millions of persons directly involved. It carries implications as well for the larger relationship between the ordinary citizen and his government in a time when the rights and responsibilities of each are undergoing serious reappraisal.

Gradually over the last half-century, and more markedly since the depression of the 1930's, the concept of public welfare—popularly suggested by the phrases "freedom from want" and "freedom from fear"—has come to assume an important place in the roster of democratic values. It is no derogation of the welfare philosophy to point out, however, that in its reference to a social norm—the general welfare—it is of an essentially different order from the traditional civil and political rights of the individual, which have had a common center in freedom from restraint. There is of course no

Reprinted from "Social Welfare and Personal Liberty : The Problem of Casework," *Social Research*, XXII (1955), 253–274, by permission.

logical inconsistency between the concepts of social welfare and the liberties of the person; but neither, it must be said, is there any necessary consistency.

The potentiality of conflict has not gone unrecognized within the ranks of the social-work profession. As one spokesman has seen, "The great task of the twentieth century is the reconciliation of individual freedom and social security. Involved in this issue are definitions of freedom and its practical limitations in organized society, of security and the extent to which it may be realized"; and another worker adds that "The development of welfare as a major function of government sharpens if it does not create new relationships between social work practice and civil liberties."[2]

Some of the most "progressive" welfare measures inaugurated in the United States over the past generation were to be found in operation in their essential form in the authoritarian Germany of Bismarck—and in several instances were elaborated under the regime of the Nazis. It surely needs no emphasis that the assumption of governmental responsibility for the nurture, education and adjustments of all citizens, "from cradle to grave," finds its completest expression today in the Communist countries of Europe and Asia. In fact, the earliest known systems of public assistance and welfare, replete with legions of workers and administrators, were those established under the Roman emperors, and subsequently under the Holy Roman emperors.

The historic affiliation of welfare practices with authoritarian regimes does not, either in logic or fact, support a thesis that there is anything undemocratic in the recognition by government of a responsibility for minimum guarantees of security and opportunity to all citizens. On the contrary, the hard-learned lesson of the last thirty years has been that in the modern world no government, democratic or other, can hope to survive without a large assumption of such responsibility. Today it is all but universally accepted that a grant of freedom which does not include a reasonable degree of security and opportunity constitutes a dubious blessing.

But there has also been sufficient occasion over the past generation to observe that security without freedom is an even lesser virtue. The perennial problem of reconciling civil liberty with national security and public order has never been more urgent or more pervasive than it is today, reaching as it does into every area of social life and economic enterprise. The problem is not least pressing in its application to the rapidly expanding province of public welfare. Accordingly it is of immediate importance to examine closely all programs and assumptions in the welfare field which may contain a threat to the reconciliation of these democratic and human values.

THE RISE OF SOCIAL CASEWORK

Social casework had its origin in the broad reaction of the nineteenth century against mounting poverty and social disorganization, and more particularly against the harsh system of the poor laws and the lack of purpose in private charitable donations. In its early stages in Victorian England and the United States, social work was an upper-class activity which, like poor relief, viewed those in poverty as a fixed class whose failures were of personal rather than social origin and who were to be cared for in part from motives of benevolence and in part as a deterrent to rebellion. This custodial philosophy was reflected in the doctrine of "less eligibility" attached to pauper status, and in the atmosphere of trusteeship and moral reformism which pervaded early charity work.

One of the first steps towards the development of organized social casework came with the incorporation in 1848 of the Association for Improving the Condition of the Poor of New York City, which recruited hundreds of volunteer workers in a community-wide welfare service and was subsequently emulated by other cities. A generation later the Charity Organization Society, formed in London in 1869 as "The Society for Organizing Charitable Relief and Repressing Mendicity," brought to the social-work movement the sophistication of professional skill and training. The Society's program, however, advocated relief only for the "worthy" or "deserving" poor, with worthiness to be determined by scrupulous investigation of such traits as devoutness, sobriety, marital habits, and personal character generally, as well as by the willingness of the recipient to "cooperate" in a plan for self-improvement. Moreover, the workhouse test of the old poor law was retained, in modified form, and punishment for professional beggars was urged as a discouragement to vagrancy. In later years the Society came gradually to recognize the limitations of "self-improvement" and to accept the need for modest social programs to raise living conditions and health levels.

Social casework "arrived" in the United States in the 1870's and 1880's through the establishment in various cities of charity organization societies on the English model. The American programs generally followed the earlier pattern: the "worthy" poor were sifted out through intensive investigations and good-character requirements, while the social causes of poverty were largely glossed over. The welfare theory of the time was a hodge-podge of traditional assumptions concerning personal responsibility, preordained failure, and natural law—variously contributed by Calvinist piety, Malthusian ecology, and Darwinian biology.

The early development of social casework was characterized by the prevalence of the Friendly Visitors, whose self-appointed function was to "close the gulf between rich and poor" and to "bring the rich into such relation with the poor as cannot fail to have a civilizing and healing influence" (on which class was not altogether clear). Charity workers sought to guide their less fortunate "neighbors" to self-improvement through a combination of material aid and moral edification. At the same time habitual vagrants and beggars were to be severely punished; imprisonment at hard labor was recommended for trespassers on the railroads, and jailing in a "compulsory labor colony with indeterminate sentence" for the hardened vagrants.

The foundations of modern social-casework theory were laid in 1917 with the publication of Mary Richmond's *Social Diagnosis*, which reflected the growing professionalization of social work and set forth the new "diagnostic" approach derived from clinical psychology. Although the book evinced a partial recognition of the social matrix of poverty and dependency, the Victorian philosophy of worthiness and need was retained in its essentials. Evidence was to be gathered from associates of the needy individual, then evaluated and converted into a program for self-betterment. This program in turn was to be carried through in a friendly spirit by the professional caseworker, who succeeded to the role that had been successively occupied by the overseer and the Friendly Visitor. In most respects the modern theory was an elaboration of the idea, earlier proposed by the Reverend Thomas Chalmers, of replacing the ineffectual workhouse test of the poor laws by an investigation of personal circumstances to determine "worthiness."

In the 1920's the focus of social casework shifted markedly from "poverty line" cases and the relative concern for social conditions to the area of general personal problems, with emphasis on the individual and his "adjustment" to given circumstances. In part this retreat was a consequence of World War I, which had involved families of the middle class in stress situations and which gave rise to the problems of returning veterans. In part also it was due to the achievement of various social programs (workmen's compensation, child-welfare laws, mother's aid, vocational rehabilitation) which were thought to deal adequately with environmental problems of poverty. Moreover, in the relative prosperity of the twenties it was possible for social workers to believe that personal difficulties were non-economic and non-social in their origin and implications.

But possibly the most crucial factor contributing to the individualist orientation of social casework in the twenties was the influence of Freudian psychology. "After Mary Richmond," a prominent caseworker has written, "came a psychiatric deluge. It overtook casework from without in the shape of theories about human development, explanations of human behavior and relationships, and methods for changing human feelings."[3] The "diagnostic" or "organismic" theory of casework, which admitted its primary debt to Freud, took from the psychoanalysts two fundamental concepts of profound relevance to welfare theory and practice: social adjustment and psychological determinism.

SOCIAL ADJUSTMENT

The preoccupation of orthodox Freudian psychoanalysis with the subjective conflicts and biological drives of the individual, and its relative inattention to external forces and institutions, encouraged psychotherapists and social workers to take the environment for granted and to place the responsibility for neurosis, "maladjustment," and distress solely upon the client-patient. Social adjustment and psychic health, in the Freudian view, were attainable only through repression or at best sublimation of personal needs and wishes —a view which in its extreme expression called more or less openly for capitulation to the prevailing habits and conventions of society. This attitude coincided with the traditional assumption that the source of economic failure and social rejection was located in the individual. To social workers in the 1920's "those relatively few who were not getting rich, particularly those who were in poverty and needed the help of social agencies, were obviously 'maladjusted.' The thing to do with them was to turn them over to a good case worker who would 'adjust' them to the (almost perfect) social order."[4]

If the root of all evil was to be found in the personal unconscious, it followed that there was little use in attempting to modify outer circumstances. "The true springs of action," declared the president of the National Conference of Social Work, "are in the internal nature of man. Hence the uselessness of programs, particularly those dependent upon state action or force. When they succeed they are no longer needed."[5] In consequence casework came more and more to take the side of "society" against the individual, accepting environmental conditions and institutions as they were found without regard to their widely varying but always intimate effect on the person. As one psychiatrist observed, "In actual practice social work must support current standards and to the extent that it does, it symbolizes the 'cultural conscience.' Like the disciplining parent, its energies and techniques must generally be directed towards the ultimate goal of bringing the failing individual into conformity with group demands."[6]

But after the outbreak of the great depression, as it became obvious that unemployment and personal distress need not result from character defects or neurotic traits, the "laissez faire" approach to social conditions came increasingly to be challenged in social-work circles, and was partly dislodged from its theoretical eminence. As early as 1933 a commentator on "Recent Changes in the Philosophy of Social Workers" pointed to a "school of thought" separation which had cut across the various fields of social work and divided workers according to "the relative emphases they place upon individual and upon group." The newer viewpoint was forcefully expressed in the same year by Harry L. Lurie: "We are beginning to realize now that we have overstressed personal factors and influences and have disregarded or underemphasized the impersonal factors and impersonal relationships of the individual to the social and economic order. . . . All along the line we have assumed the existence of freedom of opportunity for adjustment of the individual and have blinked the gross obstacles to adjustment which exist in the social order. . . . The conclusion to be drawn . . . is that the future of social work lies more in the organization of social forces than in the methods of case work."[7]

During the thirties, with the growth of social consciousness among workers together with the development of public welfare programs, the wider-reaching fields of group work and community organization assumed increasing stature, and the question whether political and social action might not be a legitimate part of the social worker's function became a running debate—usually resolved in favor of action. Nevertheless the social-adjustment approach, with its passivity toward environment, retained a strong position in casework circles. "Social reform has become a disparaging term," wrote a prominent spokesman in 1937. "It is even implied in some authoritative quarters that to engage in it is an evidence of emotional maladjustment—the outward and visible sign of an inward and unbalanced state."[8] With the advent of World War II, as economic distress receded and renewed attention was given to psychiatric problems, the adjustment approach to casework was widely revived and reaffirmed.

A report on "The Social Caseworker's Relation to Concepts of Blindness," published in 1950, typifies the tendency to resignation in the face of rigid and discriminatory social patterns.[9] In areas where such ideas persist, according to the writer, "it is the function of the social caseworker to assist the blind person to work within these preconceived ideas. Since handicapped persons are a minority group in society, there is greater possibility of bringing about a change in an individual within a stated length of time than there is in reversing accepted concepts within the culture." The "well-adjusted" blind person, it was argued, should be able to get along in this limiting social setting, and the caseworker should concentrate on his personal adjustment since it is easier to reform the client than to reform society. Likewise, the caseworker advising the parents of a blind child should "help them accept that their child will have opportunities to select a vocation that will give him some degree of success," so that the parents may achieve emotional security. Although it was recognized that employers and the community may need ultimately to modify their attitudes, the caseworker nevertheless was advised to rely primarily on contact between the "adequate" blind person and the sighted community on an individual basis.

(How the blind person facing a likely future of dependency is to become "adequate" is presumably left to the devices of casework.)

The striking feature of this and similar articles is the absence of any acknowledgment of organized activity or programing as possible means of altering social status and broadening opportunities. Status is assumed to derive from traditional notions, which are a way "most Americans" have of introducing a basis for social prediction into an undefined situation; thus "status" is cut off from the realities of economic competition in a sighted world, from the fear of dependency on the part of clients, and from the prejudicial atmosphere associated with traditions of "rugged individualism" and "survival of the fittest." The possibility of improving social status through organized movements of the blind and other client groups, together with community programs directed toward non-discrimination, full employment, and social acceptance, is minimized where it is not ignored.

In his relationship with the client the adjustment-minded caseworker assumes that all efforts to achieve integration and self-sufficiency are on an individual basis. The acceptance of physical limitations is, of course, a realistic necessity when an irreparable physical disability has occurred; but the acceptance of fixed social and vocational boundaries is negative and defeatist in its shift of emphasis from improving the situation to improving the individual. How this approach tends to put the cart before the horse is succinctly illustrated in an observation of David S. French: "In the early days of World War II social workers saw persons whom they had not been able to help through individualized casework services suddenly become self-directing, self-supporting individuals. The reason was simple. They were wanted in the economy."[10]

PSYCHOLOGICAL DETERMINISM

The second element in the Freudian influence on casework theory has been the assumption of psychological determinism. The sources of human behavior were seen by Freud to derive from unconscious "internal stimuli" or instincts. Primary among these were the drives toward self-preservation (the life instinct) and toward procreation (the sex instinct). Eventually Freud found a third: the "death" instinct, representing an innate tendency toward destruction of the self and others. The instincts of sex and death were seen to be located in the Id, and thus beneath consciousness and inaccessible to reason—in contrast to the life instinct, which lay partially within the field of the ego and was therefore to a very limited extent subject to conscious control.

The implications for casework theory of this thoroughgoing instinctivism, with its acceptance of the essential irrationality of human behavior, are evident in an enthusiastic account written in the thirties:

The case worker's acknowledgement of the unconscious was destined to transform her whole view of reality. . . . The theory of psychic determinism, as unpalatable to man's pride in his self-knowledge and free will as Darwin's theory of his biological descent from a collateral branch of the apes, forced upon case workers a view of human nature which is essentially scientific. . . . The reverberations of a scientific orientation so alien to all the speculative systems by which man had attempted to account for his nature and his fate have been far-reaching. In the first place there was ruled out every scale of values which had habitually influenced observations, interpretations, and judgments of human behavior. Aesthetic, moral, and conventional social standards became irrelevant criteria and were instead subject to study as factors within the individual and society to be reckoned with objectively.[11]

The Freudian antithesis of man and society, issuing in the goal of adjustment, led social workers to a pessimistic view concerning the possibility of modifying outer circumstances. In its corollary assumption of the fundamental irrationality of behavior, it led to an equal pessimism concerning the ability of the individual to make sensible choices and to lead his own life unassisted. "Psychoanalysis," Frederick H. Allen has noted, "stressing as it does the unconscious motivation of behavior, stresses also the helplessness of man in dealing with present reactions, the energy for which comes from the reservoir of the past."

These assumptions run directly contrary to the traditional tenet of democratic thought that the individual is an ultimately rational and self-directing agent, both entitled to happiness and capable of pursuing it in his own way. In general, of course, casework theorists have vigorously maintained the consistency of their practice with the democratic concept of individual self-determination. But despite these assertions, as Keith-Lucas has pointed out, "self-determination . . . has had to retreat before the growing conviction of caseworkers that man is irrational." Over the years more and more categories of welfare clients have been judged incompetent to lead their own lives. Prospective clients who choose to reject services or otherwise prove uncooperative may find themselves labeled as "unstable defectives." Others, such as unmarried mothers, are declared to be "unable, if not incapable of making their own independent decisions without casework services." Again, there is what one discerning worker calls "the prejudiced assumption that parents who cannot support their children are by that token lacking in the desire and capacity to bring them up properly, and need the agency's supervision."[12] The parents of difficult children may be considered "too close" to the problem to evaluate it rationally; while the children of public-assistance clients come to be classified as "wards of the community."

As more and more groups are held incapable of controlling their destinies, the responsibility for making decisions and accommodating the client to "reality" falls by default to the caseworker. To many such workers, any lack of adjustment or evidence of distress implies a failure of the client's reality sense. In the words of an English professional: "The difficulty is one of knowing reality, but this is also one approach towards the measure of maladjustment. All have to admit difficulty in being entirely objective. All tend to see situations colored by strong subjective feelings, by disappointment with what is found, by beliefs about what may be expected or how things ought to be . . . But without a certain degree of reality sense the commonest form of constructive activity becomes impossible and any client may, or may not, have sufficient objectivity to assess a real situation to make use of whatever social service is available to him."[13] On the other hand "reality," as Keith-Lucas observes, "is something which the caseworker knows because of his scientific training." Noting the view of one worker that "the client's right of self-determination exists until it is demonstrated that the exercise of this right would be highly detrimental to himself and others," the same critic points out that it is the caseworker who decides "whether a citizen may exercise what is in the same sentence described as a right".

The influence of psychoanalytic thinking is further apparent in the disposition of caseworkers to assume a therapeutic responsibility for the client. The clinical techniques of treatment and diagnosis have been taken over virtually intact from the field of psychotherapy and applied to the client-worker relationship, often with little regard for the essential differences between the two fields. "Unlike psychoanalysis," one writer has warned, "case work has always had to deal exclusively with the conscious ego; this was its immediate unavoidable task. This task has, however, been obscured by the fascination of peering into the unconscious." In their fascination some caseworkers tend to forget that a little psychiatric knowledge is a dangerous thing. "It is not uncommon," wrote a close observer in the thirties, "to see an emotionally dependent social worker attempting to be a parent surrogate to a man or woman who is much more mature than the worker in all things except social work theory." The authority lodged in the hands of the caseworker by this relationship—together with the deterministic assumption of the weakness of clients—creates an ever-present temptation to extend the power of the one and to magnify the helplessness of the other. In the words of a psychiatrist: "Practice based on authority consciously or unconsciously utilizes the weaker or submissive side of the self. Emphasis usually gets placed on the sickness of the one who receives and the strength of the other who gives. . . . The assumption is that an individual or a family group needs to be directed and relieved of the responsibility for planning."[14]

In the service of this therapeutic cause, as Keith-Lucas remarks, "the diagnostic school accepts not only responsibility for the whole client, but whole responsibility for him." Whatever the legitimate scope of the service offered—such as that of public assistance, which legally authorizes only the determination of eligibility and need—increasing numbers of diagnostically oriented workers have come to see their duty as that of solving all the personality problems that turn up in the course of inquiry. "Treatment of various problems," according to one account, "calls for the application of a wide range of ameliorative measures, from the provision of material goods to treatment of serious disturbances in social adaptation." In so far as this implies merely a recognition of the interrelationship of the client and his environment, and hence the need for modifying depriving circumstances and extending the field of opportunity, it is wholly legitimate; unfortunately, what seems often to be intended is that the agency should manage if not subsume the normal and traditional roles of such institutions as the family, the school, the church, and even the law. What is forgotten, as Emery has pointed out, is that "few clients wish to be changed. What they wish is usually relief from that which pains them." Without a clear awareness of its own limitations, "casework carries the possibility of being a peeking, prying, eavesdropping inquisition."[15]

For the most part, in deference to democratic values, writers in the casework field have been careful to stress the voluntary nature of client participation, insisting that services should not be forced upon people and that clients remain free to reject aid or terminate it at any time. In recent years, however, these traditional rights of the recipient have been openly challenged by workers advocating an "aggressive" approach to casework which in many instances would impose services regardless of the willingness of individuals or families to receive them. Thus one worker writes (in a project report on child services significantly entitled "Serving Families Who Don't Want Help"): "We were, of course, reluctant to go where we were not wanted, but we had no choice. We had to go out to these families because they would not come to us." The extent of "aggressiveness" involved is indicated by this statement concerning one parent whose uncooperative attitude led to his being designated an "unstable defective": "The father had vigorously resisted the frequent and repeated efforts made by the agency to get him a job. In fact, the father was so hostile that at one time the public assistance worker had to get a police escort to gain entry into the home."[16]

The case against the diagnostic school of casework, in its acceptance of the irrationality of the client and his therapeutic dependence on the social worker, has been well summarized by Keith-Lucas:

> Diagnostic social work . . . believes that it has, or will be able to find, the ultimate explanation of man's nature in psychoanalytic theory. Although it professes a belief in democracy, the freedom to which it looks

forward is a freedom from neurosis and its goal is a person who makes "satisfying social relationships" or is "adapted to reality" and is therefore presumably more rational than he would be if left alone. This implies that those who need the services of the state in any social matter are sick and can only be made well through the help of a class of trained, objective, neurosis-free officials. In this only the social worker or the psychiatrist is effective. Other disciplines, such as education, the law, and the church are reduced to the status of tools to be used by the social worker as instruments in this "freeing" process.[17]

THE FUNCTIONAL APPROACH

Thus far the present discussion of the client-worker relationship, and of its implications for the wellbeing of the individual, has been based upon the theories and practices arising from classical psychoanalytic doctrine—as institutionalized in the diagnostic school of casework. Not all social workers, of course, have subscribed to this theoretical approach or have accepted its interpretation of the nature of casework, the character of the client, and the communicative process of counseling. An alternative conceptual framework, which for decades has warmly contested the field with the Freudians, is that of "functionalism." Derived to some extent from the psychotherapy of Otto Rank, the functionalist approach reflects several of the distinctive insights which led Rank to his dramatic and traumatizing rupture with Freud after many years of intimate association and discipleship.

Chief among these characteristics, in Rank's idiosyncratic system of will therapy, was his emphasis upon the communicative *relationship* between therapist and patient, which he came to regard as more crucial for the outcome of treatment than any formal theory or professional knowledge. More especially, Rank insisted upon respect by the therapist for the patient's "own will," i.e., for his conscious resources and capacity to work through the problems besetting him. "A central feature of Rank's 'helping' therapy was his insistence upon subordinating the will (and the interpreting mind) of the therapist to that of the patient. The essential task became that of *freeing* the patient's will from the coercions alike of instinct (id) and of culture (superego). . . . Through all the shifts and transitions of his developing perspective—even when, in his last years, he searched beneath consciousness for deeper sources of willing—Rank's most persistent theme remained this stress upon the liberation of the human powers of creativity, responsibility, autonomy."[18]

The influence of Rank upon the thinking of American caseworkers was reinforced by two lecture tours in 1928 and 1930 which brought him directly to the attention of workers in New York and Pennsylvania; subsequently it was the Pennsylvania School of Social Work, under the leadership of Kenneth Pray and Jessie Taft, which became the unofficial headquarters of the functionalist persuasion.[19] For all his relevance, however, Rank was only one of several theoretical influences which shaped the development of this alternative approach to the client-worker relationship. The writings of Virginia Robinson, from within the profession, had a great and lasting effect;[20] while on the outside, during the thirties, a strikingly parallel movement was taking form in psychoanalysis itself with the rise of the neo-Freudian heresies of Erich Fromm, Karen Horney, Harry Stack Sullivan and Frieda Fromm-Reichmann.[21] Somewhat later, functionalist theory found an impressive and influential source of confirmation in the work of a brilliant American psychotherapist, Carl. R. Rogers.[22]

The chief distinguishing characteristic of functionalism is what may be called the *displacement of authority* for decision-making from caseworker to client; in this setting the worker's responsibility, far from being total, is reduced to a bare minimum (as suggested by Rogers' well-known adjectives "nondirective" and "client-centered"). The significance of this emphasis has been clearly expressed by Pray:

> This approach clings steadily to the conception that [the] individual . . . carries responsibility for his own life as a whole and must continue to carry it. . . . It is his own will, his own capacity for growth and change, his own selective use of his experience . . . that determine the outcome. The worker, with all his knowledge and skill, cannot determine—cannot even predict—that outcome. The worker can only accept responsibility for rendering a service which the applicant sees as appropriate to his need, and for initiating and sustaining a process, within the service relationship, which enables the client to exercise his will and use his powers with greater freedom, with less fear, with more insight and clarity, as to both the purpose and consequence of action.[23]

This firm commitment to client self-determination, with its evident respect for the dignity and rights of the person, falls securely within the democratic tradition. Taken together with similar declarations by other functionalist spokesmen, the viewpoint offers a corrective to the tendency among diagnostic caseworkers to doubt the rational capacity of the client and hence to take "whole" responsibility for him. The citizen who comes voluntarily to the agency seeking a specific service, whatever the extent of his deprivation and need, is neither custodialized nor patronized but *respected* as a self-governing agent capable of exercising the full range of rights and responsibilities which accrue to citizens in a free society. In this perspective the communicative transaction of casework—the "helping" relationship—ceases to be a one-sided monologue of coercive persuasion and takes on the fruitful dimensions of dialogue. What has happened, from the standpoint of the worker, is that he has (in Martin Buber's words) "stepped forth out of the role of professional superiority, achieved and guaranteed by long training and practice, into the elementary situation between one who calls and one who is called."[24]

CONCLUSION

The needs of the welfare client in a democratic society are the needs of the ordinary citizen, fully articulated in the constitutional guarantee of access to life, liberty, and the pursuit of happiness. It is true that persons in deprived circumstances, whether through misfortune, accident or disability, require help; but, in a timeworn yet accurate phrase, the help they need is only to help themselves. The greatest requirement of welfare and public-assistance recipients is for a rational arrangement of the social and economic environment which will afford them an equal start and an open field in the common pursuit of happiness.

In this conception lies the major challenge to social work, not alone with respect to existing clientele but with respect to all members of the community. "In a long evolutionary struggle," as Gordon Hamilton has seen, "the welfare premise gradually coming to be accepted is that the basic needs of all children, of all persons, irrespective of class and caste, of nation and race, should be met, not ignored and frustrated." It has been argued that these needs cannot be met, if indeed they can be perceived at all, through individualized casework services focused inwardly upon the unconscious. In the words of Grace L. Coyle: "It has been said that the function of the caseworker is helping people out of trouble. But it is not enough merely to be out of trouble. Important as that is, society must provide for its members opportunity for all kinds of experience that widens interest, develops latent capacities, increases knowledge of the world, encourages creative capacities, brings forth intelligent, socially valuable human beings."[25]

What this means, as Harry L. Lurie points out, is that "the caseworker must become more of a social worker intent upon the solution of social problems and less of a technician skilled in methods of adapting individuals to the status quo." Working together with his colleagues in group work and community organization, he can do much to "help the community constructively to relate its institutions and arrangements and services to the fundamental needs of human beings as these are disclosed in our service relationships."[26] The principal task of social welfare, in this perspective, becomes that of organizing the resources of the family, the community and the nation—and eventually, one may dare to hope, of the world—toward the goal of releasing the full creative capacities of all people and guaranteeing the exploitation and exclusion of none. This objective has been nowhere more clearly seen or affirmatively stated than in the 1950 report of the Social Commission of the United Nations Economic and Social Council:[27]

> ... social work, by fixing attention on specific social ills and pointing to the need for appropriate remedial and preventive service, seeks to maximize the resources available in the community for promoting social well-being. The well-trained social worker tends to become a "social diagnostician" for the community, i.e., his day-to-day work enables him to identify classes of problems requiring orderly solution by the community, or classes of persons who can be brought to normal social and economic functioning only through the creation of special community resources. The social worker here performs a primarily technical and instrumental function calculated to make more rational, more intelligent, and more effective (a) the efforts of the community in promoting social well-being, and (b) the efforts of individuals, families and groups to overcome obstacles to productive and satisfying living.

In the recognition of this welfare objective there is no place for passive resignation before the supposed immutability of social attitudes and relationships, which would compel the submission of the individual to fixed systems of status and role. Nor is there any room for authoritarian assumptions of the irrationality or weakness of welfare clients, which in the name of one "right" would take away the remaining rights and liberties of the person. Social work properly understood, to quote Miss Hamilton once more, "considers the worth of the individual to be a basic value, and believes that the individual should not be sacrificed for the State. Democracy teaches that the more an individual finds himself the more he becomes a contributing member of his society.... The right one must believe in is the right to equal opportunity for the good life and the responsibility of a good society to remove or reduce unnecessary hardships for all."[28]

The right to opportunity is by no means adequately realized as yet in the programs and policies of public welfare, which still in crucial respects embody the poor-law principle of custody and pervasive authority. The right to opportunity presupposes, moreover, a right to privacy and freedom from restraint. Gradually and grudgingly, over recent years, this basic civil liberty has gained partial recognition in welfare philosophy, through the establishment of specific rights to the confidentiality of interviews and case material; to money payments made directly to the individual and unrestricted in their use; to a fair hearing of grievances before the final authority in the state; to voluntary choice by the client as to the acceptance of services or their termination; and through the recognition of other rights of a similar nature.

Yet the most important of these rights are either lacking at crucial points of the welfare system or placed in jeopardy by its underlying philosophy. The right to free consumption choice by recipients of public assistance is vitiated by elaborate and arbitrary requirements whose enforcement has all the characteristics of compulsion. The right to accept or reject services freely is threatened by aggressive caseworkers intent upon applying remedies to persons who do not seek them. The right to equal opportunity and normal livelihood by those of insecure status is denied through efforts to adjust them to roles of permanent inferiority and dependence. And the most fundamental of all rights of the person—that of living his own life and pursuing happiness in his own way—is increasingly endangered by workers and administrators proceeding on assumptions of the irrationality and incompetence of the human person.

NOTES

1. Alan Keith-Lucas, "The Political Theory Implicit in Social Casework Theory," in *American Political Science Review*, vol. 47, no. 4 (December, 1953), p. 1076.

2. Katharine F. Lenroot, "Social Work and the Social Order" (1935), reprinted in *Readings in Social Case Work, 1920–1938*, edited by Fern Lowry (New York, 1939) p. 54; Pauline Miller, "The Confidential Relationship in Social Work Administration," paper presented at the National Conference of Social Work, 1942 (mimeographed) p. 7.

3. Grace F. Marcus, "The Status of Social Case Work Today," in *Compass*, vol. 16, no. 9 (June, 1935) p. 8.

4. Marshall E. St. Edward Jones, "Case Work and Social Work: The Function of Social Service" (1937), in *Readings* (cited above, note 2) p. 541.

5. Miriam Van Waters, "Philosophical Trends in Modern Social Work" (1930), in *Readings* (cited above, note 2) p. 53.

6. E. van Norman Emery, "First Interviews as an Experiment in Human Relations" (1936), in *Readings* (cited above, note 2) p. 189.

7. Harry L. Lurie, "Case Work in a Changing Social Order," in *Survey*, vol. 69, no. 2 (February 1933) pp. 61, 63.

8. Grace L. Coyle, "Social Workers and Social Action," in *Survey*, vol. 73, no. 5 (May 1937) p. 138.

9. Dorothy K. Anderson, "The Social Caseworker's Relation to Concepts of Blindness," in *Social Casework*, vol. 31, no. 10 (December 1950) pp. 417–18.

10. David G. French, *Measuring Results in Social Work* (New York, 1952) p. 38.

11. Marcus, *op. cit.*, p. 9.

12. Grace F. Marcus, "Worker and Client Relationships," in *Proceedings of the National Conference of Social Work*, 1946 (New York, 1947) p. 343.

13. Elizabeth Howarth, "The Scope of Social Casework in Helping the Maladjusted," in *Social Work*, vol. 6, no. 3 (July, 1949) p. 326.

14. Frederick H. Allen, "The Influence of Psychiatry on Social Work" (1935), in *Readings* (cited above, note 2) p. 700.

15. Emery, *op. cit.*, p. 198.

16. Alice Overton, "Serving Families Who Don't Want Help," in *Social Casework*, vol. 34, no. 7 (July 1953), pp. 304, 306.

17. Keith-Lucas, *op. cit.*, p. 1090.

18. Floyd W. Matson, *The Broken Image: Man, Science and Society* (New York, 1964), p. 220.

19. Jessie Taft has made clear the congruence of Rank's psychotherapeutic theories with those of functionalism, but chooses to minimize his responsibility for developments in the social work field. See Taft, *Otto Rank* (New York, 1958), pp. 228–229.

20. Virginia Robinson, *A Changing Psychology in Social Case Work* (Chapel Hill, 1939).

21. See Matson, *The Broken Image*, pp. 221 ff.

22. His works include *Counseling and Psychotherapy* (Boston, 1943); *Client-Centered Therapy* (Boston, 1951); and *On Becoming a Person* (Boston, 1961).

23. Kenneth Pray, *Social Work in a Revolutionary Age* (Philadelphia, 1949), p. 249.

24. Martin Buber, *Pointing the Way* (New York, 1957), pp. 94–95.

25. Grace L. Coyle, "Case Work and Group Work," in *Survey*, vol. 73, no. 4 (April 1937), p. 103.

26. Kenneth Pray, "Social Work and Social Action," in *Proceedings of the National Conference of Social Work, 1945* (New York, 1945), p. 353.

27. United Nations, *Training for Social Work: An International Survey*, E/CN, 5/196, UNESCO (New York, 1950, mimeo), pp. 19–20.

28. Gordon Hamilton, "Helping People—the Growth of a Profession," in *Social Work as Human Relations* (New York, 1949), pp. 5–6.

part seven

CULTURE AS COMMUNICATION: THE PERSPECTIVES OF ANTHROPOLOGY

COMMUNICATION, EVOLUTION, AND EDUCATION

Ashley Montagu

*I*t has been remarked that almost every tragedy represents a failure in communication. In most cases, we may surmise, the failure is due not so much to what has *not* been said, as to what *has* been said; said, and misunderstood. The truth is that communication is an art, the art of addressing humanity, the art of cooperation in purest form. It was Sophocles who wrote:

> *Of all the wonders, none is more wonderful than man,*
> *Who has learned the art of speech, of wind-swift thought,*
> *And of living in neighborliness.*

Communication is an art not easily come by in a world in which we need to know less and understand so much more. Since it is or should be the principal purpose of education to teach the art of communication, it will always be worth inquiring anew into the meaning of human communication.

It is probable that all animals, even unicellular organisms,[1] communicate with one another, but speech is man's alone, man's unique and unparalleled accomplishment. Man, indeed, is man because he speaks. Man's nearest relations, the anthropoid apes, do not speak, and I fear, it remains true that:

> *When anthropoids began to walk,*
> *They took the step that led to talk,*
> *But while ably learning to walk erectly,*
> *They never learned to talk circumspectly.*

That is to say, the apes that became men. The great apes, while they appear to possess the necessary vocal organs, and the chimpanzee has been recorded as capable of making 44 different sounds, a number more than enough to constitute the elements of a complex spoken language, nevertheless do not speak. All attempts to teach them to do so have met with failure.[2]

It would appear that apes lack the necessary genetic potentialities, which man alone possesses, for speech. Evidently, the most important part of the genetic system underlying the capacity for speech is not that which subserves the vocal organs, but the capacity for abstraction, for learning. Learning and the capacity for abstraction are simply different aspects of the same process. Abstract learning is, perhaps, the most astonishing product of the evolutionary process, reaching its highest development in man. It is his abstract-learning ability which enables man to use his vocal apparatus as a tool in the service of communication by means of organized segments of sound.

The apes are capable of grunts, cries, screams, squeaks, and hoots, and these vocalizations undoubtedly convey meanings to other apes; but such meanings are not the result of an organized system of communication, and far from being abstract, are concrete and categoric, of the "Stop, Look, Listen" variety. Such communication is rather more of the nature of signalling than symbolling. The apes use the sounds they utter as signs. Man uses the sounds he makes as symbols. A sign is a concrete denoter: it signals "This is it. Do something about it." A symbol, on the other hand, is abstract, connotative, contemplative, knowing, knowledgeable. A sign is external. A symbol is internal. Signs relate mostly to the world of things, symbols to the world of ideas. A symbol is an abstract meaning of value conferred by those who use it upon anything, tangible or intangible. A sign, on the other hand, is a physical thing which is apprehended as standing for something else.

Human learning consists principally in the process of building up new systems of symbol relations and integrating them with already existing ones. Thought is essentially the process of educing relations from symbol correlates. Mind arises through the communication of such symbol relational meanings in a social process or context of experience. By means of these symbol-using abilities the individual, through his experience, actual and vicarious, may build up a huge depositary of such symbols which can be brought to bear upon present and future problems. This use of symbols is largely limited to human beings. Animals can remember, but usually only when they experience the appropriate conditioned stimuli. Human beings, however, can draw upon an immense reservoir of symbols, which is one of the principal reasons for their high ability to solve problems.

In short, then, as a communicator man differs from all other animals by his highly developed capacity for conceptual thought, in his capacity for abstraction, for symbol making and symbol usage. Man is what he is because of his capacity to create in his mind, by the use of symbols, an idea about something which has no existence outside his mind, and with that idea proceed to create something according to the instructions given or the pattern constituted by that idea. In this manner ideas, symbols, create realities, give them an existence outside the mind. Symbols objectify subjective processes. Essentially a symbol is a meaning. And it is essentially because man is a symbol-using creature that he means so much. The human world, the world man has created, is the world of meanings, of symbols, and their realization. That realized and realizing world of meanings, the ideas, institutions, pots, pans, and everything else that man has created, the anthropologist calls *culture*, the man-made part of the environment.

Culture represents the new zone of adaptation, the new dimension of experience, into which man has moved as a consequence of his becoming a symbol-using primate. Every culture, that is to say, the way of life of every people, constitutes an intricate communications network. Every member of a culture is himself a complex communications system, and the form that that communication system takes, depends virtually entirely upon the cultural conditioning which the individual undergoes within his culture.

Culture consists of patterns or regularities of and for behavior, overt (as mores) or felt (as folkways), acquired and transmitted by symbols through the interactions of human beings, constituting the traditional (historically derived and selected) ideas and especially their associated values. In short, culture is whatever man learns as a member of society. Culture is what remains of men's past working on their present, to shape their future.

Almost all animals have some rudiments of culture, but those rudiments are very rudimentary indeed compared with man's culture. Man differs from all other animals in having moved virtually entirely into the cultural dimension as a way of adaptation. In contrast, other animals live largely in the world of physical adaptation, with comparatively few and simple cultural adaptations.

How, then, did man's unique cultural mode of communication come about? The answer to that question is the story of the evolution of man himself. It is a most illuminating story, for it throws a flood of light not alone upon the nature of communication, but upon the very nature of human nature, and hence, upon the nature of the materials with which the educator has to work, as well as upon the nature of education itself.

The story begins in the Pliocene, a period which lasted some 12 million years, and which came to an end about two million years ago, when the Pleistocene began. The Pleistocene came to an end about 15,000 years ago. During the Pliocene, considerable oscillations in the climate occurred in Africa, resulting periodically in marked reductions in the rainfall, with consequent extreme desiccation. In this manner vast areas of land were deforested, and the land which was once heavily wooded was transformed into plains with low and sparse vegetation and few trees. Such a plain is called a savanna; it is a sort of cross between a woodland and a desert. As a result of such climatic changes, extending over tens of thousands of years, forest-dwelling manlike apes found themselves abandoned by the trees, and therefore forced to take to a new way of life. It was not that man's ancestors abandoned the trees, but that the trees abandoned them.

The world of the forest and the world of the plains are two very different universes. In the forest the table is, as it were, laid. All that is required is to stretch out a hand and pick some succulent plant and eat. The challenges are not very great and tend to be relatively unvarying. The habitat of the primates, the order of mammals to which, in common with the monkeys and apes, man belongs, over the seventy million years of their evolution, has mainly been the forest. In that environment the several hundred different species of primates have done extremely well. Man is the only member of the order primates who has undergone evolution outside the forest. It was the savanna environment that produced the pressures which transformed an ape into a man.

In the savanna, man's precursors were confronted with a novel series of challenges. For example, all primates up to this time were predominantly herbivorous foodgatherers, but since the savannas no longer supplied a sufficient quantity of vegetable food, the savanna-dwelling anthropoids were forced to extend their foodgathering activities to animals. At first this would be restricted to the collection of the juvenile and slow-moving animals. This, in fact, we know to have been the case from the important find, in 1959, of one of the earliest discovered manlike forms together with the remains of his food. That form is *Zinjanthropus boisei*, found at Olduvai Gorge in Kenya Colony, East Africa. The skeletal remains of *Zinjanthropus* tell us that he walked erectly, and that he had a cranial capacity of about 600 cubic centimeters (adult modern man has an average cranial capacity of about 1,400 cubic centimeters). Furthermore, *Zinjanthropus* was a tool-maker, for the most primitive known stone tools were found in association with his skeletal remains. These stone tools are known as Oldowan, after the type site at which they were found. The remains of his food discovered in association with *Zinjanthropus* consisted of the small, juvenile and immature of larger animals, and of slow moving creatures like the tortoise and the shallow-water catfish.

The fact that these tools have recently been attributed to a more advanced Early Pleistocene form, *Homo habilis*, is of no great moment here.

Tools were almost certainly manufactured in consequence of the adoption of an omnivorous diet, leading to the killing and preparation of the bodies and skins of animals.

Quite possibly stones would have been thrown at cornered animals. Frequently hitting a rock rather than the prey, such stone missiles would flake and present sharp edges. In various forms and in various ways such broken flaked stones can be used as knives, scrapers, and choppers. Tools at first made adventitiously in this way, can then be used as models and manufactured deliberately, especially for use in regions in which stone does not naturally occur. This was the case at Olduvai. The tools found in association with *Zinjanthropus* were made by him or *Homo habilis* on the spot, as is evident from the many flakes found with the stone tools from which they had been struck.

In the manufacture of tools, hand, eye, and brain develop in a novel and integrative manner to shape the function of each in an interactively feedback relation. The gathering of animal foods, foods which are no longer sessile, stationary, but which are mobile, does not simply represent an extension of the previous herbivorous existence of man's forest-dwelling precursors, but a totally different way of life. Man's vegetarian ancestors did not *gather* food, they simply plucked and ate. Man's precursors did gather their food, and that food frequently had to be pursued and caught. And when these small animals are finally caught they have to be killed, skinned, and cut up. Small animals could in this way be gathered and brought back to the group to be shared, with the women, children, and infirm. In this manner the adult males, for the first time, would begin to provide food for their dependents. No other primate does this. It is the females who provide the nutrition for the infants until they can provide for themselves. The attachment of the male to a particular female develops not alone from the sexual advantages to the male of the development of a continuously potential sexual receptivity, but from the necessity also of providing the essential nutriment for the female, who must nurse their child. Thus, the nuclear or biological family comes into being in the human species, with all its attendant consequences.

Gradually, from the gathering and pursuit of small animals, man began to hunt the larger ones. It is at this stage of his evolution that the challenges presented by this new way of life, *hunting*, literally multiplied by leaps and bounds. It is probable that the adoption of this new way of life, hunting, was responsible for the initiation of more physical and cultural evolutionary changes in man than almost all his other activities put together. To name those physical and cultural changes would be to name virtually all of man's distinguishing traits.

Hunting presents so many problems to the hunter for solution, so many stimulations and challenges to him, that they are almost never-ending. Hunting is the essential problem-solving situation. In the midst of it, it is soon discovered that the hunt is most likely to be successful when it is pursued in cooperation with others. In this manner hunting became a cooperative enterprise, with a high selective value placed on cooperative behavior. The rapidly changing conditions during the hunt, and the necessity of making the appropriately successful responses to those conditions, placed a high premium upon problem-solving abilities, that is, upon intelligence. Instincts, automatic reactions, in such situations are worse than useless; they are handicapping. And so a negative selection against instincts occurs concomitantly with the positive selection pressure favoring genotypes with the necessary intelligence potentials. In this manner man came to lose his instincts and to rely principally upon his problem-solving capacities for making his way in the world. Intelligence requires an increasingly larger brain in order to house the necessary neurological structures it apparently requires. Loss of instincts necessitates a prolonged dependency period, during which the child must learn the behavior which enables it to learn those further behaviors which will enable it to function as a human being in the human world. The most important agency through which the child learns to become human is communication, verbal and also nonverbal. The long dependency period requires mothers who are well-endowed with the capacity to minister to the needs of the dependent infant; hence, those females were naturally selected for survival who possessed a highly developed capacity for love. Love is essentially the communication to others of the feeling of deep involvement in their welfare. Briefly, love is behavior calculated to confer survival benefits upon others in a creatively enlarging manner. Communication is the vehicle of love. It is the essence of the human situation. And it is for this reason, as I have already said, that it should be the first of the arts, the art of communicating humanity.

The unique and infinitely various form that communication takes in man is speech. And it is to this form of communication that we must return here. What is speech? Speech is thought and feeling made explicit. Speech is the expression or communication of thoughts and feelings by discrete vocal sounds having meanings, a complex set of bodily habits which have to be learned. It is an interesting fact that while almost all the other muscles of the body are steered by proprioception, that is, from the position and movement of the body and its parts, the muscles subserving the functions of speech obtain their control from the spoken sounds. The learning of speech takes a considerable amount of time, and involves the coordination of larynx, pharynx, cheeks, tongue, soft palate, lips, and nose. The congenitally deaf fail to speak properly if at all, because they cannot hear the spoken sounds upon which the learning of speech is dependent. They are deaf-mute.

So pervasive is the functional importance of speech that virtually every part of the gray matter, the cortex, of the brain is somehow involved in this function. It used to be thought that there were special localized areas in the brain for speech, Broca's area in the left frontal lobe, and Wernicke's area in the left temporal lobe; but since Broca's area, at least, can be removed without affecting speech, while extirpation of almost any area of the cortex is capable of affecting speech, our ideas concerning the neurophysiology of speech must be revised.

A vocal sound having a relatively stable meaning, and used as a unit of communication, is known as a *morpheme*. A morpheme is the smallest structural unit that has lexical or grammatic meaning. For example, the sound "s" at the end of a word is a morpheme, having the meaning "plural." Some birds can chop vocal sounds into discrete segments, but they do not communicate thoughts by such means, for it is man alone who produces cerebrated symbols by means of speech.

It is important to distinguish between communication, language, and speech. These words may, of course, be used synonymously, but strictly speaking communication refers to the transmission or reception of a message, while language, which is usually used interchangeably with speech, is here taken to mean the speech of a population viewed as an objective entity, whether reduced to writing or in any other form. Thoughts and feelings may be communicated in non-verbal ways, as through movements of the body. This is the study of *kinesics*. Kinesic communication is a highly efficient form of non-verbal communication. Communication, then, includes all those processes by which people influence one another, speech being the most important of all the special forms of influencing human beings. How, then, did this most human of all traits come into being?

As I have already indicated, man's nearest relations, the great apes, communicate with one another by means of body movements and by sounds. But the sounds are almost entirely communicative of emotional states. Such communication is known as *mood convection* and is common among birds and non-human mammals. Among the primates, man is the only creature who has become a hunter, and because he became a hunter he got up on his feet, stood erectly, and spoke. Man is not only the only primate that stands alone because he speaks, but who speaks because he stands.

In the hunting situation it is not only of the greatest advantage to be able to run fast—the quadrupedal apes can also run fast—but it is highly advantageous to be able to run in the erect position, bipedally. Such bipedal running affords superior visualization of the situation and at the same time leaves the upper extremities free for carrying and hurling missiles, and for carving up and carrying the kill back to the group. What is more important than running is the ability to stand for prolonged periods of time, for in stalking animals it is necessary to stand quietly for long periods of time in order not to disturb the quarry. Under such conditions non-vocal communication would tend to be developed precisely as we see it at work among living hunting peoples. Once the quarry scents danger and takes off, it is necessary to give chase, and under the kaleidoscopically changing conditions of the chase, it is of the greatest advantage for the hunters to be able to communicate with each other while they are still within earshot. Vocalizations, rather than gestures, would be most efficient under such conditions. Such vocalizations, endowed with specific activating meanings, quickly become established and adopted by the whole group. The elaboration of such words and phrases in conversation would quickly develop a full blown language, a system of verbalized meanings designed to influence behavior.

Thus, from the very birth of language the meaning of a word was the action it produced, and that is still the meaning of a word. Speech, born in a cooperative context for cooperative purposes, is the great ligature that binds human beings together. The natural purpose of words is to put man in touch with his fellow man. Indeed, as Henry James remarked, "All life comes back to the question of our speech—the medium through which we communicate."

In the individual development of the child, the earliest and consistently maintained cooperative behaviors he experiences are associated with the sound of the human voice. The child learns to become a human being, by being spoken *to*, and as he begins to respond—much earlier than most people know—we speak *with* him. And this is the nature of language which always speaks with two voices, *to* and *with*, to purposes and with involvements.

Speech, important as it is, is not, as I have already mentioned, the only means of communication. I have already made references to non-verbal kinesic communication through movements of the body. These are extremely important communicative influences. A good beginning has been made in the investigations of this fascinating field. However, a fundamentally important means of communication, such as that which occurs through the skin, cutaneous communication, has not yet been adequately explored. And yet, cutaneous communication constitutes a basic series of processes in the development of human beings. In influencing the physical, psychological and cultural development of the individual, cutaneous communication plays a substantive role.

The skin is the largest organ of the body. It is the organ of the body most immediately related to the environment. As a sense organ—and the skin is, of course, much more than that—the sensations experienced through the skin are, within its own modalities, not less important than those experienced through the other sense organs. In an age of psychosomatic medicine we know that what goes on in the mind may express itself through the skin, but we seem to be unaware of the fact that what is or is not communicated through the skin may affect the development of the mind, not to mention other organ functions. We do talk about "stroking people the right way," and "rubbing them the wrong way," "getting under their skin," and the like, phrases which indicate a vague recognition of the skin as an organ of communication. We like to have our backs scratched, and we have observed babies enjoying their baths, and the great reluctance they exhibit when being removed from that ecstatic experience; but we have not, for the most part, cottoned on to the significance of these experiences.

For the greater part of man's history, mother and infant—not to mention others—have been in close cutaneous relation with one another, in the nursing situation, the child carried by the mother on her foodgathering and visiting expeditions, held by her, and by others, caressed, stroked, and patted—all this, largely in the nude. Through such tactile experiences the child learns a great deal concerning both the human and the physical world. Indeed, the child's body-image and its image of the various worlds in which it lives are constituted from such experiences. The reality that human beings come to know is entirely built up through and maintained by such communications. In fact, reality is communication—and there is no reality without communication. Through communication the unreal may be made real, and the real unreal.

There are many levels of communication. It is interesting that on at least one of these levels we believe nothing that we cannot touch or grasp. We want "tangible" evidence. What is "tangible" and what "intangible" is conditioned through communication, and the intangible is usually made tangible through communication. This is what Maxwell's equations did for what ultimately became television, and what Alexander Graham Bell "palpably" did for what eventually became the telephone. Abstractions, symbols, in a man's head are transformed into instruments, realities, the like of which never before existed. By the same means man discovers the unknown realities, such as Kekule's magnificent envisagement of the structure of the benzene ring. Such processes have something of the character of stereognosis, perception of form by touch—as when we say, "He has the 'feel' of it."

In cultures such as ours which interpose several layers of apparel between our own skin and that of others, especially that of the small infant, in addition, in his case, to the fact that breastfeeding has now become the exception rather than the rule, we deprive the developing individual of experiences which, I venture to suggest, are essential for his healthy development, both physically and mentally. Consider the following "touching" recollections of a Kikuyu chief. Kabongo, at 80 years of age, recalls:

"My early years are connected in my mind with my mother. At first she was always there; I can remember the comforting feel of her body as she carried me on her back and the smell of her skin in the hot sun. Everything came from her. When I was hungry or thirsty she would swing me round to where I could reach her full breasts; now when I shut my eyes I feel again with gratitude the sense of well-being that I had when I buried my head in their softness and drank the sweet milk that they gave. At night when there was no sun to warm me, her arms, her body, took its place; and as I grew older and more interested in other things, from my safe place on her back I could watch without fear as I wanted, and when sleep overcame me I had only to close my eyes."

The contrast with our own way of doing or rather not doing these things requires no comment from me. Kabongo's words speak more eloquently to the point than anything I could say. In the name of progress, of greater knowledge, we have suffered a serious deprivation. What we need is not more knowledge, but more understanding. The bottle is no substitute for the breast, and the bassinette no surrogate for the shelter of the bosom. "The bosom of the family." What an archaic, old-fashioned phrase! We no longer belong in the bosom of the family, because the bosom has been removed from the family and now serves quite other and extraneous purposes. There has been a loss of communication, and that loss is nothing short of a tragedy.

We have removed human beings from the warm sheltering ambience of each other and are then amazed to find so many of them cold, shivering, alone, melancholy, unloved, and unloving. We know all this and much more, but we do not understand. We have lost touch with one another and wander like lost infants crying in the wilderness, alone and afraid. But is it really true that:

> *the world, which seems*
> *To lie before us like a land of dreams,*
> *So various, so beautiful, so new,*
> *Hath really neither joy, nor love, nor light,*
> *Nor certitude, nor peace, nor help for pain;*
> *And we are here as on a darkling plain*
> *Swept with confused alarms of struggle and flight,*
> *Where ignorant armies clash by night.*

Yes, it is really true, and it will continue to be true, if we go on as we have been doing. But it need not be true, if the educator will assume responsibility for what he should be doing. And what should he be doing? He should be reopening the channels of communication which will serve not only to restore his humanity to man, but will serve also to enlarge it. He should be enabling his charges to fulfill themselves in a creatively enlarging manner. He should learn what human beings are born as, in order that he should understand what they are born for. And he, the educator, should begin to take some measure of his real importance in the world, as one of its acknowledged legislators, engaged in the most important of all tasks: the making of human beings. Toward that end he must familiarize himself with the facts concerning the evolution of man's nature. Once he has done that he will understand that it is the purpose of the educator to assist each human being to realize his evolutionary destiny: which is, to live as if to live and love were one.[3]

I have already dealt with the evolution of man's unique traits. Let me go over them once more in relation to the purposes, or what in my view should be the purposes of education.

Man's educability, his capacity for learning, is his outstanding characteristic. He needs and wants to learn to think, and to think soundly, and thinking is as necessary to his healthy development, sound thinking, as is breathing. His greatest need as a human being is to become one, that is, to be a loving human being, to love and to be loved. And he learns to love only by being loved. As Pestalozzi and other great teachers long ago have shown, it is through love that human beings are taught and learn best. To put it in Pestalozzi's own words, "The essence of training man's nature is to educate mankind to understanding love. . . . Love is the sole and ever-lasting foundation on which our nature can be trained to humaneness."[4] In short, the purpose of education should be to enable the individual to relate himself in a creatively enlarging manner to others.

Is this a dream? It may be at the present time, but educators can make it a reality.

NOTES

1. H. S. Jennings, *Behavior of the Lower Organisms*, New York, Columbia University Press, 1906. Reprinted, Bloomington, Indiana University Press, 1962.

2. Cathy Hayes, *The Ape in the House*, New York, Harper & Bros., 1951; A. L. Bryan, *The Essential Morphological Basis For Human Culture. Current Anthropology*, 4: 297–306, 1963.

3. Ashley Montagu, *The Human Revolution*, Cleveland, World Publishing, Co., 1965.

4. Heinrich Pestalozzi, *The Education of Man: Aphorisms*, New York, Philosophical Library, 1951.

PARALINGUISTICS, KINESICS, AND CULTURAL ANTHROPOLOGY*

Weston La Barre

RANGE AND SCOPE

When Bateson states that all culture is communication (and I agree in the sense that he means this), the cultural anthropologist is overwhelmed by the flood of suggestions and ideas that come to mind. To systematize all culture as communication is here manifestly impossible. This "state of the art" work-paper will therefore aim at the provocation of ideas rather than large (and doubtless premature) synthetic theory, and comprehensiveness of sampling rather than exhaustiveness.

BASIC BIBLIOGRAPHY

Despite the potential riches in the approach, the usable sources are limited in number:

Allport, G. W. and P. Vernon, *Studies in Expressive Movement* (New York, 1933), a psychological approach to gesture, gait, and many other semantic motor acts.

Birdwhistell, R. L., *Introduction to Kinesics* (Louisville, 1952), by the pioneering taxonomist and lexicographer of kinesics, who has devised that initial tool of study: a method of recording kinesic data.

Crichtley, MacDonald, *The Language of Gesture* (London-New York, 1939), an older work but still usable, including gestures and speech, deaf-mute language, and gesture as a precursor to language.

Darwin, Charles, *The Expression of the Emotions in Man and Animals* (New York, 1955), a statement of what might be called the traditional instinctivist theories of kinesic expression.

* Reprinted from T. A. Sebeok, A. S. Hayes, and M. C. Bateson, eds., *Approaches to Semiotics*, 1964, by permission of Mouton & Co., n.v., publishers.

Feldman, S., *Mannerisms of Speech and Gesture* (New York, 1959).

Hall, E. T., *The Silent Language* (New York, 1959), a very readable and justly popular book on cultural semantics, the fundamental and indispensable primer for all modern studies.

Hayes, F., "Gestures: A Working Bibliography," *Southern Folklore Quarterly*, 21 (1957), 218–317, an excellent source which does not pretend to be exhaustive.

Hewes, G. T., "The Anthropology of Posture," *Scientific American*, 196 (Feb. 1957), 123–132, the only systematic, traditional distribution-study, a pioneering work that sacrifices depth for range, along with "World Distribution of Certain Postural Habits," *American Anthropologist*, 57, #2, pt. 1 (April 1955), 231–244.

La Barre, W., "The Cultural Basis of Emotions and Gestures," *Journal of Personality*, 16 (1947), 49–68, an argument against "instinctive gesture" and summarizing statement of an anthropological view that, like any form of social behavior, kinesic codes must be learned.

Mira y Lopez, E., *Myokinetic Psychodiagnosis* (New York, 1958), one of the first "applied" works on kinesics.

Paget, Sir Richard A. S., *Human Speech* (New York-London, 1930), a fundamental work in gesture study, perhaps the best statement of the view that speech arises from nativistic gesture, a currently unfashionable position but one not to be ignored.

Ruesch, J., and Bateson G., *Communication, the Social Matrix of Society* (New York, 1951), a richly suggestive fusion of analytic psychiatry, cultural anthropology, and the "information theory" of communications engineers.

———, and Kees, W., *Nonverbal Communication* (Berkeley, 1956), an objectivist and naturalistic approach, of many details of which the cultural anthropologist may be critical, but not to be overlooked.

Schilder, P., *The Image and Appearance of the Human Body* (New York, 1950), an odd, pioneering, brilliant, sometimes incomprehensible book, but a psychiatric classic nonetheless.

Young, P. T., *Emotion in Man and Animals* (New York, 1943).

A few other items may need to be added, but this brief list embodies most of our basic working library, though other fundamental works exist on slightly more specialized subjects.

LACK OF MASSIVE "LEXICOGRAPHICAL" DATA

Gordon Hewes' two papers are fine distribution studies, but largely limited to nonsemantic kinesics such as postural and motor habits; it is a pioneering and monumental effort to glean sporadic data from ethnographic monographs which largely neglect to cover the subject except incidentally.

Two tribal "kinesic lexicographies," to my knowledge, stand alone: Flora
L. Bailey's "Navaho motor habits" [*American Anthropologist* 44 (1942),
210–234], and George Devereux's "Some Mohave gestures" [*American
Anthropologist* 51 (1949), 325–326] a brief lexicon of 8 types of gestures
accompanying speech. The best work, of course, is Birdwhistell's on our
own society; the linguists, as usual, are ahead of the cultural anthropologists in these studies. The paralinguistic studies of McQuown, Pike,
Hockett, Smith, Trager, Hall, Sebeok, Wells (and others whom, as a non-
linguist, I may not know) are fundamental, and the cultural anthropologist
can glean much from their cues, but this large subject is beyond the scope
of the present study. Basic lexicographies are adequate for such kinesic or
allelo-languages as the Plains Indian sign language (West, Kroeber, Carl
and Florence Voegelin, and J. P. Harrington, restudying older sources);[1]
the sign language of Australian aborigines,[2] the silent gestural language of
European monks, designed to avoid interrupting the meditations of others,
an allegedly international language of traveling medieval monks, reliably
dated from, at the latest, the fourth century A.D. onward;[3] the hand-
language of deaf-mutes and those who would communicate with them;[4]
the gestural argots or kinesic trade-jargons of truck drivers, Hindu merchants, Persians, gypsies, carnival folk, burglars, street urchins, tobacco
auctioneers, and others;[5] the elaborate gestural language of the Hindu
natya dance-dramas;[6] the ritual hand-poses or *mudrās* of Buddhist and
Hindu priests in Bali;[7] the drum languages of West Africa and Central
Africa, the Jivaros, Melanesians, Polynesians, and Javanese; the "whistling
language" of the Canary Islanders and some West Africans; the special
camphor-gathering language of the Jakun, and the allusive communications
of Patani fishermen and many other hunting peoples—but these are beyond
the scope of the present preliminary work-paper. The Mediterranean
peoples are rich in kinesic communication and on the ancient Hebrews, the
Ashkenazi Jews, and Neapolitans we have something like adequate lexico-
graphic materials to work on.[8] Gestures pictured in the Mayan codices
might well be studied by linguists as an aid in breaking this refractory code;
and Andrea de Jorio makes the reasonable proposition that if we understood
the gestures of modern Neapolitans, we might with some success interpret
the gestures of the ancient Greeks, especially those on classical vases. The
covert signs of bidders at auction and those persons working in noisy
situations (hand-gestures of those directing crane-operators and earth-
mover operators, etc.) might also be worthy of scholarly attention.

HUMAN ETHOLOGY AND CULTURAL KINESICS

One fundamental question that needs to be investigated in kinesics is
the precise boundary line between instinctual movements, expressions, and

acts *versus* the numerous culture-based kinesic codes that must be learned like any arbitrary, invented, symbolic system. A great deal of speculative nonsense has been indulged in by the older instinctivist theorists and much of what they uncritically attributed to innate inherited responses can now be clearly seen to be culturally-learned responses—but the question is by no means finally settled at our present stage of knowledge. It is obvious that many body motions—for example, breathing and heartbeat—are basically structural-functional, for all that non-physiological modalities (psychological and cultural) can plainly be seen to cause a change of rate in both. The sucking-reflex, the grasping-reflex, and the startle-reflex are about as close to anything we know that we would wish to call "instinctual" in humans. They are present in the neonate as muscular movements, long before the myelination of other tracts is completed at about the age of 36 months; and they serve (or served in ancestral primates) adaptive purposes. And although eye-movements and eye-focusing are sometimes present in very young babies, it would appear that these muscular movements are already an intimate mixture of structurally-given and environment-induced learning. Eye-blinking at the approach of a noxious stimulus and "automatic" retroflexion of limbs from painful stimuli would appear to involve even more of the learned response.

The fruitful work of modern animal ethologists might well be animadverted to at this point. Overly-facile extrapolation can easily commit the "animal series fallacy" here, and the marked neoteny of man indicates that, with the very long-delayed maturation of the human infant, a change of phase has occurred between humans and infrahumans, so that man is predominantly a learning animal. Man has certainly very little of the species-specific motor acts such as we observe in the courting and fight-or-flight reactions of sticklebacks, birds, and some quadrupeds. Birds, goats, and monkeys appear to have definable periods, within which internally-given and environmentally-stimulated elements join to give adaptive responses, and outside of which periods (both before and after) environmental stimulation produces no adaptive learning. Perhaps human speech itself is one of these: for all that speech is admittedly everywhere cultural in its content (phonemics, lexemics, and syntactics), our meager data on feral children would seem to indicate that there is an optimal period for learning to talk, after which, in the absence of prior environmental stimulation, the individual can never learn to talk. Perhaps the psychiatrists might join me here in speculating that something like this may happen in the complex phatic-semantics of mother-child relationships in some schizophrenics traumatized in the early oral, pre-verbal epochs of their lives. Furthermore, the abundant psychoanalytic materials on "fixation" convince me that there are maturational stage-of-preparedness in the individual during which, in the absence of appropriate environmental stimuli, there can be the grievous and "fixated" mis-learnings that we call neuroses and psychoses. A clinical exposure to the data would, I believe, convince anyone that Karl Abraham[9] was essentially correct in correlating the symptomatology of the major psychoses and neuroses with traumata in specific maturational stages of the individual life-history. But here I approach the borderline of the territory of other specialists and must be content to indicate at least one cultural anthropologist's willingness to learn from these specialists.

The complexity of the matter, on this other borderline of human ethology and cultural kinesics, is indicated in the fact of walking. For all that I have seen of the modern students insistent upon man's bipedality, both on physical anthropological and evolutionary grounds, I am still not prepared precipitately to conclude that walking in humans is a simple instinctual matter. It really belongs in the area of human ethology. Structurally, the physical anthropologist Thieme[10] has argued that the lumbar curve is onto-genetic rather than phylogenetic in man; and functionally, again the meager evidence we have on feral children would seem to indicate that anatomically the young child, bereft of the broad cue of bipedal adults in the environment, can get about quadrupedally about as well as other children can make it bipedally, and perhaps even better. Furthermore, experienced field workers will be unregenerate kinesiologists in this matter: people simply do walk differently in different societies. There are culture-induced *styles of walking*. Old hands in Burma, during the last war, could detect the difference between the lowland Shan walk (arms are swung in planes parallel to the sagittal plane of the body) and the highland Kachin and Palaung walks (arms swung in arcs obliquely forward of the body). In my observation, the Bengali walk differently (all elbows and knees, with considerable foot-lifting) from the Punjabi (with a more puppet-like rigidity and verticality), south Chinese very differently from the Singhalese even when both are barefooted—for all that the difference in walk between the Amerindians and other American males might be imputed, in part, to differences in terrain and footgear. Amazonian men and women have very different styles of walking that may *not* be imputed to differences in tro-chanters, but rather to sex-dichotomized styles.[11] And even in the lower East side of New York one can still see what I have called the "Ashkenazi shuffle" in Jews of Eastern European origin. I would even go so far as to argue "idiolects" in walking: by purely auditory cues I am able to identify the walk of any member of my family, and even to surmise something about their emotional states. If McQuown, Newman, Trager, and other linguists can diagnose psychiatric syndromes purely on the basis of intonation, so also can psychiatrists like Kempf, Ostwald, Sullivan, and Schilder on purely kinesic grounds. My good friend Birdwhistell is so uncannily perceptive in this area that he could probably tell you what the patient wants for dinner! Walking styles undoubtedly have semantic-kinesic functions.

For example, the jointless glide (as if on wheels) to indicate the oriental woman in a movie; in my judgment, Myrna Loy could do this best, in a manner most similar to the Singhalese walk of those that I have observed. Also, in American movies, the suggestion of a sinister inhuman monster—see any Frankenstein-monster movie—is gained by a peculiarly stereotyped, stiffly wooden and deliberate gait.[12] Any addict of Western movies, I believe, can quickly decide which is the hero and which the villain by the position of the pelvis in walking and motor tempo and use of the eyes and head (plus-or-minus a dangling cigarette). Styles of standing change historically too: it is amusing to note that the modern "hood slouch" is not unlike the stylish posture of debutantes in the 'twenties in its loose pelvic forward thrust, and both are similar to the aristocratic manner of standing observable for eighteenth-century Kandyan Singhalese nobles (male) and still earlier in the Sigiriyan frescoes of females in Hinayana Buddhist paintings. The approved pose of "attention" has also differed markedly from World War I to World War II: in the former, the lumbar curve was maximized; in the latter, minimized. Stylized differences in the "dress parade walk" of the British, Americans, and Germans (describable in terms of degree of knee flexion: marked for Americans, minimal for British, absent for the German "goose-step") need only to be alluded to to be remembered.

ETHOLOGICAL KINESICS

Acts perhaps closer to the strictly ethological in humans may be seen in laughing and crying (or, more specifically, lachrimation). Gorillas cannot weep, but human babies can and do. Ashley Montagu has advanced the brilliant and provocative theory that lachrimation is a species-specific adaptive act in humans.[13] Because of its extravagantly infantile helplessness, the human baby must needs summon succor from adults, often from a distance, loudly, and for a long time. To be sure, the vocables adults use may be learned vocal segregates; vociferous, phonemically indiscriminate vocalization is sufficient for the infant's purpose: technical "noise" or something appallingly close to it would do. But prolonged crying means that large masses of air must pass over the nasal membranes, tending to dry them out, whereas sensitive olfactory membrane cells must be kept moist or they quickly die. Lachrimation, therefore, has the adaptive function of keeping cells moist that are threatened by the adaptive necessity of the helpless infant's summoning attention and aid. I would add that, because large masses of desiccating air are also involved in prolonged adult laughter, Montagu's theory has the advantage of explaining that otherwise inexplicable phenomenon of "laughing until you cry."

Laughter, as a kinesic phenomenon, is also probably panhuman, but more complex. I consider that laughter is the kinesic concomitant of "letting the cat out of the bag" of cultural repression, a tension-release of now "innocently permitted" expression of otherwise forbidden aggressive, erotic (and possibly also fearful and embarrassed) states of mind—though just why this kinesic modality is used remains a mystery to me, except that it utilizes an inveterate and habituated oral modality in humans (perhaps higher primates "laugh" also). But laughter is deeply embedded in the specific cultural context of the person who is laughing—Japanese and African and American Negro laughter are sufficient cases in themselves alone to demonstrate this point. Furthermore, the things that people laugh at, in this "return of the repressed" or the "discomfiture at incongruity" will vary depending upon what cats have, by enculturation, been put into what cultural bags.[14] Humor is notoriously as difficult to export as ethos, and for much the same reasons.

Smiling, as opposed to laughter, I consider an as yet unexplained phenomenon. Older theorists, whom we would now classify with the ethologists, were sure that the smile was a disguised snarl, symbolically exposing the canine teeth; but hominid canines haven't been much use for fighting since phylogenetically remote times, nor is it clear why a hostile gesture should be used as a friendly one. The behaviorist psychologist E. B. Holt "physiologized" the smile as being ontogenetically understandable as the relaxation of facial muscles in the infant replete from nursing. But this leaves me unconvinced, when the same infant will make the same "smile" in its sleep, from the *pain* of colic, as well as the *pleasure* of amusement.

As for other physiological modalities in man—defecation, micturition, coitus, and even childbirth—these kinetic acts surely have their anatomical substrates, but they just as surely have their kinemic contexts when they become loaded with cultural semantics and stylization, as every good and complete ethnographic monograph should indicate they do.[15] In the approved kinetic and parakinetic styles of these acts, Havelock Ellis, Malinowski and others have adequately edified us; and Kinsey has sufficiently adumbrated class-differences in these phenomena in America. Obviously, like ballroom dancing, all the above have their sex-dichotomized aspects as well; and Kinsey, in one of his rare truly cross-cultural excursions, has stated that there are even preferred modalities in perverse acts among British (sodomy), American (fellation), and French (mutual onanism) homosexuals. In this section of the present paper, then, the gamut from weeping to sexuality shows a complete range from the rather purely ethological to the clearly ethnological. One's guess is that this may be, in part, a function of the chronological *time of appearance* of the phenomenon: the child's cry at birth, at its first breathing, is most clearly cut-and-dried physiology; whereas sexual behavior already at adolescence has long since been sicklied o'er by the pale cast of culture and ontogenetic conditionings.

CULTURAL KINESICS

We enter more firmly onto sure cultural ground with such motor sememes or kinesic isolates as pointing and head-movements (for "yes" and "no"). Though man is everywhere a notably "handed" animal, pointing with the forefinger and other fingers curled palmward is a limitedly cultural phenomenon, probably of Old World origin and dispersion (American Indians, on both New World continents, point with the lips, as also do Shans and other Mongoloid peoples; in other groups, pointing is done with eye-movements, or nose- or chin-and-head movements, or head-movements alone). As for negation and affirmation kinemes, behaviorists and other psychologists have sought to explain our "yes" nod as the movement of the infant seeking the breast, the "no" as avoiding it. But here the psychologists have reckoned without their cultural hosts: they have an elegantly universalistic explanation for a phenomenon which is not humanly universal, a common pitfall for any social scientist who ignores culture. Cultural anthropologists can supply us with many alternative kinemes for "yes" and "no" in various cultures.[16] For example, shaking the hand in front of the face with the forefinger extended, is the Ovimbundu sign of negation, while Malayan Negritos express negation by casting down the eyes. The Semang thrust the head forward in affirmation. In fact, there are even regional "dialects" of affirmation in the Indic area: crown of the head following an arc from shoulder to shoulder, four times, in Bengal; throwing the head back in an oblique arc to the left shoulder, one time, somewhat "curtly" and "disrespectfully" to our taste, in the Punjab and Sind; curving the chin in a downward leftward arc in Ceylon, often accompanied by an indescribably beautiful parakineme of back-of-right-hand cupped in upward-facing-palm of the left hand, plus-or-minus the additional kineme of a crossed-ankle curtsey.

Greeting kinemes vary greatly from culture to culture. In fact, many of these motor habits in one culture are open to grave misunderstanding in another. For example, the Copper Eskimo welcome strangers with a buffet on the head or shoulders with the fist, while the northwest Amazonians slap one another on the back in greeting. Polynesian men greet one another by embracing and rubbing each other's back; Spanish-American males greet one another by a stereotyped embrace, head over the right shoulder of the partner, three pats on the back, head over reciprocal left shoulder, three more pats. In the Torres Straits, the old form of greeting was to bend the right hand into a hook, then mutually scratching palms by drawing away the rigid hand, repeating this several times. An Ainu, meeting his sister, grasped her hands in his for a few seconds, suddenly released his hold, grasped her by both ears and grave the peculiar Ainu greeting cry; then they stroked one another down the face and shoulders. Kayan males in Borneo grasp each other by the forearm, while a host throws his arm over the shoulder of a guest and strokes him endearingly with the palm of his hand. When two Kurd males meet, they grasp one another's right hand, raise them both, and alternately kiss the other's hand. Andamanese greet one another by one sitting down in the lap of the other, arms around each other's necks and weeping for a while; two brothers, father and son, mother and daughter, and husband and wife, or even two friends may do this; the husband sits in the lap of the wife. Friends' "goodbye" consists in raising the hand of the other to the mouth and gently blowing on it, reciprocally. At Matavai a full-dress greeting after long absence requires scratching the head and temples with a shark's tooth, violently and with much bleeding. This brief list could be easily enlarged by other anthropologists,

Kissing is Germanic, Graeco-Roman, and Semitic (but apparently not Celtic, originally). Greek and Roman parents kissed their children, lovers and married persons kissed one another, and friends of the same or different sexes; medieval knights kissed, as modern pugilists shake hands, before the fray. Kissing relics and the hand of a superior is at least as early as the Middle Ages in Europe; kissing the feet is an old habit among various Semites; and the Alpine peasant kisses his own hand before receiving a present, and pages in the French court kissed any article given them to carry.[17] Two men or two women exchange the "holy kiss" in greeting before meetings, in the earlier Appalachian-highland version of the snake-handling cult of the Southeast; the heterosexual kiss is a secular one, not used in public. Another admired gambit is to move the rattlesnake or copperhead back and forward across the face, and closer and closer, until the communicant's lips brush the flickering-tongued mouth of the snake; one Durham minister once offered to kiss the police officers who had raided a snake-handling meeting, to show "no hard feelings," but this offer was not accepted. Kissing, as is well known, is in the Orient an act of private lovemaking, and arouses only disgust when performed publicly: thus, in Japan, it is necessary to censor out the major portion of love scenes in American-made movies. Tapuya men in South America kiss as a sign of peace, but men do not kiss women (nor women, women) because the latter wear labrets or lip plugs. Nose-rubbing is both Eskimo and Polynesian. Djuka Negroes of Surinam show pleasure at a particularly interesting or amusing dance step by embracing the dancer and touching cheek to cheek, now on one side, now on the other—the identical attenuation of the "social kiss" (on one cheek only, however) between American women who do not wish to spoil each other's make-up. And one of the hazards of accepting a decoration in France is a bilateral buss in the name of the Republic. Ona kissing in Tierra del Fuego is performed only between certain close relatives and young married couples or lovers; and not lip-to-lip, but by pressing the lips to the head, cheek, or arm of the other, accompanied by a slight inward sucking.[18]

Sticking out the tongue is a kineme with indisputably diverse significance in varied cultures. In Sung Dynasty China, tongue protrusion was a gesture of mock terror, performed in ridicule; the tongue stretched far out was a gesture of surprise (at the time of the novel, *Dream of the Red Chamber*); in modern south China at least (Kunming), a quick, minimal tongue-protrusion and -retraction signifies embarrassment and self-castigation, as at some social *faux pas* or misunderstanding; it can vary in context from the humorous to the apologetic. Among the Ovimbundu of Africa, bending the head forward and sticking out the tongue means "you're a fool." In India, the long-protruding tongue in the statues of the goddess Kali signifies a monumental, welkinshattering rage, a demon-destroying anger as effective as a glance from the Saivite third eye in the forehead. In New Caledonia, in wooden statues of ancestors carved on houses, the protruded tongue means wisdom, vigor, and plenitude, since the tongue "carries to the outside the traditional virtues, the manly decision, and all the manifestations of life which the word bears in itself." Perhaps this is the meaning, in part, of similar New Zealand carvings, although here there may be other overtones of ancestral fertility, etc. (the meaning of the connecting of the elongated nose and mouth to umbilicus and genitals in Melanesian carvings is unknown to me). In the Carolines, however, the gods are disgusted at the lolling tongues of suicides by hanging, and for this reason refuse entry to the souls of such among the deities. In at least one of the eighteen "Devil Dance" masks in Ceylon, specialized for the exorcistic cure in specific illnesses, the black mask has a protruding red tongue, probably synergistic (to judge from other cognates in the India area) with the extremely exophthalmic eyes which are characteristic of all eighteen of these masks: to frighten out the demons regarded as causing the specific diseases. In Mayan statues of the gods, the protruded tongue signifies wisdom. In Tibet, the protruded tongue is a sign of polite deference, with or without the thrust-up thumb of the right hand, scratching the ears, or removing the hat.[19] Marquesans stick out the tongue as a sign of simple negation. In America, of course, sticking out the tongue (sometimes accompanied by "making a face") is a juvenile quasi-obscene gesture of provocative mockery, defiance, or contempt; perhaps the psychiatrists can explain why this is chiefly a little girl's gesture, though sometimes used playfully by adult women, or by effeminate men. One might also conjecture a European "etymology" behind this gesture in American child-culture, based on this chronological sequence: apotropaic (a stone head with thrust-out tongue and "making a face" on a Roman fort in Hungary, although this etymon may also include a note of defiance as well), protective-defiant (gargoyles with thrust-out tongue on Gothic cathedrals), mock-affirmative (the subordinates of the demon Malcoda in Dante acknowledge a command by sticking out their tongues and making a rump-trumpet)—all with an obscure overtone of the obscenely phallic—whence the modern child-gesture of derision (and there comes to mind a similar "shame on you gesture," using the left-hand pointing gesture and using the similarly held right hand in an outward whittling movement, repeated). But such precarious kinemic "etymologies" must await more adequate ethnographic documentations, and these we largely lack. The Eskimo curl up the tongue into a trough or cylinder and protrude the tongue slightly, but this is not a kineme; it is rather a motor habit, used to direct a current of air when blowing a tinder into flame.

Gestures of contempt are a rich area for study also. A favorite Menomini Indian gesture of contempt is to raise the clenched fist palm downward up to the level of the mouth, then bringing it downward quickly and throwing forward the thumb and the first two fingers. Malayan Negritos express contempt or disgust by a sudden expiration of breath, like our "snort of contempt." Neapolitans click the right thumbnail off the right canine in a downward arc. The *mano cornudo* or "making horns" (first and little fingers of the right hand extended forward, thumb and other fingers folded) is primarily used to defy the "evil eye." The *mano fica* (clenched right fist with thumb protruding between the first and second fingers) is an obscene kineme symbolizing the male genitals; in some contexts its meaning is the same as the more massive slapping of the left biceps with the right hand, the left forearm upraised and ending in a fist;[20] a less massive, though no less impolite, equivalent is making a fist with all save the second ("social finger") and thrusting it upward. Mediterranean peoples are traditionally rich in such gestures; I believe, though with admittedly unsatisfactory evidence, that the "cocked snout" came from Renaissance Italy as a gesture of contempt about the same time as the fork arrived in England in the reign of Elizabeth.

Beckoning gestures have been little collected. In a restaurant, an American raises a well-bred right forefinger to summon a waiter. To express "come here!," a Latin American makes a downward arc with the right hand, almost identical with an American jocular gesture of "go away with you!" The Shans of Burma beckon by holding the palm down, moving the fingers as if playing an arpeggio chord. The Boro and Witoto beckon by moving the hand downward, not upward, as with us, in our face-level, wrist-flexing, cupped-hand "come here!" signal.

Gestures of politesse are equally sparse in ethnographic sources. The Hindu palms-together, thumbs about the level of the chin, is a greeting, a "thank you," and a gesture of obeisance, depending on the context. A Shan, on being done a kindness, may bend over and sniff the sleeve of the benefactor's coat; the meaning is "how sweet you smell," not entirely unlike the Indian "shukriya" (sweetness) meaning "How sweet you are!" Curtseys and bows (almost infinitely graded in depth of bend in the Orient, to express a wide gamut of deference or mock-deference, depending on the social context) are both European and Asiatic. Indic and Oceanic peoples sit down to honor a social superior; Europeans stand up. In both Africa and Melanesia, hand-clapping is a gesture of respect to chiefs and kings. Covering and uncovering the head in deference to gods, kings, and social superiors, is complex, and sometimes contradictory in nature, in Europe and Asia. Taking off or putting on articles of clothing is also full of subtleties of politesse: in classic south India a woman uncovers the upper part of her body in deference, but in America a man puts on his coat to show respect to a lady. The psychology of clothes[21] and the motor habits in handling one's clothing can benefit from much more study: a Plains Indian warrior, for example, could express a wide variety of emotional states, simply through the manner in which he wore his outer robe or cloak. Quite as many gentlemen object to ladies hiking down their skirts or girdles, as ladies object to gentlemen hiking up their pants; and I once witnessed the interview with a young psychiatrist of a female hysteric in which a lively and wholly unconscious colloquy was carried on: she with various tugs at her bodice, skirt-hem, and other parts of her dress and underclothing, he with corresponding "business" with his tie, trousers, etc.[22] Hands were veiled in the clothing before a superior in ancient Rome; traces of this are found in Christian art; and when cardinals approach the Pope to do homage or to receive the hat, they veil their hands in their capes; Moslems also cover the hands before a person of higher rank or when making a visit. The vast folklore on clothing and nudity, the various and changing erotizations of body parts can only be alluded to here; but much of it has relevance to kinesics and paralinguistics.

Conventionalized motor acts in both Occidental and Oriental acting are of relevance to kinesics also. Chinese opera is full of them; Hindu epic drama is a whole gesture language in itself; American silent movies are an excellent source, as are the pantomimes from Chaplin to Marcel Marceau. Stage and movie motor-"business" in modern Russian acting (e.g., in the films "Alexander Nyevski" and Dostoievsky's "The Idiot") seem extravagant and ludicrous to American audiences. Notable in American films are the rapid changes of style in motor acts, so that they are quickly out of date and soon absurd (as also with the gestural tics of some television performers such as Ed Sullivan, used to express affability or endearingly folksy pseudo-embarrassment); notable in oriental drama is the stability of conventionalizations, such that they remain the same for centuries and over many countries.

Conversational gestures are multitudinous: the shaken right forefinger of accusation, sharp criticism, and threat; the recriminatory gesture of right hand thrust out and shaken palm upward (also used for subjective disincrimination with a slight variation, lifting in an upward, outward arc, sometimes with head movements); the eighteenth-century tapping of the right nostril with the right forefinger to express extravagant and amused incredulity; the forefinger spiral above the right cranial hemisphere, to express much the same thing, plus grave doubts about the speaker's mental status; the arched eyebrow for interest, surprise, disbelief. In Indo-Persian art, biting of the fingers expresses surprise. The Argentine "ademanes" are a particularly complete repertoire available for editorial comment on another speaker or the passing scene: kissing upward-held bunched fingers ("Magnifico!"), shaking the bunched fingers ("What a crowd!"), touching beneath the eye with a forefinger ("Do you take me for a sucker?"), stroking beneath the chin with the back of the palm ("I haven't the faintest idea about it" plus-or-minus "And I couldn't care less!"), moving the hand forward, palm down, fingers out lackadaisically ("Don't be spastic! Take it easy! Relax! No sweat! *Mañana!*")—and so on.

"ETHNIC" GESTURE

Much nonsense, in racist terms, has been uttered on this matter; and yet, at different times and places, social groups display quite varying volubility kinemically. "Anglo-Saxons" in a long-current stereotype are supposed to be both rigid and impoverished in kinesic communication (at least intentionally); and yet Englishmen of the first half of the eighteenth century gesticulated freely, and their American counter-parts were, if anything, even less inarticulate kinemically in frontier times. The "grand manner" of oratory lasted until the mid-nineteenth century in England at least, so far as elocutionary gesture is concerned, and has survived even later in some rural areas in America. The Sephardic Jew D'israeli spoke with great economy of gesture and is credited with introducing the more restrained "Victorian" style, although another stereotype has it that Jews as such are highly gesticulatory (what is meant is that, at least in modern times, many Ashkenazi Jews are). The French are also thought to be great gesturers; but they were not in the sixteenth century! French courtiers, before the arrival of the Italian Catherine de Medici, made few gestures and thought them vulgar, but "âmes sensibles" of the Restoration gesticulated freely. Historically, Italy (and those areas, I believe, under ancient Greek influence especially, and not the mid-northern nucleus of early Rome) has been a major source of European gestures. Sicilians are reputed to have first elaborated a gesture language under the tyrant Denys l'Ancien in which they could communicate entirely without words; "legend has it that all the details of the bloody 'Vespro Siciliano' (Sicilian Eve), 1282, in which the people of Palermo massacred several thousand officers and soldiers of the French Army of occupation, were discussed and arranged on the streets by means of gestural signs and symbols only."[23] De Jorio collected an exhaustive "vocabulary" of traditional Neapolitan gesture (some of which I consider goes back to Greek sources).

Psychologists have done some excellent work on kinesics. The foremost among these, undoubtedly, is M. H. Krout.[24] More recently D. Efrón has made a careful comparative study of the gestures of Jews and Italians.[25] His general conclusions are as follows :

> The radius of the gestures of the ghetto Jew seems to be much more confined than that of the Southern Italian. A great deal of his gestural activity appears to be taking place within the immediate area of his chest and face. Whereas in the Italian the gestural sweep often coincides with his arm's length, in the Jew it very seldom reaches a limit above the head or below his hips. In the ghetto Jew the upperarm participates seldom in the movement, and often is more or less rigid and attached to the side of his body. The axis of gestural motion is often centered at the elbow.

(An old joke is to grab the wrists of a person to "shut him up" ; "I talked my arm off" is scarcely a mere figure of speech). The contrasts (extracted *passim* from Efrón) could be summarized as follows :

Jew	*Italian*
Frontal plane, depth, centripetal	Lateral, centrifugal surface plane away from body
One hand	Symmetrical, both
Choppy	Sweeping
"Address"	"Display"
Staccato	Legato
"Familiarity" with person of interlocutor (grabs lapels)	Manipulates, touches part of own physique
Disjunctive	Synergic
Crowds interlocutor	No contact with interlocutor
Gestures punctuate	Gestures "illustrate"
Nervous energy	Animal force
Restricted	Spacious, ample
Elbow pivot	Shoulder pivot, even with finger gestures
Simultaneous, both persons, dual monologue	Alternating, dialogue
Emphatic "attention !" intensificatives	At least 125 manual "words"

Samples of Italian gestures are : "What do you want?" (bunched fingers of both hands before, move upward toward body); good, sweet, pretty (gesture of drinking thumb ; or moustache twisting—the latter identical with a classic *natya* gesture in India); "I don't care" or "La Barbe" (more exactly, "Je m'en fiche" or "Je m'en fou" = fingernails under chin, flip open and out with pivoted hand [sometimes with a "bouche mouée"] ; and "The

Pepper" = "he's nuts" (left fingertips bunched at right elbow, right arm vertical, rotate right hand with fingers slightly bunched).[26]

KINESICS AND THE ORIGIN OF SPEECH

With gesture so clearly a paralinguistic, meaning-bearing phenomenon, it is not surprising that one of the theories of the origin of language should be that speech originated in gesture. The theory is of venerable antiquity. Most recently of anthropologists, La Barre has cautiously suggested that speech may have originated from the *vocal* gestures of higher primate "phatic" communication, i.e., those vocalizations involved with danger-warning, territorialism, fighting, courtship, and the like—vocalizations "international" from ape group to ape group, communicating no more than the affective or hormonal state of the utterer (a statement about the subjective, not the objective, world, as in semantic speech), a "social hormone" that readies the ape group for synergistic action. The notion is one owed to Edward Sapir; but before him the chain of theorists in this vein include Rousseau, Vico, Lucretius, Epicurus, and Democritus. It is important to note, however, that in the later theorists at least the notion always implies primate and hominid *vocalization* or "vocal gesture," that is, the change from "phatic" cries to semantic speech. The relevant quotation from Sapir is that:

> It is likely that most referential symbols go back to unconsciously evolved symbolisms saturated with emotional quality, which gradually took on a purely referential character as the linked emotion dropped out of the behavior in question. Thus shaking of the fist at an imaginary enemy becomes a dissociated and finally a referential symbol for anger when no enemy, real or imaginary, is actually intended. When this emotional de-nudation takes place, the symbol becomes a comment, as it were, on anger itself and a preparation for something like language. What is ordinarily called language may have had its ultimate root in just such dissociated and emotionally denuded cries, which originally released emotional tension.[27]

But this is not what is meant by the psychological theorists, i.e., that *speech* originated from *gesture*. The foremost theorists of this tradition are Paget and Johannesson.[28] The notion would be that "ideas," like the "subsistential entities" of the New Realist philosophers, are all neurological or perhaps *motor sets*—operational (or sub-acute) thought-tonuses in an organism whose life-interests are served thereby and therethrough. No external reality totally corresponds to them; they are nevertheless existential in the sense that muscular tonuses and subacute or residual electrical potentials are existential. These ideas are "motor sets" so long as they are unspoken, i.e., verbalized, expressed overtly; they are a species of "emotive language." (I am aware that, as "devil's advocate," I may have added physiological rationales that, for me, would be required to give plausibility to this kind of theory.) However, for all that speech is after all a motor act, the theory has the wide chasm to jump between purely muscular gesture to specifically *vocal* muscular behavior, and I am unable to surmise how this might occur; at the very least, one would have to postulate some kind of meaningful vocalization as an intermediary step, hence the theory has more technical problems to solve than the speculations of Sapir which, in any case, remain in the area of vocalization. I do not find the Paget-Johannesson theory convincing, because as a cultural anthropologist I find difficulty in discovering anything like "instinctual gesture" in any kineme (which an absolutist "Babel" theory would seem to require), and because semantic gesture often appears to be a back-formation exploiting logically prior linguistic locutions; but perhaps it is better to leave this specialized problem to our colleagues, the linguistic experts.

KINESICS AND MOTOR ACTS INVOLVING THE PRODUCTION OF SOUNDS

One very provocative variant of this kind of thinking is the theory of S. F. Nadel that music came into existence from the wish of primitive peoples to have a special means other than ordinary speech for the purpose of communicating with the supernatural.[29] That is, music is a kind of allelo-language. To my mind, however, music does not appear to have sufficiently fixed and conventionalized meanings certainly to have *accomplished* this end. To be sure, some musical meaning *is* conventionalized, e.g., the *leitmotifs* in Wagnerian music, but these are mainly musically-repetitive melodies that serve as "cognomens" of characters, or musical allusions to other scenes in the musical drama of the Ring.[30] On the other hand, it is my private impression that, in the music of Tschaikovsky, there is a probably unconscious use of horns in orchestration to indicate the blatant and harshly disruptive entrance of the forbidding or commanding father into the languishing violins indicating the mother-relationship—but this is a question of one composer and not Western music at large, the responses of perhaps only one listener and not of a sophisticated musical audience at large (both of which would seem to be required if music is to be a sufficiently "tight" system of meaning-communication). Similarly I know the musically sophisticated wife of an analyst who says of Ravel's "Valse," "This expresses exactly what I feel about life." (I would paraphrase her opinion something like this: "It is an Existentialist piece of music. It starts off singing its melody with childlike innocence and confidence, then BANG! some trauma enters the psychological Eden; afterward the melody picks itself up and sings again, somewhat waveringly, but more or less intact; then

WHAM! the cold winds of the cosmos crash in and knock the melody sprawling, this time rather maiming the melody, which nevertheless gathers itself together bravely, somewhat fragmentarily singing its song again and gradually gaining confidence, but now with the knowledge that further vicissitudes are in store before the final catastrophe.") But, again, this is a private apperception of the music. Music, I believe, is rather more a tonal Rorschach, inviting us to private fantasy, than it is a firmly semantic system of "communication."

Nevertheless, I once had a musically and otherwise very sophisticated student (now a New York psychiatrist) who, on entering an acquaintance's room would look, not at the books, but at the music he found there. For him, the presence of much Bach was indicative of an intricate, orderly, compulsive personality (engineers, he believed, have the neat and mathematical minds that commonly prefer Bach). Mozart indicated the "oral personality," Beethoven "masculine protest," Wagner the exhibitionistic and narcissistic "phallic personality," and Tschaikovsky the hysterical and perverse with much problem concerning father-figures. I can agree with much of what he says, but once again this is primarily of diagnostic significance, at best; and, like the reading of a Rorschach protocol, is mere methodological window-dressing for psychiatric insight which may in fact derive from other cues such as knowledge of the biography and personality of the composer, which is methodologically illegitimate. Furthermore, composers often give their own verbal explications of their intentions and meanings, which is again methodologically illegitimate if we are supposed to obtain sure "communication" directly from the music itself. Most experienced listeners tend to prefer "absolute" music rather than "programmatic" music such as, e.g., Tschaikovsky's "Nutcracker Suite" (here one also has to take the nauseatingly saccharine timbre of the celesta in the "Dance of the sugar-plum fairy"); though there exist other more interesting programmatic compositions like Moussorgsky's witty "Pictures at an Exhibition," Respighi's "Fountains" and "Pines of Rome," or Copland's "Billy the Kid" and "Appalachian Spring." Similarly, I am content to listen, as instructed, to an ancient Russian fertility dance in Stravinsky's "Sacre du printemps," but find my teeth set on edge by Walt Disney's reprogrammatizing of this in *Fantasia* as the evolution of cartooned dinosaurs (Beethoven's "Pastorale" is spoiled for me because I cannot avoid seeing cartooned centaurs lolloping over the landscape: my own apperceptive fantasies are better than Disney's!). In the 'twenties and earlier, program notes to concerts contained an immense amount of apodictic aestheticist nonsense about what one was supposed to hear in a given piece of music; this condescending snobbism was often a mere vehicle for the would-be literary exhibitionism, and not very good at that, of the musical poseur. And for all that, perhaps anyone's apperceptive comments on music may grate on the ears of another listener busy with his own preferred fantasies, just as many listeners "can't stand" the personalities of Wagner, Strauss, Bruckner, or Liszt, as revealed in their music.

Nevertheless, in societies other than our own, music *does* have more fixed semantic conventions. For the Greeks, modes (or tonal key-progressions or "scales") had well-recognized and distinct emotional significance or "ethos." Thus the Dorian mode was virile, vigorous, masculine and martial, whereas the Lydian mode was soft, cloying, enervating, and effeminizing in its very femininity. The intricate Hindu *raga* system is also elaborately conventionalized in its connection with context, god addressed, mood, time of day to be used, etc. Arabic *maqāms* or "melody types" have ethos of a sort also. It is a puzzle to Westerners just how Greeks were able to discern modal differences (e.g. Hypomixolydian from Lydian), for these are not like pianoforte "keys" in successively higher pitches, are far more complex than our major-minor key dichotomy, and depended upon perception of pure configuration for perhaps a score of authentic and their derived plagal modes.

On the other hand, Hindu *raga* music contains the helpful cues of the *alapa* (preliminary statement of the unmodified *raga* "scale," which is then freely improvised upon just as, in American jazz, the "melody type" or composition [e.g., "St. Louis Woman" or "Tiger Rag"] is stated before being improvised upon by instrumentalists, alternating in melody versus accompaniment roles, in otherwise unrecognizable ways), as well as conventionally associated instrumental ornamentations (e.g., *portamento* for one *raga*, slow and increasingly rapid *tremolo* for another, etc.), appropriate instruments (e.g., the *vina* for the goddess Sarasvati, flute for Krishna, etc.), and other helpful contextual cues such as place, time of day, season, etc. Balinese music, because of different levels of acculturational style (Old Polynesian, Hinduist, Chinese, Moslem, European) has many recognizable styles such as *pelog* (narrow-interval scale) and *selendero* (wide-interval pentatonic scale), varied further in tempo, etc.[31]

Like the Hindu *raga* music, Chinese classical music, from the Confucian period onward, also had "ethos" and of a distinctly moral tone, but connected in China with numerology, magic, and government. There was, for instance, the fabled "yellow bell" or *haung chung*, whose sacred absolute pitch a ruler had to ascertain before he could be sure his regime was firmly established in the cosmic scheme. "It was said that the morals and even the future of the state could be known by examining its music, so that the king might use this means of learning whether his vassals ruled their territories well or ill."[32] Native-discerned musical categories are of course notable for the Japanese also; but the categories of such American Indians as the northern Athapaskans were *functional* categories (for hunting, ceremonies, love, canoe-songs, etc.)—long before Bartok's "Gebrauchsmusik"—and not in the present sense stylistically different; indeed, only two musical "styles" are found in the whole of North America (standard and Yuman, characterized by rests and change of register), although in my inexpert opinion I believe to have discerned distinct styles in Amazonian music quite different, of example, from familiar Andean style.

What needs to be emphasized, however, is that the ethos of all these mode-systems had to be learned, and were in no sense "racially" innate.[33] Similarly, the musical signals of specific groups have to be learned. For example,

> . . . in the days when raids by Burman dacoits were common, the scattered Karen who were hiding in the jungle, fearing lest some of their foes were still in ambush, would signal to one another by playing certain notes on . . . jew's-harps. Familiar with the sounds thus produced, which were unintelligible to their enemies, they were able to find one another and come together again.[34]

The Mura, also, when separated by a wide river could, allegedly, "carry on a conversation" by the use of the Quechuan fivestopped flute.[35] But these conventionalizations in musical communication are strictly on a par, so far as their arbitrariness is concerned, with the gestural kinemes of the many Bantu and Sudanic Negroes who have a rich quasi- "sign language."[36] Probably the repertoire of such sporadic "musical languages" is no greater than that of our own military bugle calls (i.e., a limited number of sound-configurations or "tunes" to which conventionalized word meanings have later become attached, though all but the tone-deaf should be able to apprehend the meaning by pitch and rhythm patterns alone). Likewise, I have not encountered evidence to convince me that any African group had a sign language in the sense that the Plains Indians did: African gestures appear to have about the same level of complexity as American Indian trail signs, and no more.

On the other hand, West Africans in particular are rich in symbolic allusiveness. Each Ashanti gold weight refers to a moralistic proverb (e.g., one figure in which two crocodiles at right angles to each other have separate heads and tails but the same body means family food-sharing since there is only one stomach; and another of a man smoking and carrying a powder-keg on his head refers to a proverb roughly translatable as "Discretion is the better part of valor"). In Dahomey a gift of parrot eggs was a delicate hint to an aging divine king that he should commit suicide for the good of his people.[37] However, the cowrie language, for example, had a considerable elaboration. For the Yoruba, sending one cowrie shell with a hole in the back meant defiance; two cowrie shells fastened face to face meant "I want to see you," though when tied back to back, "Go away and stay away." Up to forty cowries were used in messages of the powerful Ogboni league, the meaning depending on the number of shells used, the method of stringing, and the nature of objects placed between the cowries, e.g. a piece of charcoal meant that the prospects of the sender were gloomy. A piece of wood such as was used to clean the teeth meant "As I remember my teeth in the early morning, and during the day, so I remember you as soon as I get up, and often afterwards." A kola nut means peace, welcome, and good health. A bit of sugar signifies "There is no enmity between us."[38] The Uraons of India also have a symbolism of objects; water and mango, "life"; rice, nuts, dates, "fertility"; grinding stone, "home" (cf. our "hearth"); the color blue, "opulence"; bamboo, paddy, "marriageable girl", etc.[39]—a list which the cultural anthropologist could extend almost indefinitely, but which belongs more properly with symbolism rather than kinesics, or, strictly speaking, paralinguistics.

WHISTLING AND DRUM LANGUAGES

More relevant to our subject, perhaps, are the kinetic-semantic systems which embody more elaborate symbolisms and more sustainedly articulate communications. Some of these are not adequately known: the drum-language of the Maya; the whistle language and slit-gong xylophone "talk" of the northern Chin of Burma; Kwoma communication by drumming on tree-roots; humming "language" of the Chinese of Chekiang; whistling communication of the Mazatec, Ibo, Veda, and perhaps also Zapotec and Tlapanec. Perhaps we should mention here syllabic substitution (*Fernruf*) for the Lokele, Duala, and Yaunde, Jabbo falsetto, and Alpine yodelling. The Mexican Kickapoo are said to have some sort of whistling system, but we have no examples of it.[40] It is probable that the whistling systems vary all the way from simple conventionalized signal-isolates, to fairly complete replications of speech. For example, a man in Ashanti wanted his tobacco pipe and told the messenger in whistled tones exactly where the pipe would be found; Lobi and Builsa men also employed a whistling language.[41] Although not enough is reported to be certain of the point, it is probable that the African whistling languages exploit the tonemic patterns in language similarly to drum language. The Canary Islanders' whistled language, however, whatever its aboriginal form, now operates by whistling substitutes for the actual phonemes of spoken Spanish (i.e. not tonemes)—a complete speech surrogate.

The musical and other instruments on which semantically-configurated sounds are transmitted, comprise a wide variety: whistles and horns (Chin of Burma; horns only, Kru of Africa), flutes (Lhota Naga), hollow-seed membranophone (Chinese boys of Fukien), lute (Olombo of the Congo), musical bow and zanza (Africa), membrane drums, iron gongs, slit gongs, and xylophones (Africa, Maya, and perhaps tropical South America), wood troughs (Haka Chin), wooden canoes (Fiji, Choco of Colombia), canoe paddle shaft used as a two-toned instrument (Congo), buttress roots of trees (Melanesia and Indonesia).[42] It is of course well known both to linguists and to communications engineers that any medium whatever can communicate any information whatever through the use of only two differentiated signals or, indeed, only one (present/absent, as in electronic computers with a two digit system of on/off).

The best known systems, of course, are the drum languages of West Africa. Communication in these, basically, replicates the tonemic patterns of oral language in two musical tones or drum-timbres; but it also contains a number of "short-hand" arbitrary conventionalizations. For example, "So close is the articulation between speech and abridged communication among the Tumba (Congo) that the drummer often hums the message he is sending."[43] On the other hand, the Ewe (Togo) have adopted drum-signalling from their Ashanti neighbors, and have taken over signal-messages based on spoken Tshi, i.e., set sentences that become conventionalized; similarly, in another case, when a man signals his wife, "I feel hungry," the three-syllable spoken utterance takes seventeen syllables when drummed; and in the four-toned system of horn signal-melodies, not speech-melody but its abstractions are transmitted.[44] But drum languages should properly be left to the linguists, and need only to be alluded to here.

Non-verbal, muscle-communication, again, has become so familiar in the work of Birdwhistell that it requires no more than mention here. These are of the sort also discussed by Ashley Montagu: the (unconscious) flexing of the foot upon the lower leg in a context of embarrassment; also, marked voluntary contraction of the external sphincter ani muscle; inflation of the vestibule of the lips; lowering of the head when standing, crouching low when sitting; lowering the head, half covering the eyes with the hand; contraction of the muscles of the throat; and elevation of the left shoulder and slight lowering of the head, etc.[45]

MISCELLANY OF SEMANTIC MOTOR ACTS

The fields of kinesics and paralinguistics, though relatively new, are so rich in suggestions for the cultural anthropologist that one almost apologizes for the amount of material one needs at least to allude to, even in passing. The present section is a potpourri of examples which may stimulate the ideas of experts.

Many primitives believe that motor acts of the wife at home will affect the luck of the hunter: Old Stone Age drawings in Africa and Europe often show a line running from the hunter to the woman very likely expressing this notion (sometimes from the bow, weapon, or male genitals to the female genitals, suggesting a symbolic equation of weapon and phallus, or hunting and coitus, which, indeed, is attested to in some American Indian legends, as of a hunter drawing a bow whereupon the deer he is to shoot turns into a beautiful woman whom he marries).[46] Peruvian ceramic art, New Zealand wood carving, ancient Hindu art, and a famous temple in Benares all portray motor acts, often of an erotic nature.

The Balinese have a marked kinesthetic need to remain oriented to the directions "mountainward" versus "seaward," so much so that they become anxious when this habitual orientation is inadvertently lost. Calvin Coolidge is said to have had the presidential bed in the White House oriented north-south and placed on glass saucers, in order to obtain the health benefits of terrestrial magnetism.

> The Hebrew imagines himself to be facing east and describes east, west, north, south by the expressions "before," "behind," "left," "right".... The Indo-European peoples picture themselves as facing north and call the hand towards the rising sun the better hand, the dexterous one, and the other (although the Greek veiled it by euphemisms) the sinister. The Etruscans, on the contrary, thought of themselves as looking south; the Roman augurs continued the tradition and considered the left the lucky hand.[47]

For this reason, "thunder on the left" had a different significance as an omen for the Greeks and the Romans. In Eskimo engravings on ivory, time-sequence in drawings goes from right to left (rather than as in, for example, American cartoons, from left to right, in accordance with the linear sequence of our writing), *viz.*, a running reindeer, then one shot with an arrow, then one fallen, the hunter, the winter hut, and finally hides drying on poles.[48] The various directions of writing, including the Greek "boustro-phic" (back and forth as the ox plows), will of course be familiar to linguists —left to right writing perhaps being dictated by the necessity, in pen and ink writing, of not smudging the part already written (given the normal right-handed person). The predominance of right-handedness even in ancient humans, incidentally, is indicated by positive and negative hand paintings on Old Stone Age cave walls; the matter is not without import-ance because of the left-brain position of the speech center.

A chased silver flask, made in Kashmir, which I obtained in the present Pakistan, has a stopper which opens by unscrewing clockwise, and closes by screwing counter-clockwise—a matter which has alerted me to the fact that many motor habits in India are "backwards" when judged in terms of our own. Sir George Watts has written on this matter that

> There is a peculiarity of all Indian needlework that may in passing be mentioned in this place since it doubtless has something to say to the styles of work produced, namely, the fact that the needle is pulled away from, not drawn toward, the operator. In other words, the action of sewing adopted in India is just the opposite to that pursued in Europe. The persistence with which the inhabitants of Eastern countries work

in this so-called "opposite direction" seems due to the lesser development of the extensor muscles of the body and not a perversity of character. To the same circumstance is due the crouching gait of the people, of the plains of India more especially—the leg being swung, not pulled forward, and in consequence is never fully extended. Of the same nature is the overhead habit of swimming and the jerking of the playing marble by the forefinger of the right hand from between the forefinger and thumb of the left, instead of being propelled by the forcible extension of the thumb. Hence to the same cause also, whatever it may be, must be attributed all the agricultural and industrial operations where strength and skill are put forth in pulling and drawing, not in pushing or propelling.[49]

The matter is perhaps, on occasion, of considerable practical importance, in such concerns as industrial design, the manufacture of tools and implements, etc.

The various kinds of "arrow release" will be familiar to all Americanists. Motor habits in canoeing, etc., might be worthy of study, but have not yet, to my knowledge, been examined. Clockwise and counterclockwise movements in the Sun Dance and other rituals are well documented; in the peyote cult, the proper over-and-under passing of staff and water drum is rigorously specified by purists, because of the symbolisms involved. Motor habits of specific tribes in making artifacts might possibly have some diagnostic value for archaeologists, if these can be detected in the artifact in question (weaving, pottery, core flints, knives, awls, skin scrapers, etc.). Sex dichotomized motor acts might be studied more fully also, e.g., all Yahgan women can swim, but this is a skill unknown to males.[50]

Art conventions, with respect to positioning, perspective, duplication of view, and the like, of objects in visual art, are known to all students of primitive art. Distortion of body parts (e.g. of the lower leg, thigh, etc. to indicate strength or speed) is notable in Bushman-Hottentot art, and is almost in itself diagnostic of this style. Body-proportion distortions, indeed, are a significant feature of all West African art, in properly diagnosing the tribal style involved. A Yoruba *ibeiji* figure, for example, can be instantly recognized because of the convention of not joining the lips at the edges on the carving. The leaving unfinished of a weaving sequence, when a ritual design is put on a secular trade article, will come to mind to all students of Southwestern Indians.

A paper by Doris Webster has long aroused my admiration because of her uncanny ability to make sense of the signs of the zodiac in terms of the body image and the position of body parts (the Fishes, crossed feet; Libra, arms extended, as in balancing; Saggitarius, arch of one foot placed on the knee in a sideways plane of the other leg, etc.).[51] The paranoid science of astrology with its delusions of reference could relevantly be studied in the light of her paper. The classic paper by Tausk[52] on the "schizophrenic influencing machine" as a symbol of parental coitus should also be mentioned here. Treatment of body parts in ancient and primitive art has been used with great brilliance diagnostically in the study of both Stone Age figurines and Maya statues.[53] Diagnostic signs of depression have likewise been discerned through the study of sculpture; and the art expert André Schoeller maintains that the motor "language" in the brush strokes of a painter is as crammed with personal quirks as handwriting. The psychoanalyst, Ernst Kris, diagnosed the Viennese Baroque sculptor Messerschmidt as paranoid, largely on the basis of examples of his curiously distorted busts, a diagnosis easily confirmed by an examination of the sculptor's letters and reports from his acquaintances.[54]

The Chinese have a complex gestural language of assignation, and most of the courtesans are very expert in their interpretation. A forefinger rubbed below the nose means that a man finds a woman attractive and would like to make a more intimate acquaintance; a forefinger tapping the tip of the ear means "No!" while the right hand slapping the back of the left hand means the same. Closed fists, but with the forefingers and second fingers of both extended and rubbed together as if sharpening knives, or putting the two hands together and shaking them like castanettes, have meanings easily imagined. The most infamous of these signs would only be used by the most vulgar of coolies: shoving the right forefinger in and out of the closed palm of the left hand. By means of signs the price and the hour of meeting are also communicated; or else the fan is used to indicate the appropriate information. I have no doubt that similar signs are used on the Spanish Steps in Rome, but I do not know these; the "language of the fan" was known to all coquettes in eighteenth-century court circles in France. In Calcutta I was taught a gesture which effectively got rid of the beggars that besiege Americans as insistently as flies, but unfortunately I never learned what it means.

In advertising, the hand symbol for a well known beer (to indicate "Purity, Body, Flavor" by touching forefinger and thumb, the last three fingers extended) is a gesture equally well known to kinesiologists as an ancient and obscene European gesture for coitus. Kinsey has also made a minor contribution to kinesiology in the following passage:

> The toes of most individuals become curled or, contrariwise, spread when there is erotic arousal. Many persons divide their toes, turning their large toes up or down while the remaining toes curl in the opposite direction. Such activity is rarely recognized by the individual who is sexually aroused and actually doing these things, but the near universality of such action is attested by the graphic record of coitus in the erotic art of the world. For instance, in Japanese erotic art curled toes have, for at least eight centuries, been one of the stylized symbols of erotic responses.[55]

The erotization of body parts (foot, nape of neck, ear, etc.), on the other hand, appears to vary ethnographically quite widely.[56]

To my mind, the artist William Steig has an uncanny ability to portray psychiatric syndromes (especially in his classic, *The Lonely Ones*) largely through the postural tonuses of his figures.[57] From a study of daily column-wide wordless cartoons entitled "Tall Tales" that have appeared during the last two years, I am prepared to give, with exhaustive proofs, and in the appropriate context, a fairly complete psychiatric profile of the artist, Jaffe; I would venture the same, on the same grounds, for Gladys Parker of the series "Mopsy," and for Charles M. Schulz of "Peanuts." One of my students, expert in the Goodenough "Draw-a-Man" projective technique, applied this to the study of "Little Orphan Annie" with extraordinary results; and another has done a brilliant study on the psychological complexes of Pablo Picasso, through a study of his paintings.

The gesture language of the Japanese "tea ceremony" has been adequately described by ethnographers, but never sufficiently analyzed by kinesiologists.

A study of the approved stances and motor modalities in various sports might well be made from the point of view of kinesiology. Particularly absorbing to me has been the observation of the motor "business" and mannerisms of baseball, as observed in the Little League playing of my second son. Various athletes, I maintain, can be matched with their sport, by merely noting the way they sit in classrooms or walk across the campus; and like many other local fans I particularly admire the walking style of the Duke runner, David Sime, especially after he gave up football.

Abbé Dubois made an exhaustive study of the motor acts of an orthodox Brahman, in connection with attendance to excretory acts.[58] Sex-dichotomized motor habits of this sort for men and women are well known to everyone in our society; but these are by no means the same for the appropriate sex in all societies.

Spitting in many parts of the world is a sign of utmost contempt; and yet among the Masai of East Africa it is a sign of affection and benediction, while the spitting of an American Indian medicine man is one of the kindly offices of the healer. The enormous variety and flexibility of male punctuational and editorial-comment spitting is especially rich, I believe, in Southern rural regions. Urination upon another person (as in a famous case at the Sands Point, Long Island, country club, involving the late Huey P. Long) is a grave insult among Occidentals,[59] but it is a part of the transfer of power from one medicine man to another in Africa, or to the patient in curing rituals and initiations.

Hissing in Japan (by sudden breath-intake) is a *politesse* to social superiors, implying the withdrawal of the subject's inferior breath in the presence of the superior person thus complimented. The Basuto applaud by hissing; but in England hissing is rude and public disapprobation of an actor or a political speaker.

The extraordinary complexity of motor and paralinguistic acts involved with drinking liquids in Africa is the subject of an article by A. E. Crawley.[60] The elaborate modesties of eating are also known to ethnologists with respect to India, Polynesia, and Africa.

The kinesic use of interpersonal physical distance will be familiar to this audience from the work of Edward T. Hall's indispensable text for all kinesiologists and paralinguists.[61]

APPLIED KINESIOLOGY

It is easy to ridicule[62] kinesiology as an abstruse, pedantic, and unimportant study by pure scientists. But I believe kinesiology is, on the contrary, one of the most important avenues for better understanding internationally. Consider, as one small example, how Chinese hate to be touched, slapped on the back, or even to shake hands; how easily an American could avoid offense by merely omitting these intended gestures of friendliness![63] Misunderstanding of nonverbal communication of an unconscious kind is one of the most vexing, and unnecessary, sources of international friction. (Consider, for example, the hands-over-the head self-handshake of Khrushchev, which Americans interpreted as an arrogant gesture of triumph, as of a victorious prize-fighter, whereas Khrushchev seems to have intended it as a friendly gesture of international brotherhood.)

Gregory Bateson taught me in Ceylon the great value of attending Indian-made movies as an inexpensive kind of easily available fieldwork; and I have since, gratefully, assiduously attended foreign movies of all kinds. I should like to conclude, as a penultimate example, with some conjectures based on the Russian movie, "The Cranes Are Flying," which I believe explain somewhat the famous United Nations episode of Khrushchev's banging his shoe on a desk in the presence of that august body. I do not understand Russian, so that my comments are based entirely upon observation of the motor acts of the characters in two scenes of this movie. First scene: a soldier in a military hospital receives news that his sweetheart has married another man. Much uncontained total emotion, kinemically; raging, tearing at bandages with the teeth, so that there is potential danger to his war wounds; hospital manager is summoned in person to quell the one-man riot, and bring the social situation back to normal. No stiff-upper-lip Anglo-Saxonism here! The assumption seems to be that the mere feeling of an emotion by a Russian is sufficient legitimation for the expression of it.[64] Anyone, even the highest authority in the context, it is assumed, can legitimately be called upon to help contain it, since the experiencer of the emotion cannot, need not, or is not expected to. (In this connection one recalls the finding of Gorer that the Russian infant is swaddled because, despite his small and unthreatening size, he is regarded as a center of dangerous and uncontained emotion; whereas Polish swaddling is done because the human being is an infinitely precious and fragile thing, in need of this protection.)

Second scene: a little raggamuffin boy, quite self-contained and stolid as a street-urchin alone in the snow, comes into a warm canteen full of Russian women; some minor contretemps in which the little boy's wish is crossed, then: not merely a simple temper tantrum in the child (panhuman phenomenon) *but* all the women begin running around, dropping everything else, as if it were the most natural and necessary thing in the world to help the exploding individual contain his emotion through attention and pacification. Hypothesis: if this is the expectancy of the Russian child in the enculturation experience and evidenced both in his behavior and in that of the soldier, is it possible that Khrushchev was unconsciously using a coercive modality, plausible and understood and unconsciously taken for granted in Russian culture, that wholly missed its mark, certainly for the Anglo-Saxon expectancies of Americans and British present? My reasoning is tenuous; it needs to be supported by masses of ethnographic fact before even being respectfully listened to. But the point I wish to make is that such kinesic and paralinguistic communication is of paramount importance in international relations. Would Pearl Harbor have occurred if we had been able to read the "Japanese smile" of the diplomats as they left their last fateful meeting with Secretary of State Cordell Hull?

My last example has to do with a more modest and homely matter, the act of dunking doughnuts. During the last War there appeared in the North African edition of *Stars and Stripes* a news picture, purporting to portray an American GI teaching an Arab the gentle art of dunking doughnuts. The American is obviously much self-amused, and the whole context of the picture is "See how good Americans make friends with anybody in the world!" by teaching the foreigner a homely aspect of the American's own culture. But, protests the cultural anthropologist, is this what is actually happening here? Is the GI really teaching, or even essentially teaching, the Arab *all there is to know* about doughnut-dunking? For doughnut-dunking also evokes Emily Post, a male vacation from females striving for vertical social mobility, Jiggs and Maggie, the revolt of the American he-man from "Mom" as the modern introject-source for manners in a neomatriarchate— and much else besides. The archly bent little finger (some obscure kineme? wonders the Arab) is an American lampoon of the effete tea-drinking Englishman and reminds us of 1776—and who, after all, won *that* war. It implies the masculine frontier, class muckerism, and effeminately tea-drinking Boston versus the coffee-drinking rest of the country. There may even be an echo of a robust Anglo-Saxon parody of Norman-French manners in Montmorencys and Percivals, and thus recall 1066 and all that. Underlying it all is the classless American society—in which everyone is restlessly struggling to change his social status, by persuading others that he is a "good guy" and a good average nonconformist-conformist. Doughnut-dunking is all this—and more!

Is the Arab, in fact, actually being "taught" all these intricate culture-historical implications of an alien tradition—about which, in all probability, our GI (who only finished high school) is neither conscious nor articulate? On the contrary, the Arab brings to the event his own cultural apperceptions and interpretations. To be sure, Arabs know all about coffee (and sugar too, for that matter) and knew it long before Europeans; in fact, the common European names for these two substances are all derived from the Arabic. The Arab is far more likely to be worried about another matter: is this oddly shaped breadstuff perhaps cooked (O abomination!) in pork-fat; thus is this eating not so much naughty-humorous as filthily blasphemous! But perhaps he may be reassured that the cooking fat does not derive from an unclean animal, and the Arab can be happy that it is cottonseed oil from good old South Ca'lina, or peanut oil, possibly laced with Tay-ex-us beef suet—none of which were prohibited by the Prophet. Where, then, can he search for an explanation of the GI's manifest amusement at himself in his doughnut-dunking? Ah! At last it is clear: the doughnut is an obscene symbol for the female (such as is common in Arab life), with coffee "black as night, hot as hell, and sweet as a woman," as the Arab prefers it. Now, perhaps, in universal male confraternity, the Arab can join with his GI friend in tasting the sweetness of women (O, of course, that powdered sugar is intended to symbolize the face powder of those obscenely bare-faced Christian women!). But these outlandish paynim kaffirs are certainly peculiar buzzards in their symbolisms! However, let us be reassured, for these are the Arab's ratiocinations, not ours. For all that we have been doing, the whole time, is sitting quietly here, with the best of good intentions, purely and simply dunking doughnuts!

NOTES

1. These older sources are: W. P. Clark, *Indian Sign Language* (Washington-Philadelphia, 1885); L. F. Hadley, *Indian Sign Talk* (Chicago, 1893); S. H. Long, "The Indian language of signs," *Expedition to the Rocky Mountains*, vol. I (1832), pp. 378–394; G. Mallery, "Sign language among North American Indians," *Bureau of American Ethnology*, I (1870–1880), 263–552, and "A collection of gesture-signs and signals of the North American Indians with some comparisons," *Bureau of American Ethnology Miscellaneous Publications*, 1 (1880); H. L. Scott, "The sign language of the Plains Indians of North America," *Archives of the International Folk-Lore Association*, 1 (1893), 1–206, and W. Tomkins, *Universal Indian Sign Language of the Plains Indians of North America* (San

Diego, 1926). In this context should be mentioned J. E. Ransom's paper on "Aleut semaphor signals," *American Anthropologist*, 43 (1941), 422–477.

2. It might serve the convenience of linguists to have main ethnographic sources listed here: R. M. Berndt, "Notes on the sign language of the Jaralde tribe of the lower River Murray, South Australia," *Royal Society of South Australia, Transactions and Proceedings and Report*, 64 (1940), 267–272. A. C. Haddon, "The gesture language of the Eastern Islanders [of Torres Straits,]" *Reports of the Cambridge Anthropological Expedition to the Torres Straits*, vol. 3 (1907), 261–262. A .W. Howitt, *Native tribes of Southeast Australia* (London-New York, 1904), pp. 723–735. M. Meggitt, "Sign language among the Walbiri of Central Australia," *Oceania*, 25 (1954), 2–16. C. P. Mountford, "Gesture language of the Ngada tribe of Warburton Ranges, Western Australia," *Oceania*, 9 (1938), 152–155. C. G. Seligman and A. Wilkin, "The gesture language of the Western Islanders," *Report of the Cambridge Anthropological Expedition to the Torres Straits*, vol. 3 (1907), 255–260, and E. C. Stirling, *Report of the Work of the Horn Scientific Expedition to Central Australia*, part IV (London-Melbourne, 1896), pp. 111–125.

3. Rijnberk, G., *Le Language par Signes Chez lez Moines* (Amsterdam, 1953).

4. An excellent bibliography may be found in F. Hayes, "Gestures: A working bibliography," *Southern Folklore Quarterly*, 21 (1957), 218–317 *passim*.

5. Lexicon of trade jargon, *Federal Writers' Project, Mss.* in the Library of Congress, Washington: C. G. Loomis, "Sign language of truck drivers," *Western Folklore*, 5 (1956), 205-206; D. C. Phillot, "A note on the mercantile sign language of India," *Journal and Proceedings, Royal Asiatic Society of Bengal*, N.S., 3 (1906), 333–334, and idem, "A note on the sign-, code-, and secret-languages, etc., amongst the Persians," *Journal and Proceedings, Royal Asiatic Society of Bengal*, N.S., 3 (1907), 619–622; O. Ribsskog, *Hemmilige Språk og Tegn. Tatersprâk, Tivolifolkenes språk, Forbrytersprâk, Gattegutsprâk, Bankersprâk, Tegn, Vinkelog Punktskrift* (Oslo, 1945); Anon., "Tobacco auctioneer gestures" *Greensboro* [N.C.] *Daily News*, 29 September 1944; see also painting of similar gestures in U.S.A. national magazines in advertisements for Lucky Strike cigarettes in 1942.

6. Coomaraswamy, A. and G. (translators), of Nandikesvara, *The Mirror of Gesture*, second edition (Cambridge 1936), and Russell Meriwether Hughes [La Meri, pseud.], *The Gesture Language of the Hindu Dance* (New York, 1941).

7. Tyra af Kleen, Mudras, *The Ritual Hand-Poses of the Buddha Priests and the Shiva Priests of Bali* (1924).

8. R. Young, *Analytical Concordance to the Bible* (New York, 1936) (vid. sub "Hand," "Embrace," "Greet," "Kiss," "Salute," "Bless," "Head," etc.); D. Efrón, *Gesture and Environment: A Tentative Study of Some of the Spatio-Temporal and "Linguistic" Aspects of the Behavior of Eastern Jews and Southern Italians in New York City* (New York, 1941); A. de Jorio, *La Mimica Degli Antichi Investigata nel Gestire* (Naples, 1832). The profusely-illustrated work of F. T. Elworthy, *Horns of Honour*, (London, 1900), is world-wide in scope, occasionally overspeculative, but it is an indispensable source for kinesiologists.

9. Abraham, K., "A short study of the development of the libido, viewed in the light of mental disorders," in *Selected Papers of Karl Abraham* (London, 1927), pp. 418–501.

10. Thieme, F. P., "Lumbar breakdown caused by the erect posture in man," *Anthropological Papers, Museum of Anthropology, University of Michigan,* 4 (1950).

11. La Barre, W., "The cultural basis of emotions and gestures," *Journal of Personality,* 16 (1947), 49–68, pp. 62–63.

12. Dr. Sebeok has made to me, in correspondence, the interesting suggestion that this stereotyped kineme may be traced to an old German silent film of *The Golem,* which deals with a medieval Jewish legend. Sebeok also maintains that there is a quite distinctive urban-Swedish style of walking, but I have not had opportunity to study this. It is my impression also, from seeing numerous Italian movies, that there is a distinctive Roman walk.

13. Montagu, M. F. A., "Natural selection and the origin and evolution of weeping in man," *Science,* 130 (1959), 1572–1573. See also his paper "Why man laughs," *Think,* 26, 4 (April 1960), 30–32.

14. Examples of this are discussed in W. La Barre, "Obscenity: An anthropological appraisal," *Law and Contemporary Problems,* 20 (1955), 533–543.

15. Ellis, H., *Studies in the Psychology of Sex,* 4 vols. (New York, 1936), 3, 393 ff., gives numerous examples indicating that coitus, micturition, defecation, and walking are culture-conditioned, as also is childbirth.

16. A number of examples are given in La Barre, *Cultural basis,* pp. 50–51.

17. E. Crawley has a chapter on "The nature and history of the kiss," in his *Studies of Savages and Sex* (New York, n.d.), 113–136.

18. Cooper, J. M., "The Ona," 143 *Bulletin, Bureau of American Ethnology,* I, 107–125, esp. p. 118.

19. The desirability of multiple sources on such a matter is indicated here: R. D. Mallery (ed.), *Masterworks of Travel and Exploration* (New York, 1948), p. 271 (Tibetans put out their tongue in polite deference to a police official in Lhasa investigating their provenience and purposes); p. 275 (Tibetans scratched their ears and put out their tongues at Europeans when they break out their pictures, microscopes, etc., some with mouths open in awe); Hayes, *op. cit.,* p. 223 ("In Tibet, customary greeting to a fellow traveller: thrust up thumb of right hand and thrust out the tongue"); H. Bayley, *The Lost Language of Symbolism,* 2 vols. (London, 1912), 2,128, noted in Hayes, p. 226: "In Tibet a respectful salutation is made by removing hat and lolling out the tongue." See also: A. Sakai, *Japan in a Nutshell,* 2 vols. (Yokohama, 1949), 1,131—"Formerly every *Sambaso* [a kind of prologue in a classical play, Kabuki as well as Bunraku] doll or mask had its tongue thrust out in accordance with the greatest obeisance performed in Tibet, from which, according to the late Rev. Ekai Kawaguchi, *Sambaso* was introduced."

20. The Boro Witoto of Amazonia have a sign to express desire for coitus, but this is a mere jest or ribald suggestion: the right elbow is grasped with the left hand, the elbow being flexed so as to have the right hand extend upwards; it is, in fact, the letter Z of the deaf-and-dumb

alphabet. Note that this is somewhat the opposite of the American obscenity, so far as right and left are concerned.

21. The British psychoanalyst, J. C. Flügel has shown an exquisite sensitivity to meanings in his monograph, *The Psychology of Clothes* (London, 1930). I have not seen E. B. Hurloch, *The Psychology of Dress*, (1929), or F. A. Parsons, *Psychology of Dress* (1921).

22. In this same psychiatric clinic, at another time, I also observed a self-justifying male patient giving a long song-and-dance about himself, while slightly to his rear beside him, his psychiatrist (of German origin) gave a complete editorial comment on his patient's story, entirely through facial gestures and motions of his head—fully as skillful a performance as John O'Hara's in the original short story version of "Pal Joey" in which a self-justifying heel condemns himself out of his own mouth.

23. Efrón, D., *Gesture and Environment* (New York, 1941), pp. 25, 30–31, 38, 59.

24. The major relevant works of Krout are as follows: "Autistic gestures," *Psychological Monographs*, 46 (1935), 1–126; *Introduction to Social Psychology* (New York, 1942), esp. 313 et seqq.; "Symbolic gestures in clinical study of personality," *Transactions of the Illinois State Academy of Science*, 24 (1931), 519–523; "The social and psychological significance of gestures," *Journal of Genetic Psychology*, 47 (1935), 385–412; "A preliminary note on some obscure symbolic muscular responses of diagnostic value in the study of normal subjects," *American Journal of Psychology*, 11 (1931), 29–71; "Further studies in the relation of personality and gesture: A nosological analysis of autistic gestures," *Journal of Experimental Psychology*, 20 (1937), 279–287, "Understanding human gestures," *Scientific Monthly*, 49 (1939), 167–172.

25. Efrón, *op. cit.*, p. 43, for quotation.

26. Anthropologists should not neglect other contributions of psychologists to kinesics. "Numerous experiments based on the meaning of gesticulation have been made and reported on, especially since about 1920. A selected number of these are included in the [Hayes] bibliography. Students of folk gestures will find a mine of valuable information in the Psychological Abstracts," published monthly by the American Psychological Association [see under entries: Gesture, Face, Hand, Emotion, etc.] (Hayes, *op. cit.*, p. 292).

27. W. La Barre, *The Human Animal* (Chicago, 1954), pp. 169, 349 (361 in the 4th and subsequent printings).

28. Sir Richard A. S. Paget, "Gesture language," *Nature*, 139 (1937), 198; "Gesture as a constant factor in linguistics," *Nature*, 158 (1946), 29; *Human Speech* (New York-London, 1930), "Sign language as a form of speech," Paper read at the Royal Institute of Great Britain (1935), *Babel, or the Past, Present and Future of Human Speech* (London, 1930), esp. ch. I; *This English* (London, 1935); and "Origin of language, gesture theory," *Science*, 99 (1944), 14–15; A. Johannesson, *Origin of Language* (Reykjavik, 1949); *Gestural Origin of Language* (Reykjavik-Oxford 1952); "Origin of language," *Nature*, 157 (1946), 847–8, and "Origin of language (in imitation of gestures)," *Nature*, 162 (1948), 902.

29. Nadel, S. F., "The origins of music," *Musical Quarterly*, 16 (1930), 538–542.

30. Of course, Nadel's theory does not suffer from the necessity of

explaining *written* music, which is a phenomenon after the fact of actual vocally- or instrumentally-produced music. Musical notation, it is true, is an internationally-understood symbolic system with *instructions to action* (apart from the largely Italian expressive instructions which are purely linguistic), and as such are chronologically and logically *posterior* symbolic systems, strictly of the order of Laban's dance notation and Birdwhistell's system of descriptive kinesic notation.

31. It is interesting that, on much the same historical and classbound grounds, Western music also has musical "vocabulary-categories" similar to those of words (Norman genteel, Anglo-Saxon vulgar, neo-Latin and neo-Greek intellectual and scholarly words, advertising neologisms sometimes woefully aping these, profanity, obscenity, jocular profanity- and obscenity-avoiding circumlocutions, book-writing vocabularies, cant, trade and other jargons, colloquialisms, dialect-regional words and phrases instantly identifiable, oratorical words, baby talk, etc.)—of which every careful stylist must be constantly aware—those in music being classical (infinitely subdivisible by periods and composers from meterless ictus of pure-melody Gregorian plainsong to successively discernible types so real that they can be satirized, whether by Prokofief or Alec Templeton), jazz (again subdivided by the knowledgeable into blues, ragtime, swing, bebop, etc. by technical scale-differences, tempo, timbre, ornamentation, etc.), as well as "hill-billy" (used in both sacred and secular contexts), oldtime-popular of several periods (Stephen Foster *versus* "Dardanella" *versus* "Smoke Gets in Your Eyes" *versus* "The Peppermint Twist" which last is immediately known as contemporary and which must dubiously wait for immortality), children's sing-song verses (often of great antiquity), etc., most of which musical categories are instantly recognized by most persons in our culture.

32. Creel, H. G., *The Birth of China* (New York, 1937), p. 331. Confucius (*Analects* xv, 10) urged as a model the music of the ancient Succession Dance, "for the tunes of Chêng are licentious"; the Prince of Wei, however, liked the music of Chêng and Wei because they at least kept him from falling asleep in his full ceremonial gear, which the traditional music did not. L. C. Goodrich, *A Short History of the Chinese People*, 2nd ed. (New York-London, 1943), p. 52, fn. 20.

33. For example, a Chinese gentleman once remarked that he found Sousa's march "The Stars and Stripes Forever" embarrassing because of its marked "erotic" rhythms (which is not our apperception!: virile, aggressive, soldierly, patriotic). On the other hand, I have heard Chinese operas in which the libretto indicates a father's grief at the death of a son but the music a wholly inappropriate "jaunty" tempo as of joy. Naïve travelers' apperception of the "sad" or "minor" key music of primitives is largely nonsense, therefore; the natives merely have different scale systems which we mis-hear.

34. Marshall, H. T., "The Karen people of Burma," *Ohio State University Bulletin*, 26, 13 (1922), p. 163.

35. Church, G. E., *Aborigines of South America* (London, 1912), p. 138.

36. Since these are not so well known as some other gestural systems, it may be well to describe a few of these for the Ovimbundu. Among them, gestures of anger and contempt are common, and certain actions are used to communicate with deaf persons. Counting can be done from

one to ten with a moderately complex system of finger gestures. An insulting gesture is made by holding up the left arm with the fist closed, the left wrist grasped and shaken by the right hand (meaning that one is so angry that he can't find words). Drawing the right index finger across the mouth means completion, as also does rubbing the palms quickly together. "Go away" is an extended arm, flipping the fingers outward; "Come here" is a scratching motion of the fingers on the extended hand (W. D. Hambley, *Source book for African Anthropology* [= *Field Museum of Natural History, Anthropological Series*, 26], 1957, 318–319).

37. This is to be compared with the European "language of flowers," in which such flowers as the forget-me-not, lily, rose, pansy, rue, Parma violet, etc., have a symbolic significance. The Palaung of Burma have a similar "language of leaves," used in lovemaking and courtship. To be compared also are color-symbolisms such as the red-green-yellow of navigation lights and traffic signals, "yellow," "blue," "black-hearted," "green with envy," red (for passion), black (for mourning), white (for purity), yellow (signifying in late-Medieval England, I believe, "carrying the torch" of unrequited love), as well as the rich color-symbolisms of, especially Southwestern, American Indians (often connected with ritual objects, gods, directions), and also the color symbolisms of many other peoples. Compare also the elaborate ways in which feathers of specific birds are notched, dyed, and tipped, to indicate further information on the Plains Indian war-bonnet. But these symbolisms are connected with specific *objects*, used or worn or sent, and are not kinemically significant with respect to motor acts as such, hence are beyond the scope of the present paper.

38. Hambley, *op. cit.*, p. 320. In such *object*-communication via conventionalized symbols, animals are often used to indicate human characteristics. For example, among the Boro of Amazonia, the snake symbolizes evil; the tapir, blindness and stupidity; dog, cunning deceit; agouti or cabybara, wit and practical joking (since it is a trickster like the American Indian coyote, or the African hare, both of whom outmaneuver others); boa constrictor, silence and strength; parrot, irresponsibility (as in chattering women who betray secrets); peccary, constancy; tiger, bravery; monkey, tenacity of life (because, when shot, it may hang onto a limb with its hands for some time after death); sloth, laziness; hawk, cunning; etc. (T. Whiffen, *The North-West Amazons*, London, 1915, p. 243). Similarly, among the Singhalese, the hamsa or sacred goose of Hinduism, stands for discrimination (since it is supposed to be able to drink milk only from a bowl of mixed milk and water), and (unaccountably!) for a beautiful gait; and, in erotic poetry, for the breasts of women. The lion, the mythical ancestor of the Singhalese, stands for majesty and power (A. K. Coomaraswamy, *Medieval Singhalese Art*, 1908, 81 ff.). In the Indic culture sphere, the elephant stands for the male, royalty, or the god Indra (for whom elephants, monsoon clouds, are the *vahana* or vehicle, much as the bull is Shiva's *vahana*, the peacock Saraswati's, the mouse Ganesha's, etc.); in legends of Krishna, the elephant's head and trunk symbolizes male genitals; since Buddhist times, the lotus symbolizes the female in India.

39. MacE. Leach, review of W. G. Archer's book on Oraon poetry, in *American Anthropologist*, 57 (1955), 183–184, esp. p. 184.

40. Stern, Th., "Drum and whistle 'languages': An analysis of speech surrogates," *American Anthropologist*, 59 (1957), 487–506.

41. Hambly, *op. cit.*, p. 318.

42. Stern, *op. cit.*, pp. 492, 493.

43. Stern, *op. cit.*, p. 488.

44. Stern, *op. cit.*, pp. 490, 491, 496.

45. Montagu, M. F. A., review of an article by L. A. Dexter, in *Psychiatry*, 6 (1943), pp. 255–256.

46. "Ikpakhuak had bad luck in hunting one day, and Higilak discovered through her familiar spirit that she had been sewing too much deerskin clothing, while Ikpakhuak had also been at fault by hammering too much on the stones loosening them for caches, neither of which things should be done to excess on the pack of the migration [of caribou]" (Jenness, D., "The Life of the Copper Eskimo," *Report of the Canadian Arctic Expedition*, 12, 1923, p. 185).

47. *Hastings Encyclopedia of Religion and Ethics*, 10: 73–74.

48. See Figure 24, Singer *et al.*, *History of Technology*, 1: 41.

49. Watts, Sir George, *Indian Art* (London, 1904), pp. 370–371.

50. Review by R. H. Lowie, in *American Anthropologist*, 40 (1938), 495–503, esp. p. 496.

51. Webster, D., "The origin of the signs of the zodiac," *American Imago*, 8 (1951), 31–47.

52. Tausk, V., "On the origin of the influencing machine in schizophrenia," *Psychoanalytic Quarterly*, 2 (1933).

53. Heilbronner, P., "Some remarks on the treatment of the sexes in palaeolithic art," *International Journal of Psychoanalysis*, 19 (1938), 441; Wallace, A. F. C., "A possible technique for recognizing psychological characteristics of the ancient Maya from an analysis of their art," *American Imago*, 7 (1951), 3–22.

54. Boyer, L. B., "Sculpture and depression," *American Journal of Psychiatry*, 106 (1950), 606–615. *Time* magazine, XLIX, 23 (9 June 1947), p. 45. Kris, E., "Ein geisteskranker Bildhauer," *Imago*, 19 (1933), 384–411.

55. Kinsey, A., *et al.*, *Sexual Behavior in the Human Female* (Philadelphia–London), p. 620.

56. La Barre, W., "The erotization of body parts in various cultures," address to the Yale Anthropology Club (1936).

57. La Barre, W., "The apperception of attitudes, responses to *The Lonely Ones* of William Steig," *American Imago*, 6 (1949), 3–43.

58. Dubois, Abbé J. A., *Hindu Manners, Customs and Ceremonies*, 3rd ed. (Oxford, 1906).

59. See, in this connection, the paper by Karl Abraham, comprising chapter XIII of his *Selected Papers* (London, 1927), pp. 280–298; and also the references on the urethral personality in W. La Barre, *They Shall Take up Serpents: Psychology of the Southern Snake Handling Cult* (Minneapolis, 1962), p. 197, note 120.

60. Crawley, A. E., "Drinks and drinking," *Hastings Encyclopedia of Religion and Ethics*, 5: 72–82.

61. Hall, E. T., *The Silent Language* (New York, 1959).

62. *Horizon* magazine, in 1959–1961, in a reference I cannot locate.

63. Consider, indeed, that the atomic bomb need never have been dropped, if an interpreter had only properly translated the Japanese word *mokusatsu* (W. La Barre, *The Human Animal*, pp. 171, 348 [p. 360 in 4th and later printings]).

64. Is there any remote connection here with the Siberian "olonism" that S. M. Shirokogoroff (*Psychomental Complex of the Tungus*, London, 1935) writes of: when the underprivileged underdog expresses the most violent and psychotic emotions, and the whole society turns out to recapture the run-away "wild man" in the forest and then attempts to pacify him? If he succeeds in influencing the people, he may become a shaman; if not, he is a psychotic, in need of cure by an established shaman.

SILENT ASSUMPTIONS IN SOCIAL COMMUNICATION*†

Edward T. Hall

*t*he investigations reported briefly in this paper deal with *proxemics*, the study of ways in which man gains knowledge of the content of other men's minds through judgments of behavior patterns associated with varying degrees of proximity to them. These behavior patterns are learned, and thus they are not genetically determined. But because they are learned (and taught) largely outside awareness, they are often treated as though they were innate. I have found this type of behavior to be highly stereotyped, less subject to distortion than consciously controlled behavior and important to individuals in the judgments they form as to what is taking place around them at any given moment in time.

Thoreau wrote *Walden* (1) over 100 years ago. Yet in a section entitled "Visitors" he describes how conversational distance and subject matter are functions of each other and, what is even more remarkable, he names some of the variables by means of which people unconsciously set distances.

"One inconvenience I sometimes experienced in so small a house, is the difficulty of getting to a sufficient distance from my guest when we began to utter the big thoughts in big words. You want room for your thoughts to get into sailing trim and run a course or two before they make their port. The bullet of your thought must have overcome its lateral and ricochet motion and fallen into its last and steady course before it reaches the ear of the hearer, else it may plough out again through the side of his head. Also our sentences wanted room to unfold and form their columns in the interval. Individuals, like nations, must have suitable broad and natural boundaries, even a considerable neutral ground, between them. I have found it a singular luxury to talk across the pond to a companion on the opposite

* Reprinted from *Disorders of Communication*, Vol. XLII, Research Publications, A.R.N.M.D., by permission.

† Research supported under grants from the National Institute of Mental Health and the Wenner-Gren Foundation.

side. In my house we were so near that we could not begin to hear—we could not speak low enough to be heard; as when you throw two stones into calm water so near that they break each other's undulations. If we are merely loquacious and loud talkers, then we can afford to stand very near together, cheek by jowl, and feel each other's breath; but if we speak reservedly and thoughtfully we want to be farther apart, that all animal heat and moisture may have a chance to evaporate. If we could enjoy the most intimate society with that in each of us which is without, or above being spoken to, we must not only be silent, but commonly so far apart bodily that we cannot possibly hear each other's voice in any case. Referred to this standard, speech is for the convenience of those who are hard of hearing; but there are many fine things which we cannot say if we have to shout. As the conversation began to assume a loftier and grander tone, we gradually shoved our chairs farther apart till they touched the wall in opposite corners, and then commonly there was not room enough."

The insights and sensitive observations of Thoreau are helpful in pointing up certain consistencies in behavior in heretofore unsuspected areas, such as perceptions of body heat. They strengthened my original premise that man's behavior in space is neither meaningless nor haphazard. Yet there are paradoxes associated with proxemic behavior that need explaining.

SOME PARADOXES

A casual observer confronted with American reactions to being touched or approached too closely by foreigners is likely to dismiss such reactions as minor annoyances that will disappear as people get to know each other better. More careful investigation reveals, however, several puzzling questions, or anomalies, which suggest that there is more to behavior patterns based on interpersonal distance than meets the eye.

An anthropologist becomes accustomed to resistance to and denial of the idea that there are regularities in human behavior over which the individual has little or no control. But why do so many people, when faced with other people's behavior, take "interference" with space patterns so personally? And why is there apparently so little that they can do to relieve their feelings?

One of my interview subjects, a colleague, quite typically explained that, after 12 years of working with French culture, he still could not accustom himself to the French conversational distance. He found it "uncomfortably" close, and he found himself annoyed with Frenchmen, possibly because he felt they were getting too familiar. Like other Americans who have been brought up to resent being crowded, he used the device of barricading himself behind his desk.

Another anomaly is associated with architecture. Why is it that, even with a history of building dating back to predynastic Egypt, with surveying developed somewhere around 2500 B.C. and with the magnificence of the Parthenon achieved by the fifth century before Christ, architects have failed to develop a way of describing the experience of space? Recently Philip Thiel (2) published a notation system for describing open spaces.

By what means do people make spatial distinctions? How do people judge distance from each other and teach it to their young with such uniformity and still apparently not know that they are teaching it at all? Technically the work of transactional psychologists answered some questions and raised others (3), while Gibson's (4) approach is the most comprehensive treatment of how man perceives space visually. Asking subjects how they differentiate between distances or why they feel so strongly about matters of space, doesn't help—even the most cooperative subjects can give you only bits of information. Most people have only the vaguest notion of the rules governing the use of their immediate and distant receptors.

In approaching any new problem, the anthropologist must constantly remind himself that, even though he is faced with complexity on all sides, the components that go to make up the complexity must of necessity not be overly complex. Cultural systems are organized in such a way that the basic components (structure points) can be controlled by all *normal* members of the group. For example, varied and rich as languages are, all normal members of a group learn to speak and understand them.

In essence, one looks for simple distinctions that can be made by any normal person and go beyond individual differences.

This is a report of a study in progress. Additional data will undoubtedly result in revisions. If the data seem obvious, I can only say that to me they seemed obvious *after* I had identified the principal structure points of the system. Then I wondered why it had taken so long to reach this particular point. Recently Bruner (5) stressed something the linguistic scientist has known for a long time: that people do not necessarily have to know the structure of a system of behavior in order to control it.

RESEARCH STRATEGY

A combination of research strategies was employed during this study. Techniques included observation, participant's observations, interviews—structured and unstructured—and biweekly sessions with four blind subjects.* Normal subjects were drawn predominantly from the Washington area from the educated-professional group. Fifteen Americans and 18 foreign subjects were interviewed in depth. Interviews lasted from 3 to 15 hours in increments of 2 to 3 hours. Data were gathered from 100 additional

* These sessions were conducted in cooperation with Dr. Warren Brodey of the Washington School of Psychiatry in the winter of 1961 to 1962.

subjects in unstructured, natural situations. Foreign subjects included English, French, German, Swiss, Dutch, Spanish, Arab, Armenian, Greek and West Africans studying in the United States. These subjects were used in much the same way as subjects are used by the linguist, *i.e.*, as examples of their own particular systems. A few hours with one subject does little more than provide some of the basic and most obvious structure points as well as contrasting examples of proxemic behavior.

Since people apparently cannot describe the patterns that enable them to discriminate between one distance and another, it is next to useless to question them directly about how they go about perceiving spatial relations. It has been necessary to resort to various projective-type devices as a means of getting subjects started thinking about their own spatial experiences. Some of the most valuable leads were gathered as a result of casual conversations when a subject would "warm up" and begin talking about an experience he had had with a particular person.

"Boy, you ought to see a guy we have in our office; everybody talks about it. They even kid him a lot. He comes right up to you, breathes in your face. I sure don't like seeing his face so close, with pop eyes and nose distorted all over the place. He feels you a lot, too. Sometimes we wonder if there isn't something wrong with him."

"He breathes down my neck; why can't he keep his hands off you?"

"Did you ever notice how close he stands to you—it gives me the willies."

"She's one of those who's always pawing you; did you ever notice how some people stand much too close?"

Many of these utterances are virtually stream-of-consciousness. They are valuable because they provide clues to what specific events in other people's behavior stand out as significant.

The Arabs and the English complain (for different reasons) because Americans do not listen. Greeks experience a great flatness in our interaction with them—like eating unsalted rice, they say. In each complaint there lie valuable data concerning the nature of the feedback mechanisms used by *both* parties.

In research of this sort one is faced with a paradox, namely, it is the commonplace that makes the difference when confronted with someone else's "commonplace." Another paradox is that, in writing and talking about one's reactions to being touched and breathed upon by a stranger, the description loses much of the immediate effect. The reactions are so obscure, so small and so seemingly inconsequential that at times it is difficult to realize they may add up to something.

The distinction that Hediger (6) makes between "contact" and "noncontact" species can also be made for man or groups of men. Indeed, it seems to be the first and possibly the most basic distinction between groups.

As the term implies, the "contact" group is characterized by considerable touching, both in private and public. The "non-contact" group perceives the contact group as overly familiar and sometimes "pushy," while the contact group refers to the non-contact as "standoffish," "high-hat," "cold" or "aloof."

In addition to the contact, non-contact category, man seems to share a number of features of the generalized mammalian pattern described by Hediger (6). Personal distance and social distance are certainly present though—inasmuch as a certain amount of confusion exists because of misunderstanding of Hediger's terminology—it may eventually become necessary to define operationally what is meant by these terms. The observations which follow refer to the non-contact group.

DISTANCE SETS

For the American non-contact group, and possibly for others as well, four distance sets seem to encompass most, if not all, behavior in which more than one person is involved. These are referred to as intimate, casual-personal, social-consultative, and public. Each distance set is characterized by a close and a far phase.

The perception of distance and closeness apparently is the result of an interplay of the distant and immediate receptor systems (visual, auditory, olfactory), the systems in the skin that record touch and heat flow and those in the muscles that feed back information concerning where a part of the body is at any given moment in time. *The transition from one group of receptors to another is the boundary point between sets*, as will be shown subsequently.

For Americans, space judgments seem to depend principally on the tactile-kinesthetic and visual senses, although the olfactory, heat-radiation and oral-aural systems are also involved.

The two most commonly observed sets are *casual-personal distance* and *social-consultative distance*.* The descriptions which follow are idealized stereotypes for subjects in non-excited or non-depressed states with 20–20 vision, without excessive background noise, and at average comfortable temperature (55° to 85° F.).

Social-Consultative Distance

The distinguishing features of this distance (close phase: 4 to 7 feet plus or minus 6 inches at each end; far phase: 7 to 12 feet plus or minus

---

* Not to be confused with "social distance," a term used by both Hediger (6) and Bogardus (7). "Social-consultative distance" as used here is not at all like Bogardus' "social distance," which is the distance separating two members of a group in a social hierarchy. It is much closer in meaning to Hediger's term "social distance."

6 inches at each end) are that intimate visual detail in the face is not perceived and that nobody touches or expects to touch unless there is some
special effort. Voice level is normal for Americans. There is little change
between the far and the close phases, and conversations can be overheard
at a distance of up to 20 feet. (There is no loudness scale for the voice that
is adaptable to descriptions such as these.)

I have observed that in over-all loudness, the American voice at these
distances is under that of the Arab, the Spaniard, the South Asian Indian
and the Russian; and it is somewhat above that of the English upper class,
the Southeast Asian and the Japanese.

CLOSE PHASE: SOCIAL-CONSULTATIVE DISTANCE. The boundary between social-consultative and casual-personal distance lies at a point
just beyond where the extended arms can no longer touch (4 to 7
feet).

Foveal vision (area of sharpest focus of the eye) at 4 feet covers an area
of just a little larger than one eye (table 1); at 7 feet the area of sharp focus
extends to nose and parts of eyes, or mouth, eye and nose are sharply seen.
In many Americans, this sharp vision shifts back and forth, or around the
face. Details of skin texture and hair are clearly perceived. At 60° visual
angle, head, shoulders, and upper trunk are seen at 4 feet distance; the
same sweep includes the whole figure at 7 feet. Feet are seen peripherally,
even if standing. Head size is perceived as normal. As one moves
away from the subject, the foveal area can take in an ever-increasing
amount.

A good deal of impersonal business takes place at this distance. In the
close phase there is much greater implication of involvement than in the
distant phase. People who work together a good deal tend to use close
social-consultative distance. It is also a very common distance for people
who are attending a casual social gathering.

Looking down at a person at this distance is to dominate him almost
completely, as when a man talks to his secretary or receptionist on leaving
or entering the office.

DISTANT PHASE: SOCIAL-CONSULTATIVE DISTANCE. Business and social
discourse conducted at this distance (7 to 12 feet) has a more formal character than in the close phase. Desks in offices of "important" people are large
enough to hold anyone at this distance. In most instances, even with more
or less standard desks, the chair opposite the desk is at about 8 or 9 feet
from the man behind the desk.

At social-consultative distance, the finest details of the face, such as the
capillaries in the eyes, are lost. Otherwise skin texture, hair, condition of
teeth and condition of clothes are all readily visible. Neither heat nor odor
from another person's body is apparently detectable at this distance. At
least, none of my subjects mentioned either factor.

TABLE I. Areas covered at Eight Distances by Four Visual Angles

Distances		1°*	15° × 3°**	60° sweep†	180°
Intimate					
	6″	0.1″	2.5″ × 0.3″ eye, mouth	6″ the face	Head and shoulders
	18″	0.3″ central iris	3.75 × 1″ upper or lower face	18″ head	Upper body and arms
Casual-personal					
close	30″	0.5″ tip of nose	6.25″ × 1.5″ upper or lower face	30″ head, shoulders	Whole figure
far	48″	0.8″ one eye	10″ × 2.5″ upper or lower face	48″ waist up	
Social-consultative					
close	7′	1.7″ mouth, plus nose; nose plus parts of eye	eye 20″ × 5″ the face	7′ whole figure	
far	12′	2.5″ two eyes	31″ × 7.5″ faces of two people	12′ figure w/ space around it	
Public					
	30′	6.3″ the face	6′3″ torso of 4 or 5 people	30′	
	340′	6′			
	500′	9′			
	1500′	26′			

The full figure—with a good deal of space around it—is encompassed in a 60° angle. This is the distance which people move to when someone says "Stand away so I can look at you." Also, at around 12 feet, accommodation convergence ceases (4, 8); the eyes and the mouth are contained in the area of sharp vision so that it is not necessary to shift the eyes to take in the face. During conversations of any significant length, visual contact has to be maintained and subjects will peer around intervening objects.

If one person is standing and another seated, the seated person may push his or her chair back to about 12 feet in order to reduce the tilt of the head. Several subjects mentioned that "looking up" accentuated the higher status of the other person. In the days of servants it was taken for granted that none would approach a seated employer so close as to make him look

* Computed to nearest 0.1 inch.
** Computed to nearest 0.25 inch.
† Varies with culture

up. Today it may be that motorcycle policemen use the device of resting one foot on a running board and looking down on an offender as a way of increasing their psychological leverage. Judges' benches often accentuate differences in elevation.

The voice level is noticeably louder than for the close phase and can usually be heard easily in an adjoining room if the door is open. As the term implies, social-consultative distance is employed for professional and social transactions as long as there is an emotionally neutral effect. Raising the voice or shouting can have the effect of reducing social-consultative distance to personal distance.

I have observed some interviews start at the far end of this scale and move in; in others this process is reversed.

One of the functions of this distance is to provide for flexibility of involvement so that people can come and go without having to talk.* A receptionist in an office can usually work quite comfortably if she is 10 or more feet from people waiting to see her boss; if she is any closer, she will feel she should talk to those waiting.

A husband coming back from work often finds himself sitting and relaxing reading the paper at 10 or more feet from his wife. He may also discover that his wife has arranged the furniture back-to-back (favorite device of the cartoonist, Chick Young, creator of *Blondie*). The back-to-back arrangement is an appropriate solution to minimum space, or a shortage of reading lights.

The social-consultative distance has the advantage of permitting an easy shifting back and forth between one's activity and whoever else is in the room. Participation with others at this distance is spotty and brief. Questions and answers and introductory or opening remarks are what one hears most often. Likewise, it is easy for one of several participants to disengage himself without offending.

Casual-Personal Distance

"Personal distance" (close phase: 18 to 30 inches; far phase: 30 to 48 inches), is the term originally used by Hediger to designate the distance consistently separating the members of non-contact species. It might be thought of as a small protective sphere that an organism maintains between itself and others (6).

FAR PHASE: CASUAL-PERSONAL DISTANCE. Keeping someone "at arm's length" is one way of expressing this distance ($2\frac{1}{2}$ to 4 feet). It begins at a point that is just outside easy touching distance on the part of one person to a point where two can touch easily if they extend both arms.

* In other countries the circle of involvement cannot be counted on to be the same as in the United States.

Details of subject's features are clearly visible. Fine detail of skin, gray hair, "sleep" in eye and cleanliness of teeth are easily seen. Head size is perceived as normal.

Foveal vision covers only an area the size of the tip of the nose or one eye, so that the gaze must wander around the face; 15° clear vision covers the upper *or* lower face. Details of clothing—frayed spots, small wrinkles or dirt on cuffs—can be seen easily; 180° peripheral vision takes in the hands and the whole body of a seated person. Movement of the hands is detected, but fingers cannot be counted.

The voice is moderately low to soft.

No body heat is perceptible. The olfactory factor is not normally present for Americans. Breath odor can sometimes be detected at this distance, but Americans are trained to direct it away from others.

The boundary line between the far phase of the casual-personal distance and the close phase of social-consultative distance marks, in the words of one subject, "the limit of domination."

This is the limit of physical domination in the very real sense, for beyond it, a person cannot easily get his hands on someone else. Subjects of personal interest and involvement are talked about at this distance.

For a woman to permit a man inside the close personal zone when they are by themselves makes her body available to touch. Failure to withdraw signifies willingness to submit to touching.*

CLOSE PHASE: CASUAL-PERSONAL DISTANCE. There appears to be a distinct shift from the far phase to the close phase of casual-personal distance (1½ to 2½ feet). The distance roughly is only half that of the former. Olfaction begins to enter in, as well as heat gain and loss from the other person. The kinesthetic sense of closeness derives from the possibilities that are opening up in regard to what each participant can do to or with the other's body. At this distance one can hold or grasp the extremities.

A visual angle of 15° (clear vision) takes in the upper or lower face which is seen with exceptional clarity. The planes of the face and its roundness are accentuated; the nose projects and the ears recede; fine hair of the face and back of neck, eyelashes and hair in nose, ears and pores are clearly visible.

This is as close as one can get without real distortions of the features. In fact, it is the distortion and the enlargement of the features that one encounters in the next closer zone—the intimate—that make it intimate.

Intimate Distance.

At intimate distance (full contact to 18 inches), two subjects are deeply involved with each other. The presence of the other person is unmistakable

---

* One female subject from a Mediterranean country repeatedly miscued American men who misinterpreted her failure to respond quickly (virtually with reflex speed) to a reduction in distance from *personal* to *close-personal*.

and may at times be overwhelming because of the greatly stepped-up sensory inputs. Olfaction, heat from the other person's body, touch or the possibility of touch, not only by the hands but also by the lips and the breath, all combine to signal in unmistakable ways the close presence of another body.

FAR PHASE: INTIMATE DISTANCE. Hands can reach and grasp extremities but, because of the space between the bodies (6 to 18 inches), there is some awkwardness in caressing. The head is seen as enlarged in size and its features are distorted.

Ability to focus the eye easily is an important feature of this distance for Americans.*

In foveal vision the iris of the eye is enlarged over life size. Small blood vessels in the sclera are seen. Pores are enlarged. This is the distance at which personal services, such as removal of splinters, are provided. In apes it is the "grooming distance."

Fifteen degree clear vision includes the upper or lower portion of the face which is perceived as enlarged. When looking at the eye, the nose is overlarge, distorted and exaggerated. So are other features, such as lips, teeth and tongue. During conversations, the hands tend to come in and move up toward the face so they will be included in the peripheral field.

Peripheral vision, 180°, includes the outline of head and shoulders and very often, hands.

The voice is normally held at a low level, and Joos' (9) "intimate style"† prevails.

Heat as well as odor of breath may be detected, even though it is directed away from subject's face. Heat loss or gain from other person's body begins to be noticed by some subjects if their attention is directed to heat.

Sensory input from all previously used sources has been stepped up considerably. New channels (such as the olfactory) are just beginning to come into play.

CLOSE PHASE: INTIMATE DISTANCE. This is the distance (full contact to 6 plus or minus 2 inches) of lovemaking and wrestling, comforting and

---

* American Optical Company Phoroptor Test Card no. 1985-IA (20–20 vision at 0.37 M.) was used to test subjects in a variety of situations including subjects chosen from audiences during lectures. The distance at which the smallest type (0.37 M.) could be read was in all cases the same distance at which the investigator was told that he was now "too close." Twenty diopter lenses fitted to the eye reduced this distance from 15 inches to 19 inches to as little as 7 inches. Subjects were chosen in the 35 to 45 year age bracket. Two subjects with presbyopia failed to respond in this way. With them sharp vision ceased to be featured in the intimate zone.

† ". . . an intimate utterance pointedly avoids giving the addressee information from outside of the speaker's skin. The point . . . is simply to remind (hardly 'inform') the addressee of some feeling . . . inside the speaker's skin."

protecting. Physical contact is featured. Use of the distance receptors is greatly reduced except for olfaction and sensitivity to radiant heat, both of which are stepped up.

Vocalization at intimate distances plays a very minor part in the communications process, which is carried mainly by other channels. A whisper has the effect of expanding the distance. The moans, groans and grunts that escape involuntarily during fighting or sex are produced by the action. The two parties act as one as it were.

In the most close (maximum contact) phase, the muscles communicate. Pelvis, thighs and head can be brought into play, arms can encircle. Except at the outer limits, sharp vision is blurred at this distance, although this is not true of the highly plastic eye of the very young or of the extraordinarily nearsighted.

Much of the physical discomfort that Americans experience when others are inappropriately inside the intimate sphere is expressed as distortions of the visual system. One subject said in regard to people that got "too close"—"these people get so close, you're crosseyed! It really makes me nervous they put their face so close it feels like they're *inside you*."

The expressions, "get your face out of mine," and "he shook his fist in my face" apparently express how many Americans perceive their body boundaries. That is, there is a transition between inside and the outside. At that point where sharp focus is lost, one feels the uncomfortable muscular sensation of being crosseyed from looking at something too close.

When close vision is possible within the intimate range—as with the young—the image is greatly enlarged and stimulates a significant portion (if not the total) of the retina. The detail that one sees at this distance is extraordinary. This, plus the felt pull of the eye muscles, structures the visual experience in a way that it cannot be confused with the less intense personal, social-consultative and public distances.

Intimate distance is not favored in public among the American middle class. However, it is possible to observe the young in automobiles and on beaches using intimate distances. Crowded subways and buses may bring strangers into what would ordinarily be coded as intimate spatial relations, if it were not for several characteristically isolating compensatory devices. The correct behavior is to be as immobile as possible and, when part of the trunk or extremities contact another, to withdraw if possible. If this is not possible, the muscles in the affected area are kept tense. For members of the non-contact group it is taboo to relax and enjoy the contact. In crowded elevators, the hands are kept at the side or used to steady the body by grasping railings and overhead straps. The eyes are fixed at infinity and should not be brought to bear on anyone for more than a passing glance. Men who take advantage of the crowded situation in order to feel or pinch women violate an important cultural norm dealing with the privacy of the body and the right of a person to grant or withhold from others access to it. Middle Eastern subjects do not express the outraged reactions to palpation in public places that one encounters among the non-contact American group.

Public Distance: Outside the Circle of Involvement

Several important shifts occur in the transition from the personal, consultative and social distances to public distances (close phase: 12 feet to 25 feet plus or minus 5 feet; far phase: 30 feet to maximum carrying distance of voice).

CLOSE PHASE: PUBLIC DISTANCE. In this phase of public distance (12 to 25 feet) participants cannot touch or pass objects to each other. Possibly some form of flight reaction may be present subliminally. At 12 feet an alert subject can take evasive or defensive action if a threatening move is made.

The voice is loud but not full volume. Rice (10) suggests that choice of words and phrasing of sentences is much more careful and there may be grammatical (or syntactic) shifts that differentiate speech at this distance from the closer, less formal distances. Joos' (9) choice of the term "formal style" is appropriately descriptive: "formal texts . . . demand advance planning . . . the speaker is correctly said to think on his feet."

Because angular accommodation of the eyes is no longer necessary, there is an absence of feedback from the ocular muscles. The angle of sharpest vision (1°) covers the whole face. Fine details of the skin and eyes are no longer visible. The color of the eyes begins to be imperceivable (at 16 feet only the whites of the eyes are visible.) Also at 16 feet the body begins to lose its roundness and to look flat.

Head size is perceived as considerably under life size. The 15° cone of clear vision includes the faces of two people (at 12 feet), 60° the whole body with a little space around it. Peripheral vision includes other persons if they are present.

FAR PHASE: PUBLIC DISTANCE. The far phase of public distance begins somewhere around 30 feet. It is the distance that is automatically set around important public figures. White's description of the spatial treatment accorded John F. Kennedy when his nomination became certain is an excellent example:

"Kennedy loped into the cottage with his light, dancing step, as young and lithe as springtime, and called a greeting to those who stood in his way. Then he seemed to slip from them as he descended the steps of the split-level cottage to a corner where his brother Bobby and brother-in-law Sargent Shriver were chatting, waiting for him. The others in the room surged forward on impulse to join him. Then they halted. A distance of perhaps 30 feet separated them from him, but it was impassable. They stood apart, these older men of long-established power, and watched him. He turned after a few minutes, saw them watching him, and whispered to his brother-in-law. Shriver now crossed the separating space to invite them over. First Averell Harriman; then Dick Daley; then Mike DiSalle; then, one by one, let them all congratulate him. Yet no one could pass the little open distance between him and them uninvited, because there was this thin separation about him, and the knowledge they were there not as his patrons but as his clients. They could come by invitation only, for this might be a President of the United States" (11).

At this distance body stance and gestures are featured; facial expression becomes exaggerated as does the loudness of the voice. The tempo of the voice drops; words are enunciated more clearly. Joos' (9) *frozen style* is characteristic: "Frozen style is for people who are to remain strangers." The whole man may be perceived as *quite small* and he is *in a setting*. Foveal vision takes in more and more of the man until he is entirely within the small cone of sharpest vision. At this point, contact with him as a human being begins to diminish.

The 60° cone of vision takes in the setting. Peripheral vision seems to have as its principal function the alerting of the individual to movement at the side, which may represent danger.

MEANING AND DISTANCE

What significance do people attach to different distances? The very term "closeness" conjures up different images than "distance." "Getting *next* to" someone implies a number of things about your relationship. The expression, "I can't get together with him on that," has a literal, in addition to a figurative, meaning. In the world of actions from which words take their meaning, a wife who sees another woman standing too close to her husband gets the message loud and clear.

For that matter, anyone confronted with a person whose space pattern varies from his own, finds himself asking the following questions: Who does this man think he is? What is he trying to say? Is he trying to push me around, or why does he have to be so familiar?

Yet one of the first things one discovers in this research is that very similar spatial relationships can have entirely different meanings. What one makes of how others treat him in space is determined by one's ethnic past. This is *not* a matter, however, of generalizing about Latino's standing closer than North Americans, of moving each space zone up a notch as it were. Rather it is a matter of entirely different systems, in which some items are shared but many others are not, including the order and selection of transactions that occur in the different distance sets (12). Thus, it does not necessarily imply any existing or intended relationship if an Arab walks up and places himself inside one's personal sphere in a public place. It may only mean that he wants the spot you are standing on for himself. Since there is no relationship or chance of one, he does not care what you think. The point, however, is so basic and so subtle that it is apt to be lost.

SUMMARY

This paper has dealt with some rather specific aspects of how we gain knowledge as to the content of the minds of other men by means which function almost totally outside awareness. Proxemics represents one of several such out-of-awareness systems which fall within the general rubric of paracommunication.*

Communication of this sort, operating outside awareness as it does, appears to be an extraordinarily persistent form of culturally specific behavior which is responded to with considerable effect whenever people encounter patterns which are at variance with their own. It is also apparently a rather basic form of communication, many features of which are shared with other vertebrates.

How man codes distance is a function of which combinations of receptors he uses. These do not always seem to be the same from culture to culture and vary even within subcultures. Visual and kinesthetic cues are prominent in non-contact Americans. Olfactory and tactile cues are emphasized in Eastern Mediterranean urban Arab culture.

Recording to cues used to distinguish one distance from another is possible. It should be noted, however, that proxemic research is in its infancy and suffers from many obvious flaws. This report represents a summary of some of what has been accomplished to date rather than a definitive statement of the field.

REFERENCES

1. Thoreau, H. D., *Walden*. The Macmillan Company, New York, 1929.

2. Thiel, P., "A sequence-experience notation for architectural and urban space." *Town Planning Review*, April 1961.

3. Kilpatrick, F. P., ed., *Explorations in Transactional Psychology*. New York University Press, New York, 1961.

4. Gibson, J. J., *The Perception of the Visual World*. The Riverside Press, Cambridge, 1950.

* Paracommunication is the term suggested as an appropriate designation by Joos (9) and George Trager (13) to refer to communicative behavior which does not have its base in language but is often synchronized with linguistic and paralinguistic phenomena.

5. Bruner, J., *The Process of Education*. Harvard University Press, Cambridge, Mass., 1959.

6. Hediger, H., *Studies of the Psychology and Behavior of Captive Animals in Zoos and Circuses*. Butterworth Scientific Series, London, 1955.

7. Bogardus, E. S., *Social Distance*. Antioch Press, Yellow Springs, Ohio, 1959.

8. Whitcomb, M., Vision Committee, National Academy of Sciences, personal communication.

9. Joos, M., "The five clocks." *Internat. J. Am./Linguistics*, April, 1962.

10. Rice, F., Institute for Applied Linguistic Research, personal communication."

11. White, T. H.: *The Making of the President* 1960. Atheneum House, Inc., New York, 1961. (Reprinted by permission of the publisher.)

12. Hall, E. T., "Sensitivity and Empathy at Home and Abroad." Three Leatherbee Lectures, given at Harvard University Graduate School of Business Administration, Boston, Spring, 1962.

13. Trager, G. L., "Paralanguage: a first approximation." *Stud. Linguistics, 13:* 1–12, 1958.

part eight

OTHER VOICES, OTHER MINDS:
THE PHILOSOPHY OF COMMUNICATION

NATURE, COMMUNICATION AND MEANING*

John Dewey

Of all affairs, communication is the most wonderful. That things should be able to pass from the plane of external pushing and pulling to that of revealing themselves to man, and thereby to themselves; and that the fruit of communication should be participation, sharing, is a wonder by the side of which transubstantiation pales. When communication occurs, all natural events are subject to reconsideration and revision; they are re-adapted to meet the requirements of conversation, whether it be public discourse or that preliminary discourse termed thinking. Events turn into objects, things with a meaning. They may be referred to when they do not exist, and thus be operative among things distant in space and time, through vicarious presence in a new medium. Brute efficiencies and inarticulate consummations as soon as they can be spoken of are liberated from local and accidental contexts, and are eager for naturalization in any non-insulated, communicating, part of the world. Events when once they are named lead an independent and double life. In addition to their original existence, they are subject to ideal experimentation: their meanings may be infinitely combined and re-arranged in imagination, and the outcome of this inner experimentation—which is thought—may issue forth in interaction with crude or raw events. Meanings having been deflected from the rapid and roaring stream of events into a calm and traversible canal, rejoin the main stream, and color, temper and compose its course. Where communication exists, things in acquiring meaning, thereby acquire representatives, surrogates, signs and implicates, which are infinitely more amenable to management, more permanent and more accommodating, than events in their first estate.

By this fashion, qualitative immediacies cease to be dumbly rapturous, a possession that is obsessive and an incorporation that involves submergence: conditions found in sensations and passions. They become capable

* Reprinted from John Dewey, *Experience and Nature*, The Open Court Publishing Company, La Salle, Illinois.

of survey, contemplation, and ideal or logical elaboration; when something can be said of qualities they are purveyors of instruction. Learning and teaching come into being, and there is no event which may not yield information. A directly enjoyed thing adds to itself meaning, and enjoyment is thereby idealized. Even the dumb pang of an ache achieves a significant existence when it can be designated and descanted upon; it ceases to be merely oppressive and becomes important; it gains importance, because it becomes representative; it has the dignity of an office.

In view of these increments and transformations, it is not surprising that meanings, under the name of forms and essences, have often been hailed as modes of Being beyond and above spatial and temporal existence, invulnerable to vicissitude; nor that thought as their possession has been treated as a non-natural spiritual energy, disjoined from all that is empirical. Yet there is a natural bridge that joins the gap between existence and essence; namely communication, language, discourse. Failure to acknowledge the presence and operation of natural interaction in the form of communication creates the gulf between existence and essence, and that gulf is factitious and gratuitous.

The slight respect paid to larger and more pervasive kinds of empirical objects by philosophers, even by professed empiricists, is apparent in the fact that while they have discoursed so fluently about many topics they have discoursed little about discourse itself. Anthropologists, philologists and psychologists have said most that has been said about saying. Nevertheless it is a fact of such distinction that its occurrence changed dumb creatures—as we so significantly call them—into thinking and knowing animals and created the realm of meanings. Speaking from the standpoint of anthropology Franz Boas says: "The two outer traits in which the distinction between the minds of animals and man finds expression are the existence of organized articulate speech in man and the use of utensils of varied application."[1] It is antecedently probable that sole external marks of difference are more than external; that they have intimate connection with such intrinsic differences as religion, art and science, industry and politics. "Utensils" were discussed in the last chapter, in connection with the useful arts and knowledge, and their indispensable relation with science pointed out. But at every point appliances and application, utensils and uses, are bound up with directions, suggestions and records made possible by speech; what has been said about the role of tools is subject to a condition supplied by language, the tool of tools.

Upon the whole, professed transcendentalists have been more aware than have professed empiricists of the fact that language makes the difference between brute and man. The trouble is that they have lacked a naturalistic conception of its origin and status. Logos has been correctly identified with mind; but logos and hence mind was conceived supernaturally. Logic was thereby supposed to have its basis in what is beyond human conduct and relationships, and in consequence the separation of the physical and the rational, the actual and the ideal, received its traditional formulation.

In protest against this view empirical thinkers have rarely ventured in discussion of language beyond reference to some peculiarity of brain structure, or to some psychic peculiarity, such as tendency to "outer expression" of "inner" states. Social interaction and institutions have been treated as products of a ready-made *specific* physical or mental endowment of a self-sufficing individual, wherein language acts as a mechanical go-between to convey observations and ideas that have prior and independent existence. Speech is thus regarded as a practical convenience but not of fundamental intellectual significance. It consists of "mere words," sounds, that happen to be associated with perceptions, sentiments and thoughts which are complete prior to language. Language, thus, "expresses" thought as a pipe conducts water, and with even less transforming function than is exhibited when a wine-press "expresses" the juice of grapes. The office of signs in creating reflection, foresight and recollection is passed by. In consequence, the occurrence of ideas becomes a mysterious parallel addition to physical occurrences, with no community and no bridge from one to the other.

It is safe to say that psychic events, such as are anything more than reactions of a creature susceptible to pain and diffuse comfort, have language for one of their conditions. It is altogether likely that the "ideas" which Hume found in constant flux whenever he looked within himself were a succession of words silently uttered. Primary to these events there was, of course, a substratum of organic psycho-physical actions. But what made the latter identifiable objects, events with a perceptible character, was their concretion in discourse. When the introspectionist thinks he has withdrawn into a wholly private realm of events disparate in kind from other events, made out of mental stuff, he is only turning his attention to his own soliloquy. And soliloquy is the product and reflex of converse with others; social communication not an effect of soliloquy. If we had not talked with others and they with us, we should never talk to and with ourselves. Because of converse, social give and take, various organic attitudes become an assemblage of persons engaged in converse, conferring with one another, exchanging distinctive experiences, listening to one another, over-hearing unwelcome remarks, accusing and excusing. Through speech a person dramatically identifies himself with potential acts and deeds; he plays many roles, not in successive stages of life but in a contemporaneously enacted drama. Thus mind emerges.

It is significant of the differences between Greek and modern experience, that when their respective philosophers discovered discourse, they gave such different accounts of it. The moderns made of it a world separate from spatial and material existences, a separate and private world made of sensations, images, sentiments. The Greeks were more nearly aware that it was *discourse* they had discovered. But they took the structure of discourse for the structure of things, instead of for the forms which things assume under the pressure and opportunity of social cooperation and exchange. They overlooked the fact that meanings as objects of thought are entitled to be called complete and ultimate only because they are not original but are a happy outcome of a complex history. They made them primitive and independent forms of things, intrinsically regulative of processes of becoming. They took a work of social art to be nature independent of man. They overlooked the fact that the import of logical and rational essences is the consequence of social interactions, of companionship, mutual assistance, direction and concerted action in fighting, festivity, and work. Hence they conceived of ideal meanings as the ultimate framework of events, in which a system of substances and properties corresponded to subjects and predicates of the uttered proposition. Things conformed naturally and exactly to parts of speech, some being inherently subject-matter of nouns, proper and common; others of verbs, of which some expressed self-activity, while others designated adjectival and adverbial changes to which things are exposed on account of their own defects; some being external relations in which substances stand to one another, and subject-matter of prepositions.

The resulting theory of substances, essential properties, accidental qualities and relations, and the identification of Being (by means of the copula "is"), with the tenses of the verb (so that the highest Being was, is now, and ever shall be, in contrast to existence now and then, occasional, wholly past, merely just now, or possibly at some passing time in the future), controlled the whole scheme of physics and metaphysics, which formed the philosophic tradition of Europe. It was a natural consequence of the insight that things, meanings, and words correspond.

The insight was perverted by the notion that the correspondence of things and meanings is prior to discourse and social intercourse. Hence, every true affirmation was an assertion of the fixed belonging to one another of two objects in nature; while every true denial was an assertion of intrinsic exclusion of one object by another. The consequence was belief in ideal essences, individually complete, and yet connected in a system of necessary subordinations and dependencies. Dialectic of their relationships, definition, classification, division in arranging essences, constituted scientific truth about the inmost constituents of nature. Thus a discovery which is the greatest single discovery of man, putting man in potential possession of liberation and of order, became the source of an artificial physics of nature, the basis of a science, philosophy and theology in which the universe was an incarnate grammatical order constructed after the model of discourse.

The modern discovery of inner experience, of a realm of purely personal events that are always at the individual's command, and that are his exclusively as well as inexpensively for refuge, consolation and thrill is also a great and liberating discovery. It implies a new worth and sense of dignity in human individuality, a sense that an individual is not a mere property of nature, set in place according to a scheme independent of him, as an article is put in its place in a cabinet, but that he adds something, that he marks a contribution. It is the counterpart of what distinguishes modern science, experimental, hypothetical; a logic of discovery having therefore opportunity for individual temperament, ingenuity, invention. It is the counterpart of modern politics, art, religion and industry where individuality is given room and movement, in contrast to the ancient scheme of experience, which held individuals tightly within a given order subordinated to its structure and patterns. But here also distortion entered in. Failure to recognize that this world of inner experience is dependent upon an extension of language which is a social product and operation led to the subjectivistic, solipsistic and egotistic strain in modern thought. If the classic thinkers created a cosmos after the model of dialectic, giving rational distinctions power to constitute and regulate, modern thinkers composed nature after the model of personal soliloquizing.

Language considered as an experienced event enables us to interpret what really happened when rational discourse and logic were discovered by the ancients, and when "inner" experience and its interest were discovered by moderns. Language is a natural function of human association; and its consequences react upon other events, physical and human, giving them meaning or significance. Events that are objects or significant exist in a context where they acquire new ways of operation and new properties. Words are spoken of as coins and money. Now gold, silver, and instrumentalities of credit are first of all, prior to being money, physical things with their own immediate and final qualities. But as money they are substitutes, representations, and surrogates, which embody relationships. As a substitute, money not merely facilitates exchange of such commodities as existed prior to its use, but it revolutionizes as well production and consumption of all commodities, because it brings into being new transactions, forming new histories and affairs. Exchange is not an event that can be isolated. It marks the emergence of production and consumption into a new medium and context wherein they acquire new properties.

Language is similarly not a mere agency for economizing energy in the interaction of human beings. It is a release and amplification of energies that enter into it, conferring upon them the added quality of meaning. The quality of meaning thus introduced is extended and transferred, actually and potentially, from sounds, gestures and marks, to all other things in nature. Natural events become messages to be enjoyed and administered, precisely as are song, fiction, oratory, the giving of advice and instruction. Thus events come to possess characters; they are demarcated, and noted. For character is general and distinguished.

When events have communicable meaning, they have marks, notations, and are capable of con-notation and de-notation. They are more than mere occurrences; they have implications. Hence reference and reasoning are possible; these operations are reading the message of things, which things utter because they are involved in human associations. When Aristotle drew a distinction between sensible things that are more noted—known— to us and rational things that are more noted—known—in themselves, he was actually drawing a distinction between things that operate in a local, restricted universe of discourse, and things whose marks are such that they readily enter into indefinitely extensive and varied discourse.

The interaction of human beings, namely, association, is not different in origin from other modes of interaction. There is a peculiar absurdity in the question of how individuals become social, if the question is taken literally. Human beings illustrate the same traits of both immediate uniqueness and connection, relationship, as do other things. No more in their case than in that of atoms and physical masses is immediacy the whole of existence and therefore an obstacle to being acted upon by and effecting other things. Everything that exists in as far as it is known and knowable is in interaction with other things. It is associated, as well as solitary, single. The catching up of human individuals into association is thus no new and unprecedented fact; it is a manifestation of a commonplace of existence. Significance resides not in the bare fact of association, therefore, but in the consequences that flow from the distinctive patterns of human association. There is, again, nothing new or unprecedented in the fact that assemblage of things confers upon the assembly and its constituents, new properties by means of unlocking energies hitherto pent in. The significant consideration is that assemblage of organic human beings transforms sequence and coexistence into participation.

Gestures and cries are not primarily expressive and communicative. They are modes of organic behavior as much as are locomotion, seizing and crunching. Language, signs and significance, come into existence not by intent and mind but by over-flow, by-products, in gestures and sound. The story of language is the story of the *use* made of these occurrences; a use that is eventual, as well as eventful. Those rival accounts of the origin of language that go by the nick-names of bow-bow, pooh-pooh, and ding-dong theories are not in fact theories of the origin of *language*. They are accounts, of some plausibility, of how and why certain sounds rather than others were selected to signify objects, acts and situations. If the mere existence of sounds of these kinds constituted language, lower animals might well converse more subtly and fluently than man. But they became language only when used within a context of mutual assistance and direction. The latter are alone of prime importance in considering the transformation of organic gestures and cries into names, things with significance, or the origin of language.

Observable facts of animal experience furnish us with our starting point. "Animals respond to certain stimuli . . . by the contraction of certain muscles whose functioning is of no direct consequence to the animal itself, but affects other animals by stimulating them to act. . . . Let us call this class the signaling reflexes. A few, but very diversified examples of the signaling reflexes, are the lighting of a fire-fly, the squeezing out of a black liquid from the ink bladder of a cuttle-fish, the crowing of a rooster . . . the spreading of its tail by a peacock. These reflex activities affect other animals by stimulating them. . . . If no other animals are present, or these other animals fail to respond by their own reflexes, the former reflex actions are completely wasted."[2]

Sub-human animals thus behave in ways which have no *direct* consequences of utility to the behaving animal, but which call out certain characteristic responses, sexual, protective, food-finding (as with the cluck of a hen to her chicks), in other animals. In some cases, the act evoked in other animals has in turn an important consequence for the first agent. A sexual act or a combined protective act against danger is furthered. In other cases, the consequences turn out useful to the species, to a numerically indeterminate group including individuals not yet born. Signaling acts evidently form the basic *material* of language. Similar activities occur without intent in man; thus a babe's scream attracts the attention of an adult and evokes a response useful to the infant, although the cry itself is an organic overflow having no intent. So too a man's posture and facial changes may indicate to another things which the man himself would like to conceal, so that he "gives himself away." "Expression," or signs, communication of meaning, exists in such cases for the observer, not for the agent.

While signaling acts are a material condition of language they are not language nor yet are they its *sufficient* condition. Only from an external standpoint, is the original action even a signal; the response of other animals to it is not to a sign, but, by some preformed mechanism, to a direct stimulus. By habit, by conditioned reflex, hens run to the farmer when he makes a clucking noise, or when they hear the rattle of grain in a pan. When the farmer raises his arms to throw the grain they scatter and fly, to return only when the movement ceases. They act as if alarmed; his movement is thus not a sign of food; it is a stimulus that evokes flight. But a human infant learns to discount such movements; to become interested in them as events preparatory to a desired consummation; he learns to treat them as signs of an ulterior event so that his response is to their meaning. He treats them as means to consequences. The hen's activity is ego-centric; that of the human being is participative. The latter puts himself at the standpoint of a situation in which two parties share. This is the essential peculiarity of language, or signs.

A requests *B* to bring him something, to which *A* points, say a flower. There is an original mechanism by which *B* may react to *A*'s movement in pointing. But natively such a reaction is to the movement, not to the *pointing*, not to the object pointed out. But *B* learns that the movement *is* a pointing; he responds to it not in itself, but as an index of something else. His response is transferred from *A*'s direct movement to the *object* to which *A* points. Thus he does not merely execute the natural acts of looking or grasping which the movement might instigate on its own account. The motion of *A* attracts his gaze to the thing pointed to; then, instead of just transferring his response from *A*'s movement to the native reaction he might make to the thing as stimulus, he responds in a way which is a function of *A*'s *relationship*, actual and potential, to the thing. The characteristic thing about *B*'s understanding of *A*'s movement and sounds is that he responds to the thing from the standpoint of *A*. He perceives the thing as it may function in *A*'s experience, instead of just ego-centrically. Similarly, *A* in making the request conceives the thing not only in its direct relationship to himself, but as a thing capable of being grasped and handled by *B*. He sees the thing as it may function in *B*'s experience. Such is the essence and import of communication, signs and meaning. Something is literally made common in at least two different centers of behavior. To understand is to anticipate together, it is to make a cross-reference which, when acted upon brings about a partaking in a common, inclusive, undertaking.

Stated in greater detail; *B* upon hearing *A*, makes a preparatory reaction of his eyes, hands and legs in view of the consummatory act of *A*'s possession; he engages in the act of grasping, carrying and tendering the flower to *A*. At the same time, *A* makes a preparatory response to *B*'s consummatory act, that of carrying and proffering the flower. Thus neither the sounds uttered by *A*, his gesture of pointing, nor the sight of the thing pointed to, is the occasion and stimulus of *B*'s act; the stimulus is *B*'s anticipatory share in the consummation of a transaction in which both participate. The heart of language is not "expression" of something antecedent, much less expression of antecedent thought. It is communication; the establishment of cooperation in an activity in which there are partners, and in which the activity of each is modified and regulated by partnership. To fail to understand is to fail to come into agreement in action; to misunderstand is to set up action at cross purposes. Take speech as behavioristically as you will, including the elimination of all private mental states, and it remains true that it is markedly distinguished from the signaling acts of animals. Meaning is not indeed a psychic existence; it is primarily a property of behavior, and secondarily a property of objects. But the behavior of which it is a quality is a distinctive behavior; cooperative, in that response to another's act involves contemporaneous response to a thing as entering into the other's behavior, and this upon both sides. It is difficult to state the exact physiological mechanism which is involved. But about the fact there is no doubt. It constitutes the intelligibility of acts and things. Possession of the capacity to engage in such activity is intelligence. Intelligence and meaning are natural consequences of the peculiar form which interaction sometimes assumes in the case of human beings.

NOTES

1. *The Mind of Primitive Man* (1911), p. 98.
2. Max Meyer, *The Psychology of the Other One* (1922), p. 195; a statement of behavioristic psychology that has hardly received the attention it intrinsically deserves.

TRUTH AS COMMUNICABILITY*

Karl Jaspers

INTRODUCTION: FROM THE AMPLITUDE OF THE ENCOMPASSING TO THE BOND THROUGH COMMUNICATION

*t*he question of truth can be posed in its greatest amplitude through the knowledge of the modes of the Encompassing which we have discussed in the last lecture. In each of these modes Being and truth have a proper and distinct sense. We only grasp truth if we experience it in every horizon and omit none of its modes.

But in each of these modes there occurs a retraction from the vastness of the Encompassing, which as mere vastness would tend to sink into nothingness, through that binding which grows out of what is common to all truth in all modes of the Encompassing: that to be genuinely true, truth must be communicable.

We represent this original phenomenon of our humanity thus: we are what we are only through the community of mutually conscious understandings. There can be no man who is a man for himself alone, as a mere individual.

A. Comparison of Man with Animal

Animals either are what they are as individuals, in all their generations always the same through heredity and natural growth; or they build communities into which they are unconsciously absorbed through their instincts, bringing forth repeatable, identical, non-historical structures according to strict natural law; they are indifferently replaceable functions of

* Reprinted from *Reason and Existenz*, by Karl Jaspers, translated by William Earle, by permission of Farrar, Straus & Giroux, Inc., and of Routledge & Kegan Paul, Ltd. Copyright © 1955 by The Noonday Press.

the whole. Thus animals on the one hand pass into the immediate actuality of a community which is tightly held together, or on the other hand they run independently of one another as if nothing had happened—natural processes always dominated by the moment's instinct. Animals make themselves understood instinctively. That they find themselves together, give something like signs to one another, even, as individuals, bind themselves fast to one another does not mean that they are bound together in a human bond in which men, to some degree, express themselves. With animals it is always a consequence of an unconscious and, in its meaning to men, inaccessible biological order, always in an unhistorical identity with simply other examples.

Man, on the other hand, is comparatively more detached as an individual than many animals, but his community also conditions him more decisively, and this community is essentially different from that of the animals.

The human community in analogy to the animal is weak from the point of view of supplying a natural and reliable bond. Purely biologically, man here, as everywhere, is below the animals. His community is, first of all, no state of immediacy, but is mediated through a relation to something else: through a relation to common conscious purposes in the world, through a relation to truth, and through relation to God.

Secondly, human communication is continually moved in its relation to these changing potential contents; it finds no resting place and, unlike that of the animals, has no repeating final goal. It is historical and on a path of unceasing change of which the beginning and end are not visible, a change through the recollection and appropriation of the past as well as through ever new planning for a future. Human communities, therefore, stand in opposition to those of the animals in their potentiality for an incalculable continuity in unfolding and gathering together out of the past and present. Thus, through this movement, it is a continually insecure and endangered reality which must always re-establish itself, limit and expand itself, test itself, and push on. In its true being it does not possess its final state, but rather is only directed toward it. It exists therefore in the tension of detours, errors, somersaults, and recoveries.

Thirdly, because of this manner of movement, human nature is not solely a matter of heredity, but also of tradition. Every new human being begins in communication, and not merely with his biological nature. This is externally visible in the unfortunate cases of deaf mutes in the past, who, in consequence of an inborn or early acquired deafness (and lacking modern education which today brings them to complete humanity), remained undeveloped; since they could not hear it, speech was without influence upon them, and thus they could not participate in tradition. They were hardly distinguishable from real idiots.

This comparison of man and animal only points to communication as the universal condition of man's being. It is so much his comprehensive essence that both what man is and what is for him are in some sense bound up with communication. The encompassing which we are is, in every form, communication; the Encompassing which is Being itself exists for us only insofar as it achieves communicability by becoming speech or becoming utterable.

B. *Truth in Communication*

Truth therefore cannot be separated from communicability. It only appears in time as a reality-through-communication. Abstracted from communication, truth hardens into an unreality. The movement of communication is at one and the same time the preservation of, and the search for, the truth.

In general then, it applies to my being, my authenticity, and my grasp of the truth that, not only factually am I not for myself alone, but I can not even become myself alone without emerging out of my being with others.

I.

A. *Communication in the Encompassing Which We Are: Communication in Empirical Existence, in Consciousness as Such, and in Spirit*

Truth is not of one sort, single and unique in its meaning. It has as many senses as there are modes of communication in which it arises. For what truth is, is determined by the character of the Encompassing within which communication takes place; for example, communication from one empirical existent to another, or in consciousness as such, or in the idea of spirit; and then further, it is determined by whether it is achieved in the binding together of these modes of the Encompassing in reason, and its basis, Existenz. The truth which is ever valid is determined by the Encompassing in which we stand in communication, by who communicates, and by whom the communication is understood.

We shall analyze the modes of the Encompassing by inquiring into the kind of communication which occurs in them, characterizing them singly as though they were separable.

1. The Encompassing of our mere empirical existence is not identical with our empirical existence as already scientifically known; rather it remains as a problem for advancing knowledge through all our acquired knowledge of its physiological, psychological, and sociological character.

This empirical existence of ours has the will to preserve and develop itself without limits; it wills satisfaction and happiness. To achieve these goals, the Encompassing of empirical existence demands the communication of a community which can preserve life. Interest (or rather what each holds to be his interest) is again found in the other. Need binds them all together against nature, which threatens all in common, and against other communities. The private interests of each individual existent at the same time stand in tension toward this bond, almost always ready to break out of the community when there is any slackening of the need. According to Kant, "unsocial sociability," in which none can dispense with yet none tolerate the other, is the basic feature of empirical existence. Communication on this level of empirical existence can be characterized as follows:

Danger forces everyone quickly and easily to comprehend what is necessary. But how this is understood is based upon the experience of the majority, the average, that which when it is said is understood by everybody. The similarity within the species defines what happiness or satisfaction is, what is necessary for life.

Further, on this level of communication, the greater the danger, the more decisively is the unity of the will of all necessary. And this is only to be secured through obedience. Hence not every individual can decide what it is necessary to do to fulfill the interests in sheer existence.

How this is to occur gives rise to the many forms of government. In the communication of the community, we do not find a simple relation between a single omniscient commander and the masses of everybody else who unthinkingly obey; rather there are always many together in a complex organization who in mutual understanding work out their decision.

In the empirical community, therefore, insofar as we isolate it in its meaning, it is the pragmatic concept of truth which is valid: truth does not lie in something already known, or something finally knowable, or in an absolute, but rather in what arises and comes to pass. Here there is only a relative and changing truth, for empirical existence itself changes. This process can run so that my opponent's standpoint which for me today is wrong, tomorrow, in a changed situation, may be relevant to my purposes. Constructive acts in the community are perpetual compromises. Compromise is the truth which does not forget that every standpoint, no matter how right it seems, can also be refuted through the very fact of process. Accordingly, for the continuity of a living community the art of conversation must be developed.[1]

2. The communication of consciousness as such [*Bewusstsein überhaupt*] is that between point-consciousnesses, indifferently replaceable, dissimilar yet agreeing, which, through the dichotomies of the knowable (subject-object, form-matter, anything and its other), by means of all the logical categories, grasp in affirmation and denial that which is valid for everybody. It is the communication of a self-identical consciousness dispersed into the multiplicities of its empirical existence. The communication occurs in a

disinterested attention upon some matter one is inquiring into, either into its factual character or into its validity through agreed-upon methods of argument.

3. The communication of spirit is the emergence of the Idea of a whole out of the communal substance. The individual is conscious of standing in a place which has its proper meaning only in that whole. His communication is that of a member with its organism. He is different, as all the others are, but agrees with them in the order which comprehends all. They communicate with one another out of the common presence of the Idea. In this communication, it is as though some whole not clearly knowable by consciousness as such spoke, limited itself, and gave indications of whence it came. When the communication is not enlivened with the actual content of this whole, to that extent it slips into the indifferent and trivial.

B. *Comparison of Meanings of Truth*

In each of these three modes of the Encompassing which we are— empirical existence, consciousness as such, and spirit—there is always an appropriate sense of truth. Truth for empirical existence comes from usefulness of consequences for action, and from custom. It is a function of self-preserving and developing existence. Here truth is not based upon its own independent grounds, but arises out of action and exists for action in a mobility of generation and preservation which ultimately is purposeless. In the medium of consciousness as such, truth is a cogent correctness. As pure understanding, everyone insofar as he understands at all must see this correctness. The evidence pertains to the understanding itself as a function of its grasp of the timeless rightness of what is universally valid. In the medium of spirit, it is conviction which counts, a conviction which is confirmed out of the Idea. Out of the substance of a whole, I recognize as true from my place in the community of the whole that which belongs to an historical totality.

Intended pragmatic endurance, cogent evidence, and full conviction are the three senses of truth in these three forms of the Encompassing. A further comparison of communication in the three modes will be concerned with the nature of him who communicates, and who he is. For, in fact, we are not always identical on every level of meaning in our speaking. In the multiplicity of speeches, and assertions which so often are no longer understood, the question: who speaks? is clarifying.

If it is empirical existence that speaks, it is not a question of truth in all earnestness, but rather, whether hidden or clear, of what appears to this empirical existence as relevant to his interests and desires, of what he seeks to satisfy him in the world of the senses, of wealth, power, or whatever other form the inevitably ambiguous "happiness" appears to him.

If consciousness as such speaks, then an absolutely universal, possible understanding must occur in both speech and reply for the speaking to be meaningful. A meaningful argument therefore requires that the words describe something definite, that they not be equivocal, and the recognition that the contradictory cancels itself. It is therefore impossible to have a discussion which aims at something universally valid with someone who does not regard the identity of consciousness as such as the speaker. Such a one is entangled in the empirical existence of a living being, "almost like the plants" (Aristotle), and is to be regarded either as such, or as a vital will which is concealing itself. But when consciousness as such speaks, it is, in that respect, like an empty, indifferently replaceable point.

For communication of spirit to be possible, it is not sufficient that I as a pure understanding recognize and follow the principles of identity and contradiction. Who speaks and understands here speaks out of the substance of an Idea. He must be filled with something which is not merely an object in the world which could be known by consciousness as such. Only out of this new source can the meaning of what is said be grasped and developed.

If we call a community which understands itself a "community of minds," then such a community has a threefold sense:

Empirically, it is a community of vital sympathies and interests; it is continually mobile, always delimiting itself against others, expanding, and then again breaking up into smaller parts.

On the level of consciousness as such, it is the universality of the general, that which binds all men together identically as understandings in an impersonal community which has no actual power and which is determined by the merely valid.

As a community of the spirit, the members are united through the knowledge of a whole into the community of its Idea. It is always *a* whole, never *the* whole, and it must as a whole relate itself to other wholes and always remain uncompleted in its own actual existence.

II.

A. *The Will to Communicate of Reason and Existenz; Unsatisfactoriness of the Three Modes of Communication*

The representation of the human community in these three modes of the Encompassing does not yet show what truth really is, even though truth plays a role in each of the moments we have touched upon. And it has not yet shown the final ground and basis for the possibility of communication.

Community through communication is found, to be sure, already among the merely living existences; it is in consciousness as such, and it is in spirit. However, on the level of mere vitality, it can remain instinctive sympathies or interests limited to certain purposes. In consciousness as such, it can remain an unconcerned agreement upon what is correct or valid; in spirit, a deceptive consciousness of totality which however suddenly breaks off fellowship.

There is an insufficiency in every mode of the Encompassing, an insufficiency as much in communication as in truth. This insufficiency can be made intelligible initially by pointing out the limits which show that no mode of the Encompassing can stand by itself:

Mere empirical existence seeks gratification, survival, happiness. Its limit however is that the nature of happiness remains both unclear and questionable. A man whose every wish was fulfilled would be destroyed in consequence. No happiness is permanent, and every fulfillment is deceptive. The meaninglessness of the will which is forever desiring yet which has no goal is an old theme in philosophy.

Consciousness as such touches on the universally valid truth. But its limit is that these indubitable validities as such are trivialities, and they can be heaped up in a senseless infinity.

Spirit grasps the Idea of the whole. Its limit however is that which can not be absorbed into spirit, the reality of the less-than-total, of the contingent, of the merely factual.

If one level of the Encompassing is absolutized, we must always question those characteristic phenomena which appear when the other modes of the Encompassing are neglected and the limits of this one ignored.

1. What happens when natural existence as such is not only regarded as Being itself but also when one so acts? What happens, in other words, when such a naturalistic idea is not only uttered, but when the idea is practiced, when the absolutizing of the level of empirical existence is accomplished in fact?

When this happens there occurs a surrender of both the universally valid truth of consciousness in general and the Ideas of the spirit. To be sure, in the beginning there still can be present a certain honesty which grasps the deceptiveness of merely intellectual thinking detached from reality, of a detached and merely cultured spirit. In fact, many times a passionate "idealism" which strives for Substance can be found working in a new "materialism." But afterwards, through the influence of the contents of the thought insofar as their consequences are actually drawn, the meaning of the hidden source of truth becomes lost, a meaning which was still present as a negative truthfulness in a self-deceived will to authentic being. Then it might happen that, recklessly following the contingencies and laws of empirical existence, I would will nothing else, I would renounce communication on the level of valid and intelligible truth or effective Ideas in general. Or perhaps I would merely savor them as attitudes or charming efforts in realms irrelevant to and unaffected by the conflict of existence where force and cleverness rule, attitudes which have no real influence upon the will to know or communicate. Thus conceived they are fraudulent experiences.

The confidence in nature, whose origin is a metaphysical confidence in the grounds of Being, is changed into a confidence in those insufficient, known, yet always questionable, regularities which scientific investigation wrings out of appearance. The essence of man is lost in this blind reliance upon nature, where his existence seems identical with nature, and nature identical with knowable regularities. For even if those regularities or laws were exhaustively known, they would only make matter and biological life comprehensible, not man—only man as a species of animal, which could then be called the endangered, the sick animal. When human consciousness becomes the only possibility in the known world, man loses himself in the simple affirmation of his impulses which, however, he can not let work with animal naturalness or unquestioned simplicity of meaning. Thus, in the helpless confusion of his empirical existence which ensues, his thought and spiritual possibilities vanish into a thoughtless obedience to incomprehensible forces above or in him, simply in order to exist here and now.

If we extrapolate such a tendency to its limit in a distant future, it would be possible for man to relapse into an animal-like existence which preserved a technical apparatus like ants, but an apparatus which arose in another mental world and remained as a residue. It would be only a self-repeating, non-historical species of living thing, the result of an astonishing, but now forgotten, intermediary moment of humanity. What was once incorporated and proven in the struggle for existence to be useful for the preservation and expansion of existence would now have become instinct. In all the chaos of natural existence, it could last a long time like other forms of life until, with a thorough change in the living conditions on the surface of the earth, final catastrophe would also come to this species.

2. When the thinking of consciousness as such circles around in self-sufficiency, then it is taking its timeless validities as absolute, as though the truth and Being itself were thereby grasped, as though it had read off the order and laws of things beyond all relativity. Through the abstraction of the thinking consciousness from Being, responsibility ceases for the being which is living being and spirit. The empty play of a dissolving intellectualism begins, a play which in fact is actually directed by psychologically knowable impulses.

3. The absolutizing of spirit in a wealth of merely understood contents is simply an intensified mode of the isolation of thinking. In its self-satisfaction it creates a hollow world of culture under contingent, favorable conditions, an object of pleasure, of unreal longing, a realm of flight and negativity.

What is unsatisfactory in the communication of the true in all these hitherto mentioned modes of the Encompassing could lie in the isolation of single modes. From this standpoint, true communication is already under the following demands: none of the modes can be ignored; to play off one against the other is to miss the ground of their connection. For true communication it is important to perceive the limits of every level and therewith their inability to be completed in themselves, and further, not to deceive oneself by a fixation on one of the levels over the possibility of a communication which goes through all.

The binding together of the modes of the Encompassing is here in the form of a rising series where the succeeding can be real only under the conditions set by the preceding. The termination of the preceding in isolation against the succeeding always means a specific break-off of communication. Thus a two-fold formal requirement is laid upon communication: 1) The lower level is to be limited so that it is conditioned by the possibility of the higher. For example, communication on the level of mere existence must be under the condition that evident truth remains valid and under the Ideas of spirit. 2) The higher level can not be actualized for itself in isolation, but only under the presuppositions of the lower which it delimits and breaks through but to which it must hold fast. Thus the will to knowledge must not forget its incorporation as science in the community of human beings, nor must the spirit forget its entire dependence upon empirical existence if they are not forthwith to disappear.

The higher levels are made possible by the effects of the lower and, perhaps, influenced by them. The lower on the other hand are given direction by the higher in always determinate ways.

In empirical existence the higher levels are the weaker. For the lower levels can stand without the higher, not in their authentic truth, but still as sheer existents. From this two consequences follow: First, there is something like guilt toward empirical existence when I blindly rely upon univocal obligations of higher levels of the Encompassing without considering their relation to empirical existence, letting these higher obligations themselves be destroyed by more powerful existences. Thus Max Weber in the political sphere opposed an ethics of principle which would let itself be pushed to destruction through adherence to some single law (acting unconditionally according to moral axioms and justifying itself by having willed the good and trusting in God for the result). He argued instead for an ethics of responsibility where one is concerned also for the consequences (even though the formulations of such an ethics can be misused arbitrarily). I let myself and my friends be pushed into the position of the weaker, the impotent, the ruined, by holding to attitudes which may be valid on their own level; but, where I am not acting on this level, I simply am misused and abandoned to the cleverness of others.

Secondly, endless duration of empirical existence as such can not be a meaningful goal. Man can endure as a sheer existent, but he ceases thereby to be man, just as every living being can die, and dead matter have the victorious duration. The lower in rank, the greater the durability of a being. The higher levels are the more mobile, more imperiled, more perishable. The will to endure in time, except through the limited continuity of a changing and fulfilling historicity, is a misunderstanding of the meaning of these higher levels.

Thus everywhere we see how the absolutization and isolation of one mode of the Encompassing shows its limits and at the same time the falseness which arises therewith. The unsatisfied will to communicate can be satisfied only according to the formula: every mode of communicability has its right, none can be omitted. It would always be a fault in the realization of my will to communicate if I were to ignore any level as unimportant.

Further, since the modes of the Encompassing are not separate things which can be set alongside one another and which together as a sum make up what I am as a whole, it is inadequate to present them as alternatives for some supposed choice. Rather it is necessary to apprehend them in their order of rank.

But this whole way of looking at things still leaves something in us unsatisfied. It is as though the essential had not yet been said. What is decisively unsatisfactory can be felt first of all in this: that the modes of the Encompassing in no way lead to the unity of a self-completed whole. Neither can the essential differences in the meaning of communication and truth in the three modes be effaced; nor can they be reduced to a knowable totality. It would be a deception to suppose that the modes of the Encompassing and the kinds of communication could grow into one another so that a harmonious whole would be possible in temporal existence.

Secondly, this dissatisfaction of ours, that first strove to grasp all the modes of communication together and then experienced its impossibility, sprang out of an impulse which, in its unlimited dissatisfaction and its open readiness for all sides, itself belongs to none of the three modes of the Encompassing. Even the will to communicate in these three modes holds its own energy at the service of a universal will to communicate which comes out of reason and Existenz. Let us now characterize this further.[2]

B. *Existential and Rational Communication*

If even the basic problem for empirical existents, which can endure only through community, is how one is to understand the other, how we can think and will the same things so that we can be actively bound together, then the authentic human essence, Existenz and reason, can nowhere be touched as deeply as by the question of its communication.

The communication of Existenz is accomplished through membership in the spirit, through the universality of consciousness as such, through proving itself in empirical existence, but also by breaking through these, passing beyond them in the loving struggle of those who will to become themselves. In contrast to the communication of identical and indifferently replaceable points of consciousness as such, this existential communication is between irreplaceable individuals. In contrast to the struggle for existence over power, superiority, and annihilation, here the struggle over the content of Existenz is without the will to power in the same sense; it is a struggle where every advance of the individual comes only if the other advances too, and every destruction of the other is my own. In contrast to spiritual community, where there is security in the comprehensive Idea, it does not overlook the crack in Being for us, and it is open for Transcendence. It expresses the inevitability of struggle in temporal existence and the inability of truth to be completed by unceasingly pushing the movement of communication forward as the authentic appearance of truth. To be self and to be true are nothing else than to be in communication unconditionally. Here in the depths, to preserve oneself would be precisely to lose oneself.

Existenz then, only becomes apparent and thereby real if it comes to itself through, and at the same time with, another Existenz. What is authentically human in the community of reason and Existenz is not, as before in physical life, simply present in a plurality of naturally generated examples, which then find one another and bind themselves together. Rather communication seems to produce for the first time that which is communicating: independent natures which come to consciousness of themselves, however, as though they were not touched by the contingencies of empirical existence, but had been bound together eternally.

Since this occurs in historical situations which are always new, every form of Existenz which unfolds itself in communication is both the revelation of an irreplaceable (because historical) and essentially never repeatable selfhood, and also an unconditional binding together of historical men.

Now, in existential communication, reason is what penetrates everything. Existenz as the ground bears in its depths the organ which is present in all modes of the Encompassing, which is the universal bond as well as the unrest which disturbs every fixation. Reason, having its substance in Existenz, arises from the authentic communication of one nature with another, and it arises in such a fashion that empirical existence, consciousness as such, and spirit are, so to speak, the body of its appearance. Not for an instant is reason without these, and they are all moved and changed by it.

Reason is potential Existenz which in its thinking is continually directed upon another, upon the Being which we are not, upon the world, and upon

Transcendence. What these are then becomes communicable and, therewith, being-for-us, but in the formality through which they authentically touch Existenz. Reason is present as an unlimited drive in empirical existence, in consciousness as such, and in the spirit. No range is sufficient for it; as a passionate will-to-know oriented toward the world, it reaches no end. How Existenz is shipwrecked upon Transcendence becomes clear through reason. Reason moves toward rendering all Being transparent to itself only to experience the shock of the absolutely opaque, which as such is accessible only to the clearest reason. The content of the other made present by reason is at the same time the measure of the depths of the communication which is possible, and of the character of men who are altered therein and unfold in rank in innumerable ways.

The higher sense of the word reason should be preserved. It should not sink to mean mere comprehensibility, spirituality, or the necessities of empirical existence. Its sense however can not be immediately expressed or pointed out in a fixed definition but only through the movement of a philosophical logic.

Communication remains original and unrestricted only where reason is dependably present, a reason which as a source can not be objectified nor directly perceived in any argumentation. It is truth itself, the total will-to-communicate.

That man always holds himself still in reserve, or, so to speak, hovers over what he knows, does, is, somewhere has its limits if he is not nothing, or if he is not merely the formal empty point of this hovering. The limits are there where he is; he is himself as reason, and he is reason as potential Existenz. But, as a consequence, reason and Existenz can not be objectified like the modes of the Encompassing. Where thought transcends to reason and Existenz, nothing is reached except the inner perception of the possibility of this unknowable selfhood, which is only as the communication of Existenz through reason.

The way in which reason and Existenz belong together is not, however, that of mere identity. If Existenz finds the limit of what is counter-rational in every sense, which coincides with the break-off of all communication, still, it can perceive this possibility in itself only through reason. This negative Existenz, to which no thought and being can follow, remains true— that is, does not collapse into the restrictions of a definite mode of the Encompassing, but remains as something lost and without a world before an incomprehensible Transcendence—only by a path which leads above the full realization of the reason which it has finally surrendered.[3]

C. *Résumé of Meanings of Truth*

If Existenz and reason are, so to speak, the ground and bond of the three modes of the Encompassing which we are, we now can summarize our comparisons of the senses of truth in these three modes:

1. We distinguish among the senses of truth pragmatic preservation of empirical existence, cogent evidence for consciousness as such, and conviction in the spiritual Idea. As Existenz, I experience truth in faith whose truth however is not yet comprised in those three. Where there is no effective preservation of existence, no demonstrable certitude, no longer any saving wholeness, there I come upon a depth of truth where, without leaving that whole which is my actual world, I break through it in order to return to it out of the experience of Transcendence, at one and the same time in and out of it.

2. We distinguish in these meanings of truth who it is that speaks in communicating the truth. In existential and rational communication, it is the existing man who speaks decisively—the man who is not merely living vitality, nor merely an abstract understanding, but who is himself in all of these.

3. We distinguish modes in the community of mind. Existenz finds itself in a realm of mind which can not be closed, of Existenz open before Transcendence. Out of such a realm, the forms of community which develop in the modes of the Encompassing first derive their soul, while these forms always remain the indispensable appearance, the condition for the actualization of Existenz—a condition which must be both participated in and broken through.

III.

A. *The Meaning of Truth and the Will to Total Communication*

The dissatisfaction with every particular mode of communication leads to a will to total communication, a will which can only be one and which is the authentically driving and binding force in all the modes of communication.

But this will to communicate, which actualizes itself out of potential Existenz through reason in the three modes of the Encompassing, itself does not reach fulfillment. For it is continuously bound within the three modes, and, although aroused and moved, yet it is, so to speak, muddied in its mode. And, finally, it finds itself limited through its own, as well as through others', historicity. This historicity both brings communication in its depths before the multiplicity of truth and also lets it be wrecked.

From this situation of Existenz in time, it follows first that, if truth is bound up with communication, truth itself can only *become*—that, in its depths, it is not dogmatic but communicative. Out of the consciousness of a becoming truth, first springs the possibility of a radical openness of the will to communicate in actuality—a will, however, that can never fulfill itself except in an historical moment which, precisely as such, becomes incommunicable.

There follows secondly, in being wrecked by the multiplicity of truth, a self-recovery of the unlimited will to communicate in an attitude which just as resolutely envisages failure in the whole while it nevertheless holds to its path, not knowing where it leads.

It follows thirdly that, if truth in communication can never be definitively won and established—truth like communication seeing itself, so to speak, disappear before Transcendence, change before Being—nevertheless, its resolute actualization brings forth also the deepest openness for Transcendence.

B. *The Double Sense of Truth in Time (Dogmatic and Communicative Truth)*

The question is, how far total communication is the reality of truth, our truth in time. The question will become clear by distinguishing two senses of truth in time:

When truth seemed to be grasped historically and conclusively in object, symbol and expression, then the question still remained how such a truth, attained and now present, was to be transmitted to all men. Such truth was closed in itself, timeless in time, and therefore complete to itself and independent of men. But men had their value dependent upon it. Communication from man to man then began which was not a cooperative production, but rather a giving of a possessed truth, to which they referred, but in which they did not participate. And therewith began the process by which this truth changed. For they took it in, understood it in itself, but in fact there was no surrender to it. The truth, instead of being given to men while it itself remained in its original purity, was watered down and perverted, or, in the transformation, became something totally different out of new origins. Its spread among men in such forms went to the limits beyond which its further spread was factually impaired.

The truth which from the first would bind itself to communication would be different. It would not be found outside of its incorporation in communication. In itself, it would neither be nor be complete. As conditions, it would have changes, not only in the men to whom it would be communicated, but also in the men who would communicate, in consequence of their readiness and ability to communicate—their resolute capacities for speaking and hearing and their inward perception of all modes and levels of communication. It would be a truth which would arise for the first time in communication, which would become actual only in and through it; it would be a truth which is neither already here to be transmitted to another, nor which presents us with a methodically attainable end in which it could be valid without communication.

Historically, permanent truths have been developed into philosophical and religious techniques for the formation of men. All those *exercitia spiritualia*, yoga exercises, and mystic initiations have sought to transform the individual into a perception of the truth, not by communication, but by a self-sufficient discipline. But if one will not remain satisfied with such fixed, leveling, final, and therefore degenerative types of man as his supposed fulfillment, even though they may have their own magnificence, he will need a deeper discipline of a communication continually exercised with perspicuity. That which was often reached by restriction to rationally clear ends but which beyond that accomplished little in historical communities and that little always questionable—that must be the beginning: what is required is the bringing forth of humanity under the conditions of a communication which is not deceptive, not superficial, not degenerating, but limitless clarifying.

But, even in this communication, falsehood must also be present insofar as truth, in its movement, is never complete, but in every factual completion also remains continuously open.

Again, there is a radical abyss between the dogmatic and the communicative modes of knowing the truth:

If the presupposition is made of a permanent truth which as such is accessible to us, and if it is valid as something fixed outside of me that is already there needing only to be found, then our problem is simply to discover it, and not to produce it. Then, either there would be a single world-order of a purely immanent sort and our problem would be to set it up, or there would be a Beyond which is only like another world in safer prospect.

If, however, truth for us in every form remains a limit in the realization of communication, then the insurmountable incompleteness of the world and all worldly, knowable truth is final for immanence. Every form of truth must be shipwrecked in the world, and none can substitute itself absolutely for the truth.

If, therefore, there is truth in this last way, then it can only be in the Transcendence which is not some Beyond as a mere second world, or this world taken again as a better world. The idea which grasps Transcendence from the unfulfillment of all communication and from the shipwrecking of every form of truth in the world is like a proof of God: from the unfulfillment of every sense of truth and under the assumption that truth must be, thought touches upon Transcendence. Such an idea is valid only for Existenz which is an absolute concern for truth, and to whose honesty truth, as a single, unique, and static possession of timelessness, never shows itself in the world.

C. *The Openness of the Will-to-Communicate on its Path Through Existence*

Philosophically, to become conscious of communicative truth comes to this: so to think through all the modes of the Encompassing that potential

Existenz has the largest space in the world. Existenz, as irremediably a movement in time, should hold itself open before the whole range of possibilities and actualities. Only then can that radical will-to-communicate which springs out of reason and Existenz work; whereas the possession of truth as though it were conclusively asserted in fact breaks communication off.

The openness in the will-to-communicate is a double one: first, openness to the knowability of what is not yet known. Since that which is not communicable is as though it were not at all, openness strives to bring every possibility into the medium of communication so that it might attain being for us. Secondly, this openness must be ready to encounter the substance of every being that really communicates with me as another who I am not, but in solidarity with whom I can without limit will to become myself. This loving search of men reaches no termination.

My consciousness however remains continually restricted: in the first place, by that being which, lacking communicability, is not for me but which, unnoticed by me, works upon my existence and my world; and, in the second place, by the empirical existence and Existenz of others who are not identical with me and do not think in the same way, but who through their communication also determine my empirical existence without my knowing it, and whose communication can bring me still closer to myself. Hence my consciousness is never the absolutely true consciousness for it is never the whole. Through this unexpected effect, I am continually reminded not to stop in the movement toward truth; otherwise my own truth will discover that matters themselves have gone beyond me. Truth, said Hegel, is in league with reality against consciousness. This reality is given in the workings of what is not communicated, and perhaps is incommunicable, in the world, as that which we hear without understanding what comes between us, and as what we can only suffer. The unlimited will-to-communicate, then, never means simply to submit oneself to the other as such, but rather to know that other, to hear him, to will to reckon with him even unto the necessity of a transformation of oneself.

Living in the totality of the Encompassing in which I find myself is therefore necessarily a venture. Clarification itself shows me in a situation of venture, not because I seek danger out of bravado, but because I must venture. Only a life which remains blind can mask from itself this standing risk and remain between the polarity of supposed safety and a rising, but then immediately forgotten, anxiety. It is risk to see the possible pushed to its highest degree, to dare to entice it out at the risk of one's own openness and bearing responsibility for which men I trust and how I trust myself— and knowing that on every level communication is only possible among equals. I must assume responsibility for failure and deception, perhaps as a crisis in which communication can for the first time grow, perhaps as a disaster which I can not understand.

D. *The Many-Fold Existential Truth for the Radical Will-to-Communicate*

Where the Encompassing remains present in every form, the will-to-communicate can be genuinely total; and there Existenz stands before its final limits: that there are many truths in the sense of existential absolutes.

To recognize philosophically this multiplicity of truths can seem fickle. One can object: only a single truth is the truth absolutely, if not for God at least for man; man can not act categorically if he does not believe his truth to be the only one.

To this there is a reply. Since it is impossible for man to have Transcendence in time as a knowable object, identical for everybody like something in the world, every mode of the One Truth as absolute in the world can in fact only be historical: unconditional for this Existenz but, precisely for this reason, not universally valid. For, since it is not impossible, but only psychologically infinitely difficult, for a man to act according to his own truth, realizing at the same time the truth of others which is not truth for him, holding fast to the relativity and particularity of all universally valid truths—since it is not impossible, he must not shirk this highest demand of truthfulness which is only apparently incompatible with that of others. The Idea of man can not be projected too high so long as the absolutely impossible is avoided, that which contradicts his finitude in time. The empirically improbable, i.e., that which is improbable in the light of the actual, average, observable human species, is not valid before the Idea of a communication ready for anything, which is possible in the basis of human nature. Before the empirical reality such an Idea changes itself into an unending problem whose limits of accomplishment are not foreseeable.

The most radical disruption of communication lies close to the existential recognition of the plurality of truths. Yet the total will-to-communicate, once it is on its way, can not surrender itself. It has a confidence in itself and in possibilities in the world which may be deceived again and again, but it can doubt only its limited expressions, never its own principle. It trusts the truth of others which is not its own, but which, as truth, must contain a possibility of communication. Thus it can not collapse absolutely under the burden of failure. Perhaps a courageous modesty suits it best, where it projects a vision of its path as an Idea, to be sure without any extensive reality, but as an expression of a possibility which never betrays itself.

For example, the greatest extremes of clarity and truth can still enter into warring enmity if, in the struggle for existence, fundamentally and essentially different Existenzen apprehend unavoidably diverse destinies. Out of their potential communication, they may put the struggle under rules, thereby ceasing to be concealed beasts, and fight chivalrously, that is, under laws which presuppose potential Existenz on both sides, and which do not make genuine future communication impossible. Yet, if this were attained, the leap to genuine communication would already in fact have been accomplished; the struggle would be subordinated to conditions, no longer a course of events flowing from the necessities of empirical existence, but rather like a play, even though a play which is portentous, life-imperiling, and perhaps life-destroying.

Only thus would an unlimited will-to-communicate be honestly maintained. A humanity might arise which would not be weak, but rather capable of unforeseeable growth through openness, touched by every real Substance, a unique consciousness of limits where the reality of action points, not to some dogmatically hardened, but rather to a genuine Transcendence.

Only thus can the genuine strength of man be developed. The power of the absolute in man tested in every possibility of struggle and questioning no longer needs the power of suasion, hatred, and cruelty in order to become active; nor the intoxication of magniloquent words and unintelligible dogmas in order to be believed in. And in such ways it would only become rough, harsh, and disillusioned. Only thus can self-deception disappear without man also being destroyed through the destruction of his vital lies. Only thus does the genuine Ground reveal itself unmasked out of the depths.

On the other hand, falseness sets in with the assertion of a single truth as valid for all men, despite the greatness of the men who lived thereby and the greatness of their history.

This is shown by the most manifold connections. If this one truth in the form of an intuitive, universal validity is taken as the form of all truth and for the work of reason, or inversely as a super-rational or counter-rational matter of faith, then everyone must bow before such a mighty truth without thereby being able to be himself. Thus, as a consequence of the false presupposition of a unique form of truth accessible to man, and as a consequence of what is connected therewith—the perversion of the multiplicity of the Encompassing—an incomprehension continually arises at the limits of what does not agree with one's own truth. Then suddenly a fanaticism appears which disrupts all communication. In the apparently free medium of speech, communication, listening, showing, and the giving of reasons, secretly the brutal force of what is momentarily the most powerful in existence is deciding.

However, a doctrine of the plurality of truths would have the same effect in producing falseness, if it appeared as a dogma of the deplorable multiplicity of truths instead of being an attitude of unlimited willingness to communicate one's own possible truth. The plurality of truths is untrue at the moment when they are seen externally as many, as determinable standpoints; for every standpoint can also absorb him who thinks it. They become even more untrue when they become mutually indifferent and simply rest alongside one another. What will not and what can not become the same, nevertheless, become related through Transcendence which touches the One, which, even if our gods be different, beyond all closer gods, discovers the distant God, which requires of us not to relapse into the distraction of warring multiplicities related only by indifference or the struggle over room to exist. There is the sophistry of an easy tolerance which wishes to be valid, but not to be really touched. On the other hand, there is the truth of tolerance which listens and gives and enters into the unpredictable process of communication by which force is restrained; in such a process, man reaches from his roots to the heights possible for him. The very highest arrives only through a transforming appropriation, through a knowledge which, even though it repudiates itself, searches into everything which can be encountered in the world.

To demand fulfillment and salvation in time, or even the picture of salvation, would be to cancel the problem of men, who must always become themselves through communication. It comes to this: never close off authentic possibilities of human development by anticipation.

Our horizon is not closed off with the contents of completed pictures. What is final for us philosophically is the forms of our attitude, sketches of a project which itself is to be thought of only as form, truths which are experienced only in their tendency, not alien impossibilities, but rather possibilities which are just beginning to speak even when they also appear to sink away again.

E. *Transcendence: Appearance of Temporal Existence as Communication*

The unfulfillment of communication and the difficulty of bearing its ship-wreck become the revelation of a depth which nothing other than Transcendence can fill. If God is eternal, still for man truth is as a developing truth, indeed, a truth developing in communication. Abstracted from this as something permanent, truth instead of remaining itself degenerates into determinate knowledge, into a finished contentment instead of a demand that consumes temporal existence.

Before Transcendence, however, the unfulfillment of communication disappears as the temporal appearance of truth. Our communication is, so to speak, animated by something which is expressed in the play of some metaphysical ideas: a pretemporal origin of a temporal need to communicate, or a final fulfillment which surpasses communication. Such ideas can not make anything clearly knowable, but in their collapse they can touch for a moment the overwhelming impulse which is the actual power in genuine communication.

In the beginning was the One, the Truth as it is inaccessible to us. But it is as though the lost One should be recovered from its dispersion by communication; as though the confusion of the many could resolve itself into rest through conjunction; as though a forgotten truth could never again be wholly attained.

Or, Truth lies in the future. In temporal existence, to be sure, there is an awareness of limits: what is not communicable is as though it were not, since it is not for any consciousness or knowledge. But precisely in communication the drive goes out beyond these limits, not at all to fall back into stupor, but to go onwards into unlimited disclosure so that what is can show itself by entering into communication. But then the drive goes beyond the greatest existential clarity, for there always remains something unsatisfied in it. The high moments of seemingly perfect agreement of communication in the thoroughgoing presence of all modes of the Encompassing, of the knowable, and of Transcendence show themselves even in time either to be false, or to be seeds again for new efforts toward disclosure, toward continuity in time. They are like anticipations of a possible fulfilled communication, which would mean at the same time completed truth and a timeless unity of the soul and the cosmos. The idea of such an unreality as a communication which reaches its goal means the elevation of communication into a transcendent perfection where there is no longer any need to communicate. The question whether, insofar as we have an unlimited will-to-communicate out of Existenz and reason, we do not already live out of this guiding and communicationless Being—such a question is not to be answered. Either the question asks something that is for us perfectly empty or it becomes an unquestionable certitude which dispenses with communication and, falsely expressed, only destroys itself. That is, it would paralyze the working of an unconditioned will-to-communicate by a specious knowledge about perfect communication.

If all communication must be thought of as canceled in Transcendence, as a lack in temporal existence, then all conceivability in general is also canceled. For example, I think upon the old proposition that God is the Truth. Then such a Truth has nothing to correspond with, since it is undivided and without opposition, whereas all other truths are modes of agreement. In fact, such an idea is empty and can only be felt existentially by me historically. Here where I can not penetrate, truth can retain no thinkable sense. The shipwrecking of all thinking about truth can shake one in his depths, but can not provide a tenable thought.

The stillness of the being of truth in Transcendence—not by abandoning the modes of the Encompassing, but in surpassing their worlds—such is the boundary where what the Whole is beyond all division can momentarily flash out. But this illumination is transitory in the world and, although of decisive influence upon men, incommunicable; for when it is communicated it is drawn into the modes of the Encompassing where it is ever lacking. Its experience is absolutely historical, in time out beyond time.

One can speak out of this experience, but not of it. The ultimate in thinking as in communication is silence.

NOTES

1. E. Baumgarten has shown this in an interesting study on Franklin ("Benjamin Franklin und die Psychologie des amerikanischen Alltags," in *Neue Jahrbücher für Wissenschaft und Jugendbildung*, February, 1933, pp. 251 ff.). He shows how Franklin had developed principles for this type of communication which always went beyond merely factual communication. The sensitiveness of men in their stubbornness and hidden interests requires from anyone who thinks he possesses the truth with certitude and knows what is now right an urbane attitude, a willingness of both to listen to the other and to question seriously what one has oneself thought out and planned. All direct communications of the truth, instead of a questioning of it, destroy communication; the other does not really listen since he is no longer even questioned. Therefore the principles for communicating the truth are not less important than the communicated truth itself. Genuine and effective respect does not mean that we both remain unchanged in our opinions; perhaps later the opinion of the other will be more adapted to change mine. Cooperation demands, further, that one come to understand the defects of the matter. To wish to set up something finished and completed is to misunderstand the potentialities which lie in the concrete and, instead of perfection, ends in confusion. Only by granting room for free play can there be any union and, consequently, any perception of how the concrete matter is to be changed. So, it can even be required that we pass ourselves by, suspend all our opinions, in order to make an action possible which for the moment seems necessary.

2. Cf. my *Philosophie*, vol. II, pp. 50–117, on "Kommunikation."

3. Cf. my *Philosophie*, vol. III, pp. 102–116, on "Das Gesetz des Tages und die Leidenschaft zur Nacht."

KNOWLEDGE OF OTHER MINDS*

William Ernest Hocking

...i have sometimes sat looking at a comrade, speculating on this mysterious isolation of self from self. Why are we so made that I gaze and see of thee only thy Wall, and never Thee? This Wall of thee is but a movable part of the Wall of my world; and I also am a Wall to thee: we look out at one another from behind masks. How would it seem if my mind could but once be *within* thine; and we could meet and without barrier be with each other? And then it has fallen upon me like a shock—as when one thinking himself alone has felt a presence—But I *am* in thy soul. These things around me are in thy experience. They are thy own; when I touch them and move them I change *thee*. When I look on them I see what thou seest; when I listen, I hear what thou hearest. I am in the great Room of thy soul; and I experience thy very experience. For *where art thou?* Not there, behind those eyes, within that head, in darkness, fraternizing with chemical processes. Of these, in my own case, I know nothing, and will know nothing; for my existence is spent not behind my Wall, but in front of it. I am there, where I have treasures. And there art thou, also. This world in which I live, is the world of my soul: and being within that, I am within thee. I can imagine no contact more real and thrilling than this; that we should meet and share identity, not through ineffable inner depths (alone), but here through the foregrounds of common experience; and that thou shouldst be —not behind that mask—but *here*, pressing with all thy consciousness upon me, *containing* me, and these things of mine. This is reality: and having seen it thus, I can never again be frightened into monadism by reflections which have strayed from their guiding insight. . . .

Any experience of an Other Mind which I could either wish or fancy must contain in it, we have thought, a World, full of sense and variety, full of obstinacy, and with substance at the back of it—like this present world.

* Reprinted from *The Meaning of God in Human Experience*, by William Ernest Hocking, by permission of Yale University Press.

In a truly social experience, such a world would be known *as being the world of the Other Mind.* That world would be known by me; but as it were through the eyes of the Other Mind. It would be in some sense a world common to both of us; known by both at once.

And though it would be perhaps conceivable that we might carry on mutual relations, each of us having his own separate world (as, for example, I might imagine myself in dream conversing with some resident of heaven or hell, having at the same time a vision of that spirit's world and reaching some understanding of him thereby): yet all real understanding and mutual measurement, mutual judgment, appreciation of character and so even of self-knowledge, must come through having the same world with him throughout. A perfect social experience would require that this present world of Nature should be known as being the World of the Other, precisely as it is my World.

And here begins our final enquiry. For as it seems to me, this present World of Nature *is* known by me as being, in just this sense, a common World: it seems to me, indeed, that it is *not otherwise known*—that is, that a knowledge of Other Knower is an integral part of the simplest knowledge of Nature itself.

It is more readily granted that social consciousness involves nature-consciousness, than that nature-consciousness involves social consciousness. If for no other reason, at least for this: that our experience of Nature is constant; whereas our social experience is, at best, *intermittent*—we can and often do experience Nature by itself. It is enough if we can find a genuine social experience now and then—we have not yet done so much as this—but to make such experience an organic part of nature-experience would be to make it perpetual.

Yet I confess that I cannot find a genuine social experience at all, except as a continuous experience. It appears to me that all three types of object are intermittent in the same sense, and continuous in the same sense. Intermittent enough is self-consciousness; yet self-consciousness is always with us. Intermittent is also the consciousness of Nature, as an object of direct attention; yet the undertone of Nature's presence never deserts me, even in deep sleep. In a way closely similar to that persistent awareness of my Self, which is compatible with the most fitful movements of attention to Self, is the awareness of Other Mind persistently present in experience, though doubtless less readily discoverable than any other. Inseparably bound up as I think with the continuous experience of Nature. And such continuous experience is the foundation of all the rest. I shall attempt, first of all, to make clear that *there must be such continuity, if there is to be any social experience at all.*

The chief elements of intermittency in social experience are removed when we look away from the body of the Other and regard his environing world of objects. It is in these, we have said, that we know him, quite as much as in his body. His body appears and disappears to our sight; but his environment does not disappear. It is true that these immediate objects of mine do cease, when he is gone, to occupy his consciousness, and can no longer be counted in his environment. But his experience of Nature was not limited to immediate objects, and never is so limited. Any idea of a thing, is an idea of that thing *placed* in a world of space and energy which remains a constant object. Our Space does not move as we move about in it, nor does our idea of it alter; our placings are successful, coherent, unconfused, and for any moment absolute, only because our ideas reach an unvarying field for these varying locations. If, therefore, at any time I have known an Other; and in knowing him have known Nature as his object; then this same Nature—with its Space-field, Force-field, and the like—does not cease to be *his Object* when he disappears.

As my own physical world is not bounded, at any time, by the partition or forest or hill that happens to limit my vision, but extends with my Space in all directions indefinitely—so does his physical world indefinitely extend, wherever he may be—reaches throughout my Space, reaches me and my place, reaches Substance—that same Substance which I also reach as my ultimate object. If I have once got into his world, I cannot get out of it while he endures—any more than he can get out of my world, so long as I can mean him; and these fundamental objects of mine, which I sum up in the word Nature, if they have ever been common objects, common to him and me, can never thereafter cease to be common objects. If my own continuous experience of Nature has ever been a *social* experience it can never thereafter lose its social reference.

But I seem to imply that there can be a *beginning* of social experience, and so a time when it was not—a time when my experience of Nature was mine alone. What I am required to show is that social experience *has no beginning*, except with physical experience itself: that my knowledge of Nature and of Other Mind are in their whole history interlocked, and inseparable. If Nature is ever common object, *it has always been* common object.

Let us consider how a social experience might be supposed to begin, as at times it does appear to begin, even abruptly. I think myself alone, for example, and with uncomfortable surprise find myself observed. It seems to me that I experience a jarring change of scene: my various objects have now to be connected up, in swift series, with the intruder's eyes. They have been exclusive objects; they have suddenly and perforce become common. They are all seared with this new relationship, as with a running breath of flame, and delivered over to joint ownership. Such readjustments often take perceptible *time* to effect. Have we not here a sufficient contrast between solitude and society, showing that social experience may *begin*—being imposed as an addition upon an experience not social?

What such a transition does unmistakably show is that exclusive property in the contents of experience is possible and may have distinct value
attached to it. Such exclusive property is made possible by sensible barriers,
such as opaqueness and distance. When I say, "I am entirely alone and
unobserved," I am putting my trust in these barriers. But when I resort to
a barrier, I confess that the objects which I thereby seek to monopolize or
conceal are in some danger of being known by Others. They are already
thought of by me as being sharable. And if they are sharable, it is because
they are already in the World of an Other Mind; there are continuous lines
through space between him and me; our world of Nature is already common. Is it not clear that when I suppose myself alone, and regard my
solitude as an achievement, I am in that very thought acknowledging my
world of Space and Nature to be a world common to me and Others?
My negative sociability has a very positive social consciousness at its
basis.

What such experiences imply and illustrate may be more compactly
stated in terms of the logic of communication, as follows: *In order that any
two beings should establish communication, they must already have something
in common.* For when I consider the two beings, prior to their communication, as apart from one another, I must consider at the same time the field
through which they must pass to approach each other: and this field is
already a common field. Two beings wholly independent, having no common region to measure their distance from one another, having between
them no continuity through which to travel *toward* each other, are lacking
in any "toward"—are unable therefore to *approach* each other, cannot come
together. All actual approach implies a deeper-going *presence* as an accomplished fact.

Given a minimal core of communication, and further communication
may spin itself out upon that core, may grow intense and varied, develop its
ups and downs, its relative presences and absences. But given nothing at
all—nothing at all can happen. If then, experience ever becomes actually
social, it has, in more rarefied condition, always been so; and hence is, in
the same fundamental sense, continuously so.[1]

There is some satisfaction in reducing our question to this alternative:
that social experience is either always present or never present. If now we
can show that we have at any time a veritable experience of Other Mind, we
show that we have such experience continually. I believe that this can be
shown.

For suppose that experience is never social. In making this supposition,
we mean to contrast the supposed non-social experience with a supposed
social experience. In imagining my experience to be confined to myself and
my objects, I admit or assume that I have an Idea of my experience not-so-
confined; that I know what a social experience would be like. Now I submit

that *this Idea of a social experience would not be possible, unless such an experience were actual.* Otherwise stated—In any sense in which I can imagine, or think, or conceive an experience of Other mind, in that same sense I *have* an experience of Other Mind, apart from which I should have no such Idea.

For every supposition we may make to the effect that our idea of Other Mind is a "mere idea" to which no real experience corresponds—that our supposed social experience is, in reality, subjective—implies that we have in mind a type of experience in comparison with which we can condemn our supposed social experience as merely subjective. But the only type of experience in comparison with which any experience can be judged as merely subjective, is a non-subjective experience. *The only point of view from which our supposed social experience can be criticized as incomplete is the point of view of social experience itself.* The only ground upon which this idea can be judged a "mere idea" is the ground of this same idea as *not mere*, namely, as actually bringing me into presence of Mind which is not my own.

Leibniz, for example, judges that all experience is monadic, and that monads do not in actuality experience each other, though to themselves they seem to do so. In making this hypothesis, Leibniz presents to himself the world of monads, and *he* knows their relations to be other than they seem: *he* at any rate occupies a non-monadic position, is for the time being an inter-monadic Mind. And any one who judges that he—and God—know the actual reach of ideas to fall short of their apparent reach, does thereby assert that *his* idea has not thus fallen short. There is no degree of outwardness of which we can think; no degree of reality which we incline to *deny* to idea. Let me represent to myself the Other Subject, his living center, as inaccessible to my experience; then either I deny myself nothing conceivable, or else I have that which I deny.

An objection (or, let me say, *the* objection): may not this idea of a genuine social experience, which you say guarantees the experience, be an *ideal*, i.e., a conception of something we may desire and think of, which we may well use to criticize what we have, admitting that we have it *not*? Surely, not every ideal implies the experience, but rather the contrary.

Answer: An ideal is either an extension of experience as given, or an innate standard.

The idea of a genuine experience of Other Mind is not an extension of other types of experience. Imagination has its ways of building improvements on experience by combining, enlarging, extending what is given, according to known types of relation. But if the idea of Other Mind were not already given, it could not be built up in this way. Certainly not by any arrangement of physical ideas in physical relations; nor yet by any arrangement of psychical ideas in psychical relations; nor by any union of physical and psychical. To reach the idea from these, we must use the special relation of Other-self-hood, which is the idea itself. Since my idea of social experience is uniquely different from all such constructions within the physical and psychical worlds, it is not an ideal based on them. It is not an ideal by construction at all; what we seek is simply the thing, social experience, in its unique difference from all immanent variations of other fields of experience. If this unique difference is an ideal merely, it is not an ideal by imaginative construction—it must be innate.

To say than an idea is innate, in Cartesian fashion, may mean simply that it is once for all there, and there is nothing more to be said about it. Or it may mean that the idea is due ultimately to some outer source (ancestral or divine); whereby we only reinvest in that Outer Source the difficulty of the idea in question—namely, how my ideas can reach that which is not-myself. Or, in may mean, in Kantian fashion, that the idea is a native and necessary form by which the Self orders the material of its experience, as otherwise given. Of these, the Kantian form is doubtless the strongest: and our social experience does most closely resemble, as we have noticed, a form of interpretation, a successful hypothesis clothing our manifold experience-stuff—ultimately sensation—with social meaning.

As an hypothesis our idea of Other Mind has certain interesting peculiarities. That it is not framed imaginatively of materials taken elsewhere from experience, we have observed. But further, there is no way in which it could be proved false, or even brought to other test than its use. There are various ways in which my social judgments may err, and suffer correction in experience. Thus I may impute to a friend a false motive, accepting his statement that I am in error. This judgment clearly relies on the more authentic social experience for correction. So with other errors, as by mistaking the identity of a person, or by mistaking a post for a man; these are corrected with reference to a better social experience. There is no type of error to which social experience is subject which can refer me away from social experience for correction—none which can send me back into myself for final court of appeal. As an hypothesis, the idea of Other Mind cannot be tested—nor can it be withdrawn.

But now, when we suppose that this idea of ours is an hypothesis *only*, what more than hypothesis do we think it might be? We think, do we not, that it might be a genuine social experience, and no mere hypothesis? But "genuine social experience" is the hypothesis itself, if it is such. And the contrast between real and apparent in social experience is only such contrast as social experience has already furnished us with. My idea of social experience is then, of social experience *as it is*: my ideal and my idea are the same—they refer me to what I have.

But let me make clear that in referring our idea of Other Mind to experience, I do not mean that it is derived, in Humian fashion, as a copy from a *previous impression*. It would be as little to the point to suggest that my idea of myself is derived from a previous impression of myself. My idea of myself is *at the same time* an experience of myself (unless my idea flies wild). So, unless as frequently happens I use some paper currency in referring to Other Mind, *my idea of Other Mind is at the same time an experience of Other Mind*. Let me but think what I mean by the Other Mind, and there, as I find my Self, I find the Other also. As an idea of a fundamental and constant experience, bound up with my equally permanent experiences of Self and Nature, this idea is not *prior* to experience; but is indeed prior to all *further* social experience, to all such as is intermittent and subject to error. This fundamental experience, and its idea, deserve, from their position in knowledge, to be called a *concrete a priori* knowledge.

Of the logic of this proof that we have actual experience of Other Mind I shall have more to say in a later chapter. It stands before us now somewhat barely. Unconvincingly, too, unless we can clothe with some living sense that strange assertion that Nature is always present to experience *as known* by an Other. That we cannot genuinely conceive ourselves as mentally alone in this cosmos, though we can well imagine ourselves bodily alone. That the inherent publicity of Nature, the fitness of all its objects to be communally experienced, is no empty potentiality, but a potentiality, founded (like other potentialities) on some actuality. We must now try to bring that experience more vividly before us; for we can hardly believe in an experience which we are yet unable to disentangle, or verify in ourselves. But let this conviction stand as a firm ground in our further search: that we should have no idea of an Other Mind or of a social experience unless we had the experience itself. That in whatever sense we can think, or imagine, or even *deny*, the reality of that experience—in that same sense it must be and is real to us.

There are, I think, three natural difficulties in the way of distinguishing the undertone of social experience amid the general rumble of the ground-levels of experience. First, that we cannot identify that constant Other with any *particular* individual, yet an Other must be an individual. Second, we cannot help regarding the experience of Nature as sufficient in itself, the presence of Others in the world being additional and wholly separable fact —that the experience of Nature *may* be at the same time a social experience we can more readily believe than that it must be. Third, that we cannot verify the social experience *socially*, in the same way that we verify the facts of Nature.

An object of knowledge or experience is, for the most part, a thing which you and I can verify together. I assert that something is true, in history, in physics, in mathematics; and when I make such statements *to you*, I mean that you also can go to the same facts and experiences and find the same thing that I have found. The truth of my assertion means that it is valid for you and other real persons in the same way that it is valid for me.

This association of minds which we call "we," accustomed as it is to sit in united judgment upon facts external to itself, cannot in like fashion sit in judgment upon itself. If we doubt "we," we know not to whom to appeal. We can hardly find our fundamental sociality, because we can hardly get so far away from it as to doubt it.

Nature is pre-eminently the world of socially verifiable things, the world of scientific research—which is general human collaboration on a common object. We look at Nature through the eyes of a social world. As we look at physical things through two eyes at once, and our prospect thereby acquires something in solidity and depth; so in quite similar fashion we see objects and truths in general through two *pairs* of eyes, through indefinite multitudes of eyes, and thereby acquire that deepest solidity of judgment which we call "universality." Universality is a social habit; the necessary habit of looking at any truth as if not I alone but the whole conscious universe were looking at it with me. The simplest judgment of physical things is universal in this sense; the most particular matter of fact, as I place it in my world of Nature, is so placed by help of this deep sense of the "cloud of witnesses" to whom this fact belongs, as well as to myself. Without this habitual democracy of judgment, this habitual loss of my life in the universal judgment, I can have no life at all in Nature or in the world of truth.

And just because my social consciousness is *that with which* I am thinking my world, I am not at the same time and in the same way thinking *of* it —as one does not see his own eyes in the usual processes of seeing things. When we speak of *experience*, what is called to mind is usually experience with the experiencers left out; experience just so far as it can easily be common object and no farther. Hume, in his examination of experience, found no Self; he had gone out of his house, as one noted rejoinder had it, and looking in at the window was unable to find himself at home. In truth it is not I alone, but *we* who go out, and cannot be discovered by ourselves in that house. And that same reflexive turn of consciousness which takes notice of Self, as of something always present, must, if we are right, discover the Other also, my other I, perpetual sustainer of universality in my judgments of experience.

When, then, we think of "experience" as something solitary and subjective, we are cutting it off from ourselves, and calling upon the Other Mind to view it so, together with us. Holding it thus, at arm's length, we criticize it, and as we thought, by means of an idea of something better: we criticize our solitary experience by the standard of a conceived social experience which would be more comprehensive. And this idea of a better, we thought, confessed the reality of that better. In truth, we should read the situation the other way. That experience, thus held off at arm's length and criticized, is not the Real Experience, judged by standard of an Idea of a better. That criticized experience is but a conceptual part of reality, abstracted from its context, and criticized not by idea (alone) but by the reality itself. The real and the conceptual have changed places. It is through my present inseparable community with The Other that I know that abstracted "experience" to be incomplete.

NOTES

1. There is indeed no sufficient reason for supposing that the sociality of my nature-experience continues to exist after my fellow has gone in any different sense than before he appeared. The episode of his coming and going does not change the physical aspect of my world; those objects of Nature seem intrinsically *ready to be observed* by an Other Mind, to be essentially public in their constitution. If I were actually alone in this same cosmos, it is difficult to think that I should be without the idea of possible Others, conceived of as sharing it with me; it is difficult to believe that Nature could be experienced as simply *meine Vorstellung*—for the physical object itself, the common *thing*, seems to present itself as numerously knowable, having many unused knowable aspects or valencies which I with my single point of view can never exhaust. Nature seems *structurally* common, or let us say *commune*; made up with reference to many co-experiencing minds. My thought of Nature suffers no jar as men come and go, for soci-ability is its element. In experiencing it, I am potentially experiencing the Other, and continuously.

ON A NEW DEFINITION OF "SYMBOL"*

Susanne K. Langer

*I*n every age, philosophical thinking exploits some dominant concepts and makes its greatest headway in solving problems conceived in terms of them. The seventeenth- and eighteenth-century philosophers construed knowledge, knower, and known in terms of sense data and their association. Descartes's self-examination gave classical psychology *the mind and its contents* as a starting point. Locke set up sensory immediacy as the new criterion of the real, namely, the "really given"—James's and Whitehead's "stubborn, ineluctable fact." Hobbes provided the *genetic method* of building up complex ideas from simple ones, as one builds a wall of bricks or a puzzle picture from many pieces. So Berkeley and Hume built tables out of squareness and brownness (Russell took a final fling at this job by using "soft data" as his logical glue); and in another quarter, still true to the Hobbesian method, Pavlov built intellect out of conditioned reflexes and Loeb built life out of tropisms.

The next century, opening with the accomplished work of Kant, had a new dominant notion, the transcendental sources of experience. This begot the problems of subject and object, concept and percept, and worst of all, form and content. Empiricism and transcendentalism went their respective ways, one panting after the headlong advance of science, the other sidling toward religion; and each repudiated the very issues that seemed obvious and pressing to the other.

We inherit both lines of thought. Forty years ago this legacy seemed enough to make philosophers schizophrenic. But since then a strange development (which had already started even at the worst time of schism, the turn of the century) has become apparent: empiricism as well as transcendentalism uncovered a new level of philosophical problems, below

Reprinted from *Philosophical Sketches*, by Susanne K. Langer, by permission of the Johns Hopkins Press.

the superficial divergent "isms." Both struck the rich vein of *semantic* issues.

The concept of meaning, in all its varieties, is the dominant philosophical concept of our time. Sign, symbol, denotation, signification, communication—these notions are our stock in trade. The changing frame of scientific thought inspired the semantic shift from attributive to operational definition. The bold expansion of mathematics broached some tricky problems of incomplete symbols, purely structural signs, variable context, variable sense, indirect reference; modern symbolic logic has advanced chiefly under the goad of such puzzling ideas. It has become the basic technique of the most modern philosophical thinking, and a technique is a natural measure of a so-called "field of study." To lend meaning to mathematics has been the first aim of our semantic labors, and the concepts developed in symbolic logic—concepts like "element," "relation," "proposition," "class," and the directive notions of "assertion," "definition," "substitution," and so on—have served to organize the new realm. But mathematics has not remained the only challenger; an even greater task has arisen for the philosopher with the growth of the physical sciences, whereof mathematics is the handmaid (a highly modern, independent maid—rather an Amazon). It is with regard to the sciences of nature that all the problems of *reference* arise; and these in turn entail epistemological questions of truth, fact, knowledge, and—coming full circle back to semantics—communication of knowledge.

Every new venture in philosophy has a furiously active phase, reaches a crest of important production, and then slows to a more sober sort of work as its inherent paradoxes, its difficulties of conception, come to light. Then it either elicits a real growth of people's intellectual faculties, an advance of imagination, like the shift from substance-attribute thinking to functional thinking that marks scientific imagination today, and enlarges its field by bold extensions of its generative concepts, or it bogs down on its paradoxes, as even very ardent philosophical speculations—notoriously social and ethical ones—have often done.

Semantic theory has, I think, already passed its first crest. Its paradoxes have appeared, and the desire to evade them tends to narrow the field of inquiry to a few carefully put subjects. If you run back the table of contents of a journal like *Mind* from the current number to the 1920's, there is no great change in the titles. John Wisdom on "denoting" might be 1928, 1938, or 1948. The new contributors of the Cambridge school are fending off rather than attacking semantic problems—rolling them all up again in the careless colloquial language of common sense, from which they were originally extricated. That is one way of dealing with paradoxes.

The whole study of symbols and meaning seems to me to be temporarily exhausted, and bogging down. At the same time, an outside danger besets what conquests have been made, for the interest in symbols is not limited to the critique of science and interpretation of mathematics, but is stirring in fairly remote quarters—psychology (after two kinds), ethnology, and philology. In some of these contexts the very conception of "symbol" is different from that used by a mathematician or scientist. A symbol may be a myth, a root metaphor, or a clinical symptom. "Meaning," likewise, is neither signification nor denotation. It is anything from a stimulus-response relation, to the wish behind a dream.

There is little the poor epistemologist can do about such encroachments of the jungle on his garden. All he can say is that these are loose and illicit uses of the words "symbol" and "meaning." Yet the uses go on, and even develop techniques, in which it is hard to see a mere loose treatment of ideas once belonging to logic. The symbol concept of dynamic psychology, for instance, is obviously of different origin from that employed by Whitehead and Russell in *Principia mathematica*. The fact is that several major lines of thought have arrived almost simultaneously at the recognition of the basic mental function that distinguishes man from nonhuman creatures—the use, in one way or another, of symbols to convey concepts.

It must be admitted that one way is very different from another. Now, any phenomenon that can serve in such diverse ways must be fairly complex. It is likely to have many interrelated functions. In any given context, some of its functions are likely to be more important or more obvious than others, and the concept of the phenomenon itself (here, the concept of "symbol") will be defined with reference to its relevant properties. The definition establishes but also restricts it; and it may happen that the most adequate and economical definition we can make in a fairly precise context, such as the context of logical discourse in which "symbol" has been defined, is incapable of yielding any derivative concepts that might serve other interests. It allows of no generalization, no *wider sense*. Therefore it cannot be extended to any very different frames of reference.

It was in reflecting on the nature of art that I came on a conception of the symbol relation quite distinct from the one I had formed in connection with all my earlier studies, which had centered around symbolic logic. This new view of symbolization and meaning stemmed from the Kantian analysis of experience, and had been highly developed in Cassirer's *Philosophie der symbolischen Formen*. In many years of work on the fundamental problems of art I have found it indispensable; it served as a key to the most involved questions. But this symbol concept, as it emerges in use, in the course of work—which, after all, is the most authentic source of all concepts—cannot be defined in terms of denotation, signification, formal assignment, or reference. The proof of a pudding is in the eating, and I submit that Cassirer's pudding is good; but the recipe is not on the box. Cassirer himself considered the semantic functions that belong to scientific symbols as a special development, which occurred under the influence of language, by virtue of its inherent *generality* together with its *signific* character. But symbolization as such he traced further back. His notion of "symbol" was more primitive than that of a sign used by common consent to stand for an associated concept; in his sense of the word, a sound, mark, object, or event could be a symbol to a person, without that person's consciously going from it to its meaning. This is the basic concept in his theory of myth.

A similar idea meets us in Freud's theory of dreams. Cassirer opposed that theory vehemently. It was, however, not Freud's symbol concept he rejected, but the subjective nature of the meaning Freud attributed to it. We need not go into this question; what is relevant here is merely that two thinkers with different interests and aims have worked extensively and effectively with a concept that logicians and philosophers of science find unintelligible.

The fact that three large subjects—myth, art, and dynamic psychology —are made accessible to progressive study by the use of a wide, but logically questionable conception of "symbol," and consequently of "meaning," "knowledge," and other *definienda* connected with "symbol," makes me suspect that the terms in which our semantic definitions are traditionally couched militate against their generalization, and thereby against legitimate extensions of our metalogical concepts. If the formally defined sense of "symbol" and the problematical sense derived from new uses cannot be commensurated, they will simply diverge until the word has two unrelated meanings—not a desirable prospect, in an age that dreams of the unity of science. Above all, such a practice would court the danger that where the word "symbol" is simply left undefined, it will increase without limit in vagueness, and collect the aura of emotional values that usually accrues to illicitly extended terms. My recommendation, therefore, is to try a new definition altogether, that may lend itself to wider uses, but allow the closest specification in formal contexts.

Most semanticists have approached the study of symbols with a primary interest in discursive thought and its communication, i.e., their obvious functions in discourse. During recent years the emphasis has shifted more and more toward communication. There are some interesting reasons for this tendency, but they do not concern us here. What concerns us is the stress which has thereby been laid on two properties of symbols that are usually taken as essential characteristics: the function of *reference*, or direction of the user's interest to something apart from the symbol, and the *conventional* nature of the connection between the symbol and the object to which it refers, by virtue of which connection the reference occurs. Ernest Nagel has defined the scientist's concept of "symbol" in the statement: "By a symbol I understand any occurrence (or type of occurrence), usually linguistic in status, which is taken to signify something else by way of tacit or explicit conventions or rules of language."[1]

This is, I think, a sufficient characterization of "symbol" for all purposes of science, and indeed all literal uses of language, including idiomatic and colloquially figurative uses. The rules of using language need not be strict to be publicly though tacitly accepted conventions. In most cases of figurative statement, the literal equivalent is directly understood, and could be readily produced by the speaker or writer using the figure of speech, which is itself a further convention.

Nagel is quite aware of the fact that the word "symbol" has some uses to which this definition would not be adequate, and takes care to point it out. In the essay from which I just quoted, he does not censure those other uses as illicit, though he has questioned their credentials elsewhere. But the thing that concerns me here is precisely the ground on which he could and did question them—namely, that a symbol concept appropriate to those other uses cannot be derived by any modification of the scientific concept. No generalization of the definition he has given, followed by a different specification, will yield a meaning of "symbol" usable in the contexts where obviously a different meaning obtains.

Our interest in communication had led us to note, above all, those kinds of symbol that lend themselves to this purpose; some semantic theories, especially the classic doctrines that go back to the eighteenth century, treat communication as the original function of language, and indeed of all symbolization. Modern psychological studies of language often present symbols as glorified signals (what Nagel distinguishes as "natural signs"), in the hope of finding their prototypes in animal communication. The importance of language as a human communicative device is certainly patent.

But this paramount use has made us neglect another aspect of symbols, which is less obvious, but perhaps, at some levels of our mental evolution, equally important—the *formulation* of experience by the process of symbolization. This aspect has not gone entirely unrecognized. It is the great insight of those epistemological thinkers who take their inspiration from Kant. Kant, of course, realized and declared that the human mind puts its stamp on experience, that it receives no raw data for its perceptions, but that everything humanly perceivable, is already held in the mold of the humanly conceivable. The innate schema, however, is transcendental, common to all human consciousness; it furnishes no principle of conceptual advance, no phenomenal means of conception. Its imposition is not a phenomenal process. Yet the formulation of experience is a phenomenal process. Again it was, above all, Cassirer who recognized the part which *symbolization*, or symbolic expression, plays in the formulation of things and events and the natural ordering of our ambient as a "world."

This formulative function is common to all symbols, though in some it is very elementary. Any sign—for instance, the little noise that a word physically is—by being conventionally *assigned* to any object, event, quality, relation, or what not that it is to signify, bestows a conceptual identity on that designated item. Symbolization gives it form.

The perception of form arises, I think, from the process of symbolization, and the perception of form is abstraction. Abstraction is usually treated as a difficult, unnatural process—Bergson would have us believe, indeed, that it is an antinatural process of perceptual distortion. But from the naturalistic view which, for better or worse, I find compelling, it is hard to understand how anyone could have started any abstractive practices if abstraction were not natural to human minds.[2] The fact is, I think, that the perception of forms, or abstraction, is intuitive, just as the recognition of relations, of instances, and of meaning is. It is one of the basic acts of logical intuition, and its primitive and typical occurrence is in the process of symbolization.

I should like to propose a definition of "symbol" based on this formulative function, by means of which some sort of *conception* is always abstracted from any symbolized experience. In a book published only three years ago [1953], I defined a symbol as "any device whereby we are enabled to make an abstraction." I am already doubtful of that definition in its simple, initial form, though it may prove to be tenable. On the other hand, it may be that some devices whereby we make an abstraction are not complete, bona fide symbols, but that it is safer—at least tentatively—to say: "Any device whereby we make an abstraction is a symbolic element, and all abstraction involves symbolization." Whatever the precise wording should finally be, the reasons for trying some such new definition are easy enough to present.

In the first place, there may be many ways of making abstractions, and therefore many kinds of symbols. Abstraction is a process that allows of steps, incomplete phases, to which all sorts of protosymbolic phenomena, such as Cassirer adduces in his great *Philosophy of Symbolic Forms* (esp. Vol. II), might be related. Works of art, which I am sure have *import*, but not genuine *meaning*, are symbols of a sort, but not of the sort Nagel defined; for neither do they point beyond themselves to something thereafter known apart from the symbol, nor are they established by convention. It is their powerful articulation of form that enables us to perceive the form in its single instance. But they are, I think, quasi-symbols; they have some but not all the functions of genuine symbols. Melvin Rader suggested that one should speak of a work of art as an "expressive form" rather than as an "art symbol," and although I think the latter term perfectly defensible, I have used his term alternatively ever since.

Similar considerations apply to the dream elements which Freud classes as symbols. Surely they are not established by any convention; and although they are related to quite other ideas, which they are said to "mean," they are not in any usual sense employed to refer to those ideas. They do not denote them for the dreamer as words denote their objects. Yet the relation of dream figments to their meanings is one of *formulation* of the supposedly unconscious "dream thought," and in fact a rather complex abstraction of the emotional aspects of experiences; and the element common to symbol and "meaning" is a formal one—an abstract element.

Finally, the abstractive character of symbols is what gives them their scientific value. In science we have a highly developed special use of symbols, built on conventions, and resulting in the boldest abstractions that have ever been made. Scientific symbolization is, I think, always genuine *language*, in the strictest sense, and the symbolism of mathematics the greatest possible refinement of language; and language as such is the paradigm of symbolism, as its content—discursive thought—is of conception.

Whatever the difficulties of the proposed redefinition of "symbol," I think the direction is right; only a radical shift of approach can give us a basic concept elastic enough to allow the widely diverse definitions we want to derive, in essential relation to each other.

NOTES

1. "Symbolism and Science," in *Symbols and Values: An Initial Study* (Thirteenth Symposium on Science, Philosophy and Religion; New York, 1954).

2. For a further treatment of this problem, see "Emotion and Abstraction" (No. 4) [in S. K. Langer, *Philosophical Sketches*, New York: Mentor, 1964].

RULES, PERCEPTION, AND INTELLIGIBILITY*

F. A. Hayek

1. RULE-GUIDED ACTION

*t*he most striking instance of the phenomenon from which we shall start is the ability of small children to use language in accordance with the rules of grammar and idiom of which they are wholly unaware.** "Perhaps there is," Edward Sapir wrote thirty-five years ago, "a far-reaching moral in the fact that even a child may speak the most difficult language with idiomatic ease but that it takes an unusually analytical type of mind to define the mere elements of that incredibly subtle linguistic mechanism which is but a plaything in the child's unconscious.†

The phenomenon is a very comprehensive one and includes all that we call skills. The skill of a craftsman or athlete which in English is described as "know how" (to carve, to ride a bicycle, to ski, or to tie a knot) belongs to this category. It is characteristic of these skills that we are usually not able to state explicitly (discursively) the manner of acting which is involved. A good example is given in another connexion by M. Friedman and L. J. Savage:

> * Reprinted from *The Proceedings of the British Academy*, Vol. XLVIII, 19, by permission of The British Academy.
>
> ** Cf. particularly Michael Polanyi, *Personal Knowledge, Towards a Post-Critical Philosophy*, London, 1959, especially the chapters on "Skills" and "Articulation," and see also the penetrating observation in Adam Ferguson, *An Essay on the History of Civil Society*, London, 1766, p. 50.
>
> † E. Sapir (52, p. 549). Further insight into the nature of grammatical order makes this achievement of children appear even more remarkable, and R. D. Lees was recently moved to observe (32, p. 408) that "in the case of this typically human and culturally universal phenomenon of speech, the simplest model that we can construct to account for it reveals that a grammar is of the same order as a predictive theory. If we are to account adequately for the indubitable fact that a child by the age of five or six has somehow reconstructed for himself the theory of this language, it would seem that our notions of human learning are due for some considerable sophistication." Numbers in footnotes refer to the Bibliography at the end.

Consider the problem of predicting, before each shot, the direction of travel of a billiard ball hit by an expert billiard player. It would be possible to construct one or more mathematical formulas that would give the directions of travel that would score points and, among these, would indicate the one (or more) that would leave the balls in the best positions. The formulas might, of course, be extremely complicated, since they would necessarily take account of the location of the balls in relation to one another and of the cushions and of the complicated phenomena induced by "english." Nonetheless, it seems not at all unreasonable that excellent predictions would be yielded by the hypothesis that the billiard player made his shots *as if* he knew the formulas, could estimate accurately by eye the angles, etc., describing the location of the balls, could make lightning calculations from the formulas, and could then make the ball travel in the direction indicated by the formulas.*

(A being endowed with intellectual powers of a higher order would probably describe this by saying that the billiard player acted as if he could think.)

So far as we are able to describe the character of such skills we must do so by stating the rules governing the actions of which the actors will usually be unaware. Unfortunately, modern English usage does not permit generally to employ the verb "can" (in the sense of the German *können*) to describe all those instances in which an individual merely "knows how" to do a thing. In the instances so far quoted it will probably be readily granted that the "know how" consists in the capacity to act according to rules which we may be able to discover but which we need not be able to state in order to obey them.** The problem is, however, of much wider significance than will perhaps be readily conceded. If what is called the *Sprachgefühl* consists in our capacity to follow yet unformulated rules,† there is no reason why,

---

* M. Friedman and L. J. Savage (8, p. 87).

** Cf. Gilbert Ryle (48) and (49, chapter 2). The almost complete loss of the original connotation of "can" in English, where it can scarcely any longer be used in the infinitive form, is not only an obstacle to the easy discussion of these problems but also a source of confusion in the international communication of ideas. If a German says "Ich weiß, wei man Tennis spielt" this does not necessarily imply that he knows how to play tennis, which a German would express by saying "Ich kann Tennis spielen." In German the former phrase states the explicit knowledge of the rules of the game and may—if the speaker had made special motion studies—refer to the rules by which the skill of a player can be described, a skill which the speaker who claims to know these rules need not possess. German, in fact, has three terms for the English "to know": *wissen*, corresponding to "know that," *kennen*, corresponding to "be acquainted with," and *können*, corresponding to "know how." See the interesting discussion in H. Helmholtz (21, pp. 92 et seq.). The passage is inevitably rendered only imperfectly in the English translation of this work.

† Cf. F. Kainz (23, p. 343): "Die Normen, die das Sprachverwenden steuern, das Richtige vom Falschen sondern, bilden in ihrer Gesamtheit das Sprachgefühl."

for example, the sense of justice (the *Rechtsgefühl*) should not also consist in such a capacity to follow rules which we do not know in the sense that we can state them.*

From these instances where action is guided by rules (movement patterns, ordering principles, &c.) which the acting person need not explicitly know (be able to specify, discursively to describe, or "verbalize"),** and where the nervous systems appears to act as what may be called a "movement pattern effector," we must now turn to the corresponding and no less interesting instances where the organism is able to recognize actions conforming to such rules or patterns without being consciously aware of the elements of these patterns, and therefore must be presumed to possess also a kind of "movement pattern detector."

2. RULE-GUIDED PERCEPTION

Again the capacity of the child to understand various meanings of sentences expressed by the appropriate grammatical structure provides the most conspicuous example of the capacity of rule-perception. Rules which we cannot state thus do not govern only our actions. They also govern our perceptions, and particularly our perceptions of other people's actions. The child who speaks grammatically without knowing the rules of grammar not only understands all the shades of meaning expressed by others through following the rules of grammar, but may also be able to correct a grammatical mistake in the speech of others.

This capacity of perceiving rules (or regularity, or patterns) in the action of others is a very general and important phenomenon. It is an instance of *Gestalt* perception, but of a perception of configurations of a peculiar kind. While in the more familiar instances we are able to specify (explicitly or discursively to describe or explicate) the configurations which are recognized as the same, and therefore also are able deliberately to reproduce the stimulus situation which will produce the same perception in different people, all we often know in the instances which belong here and which will be the main subject of this paper is that a particular situation is recognized by different persons as one of a certain kind.

To these classes of structures of events which are "known by none, and

---

* Cf. L. Wittgenstein (66, p. 185): " 'Knowing' it means only: being able to describe it."

** Since the meaning of many of the terms we shall have to use is somewhat fluid, we shall occasionally resort to the device of cumulating near synonyms which, although not identical in their meaning, by the range of overlap of meaning define more precisely the sense in which we use these terms.

understood by all"* belong in the first instance gestures and facial expressions. It is significant that the capacity to respond to signs of which we are
not conscious decreases as we move from members of our own culture to
those of different cultures, but that in some measure it also exists in our
mutual relations to and also between higher animals.** The phenomenon
has in recent years received a good deal of attention under the heading of
"physiognomy perception";† it seems, however, to be of much wider
occurrence than this term at first suggests. It guides not only our perception of expression but also our recognition of action as directed or purposive;†† and it colours also our perception of non-human and inanimate
phenomena. It would lead too far to consider here the important contributions made to the knowledge of these phenomena by ethology, particularly
by the studies of birds by O. Heinroth, K. Z. Lorenz, and N. Tinbergen,§
though their descriptions of the "infective" character of certain types of
movement and of the "innate releasing mechanism" as a "perceptual
function" are highly relevant. We shall on the whole have to confine ourselves to the problems in man with an occasional look at other mammals.

3. IMITATION AND IDENTIFICATION

The main difficulty which has to be overcome in accounting for these
phenomena is most clearly seen in connexion with the phenomenon of
imitation. The attention paid to this by psychologists has fluctuated much

* E. Sapir (52, p. 556): "In spite of these difficulties of conscious analysis,
we respond to gestures with an extreme alertness and, one might almost say, in
accordance with an elaborate and secret code that is written nowhere, known
by none, and understood by all." Compare also Goethe's expression "Ein jeder
lebt's, nicht allen ist's bekannt."

** Wolfgang Köhler (27, p. 307) reports that the chimpanzee "at once
correctly interprets the slightest changes of human expression, whether menac-
ing or friendly"; and H. Hediger (18, p. 282) writes: "Im Tierreich, namentlich
bei den Säugetieren, besteht eine weitvertreitete und überraschend hohe
Fähigkeit, menschliche Ausdruckserscheinungen ganz allgemein aufs feinste
zu interpretieren." R. E. Miller and his collaborators (37, p. 158) have shown
"that the effect of fear and/or anxiety can be perceived or discriminated by
rhesus monkeys in the facial expression and posture of other monkeys." For
an illustration of the reverse relation, man recognizing the actions of apes as
meaningful, see the description of observations of chimpanzees in the wild in
A. Kortlandt (30).

† See H. Werner (63 and 64), F. Heider (19), and now J. Church (7) where,
after completing this paper, I found much support for its argument.

†† See, particularly, F. G. From (9) and E. Rubin (50), as well as G. W.
Allport (2, p. 520), who sums up by saying that "the key to person perception
lies in our attention to what the other is *trying to do*."

§ See 20, 33 and 34, and 58.

and after a period of neglect it seems again to become respectable.* The aspect which concerns us here probably has not again been stated more clearly since it was first pointed out at the end of the eighteenth century by Dugald Stewart.** It concerns a difficulty which is commonly overlooked because imitation is most frequently discussed in connexion with speech where it is at least plausible to assume that the sounds emitted by an individual are perceived by him as similar to those produced by another.

The position is very different, however, in the case of gestures, postures, gait, and other movements and particularly in that of facial expressions, where the movements of one's own body are perceived in a manner altogether different from that in which the corresponding movements of another person are perceived. Whatever in this respect may be the capacities of the newborn infant,† there can be no doubt that not only do human beings soon learn to recognize and to imitate complex movement patterns, but also that the various forms of "infection" which occur in all forms of group life presuppose some such identification of the observed movements of another with one's own movements.†† Whether it is the bird which is induced to fly (or preen, scratch, shake itself, &c.) by the sight of other birds doing so, or man induced to yawn or stretch by seeing others doing the same, or the more deliberate imitation practised in mimicry or learning a skill, what happens in all these instances is that an observed movement is directly translated into the corresponding action, often without the observing and imitating individual being aware of the elements of which the action consists or (in the case of man) being able to state what he observes and does.*

* For a survey see N. E. Miller and J. Dollard (36, especially Appendix 2), and cf. also H. F. Harlow (14, p. 443), K. Koffka (28, pp. 307–19), and G. W. Allport (2, chapter 1).

** Dugald Stewart (56, chapter on "Sympathetic Imitation").

† For the latest experimental results and the earlier literature on the smiling response of infants see R. Ahrens (1), K. Goldstein (11), H. Plessner (44), and F. J. J. Buytendijk (6).

†† Cf. Dugald Stewart (56, p. 139): "To bestow upon [this theory of imitation] even the shadow of plausibility, it must be supposed further, that the infant has the aid of a mirror, to enable it to know the existence of its own smile, and what sort of appearance these smiles exhibit to the eye . . . this throws no light whatever on the present difficulty till it is further explained by what process the child learns to *identify* what it feels, or is conscious of, in its own countenance, with what it sees on the countenance of others." (Italics added and original italics omitted.)

* Cf. P. Schilder (53, p. 244): "real imitation actions . . . are due to the fact that the visual presentation of the movement of another is apt to evoke the representation of a similar movement of one's own body, which, like all motor representations, tends to realize itself immediately in movements. Many of the imitation movements of children are of this class."

Our capacity to imitate someone's gait, postures, or grimaces certainly does not depend on our capacity to describe these in words. We are frequently unable to do the latter, not merely because we lack the appropriate words but because we are unaware both of the elements of which these patterns are made up and of the manner in which they are related. We may well have a name for the whole,* or sometimes use comparisons with movements of animals ("creeping," "ferocious") and the like, or describe conduct as expressive of an attribute of character such as "furtive," "timid," "determined," or "proud." In one sense we thus know what we observe, but in another sense we do not know what it is that we thus observe.

Imitation is of course only one particularly obvious instance of the many in which we recognize the actions of others as being of a known kind, of a kind, however, which we are able to describe only by stating the "meaning" which these actions have to us and not by pointing out the elements from which we recognize this meaning. Whenever we conclude that an individual is in a certain mood, or acts deliberately or purposively or effortlessly, seems to expect** something or to threaten or comfort another, &c., we generally do not know, and would not be able to explain, how we know this. Yet we generally act successfully on the basis of such "understanding" of the conduct of others.

All these instances raise a problem of "identification," not in the special psycho-analytical but in the ordinary sense of the term, i.e., in the sense that some movement (or posture, &c.) of our own which is perceived through one sense is recognized as being of the same kind as the movements of other people which we perceive through another sense. Before imitation is possible, identification must be achieved, i.e., the correspondence established between movement patterns which are perceived through different sense modalities.

4. THE TRANSFER OF LEARNT RULES

The recognition of a correspondence between patterns made up of different sensory elements (whether belonging to the same or to different sense modalities) presupposes a mechanism of sensory pattern transfer, that is, a mechanism for the transfer of the capacity to discern an abstract order or arrangement from one field to another. That such a capacity should exist seems not implausible as a similar transfer of learning in the motor sphere is a well-established fact: skills learnt with one hand are readily transferred

* G. Kietz (24, p. 1) lists 59 verbs and 67 adjectives which are used in the region of Leipzig to describe distinguishable kinds of gait.

** Even the author of *A Glossary of some Terms used in the Objective Science of Behavior* (61, s.v. "expect") finds himself forced to say that "If one does not 'intuitively know' what *expect* means, one is lost."

to the other, &c*. It has recently also been demonstrated that, for example, monkeys trained to respond to differences in simple rhythms of light signals (opening a door on two signals of equal duration and not opening it on two signals of unequal duration) at once transferred this response to the corresponding rhythms of sound signals.** In the field of perception many of the Gestalt phenomena, such as the transposition of a melody, also imply the operation of the same principle. The prevalent views on the nature of perception, however, do not supply us with an adequate account of how such a transfer is brought about.†

Such a mechanism is not difficult to conceive. The main point to keep in mind is that in order that any two different sensory elements ("elementary sense qualities" or more complex percepts) should be capable of taking the same place in a pattern of a certain kind, they must have certain attributes in common. Unless both can vary along some such scale as large: small, strong: weak, of long duration: of short duration, &c., they cannot serve in the same place as constituents of similar patterns. The most important of these common properties of different kinds of sensations which enables them to take the same place in a pattern of a certain kind is their common space-time framework: while visual, tactile, kinesthetic, and auditory sensations may have the same rhythm, and the first three of them also form the same spatial patterns, this is not possible for sensations of smell and taste.††

---

* A convenient survey of the facts is given by R. S. Woodworth and H. Schlossberg (67, chapter 24), where also instances of the transfer of "perceptual skills" are given. See also K. S. Lashley (31), a paper full of significant suggestions on our problem.

** L. C. Stepien and others (55, pp. 472–3).

† In modern discussions of these problems resort is generally had to the somewhat vague conception of the "schema." For recent discussions of this see R. C. Oldfield and O. L. Zangwill (42), R. C. Oldfield (41), and M. D. Vernon (60). We shall not use it here as a technical term because by its various uses it has acquired a penumbra of undesirable connotations.

†† It is also becoming increasingly clear that even the perception of spatial patterns, which we are inclined to ascribe to the simultaneous occurrence of the sensory elements from which the patterns are made up, rests largely on a process of visual or tactual scanning and on the perception of "gradients," i.e., on the particular sequence of stimuli being recognized as following a rule. Hence, as K. S. Lashley has pointed out (31, p. 128), "spatial and temporal order thus appear to be almost completely interchangeable in cerebral action." It would seem as if the task of the theory of perception were increasingly becoming the discovery of the rules according to which various constellations of physical data are translated into perceptual categories so that a great variety of sets of physical facts are interpreted as the same phenomenal situation. This development traces back to H. Helmholtz's conception of the "unconscious inference" (21), has been developed particularly by J. C. Gibson (10), and has recently produced the most remarkable results on Ivo Kohler's demonstration (29) of the "general rules" by which the visual system learns to correct exceedingly complex and variable distortions produced by prismatic spectacles when the eye or the head moves.

These common attributes that the separate sensations must possess in order to be capable of forming the same abstract patterns must evidently have some distinct neutral correlates (impulses in particular groups of neurons which represent them), because only thus can they in some respect have the same effect on our mental processes and actions: if different sensations lead us to describe them as "large" or "intense" or "long," the impulses corresponding to them must at some stage of the hierarchical order of evaluation (classification)* reach the same pathways. Once, however, we recognize that in order to possess similar attributes the sensations caused by different nerve impulses must have some identical elements among the "following"** which determines their quality, the problem of the transfer of a pattern that has been learnt in one sensory field to another presents no serious difficulty.

If a certain order or sequence of sensory elements possessing given attributes has acquired a distinctive significance, this significance will be determined by the classification as equivalent of the neutral events standing for those attributes and it will thus automatically apply to them also when they are evoked by other sensations than those in connexion with which the pattern has been learnt in the first instance. Or, to put this differently, sensations which have common attributes will be capable of forming elements of the same pattern and this pattern will be recognized as one of the same kind even if it has never been experienced before in connexion with the particular elements, because the otherwise qualitatively different sensations will have among the impulses determining their quality some which uniquely determine the abstract attribute in question; and whenever the capacity of recognizing an abstract rule which the arrangement of these attributes follow has been acquired in one field, the same master mould will apply when the signs for those abstract attributes are evoked by altogether different elements. It is the classification of the structure of relationships between these abstract attributes which constitutes the recognition of the patterns as the same or different.

5. BEHAVIOUR PATTERNS AND PERCEPTION PATTERNS

In the course of its development† any organism will acquire a large repertoire of such perceptual patterns to which it can specifically respond, and among this repertoire of patterns some of the earliest and most firmly embedded will be those due to the proprioceptive (kinesthetic) recording

* For a systematic exposition of the theory underlying this statement see F. A. Hayek (15).

** See 15, par. 3.34.

† The expression "development" is used to include not only ontogenetic but also phylogenetic processes.

of movement patterns of its own body, movement patterns which in many instances will be guided by innate organization and probably be directed sub-cortically yet reported to and recorded at higher levels. The term "movement pattern" in this connexion hardly suggests the complexity or variety of the attributes of the movements involved. Not only does it include relative movements of rigid bodies and various bending or elastic movements of flexible bodies, but also continuous and discontinuous, rhythmic and rhythmic changes of speed, &c. The opening and closing of jaws or beaks or the characteristic movements of limbs are relatively simple instances of such patterns. They can generally be analysed into several separate movements which together produce the pattern in question.

The young animal for which every day begins with the sight of his elders and siblings yawning and stretching, grooming and defecating, scanning the environment, and so on, and who soon learns to recognize these basic schemata as the same as its own innate movement patterns connected with certain moods (or dispositions, or sets), will tend to place into these perceptual categories everything which approximately fits them. These patterns will provide the master moulds (templates, schemata, or *Schablonen*) in terms of which will be perceived many other complex phenomena in addition to those from which the patterns are derived. What at first may have originated with an innate and fairly specific movement pattern may thus become a learnt and abstract mould for classifying perceived events. ("Classifying" stands here, of course, for a process of channelling, or switching, or "gating," of the nervous impulses so as to produce a particular disposition or set.)* The effect of perceiving that events occur according to a rule will thus be that another rule is imposed upon the further course of the processes in the nervous system.

The phenomenal (sensory, subjective, or behavioural**) world in which such an organism lives will therefore be built up largely of movement patterns characteristic of its own kind (species or wider group). These will be among the most important categories in terms of which it perceives the world and particularly most forms of life. Our tendency to personify (to interpret in anthropomorphic or animistic terms) the events we observe is probably the result of such an application of schemata which our own bodily movements provide. It is they which make, though not yet intelligible, at least perceivable (comprehensible or meaningful) complexes of events which without such perceptual schemata would have no coherence or character as wholes.

It is not surprising that the explicit evoking of these anthropomorphic interpretations should have become one of the main tools of artistic expression by which the poet or painter can conjure up the character of our

* See 15, chapter iii.

** In contrast to objective, physical, scientific, &c. See 15, para. 1.10.

experiences in an especially vivid manner. Expressions such as that a thundercloud leans threateningly over us, or that a landscape is peaceful or smiling or sombre or wild, are more than merely metaphors. They describe true attributes of our experiences in the terms in which they occur. This does not mean that these attributes belong to the objective events in any other sense than that we intuitively ascribe them to those events. But they are nevertheless part of the environment as we know it and as it determines our conduct. And, as we shall see, if our perceptions in those instances do not in fact help us to understand nature, the fact that sometimes those patterns we read (or project) into nature are all that we know and all that determines our action makes it an essential datum in our efforts to explain the results of human interaction.

The conception that we often perceive patterns without being aware of (or even without perceiving at all) the elements of which they are made up conflicts with the deeply ingrained belief that all recognition of "abstract" forms is "derived" from our prior perception of the "concrete": the assumption that we must first perceive particulars in all their richness and detail before we learn to abstract from them those features which they have in common with other experiences. But, although there exists some clinical evidence that the abstract is often dependent on the functioning of higher nervous centres and that the capacity to form abstract conceptions may be lost while more concrete images are still retained, this is clearly not always so.* Nor would it prove that the concrete is chronologically prior. It is at least highly probable that we often perceive only highly abstract features, that is, an order of stimuli which individually are not perceived at all or at least are not identified.**

6. SPECIFIABLE AND NON-SPECIFIABLE PATTERNS

The fact that we sometimes perceive patterns which we are unable to specify has often been noticed, but it has scarcely yet been given its proper place in our general conception of our relations to the outside world. It will therefore be useful to contrast it explicitly with the two more familiar ways in which patterns play a role in the interpretation of our surroundings. The instance which is familiar to everybody is that of the sensory perception of patterns, such as geometrical figures, which we can also explicitly describe. That the ability intuitively to perceive and the ability discursively to describe a pattern are not the same thing, however, has become evident in the

---

* Cf. Roger W. Brown (3, pp. 264–98), and (15, paras. 6.33–6.43).

** Cf. J. Church (7, p. 111): "It is perfectly possible to see something well enough to sense that it is something dangerous or something attractive but not well enough to know what it is."

course of the advance of science which has increasingly led to the interpretation of nature in terms of patterns which can be constructed by our intellect but not intuitively pictured (such as patterns in multidimensional space). Mathematics and logic are largely occupied with the making of new patterns which our perception does not show us but which later may or may not be found to describe relations between observable elements.*

In the third case, the one which interests us here, the relation is the reverse: our senses recognize (or better: "project," or "read into" the world) patterns which we are in fact not able discursively to describe** and perhaps may never be able to specify. That there exist instances where we do recognize such patterns intuitively long before we can describe them the instance of language alone sufficiently demonstrates. But once the existence of some such is demonstrated, we must be prepared to discover that they are more numerous and significant than we are immediately aware of. Whether in all such instances we shall, even in principle, be able explicitly to describe the structures which our senses spontaneously treat as instances of the same pattern we shall have to consider at the end of this paper.

The fact that we recognize patterns which we cannot specify does, of course, not mean that such perceptions can legitimately serve as elements of scientific explanation (though they may provide the "intuitions" which usually precede the conceptual formulation).† But, though such perceptions do not provide a scientific explanation, they not only raise a problem for explanation; we must also take into account in explaining the effects of men's actions that they are guided by such perceptions. We shall have to return to this problem later. At this stage it should merely be pointed out that it is entirely consistent, on the one hand, to deny that "wholes" which are intuitively perceived by the scientist may legitimately figure in his explanations and, on the other, to insist that the perception of such wholes by the persons whose interactions are the object of investigation must form a datum for scientific analysis. We shall find that perceptions of this sort, which the radical behaviourists wish to disregard because the corresponding stimuli cannot be defined in "physical terms," are among the

---

* Cf. F. A. Hayek (17).

** Compare Goethe's remark that "Das Wort bemüht sich nur umsonst, Gestalten schöpferisch aufzubauen." See also E. H. Gombrich (12, pp. 103–5 and 307–13) and particularly his observation (p. 307) that "it almost looks as if the eye knew of meanings of which the mind knows nothing."

† It is a different matter that in medical and other diagnoses "physiognomy perception" plays a very important role as a guide to practice. Even here, however, it cannot directly enter theory. On its role cf. M. Polanyi (45). See on these problems also H. Klüver (25, pp. 7–9) and K. Z. Lorenz (34, p. 176) who suggests that "no important scientific fact has ever been 'proved' that has not previously been simply and immediately seen by intuitive Gestalt perception."

chief data on which our explanations of the relations between men must be built.*

In a certain sense it is generally true that the requirement that the terms in which an explanation runs must be fully specifiable applies only to the theory (the general formula or the abstract pattern) and not to the particular data which must be inserted in place of the blanks to make it applicable to particular instances. So far as the recognition of the particular conditions is concerned to which a theoretical statement is applicable, we always have to rely on interpersonal agreement, whether the conditions are defined in terms of sensory qualities such as "green" or "bitter," or in terms of point coincidences, as is the case where we measure. In these familiar instances this raises in general no difficulty, not only because agreement between different observers is very high, but also because we know how to create the conditions in which different persons will experience the same perceptions. The physical circumstances which produce these sensations can be deliberately manipulated and generally assigned to defined space-time regions which are for the observer "filled" with the sensory quality in question. We will also find in general that what appears as alike to different people will also have the same effects on other objects; and we regard it as a rather surprising exception if what appears as alike to us acts differently on other objects, or if what appears different to us acts alike on other objects.** Yet we can experiment with the stimuli to which such perceptions are due, and though in the last resort the applicability of our theoretical model also rests on agreement on sense perceptions, we can push these, as it were, as far back as we wish.

The situation is different where we cannot specify the structures of elements which people in fact treat as the same pattern and call by the same name. Though in one sense people know in those instances what they perceive, in another they do not know what it is that they thus perceive. While all observers may in fact agree that a person is happy, or acts deliberately or clumsily, or expects something, &c., they cannot for persons

---

* It is difficult to say how far such perceptions of non-specifiable patterns fit the usual conception of "sense data," "data of observation," "perceptual data," "empirical ultimates," or "objective facts," and perhaps even whether we can still speak of perception by the senses or should rather speak of perception by the mind. It would seem as if the whole phenomenon we are considering could not be fitted into the sensualist philosophy from which those conceptions derive. It is clearly not true, as is implied in those terms, that all we experience we must also be in a position to describe. Though we may have a name for such unspecifiable perceptions which our fellows understand, we should have no way of explaining what they are to a person who does not already in some sense perceive the same complexes of events of which we cannot further explain what they have in common.

** See 15, paras. 1.6–1.21 and 14, pp. 18–24.

who do not know what these terms mean provide an "ostensive" definition because they cannot point to those parts of the observed environment from which they recognize those attributes.

The intelligibility of communications intended to be understood (or the comprehension of their meaning) on the basis of the perception of the rules which they follow is merely the most conspicuous instance of a phenomenon of much wider occurrence. What we perceive in watching other people, and in some measure also in watching other living things,* is not so much particular movements but a purpose or mood or attitude (disposition or set) which we recognize from we do not know what. It is from such perceptions that we derive most of the information which makes the conduct of others intelligible to us. What we recognize as purposive conduct is conduct following a rule with which we are acquainted but which we need not explicitly know. Similarly, that an approach of another person is friendly or hostile, that he is playing a game or willing to sell us some commodity or intends to make love, we recognize without knowing what we recognize it from. In general, we do not know in those instances what psychologists call the "clues" (or "cues") from which men recognize what to them is the significant aspect of the situation; and in most instances there will in fact be no specific clues in the sense of single events but merely a pattern of a certain kind which has a meaning to them.

7. THE MULTIPLE CHAIN OF RULES

We have called the phenomena we are discussing "rule perception" (though "regularity perception" would perhaps be more exact).** That expression has the advantage over such terms as "pattern perception" and the like that it more strongly suggests that such perceptions may be of any degree of generality or abstractness, that it clearly includes temporal as well as spatial orders, and that it is compatible with the fact that the rules to which it refers interact in a complex structure. It is also helpful in bringing out the connexion between the rules governing perception and the rules governing action.†

No attempt will be made here to define "rule." It should be noted, however, that in describing the rules on which a system acts, at least some

---

* If the vitalists find causal explanations of the phenomena of life so unsatisfactory, it is probably because such explanations do not fully account for those features by which we intuitively recognize something as living.

** Cf. O. G. Selfridge (54, p. 345): "A pattern is equivalent to a set of rules for recognizing it"; and (p. 346): "By pattern recognition is meant classifying patterns into learnt categories."

† The crucial significance of the concept of rule in this connexion was brought home to me by reading T. S. Szasz (57) and R. S. Peters (43) which helped me to bring together various strands of thought starting from different origins.

of these rules will have to be given the form of imperatives or norms, i.e., the form "if A, then do B," though once a framework of such imperatives has been established, within it indicative rules such as "if A, then B" may be used to determine the premisses of the imperative rules. But while all the indicative rules could be restated as imperative rules (namely in the form "if A, then do as if B"), the reverse is not true.

The unconscious rules which govern our action are often represented as "customs" or "habits." These terms are somewhat misleading because they are usually understood to refer to very specific or particular actions. The rules of which we are speaking, however, generally control or circumscribe only certain aspects of concrete actions by providing a general schema which is then adapted to the particular circumstances. They will often merely determine or limit the range of possibilities within which the choice is made consciously.* By eliminating certain kinds of action altogether and providing certain routine ways of achieving the object, they merely restrict the alternatives on which a conscious choice is required. The moral rules, for example, which have become part of a man's nature will mean that certain conceivable choices will not appear at all among the possibilities between which he chooses. Thus even decisions which have been carefully considered will in part be determined by rules of which the acting person is not aware. Like scientific laws,** the rules which guide an individual's action are better seen as determining what he will not do rather than what he will do.

The relations between rules of perception and rules of action are complex. So far as the perception of actions of other individuals is concerned we have seen that in the first instance the perceiving individual's own action patterns provide the master moulds by which the action patterns of other individuals are recognized. But recognizing an action pattern as one of a class determines merely that it has the same meaning as others of the same class, but not yet what that meaning is. The latter rests on the further pattern of action, or sect of rules, which in response to the recognition of a pattern as one of a certain kind the organism imposes upon its own further activities.† Every perception of a rule in the external events as well as every

* Cf. G. Humphrey (22, esp. p. 255) who distinguishes with respect to habits between the fixed strategy and the variable tactics.

** Cf. K. R. Popper (46).

† I presume that it is this circular connexion between action patterns and perception patterns which V. von Weizsäcker has in mind in speaking of the *Gestaltkreis* (65). In this connexion it should be mentioned that, apart from the Gesalt theorists, those who have given most attention to the phenomena discussed here were mainly students influenced by phenomenologist and existentialist conceptions, though I find myself unable to accept their philosophical interpretations. See particularly F. J. J. Buytendijk (5), M. Merleau-Ponty (35), and H. Plessner (44). Cf. also 15, paras. 4.45–4.63 and 5.63–5.75.

single perceived event or any need arising out of the internal processes of the organism, thus adds to or modifies the set of rules governing its further responses to new stimuli. It is the total of such activated rules (or conditions imposed upon further action) which constitutes what is called the "set" (disposition) of the organism at any particular moment; and the significance of newly received signals consists in the manner in which they modify this complex of rules.*

The complexity of the arrangement in which these rules may be super-imposed and interrelated is difficult briefly to indicate. We must assume that there exists not only on the perceptual side a hierarchy of superimposed classes of classes, &c., but that similarly also on the motor side not merely dispositions to act according to a rule but dispositions to change disposi-tions and so on will operate in sometimes long chains. Indeed, in view of the interconnexions between the sensory and the motor elements on all levels, it becomes impossible clearly to distinguish between an ascending (sensory) and descending (motor) branch of the process; we should con-ceive of this process rather as one continuous stream in which the con-nexion between any group of stimuli and any group of responses is effected by many arcs of different length, with the longer ones not only controlling the results of the shorter ones but in turn being controlled by the ongoing processes in the higher centres through which they pass. The first step in the successive classification of the stimuli must thus be seen as at the same time the first step in a successive imposition of rules on action, and the final specification of a particular action as the last step of many chains of suc-cessive classifications of stimuli according to the rules to which their arrangement correspond.**

It would seem to follow from this that the meaning (connotation, intension) of a symbol or concept will normally be a rule imposed on further mental processes which itself need not be conscious or specifiable. This would imply that such a concept need not be accompanied by an image or have an external "referent": it merely puts into operation a rule which the organism possesses. This rule imposed upon the further processes must, of course, not be confused with the rule by which the symbol or action having the meaning is recognized. We must also not expect to find any simple correspondence between the structure of any system of symbols and the structure of meaning: what we have to deal with is a set of relations

---

* That the arrival of additional modifiers of an action that may already be sufficiently determined by other circumstances does not lead to overdetermina-tion presupposes an organization more complex than that represented, for example, by a system of simultaneous equations, something in which a "normal" (general purpose or routine) instruction can be superseded by another containing more specific information.

** Cf. 15, paras. 4.45–4.63 and 5.63–5.75.

between two systems of rules. A great part of the current philosophies of "symbolism" seem in this respect to be barking up the wrong tree—not to speak of the paradox of a "theory of communication" which believes that it can account for communication while disregarding meaning or the process of understanding.

8. ΓΝΩΣΙΣ ΤΟΥ ΟΜΟΙΟΜ ΤΩ ΟΜΟΙΩ

We still have to consider more closely the role which the perception of the meaning of other people's action must play in the scientific explanation of the interaction of men. The problem which arises here is known in the discussion of the methodology of the social science as that of *Verstehen* (understanding). We have seen that this understanding of the meaning of actions is of the same kind as the understanding of communications (i.e., of action intended to be understood). It includes what the eighteenth-century authors described as sympathy and what has more recently been discussed under the heading of "empathy" (*Einfühlung*). Since we shall be concerned chiefly with the use of these perceptions as data for the theoretical social sciences, we shall concentrate on what is sometimes called rational understanding (or rational reconstruction), that is, on the instances where we recognize that the persons in whose actions we are interested base their decisions on the meaning of what they perceive. The theoretical social sciences do not treat the whole of a person's actions as an unspecifiable and unexplainable whole but, in their efforts to account for the unintended consequences of individual actions, endeavour to reconstruct the individual's reasoning from the data which to him are provided by the recognition of the action of others as meaningful wholes. We shall indicate this limitation by speaking of *intelligibility* and of *comprehending the meaning* of human action rather than of understanding.*

The chief question we shall have to consider is that of what, and how much, we must have in common with other people in order to find their actions intelligible or meaningful. We have seen that our capacity to recognize action as following rules and having meaning rests on ourselves already being equipped with these rules. This "knowledge by acquaintance" presupposes therefore that some of the rules in terms of which we perceive and act are the same as those by which the conduct of those whose actions we interpret is guided.

> * See L. von Mises (38 and 39), who distinguishes between *Begreifen* and *Verstehen*, though I prefer to render his *Begreifen* by "comprehension" rather than his own English term " conception." To the first of his works cited I owe also the quotation from Empedocles used as the heading of this section, which is derived from Aristotle, *Metaphysics*, ii. 4, 1000^b5. A careful analysis of the whole problem of *Verstehen* which deserves to be better known will be found in H. Gomperz (13).

The contention that intelligibility of human action presupposes a certain likeness between an actor and the interpreter of his actions has led to the misunderstanding that this means that, for example,"only a war-like historian can tackle a Genghis Khan or a Hitler." *This, of course, is not implied in the contention. We need not be wholly alike or even have a similar character with those whose communications or other actions we find intelligible, but we must be made up of the same ingredients, however different the mixture may be in the particular instances. The requirement of likeness is of the same kind as in the case of understanding language, although in the latter case the specificity of languages to particular cultures adds an extra requirement which is not needed for the interpretation of the meaning of many other actions. One need clearly not be frequently or even ever violently angry to be familiar with the rage pattern or to recognize and interpret a choleric temper.** Nor need one be at all like Hitler to understand his reasoning in a way one cannot understand the mental processes of an imbecile. Nor does one have to like the same things as another to know what "liking" means.* Intelligibility is certainly a matter of degree and it is a commonplace that people who are more alike also understand each other better. Yet this does not alter the fact that even in the limiting case of the restricted understanding which occurs between men and higher animals, and still more in the understanding between men of different cultural backgrounds or character, intelligibility of communications and other acts rests on a partial similarity of mental structure.

It is true that there is no systematic procedure by which we are able to decide in a particular instance whether our comprehension of the meaning of the action of others is correct, and also that for this reason we can never be certain of this sort of fact. But of this those who guide their action by physiognomic perceptions are generally also aware, and the degree of confidence they attach to their knowledge of the meaning of another man's action is as much a datum by which they orient themselves as the meaning itself, and must therefore in the same manner enter our scientific account of the effects of the interactions of many men.

* J. W. N. Watkins (62, p. 740).

** Cf. R. Redfield (47): "The anthropologist demonstrates the existence of human nature whenever he finds out what an exotic people are thinking and feeling. He can do this only by supposing that they have in common with him certain acquired propensities of attitude; these are human nature. To be able to find out what it is that a Zuni Indian is ashamed of, one must first know what it is to be ashamed."

† Cf. H. Klüver (26, p. 286): "It should be realized that 'emotional' or 'affective' qualities may become visible as 'physiognomic' properties without emotional states or events occurring in the observer or the observed object. We may see, for instance, 'sadness' or 'aggressiveness' in a face without being emotionally affected."

9. SUPRA-CONSCIOUS RULES AND THE EXPLANATION OF MIND

So far our argument has rested solely on the uncontestable assumption that we are not in fact able to specify all the rules which govern our perceptions and actions. We still have to consider the question whether it is conceivable that we should ever be in a position discursively to describe all (or at least any one) of these rules, or whether mental activity must always be guided by some rules which we are in principle not able to specify.

If it should turn out that it is basically impossible to state or communicate all the rules which govern our actions, including our communications and explicit statements, this would imply an inherent limitation of our possible explicit knowledge and, in particular, the impossibility of ever fully explaining a mind of the complexity of our own. Yet, though I am not able to supply a strict proof, this seems to me indeed to follow from our considerations.

If everything we can express (state, communicate) is intelligible to others only because their mental structure is governed by the same rules as ours, it would seem that these rules themselves can never be communicated. This seems to imply that in one sense we always know not only more than we can deliberately state but also more than we can be aware of or deliberately test; and that much that we successfully do depends on presuppositions which are outside the range of what we can either state or reflect upon. This application to all conscious thought of what seems obviously true of verbal statements seems to follow from the fact that such thought must, if we are not to be led into an infinite regress, be assumed to be directed by rules which in turn cannot be conscious—by a supra-conscious* mechanism which operates upon the contents of consciousness but which cannot itself be conscious.**

---

* Or better, perhaps, "meta-conscious," since the problem is essentially the same as those which have given rise to meta-mathematics, meta-languages, and meta-legal rules.

** Twenty years ago I suggested (15, p. 48) that it would seem that any mechanism of classification would always have to possess a degree of complexity greater than any one of the different objects it classifies, and if this is correct it would follow that it is impossible that our brain should ever be able to produce a complete explanation of the particular ways in which it classifies stimuli (as distinguished from a mere explanation of the principle); and ten years later I attempted to state the argument more fully (16, paras. 8.66–8.68). It now seems to me as if this would follow from what I understand to be Georg Cantor's theorem in the theory of sets according to which in any system of classification there are always more classes than things to be classified, which presumably implies that no system of classes can contain itself. But I do not feel competent to attempt such a proof.

The main difficulty of admitting the existing of such supraconscious processes is probably our habit of regarding conscious thought and explicit statements as in some sense the highest level of mental functions. While we are clearly often not aware of mental processes because they have not yet risen to the level of consciousness but proceed on what are (both physiologically and psychologically) lower levels, there is no reason why the conscious level should be the highest level, and many grounds which make it probable that, in order to be conscious, processes must be guided by a supra-conscious order which cannot be the object of its own representations. Mental events may thus be unconscious and uncommunicable because they proceed on too high a level as well as because they proceed on too low a level.

To put this differently: if "to have meaning" is to have a place in an order which we share with other people, this order itself cannot have meaning because it cannot have a place in itself. A point may have a distinct place in a network of lines which differentiates it from all other points in that network; and, similarly, a complex structure of relationships may be distinguished from all other similar structures by a place in a more comprehensive structure which gives each element of the first structure and its relations a distinct "place." But the distinguishing character of such an order could never be defined by its place in itself and a mechanism possessing such an order, though it may be able to indicate meaning by reference to such a place, can never by its action so reproduce the set of relations which defines this place as to distinguish it from another such set of relations.

It is important not to confuse the contention that any such system must always act on some rules which it cannot communicate with the contention that there are particular rules which no such system could ever state. All the former contention means is that there will always be some rules governing a mind which that mind in its then prevailing state cannot communicate, and that, if it ever were to acquire the capacity of communicating these rules, this would presuppose that it had acquired further higher rules which make the communication of the former possible but which themselves will still be incommunicable.

To those familiar with the celebrated theorem due to Kurt Gödel it will probably be obvious that these conclusions are closely related to those Gödel has shown to prevail in formalized arithmetical systems.* It would thus appear that Gödel's theorem is but a special case of a more general principle applying to all conscious and particularly all rational processes, namely the principle that among their determinants there must always be some rules which cannot be stated or even be conscious. At least all we can talk about and probably all we can consciously think about presupposes

---

* See E. Nagel and J. R. Newman (40) for a semi-popular exposition.

the existence of a framework which determines its meaning, i.e., a system of rules which operate us but which we can neither state nor form an image of and which we can merely evoke in others in so far as they already possess them.

It would lead too far if we were here to attempt an examination of the processes by which the manipulation of rules of which we are conscious may lead to the building up of further metaconscious rules, in terms of which we may then be able explicitly to formulate rules of which we were formerly unconscious. It seems that much of the mysterious powers of scientific creativity are due to processes of this sort which involve a restructuring of the supra-conscious matrix in which our conscious thought moves.

We must be content here with providing a framework within which the problem of meaning (intelligibility, significance, understanding) can be meaningfully discussed. To pursue it further would demand the construction of a formal model of a causal system capable not only of recognizing rules in the observed events and responding to them according to another set of rules, different from, yet related to the former, but also able to communicate its perceptions and actions to another system of the same sort, and the demonstration that two such communicating systems must be governed by a common set of rules which cannot be communicated between them. This, however, is a task which would exceed not only the scope of this paper but also the powers of its author.

REFERENCES

1. R. Ahrens, "Beitrag zur Entwicklung der Physiognomie- und Mimikerkenntnis," *Z. f. exp. u. ang. Psychologie*, 1954.

2. Gordon W. Allport, *Pattern and Growth of Personality*, New York, 1961.

3. Roger W. Brown, *Words and Things*, Glencoe, Ill., 1958.

4. J. S. Bruner, J. J. Goodnow, and G. A. Austin, *A Study of Thinking*, New York, 1956.

5. F. J. J. Buytendijk, *Allgemeine Theorie der menschlichen Haltung und Bewegung*, Berlin–Heidelberg, 1956.

6. ———, "Das erste Lächlen des Kindes," *Psyche*, **2**, 1957.

7. Joseph Church, *Language and the Discovery of Reality*, New York, 1961.

8. Milton Friedman and L. J. Savage, "The Utility Analysis of Choice involving Risk," (*J. of Pol. Econ.*, 56, 1948), reprinted in G. J. Stigler and K. E. Boulding (eds.), *Readings in Price Theory*, Chicago, 1952.

9. Franz G. From, "Perception and Human Action," in H. P. David and J. C. Breugelmann (eds.), *Perspectives in Personality Research*, New York, 1960.

10. James C. Gibson, *The Perception of the Visual World*, Boston, 1950.

11. Kurt Goldstein, "The Smiling of the Infant and the Problem of Understanding the 'Other,' " *J. Psychology*, **44**, 1957.

12. E. H. Gombrich, *Art and Illusion*, New York, 1960.

13. Heinrich Gomperz, *Über Sinn und Sinngebilde, Verstehen und Erklären*, Tübingen, 1929.

14. Harry F. Harlow, "Social Behavior in Primates," in C. P. Stone (ed.), *Comparative Psychology*, 3rd ed., New York, 1951.

15. F. A. Hayek, "Scientism and the Study of Society," Part II, *Economica*, N.S., 10, 1942, reprinted in *The Counter-Revolution of Science*, Glencoe, Ill., 1952.

16. ———, *The Sensory Order*, London and Chicago, 1952.

17. ———, "The Theory of Complex Phenomena," in M. Bunge (ed.), *The Critical Approach to Science and Philosophy*. Essays in Honor of Karl Popper, New York, 1963.

18. H. Hediger, *Skizzen zu einer Tierpsychologie im Zoo und im Zirkus*, Stuttgart, 1954.

19. Fritz Heider, *The Psychology of Interpersonal Relations*, New York, 1958.

20. O. Heinroth, "Über bestimmte Bewegungsweisen von Wirbeltieren," *Sitzungsberichte der Gesellschaft naturforschender Freunde*, Berlin, 1931.

21. H. Helmholtz, *Populäre wissenschaftliche Vorträge*, 2. Heft, Braunschweig, 1871.

22. G. Humphrey, *The Nature of Learning*, London, 1933.

23. F. Kainz, *Psychologie der Sprache*, 4. Band, Stuttgart, 1956.

24. G. Kietz, *Der Ausdrucksgehalt des menschlichen Ganges* (Beiheft 93 to *Zeitschr. f. ang. Psychologie u. Charakterkunde*), Leipzig, 1948.

25. Heinrich Klüver, *Behavior Mechanisms in Monkeys*, Chicago, 1933.

26. ———, "Functional Significance of the Geniculo-Striate System," *Biological Symposium*, **7**, 1942.

27. Wolfgang Köhler, *The Mentality of Apes*, New York, 1925.

28. Kurt Koffka, *Growth of the Mind*, New York, 1925.

29. Ivo Kohler, "Experiments with Goggles," *Scientific American*, 206–5, May 1962.

30. Adriaan Kortlandt, "Chimpanzees in the Wild," *Scientific American*, **206–5**, May, 1962.

31. K. S. Lashley, "The Problem of Serial Order in Behavior," in L. Jeffress (ed.), *Hixon Symposium on Cerebral Mechanism in Behavior*, New York, 1951.

32. Robert B. Lees, Review of N. Chomsky, *Syntactic Structures*, *Language*, *33*, 1957.

33. K. Z. Lorenz, "The Comparative Method in Studying Innate Behaviour," in *Physiological Mechanisms in Animal Behaviour* (Symposia of the Society for Experimental Biology, No. 4), Cambridge, 1950.

34. ———, "The Role of Gestalt Perception in Animal and Human Behaviour," in L. L. Whyte, (e.), *Aspects of Form*, London, 1951.

35. M. Merleau-Ponty, *La Structure du comportement*, Paris, 1942.

36. N. E. Miller and J. Dollard, *Social Learning and Imitation*, Yale University Press, 1941.

37. R. E. Miller, J. V. Murphy, and I. A. Mirsky, "Non-verbal Communication of Affect," *J. Clin. Psych.*, *15*, 1959.

38. Ludwig von Mises, "Begreifen und Verstehen" (1930), trsl. by G. Reisman as "Conception and Understanding," in L. von Mises, *Epistemological Problems of Economics*, New York, 1960.

39. Ludwig von Mises, *Human Action*, Yale University Press, 1949.

40. Ernest Nagel and James R. Newman, *Gödel's Proof*, New York University Press, 1958.

41. R. C. Oldfield, "Memory Mechanism and the Theory of Schemata," *Brit. J. of Psych.* (Gen. Sect.), **45**, 1954.

42. —— and O. L. Zangwill, "Head's Concept of the Schema and its Application to Contemporary British Psychology," *Brit. J. of Psych.*, **32-33**, 1942-3.

43. R. S. Peters, *The Concept of Motivation*, London, 1958.

44. H. Plessner, "Die Deutung des mimischen Ausdrucks" (1925-6), reprinted in H. Plessner, *Zwischen Philosophie und Gesellschaft*, Bern, 1953.

45. Michael Polanyi, "Knowing and Being," *Mind*, **70**, 1951.

46. Karl R. Popper, *The Logic of Scientific Discovery*, London, 1959.

47. Robert Redfield, "Social Science among the Humanities," *Measure*, **1**, 1950.

48. E. Rubin, "Bemerkungen über unser Wissen von anderen Menschen," in E. Rubin, *Experimenta Psychologica*, Copenhagen, 1949.

49. J. Ruesch and W. Kees, *Non-verbal Communication*, University of Colorado Press, 1956.

50. Gilbert Ryle, "Knowing How and Knowing That," *Proc. Arist. Soc.*, 1945-6.

51. ——, *The Concept of Mind*, London, 1949.

52. Edward Sapir, "The Unconscious Patterning of Behavior in Society," (1927) in *Selected Writings of Edward Sapir*, ed. by D. G. Mandelbaum, University of California Press, 1949.

53. Paul Schilder, *The Image and Appearance of the Human Body*, London, 1936.

54. O. G. Selfridge, "Pattern Recognition and Learning," in Colin Cherry (ed.), *Information Theory*, Third London Symposium, London, 1956.

55. L. C. Stepien, J. P. Cordeau, and T. Rasmussen, "The Effect of Temporal Lobe and Hippocampal Lesions on Auditory and Visual Recent Memory in Monkeys," *Brain*, **83**, 1960.

56. Dugald Stewart, *Elements of the Philosophy of the Human Mind*, in *Collected Works*, vol. 4, Edinburgh, 1854.

57. Thomas S. Szasz, *The Myth of Mental Illness: Foundations of a Theory of Personal Conduct*, New York, 1961.

58. N. Tinbergen, *The Study of Instinct*, Oxford, 1951.

59. M. D. Vernon, "The Function of Schemata in Perceiving," *Psych. Rev.*, **62**, 1955.

60. ——, *The Psychology of Perception*. London, 1962.

61. W. S. Verplanck, *A Glossary of some Terms used in the Objective Science of Behavior*, Supplement to *Psych. Rev.*, **64**, 1947.

62. J. W. N. Watkins, "Ideal Types and Historical Explanation," in H. Feigl and M. Brodbeck (eds.), *Readings in the Philosophy of Science*, New York, 1953.

63. Heinz Werner, *Comparative Psychology of Mental Development*, rev. ed., Chicago, 1948.

64. ——— and others, "Studies in Physiognomic Perception," *J. of Psych.*, **38–46**, 1954–8.

65. Viktor von Weizsäcker, *Der Gestaltkreis*, 3rd ed., Stuttgart, 1947.

66. Ludwig Wittgenstein, *Philosophical Investigations*, Oxford, 1953.

67. R. S. Woodworth and H. Schlossberg, *Experimental Psychology*, rev. ed., New York, 1955.

BIBLIOGRAPHY

Part One. COMMUNICATION AS SCIENCE

Ashby, W. R. *An Introduction to Cybernetics*. London: Chapman and Hall, 1956. New York: Wiley, 1956.

Berlo, D. K. *The Process of Communication*. New York: Holt, Rinehart & Winston, 1960. Chap. 2, 3, 4.

Borko, H., ed. *Computer Applications in the Behavioral Sciences*. Englewood Cliffs, N.J.: Prentice-Hall, 1962.

Cherry, C. " 'Communication Theory'—and Human Behavior." In A. J. Ayer, *et al.*, ed., *Studies in Communication*. London: Martin Secker and Warburg, 1955.

——. *On Human Communication*. Cambridge, Mass.: The Technology Press, 1957.

Dubos, R. *The Dreams of Reason: Science and Utopias*. New York: Columbia University Press, 1961.

Eisenson, J., Auer, J. J., and Irwin, J. V. *The Psychology of Communication*. New York: Appleton-Century-Crofts, 1963.

Fehr, H. F. "Communication of Scientific Thought." In P. C. Obler and H. A. Estrin, eds., *The New Scientist: Essays on the Methods and Values of Modern Science*. New York: Doubleday Anchor Books, 1962.

Harrah, D. *Communication: A Logical Model*. Cambridge: M.I.T. Press, 1963.

Harris, E. "Mind and Mechanical Models." In J. M. Scher, ed., *Theories of the Mind*. New York: Free Press, 1962.

Korzybski, A. *Science and Sanity*. Lancaster: Science Press, 1933.

Krutch, J. W. *The Measure of Man*. New York: Grosset & Dunlap, 1953.

Le Corbeiller, P. "Introduction." In *The Languages of Science: A Survey of Techniques of Communication*. New York: Basic Books, 1963.

Matson, F. W. *The Broken Image: Man, Science and Society*. New York: Braziller, 1964.

Muses, C. A. "Foreword." In J. Rothstein, *Communication, Organization, and Science*. Indian Hills, Colo.: The Falcon's Wing Press, 1958.

579

Northrop, F. S. C. *Man, Nature, and God*. New York: Simon & Schuster, Trident Press Book, 1962. Chap. 2, "The Communicants in Communication Engineering."

Osgood, C. E., Suci, G. J., and Tannenbaum, P. *The Measurement of Meaning*. Urbana: University of Illinois Press, 1957.

Polanyi, M. *Personal Knowledge: Towards a Post-Critical Philosophy*. Chicago: University of Chicago Press, 1958.

Quastler, H., ed. *Information Theory in Psychology*. New York: Free Press, 1955.

Rapoport, A. *Fights, Games, and Debates*. Ann Arbor: University of Michigan Press, 1960.

Shannon, C., and Weaver, W. *The Mathematical Theory of Communication*. Urbana: University of Illinois Press, 1949.

Turbayne, C. M. *The Myth of Metaphor*. New Haven: Yale University Press, 1962.

Von Neumann, J., and Morgenstern, O. *Theory of Games and Economic Behavior*. Princeton: Princeton University Press, 1944.

Wiener, N. *Cybernetics: Or Control and Communication in the Animal and the Machine*. 2nd ed. Cambridge, Mass.: M.I.T. Press, 1961.

Part Two. COMMUNICATION AS DIALOGUE

Buber, M. *Between Man and Man*. Boston: Beacon Paperback, 1955.

———. *I and Thou*. 2nd ed. New York: Scribner's, 1958.

———. *The Knowledge of Man*. Edited with an Introductory Essay by Maurice Friedman. New York: Harper, 1964.

———. *Pointing the Way*. New York: Harper Torchbook Edition, 1963.

Dilthey, W. *Pattern and Meaning in History: Thoughts on History and Society*. Edited with an Introduction by H. P. Rickman. New York: Harper Torchbooks, 1962.

Friedman, M. S. *Martin Buber: The Life of Dialogue*. New York: Harper Torchbooks, 1960.

———. *The Worlds of Existentialism*. New York: Random House, 1964. Part IV "Intersubjectivity".

Hartshorne, C. "Mind as Memory and Creative Love." In J. M. Scher, ed., *Theories of the Mind*. New York: Free Press, 1962.

Jaspers, K. *The Way To Wisdom*. New Haven: Yale University Press, 1960.

Jeffreys, M. V. C. *Personal Values in the Modern World*. Pelican Books, 1962. Chap. 6.

Krutch, J. W. *The Measure of Man*. New York: Grosset & Dunlap, 1953. Chaps. 10, 11.

Marcel, G. "I and Thou." In P. A. Schilpp and M. S. Friedman, eds., *The Philosophy of Martin Buber*. Wilmette, Illinois: Open Court Publishing Co., 1964.

———. *Man Against Mass Society*. Chicago: Gateway Edition, 1962.

———. *The Mystery of Being*. Vol 1, *Reflection and Mystery*. Chicago: Gateway Edition, 1960.

Montagu, Ashley. *On Being Human*. 2nd ed. New York: Hawthorn Books, 1966.

Pfuetze, P. E. *Self, Society, Existence*. New York: Harper Torchbooks, 1961.

Scheler, M. *The Nature of Sympathy*. Transl. by Peter Heath. London: Routledge and Kegan Paul, 1954.

Schrag, C. O. *Existence and Freedom*. Evanston: Northwestern University Press, 1961.

Tillich, P. *The Courage To Be*. New Haven: Yale Paperbound Edition, 1959.

———. *Theology of Culture*. New York: Oxford Galaxy Book Edition, 1964, Chaps. V. XV.

Tournier, P. *The Meaning of Persons*. New York: Harper, 1957.

Wild, John. *The Challenge of Existentialism*. Bloomington: Indiana University Press, 1955.

Part Three. PERSON TO PERSON: PSYCHOLOGICAL
APPROACHES

Allport, G. W. *Becoming*. New Haven: Yale University Press, 1955.

———. *Personality and Social Encounter*. Boston: Beacon Press, 1960.

Becker, E. *The Revolution in Psychiatry*. New York: Free Press, 1964.

Buhler, C. *Values in Psychotherapy*. New York: Free Press, 1962.

Cantril, H. "A Transactional Inquiry Concerning Mind." In J. M. Scher, ed., *Theories of the Mind*. New York: Free Press, 1962.

Cohen, J. *Humanistic Psychology*. New York: Collier Books, 1962. Chap 7 "Contact of Minds".

De Forrest, I. *The Leaven of Love: A Development of the Psychoanalytic Theory and Technique of Sandor Ferenczi*. New York: Harper, 1954.

Eisenson, J., Auer, J. A., and Irwin, J. V. *The Psychology of Communication*. New York: Appleton-Century-Crofts, 1963.

Fromm, E. *The Art of Loving*. New York: Harper & Row, 1956.

———. *Man For Himself*. New York: Rinehart, 1947.

———. *The Sane Society*. New York: Rinehart, 1955.

Fromm-Reichmann, F., and Moreno, J. L. *Progress in Psychotherapy*: 1956. New York: Grune & Stratton, 1956.

Heider, F. *The Psychology of Interpersonal Relations*. New York: Wiley, 1958.

Hoch, P. H., and Zubin, J., eds. *The Psychopathology of Communication*. New York: Grune & Stratton, 1958.

McCurdy, H. G. *Personality and Science*. Princeton: Van Nostrand, 1965. Chap, 5, 6.

———. *The Personal World*. New York: Harcourt, Brace & World, 1961.

Maslow, A. H. *Religions, Values, and Peak-Experiences*. Columbus: Ohio State University Press, 1964.

———. *Towards a Psychology of Being*. Princeton: Van Nostrand, 1962.

Miller, G. A. *Language and Communication*. New York: McGraw-Hill, 1951.

Newcomb, T. M. "An Approach to the Study of Communicative Acts," *Psychologicl Review*, 60 (1953), 393–404.

Nuttin, J. *Psychoanalysis and Personality*. Transl. by George Lamb. New York: Mentor-Omega Edition, 1962.

Progoff, I. *Depth Psychology and Modern Man*. New York: Julian Press, 1959.

Rank, O. *Will Therapy and Truth and Reality*. New York: Knopf, 1945.

Robertiello, R. C., Friedman, D. B., and Pollens, B. *The Analyst's Role*. New York: Citadel Press, 1963.

Rogers, C. R. *Client-Centered Therapy*. Boston: Houghton Mifflin, 1951.

———. *On Becoming a Person: A Therapist's View of Psychotherapy*. Boston: Houghton Mifflin, 1961.

Ruesch, J. *Disturbed Communication*. New York: Norton, 1957.

———. *Therapeutic Communication*. New York: Norton, 1961.

Ruesch, J., and Bateson, G. *Communication: The Social Matrix of Psychiatry*. New York: Norton, 1951.

Scher, J. M. "Mind as Participation." In J. M. Scher, ed., *Theories of the Mind*. New York: Free Press, 1962.

Sechehaye, M. A. *Symbolic Realization*. New York: International Universities Press, 1951.

Stern, K. *The Third Revolution*. New York: Harcourt, Brace, 1954. Chaps. VII, XII.

Storr, A. *The Integrity of the Personality*. New York: Atheneum, 1961.

Sullivan, H. S. *The Interpersonal Theory of Psychiatry*. New York: Norton, 1953.

———. *The Psychiatric Interview*. New York: Norton, 1954.

Van den Berg, J. H. *The Changing Nature of Man*. New York: Norton, 1961.

———. *The Phenomenological Approach to Psychiatry*. Springfield: Thomas, 1955.

Wheelis, A. *The Quest for Identity*. New York: Norton, 1958.

Part Four.   DEMOCRATIC DIALOGUE: THE POLITICS OF
COMMUNICATION

Arnold, T. *The Folklore of Capitalism*. Garden City: Blue Ribbon Books, 1937.

———. *The Symbols of Government*. New Haven: Yale University Press, 1935; New York: Harbinger Books, 1962.

Bailey, T. A. *The Man in the Street*. New York: Macmillan, 1948.

Bay, C. *The Structure of Freedom*. Stanford: Stanford University Press, 1958.

Becker, C. L. *Freedom and Responsibility in the American Way of Life*. New York; Knopf, 1951.

Bentley, A. F. *The Process of Government: A Study of Social Pressures*. Chicago: University of Chicago Press, 1908.

Berelson, B., and Janowitz, M., eds. *Reader in Public Opinion and Communication*. New York: Free Press, 1950.

Berelson, B., Lazarsfeld, P. F., and McPhee, W. N. *Voting: A Study of Opinion Formation in a Presidential Campaign*. Chicago: University of Chicago Press, 1954.

Buchanan, W., and Cantril, H. *How Nations See Each Other*. Urbana: University of Illinois Press, 1953.

Burdick, E., and Brodbeck, A. J., eds. *American Voting Behavior*. New York: Free Press, 1958.

Campbell, A., Gurin, G., and Miller, W. E. *The Voter Decides*. Evanston: Row, Peterson, 1954.

Cantril, H., ed. *Tensions That Cause Wars*. Urbana: University of Illinois Press 1950.

Cassirer, E. *The Myth of the State*. New York: Doubleday Anchor Books, 1955.

Chafee, Z. *Free Speech in the United States*. Cambridge, Mass.: Harvard University Press, 1941.

De Grazia, S. *The Political Community*. Chicago: University of Chicago Press, 1948.

Deutsch, K. W. *The Nerves of Government: Models of Political Communication and Control*. New York: Free Press, 1963.

Dewey, J. *The Public and Its Problems*. New York: Holt, 1927.

Friedrich, C. J. *The New Belief in the Common Man*. Boston: Little, Brown, 1942.

Galbraith, J. K. *Economics and the Art of Controversy*. New York: Vintage Books, 1959.

Kariel, H. S. *The Decline of American Pluralism*. Stanford: Stanford University Press, 1961.

Kelley, S. *Professional Public Relations and Political Power*. Baltimore: Johns Hopkins University Press, 1959.

Lasswell, H., Leites, N., *et al.*, eds. *The Language of Politics*. New York: G. W. Stewart, 1949.

Lazarsfeld, P. F., Berelson, B., and Gaudet, H. *The People's Choice: How the Voter Makes Up His Mind in a Presidential Campaign*. New York: Columbia University Press, 1948.

Lindsay, A. D. *Toleration and Democracy*. London: Oxford University Press, 1942.

Lippmann, *The Public Philosophy*. New York: Mentor, 1956.

Meiklejohn, A. *Free Speech and Its Relation to Self-Government*. New York: Harper, 1948.

Miller, H. *The Community of Man*. New York: Macmillan, 1949.

———. *Progress and Decline*. Los Angeles: Ward Ritchie, 1963.

Mills, C. W. *The Power Elite*. New York: Oxford University Press, 1956.

Montagu, Ashley. *The Direction of Human Development*. New York: Harper, 1955.

Odegard, P. H. *The American Public Mind*. New York: Columbia University, Press, 1930.

Pye, L. W., ed. *Communications and Political Development*. Princeton: Princeton University Press, 1963.

Rapoport, A. *Strategy and Conscience*. New York: Harper, 1964.

Smith, B. L., Lasswell, H. D., and Casey, R.D. *Propaganda, Communication, and Public Opinion*. Princeton: Princeton University Press, 1946.

Smith, B. L., and Smith, C. *International Communication and Public Opinion*. Princeton: Princeton University Press, 1956.

TenBroek, J., Barnhart, E. N., and Matson, F. W. *Prejudice, War, and the Constitution*. Berkeley: University of California Press, 1954. Chap. 1.

Truman, D. B. *The Governmental Process*. New York: Knopf, 1955.

White, L., and Leigh, R. D. *Peoples Speaking to Peoples*. Chicago: University of Chicago Press, 1946.

White, T. H. *The Making of the President* 1960. New York: Atheneum, 1962.

Wilson, R. B. "Freedom of Speech and Public Opinion." Unpublished Ph.D. dissertation, University of California, Berkeley, 1952.

Part Five. THE MODERN PERSUASION: THE RHETORICS
OF MASS SOCIETY

Allport, G. W., and Postman, L. *The Psychology of Rumor*. New York: Holt, 1947.

Bogart, L. *The Age of Television: A Study of Viewing Habits and the Impact of Television on American Life*. New York: Ungar, 1956.

Boorstin, D. *The Image: Or What Happened to the American Dream*. New York: Atheneum, 1962.

Brown, R. *Words and Things*. New York: Free Press, 1958. Chaps. IX, X.

Burke, K. *A Rhetoric of Motives*. New York: Prentice-Hall, 1952.

DeFleur, M. L., and Larsen, O. N. *The Flow of Information*. New York: Harper, 1958.

Denney, Reuel, *The Astonished Muse*. New York: Universal Library, 1958.

Dexter, L. A. and White, D. M., eds. *People, Society, and Mass Communications*. New York: Free Press, 1964.

Henry, J. *Culture Against Man*. New York: Random House, 1962. Chap. 3.

Hoffer, E. *The True Believer*. New York: Mentor Books, 1951.

Hovland, C. I., Janis, I. L., and Kelley, H. H. *Communication and Persuasion*. New Haven: Yale University Press, 1953.

Hovland, C. I., Lumsdaine, A. A., and Sheffield, F. D. *Experiments on Mass Communication*. Princeton: Princeton University Press, 1949.

Huxley, A. *Brave New World Revisited*. New York: Harper, 1958.

Katz, E., and Lazarsfeld, P. *Personal Influence*. New York: Free Press, 1956.

Klapper, J. T. *Effects of Mass Communication.* New York: Free Press, 1960.

Lazarsfeld, P., and Stanton, F., eds. *Communications Research, 1948–49.* New York: Harper, 1949.

Lerner, M. *America as a Civilization.* New York: Simon & Schuster, 1957. Chap. XI.

Lowenthal, L. *Literature, Popular Culture, and Society.* New York: Prentice-Hall Spectrum Books, 1961.

McLuhan, M. *Understanding Media: The Extensions of Man.* New York: McGraw-Hill, 1964.

Merton, R. K. *Mass Persuasion.* New York: Harper, 1946.

Olson, P., ed. *America as a Mass Society.* New York: Free Press, 1962.

Packard, V. *The Hidden Persuaders.* New York: McKay, 1957.

Riesman, D. *Individualism Reconsidered.* New York: Free Press, 1954.

Riesman, D., Denney, R., and Glazer, N. *The Lonely Crowd.* New Haven: Yale University Press, 1950.

Riley, J. W., and Riley, M. H. "Mass Communication and the Social System," in R. K. Merton, L. Broom, and L. S. Cottrell, Jr., eds., *Sociology Today.* New York: Basic Books, 1959.

Rosenberg, B., and White, D. M., eds. *Mass Culture: The Popular Arts in America.* New York: Free Press, 1957.

Ruesch, J. "Mass Communication and Mass Motivation," *American Journal of Psychotherapy,* 14 (1960), 250–258.

Schramm, W., ed. *Communications in Modern Society.* Urbana: University of Illinois Press, 1948.

————, ed. *Mass Communications.* Urbana: University of Illinois Press, 1960.

Seldes, G. *The Public Arts.* New York: Simon & Schuster, 1956.

Shils, E. *The Torment of Secrecy.* New York: Free Press, 1956.

Van den Haag, E. *Passion and Social Constraint.* New York: Stein and Day, 1963. Part Three.

Warshow, R. *The Immediate Experience.* Garden City: Doubleday, 1962.

Whyte, W. H., Jr. *The Organization Man.* Garden City: Doubleday Anchor Books, 1957.

Part Six. SYMBOLIC INTERACTION: THE SOCIOLOGY
OF COMMUNICATION

Back, K. W. "Influence Through Social Communication," *Journal of Abnormal Psychology,* 46 (1951), 9–23.

Bales, R. F., Strodtbeck, F. L., Mills, T. M., and Roseborough, M. E. "Channels of Communication in Small Groups," *American Sociological Review,* 16 (1951), 461–468.

Bavelas, A. "Communication Patterns in Task Oriented Groups," *Journal of the Acoustical Society of America,* 22 (1951), 725–730.

Blumer, H. "Psychological Import of the Human Group." In M. Sherif and M. O. Wilson, eds., *Group Relations at the Crossroads*. New York, Harper. 1953.

Boulding, K. *The Image*. Ann Arbor: University of Michigan, Ann Arbor Paperbacks, 1961.

Cooley, C. H. *Human Nature and the Social Order*. New York: Scribner's, 1902.

Goffman, E. *Encounters: Two Studies in the Sociology of Interaction*. Indianapolis: Bobbs-Merrill, 1961.

———. *The Presentation of Self in Everyday Life*. New York: Doubleday Anchor Books, 1959.

Goodman, P. *Growing Up Absurd*. New York: Vintage Books, 1960.

Grinker, R. R., Sr., *et al. Psychiatric Social Work: A Transactional Case Book*. New York: Basic Books, 1961.

Hayakawa, S. I. *Language in Thought and Action*. New York: Harcourt, Brace, 1949.

Hofstein, S. "The Nature of Process: Its Implications for Social Work," *Journal of Social Work Process*, 14 (1964), 13–52.

Kelley, H. H. "Communication in Experimentally Created Hierarchies," *Human Relations*, 4 (1951), 39–56.

Merton, R. K. *Social Theory and Social Structure*. New York: Free Press, 1957.

Newcomb, N. "The Study of Consensus." In R. K. Merton, L. Broom, and L. S. Cottrell, Jr., eds., *Sociology Today*. New York: Basic Books, 1959.

Nisbet, R. A. *The Quest for Community*. New York: Oxford University Press, 1953.

Parsons, T. *The Social System*. New York: Free Press, 1951.

Parsons, T., and Shils, E. A., eds. *Toward a General Theory of Action*. Cambridge Mass.: Harvard University Press, 1952.

Pfuetze, P. E. *Self, Society, Existence*. New York: Harper Torchbooks, 1961.

Riesman, D., Denney, R., and Glazer, N. *The Lonely Crowd*. New Haven: Yale University Press, 1950.

Riessman, F. "The Revolution in Social Work: The New Nonprofessional," *Trans-Action* 2, No. 1 (Nov.-Dec., 1964).

Riessman, F., and Pearl, A. *New Careers for the Poor*. New York: Free Press, 1965.

Ross, R. *Symbols and Civilization*. New York: Harcourt, Brace Harbinger Books, 1962.

Ruesch, J., and Kees, W. *Nonverbal Communication*. Berkeley: University of California Press, 1956.

Schutz, A. "The Social World and the Theory of Social Action." In D. Braybrooke, ed., *The Philosophical Problems of the Social Sciences*. New York: Macmillan, 1965.

Simmel, G. *The Sociology of Georg Simmel*. Transl. by K. H. Wolff. New York: Free Press, 1950.

Stein, M., Vidich, A., and White, D. M., eds. *Identity and Anxiety*. New York: Free Press, 1960.

Stoodley, B. H., ed. *Society and Self*. New York: Free Press, 1962.

Strauss, A. *Mirrors and Masks: The Search for Identity*. New York: Free Press, 1959.

TenBroek, J., and Matson, F. W. *Hope Deferred: Public Welfare and the Blind*. Berkeley: University of California Press, 1959.

Whyte, W. H., Jr. *The Organization Man*. Garden City: Doubleday Anchor Books, 1957.

Part Seven. CULTURE AS COMMUNICATION: THE PERSPECTIVES OF ANTHROPOLOGY

Becker, E. *The Birth and Death of Meaning*. New York: Free Press, 1962.

Carpenter, E., and McLuhan, M., eds. *Explorations in Communication*. Boston: Beacon Press, 1960.

Erikson, E. H. *Childhood and Society*. New York: Norton, 1950.

Hall, E. T. *The Silent Language*. Garden City: Doubleday, 1959.

Hymes, D., ed. *Language and Culture in Society*. New York: Harper, 1965.

Mead, M. "Some Cultural Approaches to Communications Problems" and "A Case History in Cross-National Communications." In L. Bryson, ed., *The Communication of Ideas*. New York: Harper, 1948.

Montagu, A. *The Biosocial Nature of Man*. New York: Grove Press, 1956.

————. *The Direction of Human Development*. New York: Harper, 1955.

————. *The Human Revolution*. Cleveland and New York: World, 1965.

————. *Man in Process*. New York: Mentor Books, 1961.

————. *On Being Human*. 2nd ed. New York: Hawthorn Books, 1966.

————, ed. *Culture and the Evolution of Man*. New York: Oxford University Press, 1963.

Northrop, F. S. C., and Livingston, H. H., eds. *Cross-Cultural Understanding*. New York: Harper, 1964.

Oliver, R. T. *Culture and Communication*. Springfield: Charles C. Thomas, 1962.

Piaget, J. *The Language and Thought of the Child*. New York: Meridian Books, 1955.

Sapir, E. *Language*. New York: Harcourt, Brace, 1921.

Sebeok, T. A., Hayes, A. S., and Bateson, M. C., eds. *Approaches to Semiotics*. The Hague: Mouton, 1964.

Spitz, R. *No and Yes: On the Genesis of Human Communication*. New York: International Universities Press, 1957.

Spuhler, J. N. "Somatic Paths to Culture." In J. N. Spuhler, ed., *The Evolution of Man's Capacity for Culture*. Detroit: Wayne State University Press, 1959.

Tax, S., ed. *Horizons of Anthropology*. Chicago: Aldine, 1964.

Von Bertalanffy, L. "On the Definition of the Symbol." In J. R. Royce, ed., *The Symbol: An Interdisciplinary Symposium.* New York: Random House, 1965.

White, L. A. *The Science of Culture.* New York: Farrar, Strauss, 1949. Chap. Two ("The Symbol").

Whorf, B. L. *Language, Thought, and Reality.* Cambridge, Mass.: Technology Press, 1956.

Part Eight. OTHER VOICES, OTHER MINDS: THE PHILOSOPHY OF COMMUNICATION

Buber, M. *The Knowledge of Man.* Edited and Transl. by M. Friedman and R. G. Smith. New York: Harper, 1964.

Cassirer, E. *An Essay on Man.* Garden City: Doubleday Anchor Books, 1953.

———. *The Philosophy of Symbolic Forms.* 3 vols, New Haven: Yale University Press, 1953.

Castell, A. *The Self in Philosophy.* New York: Macmillan, 1965.

Dewey, J. *Intelligence in the Modern World.* Edited by J. Ratner. New York: Modern Library, 1939. Chaps. V, XV, XVI.

Dewey, J., and Bentley, A. F. *Knowing and the Known.* Boston: Beacon, 1949.

Fite, W. *The Living Mind.* New York: Dial Press, 1930.

Friedman, M. *Problematic Rebel: An Image of Modern Man.* New York: Random House, 1963.

Hocking, W. E. "Marcel and the Ground Issues of Metaphysics," *Philosophy and Phenomenological Research,* 14 (1954), 439–469.

———. *The Self: Its Body and Its Freedom.* New Haven: Yale University Press, 1928.

———. *What Man Can Make of Man.* New York: Harper, 1942.

Jaspers, K. *The Perennial Scope of Philosophy.* Transl. by R. Manheim. London: Routledge & Kegan Paul, 1950.

———. *The Way to Wisdom.* New Haven: Yale University Press, 1954.

Kaufman, F. "Jaspers' Theory of Communication." In P. A. Schilpp, ed., *The Philosophy of Karl Jaspers.* Wilmette, Ill.: Open Court Publishing Co., 1957.

Kwant, R. C. *Encounter.* Transl. by R. C. Adolfs. Pittsburgh: Duquesne University Press, 1960.

Langer, S. K. *Philosophy in a New Key.* New York: Pelican Books, 1948.

Macmurray, J. *The Self as Agent.* London: Faber and Faber, 1957.

Marcel, G. *Metaphysical Journal.* Transl. by B. Wall. Chicago: Regnery, 1961.

Mead, G. H. *The Philosophy of the Act.* Chicago: University of Chicago Press, 1938.

Morris, C. *The Open Self.* New York: Prentice-Hall, 1948.

———. *Signs, Language, and Behavior.* New York: Prentice-Hall, 1946.

Riezler, K. *Man Mutable and Immutable.* Chicago: Regnery 1950.

Sartre, J.-P. *Being and Nothingness.* Transl. by Hazel Barnes. New York: Philosophical Library, 1956. Part Four.

NAME INDEX